International Handbooks on Information Systems

Series Editors
Peter Bernus, Jacek Błażewicz, Günter Schmidt, Michael Shaw

Springer
Berlin
Heidelberg
New York
Barcelona
Hong Kong
London
Milan
Paris
Singapore
Tokyo

Titles in the Series

Jacek Błażewicz · Klaus Ecker
Brigitte Plateau · Denis Trystram
Editors

Handbook on Parallel and Distributed Processing

With 195 Figures
and 22 Tables

Springer

Prof. Dr. Jacek Błażewicz
Politechnika Poznanska
Instytut Informatyki
ul. Piotrowo 3a
60-965 Poznań
Poland

Prof. Klaus Ecker
Technische Universität Clausthal
Institut für Informatik
Julius Albert Str. 4
D-78678 Clausthal-Zellerfeld
Germany

Prof. Brigitte Plateau
LMC
Institut Fourier
BP 53X
100 Rue des Mathematiques
F-38041 Grenoble Cedex 9
France

Prof. Denis Trystram
Institut National Polytechniques de Grenoble
46, avenue Felix Viallet
F-38031 Grenoble Cedex
France

ISBN 978-3-642-08571-0

Cataloging-in-Publication Data applied for
Die Deutsche Bibliothek – CIP-Einheitsaufnahme
Handbook on parallel and distributed processing: with 22 tables / Jacek Błażewicz ed. ... – Berlin; Heidelberg; New York; Barcelona; Hong Kong; London; Milan; Paris; Singapore; Tokyo: Springer, 2000
 (International handbooks on information systems)

© Springer-Verlag Berlin · Heidelberg 2010
Printed in Germany

The use of general descriptive names, registered names, trademarks, etc. in this publication does not imply, even in the absence of a specific statement, that such names are exempt from the relevant protective laws and regulations and therefore free for general use.

Hardcover Design: Erich Kirchner, Heidelberg

Foreword

This book is the third of a running series of volumes dedicated to selected topics of information systems theory and application. The objective of the series is to provide a reference source for problem solvers in business, industry, government, and professional researchers and graduate students.

The first volume, Handbook on Architectures of Information Systems, presents a balanced number of contributions from academia and practitioners. The structure of the material follows a differentiation between modeling languages, tools and methodologies. The second volume, Handbook on Electronic Commerce, examines electronic storefront, on-line business, consumer interface, business-to-business networking, digital payment, legal issues, information product development and electronic business models.

The present volume is a joint venture of an international board of editors, gathering prominent authors of academia and practice, who are well known specialists in the area of parallel and distributed processing. The intention of the Handbook is to provide practitioners, scientists and graduate students with a good overview of basic methods and paradigms, as well as important issues and trends across the broad spectrum of the above area. In particular, the book covers fundamental topics such as efficient parallel algorithms, languages for parallel processing, parallel operating systems, architecture of parallel and distributed systems, management of resources in parallel systems, tools for parallel computing, parallel database systems and multimedia object servers, and networking aspects of distributed and parallel computing. Three chapters are dedicated to applications: parallel and distributed scientific computing, high-performance computing in molecular sciences, and multimedia applications for parallel and distributed systems.

Summing up, the Handbook is indispensable for academics and professionals who are interested in learning a leading expert's coherent and individual view of the topic.

This volume was supported by Project CRIT-2 and KBN Grant No 8T11F02516 Particular thanks are dedicated to Dr. Müller from the Springer Verlag for his encouragement to prepare the volume. Special thanks are addressed to Maciej Drozdowski for his excellent job in careful editing the manuscripts, Anna Błażewicz and Maciej Machowiak for proofreading and corrections, and to many others who helped to prepare the volume.

Jacek Błażewicz
Klaus Ecker
Brigitte Plateau
Denis Trystram

Table of Contents

I. Parallel and Distributed Computing: State-of-the-Art and Emerging Trends

Brigitte Plateau and Denis Trystram

Institut National Polytechnique de Grenoble, Grenoble, France

Summary. This chapter presents an introduction to the area of Parallel and Distributed Computing. The aim is to recall the main historical steps in order to present the future trends and emerging topics. Four major research areas are detailed within this perspective and discussed. They concern respectively the needs of parallel resources for solving large actual applications, the evolution of parallel and distributed systems, the programming environment and some theoretical foundations for the design of efficient parallel algorithms.

1. Introduction

1.1 Parallelism in Short

Historically, high-performance computing was a specialized market area within the computer industry, to serving the computational needs of science, engineering, and defense. However, over the last few years, a major transition could be observed from pure computation-intensive applications towards applications including also intensive communications.

Parallelism is indeed a concept known from the early days of computing and it covers now a large variety of techniques used in most areas of computer science. It appeared in various basic forms many years ago for speeding up the execution times of algorithms. The pioneers developed the fundamentals related to parallelism in the early seventies, but an explosion of the discipline took place during the mid-eighties with the appearance of the first commercially available general purpose parallel machines.

The fast development of parallel processing was encouraged by user demands. In the seventies and eighties, high-performance was based on architectures and technologies optimized to the requirements of computation-intensive applications, but they were expensive in comparison to mainstream computers. Mainly due to the consequences of the economical crisis at the end of the last decade, the interest for this type of machines was decreasing. With the arrival of powerful microprocessors used in workstations, the supercomputing market is now directed towards networks or clusters of computers which provide high computing power at very reasonable prices.

1.2 Content and Organization of the Paper

In this chapter, we discuss the state-of-art and the perspectives of parallel and distributed computing. This concerns application aspects, machine architectures and operating systems, programming, and theoretical foundations. Finally, we survey the contents of the chapters of the book.

2. The Benefits and Needs for Parallel High Performance Computing

The solutions developed in supercomputing are of significant importance in many different areas of practice such as engineering, science, economy, environment and society, to mention the more important.

The availability of parallel high performance computers has opened the gate to tackle problems that were too complex even for the most powerful sequential computers. For example, understanding natural phenomena in earth sciences like in geology, or long term climatic changes, the cause and development of pollution, and short term weather forecast require simulation of accurate and, as a consequence, large computational models. In computer aided design, complex computations during the design process e.g. of vehicles or aircrafts, and simulations for verifying and optimizing the solutions are required. Finally, in special areas, high performance parallel computers enabled considerable progresses, for example developments in chemistry, genetic analyses, and discoveries in nuclear sciences were the result of intensive computations.

Parallel computation has also stimulated the search for, and use of, new mathematical methods. Among them are the well-known domain decomposition methods which can be applied in many applications such as weather forecast, fluid dynamics, and in chemistry. These methods are still a current subject of research. Parallelism has also encouraged the user to develop algorithms suited for a parallel or distributed execution.

There are many areas where parallel high performance computing can provide further progress in the near future:

- The intelligent use of very large databases, also referred to as data mining. In a large variety of applications such as multi-media applications, expert decisions are required on the basis of a huge amount of data; to support their work, sophisticated algorithms have to operate on specialized data ranging from images and video, speech and sound, to structured data and text, very often under the condition of very short time. On a smaller scale, an individual may want to access remotely simple information about books, videos, or other data items. This requires significant improvements of data access methods in high performance information systems, and tools to help individuals to locate information and present, integrate, and transform the information in meaningful ways. In the context of telemedicine applications, powerful systems should provide expert advice based on sophisticated analysis of distributed medical information.
- Engineering. The design of complex products like cars and aircrafts, and the verification of the designs by direct computation or simulation are classical areas of Computer Aided Engineering. In particular, simulation allows the presentation of increasing accuracy of the properties of designed complex objects. The information technology has already revolutionized the entire product development design cycle. The design and realization of powerful visualization systems with 3D images for interactive real-time applications and virtual reality is a hot research subject. Finally, scene recognition systems play an important role in many areas such as security systems and automatic driving. The developments in these areas were on one hand possible due to the progresses in the management of distributed data, and on the other hand by parallel computations.
- Understanding the environment. Modeling the environment leads to very complex and large systems. Precise models are required when dealing with environmental problems such as air or water pollution or avalanche prediction, as well as with transportation systems where vehicle flows are to

be calculated, and electricity, computer and other networks. Progress in these areas depends on improvements in computational methods. This will require a major increase in the computing capability to deal with the immense size of these problems in both time and space.

- Progress in fundamental sciences. Scientists are usually at the forefront for developing and using new technologies such as parallel and distributed computing or networking, in order to solve applications of increasing size and complexity. While experiments become more and more expensive (e.g. in nuclear sciences) or even are impossible (e.g. in astronomy), we get more and more powerful computers at declining prices. Hence computations on parallel machines or in computer networks are an actual alternative. Computers play now a similar role for scientists, as large scale shared physical instruments (for example, national telescopes, microscopes, and particle accelerators) have played in the past. Key research in information technologies includes powerful computing to permit models of complex physical phenomena of a higher accuracy, visualization of complex data, and data mining techniques.

This book covers a large amount of available knowledge and technology required by the above mentioned applications. This material is also fundamental to understand further innovations in hardware technology, computer architecture, system software, algorithms, languages, programming methods and tools, and using them in practice.

3. Parallel and Distributed Systems

In the history of computing, power has been mainly increased by improvements in circuit technology and hardware concepts. Though the limits still seem to be in a far distance, we can already see that further improvements require increasing scientific and financial efforts. Another way of raising computing power is offered by parallel and distributed processing.

VLSI technology makes it possible to realize high-performance on-chip processors accompanied with local memory at a low price. By connecting processors in an array or a multiprocessor system, large parallel computers can be built. Constructing safe and reliable operating systems for parallel computers is a challenge because of the extended demands for managing processes and resources. For example, a design of memory hierarchies with acceptable access latencies and high memory bandwidths requires sophisticated resource allocation strategies as well as software that supports the automatic use of these memories. Generally, research is needed to improve the overall system efficiency by eliminating potential bottlenecks. For the latter, hardware and system software must be developed in a coordinated fashion.

As a prerequisite for distributed systems, the recent progress in communication network technology concerning both, speed and bandwidth, has been tremendous. Advances in networking are led by improvements in transmission technology (signal processing and optical and wireless transmission). The progresses in computing and communication technologies of the last decade are the basis for the rapid growth of distributed computing: interconnected computers are now systems that can be reliable, fast, scalable and cheap. The enormous advances in computing capability, the integration of computing and communications, and the reduction in the cost of these technologies led to an increase in number and size of distributed systems. This evolution has also to take into account the explosion of the internet. As the hardware (processor and communication network) structure is converging to standards, which results in the availability of cheap components, the key point is now to bring the software, including middleware, languages, tools and applications to the same quality: standardization, reliability and ease of use.

It can be observed that the developments of networks and clusters of heterogeneous computers lead to the convergence of parallel and distributed processing. They share, for example, the complex problem of efficiently using the resources that are spread over the system components.

4. Programming Environment

In the preceding sections we discussed some examples of large and complex applications which are distributed by nature or where exploiting parallelism is needed for obtaining a solution in reasonable time. In this section we turn to questions related to the programming environment. The problem here is to design programming environments which help the potential user to exploit efficiently the parallelism with a minimum effort, such that an efficient execution on any available platform is gained. In the following, an overview of various technical concepts of parallel and concurrent execution is given.

An elementary form of parallelism can be found in pipeline computers. A pipeline consists of several functional units that work simultaneously on successive components of an array of data. After a start-up time needed for initiating the pipe, a series of regular operations is realized at the speed of the clock. Pipelines have been invented at different levels of the architecture. Though there are many problems with the effective use of pipelines, as for example reducing the number of pipeline flushes, machines with this feature were for the first time able to solve large contemporary problems.

In the mid-seventies vector-computers appeared for solving scientific applications with regular computations on large arrays (vectors and matrices). These computers were essentially programmed in Fortran with specialized and powerful vector instructions.

OCCAM and the INMOS Transputers appeared in the mid-eighties and, at least in Europe, contributed to the acceptance of the parallelism paradigm. For the first time, parallel machines could be realized with little effort and at a reasonable price. The architecture of the Transputer has been heavily influenced by the high-level language OCCAM, a relatively simple language inspired by the programming language CSP (Communicating Sequential Processes).

Mainly in academic laboratories in the USA, new and interesting concepts had been developed and many of them found their realization in prototypes. Among the most significant, the Connection Machine CM2 has a specialized data parallel language called C*. The Intel Paragon Machine has dedicated routing chips and an associated library allowing to build a program as a set of communicating processes. KSR proposed a hierarchical machine which physically implemented a virtual shared-memory. The IBM SP series was one of the first parallel systems where the processors were linked through a dynamic multi-stage interconnection network. With the T3D, Cray concentrated on massively parallel systems.

On the programming side, most of the scientific and engineering soft- ware is written in Fortran. The considerable advents in the field of parallel and distributed computing led to the extension of existing languages for managing data parallelism (for example, Fortran 90 and High Performance Fortran). This concept is very efficient for problems with regular data structures, but has serious drawbacks on irregular applications. Alternatively, other approaches are based on explicit message passing.

To escape from languages dedicated to parallelism, the research area of automatic parallelisation was very active during the last decade. Some solutions have been proposed for ideal cases such as managing fine-grained parallelism within nested loops. Some practical tools have been implemented for shared-memory parallel systems. For instance, Cray's micro-tasking environment was the ancestor of modern tools like OpenMP which partially provide automatic detection of parallelism. Purely automatic tools are available for some functional expressions of parallel programs.

The success of parallel machines with distributed memories that are based on standard components has been a good answer to reach performance at a reasonable price. This tendency came along with the success of the academic library PVM at the end of the eighties. PVM became a de facto standard whose message passing paradigm provides a simple way to express parallelism by means of communicating processes. PVM is now supported by most machines in the world. A newer development is MPI with the advantage of being efficiently implemented on proprietary clusters and offering a standardized interface. For programming a parallel machine, basically a sequential language (C or Fortran) can be used, and a library offers functions to handle data movement, data concurrency and synchronization.

Following this same line of thought, OpenMP is a library which handles shared memory in symmetric multi-processors where the memory accesses are uniform. It is an emerging standard for expressing the concurrency as a set of directives on a machine with a physically shared memory. Thread technology, commonly used in operating systems to manage concurrency is now a part of the tools of application programmers. It helps to program irregular applications and makes intensive use of multiprogramming within the same application. The system scheduler is in charge of managing a complex asynchronous behavior of programs. Moreover, OpenMP allows to mask communications during computations. The standard thread library follows the Posix standard.

As a conclusion, we may say that parallel systems have become more and more accessible to common users, who are not specialists in the parallel processing area. During the last decade, advances in research offered great opportunities to test new ideas and to evaluate prototypes, and even resulted in successful realizations of some industrial applications. Only a few architectural concepts survived due to economical constraints. Today, the large variety of architectures converges towards powerful sophisticated multiprocessors with increasing size of local memories, linked through very fast interconnection networks. Cluster computing, i.e. computing on large systems connected by wide area networks, is gaining popularity and large applications sharing distant resources are already executing on such systems.

It may be interesting to recall the successive programs of the European Community concerning architectures, software, applications and transfer to the market. Nevertheless research in languages, compilers, system software, runtime libraries, debuggers, programming interfaces, and tools for tuning the performance is still needed. It should lead to better efficiency and performance and make parallel systems usable by a much larger community. The situation to avoid is to build a computer system that offers ever increasing performance, but does not support its usage by providing the corresponding software tools and algorithms.

5. Theoretical Foundations

Parallel and distributed processing differs from classical sequential computing in the wide diversity of existing supports. As pointed out before, the history highlighted the successive progresses in architecture and software and their impact on applications. Despite the potential improvements in architecture, parallel systems seem to be more or less stabilizing towards powerful processors supplied with large local memories and organized by a hierarchical multi-stage interconnection network. On the other hand, the recent emergence of cluster computing and meta-computing creates new problems. For representing this diversity, and depending at what level we are looking at the problem, researchers proposed some models to abstract the main characteristics of physical components and logical mechanisms, to be able to study and analyze more precisely the behavior of parallel applications. Three levels of abstraction are usually distinguished:

– Architectural models are low-level models introduced to simplify the complex mechanisms by identifying key parameters which reflect the global behavior of the system.
– Computational models for studying the mechanisms linked with the management of resources are of intermediate level. They are established on the basis of some functional architectural features. Despite the fact of a trade-off between universality and representation power, it is at least possible to establish a hierarchy of such models and their mutual interactions.
– Programming models are at the highest level. The idea is to propose a powerful framework to express the parallelism at this level, so that the lower levels can exploit parallelism more easily. Again, the universality of parallel and distributed computing is a dream, and a reasonable balance between simplicity of use, power of expression, efficiency and universality has to be found.

Let us notice that there is no strict border between these models. For instance, BSP (initially introduced as a programming paradigm) or LogP (introduced as a architectural model) are usually used as computational models. These models are often referenced as bridging models which describe a parallel architecture by using a set of pertinent abstract parameters. The aim is to bridge the gap between the worlds of architectures and of parallel programming.

To summarize, abstract models, whatever they are, are necessary to study the impact of parallelism. Computational (or bridging) models at an intermediate level are designed for studying resource management problems. They provide a reasonable theoretical framework for designing and evaluating efficient parallel algorithms and programs.

The recent development of clusters introduces new challenging problems. The main issues are the heterogeneity of computing resources and the difficulty of managing complex communication mechanisms. The problem of allocating parts of a parallel program optimally to the processors is known to be intractable even if restrictions are imposed on the application program or on the architecture of the targeted parallel system. A lot of work has already been devoted to design efficient heuristics for determining schedules. Computer scientists have to invent new heuristics and approximation methods. In most cases the knowledge of the structure of the program may be used at compile time for tuning the heuristics. If the structure is not known or if the parameters of the system are not fixed, we need on-line scheduling policies. In both cases, it is possible to build strong theoretical foundations which guarantee an acceptable performance of heuristics.

6. Survey of the Volume

The design of algorithms for parallel and distributed systems differs from conventional computers. Like in sequential calculations, complex applications can be decomposed into elementary bulks of the computations. Some extra canonical communication patterns which link these components together have also to be identified. Both computation and communication routines have to be implemented as best as possible.

The design of parallel algorithms is influenced by some new characteristics of parallel systems. Problems like tuning the basic software components to the right granularity, using the asynchronism of the systems for improving the execution, increasing the locality or optimizing the routing strategy, have to be solved.

There is no universal model for parallel systems for representing the diversity of parallel systems. The fundamental reference model is the well-known PRAM model designed for shared-memory parallel computers. Some alternative models have been proposed for capturing new features like distributed-memory or large grained processors. Moreover, some cost models can be used for predicting the performance of the algorithms taking into account the underlying topology of the interconnection network (ring, array, hypercube, etc.). The second chapter presents an overview of the basic models of parallel machines and algorithms. It detailes and analyzes some of the most typical problems in computer science, namely sorting, matrix multiplication and convex hull.

The parallelism is usually difficult to extract from a program. Today, it is not possible to analyze any sequential program purely automatically. Several approaches are possible to help the users to express the potential parallelism. The third chapter is devoted to some new programming paradigms that have been invented: extensions of existing languages can deal with parallelism, data-parallel languages concentrate on parallel data structures and library-based approaches may be useful for classical numerical applications.

Parallel systems are composed of processors, hierarchy of memories and interconnection networks. The evolution of these components has been very important and they are still improved, but the at different speeds. The fourth chapter focuses on hardware issues of these three directions. The evolution of technology continues and makes the processors always more powerful. Even if the performance of the memory is still increasing, the gap between processors and memory grows up. Today, several levels of cache are required to fill it. Finally, the connection between computational units is done by buses if their number is small, or by interconnection networks in the other case. This chapter details all the aspects concerned with the memory management and the interaction between processors, memory and interconnection mechanisms.

Most programmers would like to have only the view of one single memory space. Sofware is in charge of all the movements of data. Operating systems are the intermediate layer between hardware and applications. Chapter V surveys the history of Operating Systems for parallel systems. During the years of development of parallel and distributed systems, the variety of operating systems was as large as the variety of hardware installations. Today, they are converging to a set of dominating configurations based on symmetric multiprocessor systems (SMP). They are popular because the users do not have to change considerably their applications while running them in parallel. However, looking for a better performance requires more efforts. NORMA systems (*no remote memory access*) allow to run efficiently message-passing parallel programs. Finally, the scalabity issues are discussed from the point of view of Operating Systems.

Sophisticated software tools are needed for managing efficiently the resources of parallel and distributed systems. Chapter VI explores the scheduling issues, which correspond to an allocation of the resources of the system (mainly the processors) over time to perform tasks which are parts of processes. The basic definitions and results are recalled and the principal scheduling models are presented, namely, the multiprocessor tasks, the classical delay model for handling explicitly the communications and the divisible task model.

The development of large actual parallel and distributed applications involves high-level infrastructure including performance evaluation, debuging, runtime program control and program interaction. The current state of research and practical tools are discussed in Chapter VII from the performance evaluation perspective. Then, the four challenges of modeling, observability, diagnostic and perturbation, are studied.

The storage capacity in computers increased considerably during the last decade. Today, large storages are available at low prices on most computers, and in particular in parallel and distributed systems. Many new applications like data warehousing or data mining requiring large storage can be met. Multimedia is a fast growing area which also needs large storage capacity. Chapter VIII presents the state-of-the-art in the use of parallel I-O in the area of database systems and multimedia servers. It describes the basic disk performance characteristics and discusses the main performance metrics. Problems like data partioning, scheduling, reliability and fault-tolerance, are studied.

The recent development of the technology together with advances in parallel and distributed operating systems allow to envisage network computing as a promising support for developing large actual applications. Moreover, the low cost of the basic components and the availability of public domain software should be an important factor in the future. Networking is a real revolution in the way we think and solve the problems. Chapter IX describes the technological issues of networking: fast ethernet, FDDI, ATM, fiber channels and HIPPI. Some performance evaluations of network interfaces are introduced through particular cases in existing parallel systems. Then, the question of an access to networks with a specific quality of service is studied with various communication protocols.

Chapter X is an introduction to the parallel environment for scientific computing. From the beginning, most of the research in the domain of parallel processing was concerned with scientific and numerical computing. This chapter discusses the design of modern numerical algebra algorithms which are the basic bulk of most scientific programs. Efficient environments for parallel and distributed systems are obtained by the combination of three components, namely, well-designed software libraries for numercial analysis, software tools for optimized versions of basic numerical kernels tuned for specific parallel systems, and software tools that unify all separate components into efficient and easy to use services. This chapter recalls the rich history of this field and stresses new directions including the management of heterogeneous systems.

The last two chapters are dedicated to applications of parallel and distributed systems.

A high-performance implementation of a code for solving Schrödinger equation in Molecular Science is reported in the Chapter XI. The background in quantum chemistry and modeling of this problem are described in order to allow the reader to follow the parallelization process. The most natural and efficient way to obtain good performance is to use a heterogeneous parallel system composed of scalar and vector systems. The experiments show how a parallel approach was used to obtain the solution with a better accuracy for larger problems.

The final chapter introduces the domain of multimedia which becomes more and more popular. First, MPEG, the most important standard in audio and video, is presented. Then, some high-level aspects of networking are discussed. Corba and Java are discussed as the most acredited software environments for developing multimedia applications in heterogeneous systems. Finally, some representative applications are detailed, like video on demand or multimedia conferences.

12   Brigitte Plateau and Denis Trystram

References

[CT95]   Cosnard, M., Trystram, D., *Parallel Algorithms and Architectures*, International Thomson Computer Press, 1995.
[DDS+98]   Dongarra, J.J., Duff, I.S., Sorensen, D.C., van der Vorst, H.A., *Numerical Linear Algebra for High-Performance Computers*, Series: Software-Environments-Tools, SIAM, 1998.
[F95]   Foster, I., *Designing and Building Parallel Programs*, Addison-Wesley, 1995.
[H93]   Hwang, K., *Advanced Computer Architecture: Parallelism, Scalability, Programmability*, Mc Graw-Hill, 1993.
[KGG+94]   Kumar, V., Grama, A., Gupta, A., Karypis, G., *Introduction to Parallel Computing: Design and Analysis of Algorithms*, Benjamin/Cummings, 1994.
[T92]   Thomson Leighton, F., *Introduction to Parallel Algorithms and Architectures: Arrays - Trees - Hypercubes*, Morgan Kaufmann Publishers, 1992.
[TW91]   Trew, A., Wilson, G., *Past, Present Parallel: A Survey of Available Parallel Computing Systems*, Springer-Verlag, 1991.

II. The Design of Efficient Parallel Algorithms

Selim G. Akl

Queen's University, Canada

Summary. This chapter serves as an introduction to the study of parallel algorithms, in particular how they differ from conventional algorithms, how they are designed, and how they are analyzed to evaluate their speed and cost.

1. Introduction

The design and analysis of parallel algorithms is a cornerstone of parallel computation. Fast parallel algorithms are necessary if a significant reduction in running time is to be achieved when solving computationally demanding problems on parallel computers. This chapter serves as an introduction to the study of parallel algorithms, in particular how they differ from conventional algorithms, how they are designed, and how they are analyzed to evaluate their speed and cost.

One of the most striking differences between the conventional and parallel approaches to computing is the wide diversity of parallel models of computation available. We explore this rich landscape and demonstrate how it leads to a variety of new computing paradigms. Four case studies are used for illustration. In each case, a sequence of increasingly more involved algorithms is developed in order to show either how a problem can be solved on several different models or how efficient solutions to fundamental problems can be used to address more difficult ones.

The chapter is organized as follows. Section 2 is devoted to explaining the concepts of parallel model of computation and parallel algorithm and providing a brief introduction to the analysis of parallel algorithms. The problems of sorting, matrix multiplication, computing the convex hull, and manipulating pointer-based data structures, are the subject of Sections 3 – 6, along with variations and applications. In Section 7 we discuss current trends and future directions, including alternative computational models and the notion of synergy in parallel computation.

2. Parallel Models and Algorithms

Today's conventional computers comprise a single *processor*. This processor is in charge of executing *one by one* the instructions of a *program* it stores. Each instruction may be an *arithmetic* or *logical operation* on values retrieved from *memory*, or may require the *input* or *output* of data. Because the instructions are performed in sequence, conventional computers are said to be *sequential*. A *parallel computer*, by contrast, consists of several processors. Each processor is of the same type as used on a sequential computer. It has its program and executes its instructions in sequence. Thus, the processors cooperate in solving a computational problem by executing several instructions simultaneously, that is, *in parallel*.

Given that a parallel computer has several processors, it is natural to pose the following questions: How are these computers organized? How are their programs designed? How is their performance measured? Obtaining answers to these questions is greatly simplified by introducing the notions of *parallel model of computation*, *parallel algorithm*, and *mathematical analysis of algorithms*.

2.1 What Is a Parallel Model?

A *parallel model of computation* is an abstract description of a parallel computer. It ignores irrelevant implementation details and attempts to capture the most important features. As such, it allows us to focus on the issues that matter most when designing parallel solutions to computational problems. It also renders the analysis of such solutions simpler and more useful.

There are many different ways to organize the processors on a parallel computer. Consequently, a multitude of parallel models exist. One simple way to classify these models is to use two general families, namely, *shared-memory* models and *interconnection-network* models.

Shared Memory.   In this family of parallel models of computation, the processors share a common memory from which they can all read and to which they can all write. The processors treat the shared memory as a bulletin board. They use it to receive data, exchange information, and deposit the results of their computations. We now describe one example of a model in this family.

Example 2.1. The *Parallel Random Access Machine* (PRAM), illustrated in Fig. 2.1, consists of N identical processors, P_1, P_2, ..., P_N, where $N \geq 2$, sharing a memory of M locations, $U_1, U_2, \ldots, U_M$, where $M \geq 1$. (Typically, $M > N$.) Each processor has a small local memory (i.e., a fixed number of *registers*) and circuitry to allow the execution of arithmetic and logical operations on data held by the registers. Each memory location and each processor register can store a datum of constant size. The processors gain access to the memory locations by means of a *memory access unit* (MAU). This unit may be implemented as a *combinational circuit* (a description of which is deferred until Section 7.2).

The processors operate *synchronously* and execute the same sequence of instructions on different data. Each step of a PRAM computation consists of three phases (executed in the following order):

1. A reading phase in which each processor (if so required) copies a datum from a memory location into one of its registers;
2. A computing phase in which each processor (if so required) performs an arithmetic or logical operation on data stored in its registers;
3. A writing phase in which each processor (if so required) copies a datum from one of its registers into a shared memory location.

During the reading phase any number of processors can gain access to the same memory location, if so desired. In one extreme situation each of the N processors reads from a distinct memory location. In another, all N processors read from the same memory location. This is also true of the writing phase, except that one must specify what ends up in a memory location when two or more processors are writing into it. Depending on the problem

MEMORY
LOCATIONS

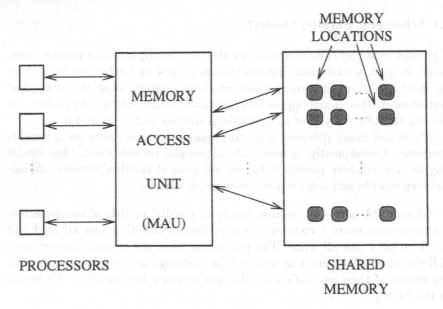

MEMORY

ACCESS

UNIT

(MAU)

PROCESSORS   SHARED
                                              MEMORY

Fig. 2.1. A parallel random access machine.

being solved, we may specify, for instance, that the *sum* of the values written
by the processors is stored, or their *minimum*, or one of the values selected
arbitrarily, and so on.

It is important to note that the processors use the shared memory to
communicate with each other. Suppose that processor P_i wishes to send a
datum d to processor P_j. During the writing phase of a step, P_i writes d in
a location U_k known to P_j. Processor P_j then reads d from U_k during the
reading phase of the following step. □

Interconnection Network.   A model in this family consists of N processors, $P_1, P_2, \ldots, P_N$, where $N \geq 2$, forming a connected network. Certain
pairs of processors are directly connected by a two-way communication link.
Those processors to which P_i is directly connected, $1 \leq i \leq N$, are called P_i's
neighbors. There is no shared memory: M locations are distributed among
the processors. Thus, each processor has a local memory of M/N locations.
When two processors P_i and P_j wish to communicate they do so by *exchanging messages*. If P_i and P_j are neighbors, they use the link between them to
send and receive messages; otherwise, the messages travel over a sequence of
links through other processors. All processors execute the same sequence of
instructions on different data. Two models in this family are distinguished
from one other by the subset of processor pairs that are directly connected.

Example 2.2. For some integer $m \geq 2$, a *binary tree* interconnection network
consists of $N = 2^m - 1$ processors connected in the shape of a complete binary

tree with 2^{m-1} leaves. The tree has m levels, numbered 0 to $m-1$, with the root at level $m-1$ and the leaves at level 0, as shown in Fig. 2.2 for $m = 4$. Each processor at level ℓ, $0 < \ell < m-1$, is connected to three neighbors: one *parent* at level $\ell + 1$ and two children at level $\ell - 1$. The root has two children and no parent while each leaf has a parent and no children. The processor indices go from 1 to N from top to bottom in the tree and from left to right on each level, such that on level ℓ, $0 \leq \ell \leq m-1$, the processors are numbered from $2^{m-\ell-1}$ to $2^{m-\ell} - 1$. $\square$

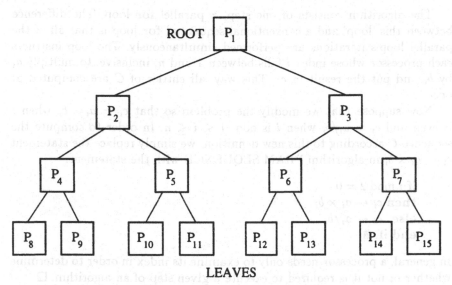

Fig. 2.2. A binary tree of processors.

2.2 What Is a Parallel Algorithm?

A *parallel algorithm* is a method for solving a computational problem on a parallel model of computation. It allows the problem to be broken into smaller parts that are solved simultaneously. Most computer scientists are familiar with *sequential algorithms*, that is, algorithms for solving problems in a sequential fashion, one step at a time. This is not surprising since these algorithms have been around for quite a long time. In order to understand parallel algorithms, however, a new way of thinking is required.

Example 2.3. Suppose that we wish to construct a sequence of numbers $C = (c_1, c_2, \ldots, c_n)$ from two given sequences of numbers $A = (a_1, a_2, \ldots, a_n)$ and $B = (b_1, b_2, \ldots, b_n)$, such that $c_i = a_i \times b_i$, for $1 \leq i \leq n$. Also, let a PRAM with n processors $P_1, P_2, \ldots, P_n$ and a shared memory with at least

$3n$ memory locations be available. The two sequences A and B are initially stored in the shared memory, one number per location. The following parallel algorithm computes the sequence C and stores it, one number per location, in the shared memory:

Algorithm PRAM SEQUENCE

    for $i = 1$ **to** n **do in parallel**
        $c_i \leftarrow a_i \times b_i$
    end for. ∎

The algorithm consists of one step, a parallel **for** loop. The difference between this 'loop' and a conventional sequential **for** loop is that all of the parallel loop's iterations are performed simultaneously. The loop instructs each processor whose index i falls between 1 and n, inclusive, to multiply a_i by b_i and put the result in c_i. This way, all entries of C are computed at once.

Now suppose that we modify the problem so that $c_i = a_i \times b_i$ when i is even and $c_i = a_i/b_i$ when i is odd, $1 \leq i \leq n$. In order to compute the sequence C according to this new definition, we simply replace the statement $c_i \leftarrow a_i \times b_i$ in algorithm PRAM SEQUENCE with the statement:

    if $i \bmod 2 = 0$
    then $c_i \leftarrow a_i \times b_i$
    else $c_i \leftarrow a_i/b_i$
    end if. ∎

In general, a processor needs only to examine its index in order to determine whether or not it is required to execute a given step of an algorithm. □

Example 2.4. A sequence $X = (x_1, x_2, \ldots, x_n)$ of numbers is given, where $n = 2^{m-1}$, for some integer $m \geq 2$. It is required to compute the sum $S = x_1 + x_2 + \cdots + x_n$ of this sequence. Here, we assume that a binary tree is available with $2n - 1$ processors. Each of the processors holds a number y_j, $1 \leq j \leq 2n - 1$. For the nonleaf processors P_i, $1 \leq i \leq n - 1$, y_i is initialized to 0. These y_i will serve to store intermediate results during the course of the computation. For leaf P_{n+i-1}, $y_{n+i-1} = x_i$, $1 \leq i \leq n$. In other words, the sequence X is initially stored one number per leaf processor. The following algorithm computes S and stores it in the root processor:

Algorithm TREE SUM

    for $\ell = 1$ **to** $m - 1$ **do**
        for $j = 2^{m-\ell-1}$ **to** $2^{m-\ell}$ **do in parallel**
            $y_j \leftarrow y_{2j} + y_{2j+1}$
        end for
    end for. ∎

The outer (sequential) **for** loop is executed once per level, for levels 1 to $m-1$ of the tree. For each level, all processors on that level execute the inner (parallel) **for** loop simultaneously, with each processor replacing the number it holds with the sum of the numbers held by its children. In this way, the global sum is computed by the root in the final iteration; in other words, $y_1 = S$.

The process implemented by algorithm TREE SUM is a *halving* process: After each iteration of the outer **for** loop, the number of values to be added up is one half of the number before the iteration. Also, the data move up the tree from the leaves to the root. In a similar way, a *doubling* process can be executed, with the data moving from the root to the leaves. Suppose that the root processor holds a value that it wishes to make known to all of the remaining processors. It sends that value to its two children, who in turn send it to their respective children, and so on until the value is received by the leaf processors. □

2.3 How Do We Analyze Parallel Algorithms?

There are several criteria that one can use in order to evaluate the quality of a parallel algorithm. In this chapter we focus on three such criteria, namely, running time, number of processors, and cost. The presentation is simplified by the use of the following notations. Let $f(n)$, $g(n)$, and $h(n)$ be functions from the positive integers to the positive reals. Then

1. The function $f(n)$ is said to be *of order at least* $g(n)$, denoted $\Omega(g(n))$, if there are positive constants k_1 and n_1 such that $f(n) \geq k_1 g(n)$ for all $n \geq n_1$.
2. The function $f(n)$ is said to be *of order at most* $h(n)$, denoted $O(h(n))$, if there are positive constants k_2 and n_2 such that $f(n) \leq k_2 h(n)$ for all $n \geq n_2$.

The Ω and O notations allow us to focus on the *asymptotic* behavior of a function $f(n)$, that is, its value *in the limit* as n grows without bound. To say that $f(n)$ is $\Omega(g(n))$ is to say that, for large values of n, $f(n)$ is bounded from below by $g(n)$. Similarly, to say that $f(n)$ is $O(h(n))$ is to say that, for large values of n, $f(n)$ is bounded from above by $h(n)$. This simplifies our analyses a great deal. Thus, for example, if $f(n) = 3.5n^3 + 12n^{2.7} + 7.4n + 185$, we can say that $f(n)$ is of order n^3 and write either $f(n) = O(n^3)$, or $f(n) = \Omega(n^3)$, thereby ignoring constant factors and lower order terms. Note that in the special case where $f(n)$ is itself a constant, for example, $f(n) = 132$, we write $f(n) = O(1)$.

Running Time.   The primary reason for designing a parallel algorithm is to use it (once implemented as a parallel program on a parallel computer) so that a computational task can be completed quickly. It is therefore natural for running time to be taken as an indicator of the goodness of a parallel algorithm.

A useful way of estimating what an algorithm's running time would be in practice is provided by mathematical analysis. Let a *time unit* be defined as the time required by a typical processor to execute a basic arithmetic or logical operation (such as addition, multiplication, AND, OR, and so on), to gain access to memory for reading or writing a datum (of constant size), or to route a datum (of constant size) to a neighbor. We measure a parallel algorithm's running time by counting the number of time units elapsed from the moment the algorithm begins execution until it terminates. We note here that in a parallel algorithm several basic operations are executed in one time unit. In fact, the number of such operations may be equal to the number of processors used by the algorithm, if all processors are active during that time unit.

The running time of an algorithm is intimately related to the *size* of the problem it is meant to solve, that is, the number of (constant-size) inputs and outputs. It is typical that the number of time units elapsed during the execution of a parallel algorithm is a function of the size of the problem. Therefore, we use $t(n)$ to express the running time of an algorithm solving a problem of size n.

A good appreciation of the speed of a parallel algorithm is obtained by comparing it to the best sequential solution. The *speedup* achieved by a parallel algorithm when solving a computational problem is equal to the ratio of two running times—that of the best possible (or best known) sequential solution divided by that of the parallel algorithm. The higher is the ratio, the better is the parallel algorithm.

Example 2.5. In Example 2.3, algorithm PRAM SEQUENCE computes the sequence C by having each processor P_i, $1 \leq i \leq n$, read two values (a_i and b_i), multiply them, and write the result in c_i. This requires a constant number of time units. Therefore, $t(n) = O(1)$. Sequentially, the best possible solution requires n iterations and runs in $O(n)$ time. Hence, the speedup is $O(n)$. $\square$

Example 2.6. In Example 2.4, algorithm TREE SUM computes the sum of n numbers by performing $m-1$ iterations, one for each level of the tree (above the leaf level). Each iteration comprises a parallel **for** loop consisting of a routing operation, a multiplication, and an assignment, and thus requiring a constant number of time units. Therefore, the total number of time units is a constant multiple of $m - 1$. Since $m - 1 = \log n$, we have $t(n) = O(\log n)$.

Another way to see this is to note that the algorithm operates by forming $n/2$ pairs and adding up the numbers in each pair, then again pairing and adding up the results, and so on until the final sum is obtained. Since we began with n inputs, the number of iterations required is $\log n$.

Sequentially, the sum requires $n - 1$ constant-time iterations to be computed and, therefore, the sequential solution runs in $O(n)$ time. In this case, the speedup is $O(n/\log n)$. □

A parallel algorithm for solving a given problem on a particular model of computation is said to be *time optimal* if its running time matches (up to a constant factor) a lower bound on the time required to solve the problem on that model. For example, algorithm TREE SUM is time optimal since its running time is of $O(\log n)$ and any algorithm for adding n numbers stored in the leaves of a binary tree and producing the sum from the root must require $\Omega(\log n)$ time.

Number of processors.   Mostly for economic reasons, the number of processors required by a parallel algorithm is an important consideration. Suppose that two algorithms, designed to solve a certain problem on the same model of computation, have identical running times. If one of the two algorithms needs fewer processors, it is less expensive to run and hence this algorithm is the preferred one. The number of processors is usually expressed as a function of the size of the problem being solved. For a problem of size n, the number of processors is given as $p(n)$.

Example 2.7. In Example 2.3, algorithm PRAM SEQUENCE uses n processors; thus, $p(n) = n$. □

Example 2.8. In Example 2.4, algorithm TREE SUM uses $2n - 1$ processors; thus, $p(n) = 2n - 1$. □

The number of processors often allows us to derive a lower bound on the running time of any parallel algorithm for solving a given problem, independently of the model of computation. Suppose that a lower bound of $\Omega(f(n))$ on the number of operations required to solve a problem of size n is known. Then any algorithm for solving that problem in parallel using n processors must require $\Omega(f(n)/n)$ time. For example, a lower bound on the number of operations required to multiply two $n \times n$ matrices is $\Omega(n^2)$. Therefore, any parallel algorithm for multiplying two $n \times n$ matrices using n processors must require $\Omega(n)$ time.

The notion of *slowdown* (by contrast with speedup) expresses the *increase* in running time when the number of processors *decreases*. Specifically, if an algorithm runs in time t_p using p processors and in time t_q using q processors, where $q < p$, the slowdown is equal to t_q/t_p.

Cost.   The cost of a parallel algorithm is an upper bound on the total number of basic operations executed collectively by the processors. If a parallel algorithm solves a problem of size n in $t(n)$ time units with $p(n)$ processors, then its cost is given by $c(n) = p(n) \times t(n)$. Cost is useful in assessing how expensive it is to run a parallel algorithm. More importantly, this measure is often used for comparison purposes with a sequential solution. The *efficiency* of a parallel algorithm for a given problem is the ratio defined as follows: The running time of the best (possible or known) sequential solution to the problem divided by the cost of the parallel algorithm. The larger is the efficiency, the better is the parallel algorithm.

Example 2.9. In Example 2.3, algorithm PRAM SEQUENCE has a cost of $c(n) = p(n) \times t(n) = n \times O(1) = O(n)$. Since the best possible sequential solution runs in $O(n)$ time, the algorithm's efficiency is $O(1)$. □

Example 2.10. In Example 2.4, algorithm TREE SUM has a cost of $c(n) = p(n) \times t(n) = (2n-1) \times O(\log n) = O(n \log n)$. The best sequential algorithm runs in $O(n)$ time; the algorithm's efficiency in this case is $O(1/\log n)$.

The efficiency can be improved by modifying the algorithm to use fewer processors as follows. Let $q = \log n$ and $r = n/q$. For ease of presentation, we assume that $r = 2^v$, for some integer $v \geq 1$. A tree with $2r - 1$ processors, of which r are leaves, is available. Each processor P_i, $1 \leq i \leq 2r - 1$, holds a value y_i. All y_i, $1 \leq i \leq 2r - 1$, are initially equal to 0. The input sequence X is presented to the tree with its entries organized as a table with q rows and r columns:

$$
\begin{array}{cccc}
x_1 & x_2 & \cdots & x_r \\
x_{r+1} & x_{r+2} & \cdots & x_{2r} \\
& & \vdots & \\
x_{(q-1)r+1} & x_{(q-1)r+2} & \cdots & x_{qr}.
\end{array}
$$

The new algorithm consists of two phases. The first phase has q iterations: During the jth iteration, $1 \leq j \leq q$, leaf processor P_{r+k-1}, $1 \leq k \leq r$, reads $x_{(j-1)r+k}$ and adds it to y_{r+k-1}. The second phase is simply an application of algorithm TREE SUM with $m = v + 1$.

The first phase runs in $O(q)$, that is, $O(\log n)$ time. The second phase requires $O(v) = O(\log(n/\log n)) = O(\log n)$ time. The overall running time is therefore $t(n) = O(\log n)$. Since the number of processors used is $2r - 1$, we have $p(n) = O(n/\log n)$, for a cost of $c(n) = O(n)$. As a result, the new algorithm's efficiency is $O(1)$. □

When the cost of a parallel algorithm for a given problem matches (up to a constant factor) a lower bound on the number of operations required to solve that problem, the parallel algorithm is said to be *cost optimal*. For example, if the cost of a parallel algorithm for sorting a sequence of n numbers is $O(n \log n)$, then that algorithm is cost optimal in view of the $\Omega(n \log n)$ lower bound on the number of operations required to sort.

3. Sorting

We begin our study of the design and analysis of parallel algorithms by considering what is perhaps the most typical of problems in computer science,

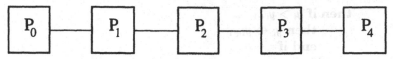

Fig. 3.1. A linear array of processors.

namely, the problem of sorting a sequence of numbers in nondecreasing order. Specifically, given a sequence of numbers $(x_0, x_1, \ldots, x_{N-1})$ listed in arbitrary order, it is required to rearrange these same numbers into a new sequence $(y_0, y_1, \ldots, y_{N-1})$ in which $y_0 \le y_1 \le \cdots \le y_{N-1}$. Note here that if $x_i = x_j$ in the given sequence, then x_i precedes x_j in the sorted sequence if and only if $i < j$. Sequentially, a number of algorithms exist for solving the problem in $O(N \log N)$ time, and this is optimal. In this section, we demonstrate how the problem is solved on various models of parallel computation in the interconnection-network family. These models are the linear array, the mesh, the multidimensional array, the hypercube, and the star. In each case we will assume that there are as many processors on the model as there are numbers to be sorted. It is important to note here that, in order to fully define the problem of sorting, an indexing of the processors must be specified such that, when the computation terminates, P_i holds y_i, for $0 \le i \le N - 1$. In other words, the set of numbers has been sorted once the smallest number of the set resides in the 'first' processor, the second smallest number of the set resides in the 'second' processor, and so on.

3.1 Linear Array

The *linear array* interconnection network is arguably the simplest of all models of parallel computation. It consists of N processors $P_0, P_1, \ldots, P_{N-1}$, placed side by side in a one-dimensional arrangement and indexed from left to right. The processors are interconnected to form a linear array such that, for $1 \le i \le N - 2$, each processor P_i is connected by a two-way communication link to each of P_{i-1} and P_{i+1}, and no other connections are present. This is illustrated in Fig. 3.1 for $N = 5$.

The sequence $(x_0, x_1, \ldots, x_{N-1})$ is sorted on a linear array of N processors as follows. We begin by storing each of the numbers in a distinct processor. Thus, initially, P_i holds x_i and sets $y_i = x_i$, for $0 \le i \le N - 1$. Now, the processors repeatedly perform an operation known as a 'comparison-exchange', whereby y_i is compared to y_{i+1} with the smaller of the two numbers ending up in P_i and the larger in P_{i+1}. The algorithm is given next.

Algorithm LINEAR ARRAY SORT

    for $j = 0$ **to** $N - 1$ **do**
        for $i = 0$ **to** $n - 2$ **do in parallel**
            if $i \bmod 2 = j \bmod 2$

> **then if** $y_i > y_{i+1}$
> > **then** $y_i \leftrightarrow y_{i+1}$
> > **end if**
> **end if**
> **end for**
> **end for.** ∎

It can be shown that this algorithm sorts correctly in N steps, that is, $O(N)$ time. The proof is based on the observation that the algorithm is *oblivious*, that is, the sequence of comparisons it performs is predetermined. Thus, the algorithm's behavior and the number of iterations it requires are not affected by the actual set of numbers to be sorted. This property allows the proof of correctness to use the 0-1 principle: If it can be shown that the algorithm correctly sorts any sequence of 0s and 1s, it will follow that the algorithm correctly sorts any sequence of numbers.

A running time of $O(N)$ for sorting n numbers in parallel is not too impressive, affording a meager speedup of $O(\log N)$ over an optimal sequential solution. However, two points are worth making here:

1. The running time achieved by algorithm LINEAR ARRAY SORT is the best that can be accomplished on the linear array. To see this note that a lower bound of $\Omega(N)$ on the time required to sort N numbers on a linear array with N processors is established as follows: If the largest number in the sequence to be sorted is initially stored in P_0, it needs $N - 1$ steps to travel to its final destination in P_{N-1}.

2. More importantly, algorithm LINEAR ARRAY SORT will play an important role in the design of algorithms for other models as shown in what follows.

3.2 Mesh

In an interconnection network, the *distance* between two processors P_i and P_j is the number of links on the shortest path from P_i to P_j. The *diameter* of the network is the length of the longest distance among all distances between pairs of processors in that network. Since processors need to communicate among themselves, and since the time for a message to go from one processor to another depends on the distance separating them, a network with a small diameter is better than one with a large diameter.

One limitation of the linear array is its large diameter. As we saw in Section 3.1, in an array with N processors, $N - 1$ steps are needed to transfer a datum from the leftmost to the rightmost processor. We therefore seek another network with a smaller diameter to solve the sorting problem.

A natural extension of the linear array is the two-dimensional array or *mesh*. Here, N processors $P_0, P_1, \ldots, P_{N-1}$ are arranged into an $m \times n$ array, of m rows and n columns, where $N = m \times n$, as shown in Fig. 3.2 for $m = 4$ and $n = 5$.

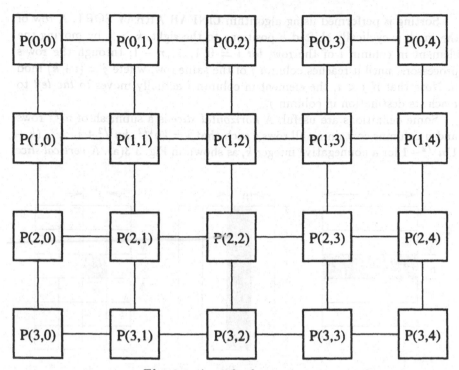

Fig. 3.2. A mesh of processors.

The processor in row j and column k is denoted by $P(j,k)$, where $0 \le j \le m - 1$ and $0 \le k \le n - 1$. A two-way communication line links $P(j,k)$ to its neighbors $P(j+1,k)$, $P(j-1,k)$, $P(j,k+1)$, and $P(j,k-1)$. Processors on the boundary rows and columns have fewer than four neighbors and, hence, fewer connections.

While retaining essentially the same simplicity as the linear array, the mesh offers a significantly smaller diameter of $m + n - 2$ (i.e., the number of links on the shortest path from the processor in the top left corner to the processor in the bottom right corner). When $m = n = N^{1/2}$, the diameter is $2N^{1/2} - 2$.

For the purpose of sorting the sequence of numbers $(x_0, x_1, \ldots, x_{N-1})$, the N processors are indexed in *row-major* order, that is, processor P_i is placed in row j and column k of the two-dimensional array, where $i = jn + k$ for $0 \le i \le N - 1$, $0 \le j \le m - 1$, and $0 \le k \le n - 1$. Initially, P_i holds x_i, for $0 \le i \le N - 1$. Since y_i will be held by P_i, for $0 \le i \le N - 1$, the sorted sequence will be arranged in row-major order.

The sorting algorithm consists of two operations on the rows and columns of the mesh:

1. Sorting a row or a column (or part thereof)
2. Cyclically shifting a row (or part thereof).

Sorting is performed using algorithm LINEAR ARRAY SORT. A row of the mesh is cyclically shifted k positions to the right, $k \geq 1$, by moving the element in column i of the row, for $i = 0, 1, \ldots, n - 1$, through the row's processors, until it reaches column j of the same row, where $j = (i + k) \bmod n$. Note that if $j < i$, the element in column i actually moves *to the left* to reach its destination in column j.

Some definitions are useful. A *horizontal slice* is a submesh of $n^{1/2}$ rows and n columns containing all rows i such that $i = kn^{1/2}, kn^{1/2} + 1, \ldots, (k + 1)n^{1/2} - 1$ for a nonnegative integer k, as shown in Fig. 3.3(a). A *vertical slice*

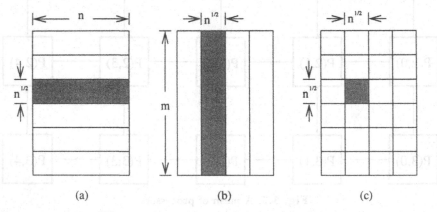

(a)   (b)   (c)

Fig. 3.3. Dividing a mesh into submeshes.

is a submesh of m rows and $n^{1/2}$ columns containing all columns j such that $j = ln^{1/2}, ln^{1/2} + 1, \ldots, (l + 1)n^{1/2} - 1$ for a nonnegative integer l, as shown in Fig. 3.3(b). A *block* is a submesh of $n^{1/2}$ rows and $n^{1/2}$ columns consisting of all processors $P(i, j)$ such that $i = kn^{1/2}, kn^{1/2} + 1, \ldots, (k + 1)n^{1/2} - 1$ and $j = ln^{1/2}, ln^{1/2} + 1, \ldots, (l + 1)n^{1/2} - 1$, for nonnegative integers k and l, as shown in Fig. 3.3(c).

The algorithm is as follows:

Algorithm MESH SORT

Step 1: for all vertical slices **do in parallel**
        (1.1) Sort each column
        (1.2) **for** $i = 1$ **to** n **do in parallel**
            Cyclically shift row i by $i \bmod n^{1/2}$ positions to the right
            end for
        (1.3) Sort each column
        end for
Step 2: (2.1) **for** $i = 1$ **to** n **do in parallel**
            Cyclically shift row i by $in^{1/2} \bmod n$ positions to the right
            end for

(2.2) Sort each column of the mesh

Step 3: for all horizontal slices **do in parallel**

(3.1) Sort each column

(3.2) **for** $i = 1$ **to** n **do in parallel**

Cyclically shift row i by $i \bmod n^{1/2}$ positions to the right

end for

(3.3) Sort each column

end for

Step 4: (4.1) **for** $i = 1$ **to** n **do in parallel**

Cyclically shift row i by $in^{1/2} \bmod n$ positions to the right

end for

(4.2) Sort each column of the mesh

Step 5: for $k = 1$ **to** 3 **do**

(5.1) **for** $i = 1$ **to** n **do in parallel**

if $i \bmod 2 = 0$

then sort row i from left to right

else sort row i from right to left

end if

end for

(5.2) Sort each column

end for

Step 6: for $i = 1$ **to** n **do in parallel**

Sort row i

end for. ■

Note that in Step 4 each horizontal slice is treated as an $n \times n^{1/2}$ mesh. The algorithm is clearly oblivious and the 0-1 principle can be used to show that it sorts correctly. It is also immediate that the running time is $O(n+m)$. To see that this time is the best possible on the mesh, suppose that $P(0,0)$ initially holds the largest number in the sequence to be sorted. When the sequence is finally sorted, this number must occupy $P(m-1, n-1)$. The shortest path from $P(0,0)$ to $P(m-1, n-1)$ consists of $(m-1)+(n-1)$ links to be traversed, thus establishing an $\Omega(m+n)$ lower bound on the number of elementary operations required to sort a sequence of mn elements on an $m \times n$ mesh. To derive the algorithm's cost, assume for simplicity that $m = n = N^{1/2}$. Therefore, $p(N) = N$ and $t(N) = O(N^{1/2})$, for a cost of $c(N) = O(N^{3/2})$, which is not optimal in view of the $O(N \log N)$ elementary operations sufficient for sorting sequentially.

3.3 Multidimensional Array

A natural extension of the mesh model is to arrange $N = n_1 n_2 \cdots n_d$ processors in a d-dimensional $n_1 \times n_2 \times \cdots \times n_d$ array, where $d \geq 3$ and $n_i \geq 2$, for $1 \leq i \leq d$. This is illustrated in Fig. 3.4 for $d = 3$, $n_1 = 2$, $n_2 = 3$, and

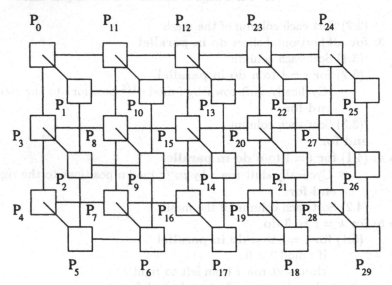

Fig. 3.4. A 3-dimensional array.

$n_3 = 5$. Each position of the d-dimensional array has coordinates $I(1)$, $I(2)$, ..., $I(d)$, where $1 \leq I(k) \leq n_k$.

Example 3.1. When $d = 3$, $n_1 = 2$, $n_2 = 3$, and $n_3 = 5$, the coordinates of the 30 positions of the $2 \times 3 \times 5$ array are as follows:

1,1,1	2,1,1	1,1,2	2,1,2	1,1,3	2,1,3	1,1,4	2,1,4	1,1,5	2,1,5
1,2,1	2,2,1	1,2,2	2,2,2	1,2,3	2,2,3	1,2,4	2,2,4	1,2,5	2,2,5
1,3,1	2,3,1	1,3,2	2,3,2	1,3,3	2,3,3	1,3,4	2,3,4	1,3,5	2,3,5. □

In dimension k, where $1 \leq k \leq d$, there are

$$n_1 \times n_2 \times \cdots \times n_{k-1} \times n_{k+1} \times \cdots \times n_d$$

(i.e., N/n_k) groups of n_k consecutive positions. The positions in each group have the same

$$I(1), I(2), \ldots, I(k-1), I(k+1), I(k+2), \ldots, I(d)$$

coordinates (in other words, they differ only in coordinate $I(k)$, with the first in the group having $I(k) = 1$, the second $I(k) = 2$, and the last $I(k) = n_k$). All the processors in a group are connected to form a linear array.

The processors are indexed in *snakelike order by dimension*. The following recursive function $snake_i$ maps the coordinates $I(1), I(2), \ldots, I(d)$ of each position of the d-dimensional $n_1 \times n_2 \times \cdots \times n_d$ array into a unique integer in the set $\{1, 2, \ldots, N\}$ according to snakelike order by dimension: $snake_1(I(1)) = I(1)$, for $1 \leq I(1) \leq n_1$, and $snake_k(I(1), I(2), \ldots, I(k)) =$

$n_1 n_2 \cdots n_{k-1}(I(k) - 1) + K$, where $K = snake_{k-1}(I(1), I(2), \ldots, I(k-1))$ if $I(k)$ is odd, and $K = n_1 n_2 \cdots n_{k-1} + 1 - snake_{k-1}(I(1), I(2), \ldots, I(k-1))$ otherwise, for $2 \leq k \leq d$, $1 \leq I(j) \leq n_j$, and $1 \leq j \leq k$. Now the index i of processor P_i, where $0 \leq i \leq N - 1$, occupying the position whose coordinates are $I(1), I(2), \ldots, I(d)$, is thus obtained from $i = snake_d(I(1), I(2), \ldots, I(d)) - 1$.

In order to sort the sequence $(x_0, x_1, \ldots, x_{N-1})$ on this array, we store x_i in P_i initially, for $0 \leq i \leq N - 1$. When the algorithm terminates, P_i holds element y_i of the sorted sequence, for $0 \leq i \leq N-1$. The algorithm consists of a number of iterations. During an iteration, the numbers are sorted either in the forward or reverse direction along each of the d dimensions in turn. Here, "sorting in the forward (reverse) direction in dimension k" means sorting the numbers in nondecreasing (nonincreasing) order from the processor with $I(k) = 1$ to the processor with $I(k) = n_k$. This sorting is performed using algorithm LINEAR ARRAY SORT.

Henceforth, we refer to each group of consecutive positions in a given dimension of the multidimensional array, as a 'row'. Thus, a row in dimension k consists of n_k consecutive positions. Let $D(k) = \sum_{r=k+1}^{d}(I(r) - 1)$, for $k = 1, 2, \ldots, d$, where the empty sum (when $k = d$) is equal to 0 by definition, and let $M = \sum_{k=2}^{d} \lceil \log n_k \rceil$. The algorithm is as follows:

Algorithm MULTIDIMENSIONAL ARRAY SIMPLE SORT

    for $i = 1$ to M **do**
      for $k = 1$ to d **do**
        for each row in dimension k **do in parallel**
          if $D(k)$ is even
          then sort in the forward direction
          else sort in the reverse direction
          end if
        end for
      end for
    end for. ∎

Example 3.2. Let $d = 4$, $n_1 = 2$, $n_2 = 3$, $n_3 = 4$, $n_4 = 5$, and let the sequence to be sorted be $(120, 119, \ldots, 3, 2, 1)$. The numbers are initially stored in the 120 processors of the 4-dimensional array, one number per processor (such that P_0 holds 120, P_1 holds 119, and so on). Once algorithm MULTIDIMENSIONAL ARRAY SIMPLE SORT has been applied, the following arrangement results:

1	2	12	11	13	14	24	23
4	3	9	10	16	15	21	22
5	6	8	7	17	18	20	19

48	47	37	38	36	35	25	26
45	46	40	39	33	34	28	27
44	43	41	42	32	31	29	30

49	50	60	59	61	62	72	71
52	51	57	58	64	63	69	70
53	54	56	55	65	66	68	67

96	95	85	86	84	83	73	74
93	94	88	87	81	82	76	75
92	91	89	90	80	79	77	78

97	98	108	107	109	110	120	119
100	99	105	106	112	111	117	118
101	102	104	103	113	114	116	115. □

As a minor implementation detail, note that each processor computes $D(k)$ over its coordinates $I(1), I(2), \ldots, I(d)$ using two variables C and D as follows. Initially, it computes $C = \sum_{r=1}^{d}(I(r) - 1)$. Then, prior to the second **for** loop, it computes $D(1)$ as $D = C - (I(1) - 1)$. Subsequently, at the end of the kth iteration of the second **for** loop, where $k = 1, 2, \ldots, d-1$, it computes $D(k + 1)$ as $D = D - (I(k + 1) - 1)$.

Analysis. We now show that M iterations, each of which sorts the rows in dimensions $1, 2, \ldots, d$, suffice to sort correctly $N = n_1 n_2 \cdots n_d$ numbers stored in a d-dimensional $n_1 \times n_2 \times \cdots \times n_d$ array. Because algorithm LINEAR ARRAY SORT is oblivious, then so is algorithm MULTIDIMENSIONAL ARRAY SIMPLE SORT. This property allows us to use the 0-1 principle. Suppose then that the input to algorithm MULTIDIMENSIONAL ARRAY SIMPLE SORT consists of an arbitrary sequence of 0s and 1s. Once sorted in nondecreasing order, this sequence will consist of a (possibly empty) subsequence of 0s followed by a (possibly empty) subsequence of 1s. In particular, the sorted sequence will contain at most one (0, 1) pattern, that is, a 0 followed by a 1. (If the input consists of all 0s or all 1s, then of course the output contains no such (0, 1) pattern.) If present, the (0, 1) pattern will appear either in a row in dimension 1, or at the boundary between two adjacent dimension 1 rows (consecutive in snakelike order) such that the 0 appears in one row and the 1 in the next.

Now consider the rows in dimension k, $1 \le k \le d$. There are N/n_k such rows. A row in dimension k is said to be *clean* if it holds all 0s (all 1s) and there are no 1s preceding it (no 0s following it) in snakelike order; otherwise, the row is *dirty*.

Suppose that an iteration of the algorithm has just sorted the contents of the rows in dimension $d - 1$, and let us focus on two such rows, adjacent in dimension d. For example, for $d = 3$, $n_1 = 2$, $n_2 = 3$, and $n_3 = 4$, the coordinates of two dimension 2 rows, adjacent in dimension 3 of the $2 \times 3 \times 4$ array, are

$$
\begin{array}{ccc}
1,1,1 & & 1,1,2 \\
1,2,1 & \text{and} & 1,2,2 \\
1,3,1 & & 1,3,2,
\end{array}
$$

respectively. Because these two dimension $d-1$ rows were sorted in snakelike order, they yield at least one clean dimension $d-1$ row when the dimension d rows are sorted. To illustrate, suppose that the two preceding dimension 2 rows contained

$$
\begin{array}{ccc}
0 & & 1 \\
0 & \text{and} & 0 \\
1 & & 0,
\end{array}
$$

respectively, after they were sorted. Then (regardless of what the other dimension 2 rows contained) a clean dimension 2 row containing all 0s is created after the dimension 3 rows are sorted. Thus, after $\lceil \log n_d \rceil$ iterations all dimension $d-1$ rows are clean, except possibly for $N/(n_{d-1}n_d)$ dimension $d-1$ rows contiguous in dimension $d-1$. All dimension d rows are now permanently sorted.

By the same argument, $\lceil \log n_{d-1} \rceil$ iterations are subsequently needed to make all dimension $d - 2$ rows clean (except possibly for $N/(n_{d-2}n_{d-1}n_d)$ dimension $d - 2$ rows contiguous in dimension $d - 2$). In general, $\lceil \log n_k \rceil$ iterations are needed to make all dimension $k - 1$ rows clean (except possibly for $N/(n_{k-1}n_k \cdots n_d)$ dimension $k - 1$ rows contiguous in dimension $k - 1$) after all dimension k rows have been permanently sorted, for $k = d, d - 1, \ldots, 2$. This leaves possibly one dirty dimension 1 row holding the $(0, 1)$ pattern. Since that row may not be sorted in the proper direction for snakelike ordering, one final iteration completes the sort. The algorithm therefore sorts correctly in

$$
\begin{aligned}
M &= \lceil \log n_d \rceil + \lceil \log n_{d-1} \rceil + \cdots + \lceil \log n_2 \rceil + 1 \\
&= O(\log N)
\end{aligned}
$$

iterations.

Finally, observe that algorithm LINEAR ARRAY SORT is used in dimensions $1, 2, \ldots, d$, and hence each iteration of the outer **for** loop in algorithm

MULTIDIMENSIONAL ARRAY SIMPLE SORT requires $\sum_{k=1}^{d} O(n_k)$ time. Since the outer loop is executed $O(\log N)$ times, the algorithm has a running time of $O((n_1 + n_2 + \cdots + n_d) \log N)$. When $n_i = n$ for $1 \leq i \leq d$, we have $N = n^d$. In this case, the number of iterations is $O(d \log n)$ and the time per iteration is $O(dn)$, for a total running time of $O(d^2 n \log n)$.

The algorithm is fairly straightforward and relatively efficient. It is nonrecursive and does not require that data be exchanged between pairs of distant processors: The only operation used, namely, 'comparison-exchange', applies to neighboring processors. Thus, because no routing is needed, the algorithm has virtually no control overhead. However, it is not time optimal. Indeed, it is easy to see that a d-dimensional $n_1 \times n_2 \times \cdots \times n_d$ array has a diameter of $\sum_{k=1}^{d} (n_k - 1)$. It follows that a lower bound of $\Omega(n_1 + n_2 + \cdots + n_d)$ holds on the time required to sort on such an array. This suggests that the running time of algorithm MULTIDIMENSIONAL ARRAY SIMPLE SORT is not the best that can be obtained on a d-dimensional array. We now show that this is indeed the case by exhibiting an algorithm whose running time is $O(n_1 + n_2 + \cdots + n_d)$.

For each n_i, let u_i and v_i be positive integers such that $u_i v_i = n_i$, $1 \leq i \leq d$. The d-dimensional lattice is viewed as consisting of $u_1 u_2 \cdots u_d$ d-dimensional $v_1 \times v_2 \times \cdots \times v_d$ sublattices, called *blocks*, numbered in snakelike order by dimension from 1 to $u_1 u_2 \cdots u_d$. Alternatively, the d-dimensional lattice consists of $u_1 u_2 \cdots u_d$ $(d-1)$-dimensional *hyperplanes* of $v_1 v_2 \cdots v_d$ processors each, numbered from 1 to $u_1 u_2 \cdots u_d$. The algorithm is given in what follows.

Algorithm MULTIDIMENSIONAL ARRAY FAST SORT

Step 1: Sort the contents of block i, $1 \leq i \leq u_1 u_2 \cdots u_d$.

Step 2: Move the data held by the processors in block i
  to the corresponding processors in hyperplane i,
  $1 \leq i \leq u_1 u_2 \cdots u_d$.

Step 3: Sort the contents of all d-dimensional
  $v_1 \times v_2 \times \cdots \times n_d$ 'towers' of blocks.

Step 4: Move the data held by the processors in hyperplane i
  to the corresponding processors in block i,
  $1 \leq i \leq u_1 u_2 \cdots u_d$.

Step 5: Sort the contents of
  (5.1) All pairs of consecutive blocks i and $i + 1$,
    for all odd i, $1 \leq i \leq u_1 u_2 \cdots u_d$.
  (5.2) All pairs of consecutive blocks $i - 1$ and i,
    for all even i, $2 \leq i \leq u_1 u_2 \cdots u_d$. ∎

The algorithm requires $O(n_1 + n_2 + \cdots + n_d)$ elementary steps (in which a datum is sent from a processor to its neighbor), and this is time optimal. However, note that, while appealing in theory due to its time optimality, algorithm MULTIDIMENSIONAL ARRAY FAST SORT is significantly more complex than algorithm MULTIDIMENSIONAL ARRAY SIMPLE SORT. Deriving a simple time-optimal algorithm for sorting on a d-dimensional array remains an interesting open problem.

3.4 Hypercube

A special case of a d-dimensional $n_1 \times n_2 \times \cdots \times n_d$ array occurs when $n_i = 2$ for $1 \leq i \leq d$. This array is commonly known in the literature as the *hypercube*, a popular model among theoreticians and practitioners of parallel computation alike. The hypercube has $N = 2^d$ processors, each of which is directly connected to d other processors. The diameter of the hypercube is also equal to d. A closer look at the hypercube is provided in Section 4.1. Our purpose here is to exhibit a very simple algorithm for sorting N numbers on the hypercube. The algorithm is readily derived from algorithm MULTIDIMENSIONAL ARRAY SIMPLE SORT and is as follows:

> **Algorithm HYPERCUBE SIMPLE SORT**
> **for** $i = 1$ to d **do**
>   **for** $k = 1$ to d **do**
>   **for** each row in dimension k **do in parallel**
>   **If** $D(k)$ is even
>   **then** sort in the forward direction
>   **else** sort in the reverse direction
>   **end if**
>   **end for**
>   **end for**
> **end for.** ∎

We note here that a row consists of two processors and that sorting a row is simply a 'compare-exchange' operation. The algorithm executes d^2 such operations. Since $d = \log N$, the algorithm has a running time of $O(\log^2 N)$. This running time is larger than the lower bound of $\Omega(\log N)$ imposed by the hypercube's diameter only by a factor of $O(\log N)$. It is not optimal, however, as there exist slightly faster (but considerably more complicated) algorithms for sorting on the hypercube. We also note here that algorithm MULTIDIMENSIONAL ARRAY FAST SORT does not appear to lead to a more efficient algorithm for the hypercube.

3.5 Star

For a positive integer $n > 1$, an *n-star interconnection network*, denoted $\mathcal{S}_n$, is defined as follows:

1. $\mathcal{S}_n$ is an undirected graph with $n!$ vertices, each of which is a processor;

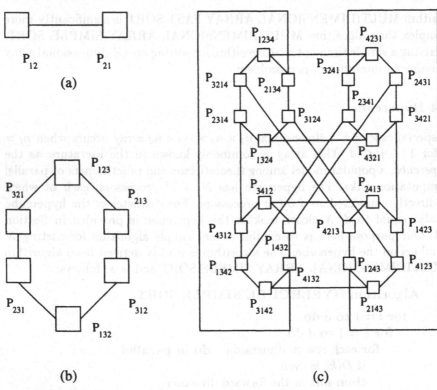

Fig. 3.5. A 2-star, a 3-star, and a 4-star interconnection networks.

2. The label v of each processor P_v is a distinct permutation of the symbols $\{1, 2, \ldots, n\}$;

3. Processor P_v is directly connected by an edge to each of $n - 1$ processors P_u, where u is obtained by interchanging the first and ith symbols of v, that is, if

$$v = v(1)v(2)\ldots v(n),$$

where $v(j) \in \{1, 2, \ldots, n\}$ for $j = 1, 2, \ldots, n$, then

$$u = v(i)v(2)\ldots v(i-1)v(1)v(i+1)\ldots v(n),$$

for $i = 2, 3, \ldots, n$.

Networks $\mathcal{S}_2$, $\mathcal{S}_3$, and $\mathcal{S}_4$ are shown in Fig. 3.5(a)–(c).

In a given interconnection network, the maximum number of neighbors per processor is called the *degree* of the network. In practice, a small degree is usually a good property for a network to possess. As pointed out earlier, a small diameter is also desirable for an interconnection network. In this regard, the n-star has a degree of $n - 1$ and a diameter of $\lceil 3(n-1)/2 \rceil$. This makes it a much more attractive network than a hypercube with $O(n!)$ processors which, by comparison, has a degree and a diameter of $O(n \log n)$.

We now consider the problem of sorting on the n-star. Specifically, given $n!$ numbers, held one per processor of the n-star, it is required to sort these numbers in nondecreasing order. The central idea of the algorithm we are about to describe is to map the processors of the n-star onto an $(n-1)$-dimensional array and then apply either of the two algorithms described in Section 3.3.

3.5.1 Ordering the processors. As we did with previous networks, we impose an order on the processors, so that the problem of sorting is properly defined. For a given permutation $v = v(1)v(2)\ldots v(n)$, let

(a) $vmax(n) = \max\{v(k) \mid v(k) < v(n), 1 \leq k \leq n-1\}$, if such a $v(k)$ exists; otherwise, $vmax(n) = \max\{v(k) \mid 1 \leq k \leq n-1\}$.
(b) $vmin(n) = \min\{v(k) \mid v(k) > v(n), 1 \leq k \leq n-1\}$, if such a $v(k)$ exists; otherwise, $vmin(n) = \min\{v(k) \mid 1 \leq k \leq n-1\}$.

Beginning with the processor label $v = 12\ldots n$, the remaining $n! - 1$ labels are arranged in the order produced by (sequential) algorithm LABELS (n, j) given in what follows. The algorithm operates throughout on the array $v = v(1)v(2)\ldots v(n)$. Initially, $v(i) = i$, $1 \leq i \leq n$, and the algorithm is called with $j = 1$. A new permutation is produced every time two elements of the array v are swapped.

> **Algorithm LABELS(n, j)**
>
>   **Step 1:** $i \leftarrow 1$
>   **Step 2: while** $i \leq n$ **do**
>   (2.1) **if** $n > 2$
>   **then** LABELS$(n - 1, i)$
>   **end if**
>   (2.2) **if** $i < n$
>   **then if** j is odd
>   **then** $v(n) \leftrightarrow vmax(n)$
>   **else** $v(n) \leftrightarrow vmin(n)$
>   **end if**
>   **end if**
>   (2.3) $i \leftarrow i + 1$
>   **end while.** ∎

The order produced by the preceding algorithm satisfies the following properties:

1. All $(n - 1)!$ permutations with $v(n) = \ell$ precede all permutations with $v(n) = \ell'$, for each ℓ and ℓ' such that $1 \leq \ell' < \ell \leq n$.
2. Consider the jth group of $(m - 1)!$ consecutive permutations in which the symbols $v(m)v(m + 1)\ldots v(n)$ are fixed, where $1 \leq j \leq n!/(m - 1)!$ and $2 \leq m \leq n - 1$. Within this group, the $m - 1$ elements of the set

$\{1, 2, \ldots, n\} - \{v(m), v(m + 1), \ldots, v(n)\}$ take turns in appearing as $v(m - 1)$, each repeated $(m - 2)!$ times consecutively. They appear in decreasing order if j is odd and in increasing order if j is even.

Example 3.3. For $n = 4$, the 4! labels, that is, the 24 permutations of $\{1, 2, 3, 4\}$, ordered according to algorithm LABELS, are as follows:

1. 1234	7. 4213	13. 1342	19. 4321
2. 2134	8. 2413	14. 3142	20. 3421
3. 3124	9. 1423	15. 4132	21. 2431
4. 1324	10. 4123	16. 1432	22. 4231
5. 2314	11. 2143	17. 3412	23. 3241
6. 3214	12. 1243	18. 4312	24. 2341. $\square$

3.5.2 Rearranging the data. An important operation in our sorting algorithms is *data rearrangement* whereby pairs of processors exchange their data. We now define this operation. Recall that a processor can send a datum of constant size to a neighbor in constant time. In S_n each processor P_v has $n - 1$ neighbors P_u. The label u of the kth neighbor of P_v is obtained by swapping $v(1)$ with $v(k + 1)$, for $k = 1, 2, \ldots, n - 1$. The edges connecting P_v to its neighbors are referred to as *connections* $2, 3, \ldots, n$. If each processor of S_n holds a datum, then the phrase "rearranging the data over connection i" means that all processors directly connected through connection i exchange their data. Specifically, each processor P_v, where $v = v(1)v(2) \ldots v(i - 1)v(i)v(i + 1) \ldots v(n)$ sends its datum to processor P_u, where $u = v(i)v(2) \ldots v(i - 1)v(1)v(i + 1) \ldots v(n)$. This is illustrated in Fig. 3.6.

3.5.3 The star viewed as a multidimensional array. The $n!$ processors of S_n are thought of as being organized in a virtual $(n - 1)$-dimensional $2 \times 3 \times \cdots \times n$ orthogonal array. This organization is achieved in two steps: The processors are first listed according to the order obtained from algorithm LABELS, they are then placed (figuratively) in this order in the $(n - 1)$-dimensional array according to snakelike order by dimension.

Example 3.4. For $n = 4$, the 24 processor labels appear in the $2 \times 3 \times 4$ array as shown in Fig. 3.7, where the arrows indicate snakelike order by dimension. A three-dimensional drawing is given in Fig. 3.8. $\square$

As a result of the arrangement just described, processor P_v, such that $v = v(1)v(2) \ldots v(n)$, occupies that position of the $(n-1)$-dimensional array whose coordinates $I(1), I(2), \ldots, I(n-1)$ are given by $I(k) = k + 1 - \sum_{j=1}^{k} [v(k+1) > v(j)]$, for $1 \leq k \leq n - 1$, where $[v(k + 1) > v(j)]$ equals 1 if $v(k + 1) > v(j)$ and equals 0 otherwise.

It should be stressed here that two processors occupying adjacent positions in some dimension k, $1 \leq k \leq n - 1$, on the $(n - 1)$-dimensional array

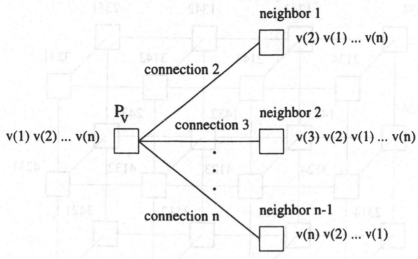

Fig. 3.6. Rearranging the data.

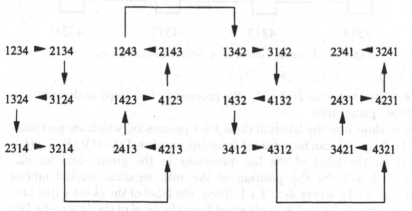

Fig. 3.7. Snakelike order by dimension.

are not necessarily directly connected on the n-star. Now suppose that in dimension k, each processor in a group of $k+1$ processors occupying consecutive positions holds a datum. Our purpose in what follows is to show that after rearranging the data over connection $k+1$, these $k+1$ data are stored in $k+1$ processors forming a linear array (i.e., the first of the $k+1$ processors is directly connected to the second, the second is directly connected to the third, and so on). To simplify the presentation, we assume in what follows that the $k+1$ consecutive positions (of the multidimensional array) occupied by the $k+1$ processors begin at the position with $I(k) = 1$ and end at that with $I(k) = k+1$ (the argument being symmetric for the case where the $k+1$ processors are placed in the opposite direction, that is, from the position with

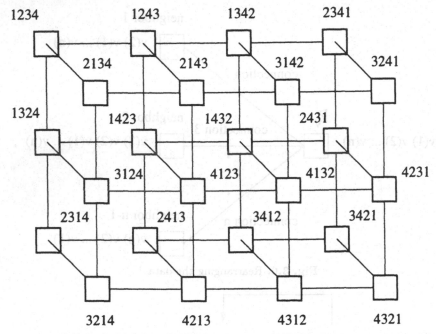

Fig. 3.8. A 4-star viewed as a 3-dimensional array.

$I(k) = k + 1$ to that with $I(k) = 1$). We proceed in two steps as described in the next two paragraphs.

First we show how the labels of these $k+1$ processors, which are permutations of $\{1, 2, \ldots, n\}$, can be obtained from one another. Let $v(1)v(2) \ldots v(k+1) \ldots v(n)$ be the label of the last processor in the group, and let d_m, $1 \leq m \leq k + 1$, be the position of the mth smallest symbol among $v(1)v(2) \ldots v(k+1)$, where $d_1 = k+1$. Then, the label of the $(k+1-i)$th processor in the group, $1 \leq i \leq k$, is obtained from the label of the $(k+1-i+1)$st processor by exchanging the symbols in positions $k + 1$ and d_{i+1}. For example, for $n = 4$, consider the four processors, occupying consecutive positions over dimension 3, whose labels are 1324, 1423, 1432, and 2431. The second of these (i.e., 1423) can be obtained from the third (i.e., 1432) by exchanging the symbol in position 4 (i.e., 2) with the third smallest symbol among 2, 4, 3, and 1 (i.e., 3). This property follows directly from the definition of the LABEL ordering.

Now consider a group of $k + 1$ processors occupying consecutive positions over dimension k, with each processor holding a datum and the label of the $(k + 1)$st processor in the group being $v(1)v(2) \ldots v(k + 1) \ldots v(n)$. From the property established in the previous paragraph, the label of the $(k+1-i)$th processor has the $(i + 1)$st smallest symbol among $v(1)v(2) \ldots v(k + 1)$ in position $k + 1$, for $0 \leq i \leq k$. Rearranging the data over connection $k + 1$ moves the data from this group to another group of $k+1$ processors in which

the label of the $(k+1-i)$th processor has the $(i+1)$st smallest symbol among
$v(1)v(2)\ldots v(k+1)$ in position 1, for $0 \leq i \leq k$. In this new group, the label of
the $(k+1-i)$th processor can be obtained from that of the $(k+1-i+1)$st by
exchanging the symbol in position 1 with that in position d_{i+1}, for $1 \leq i \leq k$.
It follows that the processors in the new group are connected to form a
linear array. For example, consider once again the four processors, occupying
consecutive positions over dimension 3, whose labels are 1324, 1423, 1432, and
2431 as illustrated in Fig. 3.8. Rearranging the data held by these processors
over connection 4 moves them to the processors whose labels are 4321, 3421,
2431, and 1432, respectively.

3.5.4 Sorting algorithms for $\mathcal{S}_n$.
In order to sort the sequence of numbers
$(x_0, x_1, \ldots, x_{N-1})$, where $N = n!$, on an n-star, we view the processors of the
n-star as an $(n-1)$-dimensional $2 \times 3 \times \cdots \times n$ virtual array. Either of the
two sorting algorithms described in Section 3.3 is now applied.

Note that in dimension k the $k+1$ processors in each group are not necessarily connected on the n-star to form a linear array. Thus, each time a linear
array operation is to be performed (such as applying algorithm LINEAR AR-
RAY SORT), the contents of the $k+1$ processors are copied in constant time
to another set of $k+1$ processors which *are* connected on the n-star as a linear array. This is done simply by rearranging the numbers to be sorted over
connection $k+1$. After the linear array operation is performed, the numbers
are brought back to the original processors, also in constant time.

As shown in Section 3.3, when sorting $N = n_1 n_2 \cdots n_d$ numbers on a d-
dimensional $n_1 \times n_2 \times \cdots \times n_d$ array, algorithm MULTIDIMENSIONAL AR-
RAY SIMPLE SORT has a running time of $O((n_1+n_2+\cdots+n_d)\log N)$, while
algorithm MULTIDIMENSIONAL ARRAY FAST SORT runs in $O(n_1+n_2+\cdots+n_d)$ time. Since the number of dimensions d of the multidimensional array (to which the processors of the star are mapped) is $n-1$, and $n_i = i+1$ for
$1 \leq i \leq n-1$, we obtain running times of $O(n^3 \log n)$ and $O(n^2)$, respectively,
when using the aforementioned algorithms.

Because $n!$ numbers are sorted optimally using one processor in time
$O(n!\log n!)$, a parallel algorithm using $n!$ processors must have a running time
of $O(\log n!)$, that is, $O(n \log n)$, in order to be time optimal. In that sense,
the $O(n^2)$-time n-star algorithm obtained in the preceding is suboptimal by
a factor of $O(n/\log n)$. However, it is not known at the time of this writing
whether an $O(n \log n)$ running time for sorting $n!$ numbers is achievable on
the n-star.

A related open question is formulated as follows. Let G be a graph whose
set of vertices is V and set of edges is E. A *Hamilton cycle* in G is a cycle that
starts at some vertex v of V, traverses the edges in E, visiting each vertex in
V exactly once, and finally returns to v. Not all graphs possess a Hamilton
cycle; those that do are said to be *Hamiltonian*. As it turns out, it is often
useful in parallel computation to determine whether the graph underlying an
interconnection network is Hamiltonian. When this is the case, the processors

can be viewed as forming a *ring*, that is, a linear array with an additional link connecting the first and last processors. Several useful operations can thus be performed efficiently on the data held by the processors. For example, one such operation is a circular shift. Now, while the n-star can be shown to be Hamiltonian, it is easily verified that the order defined on the processors by algorithm LABELS does not yield a Hamilton cycle for $n > 3$. Thus, for $n = 4$, P_{1234} and P_{2341}, the first and last processors, respectively, are not neighbors. Does there exist an efficient sorting algorithm for the n-star when the processors are ordered to form a Hamilton cycle?

4. Matrix Multiplication

We now turn our attention to the problem of computing the product of two matrices. This is a fundamental computation in many fields, including linear algebra and numerical analysis. Its importance to parallel algorithms, however, goes well beyond its immediate applications. A great many computations are performed efficiently in parallel by expressing each of them as a matrix multiplication.

The problem of matrix multiplication is defined as follows. Let A and B be two $n \times n$ matrices of real numbers. It is required to compute a third $n \times n$ matrix C equal to the product of A and B. The elements of C are obtained from

$$c_{jk} = \sum_{i=0}^{n-1} a_{ji} \times b_{ik} \qquad 0 \le j, k \le n - 1.$$

A lower bound on the number of operations required to perform this computation is $\Omega(n^2)$. This is easy to see: The result matrix C consists of n^2 elements, and that many steps are therefore needed simply to produce it as output. While this is what one might call an *obvious* lower bound, as it is based solely on the size of the output, it turns out to be the highest lower bound known for this problem. Despite concerted efforts, no one has been able to show that more than n^2 steps are required to compute C.

On the other hand, since C has n^2 entries, each of which, by definition, equals the sum of n products, a straightforward sequential algorithm requires $O(n^3)$ time. However, the asymptotically fastest known sequential algorithm for multiplying two $n \times n$ matrices runs in $O(n^\epsilon)$ time, where $2 < \epsilon < 2.38$. Because of the evident gap between the $\Omega(n^2)$ lower bound and the lowest available upper bound of $O(n^\epsilon)$, it is not known whether this algorithm is time-optimal, or whether a faster algorithm exists (but has not yet been discovered).

In the remainder of this section a parallel algorithm is described for computing the product of two matrices on a hypercube interconnection network. Applications of this algorithm in graph theory and numerical computation are then studied. We assume in what follows that $n = 2^q$, for a positive integer q.

4.1 Hypercube Algorithm

The hypercube was briefly introduced in Section 3.4. We now provide a formal specification of the model.

4.1.1 The hypercube model.

Let $N = 2^d$ processors $P_0, P_1, \ldots, P_{N-1}$ be available, for $d \geq 1$. Further, let i and $i^{(b)}$ be two integers, $0 \leq i, i^{(b)} \leq N-1$, whose binary representations differ only in position b, $0 \leq b < d$. Specifically, if

$$i_{d-1} i_{d-2} \cdots i_{b+1} i_b i_{b-1} \cdots i_1 i_0$$

is the binary representation of i, then

$$i_{d-1} i_{d-2} \cdots i_{b+1} i'_b i_{b-1} \cdots i_1 i_0$$

is the binary representation of $i^{(b)}$, where i'_b is the binary complement of bit i_b. A *d-dimensional hypercube interconnection network* is formed by connecting each processor P_i, $0 \leq i \leq N-1$, to $P_{i^{(b)}}$ by a two-way link, for all $0 \leq b < d$. Thus, each processor has d neighbors. This is illustrated in Fig. 4.1(a)-(d), for $d = 1, 2, 3$ and 4, respectively. The indices of the processors are given in binary notation. Note that the hypercube in dimension d is obtained by connecting corresponding processors in two $(d-1)$-dimensional hypercubes (a 0-dimensional hypercube being a single processor). It is also easy to see that the diameter of a d-dimensional hypercube is precisely d.

4.1.2 Matrix multiplication on the hypercube.

The hypercube algorithm for computing the product of two matrices is essentially an implementation of the straightforward sequential algorithm. In order to multiply the two $n \times n$ matrices A and B, where $n = 2^q$, we use a hypercube with $N = n^3 = 2^{3q}$ processors. It is helpful to visualize the processors as being arranged in an $n \times n \times n$ array, with processor P_r occupying position (i, j, k), where $r = in^2 + jn + k$ and $0 \leq i, j, k \leq n-1$. Thus, if the binary representation of r is

$$r_{3q-1} r_{3q-2} \cdots r_{2q} r_{2q-1} \cdots r_q r_{q-1} \cdots r_0,$$

then the binary representations of i, j, and k are

$$r_{3q-1} r_{3q-2} \cdots r_{2q}, \quad r_{2q-1} r_{2q-2} \cdots r_q, \quad \text{and } r_{q-1} r_{q-2} \cdots r_0,$$

respectively. Note that in the $n \times n \times n$ array, all processors agreeing on one or two of the coordinates (i, j, k) form a hypercube. Specifically, all processors with the same index value in one of the three coordinates form a hypercube with n^2 processors; similarly, all processors with the same index values in two fixed coordinates form a hypercube with n processors.

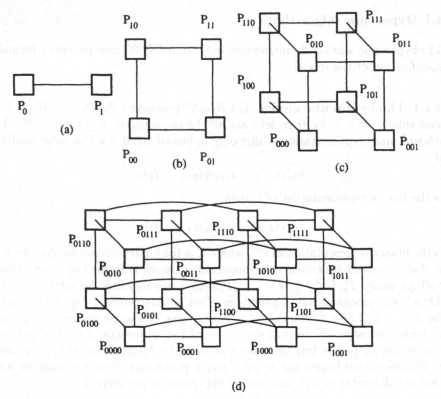

Fig. 4.1. A d-dimensional hypercube for $d = 1, 2, 3$ and 4.

We assume in what follows that each processor P_r has three registers A_r, B_r, and C_r. For notational convenience, the same three registers are also denoted $A(i, j, k)$, $B(i, j, k)$, and $C(i, j, k)$, respectively. Initially, processor P_s in position $(0, j, k)$, $0 \le j \le n - 1$, $0 \le k \le n - 1$, contains element a_{jk} of matrix A and element b_{jk} of matrix B in registers A_s and B_s, respectively. The registers of all other processors are initialized to 0. At the end of the computation, register C_s of P_s should contain element c_{jk} of the product matrix C. The algorithm is designed to perform the n^3 multiplications involved in computing the n^2 entries of matrix C simultaneously. It is given in what follows.

Algorithm HYPERCUBE MATRIX MULTIPLICATION

Step 1: The elements of matrices A and B are distributed over the n^3 processors so that the processor in position (i, j, k) contains a_{ji} and b_{ik}. This is done as follows:

(1.1) Copies of data initially in $A(0, j, k)$ and $B(0, j, k)$, are sent to the processors in positions (i, j, k), where $1 \leq i \leq n - 1$. As a result, $A(i, j, k) = a_{jk}$ and $B(i, j, k) = b_{jk}$, for $0 \leq i \leq n - 1$. Formally,

> **for** $m = 3q - 1$ **downto** $2q$ **do**
> > **for all** r such that $r_m = 0$ **do in parallel**
> > > (i) $A_{r(m)} \leftarrow A_r$
> > > (ii) $B_{r(m)} \leftarrow B_r$
> > **end for**
> **end for**

(1.2) Copies of the data in $A(i, j, i)$ are sent to the processors in positions (i, j, k), where $0 \leq k \leq n - 1$. As a result, $A(i, j, k) = a_{ji}$ for $0 \leq k \leq n - 1$. Formally,

> **for** $m = q - 1$ **downto** 0 **do**
> > **for all** r such that $r_m = r_{2q+m}$ **do in parallel**
> > > $A_{r(m)} \leftarrow A_r$
> > **end for**
> **end for**

(1.3) Copies of the data in $B(i, i, k)$ are sent to the processors in positions (i, j, k), where $0 \leq j \leq n - 1$. As a result, $B(i, j, k) = b_{ik}$ for $0 \leq j \leq n - 1$. Formally,

> **for** $m = 2q - 1$ **downto** q **do**
> > **for all** r such that $r_m = r_{q+m}$ **do in parallel**
> > > $B_{r(m)} \leftarrow B_r$
> > **end for**
> **end for**

Step 2: Each processor in position (i, j, k) computes the product

$$C(i, j, k) \leftarrow A(i, j, k) \times B(i, j, k).$$

Thus, $C(i, j, k) = a_{ji} \times b_{ik}$ for $0 \leq i, j, k \leq n - 1$. Formally,

> **for** $r = 0$ **to** $N - 1$ **do in parallel**
> > $C_r \leftarrow A_r \times B_r$
> **end for**

Step 3: The sum

$$C(0, j, k) \leftarrow \sum_{i=0}^{n-1} C(i, j, k)$$

is computed for $0 \leq j, k \leq n - 1$. Formally,

> **for** $m = 2q$ **to** $3q - 1$ **do**
>   **for all** $r \in N(r_m = 0)$ **do in parallel**
> $C_r \leftarrow C_r + C_{r(m)}$
>   **end for**
> **end for.** ∎

Analysis.   Each of Steps (1.1), (1.2), (1.3), and 3 consists of q constant-time iterations. Step 2 requires constant time. Therefore, the algorithm has a running time of $O(q)$—that is, $t(n) = O(\log n)$. Since $p(n) = n^3$, the algorithm's cost is $c(n) = O(n^3 \log n)$. This cost is not optimal since $O(n^3)$ basic operations suffice to multiply two $n \times n$ matrices by the straightforward sequential algorithm based on the definition of the matrix product.

4.2 Graph Theoretical Problems

Graphs are important modeling tools in many fields of knowledge, particularly in science and engineering. Graph theory is that branch of discrete mathematics whose purpose is the study of graphs and their algorithms. In this section we show how two problems defined on graphs can be solved efficiently in parallel through the use of matrix multiplication. We begin with some definitions.

A *graph* $G = (V, E)$ is a set of vertices V connected by a set of edges E. If the edges have no orientation, then the graph is *undirected*; thus, the edge connecting two vertices v_1 and v_2 can be traversed in either way, from v_1 to v_2 or from v_2 to v_1. By contrast, a graph is *directed* if each edge has an orientation; thus, an edge connecting v_1 to v_2 can only be traversed from v_1 to v_2. A *path* in a graph is an ordered list of edges of the form $(v_i, v_j), (v_j, v_k), (v_k, v_l)$, and so on. If, for every pair of vertices v_p and v_q in an undirected graph, there is a path leading from v_p to v_q, then the graph is said to be *connected*. A directed graph is connected if the undirected graph obtained from it by ignoring the edge orientations is connected. A *cycle* in a graph is a path that begins and ends at the same vertex.

When each edge of a graph is associated with a real number, called its *weight*, the graph is said to be *weighted*. A weighted graph may be directed or undirected. The meaning of an edge's weight varies from one application to another; it may represent distance, cost, time, probability, and so on. A *weight matrix* W is used to represent a weighted graph. Here, entry w_{ij} of W represents the weight of edge (v_i, v_j). If v_i and v_j are not connected by an edge, then w_{ij} may be equal to zero, infinity, or any appropriate value, depending on the application.

4.2.1 All-Pairs Shortest Paths. Suppose that we are given a directed and weighted graph $G = (V, E)$, with n vertices, as shown in Fig. 4.2(a). The graph is defined by its weight matrix W, as shown in Fig. 4.2(b). We assume that W has positive, zero, or negative entries, as long as there is no cycle in G such that the sum of the weights of the edges on the cycle is negative.

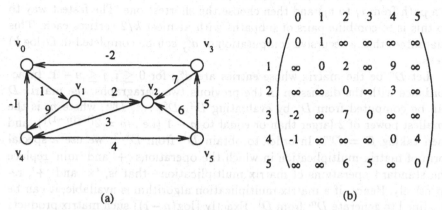

(a)   (b)

Fig. 4.2. A directed and weighted graph and its weight matrix.

The problem that we address here is known as the *all-pairs shortest paths problem* and is stated as follows: For every pair of vertices v_i and v_j in V, it is required to find the length of the shortest path from v_i to v_j along edges in E. Specifically, a matrix D is to be constructed such that d_{ij} is the length of the shortest path from v_i to v_j in G, for all i and j. Here, the length of a path (or cycle) is the sum of the weights of the edges forming it. In Fig. 4.2, the shortest path from v_0 to v_4 is along edges (v_0, v_1), (v_1, v_2), (v_2, v_4) and has length 6. It may be obvious now why we insisted that G have no cycle of negative length: If such a cycle were to exist within a path from v_i to v_j, then one could traverse this cycle indefinitely, producing paths of ever shorter length from v_i to v_j.

Let d_{ij}^k denote the length of the shortest path from v_i to v_j that goes through at most $k-1$ intermediate vertices. Thus, $d_{ij}^1 = w_{ij}$ — that is, the weight of the edge from v_i to v_j. In particular, if there is no edge from v_i to v_j, where $i \neq j$, then $d_{ij}^1 = w_{ij} = \infty$. Also, $d_{ii}^1 = w_{ii} = 0$. Given that G has no cycles of negative length, there is no advantage in visiting any vertex more than once in a shortest path from v_i to v_j. It follows that $d_{ij} = d_{ij}^{n-1}$, since there are only n vertices in G.

In order to compute d_{ij}^k for $k > 1$, we can use the recurrence

$$d_{ij}^k = \min_l(d_{il}^{k/2} + d_{lj}^{k/2}).$$

The validity of this relation is established as follows: Suppose that d_{ij}^k is the length of the *shortest* path from v_i to v_j and that two vertices v_r and v_s are on this shortest path (with v_r preceding v_s). It must be the case that the edges from v_r to v_s (along the shortest path from v_i to v_j) form a shortest path from v_r to v_s. (If a shorter path from v_r to v_s existed, it could be used to obtain a shorter path from v_i to v_j, which is absurd.) Therefore, to obtain d_{ij}^k, we can compute all combinations of *optimal subpaths* (whose concatenation is a path from v_i to v_j) and then choose the shortest one. The fastest way to do this is to combine pairs of subpaths with at most $k/2$ vertices each. This guarantees that a recursive computation of d_{ij}^k can be completed in $O(\log k)$ steps.

Let D^k be the matrix whose entries are d_{ij}^k, for $0 \leq i,j \leq n-1$. In accordance with the discussion in the previous two paragraphs, the matrix D can be computed from D^1 by evaluating D^2, D^4, ..., D^m, where m is the smallest power of 2 larger than or equal to $n-1$ (i.e., $m = 2^{\lceil \log(n-1) \rceil}$), and then taking $D = D^m$. In order to obtain D^k from $D^{k/2}$, we use a special form of matrix multiplication in which the operations '+' and 'min' replace the standard operations of matrix multiplication—that is, '×' and '+', respectively. Hence, if a matrix multiplication algorithm is available, it can be modified to generate D^m from D^1. Exactly $\lceil \log(n-1) \rceil$ such matrix products are required.

In particular, algorithm HYPERCUBE MATRIX MULTIPLICATION, appropriately modified, can be used to compute the shortest path matrix D. The resulting algorithm, to which we refer as algorithm HYPERCUBE SHORTEST PATHS, has a running time of $t(n) = O(\log^2 n)$. Since $p(n) = n^3$, the algorithm's cost is $c(n) = O(n^3 \log^2 n)$.

4.2.2 Minimum Spanning Tree. An undirected graph is a *tree* if it is connected and contains no cycles. Let $G = (V, E)$ be an undirected, connected, and weighted graph with n vertices. A *spanning tree* of G is a connected subgraph $G' = (V, E')$ that contains no cycles. A *minimum-weight spanning tree* (MST) of G is a spanning tree of G with the smallest edge-weight sum.

We now show how algorithm HYPERCUBE SHORTEST PATHS can be used to compute an MST for a given graph G. Let w_{ij} be the weight of edge $(v_i, v_j) \in E$. In what follows, we assume that all w_{ij} are distinct. (If, for two edges (v_i, v_j) and $(v_{i'}, v_{j'})$, $w_{ij} = w_{i'j'}$, then w_{ij} is considered smaller than $w_{i'j'}$ if $in + j < i'n + j'$; otherwise, $w_{i'j'}$ is considered smaller than w_{ij}.) Our algorithm uses the following property of MST edges: Edge $(v_i, v_j) \in$ MST if and only if, on every path from v_i to v_j consisting of two or more edges, there is an edge $(v_{i'}, v_{j'})$ such that $w_{i'j'} > w_{ij}$.

Example 4.1. A graph G is illustrated in Fig. 4.3, with its MST shown by thick lines. Note that edge $(v_1, v_3) \in$ MST, since every path of length 2 or more from v_1 to v_3 contains an edge whose weight is larger than w_{13}. On the other hand, $(v_0, v_5) \notin$ MST, since every edge on the path from v_0 to v_5 in MST has weight less than w_{05}. $\square$

Given G, an algorithm for computing MST is now obtained as follows: Algorithm HYPERCUBE SHORTEST PATHS is modified so that the length

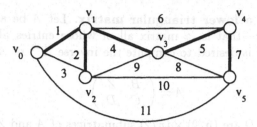

Fig. 4.3. A graph and its MST.

of a path is now equal to the longest edge it contains (as opposed to the sum of the lengths of the edges). With this new definition, all shortest paths are computed by replacing the statement

$$d_{ij}^k \leftarrow \min_l(d_{il}^{k/2} + d_{lj}^{k/2})$$

in algorithm HYPERCUBE SHORTEST PATHS with

$$d_{ij}^k \leftarrow \min_l(\max(d_{il}^{k/2}, d_{lj}^{k/2})).$$

This means that, for every path from v_i to v_j, we find the longest edge in the path, and then we determine the shortest of these edges, whose length is d_{ij}^{n-1}. It is now possible to determine those edges of E which belong in the minimum-weight spanning tree. This is done using the condition

$$(v_i, v_j) \in \text{MST} \quad \text{if and only if} \quad w_{ij} = d_{ij}^{n-1}.$$

It follows that the MST of a graph G with n vertices can be computed in $O(\log^2 n)$ time on a hypercube with n^3 processors.

4.3 Numerical Computations

Matrix operations arise most naturally in numerical computations, such as the solution of a set of linear equations, to cite a well-known example. In this section we illustrate how matrix multiplication can be used as a powerful tool to address a fundamental problem in linear algebra.

Let A be an $n \times n$ matrix whose *inverse* A^{-1} we seek to compute, such that $AA^{-1} = A^{-1}A = I$. Here I is an $n \times n$ identity matrix (whose main diagonal elements are 1, and all the rest are 0). Our derivation of a parallel algorithm for computing A^{-1} proceeds in stages. We begin by developing a parallel algorithm for inverting A in the special case where A is a lower triangular matrix.

4.3.1 Inverting a lower triangular matrix. Let A be an $n \times n$ *lower triangular matrix*—that is, a matrix all of whose entries above the main diagonal are 0. It is desired to compute the inverse A^{-1} of A. We begin by writing

$$A = \begin{pmatrix} B & Z \\ C & D \end{pmatrix}$$

where B, C, and D are $(n/2) \times (n/2)$ submatrices of A and Z is an $(n/2) \times (n/2)$ zero matrix. It follows that

$$A^{-1} = \begin{pmatrix} B^{-1} & Z \\ -D^{-1}CB^{-1} & D^{-1} \end{pmatrix}.$$

If B^{-1} and D^{-1} are computed recursively and simultaneously, a parallel algorithm for A^{-1} would have a running time of $t(n) = t(n/2) + 2r(n/2)$, where $r(n/2)$ is the time it takes to multiply two $(n/2) \times (n/2)$ matrices. Using algorithm HYPERCUBE MATRIX MULTIPLICATION, we have $r(n) = O(\log n)$. Therefore, $t(n) = O(\log^2 n)$.

4.3.2 The characteristic equation of a matrix. In order to take advantage of the algorithm just developed for inverting a lower triangular matrix, we need two definitions and a theorem from linear algebra.

Let A be an $n \times n$ matrix. When $n > 1$, we denote by A_{ij} the $(n-1) \times (n-1)$ matrix obtained from A by deleting row i and column j. The *determinant* of A denoted $det(A)$, is defined as follows: For $n = 1$, $det(A) = a_{11}$, and for $n > 1$, $det(A) = a_{11}det(A_{11}) - a_{12}det(A_{12}) + \cdots + (-1)^{1+j}a_{1j}\,det(A_{1j}) + \cdots + (-1)^{n+1}a_{1n}det(A_{1n})$. If $det(A) \neq 0$, then A is said to be *nonsingular*; in this case, the inverse A^{-1} is guaranteed to exist (and, conversely, if A^{-1} exists, then $det(A) \neq 0$).

The *characteristic polynomial* $\phi(x)$ of an $n \times n$ matrix A is defined to be

$$\begin{aligned} \phi(x) &= det(xI - A) \\ &= x^n + h_1 x^{n-1} + h_2 x^{n-2} + \cdots + h_n. \end{aligned}$$

Note, in particular, that for $x = 0$, $det(-A) = h_n$. Therefore, $det(A) = (-1)^n h_n$.

The *Cayley-Hamilton Theorem* states that every $n \times n$ matrix A satisfies its own characteristic polynomial. Thus, taking $x = A$ yields the *characteristic equation*

$$A^n + h_1 A^{n-1} + h_2 A^{n-2} + \cdots + h_{n-1}A + h_n I = 0.$$

Multiplying by A^{-1} yields

$$A^{n-1} + h_1 A^{n-2} + h_2 A^{n-3} + \cdots + h_{n-1}I + h_n A^{-1} = 0.$$

Therefore,

$$A^{-1} = -\frac{1}{h_n}(A^{n-1} + h_1 A^{n-2} + \cdots + h_{n-2}A + h_{n-1}I).$$

Now, the coefficients $h_1, h_2, \ldots, h_n$ satisfy

$$\begin{pmatrix} 1 & 0 & 0 & \ldots & 0 \\ s_1 & 2 & 0 & \ldots & 0 \\ s_2 & s_1 & 3 & \ldots & 0 \\ & & \vdots & & \\ s_{n-1} & \ldots & s_2 & s_1 & n \end{pmatrix} \begin{pmatrix} h_1 \\ h_2 \\ h_3 \\ \vdots \\ h_n \end{pmatrix} = - \begin{pmatrix} s_1 \\ s_2 \\ s_3 \\ \vdots \\ s_n \end{pmatrix},$$

or $Sh = -s$, where s_i denotes the *trace* of A^i—that is, the sum of the diagonal elements of A^i, for $1 \le i \le n$. The system of equations $Sh = -s$ can be solved for h by computing the inverse of S and writing: $h = -S^{-1}s$. Since S is lower triangular, it can be inverted using the algorithm previously developed for that purpose.

4.3.3 Inverting an arbitrary matrix. The algorithm for inverting an arbitrary $n \times n$ matrix A is now straightforward and is given next:

Step 1: Compute the powers A^2, A^3, ..., A^n of the matrix A (taking $A^1 = A$).
Step 2: Compute s_i by summing the diagonal elements of A^i for $i = 1, 2, \ldots, n$.
Step 3: Compute $h_1, h_2, \ldots, h_n$ from the equation $h = -S^{-1}s$.
Step 4: Compute $A^{-1} = (-1/h_n)(A^{n-1} + h_1 A^{n-2} + \cdots + h_{n-2}A + h_{n-1}I)$.

■

Analysis. Each of the powers A^i in Step 1 can be computed in $O(\log n) \times O(\log i)$ time with n^3 processors by repeated squaring and multiplication of matrices, using algorithm HYPERCUBE MATRIX MULTIPLICATION. Step 1 therefore requires $O(n^4)$ processors and $O(\log^2 n)$ time if all matrices A^i, $2 \le i \le n$, are to be computed simultaneously.

Step 2 is performed as follows: The elements of the matrix A^i reside in the base layer of a hypercube with n^3 processors, viewed as an $n \times n \times n$ array. In particular, the diagonal elements are held by the processors in positions $(0, j, j)$ of the array, for $j = 0, 1, \ldots, n - 1$. These processors do not form a hypercube. However, because each row of the base layer is a hypercube of n processors, the diagonal elements can be routed to the processors in positions $(0, 0, 0)$, $(0, 1, 0)$, ..., $(0, n - 1, 0)$, respectively, in $O(\log n)$ time. The latter processors, in turn, form a hypercube and can compute the sum of the diagonal elements in $O(\log n)$ time. Thus, each of the s_i can be computed in $O(\log n)$ time using n processors.

Inverting the lower triangular matrix S in Step 3 requires $O(\log^2 n)$ time and n^3 processors. This is followed by a matrix-by-vector product to obtain $h_1, h_2, \ldots, h_n$. The latter computation is easy to execute on the hypercube as a special case of matrix-by-matrix multiplication and requires $O(\log n)$ time and n^2 processors.

Finally, in Step 4, the simple operation of multiplying a matrix by a real number is immediate, while computing the sum of a collection of matrices consists in applying the method used in Step 3 of algorithm HYPERCUBE MATRIX MULTIPLICATION. Thus, Step 4 can be performed in $O(\log n)$ time using $O(n^3)$ processors.

The overall running time is therefore $t(n) = O(\log^2 n)$, while the number of processors used is $p(n) = O(n^4)$.

5. Computing the Convex Hull

Computational geometry is that branch of computer science whose focus is the design and analysis of efficient algorithms for the solution of geometric problems, that is, problems involving points, lines, polygons, circles, and the like. Solutions to such problems have applications in graphics, image processing, pattern recognition, operations research, and computer-aided design and manufacturing, to name just a few. A typical problem in computational geometry is that of computing the convex hull of a set of points in the plane. In this section, we develop a parallel algorithm for solving the convex hull problem on the PRAM model of computation. Our solution illustrates the algorithm design method of *divide and conquer*. In this method, a problem to be solved is broken into a number of subproblems of the same form as the original problem; this is the *divide* step. The subproblems are then solved independently, usually recursively; this is the *conquer* step. Finally, the solutions to the subproblems are combined to provide the answer to the original problem. In conjunction with the divide and conquer method, our solution to the convex hull problem uses a number of techniques that are interesting in their own right due to their wide applicability, namely, computing prefix sums, array packing, and sorting by merging. We begin by describing these techniques.

5.1 Prefix Sums on the PRAM

We are given a sequence $X = (x_0, x_1, \ldots, x_{n-1})$ of n numbers. For simplicity, let n be a power of 2. It is required to compute the following sums, known as the *initial* or *prefix* sums: $s_0 = x_0$, $s_1 = x_0 + x_1$, $s_2 = x_0 + x_1 + x_2$, $\ldots$, $s_{n-1} = x_0 + x_1 + \cdots + x_{n-1}$. A sequential algorithm to solve this problem reads one number at a time and executes $n - 1$ additions in sequence. The time required is $O(n)$, which is optimal in view of the $\Omega(n)$ operations required to compute just s_{n-1}.

On a PRAM with n processors $P_0, P_1, \ldots, P_{n-1}$, the problem can be solved much faster. Initially, with all processors operating in parallel, P_i reads

x_i, sets $s_i = x_i$, and stores s_i in the shared memory, for $i = 0, 1, \ldots, n - 1$. The sequence $S = (s_0, s_1, \ldots, s_{n-1})$ is assumed to be stored in an array of contiguous locations. The parallel algorithm now consists of $\log n$ steps. During each step, two numbers are added whose indices are twice the distance in the previous step. The algorithm is as follows:

Algorithm PRAM PREFIX SUMS

> **for** $j = 0$ **to** $(\log n) - 1$ **do**
> > **for** $i = 2^j$ **to** $n - 1$ **do in parallel**
> > > $s_i \leftarrow s_{i-2^j} + s_i$
> > **end for**
> **end for.** ∎

It is easy to see that each iteration yields twice as many final values s_i as the previous one. The algorithm therefore runs in $O(\log n)$ time. Since $p(n) = n$, the algorithm's cost is $c(n) = O(n \log n)$. This cost is not optimal, in view of the $O(n)$ operations that are sufficient to solve the problem sequentially.

We now show how to obtain a cost-optimal algorithm for computing the sequence $S = (s_0, s_1, \ldots, s_{n-1})$. The algorithm is based on the design technique of divide and conquer and proceeds as follows. Initially, $s_i = x_i$ for $i = 0, 1, \ldots, n - 1$.

1. The sequence S is divided into $n^{1/2}$ subsequences of size $n^{1/2}$ elements each. The prefix sums of each subsequence are now computed recursively, using $n^{1/2}$ processors. This requires $t(n^{1/2})$ time. Let the result of this computation over the ith sequence be $(s(i, 1), s(i, 2), \ldots, s(i, n^{1/2}))$.
2. The prefix sums $(s'(1, n^{1/2}), s'(2, n^{1/2}), \ldots, s'(n^{1/2} - 1, n^{1/2}))$ of the sequence $(s(1, n^{1/2}), s(2, n^{1/2}), \ldots, s(n^{1/2} - 1, n^{1/2}))$, are computed using n processors. This can be done in constant time by assigning k processors, denoted by $P(k, 1), P(k, 2), \ldots, P(k, k)$, to the computation of the kth prefix sum $s'(k, n^{1/2}) = s(1, n^{1/2}) + s(2, n^{1/2}) + \cdots + s(k, n^{1/2})$, for $1 \leq k \leq n^{1/2} - 1$. With all processors operating in parallel, $P(k, j)$ writes $s(j, n^{1/2})$ into $s'(k, n^{1/2})$, such that the *sum* of all the values written ending up in $s'(k, n^{1/2})$.
3. The sum $s'(i, n^{1/2})$ is now added to each element of the sequence $(s(i + 1, 1), s(i + 1, 2), \ldots, s(i + 1, n^{1/2}))$ for $i = 1, 2, \ldots, n^{1/2} - 1$, using $n^{1/2}$ processors per sequence. This requires constant time. ∎

The total number of processors used is therefore $O(n)$, and the running time is $t(n) = t(n^{1/2}) + a$, where a is a positive constant. Thus, $t(n) = O(\log \log n)$, for a cost of $O(n \log \log n)$.

This cost can be reduced to $O(n)$ by using only $O(n/\log \log n)$ processors. Initially, each processor is assigned $O(\log \log n)$ elements of the input sequence. With all processors operating in parallel, each processor computes the prefix sums of its assigned subsequence sequentially in $O(\log \log n)$ time. The sequence formed by the last prefix sum computed by each processor is

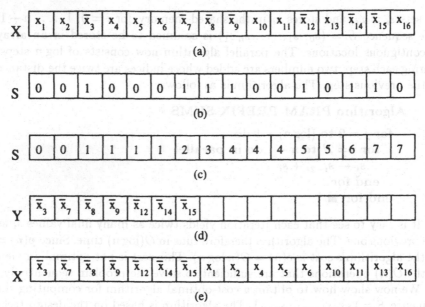

Fig. 5.1. Packing labeled and unlabeled data in an array.

now fed as input to the algorithm described in the preceding Steps 1 - 3. Each prefix sum thus computed is now added to $O(\log \log n)$ elements obtained in the initial step, as done in Step 3.

The technique described in the previous paragraph can be also be applied to obtain a cost-optimal algorithm with a lower processor requirement, namely, $O(n/\log n)$, and a higher running time, namely, $O(\log n)$.

5.2 Array Packing

Of all the applications of prefix sums computation to the design of efficient parallel algorithms, one of the most common is packing an array. Suppose that an array X of n elements is given, some of whose entries are labeled. The labeled entries are scattered arbitrarily throughout the array, as illustrated in Fig. 5.1(a) for the array $X = (x_1, x_2, \ldots, x_{16})$, where a label is denoted by a bar over x_i. Such an array may arise in an application in which a set of data is given and it is required to identify those data satisfying a certain condition. A datum satisfying the condition is labeled.

Once the data have been labeled, it is required to bring the labeled elements into contiguous positions in the same or another array. This may be necessary for a proper output of the results, or because the labeled elements are to undergo further processing and they are expected to appear in adjacent positions in the next stage of the computation.

Sequentially, the problem is solved by "burning the candle at both ends:" Two pointers q and r are used, where $q = 1$ and $r = n$ initially. The pointers are moved in opposite directions, q to the right and r to the left; q advances if x_q is a labeled element, whereas r advances if x_r is an unlabeled element. If at any time x_q is unlabeled and x_r is labeled, these two elements switch positions. When $q \geq r$, the labeled elements appear in adjacent positions in the first part of the array. This takes $O(n)$ time, which is optimal.

In parallel, we use a secondary array of n elements $S = (s_1, s_2, \ldots, s_n)$ to compute the destination of each labeled element of X. Initially, $s_i = 1$, provided that x_i is labeled, and $s_i = 0$, otherwise, as illustrated in Fig. 5.1(b). A prefix sums computation is then performed on the elements of S, as shown in Fig. 5.1(c). Finally, each labeled element x_i of X is copied into position s_i of an array Y. This is illustrated in Fig. 5.1(d). Note that the labeled elements of X occupy the first s_n positions of Y. The array S can be created with n processors in $O(1)$ time, each processor filling one positions of S. The prefix sums are computed by algorithm PRAM PREFIX SUMS in $O(\log n)$ time using n processors. Copying the labeled elements of X into Y can be done by n processors in $O(1)$ time. Therefore, this algorithm, which we call PRAM ARRAY PACKING, runs in $O(\log n)$ time and uses $O(n)$ processors. The algorithm's time and processor requirements can be reduced in a straightforward manner as described in the Section 5.1. It is interesting to observe here that, unlike the sequential solution described in the preceding, the parallel algorithm packs the labeled elements while maintaining their order (i.e., their original positions relative to one another).

In some cases, it may be necessary to pack the labeled elements of X within X itself: Once their destinations are known, the labeled elements can be copied directly into the first s_n positions of X. However, this would overwrite some unlabeled elements of X. Should this be undesirable, it can be avoided as follows:

1. The destinations of the s_n labeled elements are first computed.
2. The same procedure is then applied to the $n - s_n$ unlabeled elements.
3. Simultaneously, the labeled and unlabeled elements are copied into the first s_n and last $n - s_n$ positions of X, respectively.

This is shown in Fig. 5.1(e).

5.3 Sorting on the PRAM

As pointed out in Section 3., sorting is fundamental to computer science. For many problems, sorting a sequence of data is an inherent part of the solution, both in sequential as well as in parallel algorithms. The interconnection-network algorithms for sorting described in Section 3. can be easily simulated on the PRAM to run within the same time and processor requirements: Whenever two processors need to communicate they do so through the shared memory in constant time. In this section, however, we present a sorting algorithm that is specifically designed for the PRAM. We do so for two reasons.

First, the algorithm is based on merging and hence offers a new paradigm for parallel sorting. Second, and more important, the algorithm is significantly faster than any simulation of the interconnection-network algorithms, and in addition is cost optimal.

Suppose that a sequence of n numbers (in arbitrary order) $X = (x(1), x(2), \ldots, x(n))$ is to be sorted in nondecreasing order. The sequence X is stored in an array in shared memory, one number per array element. The array elements are thought of as being the leaves of a virtual complete binary tree T. Conceptually, the algorithm moves the numbers up the tree: At each node, the sequences received from the left and right children of the node are merged and the resulting sorted sequence is sent to the node's parent. When the algorithm terminates, the initial sequence of n values emerges from the root of the tree in sorted order. Because our aim is to achieve a total running time of $O(\log n)$, the merging process is pipelined. Thus, the algorithm works at several levels of the tree at once, overlapping the merging at different nodes over time. Henceforth, we refer to this as algorithm PRAM SORT.

Algorithm PRAM SORT. Let L_v be the sequence of values stored in the leaves of the subtree of T whose root is an internal (i.e., nonleaf) node v. At the jth time step, v contains a *sorted* sequence $Q_v(j)$ whose elements are selected from L_v. Furthermore, the sequence $Q_v(j)$ is an *increasing* subsequence of L_v. Eventually, when $Q_v(j) = L_v$, node v is said to be *complete*. Also, all leaves are said to be complete by definition. During the algorithm, a node v whose parent is not complete at the jth step sends a sorted subsequence $R_v(j)$ of $Q_v(j)$ to its parent.

How is $Q_v(j)$ created? Let w and z be the children of v. Node v merges $R_w(j)$ and $R_z(j)$ to obtain $Q_v(j)$, where $R_w(j)$ and $R_z(j)$ are themselves formed as follows:

1. If w is not complete during the $(j-1)$st step, then $R_w(j)$ consists of every fourth element of $Q_w(j-1)$.
2. If w becomes complete during the jth step, then:
    (i) $R_w(j+1)$ consists of every fourth element of $Q_w(j)$.
    (ii) $R_w(j+2)$ consists of every second element of $Q_w(j)$.
    (iii) $R_w(j+3) = Q_w(j)$.

Consequently, if w and z become complete during the jth step, then v becomes complete during step $j + 3$. It follows that the root of T becomes complete during step $3 \log n$. At this point, the root contains the input sequence of n values in sorted order, and the algorithm terminates.

The only detail left is to show how the sequences $R_w(j)$ and $R_z(j)$ are merged in constant time. Given two sequences of values, the *predecessor* of an element in one sequence is the largest element in the other sequence that is smaller than it (if such an element exists). Suppose that each element of $R_w(j)$ $(R_z(j))$ knows the position of its predecessor in $R_z(j)$ $(R_w(j))$. In that case, $R_w(j)$ and $R_z(j)$ can be merged in constant time using $|R_w(j)| +$

$|R_z(j)|$ processors, each processor directly placing one element in its final position in $Q_v(j)$. To make this possible, certain necessary information about predecessors is maintained. To wit, after step $j - 1$:

1. The elements of $R_w(j-1)$ "know" their predecessors in $R_z(j-1)$, and vice versa, these two sequences having just been merged to form $Q_v(j-1)$.
2. Each element of $R_w(j-1)$ finds its predecessor in $Q_w(j-1)$ in constant time. Consequently, all elements in $R_w(j-1)$ can determine their predecessor in $R_w(j)$, also in constant time. Note that no more than four elements of $R_w(j-1)$ have the same predecessor in $R_w(j)$. Now each element in $R_w(j)$ can determine its predecessor in $R_w(j-1)$ in constant time.
3. Each element of $R_z(j-1)$ finds its predecessor in $Q_z(j-1)$ in constant time. Consequently, all elements in $R_z(j-1)$ can determine their predecessors in $R_z(j)$, also in constant time. Note that no more than four elements of $R_z(j-1)$ have the same predecessor in $R_z(j)$. Now each element in $R_z(j)$ can determine its predecessor in $R_z(j-1)$ in constant time.
4. With the preceding "knowledge," the elements of $R_w(j)$ can determine their predecessors in $R_z(j)$, and vice versa, in constant time.

Thus, obtaining the information about predecessors required in the current step, merging, and obtaining the information about predecessors for the following step all require constant time. As mentioned before, there are $3 \log n$ steps in all, and therefore, the algorithm runs in $O(\log n)$ time. Since the sequences involved at each step contain a total of $O(n)$ elements, the number of processors needed is $O(n)$.

5.4 Divide and Conquer

Let $Q = (q_1, q_2, \ldots, q_n)$ be a finite sequence representing n points in the plane, where $n \geq 4$. Each point q_i of Q is given by a pair of Cartesian coordinates (x_i, y_i). The *convex hull* of Q, denoted $CH(Q)$, is the convex polygon with the smallest area containing all the points of Q. Thus, each $q_i \in Q$ either lies inside $CH(Q)$ or is a corner of $CH(Q)$. A set of points and its convex hull are shown in Fig. 5.2(a) and (b), respectively.

Given Q, the problem we wish to solve is to compute $CH(Q)$. Since $CH(Q)$ is a polygon, an algorithm for this problem must produce the corners of $CH(Q)$ in the order in which they appear on the boundary of the polygon (in clockwise order, for example). Sequentially, the problem is solved in $O(n \log n)$ time, and this is optimal in light of an $\Omega(n \log n)$ lower bound on the number of operations required to compute $CH(Q)$, obtained by showing that any convex hull algorithm must be able to sort a sequence of n numbers in nondecreasing order.

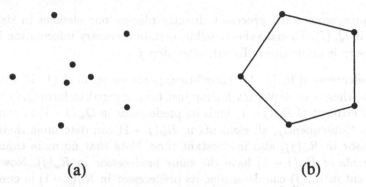

Fig. 5.2. A set of points and its convex hull.

We now describe a parallel algorithm for computing $CH(Q)$ that uses the divide and conquer approach. The algorithm consists of four steps and is given next as algorithm PRAM CONVEX HULL:

Algorithm PRAM CONVEX HULL $(n, Q, CH(Q))$

    Step 1: Sort the points of Q by their x-coordinates.
    Step 2: Partition Q into $n^{1/2}$ subsets $Q_1, Q_2, \ldots, Q_{n^{1/2}}$,
           of $n^{1/2}$ points each, separated by vertical lines,
           such that Q_i is to the left of Q_j if $i < j$.
    Step 3: for $i = 1$ to $n^{1/2}$ do in parallel
           if $|Q_i| \leq 3$
           then $CH(Q_i) \leftarrow Q_i$
           else PRAM CONVEX HULL $(n^{1/2}, Q_i, CH(Q_i))$
           end if
        end for
    Step 4: $CH(Q) \leftarrow CH(Q_1) \cup CH(Q_2) \cup \cdots \cup CH(Q_{n^{1/2}})$. ∎

Step 1 is performed using algorithm PRAM SORT. Step 2 is immediate: Since the points are sorted by their x-coordinates, it suffices to take the ith set of $n^{1/2}$ points in the sorted list and call it Q_i, $i = 1, 2, \ldots, n^{1/2}$. Step 3 applies the algorithm recursively to all the Q_i simultaneously. Finally, Step 4 merges the convex hulls obtained in Step 3 to compute $CH(Q)$. We now show how this step is implemented.

5.4.1 Merging a set of disjoint polygons. The situation at the end of Step 3 is illustrated in Fig. 5.3, where u and v are the points of Q with the smallest and largest x-coordinates, respectively. The convex hull $CH(Q)$ consists of two parts, namely, the *upper hull* (i.e., the sequence of corners of $CH(Q)$ in clockwise order, beginning with u and ending with v), and the *lower hull* (i.e., the sequence of corners of $CH(Q)$ in clockwise order, beginning with v and ending with u). This is depicted in Fig. 5.4, in which the upper hull consists of the corners u, a, b, c, and v, while v, d, e, f, and u

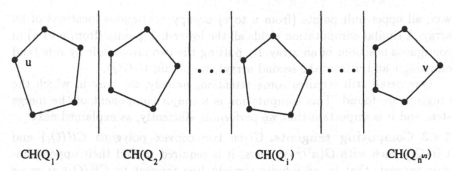

$$CH(Q_1) \qquad CH(Q_2) \qquad\qquad CH(Q_i) \qquad\qquad CH(Q_{n^{1/2}})$$

Fig. 5.3. Convex polygons to be merged in the computation of $CH(Q)$.

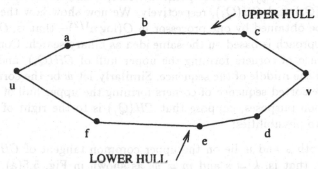

Fig. 5.4. The upper and lower hulls of $CH(Q)$.

are the corners of the lower hull. Step 4 computes the upper hull and lower hull separately and then concatenates them. Since computing the lower hull is symmetric to computing the upper hull, we only explain how the latter is performed.

5.4.2 Identifying the upper hull. Given two convex polygons, an *upper common tangent* to the two polygons is an infinite straight line that touches exactly one corner of each polygon; all remaining corners of the two polygons fall below the tangent. Suppose that n processors are available. We assign $n^{1/2} - 1$ processors to $CH(Q_i)$, for $i = 1, 2, \ldots, n^{1/2}$. Each processor assigned to $CH(Q_i)$ finds the upper tangent common to $CH(Q_i)$ and one of the remaining $n^{1/2} - 1$ convex polygons $CH(Q_j)$, $j \neq i$. Among all tangents to polygons to the left of $CH(Q_i)$, let L_i be the one with the smallest slope and tangent to $CH(Q_i)$ at corner l_i. Similarly, among all tangents to polygons to the right of $CH(Q_i)$, let R_i be the one with the largest slope and tangent to $CH(Q_i)$ at point r_i. If the angle formed by L_i and R_i is smaller than 180 degrees, then none of the corners of $CH(Q_i)$ is on the upper hull. Otherwise, all corners from l_i to r_i are on the upper hull.

These computations are done simultaneously for all $CH(Q_i)$, each yielding a (possibly empty) list of points of Q on the upper hull. The lists are then compressed into one list using algorithm PRAM ARRAY PACKING. This way, all upper-hull points (from u to v) occupy contiguous locations of an array. A similar computation yields all the lower-hull points (from v to u) in contiguous positions of an array. By putting the two arrays side by side (and omitting v and u from the second array), we obtain $CH(Q)$.

One detail still requires some attention, namely, the way in which the tangents are found. This computation is a major component of the merge step, and it is important that we perform it efficiently, as explained next.

5.4.3 Computing tangents. Given two convex polygons $CH(Q_i)$ and $CH(Q_j)$, each with $O(n^{1/2})$ corners, it is required to find their upper common tangent, that is, an infinite straight line tangent to $CH(Q_i)$ at some point k and to $CH(Q_j)$ at some point m. Here, k and m are on the upper hulls of $CH(Q_i)$ and $CH(Q_j)$, respectively. We now show how the points k and m can be obtained by one processor in $O(\log n^{1/2})$—that is, $O(\log n)$—time. The approach is based on the same idea as binary search. Consider the sorted sequence of corners forming the upper hull of $CH(Q_i)$, and let s be the corner in the middle of the sequence. Similarly, let w be the corner in the middle of the sorted sequence of corners forming the upper hull of $CH(Q_j)$. For illustration purposes, suppose that $CH(Q_j)$ is to the right of $CH(Q_i)$. There are two possibilities:

1. Either both s and w lie on the upper common tangent of $CH(Q_i)$ and $CH(Q_j)$, that is, $k = s$ and $m = w$, as shown in Fig. 5.5(a), in which case we are done;
2. Or one half of the (remaining) corners of $CH(Q_i)$ and/or $CH(Q_j)$ can be removed from further consideration as upper tangent points. An example of such a situation is illustrated in Fig. 5.5(b), in which those parts of a polygon removed from consideration are highlighted. The process is now repeated by finding the corners s and w in the middle of the remaining sequence of corners in $CH(Q_i)$ and $CH(Q_j)$, respectively.

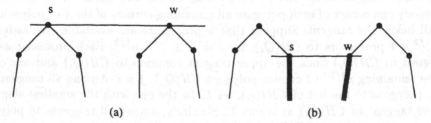

(a)   (b)

Fig. 5.5. Computing the upper tangent.

Analysis. As mentioned earlier, Step 1 of algorithm PRAM CONVEX HULL is performed using algorithm PRAM SORT. This requires $O(n)$ processors and $O(\log n)$ time. If $\{q'_1, q'_2, \ldots, q'_n\}$ represents the sorted sequence, then points q'_j, $j = (i-1)n^{1/2} + 1, (i-1)n^{1/2} + 2, \ldots, in^{1/2}$, belong to Q_i, for $i = 1, 2, \ldots, n^{1/2}$. Therefore, with n processors, Step 2 requires constant time: Processor P_j reads q'_j, then uses j and $n^{1/2}$ to compute i, and finally assigns q'_j to Q_i, $j = 1, 2, \ldots, n$. If $t(n)$ is the running time of algorithm PRAM CONVEX HULL, then Step 3 requires $t(n^{1/2})$ time, with $n^{1/2}$ processors computing $CH(Q_i)$. In Step 4, each of $(n^{1/2} - 1)n^{1/2}$ processors computes one tangent in $O(\log n)$ time. For each $CH(Q_i)$, the tangent L_i is found in constant time: The slopes of the tangents to polygons to the left of $CH(Q_i)$ are written simultaneously into some memory location, each slope written by a different processor, such that the *minimum* of all these slopes ends up in the memory location. The tangent R_i is found similarly. It also takes constant time to determine whether the corners from l_i to r_i belong to the upper hull.

Finally, array packing is done in $O(\log n)$ time using n processors. Putting all the pieces together, the overall running time of the algorithm is given by $t(n) = t(n^{1/2}) + \beta \log n$, for some constant β. Thus, $t(n) = O(\log n)$. Since $p(n) = n$, the algorithm's cost is $c(n) = O(n \log n)$ and that is optimal.

6. Pointer-Based Data Structures

The PRAM algorithms described in Section 5. manipulate data stored in *arrays* in shared memory. Specifically, the inputs to the prefix sums, array packing, sorting, and convex hull problems are known to occupy contiguous locations in memory. Thus, element x_i of an array X can be accessed directly using its index i in the array. In this section, we continue to use the PRAM model while focusing on problems whose inputs are stored in data structures that use pointers to relate their elements to one another. These data structures include linked lists, trees, and general graphs.

We begin in Section 6.1 by describing *pointer jumping*, a basic tool at the heart of all efficient parallel algorithms for pointer-based data structures. The problem of computing prefix sums on a linked list is then addressed in Section 6.2. The importance of this problem stems from the fact that a fast parallel algorithm for its solution allows a host of other computations to be performed efficiently. In fact, the scope of this algorithm extends beyond computations defined strictly on linked lists. Many computational problems occurring in the context of other data structures can be solved by transforming those structures into linked lists and then applying the prefix sums algorithm. Such a transformation is performed efficiently through the use of a powerful approach known as the *Euler tour* method, presented in Section 6.3. Finally, we show in Section 6.4 how a number of problems defined on trees are solved in parallel using the Euler tour and pointer jumping techniques.

6.1 Pointer Jumping

Consider a data structure in the form of a rooted tree where each node (except the root R) has a pointer to its parent. A certain node E, at a distance n from the root, holds a datum d. It is desired to copy d into every node on the path from E to R. Sequentially, there are n pointers to traverse and hence the computation requires $\Omega(n)$ time. In a parallel setting, we assume that each node of the tree is directly accessible to one (and only one) processor. The computation is performed in a number of iterations, with all processors operating in parallel. Let some node A point to some node B and node B point to some node C. The processor in charge of node A executes the following two steps:

1. It copies the datum d, if held by A, into node B, then
2. Modifies the pointer of node A to point to node C.

The same two steps are now repeated using the new pointers. After $O(\log n)$ iterations, all nodes on the path from E to R hold the datum d.

6.2 Prefix Sums Computation

Consider the singly linked list L shown in Fig. 6.1 and composed of *nodes* linked by *pointers*. Each node i consists of a number of fields, two of which

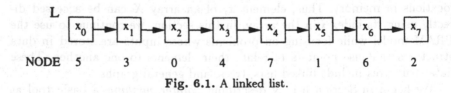

L

NODE   5   3   0   4   7   1   6   2

Fig. 6.1. A linked list.

in particular are illustrated in Fig. 6.1:

1. A value field $val(i)$ holding a number x_j.
2. A pointer field $succ(i)$ pointing to the successor of node i in L.

Since the last node in the list, the *tail*, has no successor, its pointer is equal to *nil*. It is important to note here that the index i of a node is essentially meaningless as the nodes occupy arbitrary locations in memory. The same is true of the index j of x_j since the latter is just a number. We use indices only for ease of exposition.

It is required to compute the prefix sums x_0, $x_0 + x_1$, $x_0 + x_1 + x_2$, ..., as shown in Fig. 6.2, where the symbol x_{ij} is used to denote $x_i + x_{i+1} + \cdots + x_j$. On a PRAM, we assume that processor P_i is assigned node i and is in charge of that node throughout the computation: P_i "knows" the address of node i and can gain access to its contents in $O(1)$ time. However, P_i "knows"

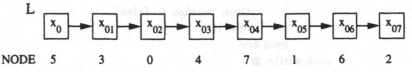

NODE   5   3   0   4   7   1   6   2

Fig. 6.2. Linked list after prefix computation on *val* field.

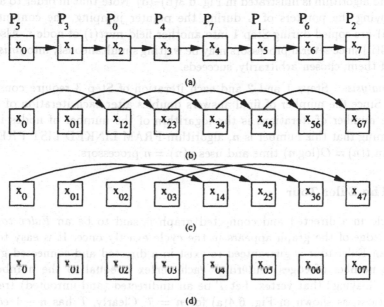

(a)

(b)

(c)

(d)

Fig. 6.3. Prefix computation by pointer jumping.

neither its position relative to the other processors nor the number of nodes in L. A processor assignment for the list of Fig. 6.1 is shown in Fig. 6.3(a).

The prefix sums of L are computed using pointer jumping by the following algorithm:

Algorithm PRAM LINKED LIST PREFIX

Step 1: for all i **do in parallel**
    $next(i) \leftarrow succ(i)$
end for
Step 2: *finished* $\leftarrow$ **false**
Step 3: while not *finished* **do**
    (3.1) *finished* $\leftarrow$ **true**
    (3.2) **for all** i **do in parallel**
        (i) **if** $next(i) \neq nil$
            then (a) $val(next(i)) \leftarrow val(i) + val(next(i))$
                  (b) $next(i) \leftarrow next(next(i))$
        end if
        (ii) **if** $next(i) \neq nil$

> **then** *finished* ← **false**
> **end if**
> **end for**
> **end while.** ∎

The algorithm is illustrated in Fig. 6.3(b)–(d). Note that in order to avoid destroying the pointers of L during the pointer jumping, the contents of $succ(i)$ are copied during Step 1 into another field $next(i)$ of node i. Also, in Step 3(ii) since several processors may be writing simultaneously into *finished*, one of them, chosen arbitrarily, succeeds.

Analysis. Steps 1 and 2 and each iteration of Step 3 require constant time. Since the number of final answers doubles after each iteration of Step 3, the number of iterations is the logarithm of the number of nodes in L. Assuming that this number is n, algorithm PRAM LINKED LIST PREFIX runs in $t(n) = O(\log n)$ time and uses $p(n) = n$ processors.

6.3 The Euler Tour

A cycle in a directed and connected graph is said to be an *Euler tour* if every edge of the graph appears in the cycle exactly once. It is easy to see that an Euler tour is guaranteed to exist in a directed and connected graph if the number of edges "entering" each vertex is equal to the number of edges "leaving" that vertex. Let T be an undirected (and unrooted) tree on n vertices, as shown in Fig. 6.4(a) for $n = 7$. Clearly, T has $n - 1$ edges. Suppose that we replace each edge (v_i, v_j) in T with two *oriented* edges (v_i, v_j) and (v_j, v_i), as shown in Fig. 6.4(b). Then the resulting directed graph is guaranteed to have an Euler tour. In what follows, we denote a directed tree such as the one in Fig. 6.4(b) by DT. An Euler tour defined on DT is denoted ET. Note that a DT with n vertices has $2n - 2$ edges, and hence ET is a sequence of $2n - 2$ edges.

We now describe an algorithm for computing an Euler tour ET of a directed tree DT. The algorithm receives DT as input, stored in the form of n linked lists, each of which containing the edges "leaving" a particular vertex. Node $< ij >$ in the linked list for vertex v_i consists of two fields, namely, a field *edge* holding the edge (v_i, v_j) and a field *next* holding a pointer to the next node in the list. A pointer $head(v_i)$ gives access to the first node in the linked list for vertex v_i. For example, the linked list for vertex v_5 of Fig. 6.4(b) is as follows:

$$head(v_5) \longrightarrow (v_5, v_1) \longrightarrow (v_5, v_6) \longrightarrow (v_5, v_7).$$

An algorithm for computing ET arranges all the edges of DT into a *single* linked list in which each edge (v_i, v_j) is followed by an edge (v_j, v_k). Also, if the first edge in ET "leaves" some vertex v_l, then the last edge in ET "enters" v_l. Such a linked list for the DT of Fig. 6.4(b) is shown in Fig. 6.5

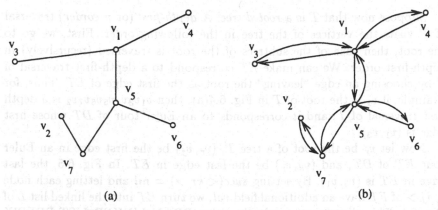

Fig. 6.4. A tree T and its directed version DT.

(in which the pointer from (v_5, v_1) to (v_1, v_3) is omitted). Note that each node in the linked list ET consists of two fields, namely, a field *edge* containing an edge and a field *succ* containing a pointer to the successor of the node.

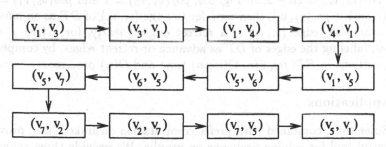

Fig. 6.5. The Euler tour as a linked list.

On a PRAM we assume that $2n - 2$ processors are available. Processor P_{ij} is in charge of edge (v_i, v_j) and determines the position in ET of node $< ij >$ holding that edge. It does so in constant time by determining the successor of $< ij >$ in the linked list as follows:

Successor of (v_i, v_j)

  if $next(< ji >) = jk$
  then $succ(< ij >) \leftarrow jk$
  else $succ(< ij >) \leftarrow head(v_j)$
  end if. ∎

Note that P_{ij} needs $next(< ji >)$ to compute $succ(< ij >)$, and obtains it from P_{ji} through shared memory. It follows that ET is computed in constant time.

Suppose now that T is a *rooted* tree. A *depth-first* (or *preorder*) traversal of T visits the vertices of the tree in the following order: First, we go to the root, then each of the subtrees of the root is traversed (recursively) in depth-first order. We can make ET correspond to a depth-first traversal of T by choosing an edge "leaving" the root as the first edge of ET. Thus, for example, if v_1 is the root of T in Fig. 6.4(a), then $v_1v_3v_4v_5v_6v_7v_2$ is a depth first traversal of T, and it corresponds to an Euler tour of DT whose first edge is (v_1, v_3).

Now let v_r be the root of a tree T, (v_r, v_j) be the first edge in an Euler tour ET of DT, and (v_k, v_r) be the last edge in ET. In Fig. 6.5, the last edge in ET is (v_5, v_1). By setting $succ(< kr >) = nil$ and letting each node $< ij >$ of ET have an additional field val, we turn ET into the linked list L of Fig. 6.1. This allows us to apply algorithm PRAM LINKED LIST PREFIX to ET.

In particular, let a prefix sums computation be applied to ET with all val fields initialized to 1. This gives the position in ET of each edge (v_i, v_j), denoted $pos(v_i, v_j)$ and stored in the val field of node $< ij >$. Thus, if (v_r, v_j) and (v_k, v_r) are the first and last edges in ET, respectively, then $pos(v_r, v_j) = 1$ and $pos(v_k, v_r) = 2n - 2$. In Fig. 6.5, $pos(v_1, v_3) = 1$ and $pos(v_5, v_1) = 12$. If $pos(v_i, v_j) < pos(v_j, v_i)$, then we refer to edge (v_i, v_j) of DT as an *advance* edge; otherwise, edge (v_i, v_j) is a *retreat* edge. Clearly, for a tree T of n vertices, labeling the edges of DT as advance or retreat edges, by computing their positions in ET, requires $O(\log n)$ time and $O(n)$ processors.

6.4 Applications

The Euler tour, combined with prefix computation on linked lists, provides a powerful tool for solving problems on graphs. We provide three examples of parallel algorithms for problems defined on trees.

6.4.1 Determining levels of vertices. The *level* of a vertex in an undirected rooted tree T is the number of (unoriented) edges on a shortest path from the root to the vertex. In an ET of DT, the level of a vertex v_j equals the number of retreat edges minus the number of advance edges following the first occurrence of v_j in ET. We compute this level as follows: First, we assign values to the val fields of ET. If (v_k, v_l) is a retreat edge, then $val(< lk >) = 1$; otherwise, $val(< lk >) = -1$. A *suffix sums* computation is now performed over the val fields using algorithm PRAM LINKED LIST PREFIX, with two changes: Each occurrence of i is replaced with $< ij >$, and Step (3.2)(i)(a) modified to be

$$val(< ij >) \leftarrow val(< ij >) + val(next(< ij >)).$$

Finally, if (v_i, v_j) is an advance edge, then

$$level(v_j) \leftarrow val(< ij >) + 1.$$

Note that if v_r is the root, then $level(v_r) \leftarrow 0$. If T has n vertices, then the computation requires $O(n)$ processors and runs in $O(\log n)$ time.

6.4.2 Numbering the vertices. The *inorder* traversal of a rooted binary tree T visits the vertices in the following order: The left subtree of the root is traversed recursively in inorder, then the root is visited, and finally, the right subtree of the root is traversed recursively in inorder. Given a binary tree T with n vertices, the Euler tour technique can be used to number the vertices of T in the order of the inorder traversal of T.

Let v_r be the root of T and ET be an Euler tour defined on T such that (v_r, v_s) is the first (advance) edge in ET, for some child v_s of the root. Values are assigned to the *val* fields of the nodes in ET as follows:

1. Let (v_i, v_j) be an advance edge; if (v_i, v_j) is immediately followed by a retreat edge, then $val(< ij >) = 1$; otherwise $val(< ij >) = 0$.
2. Let (v_k, v_l) be a retreat edge; if (v_k, v_l) is immediately followed by an advance edge, then $val(< kl >) = 1$; otherwise $val(< kl >) = 0$.

A prefix sums computation is now performed over the *val* fields. Finally,

1. If (v_i, v_j) is an advance edge immediately followed by a retreat edge, then $inorder(v_j) \leftarrow val(< ij >)$.
2. If (v_k, v_l) is a retreat edge immediately followed by an advance edge, then $inorder(v_l) \leftarrow val(< kl >)$.

The algorithm runs in $O(\log n)$ time using $O(n)$ processors.

6.4.3 Computing lowest common ancestors. Let T be a rooted complete binary tree and v_1 and v_2 two of its vertices. The *lowest common ancestor* of v_1 and v_2 is a vertex u that is an ancestor of both v_1 and v_2 and is farthest away from the root. Suppose that T has n leaves. Given n pairs of vertices (v_i, v_j), it is required to compute the lowest common ancestor of each pair. We now show that n processors can find the required n lowest common ancestors in constant time, provided that the vertices of T have been numbered in the order of an inorder traversal.

Let v_i and v_j be two vertices of T, whose inorder numbers are i and j, respectively. Further, let $i_1 i_2 \ldots i_k$ and $j_1 j_2 \ldots j_k$ be the binary representations of i and j, respectively. Now, let l be the leftmost position where $i_1 i_2 \ldots i_k$ and $j_1 j_2 \ldots j_k$ differ; in other words, $i_1 i_2 \ldots i_{l-1} = j_1 j_2 \ldots j_{l-1}$ and $i_l \neq j_l$.

The lowest common ancestor of v_i and v_j is that vertex v_m whose inorder number m has the following binary representation: $i_1 i_2 \ldots i_{l-1} 100 \ldots 0$. A single processor can obtain m in constant time.

7. Conclusions

A number of approaches to the design of efficient parallel algorithms were illustrated in the previous five sections. Our purpose in this final section is to probe some of these concepts a little further. We begin by extending the mesh interconnection network with the addition of *buses* and demonstrate the new model's flexibility and efficiency. Then it is the PRAM 's turn to be augmented with a special instruction for broadcasting. This results in *broadcasting with selective reduction*, an elegant and effective environment for designing parallel algorithms. Finally, we reflect on the power of parallelism by developing the notion of *parallel synergy*.

7.1 Meshes That Use Buses

The mesh of processors introduced in Section 3.2 is one of the most attractive models of computation in theory and in practice mainly because of its simplicity. In it, the maximum degree of a processor is four. The network is *regular*, as all rows (and columns) are connected to their successors in exactly the same way. It is also *modular*, in the sense that any of its regions can be implemented with the same basic component. These properties allow the mesh to be easily extended by the simple addition of a row or a column. However, the mesh is inadequate for those computational problems in which its diameter is considered too large. This limits its usefulness in many applications. In an attempt to retain most of the advantages of the mesh, an extension to the basic model is sought to reduce its diameter. In the most promising approach, the mesh is augmented with a certain number of *buses*. Here, a bus is simply a communication link to which some or all of the processors of the mesh are attached. Here, two processors that are not neighbors on the mesh can communicate directly through the bus to which they are both connected.

Writing a (fixed-size) datum on a bus and reading a (fixed-size) datum from the bus are considered basic operations requiring constant time. But how long does it take to traverse a bus? Let $B(L)$ represent a bus of length L, and let $\tau_{B(L)}$ be the time taken by a datum of fixed size to go from one end of the bus to the other. Clearly, $\tau_{B(L)}$ is a function of L. There are many choices for this function, depending on the technology used to implement the bus. In theoretical analyses of algorithms for meshes enhanced with buses, it is best, therefore, to leave $\tau_{B(L)}$ as a parameter when expressing the running time of an algorithm. Thus, if S steps of an algorithm use the bus, the time consumed by these steps would be $S \times \tau_{B(L)}$. However, for simplicity, we take $\tau_{B(L)} = O(1)$ in what follows. Specifically, we take $\tau_{B(L)}$ to be smaller than or equal to the time required by a basic computational operation, such as adding or comparing two numbers.

Buses can be implemented in a variety of ways. Thus, for example, they may be *fixed* (i.e., their number, shape, and length are static throughout the computation), or they may be *reconfigurable* (i.e., the buses are created dynamically while a problem is being solved). There may be one (or several) *global* bus(es) spanning all rows and columns of the mesh, or there may be one (or several) bus(es) for each row and one (or several) bus(es) for each column.

Also, a bus may be *electronic* or *optical*. On an electronic bus, *one* processor can *broadcast* a datum by placing it on the bus; the datum is now available for reading by *all* the remaining processors on the bus. An *optical bus*, by contrast, allows several processors to inject data on the bus simultaneously, each datum destined for one or several processors. This capability leads to an entirely new range of techniques for parallel algorithm design. In this section, we sketch the design and analysis of algorithms for electronic reconfigurable buses and fixed optical buses.

7.1.1 Reconfigurable buses. In a mesh-of-processors interconnection network a typical processor has four links connecting it to its neighbors. Each of these links is attached to the processor itself via an interface, commonly referred to as a *port*. A mesh processor therefore has four ports, called its north (N), south (S), west (W), and east (E) ports. Suppose that a processor is capable of connecting its ports internally in pairs in any one of the 10 configurations depicted in Fig. 7.1. These internal connections, combined with

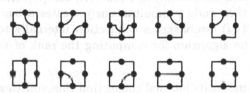

Fig. 7.1. Possible internal connections of a processor's ports.

the standard mesh links, allow for paths of arbitrary lengths and shapes to be created in the mesh, as shown in Fig. 7.2 for a 4×4 mesh in which three paths have been established. These paths are *dynamic*: They are created in constant time by the processors (and then modified if necessary) as specified by the algorithm. Each path created by a set of processors among themselves is viewed as a *bus* to which these processors are connected. It therefore possesses all the properties of (electronic) buses. Specifically, at any given time only *one* processor can place (i.e., write) on the bus a datum that takes constant time to travel from one end of the bus to the other and can be obtained (i.e., read) by *all* processors connected to the bus simultaneously. These specifications yield a new model of computation, called the *mesh with reconfigurable buses*.

We now show how this model can be used to solve a problem on linked lists, known as the *list ranking* problem. Given a linked list L of n nodes, it is required to determine the distance of each node from the end of the list. For example, in Fig. 6.1, node 7 is at distance 3 from the end of the list. Specifically, for each node i for which $succ(i) \neq nil$, we wish to compute $rank(i) = rank(succ(i)) + 1$. Of course, if $succ(i) = nil$, then $rank(i) = 0$.

The list L is mapped onto an $n \times n$ mesh with reconfigurable buses. In doing so we seek to shape a bus that reflects the topology of the list.

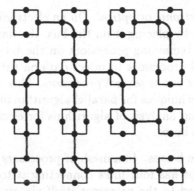

Fig. 7.2. A mesh with three configured buses.

Thus, node i is assigned to $P(i, i)$. A subbus is then implemented connecting $P(i, i)$ to $P(succ(i), succ(i))$ as follows: The bus goes vertically from $P(i, i)$ to $P(succ(i), i)$ and then horizontally to $P(succ(i), succ(i))$. Also, if $i = succ(j)$, for some node j, then node j simultaneously creates a bus from $P(j, j)$ to $P(i, i)$. Finally, $P(i, i)$ establishes a connection internally to join these two buses together. The algorithm for computing the rank of node i in L is as follows:

Step 1: $P(i, i)$ removes its internal connection thus splitting the bus in two.
Step 2: $P(i, i)$ sends a signal '$*$' on the bus connecting it to $P(succ(i), succ(i))$.
Step 3: If a processor $P(k, k)$, $1 \leq k \leq n$, receives '$*$' then it produces a 1 as output; otherwise, it produces a 0.
Step 4: The rank of node i in L is the sum of the 1s and 0s produced in Step 3 and is computed as follows:

    (4.1) All processors connect their W and E ports, thus creating a bus on each row. Processor $P(k, k)$, $1 \leq k \leq n$, broadcasts its 0 or 1 on the bus in row k. All processors in row k store the received value (i.e., 0 or 1).

    (4.2) If a processor contains a 0, it connects its N and S ports; otherwise, it connects its W and N ports and its S and E ports.

    (4.3) Processor $P(n, 1)$ places a '$*$' on the bus to which its S port is connected. If processor $P(1, j)$ receives that symbol then the the rank of node i is $j - 1$. ∎

Example 7.1. Let $n = 5$, and assume that for node i, the output of $P(k, k)$ in Step 3 is 0, 1, 1, 0, 1, for $k = 1, 2, 3, 4$, and 5, respectively. Step 4 is illustrated in Fig. 7.3, showing that the rank of node i is 3. □

By using n such $n \times n$ meshes, and running the preceding algorithm simultaneously for all nodes of L, the ranks of all nodes can be computed

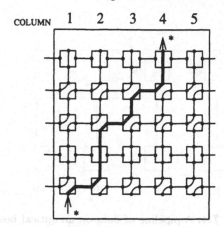

Fig. 7.3. Computing the rank of node i.

in $O(1)$ time. This requires a mesh of size $n^2 \times n$. This algorithm can be modified to use a mesh of size $O(mn \times n)$ and run in $O(\log n / \log m)$ time.

7.1.2 Optical buses. An alternative to electronic buses is provided by *optical buses*. Here, *light signals* are used instead of electrical signals. This allows the bus to have two properties, namely, *unidirectionality*, which means that a datum placed by any processor on an optical bus travels in only one (always the same) direction, and *predictability of the propagation delay per unit length*, which means that the time it takes a light signal to travel a certain distance along the bus is directly proportional to that distance. These two simple, yet important, properties lead to the definition of entirely new computational models and open up rich avenues for algorithmic design. To see this, let n processors $P_0, P_1, \ldots, P_{n-1}$ be connected to an optical bus. It is possible for *several* processors to place data on the bus simultaneously, one datum per processor. The data form a *pipeline* and travel down the bus, all in the same direction, as shown in Fig. 7.4, where d_i, d_j, and d_k are the data placed at the same time on the bus by processors P_i, P_j, and P_k, respectively. The difference between the arrival times of two data d_i and d_j at some processor P_l can be determined by the distance separating P_i and P_j.

The time taken by a light signal to traverse the optical bus from one end (at P_0) to the other (at P_{n-1})—that is, $\tau_{B(L)}$—is known as the *bus cycle*. Time is divided into bus-cycle intervals. As stated at the beginning of Section 7.1, we take $\tau_{B(L)} = O(1)$. All processors *write* their data on the bus synchronously at the beginning of each bus cycle. (Processors without any real message to send place a dummy message on the bus.) When is a processor P_j to *read* a message d_i from the bus? Since P_j "knows" the identity of the sender P_i, it skips $j - i - 1$ messages and reads the $(j - i)$th message that passes by it. In what follows we express $j - i$ using the function $wait(i, j)$.

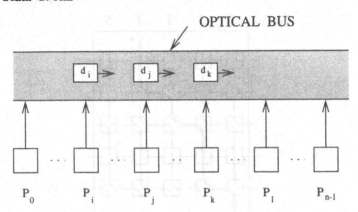

Fig. 7.4. A pipeline of data on an optical bus.

The system in Fig. 7.4 permits data to travel only in one direction. In order to allow messages to be sent in both directions, *two* optical buses are used. Data travel from left to right on one bus and from right to left on the other. Each processor can read and write to either of the two buses, as required by the algorithm. The two buses are completely independent from one another and accommodate separate pipelines. The *wait* function is now interpreted as follows: For $i \neq j$, if $wait(i, j) > 0$ then P_j reads from the left-to-right bus, otherwise it reads from the right-to-left bus.

It is now clear that any communication pattern among the processors (such as, for example, broadcasting a datum from one processor to all others, or executing an arbitrary permutation of the data) can be defined simply by specifying the *wait* function. To illustrate, consider the following general form of data distribution: For each i, $0 \leq i \leq n-1$, it is required to send datum d_i, held by P_i, to one or more processors or to no processor at all. Let $s(j)$ be the index of the processor from which P_j receives a datum, where $0 \leq j, s(j) \leq n-1$. This allows for the possibility that $s(j) = s(k) = i$, for $j \neq k$, meaning that the function s is not necessarily a permutation. In order to perform this operation, we define the waiting function as $wait(s(j), j) = j - s(j)$, for all j. Thus, the entire data distribution operation is completed in one bus cycle and hence requires constant time.

One interesting consequence of the foregoing is that the system of Fig. 7.4, consisting of n processors and $O(1)$ memory locations per processor, can simulate in constant time all (but one) of the forms of memory access allowed on a PRAM with n processors and $O(n)$ shared memory locations. This is true because memory access can be viewed as a data distribution operation. The only exception is that form of PRAM memory access (known as *concurrent writing*) where several processors write to the same memory location simultaneously (see Example 2.1). This case cannot be simulated in constant time. To see this, recall that $\tau_{B(L)}$ is assumed to be smaller than or equal to the time required by a basic operation, such as adding or comparing two numbers, whereas concurrent writing typically involves an arbitrary number of such operations. It follows that any PRAM algorithm (which does not require concurrent writing) can be performed in the same amount of time on the system of Fig. 7.4 as on the PRAM (the processors used in the two models being identical in kind and in number).

In an attempt to reduce the bus length L when the number of processors n is large, the system of Fig. 7.4 is modified so that the n processors are placed in a two-dimensional pattern with $n^{1/2}$ rows and $n^{1/2}$ columns. In this arrangement, each processor $P(i, j)$ is connected to four optical buses: Two buses on its row to send data horizontally and two buses on its column to send data vertically. A message can be sent from $P(i, j)$ to $P(k, l)$ in two bus cycles: First the message is sent from $P(i, j)$ to $P(i, l)$ and then from $P(i, l)$ to $P(k, l)$. We conclude our discussion of optical buses by showing how n numbers can be sorted on this model.

Recall that algorithm MESH SORT uses two basic operations to sort a sequence of numbers stored in a two-dimensional array, namely, sorting a row (or column) and cyclically shifting a row. Now suppose that the n numbers to be sorted are stored one number per processor in a two-dimensional array with row and column optical buses. The steps of algorithm MESH SORT are simulated as follows:

1. Whenever a row (or column) is to be sorted, the processors in that row (or column) and their two horizontal (vertical) optical buses simulate algorithm PRAM SORT.

2. Whenever a row is to be cyclically shifted, this is done using function *wait*, since a cyclic shift is a special case of data distribution.

This requires $O(\log n)$ time and n processors, for an optimal cost of $O(n \log n)$.

7.2 Broadcasting with Selective Reduction

In this section we describe a model of computation called *broadcasting with selective reduction* (BSR). This model is more powerful than the PRAM yet requires no more resources than the PRAM for its implementation. It consists of N processors, M shared-memory locations, and a memory access unit (MAU). Thus, BSR can be fully described by the diagram in Fig. 2.1 depicting the PRAM. In fact, all the components of the PRAM shown in that figure are the same for BSR (including the MAU, as we demonstrate later in this section). The only difference between the two models is in the way the MAU is exploited on BSR. Specifically, BSR's repertoire of instructions is that of the PRAM, augmented with one instruction called BROADCAST. This instruction allows *all* processors to write to *all* shared-memory locations simultaneously. It consists of three phases:

1. A *broadcasting* phase, in which each processor P_i broadcasts a *datum* d_i and a *tag* g_i, $1 \leq i \leq N$, destined to all M memory locations.

2. A *selection* phase, in which each memory location U_j uses a *limit* l_j, $1 \leq j \leq M$, and a *selection rule* σ to test the condition $g_i \ \sigma \ l_j$. Here, g_i and l_j are variables of the same type (e.g., integers), and σ is a *relational operator* selected from the set $\{<, \leq, =, \geq, >, \neq\}$. If $g_i \ \sigma \ l_j$ is **true**, then d_i is selected for reduction in the next phase; otherwise d_i is rejected by U_j.

3. A *reduction* phase, in which all data d_i selected by U_j during the selection phase are combined into one datum that is finally stored in U_j. This phase uses an appropriate binary associative *reduction operator* $\mathcal{R}$ selected from the set $\{\sum, \prod, \wedge, \vee, \oplus, \cap, \cup\}$, whose elements denote the operations *sum, product, and, or, exclusive-or, maximum,* and *minimum,* respectively.

All three phases are performed simultaneously for all processors P_i, $1 \leq i \leq N$, and all memory locations U_j, $1 \leq j \leq M$.

The instruction BROADCAST of BSR is written as follows:

$$U_j \quad \underset{1 \leq j \leq M}{\leftarrow} \quad \underset{\substack{g_i \ \sigma \ l_j \\ 1 \leq i \leq N}}{\mathcal{R}} \quad d_i.$$

This notation is interpreted as saying that, for each memory location U_j associated with the limit l_j, the proposition $g_i \ \sigma \ l_j$ is evaluated over all broadcast *tag* and *datum* pairs (g_i, d_i). In every case where the proposition is **true**, d_i is *accepted* by U_j. The set of all *data* accepted by U_j is reduced to a single value by means of the binary associative operation $\mathcal{R}$ and is stored in that memory location. If no *data* are accepted by a given memory location, the value (of the shared variable) held by that location is not affected by the BROADCAST instruction. If only one *datum* is accepted, U_j is assigned the value of that datum.

As we show at the end of this section, the BROADCAST instruction is executed in one access to memory, that is, in one traversal of the MAU. Since the BSR's MAU is identical to that of the PRAM, one access to memory on BSR takes constant time (as it does on the PRAM). Therefore, BROADCAST requires $O(1)$ time.

7.2.1 Computing a maximum-sum subsequence.

BSR is now used to solve a nontrivial computational problem. The power and elegance of the model are demonstrated by the efficiency and conciseness of the algorithm it affords. Given a sequence of numbers $X = (x_1, x_2, \ldots, x_n)$, it is required to find two indices u and v, where $u \leq v$, such that the subsequence $(x_u, x_{u+1}, \ldots, x_v)$ has the largest possible sum $x_u + x_{u+1} + \cdots + x_v$, among all such subsequences of X. In case of a tie, the leftmost subsequence with the largest sum is to be returned as the answer. Sequentially, the problem can be solved optimally in $O(n)$ time (by an algorithm which is by no means obvious).

The BSR algorithm uses n processors $P_1, P_2, \ldots, P_n$, and consists of four steps:

1. The prefix sums $s_1, s_2, \ldots, s_n$ of $x_1, x_2, \ldots, x_n$ are computed.

2. For each j, $1 \leq j \leq n$, the maximum prefix sum to the right of s_j, beginning with s_j, is found. The value and index of this prefix sum are stored in m_j and a_j, respectively. To compute m_j, a BROADCAST instruction is used, where the *tag* and *datum* pair broadcast by P_i is (i, s_i), while U_j uses j as *limit*, '$\geq$' for selection, and '$\bigcap$' for reduction. Similarly, to compute a_j, a BROADCAST is used, where P_i broadcasts (s_i, i) as its *tag* and *datum* pair, while U_j uses m_j, '$=$', and '$\bigcap$' as *limit*, selection rule, and reduction operator, respectively.

3. For each i, the sum of a maximum-sum subsequence, beginning with x_i, is computed as $m_i - s_i + x_i$. This step is implemented using a simple PRAM write, with P_i writing in b_i.

4. Finally, the sum L of the overall maximum-sum subsequence is found. Here, a PRAM concurrent-write operation suffices (with the *maximum* of the values written by the processors chosen for storing in L). Similarly, the starting index u of the overall maximum-sum subsequence is computed using a PRAM concurrent-write operation (with the *minimum* of the values written by the processors chosen for storing in u). The index at which the maximum-sum subsequence ends is computed as $v = a_u$.

The algorithm is given in what follows:

Algorithm BSR MAXIMUM SUM SUBSEQUENCE

Step 1: for $j = 1$ to n do in parallel
    for $i = 1$ to n do in parallel
$$s_j \leftarrow \sum_{i \leq j} x_i$$
    end for
end for
Step 2: (2.1) for $j = 1$ to n do in parallel
    for $i = 1$ to n do in parallel
$$m_j \leftarrow \bigcap_{i \geq j} s_i$$
end for

$$\textbf{end for}$$
$$(2.2) \textbf{ for } j = 1 \textbf{ to } n \textbf{ do in parallel}$$
$$\textbf{for } i = 1 \textbf{ to } n \textbf{ do in parallel}$$
$$a_j \leftarrow \bigcap_{s_i = m_j} i$$
$$\textbf{end for}$$
$$\textbf{end for}$$

Step 3: **for** $i = 1$ **to** n **do in parallel**
$$b_i \leftarrow m_i - s_i + x_i$$
end for

Step 4: (4.1) **for** $i = 1$ **to** n **do in parallel**
$$(i)\ L \leftarrow \bigcap_{i \geq 1} b_i$$
$$(ii)\ \textbf{if } b_i = L$$
$$\textbf{then } u \leftarrow \bigcup_{i \geq 1} i$$
$$\textbf{end if}$$
$$\textbf{end for}$$
$$(4.2)\ v \leftarrow a_u . \blacksquare$$

Each step of the algorithm runs in $O(1)$ time. Thus, $p(n) = n$, $t(n) = O(1)$, and $c(n) = O(n)$, which is optimal.

7.2.2 A MAU for the PRAM and BSR. We conclude our description of the BSR model by illustrating how the same MAU implemented as a combinational circuit can serve both the PRAM and BSR. A *combinational circuit* is a device consisting of components arranged in *stages*. A datum travels through the circuit from one end to the other in one direction: It is never allowed to backtrack midway. Once it has reached the opposite end, then (and only then) the datum is allowed (if necessary) to travel in the other direction (thus returning where it came from). Each component is a simple processor capable of performing in constant time some elementary operations such as adding or comparing two numbers. It receives a constant number of inputs and produces a constant number of outputs. The inputs to the components in each stage are received from the outside world or from components in a previous stage using direct links. The outputs from a component are sent to components in a subsequent stage or to the outside world. The *width* of a combinational circuit is the maximum number of components forming a stage. The *depth* of a combinational circuit is the maximum number of components forming a path from one end of the circuit to the other. The *size* of a combinational circuit is the total number of components it uses.

Example 7.2. The combinational circuit of Fig. 7.5 computes the prefix sums of four numbers (received as input by its leftmost stage) and produces them as output (through its rightmost stage). It can also compute the suffix sums of its inputs. As well, the circuit may be used to distribute a value received on one input line to several output lines. The circuit has a width of 4, a depth of 3, and a size of 12. $\square$

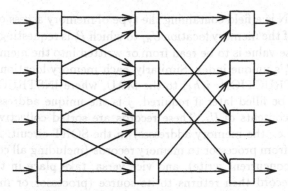

Fig. 7.5. A combinational circuit for computing prefix and suffix sums.

The combinational circuit depicted in Fig. 7.6 serves as a memory access unit for both the PRAM and the BSR models. It is made up of two circuits:

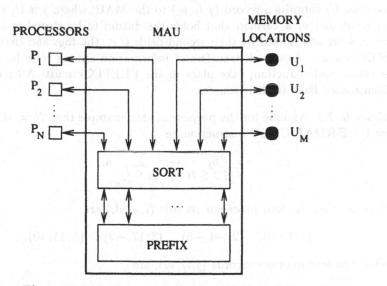

Fig. 7.6. A MAU for the PRAM and BSR models.

1. A sorting circuit (the box labeled SORT) of width $O(N + M)$, depth $O(\log(N + M))$, and size $O((N + M)\log(N + M))$, and
2. A circuit for computing prefix and suffix sums (the box labeled PREFIX). This is the circuit of Fig. 7.5 rotated 90 degrees clockwise and capable of receiving $N + M$ inputs. It has a width of $N + M$, a depth of $1 + \log(N + M)$, and a size of $N + M + ((N + M)\log(N + M))$.

On the PRAM, when a memory access operation is to be executed, each processor P_i submits a record (INSTRUCTION, a_i, d_i, i) to the MAU, where

INSTRUCTION is a field containing the type of memory access operation, a_i is the address of the memory location U_{a_i} to which P_i is requesting access, d_i is a variable whose value is to be read from or written into the memory location U_{a_i}, and i is P_i's unique index. Similarly, each memory location U_j submits a record (INSTRUCTION, j, h_j) to the MAU, where INSTRUCTION is an empty field to be filled later if required, j is the unique address of U_j, and h_j carries the contents of U_j. These records are sorted collectively by their second fields (i.e., the memory addresses) in the SORT circuit. All transfers of information from processor to memory records (including all computations required by a concurrent write), and vice versa, take place in the PREFIX circuit. Each record then returns to its source (processor or memory location) by retracing its own path through the MAU. On the BSR model, the memory access operations of the PRAM instruction repertoire are executed in the same way as just described. When a BROADCAST instruction is to be performed, each processor P_i submits a record (i, g_i, d_i) to the MAU, where i is the processor's index, g_i its *tag*, and d_i its *datum*. Similarly, each memory location U_j submits a record (j, l_j, v_j) to the MAU, where j is U_j's *index*, l_j its *limit*, and v_j a *variable* that holds the datum to be stored in U_j. These records are now sorted by their second fields (i.e., the *tags* and *limits*) in the SORT circuit. Again, all transfers of information among records, including selection and reduction, take place in the PREFIX circuit. All records are then routed back to their sources.

Example 7.3. Assume for the purpose of this example that $N = M = 4$, and let the **BROADCAST** instruction be

$$ v_j \quad \leftarrow \quad \sum_{\substack{g_i < l_j \\ 1 \le i \le N}} d_i. $$
$$ 1 \le j \le M $$

Suppose that the four processor records (i, g_i, d_i) are

$$ (1, 15, 9), \quad (2, -4, -5), \quad (3, 17, -2), \quad (4, 11, 10), $$

while the four memory records (j, l_j, v_j), are

$$ (1, 16, v_1), \quad (2, 12, v_2), \quad (3, 18, v_3), \quad (4, -6, v_4). $$

Initially, $v_j = 0$, for $1 \le j \le 4$. When the **BROADCAST** instruction is complete, we want $v_1 = 9 - 5 + 10 = 14$ (since 15, -4, and 11 are less than 16), $v_2 = -5 + 10 = 5$ (since -4 and 11 are less than 12), $v_3 = 9 - 5 - 2 + 10 = 12$ (since all *tags* are less than 18), and $v_4 = 0$ (since no *tag* is less than -6).

The processor and memory records are fed as input to the SORT circuit. They exit from it sorted (from left to right) on their second fields (i.e., the g_i and the l_j) as $\{(4, -6, v_4), (2, -4, -5), (4, 11, 10), (2, 12, v_2), (1, 15, 9), (1, 16, v_1), (3, 17, -2), (3, 18, v_3)\}$. Note that in case of equality, a memory record precedes a processor record (since the selection rule is '<' and we don't want any datum d_i to be included in the computation of v_j unless its tag g_i is strictly smaller than l_j).

The sorted sequence of records now enters a PREFIX circuit whose width is $N + M = 8$ and whose depth is $1 + \log(N + M) = 4$. This circuit computes the values of the v_j. It performs *selection* and *reduction* by computing the sum of the d_i entries of all processor records preceding v_j's record in the sorted sequence. This computation uses only the links going 'down' and 'to the right' from one stage to the next in the PREFIX circuit (again because the selection rule is '<'). Depending on whether it has one or two inputs and one or two outputs, a component of the PREFIX circuit behaves in one of the four ways illustrated in Fig 7.7.

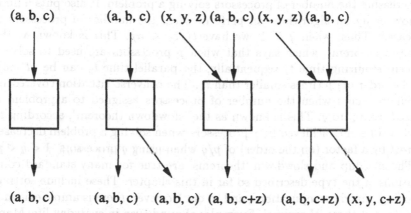

Fig. 7.7. Behavior of components in PREFIX circuit.

After the last stage of the PREFIX circuit has performed its computation, the records have become $\{(4, -6, 0), (2, -4, -5), (4, 11, 5), (2, 12, 5), (1, 15, 14), (1, 16, 14), (3, 17, 12), (3, 18, 12)\}$. Note in particular that $v_4 = 0$, $v_1 = 14$, $v_2 = 5$, and $v_3 = 12$, as required. The four memory records $(4, -6, 0)$, $(2, 12, 5)$, $(1, 16, 14)$, and $(3, 18, 12)$ now retrace their paths through the MAU to return to their respective memory locations. $\square$

When $N = O(M)$, the MAU of Fig 7.6 has a width of $O(M)$, a depth of $O(\log M)$, and a size of $O(M \log M)$. That this circuit is optimal for all three measures is seen by deriving $\Omega(M)$, $\Omega(\log M)$, and $\Omega(M \log M)$ lower bounds on the width, depth, and size, respectively, of any combinational circuits capable of implementing the simplest of the memory access operations allowed on the PRAM (namely, when each processor gains access to a distinct memory location). Finally, note that although the MAU's depth is $O(\log M)$ the time to gain access to memory on both the PRAM and BSR models is taken to be constant.

7.3 Synergy in Parallelism

A central 'belief' in the theory and practice of parallel computation is stated as follows:

> **Claim:** If a certain computation can be performed with p processors in time t_p on a given model and with q processors in time t_q on the same model, where $q < p$, then for a positive constant $\alpha \geq 1$,
>
> $$1 \leq \frac{t_q}{t_p} \leq \alpha \frac{p}{q}. \square$$

The preceding statement essentially puts a limit on how well one can do by increasing the number of processors solving a problem. It also puts a limit on how badly an algorithm can perform when the number of processors is decreased. Thus, when $q = 1$, we have $t_1/t_p \leq \alpha p$. This is known as the 'speedup theorem', which says that when p processors are used to solve a problem requiring time t_1 sequentially, the parallel time t_p can be *at most* (on the order of) p times smaller than t_1. The converse situation covered by the claim occurs when the number of processors assigned to a problem is *reduced* from p to q. This is known as the 'slowdown theorem', according to which a time of t_p achieved by p processors when solving a problem decreases *at most* by a factor (on the order of) of p/q when using q processors, $1 < q < p$.

The speedup and slowdown 'theorems' are true for many standard computations of the type described so far in this chapter. These include sorting, searching, matrix computations, and so on. However, there is ample evidence to contradict these 'theorems'. Examples abound even in everyday life. Many tasks done by one person in time t_1 are often completed by p people in time t_p, where t_p is significantly *smaller* than t_1/p. By contrast, $p/2$ people will perform those tasks in time $t_{p/2}$, where $t_{p/2}$ is a lot *greater* than $2t_p$. Huge construction jobs provide a perfect illustration.

Our purpose in this final section is to show that for a large class of computational problems, the claim that $t_q/t_p \leq \alpha p/q$, for $q < p$, does *not* hold. Specifically, we exhibit computations satisfying a computational phenomenon called *parallel synergy* and stated as follows:

> **Parallel Synergy:** There exist computations performed with p processors in time t_p on a given model and by q processors in time t_q on the same model, where $q < p$, and for which
>
> $$\frac{t_q}{t_p} \text{ is } \textit{asymptotically} \text{ greater than } \frac{p}{q}. \square$$

When parallel synergy applies, p processors can perform a computation *asymptotically* faster than t_1/p. In other words, the running time is reduced by a factor larger than the number of processors used. On the other hand, q processors, $1 < q < p$, perform such a computation *asymptotically* slower than pt_p/q. This means that, when full parallelism is not used, the running time increases by a factor larger than the processor ratio. In both cases, 'asymptotically' is used to indicate that $(t_q/t_p)/(p/q)$ is not just a constant.

Parallel synergy manifests itself in nonconventional computations arising, for example, in time-dependent applications in which a computer receives its input in real time and has to produce an output by a certain deadline, in applications where inputs vary with time, or where outputs affect subsequent inputs, and so on. We illustrate parallel synergy with the help of the following examples.

7.3.1 Independent input streams.

Suppose that a computer receives n independent and simultaneous streams of data as input. Each stream is of the form $< v_1, v_2, \ldots, v_n >$ and represents a distinct cyclic permutation of the values in the sequence $X = (x_1, x_2, \ldots, x_n)$. For example, when $n = 5$, there are five input streams as follows: $< x_1, x_2, x_3, x_4, x_5 >$, $< x_5, x_1, x_2, x_3, x_4 >$, $< x_4, x_5, x_1, x_2, x_3 >$, $< x_3, x_4, x_5, x_1, x_2 >$, and $< x_2, x_3, x_4, x_5, x_1 >$. It is also the case that within each stream value v_{i+1} arrives n time units after value v_i, $1 \leq i \leq n - 1$. Receiving a value from a stream requires one time unit. Thus, a single processor can monitor the values in only one stream: By the time the processor reads and stores the first value of a selected stream, it is too late to turn and process the remaining $n - 1$ values from the other streams, which arrived at the same time. Furthermore, a stream remains active if and only if its first value has been read and stored by a processor.

An application in which the situation just described occurs is when n sensors are used to make certain measurements from an environment. Each x_i is measured in turn by a different sensor and relayed to the computer. It takes n time units to make a measurement. It is important to use several sensors to make the same set of measurements (in different orders): This increases the chances that the measurements will be made, even if some sensors break down; furthermore, it allows parallelism to be exploited advantageously.

Suppose that the application calls for finding the smallest value in X. If the computer used is a sequential one, its single processor selects a stream and reads the consecutive values it receives, keeping track of the smallest encountered so far. By our assumption, a processor can read a value, compare it to the smallest so far, and update the latter if necessary, all in one time unit. It therefore takes n time units to process the n inputs, plus $n(n - 1)$ time units of waiting time in between consecutive inputs. Therefore, after exactly n^2 time units, the minimum value is known, and $t_1 = n^2$.

Now consider the situation when a parallel computer is used. For instance, let the computer be a complete binary tree of processors with n leaves (and a total of $p = 2n - 1$ processors). Each leaf processor is connected to an input stream. As soon as the first n values arrive at the leaves, with each leaf receiving one value from a different stream, computation of the minimum can commence. Each leaf reads its input value and sends it to its parent. The latter finds the smaller of the two values received from its children and sends it to its parent. This continues up the tree, and after $t_p = \log n$ time units, the minimum emerges from the root. It follows that $t_1/t_p = n^2/\log n$, and this is asymptotically greater than p.

What if the tree has fewer than n leaves? For example, suppose that a tree with $n^{1/2}$ leaves (and a total of $q = 2n^{1/2} - 1$ processors) is used. The best we can do is assign the $n^{1/2}$ leaf processors to monitor $n^{1/2}$ streams whose first $n^{1/2}$ values are distinct from one another. Since consecutive data in each stream are separated by n time units, each leaf processor requires $(n^{1/2} - 1)n$ time to see the first $n^{1/2}$ values in its stream and determine their minimum. The $n^{1/2}$ minima thus identified now climb the tree, and the overall minimum is obtained in $\log n^{1/2}$ time. Therefore, $t_q = (n^{1/2} - 1)n + (\log n)/2$. Clearly, t_q/t_p is asymptotically greater than p/q.

Accumulating Data. In a certain application, a set of n data is received every k time units and stored in a computer's memory. Here $2 < k < n$; for example, let $k = 5$. The ith data set received is stored in the ith row of a two-dimensional array A. In other words, the elements of the ith set occupy locations $A(i, 1), A(i, 2), \ldots, A(i, n)$. At most 2^n such sets may be received. Thus, A has 2^n rows and n columns. Initially, A is empty. The n data forming a set are received and stored simultaneously: One time unit elapses from the moment the data are received from the outside world to the moment they settle in a row of A. Once a datum has been stored in $A(i, j)$, it requires one time unit to be processed; that is, a certain operation must be performed on it which takes one time unit. This operation depends on the application. For example, the operation may simply be to replace $A(i, j)$ by $(A(i, j))^2$. The computation terminates once all data currently in A have been processed, *regardless of whether more data arrive later.*

Suppose that we use a sequential computer to solve the problem. It receives the first set of n data in one time unit. It then proceeds to update it. This requires n time units. Meanwhile, $n/5$ additional data sets would have arrived in A, and must be processed. The computer does not catch up with the arriving data until they cease to arrive. Therefore, it must process $2^n \times n$ values. This requires $2^n \times n$ time units. Hence, $t_1 = 1 + 2^n \times n$.

Now consider what happens when a PRAM with $p = n$ processors is used. It receives the first data set, stores it in $A(1, 1), A(1, 2), \ldots, A(1, n)$, and updates it to $(A(1, 1))^2, (A(1, 2))^2, \ldots, (A(1, n))^2$, all in two time unit. Since all data currently in A have been processed and no new data have been received, the computation terminates. Thus, $t_p = 2$. Clearly, t_1/t_p is asymptotically greater than p.

Finally, let the PRAM have only q processors, where $q < n$, and assume that $(n/q) > 5$. The first set of data is processed in n/q time units. Meanwhile, $(n/q)/5$ new data sets would have been received. This way, the PRAM cannot catch up with the arriving data until the data cease to arrive. Therefore, $2^n \times n$ data must be processed, and this requires $(2^n \times n)/q$ time units. It follows that $t_q = 1 + (2^n \times n)/q$, and once again, t_q/t_p is asymptotically greater than p/q.

7.3.2 Varying data. An array A of size p resides in the memory of a computer, such that $A(i) = 0$ for $1 \le i \le p$. It is required to set $A(i)$ to the value p^x, for all i, $1 \le i \le p$, where x is some positive integer constant, such that $1 < x \le p$. One condition of this computation is that at no time during the update two elements of A differ by more than a certain constant $w < p$.

A sequential computer updates each element of A by w units at a time, thus requiring $t_1 = p \times (p^x/w)$ time to complete the task. Now, let a PRAM with p processors be available. The processors compute p^x using a concurrent-write operation in one time unit: Each of the first x processors writes the value p in some memory location X; the *product* of all such values written is stored in X as p^x. All p processors now read X and prite p^x in all positions of A simultaneously in another time unit. Thus, $t_p = 2$, and t_1/t_p is asymptotically greater than p. Finally, suppose that q processors are available, where $q < p$. The PRAM now updates the elements of A in groups of q elements by w units at a time. The total time required is $t_q = (p/q) \times (p^x/w)$. It follows that t_q/t_p is asymptotically greater than p/q.

The preceding examples dramatically illustrate the tremendous potential of parallel computation. In each case, when moving from a sequential to a parallel computer, the benefit afforded by parallel synergy was significantly greater than the investment in processors. Also, any reduction in processing power resulted in a disproportionate loss. Yet, in more than one sense, these examples barely scratch the surface. Indeed, each of the aforementioned computations can in principle be performed, albeit considerably slowly, on a sequential computer. There are situations, however, were using a parallel computer is not just a sensible approach—it is the *only* way to complete successfully the computation involved. This is the case, for instance, in applications where the input data cease to exist or become redundant after a certain period of time, or when the output results are meaningful only by a certain deadline. Similarly, in each of the examples where parallel synergy occurred, the models of computation used were conventional static engines. One of the main research challenges is to study the role played by parallelism in a paradigm of computation where processors are *dynamic agents* capable of manifesting themselves within all aspects of the physical universe.

8. Bibliographical Remarks

A good introduction to the design and analysis of sequential algorithms is provided in Cormen et al. [CLR90]. The design and analysis of parallel algorithms are covered in Akl [Akl85, Akl89, Akl97], Akl and Lyons [AL93], JáJá [Jaj92], Kumar et al. [KGG+94], Leighton [Lei92], and Reif [Rei93]. Combinational circuits implementing the memory access unit of the PRAM are described in Akl [Akl97], Fava Lindon and Akl [FA93], and Vishkin [Vis84].

The sequential complexity of sorting and the 0-1 principle are studied in Knuth [Knu73] along with the design and analysis of several optimal sorting algorithms. A proof of correctness and an analysis of algorithm LINEAR ARRAY SORT are provided in Akl [Akl97]. Algorithm MESH SORT is due to Marberg and Gafni [MG88]. Algorithm MULTIDIMENSIONAL ARRAY SIMPLE SORT was first proposed by Akl and Wolff [AW97]. It can be seen as a generalization of an algorithm designed by Scherson et al. [SSS86] for sorting on a mesh. Furthermore, its idea of repeatedly going through the dimensions of the multidimensional array during each iteration of the outer for loop is reminiscent of the ASCEND paradigm (originally proposed for the hypercube and related interconnection networks [PV81]). Algorithm MULTIDIMENSIONAL ARRAY FAST SORT was discovered by Kunde [Kun87].

Algorithm HYPERCUBE SORT follows directly from the work of Akl and Wolff [AW97]. A different derivation of this algorithm appears in [Gor91] where it is shown to be equivalent to the *odd-even-merge* [Bat68] and to the *balanced* [DPR+83] sorting circuits. Other algorithms for sorting on the hypercube, including those with the same running time (i.e., $O(\log^2 M)$) as well as asymptotically faster ones, are considerably more complicated [Akl85, Lei92]. Because its degree and diameter are sublogarithmic in the number of its vertices, the star graph interconnection network has received a good deal of attention lately (see, for example, Akers et al. [AHK87], Akers and Krishnamurthy [AK87, AK89], Akl [Akl97], Akl et al. [ADF94], Akl and Qiu [AQ92, AQ93], Akl et al. [AQS92, AQS93], Akl and Wolff [AW97], Chiang and Chen [CC95], Dietzfelbinger et al. [MS91], Fragopoulou [Fra95], Fragopoulou and Akl [FA94, FA95a, FA95b, FA95c, FA95d, FA96a], Fragopoulou et al. [FA96b], Gordon [Gor91], Jwo et al. [JLD90], Menn and Somani [MS90], Nigam et al. [NSK90], Qiu [Qiu92], Qiu and Akl [QA94a, QA94b], Qiu et al. [QAM94, QMA91a, QMA91b, QMA93], Rajasekaran and Wei [RW93, RW97], and Sur and Srimani [SS91]. Algorithms for sorting on the n-star in $O(n^3 \log n)$ time are described in Akl and Wolff [AW97], Menn and Somani [MS90] and Rajasekaran and Wei [RW93]. Another algorithm for sorting on the n-star is described in [Gor91], and a lower bound of $\Omega((\log n!)^2)$ on its running time is given, but no upper bound.

A fast sequential algorithm for multiplying two matrices is described in Coppersmith and Winograd [CW87]. Several parallel algorithms for matrix multiplication on the hypercube, including the algorithm of Section 4.1, together with their applications, are presented in Dekel et al. [DNS81]. References to, and descriptions of, other parallel algorithms for matrix multiplication and their applications to graph theoretic and numerical problems, can be found in Akl [Akl89], Leighton [Lei92], Reif [Rei93], and Ullman [Ull84]. Miscellaneous hypercube algorithms are provided in Akl [Akl85, Akl89], Akl and Lyons [AL93], Blelloch [Ble90], Das et al. [DDP90], Ferreira [Fer96], Fox et al. [FJL+88], Hatcher and Quinn [Hat91], Hillis [Hil85], Leighton [Lei92], Qiu and Akl [QA97], Ranka and Sahni [RS90], Seitz [Sei84, Sei85], and Trew and Wilson [TW91].

The algorithms of Section 5.1 for computing prefix sums can be used in a more general setting where the operation '+' is replaced with any binary associative operation 'o', such as '×', MIN, MAX, AND, OR, and so on. Prefix computation plays a central role in the design of efficient parallel algorithms in a variety of applications ranging from fundamental computations such as array packing, sorting, searching, and selection, to numerical computations, graph theory, picture processing, and computational geometry. A number of such applications are described in Akl [Akl97] and Lakshmivarahan and Dhall [LD94]. Algorithm PRAM SORT was originally proposed by Cole [Col88]. Lower bounds and sequential algorithms for fundamental problems in computational geometry are provided in Preparata and Shamos [PS85]; see also Mulmuley [Mul93] and O'Rourke [ORo94]. Parallel algorithms for computational geometric problems are described in Akl and Lyons [AL93] and Goodrich [Goo97]. Algorithm PRAM CONVEX HULL was first described in Aggarwal et al. [ACG+88] and Atallah and Goodrich [AG86].

The pointer-jumping method and algorithm PRAM LINKED LIST PREFIX were originally introduced in Wyllie [Wyl79]. It is interesting to note that prefix computation can be done sequentially on a linked list of n nodes in $O(n)$ time and, consequently, the parallel algorithm's cost of $O(n \log n)$ is not optimal. However, the main advantage of the algorithm, besides its elegance and simplicity, is the fact that it adheres faithfully to the definition of a linked list data structure, namely, that the list is made up of nodes stored in arbitrary locations in memory with a pointer linking each node to its successor in the list. It is in fact possible, once this definition is modified, to design algorithms that use $O(n/\log n)$ processors and run in $O(\log n)$ time. Such algorithms are based on the assumption that the linked list is stored in an *array*, in which each node is not necessarily adjacent to its successor in the linked list. The array is divided into subarrays of $O(\log n)$ elements, with each processor receiving one such array to process. See, for example, Anderson and Miller [AM91] and Cole and Vishkin [CV86a, CV88, CV89]. Algorithms that use even fewer processors, but whose running time is higher, are given in Cole and Vishkin [CV86b, CV86c], Kruskal et al. [KRS85], Snir [Sni86], and Wagner and Han [WH86]. As is the case with prefix computation on a linear array, algorithm PRAM LINKED LIST PREFIX can be used in a variety of contexts whenever '+' is replaced by any binary associative operation. Numerous applications of this algorithm to problems defined on pointer-based data structures appear in the literature; see, for example, Abrahamson et al. [ADK+89], Chen et al. [CDA91], Eppstein and Galil [EG88], Kruskal et al. [KRS90], and Lin and Olariu [LO91]. The Euler tour method was first used effectively in Tarjan and Vishkin [TV85] and Vishkin [Vis85]. A survey of its applications is given in Karp and Ramachandran [KR90].

A tutorial survey of algorithmic aspects of meshes enhanced with buses is provided in Akl [Akl97]. There are many algorithms in the literature for meshes, and more generally multidimensional arrays, augmented with fixed electronic buses; see, for example, Aggarwal [Agg86], Bokhari [Bok84], and Stout [Sto83] for global buses, and Bhagavathi et al. [BOS+94], Chen et al. [CCC+90], and Prasanna Kumar and Raghavendra [PR87] for row and column buses. Meshes with reconfigurable buses have been extensively studied; see, for example, Alnuweiri [AC94], Ben-Asher and Shuster [BS91], and Nigam and Sahni [NS94]. Algorithms for arrays augmented with optical buses are given in Chiarulli et al. [CML87], Hamdi [Ham95], Pavel [Pav96] and Pavel and Akl [PA96a, PA96b, PA96c, PA96d, PA98].

Broadcasting with selective reduction was first proposed by Akl and Guenther [AG89]. It is shown in Akl [Akl97] that BSR is strictly more powerful than the PRAM: A certain computation can be performed in constant time on BSR using n processors, while requiring $\Omega(n)$ time on an n-processor PRAM. Several algorithms have been proposed for solving various computational problems on this model; see, for example, Akl and Chen [AC96], Akl and Guenther [AG91], Akl and Lyons [AL93], Chen [Che97], Gewali and Stojmenović [GS94], Melter and Stojmenović [MS95], Semé and Myoupo [SM97], Springsteel and Stojmenović [SS89], Stojmenović [Sto96], and Xiang and Ushijima [XU98, XU99]. Different implementations of BSR appear in Akl et al. [AFG91], Akl and Guenther [AG89], and Fava Lindon and Akl [FA93]. A generalization of BSR to allow for multiple selection criteria is proposed in Akl and Stojmenović [AS94]. An implementation of the MAU for this generalization and several algorithms for solving problems on it are described in Akl and Stojmenović [AS96].

Parallel synergy was first introduced in a restricted form in Akl [Akl93]. The concept was later generalized and extended in Akl [Akl97], Akl and Bruda [AB99], Akl and Fava Lindon [AF94, AF97], Bruda and Akl [BA98a, BA98b, BA99], Fava Lindon [Fav92, Fav96], Luccio and Pagli [LP92a, LP92b], and Luccio et al. [LPP92].

References

[ADK+89]   Abrahamson, K., Dadoun, N., Kirkpatrick, D., Przytycka, T., A simple parallel tree contraction algorithm, *Journal of Algorithms* 10, 1989, 187–302.

[Agg86]   Aggarwal, A., Optimal bounds for finding maximum on array of processors with k global buses, *IEEE Transactions on Computers* 35, 1986, 62–64.

[ACG+88]   Aggarwal, A., Chazelle, B., Guibas, L.J., Ó'Dúnlaing, C., Yap, C.K., Parallel computational geometry, *Algorithmica* 3, 1988, 293–327.

[AHK87]   Akers, S.B., Harel, D., Krishnamurthy, B., The star graph: An attractive alternative to the n-cube, *Proc. of the International Conference on Parallel Processing*, 1987, 393-400.

[AK87]   Akers, S.B., Krishnamurthy, B., The fault tolerance of star graphs, *Proc. of the International Conference on Supercomputing* 3, 1987, 270-276.

[AK89]   Akers, S.B., Krishnamurthy, B., A group theoretic model for symmetric interconnection networks, *IEEE Transactions on Computers* **38**, 1989, 555-566.

[Akl85]   Akl, S.G., *Parallel Sorting Algorithms*, Academic Press, Orlando, Florida, 1985.

[Akl89]   Akl, S.G., *The Design and Analysis of Parallel Algorithms*, Prentice Hall, Englewood Cliffs, New Jersey, 1989.

[Akl93]   Akl, S.G., Parallel synergy, *Parallel Algorithms and Applications* 1, 1993, 3-9.

[Akl97]   Akl, S.G., *Parallel Computation: Models and Methods*, Prentice Hall, Upper Saddle River, New Jersey, 1997.

[AB99]   Akl, S.G., Bruda, S.D., Parallel real-time optimization: Beyond speedup, Technical Report No. 1999-421, Department of Computing and Information Science, Queen's University, Kingston, Ontario, January 1999.

[AC96]   Akl, S.G., Chen, L., Efficient parallel algorithms on proper circular arc graphs, *IEICE Transactions on Information and Systems, Special Issue on Architecture, Algorithms and Networks for Massively Parallel Computing* **E79-D**, 1996, 1015-1020.

[ADF94]   Akl, S.G., Duprat, J., Ferreira, A.G., Hamiltonian circuits and paths in star graphs, I. Dimov, O. Tonev (eds.), *Advances in Parallel Algorithms*, IOS Press, Sofia, Bulgaria, 1994, 131-143.

[AG89]   Akl, S.G., Guenther, G.R., Broadcasting with selective reduction, *Proc. of the IFIP Congress*, 1989, 515-520.

[AG91]   Akl, S.G., Guenther, G.R., Applications of broadcasting with selective reduction to the maximal sum subsegment problem, *International Journal of High Speed Computing* 3, 1991, 107-119.

[AF94]   Akl, S.G., Fava Lindon, L., Paradigms admitting superunitary behavior in parallel computation, *Proc. of the Joint Conference on Vector and Parallel Processing (CONPAR)*, Lecture Notes in Computer Science, No. 854, Springer-Verlag, Berlin, 1994, 301-312.

[AF97]   Akl, S.G., Fava Lindon, L., Paradigms for superunitary behavior in parallel computations, *Parallel Algorithms and Applications* 11, 1997, 129-153.

[AFG91]   Akl, S.G., Fava Lindon, L., Guenther, G.R., Broadcasting with selective reduction on an optimal PRAM circuit, *Technique et Science Informatiques* 10, 1991, 261-268.

[AL93]   Akl, S.G., Lyons, K.A., *Parallel Computational Geometry*, Prentice Hall, Englewood Cliffs, New Jersey, 1993.

[AQ92]   Akl, S.G., Qiu, K., Les réseaux d'interconnexion star et pancake, M. Cosnard, M. Nivat, Y. Robert (eds.), *Algorithmique parallèle*, Masson, Paris, 1992, 171-181.

[AQ93]   Akl, S.G., Qiu, K., A novel routing scheme on the star and pancake networks and its applications, *Parallel Computing* 19, 1993, 95-101.

[AQS92]   Akl, S.G., Qiu, K., Stojmenović, I., Computing the Voronoi diagram on the star and pancake interconnection networks, *Proc. of the Canadian Conference on Computational Geometry*, 1992, 353-358.

[AQS93]   Akl, S.G., Qiu, K., Stojmenović, I., Fundamental algorithms for the star and pancake interconnection networks with applications to computational geometry, *Networks, Special Issue on Interconnection Networks and Algorithms* 23, 1993, 215–226.

[AS94]   Akl, S.G., Stojmenović, I., Multiple criteria BSR: An implementation and applications to computational geometry problems, *Proc. of the Hawaii International Conference on System Sciences* 2, 1994, 159–168.

[AS96]   Akl, S.G., Stojmenović, I., Broadcasting with selective reduction: A powerful model of parallel computation, A.Y. Zomaya (ed.), *Parallel and Distributed Computing Handbook*, McGraw-Hill, New York, 1996, 192–222.

[AW97]   Akl, S.G., Wolff, T., Efficient sorting on the star graph interconnection network, *Proc. of the Annual Allerton Conference*, 1997.

[AC94]   Alnuweiri, H.M., Constant-time parallel algorithm for image labeling on a reconfigurable network of processors, *IEEE Transactions on Parallel and Distributed Systems* 5, 1994, 321–326.

[AM91]   Anderson, R., Miller, G., Deterministic parallel list ranking, *Algorithmica* 6, 1991, 859–868.

[AG86]   Atallah, M.J., Goodrich, M.T., Efficient parallel solutions to some geometric problems, *Journal of Parallel and Distributed Computing* 3, 1986, 492–507.

[Bat68]   Batcher, K.E., Sorting networks and their applications, *Proc. of the AFIPS Spring Joint Computer Conference*, 1968, 307–314. C.L. Wu, T.S. Feng (eds.), Interconnection networks for parallel and distributed processing, *IEEE Computer Society*, 1984, 576–583.

[BS91]   Ben-Asher, Y., Shuster, A., Ranking on reconfigurable networks, *Parallel Processing Letters* 1, 1991, 149–156.

[BOS+94]   Bhagavathi, D., Olariu, S., Shen, W., Wilson, L., A unifying look at semigroup computations on meshes with multiple broadcasting, *Parallel Processing Letters* 4, 1994, 73–82.

[Ble90]   Blelloch, G.E., *Vector Models for Data-Parallel Computing*, MIT Press, Cambridge, Massachusetts, 1990.

[Bok84]   Bokhari, S.H., Finding maximum on an array processor with a global bus, *IEEE Transactions on Computers* 33, 1984, 133–139.

[BA98a]   Bruda, S.D., Akl, S.G., On the data-accumulating paradigm, *Proc. of the Fourth International Conference on Computer Science and Informatics*, 1998, 150–153.

[BA98b]   Bruda, S.D., Akl, S.G., A case study in real-time parallel computation: Correcting algorithms, Technical Report No. 1998-420, Department of Computing and Information Science, Queen's University, Kingston, Ontario, December 1998.

[BA99]   Bruda, S.D., Akl, S.G., The characterization of data-accumulating algorithms, *Proc. of the International Parallel Processing Symposium*, 1999.

[CDA91]   Chen, C.C.Y., Das, S.K., Akl, S.G., A unified approach to parallel depth-first traversals of general trees, *Information Processing Letters* 38, 1991, 49–55.

[Che97]   Chen, L., Optimal bucket sorting and overlap representations. *Parallel Algorithms and Applications* 10, 1997, 249–269.

[CCC+90]   Chen, Y.C., Chen, W.T., Chen, G.H., Sheu, J.P., Designing efficient parallel algorithms on mesh-connected computers with multiple broadcasting, *IEEE Transactions on Parallel and Distributed Systems* 1, 1990, 241–245.

[CC95]   Chiang, W.K., Chen, R.J., The (n,k)-star graph: A generalized star graph, *Information Processing Letters* 56, 1995, 259–264.

[CML87]   Chiarulli, D.M., Melhem, R.G., Levitan, S.P., Using coincident optical pulses for parallel memory addressing, *The Computer Journal* 30, 1987, 48–57.

[Col88]   Cole, R., Parallel merge sort, *SIAM Journal on Computing* 17, 1988, 770–785.

[CV86a]   Cole, R., Vishkin, U., Approximate and exact parallel scheduling with applications to list, tree, and graph problems, *Proc. of the IEEE Symposium on Foundations of Computer Science*, 1986, 478–491.

[CV86b]   Cole, R., Vishkin, U., Deterministic coin tossing and accelerating cascades: Micro and macro techniques for designing parallel algorithms, *Proc. of the ACM Symposium on Theory of Computing*, 1986, 206–219.

[CV86c]   Cole, R., Vishkin, U., Deterministic coin tossing with applications to optimal parallel list ranking, *Information and Control* 70, 1986, 32–53.

[CV88]   Cole, R., Vishkin, U., Approximate parallel scheduling, Part 1: The basic technique with applications to optimal list ranking in logarithmic time, *SIAM Journal on Computing* 17, 1988, 128–142.

[CV89]   Cole, R., Vishkin, U., Faster optimal parallel prefix sums and list ranking, *Information and Control* 81, 1989, 334–352.

[CW87]   Coppersmith, D., Winograd, S., Matrix multiplication via arithmetic progressions, *Proc. of the ACM Symposium on Theory of Computing*, 1987, 1–6.

[CLR90]   Cormen, T.H., Leiserson, C.E., Rivest, R.L., *Introduction to Algorithms*, McGraw-Hill, New York, 1990.

[DDP90]   Das, S.K., Deo, N., Prasad, S., Parallel graph algorithms for hypercube computers, *Parallel Computing* 13, 1990, 143–158.

[DNS81]   Dekel, E., Nassimi, D., Sahni, S., Parallel matrix and graph algorithms, *SIAM Journal on Computing* 10, 1981, 657–675.

[MS91]   Dietzfelbinger, M., Madhavapeddy, S., Sudborough, I.H., Three disjoint path paradigms in star networks, *Proc. of the IEEE Symposium on Parallel and Distributed Processing*, 1991, 400–406.

[DPR+83]   Dowd, M., Perl, Y., Rudolph, L., Saks, M., The balanced sorting network, *Proc. of the Conference on Principles of Distributed Computing*, 1983, 161–172.

[EG88]   Eppstein, D., Galil, Z., Parallel algorithmic techniques for combinatorial computation, *Annual Review of Computer Science* 3, 1988, 233–283.

[Fav92]   Fava Lindon, L., Discriminating analysis and its application to matrix by vector multiplication on the CRCW PRAM, *Parallel Processing Letters* 2, 1992, 43–50.

[Fav96]   Fava Lindon, L., *Synergy in Parallel Computation*, Ph.D. Thesis, Department of Computing and Information Science, Queen's University, Kingston, Ontario, 1996.

[FA93]   Fava Lindon, L., Akl, S.G., An optimal implementation of broadcasting with selective reduction, *IEEE Transactions on Parallel and Distributed Systems* 4, 1993, 256–269.

[Fer96]   Ferreira, A.G., Parallel and communication algorithms on hypercube multiprocessors, A.Y. Zomaya (ed.), *Parallel and Distributed Computing Handbook*, McGraw-Hill, New York, 1996, 568–589.

[FJL+88]   Fox, G.C., Johnson, M.A., Lyzenga, G.A., Otto, S.W., Salmon, J.K., Walker, D.W., *Solving Problems on Concurrent Processors* 1, Prentice Hall, Englewood Cliffs, New Jersey, 1988.

[Fra95]   Fragopoulou, P., *Communication and Fault Tolerance Algorithms on a Class of Interconnection Networks*, Ph.D. Thesis, Department of Computing and Information Science, Queen's University, Kingston, Ontario, 1995.

[FA94]   Fragopoulou, P., Akl, S.G., A parallel algorithm for computing Fourier transforms on the star graph, *IEEE Transactions on Parallel and Distributed Systems* 5, 1994, 525–531.

[FA95a]   Fragopoulou, P., Akl, S.G., Optimal communication algorithms on star graphs using spanning tree constructions, *Journal of Parallel and Distributed Computing* 24, 1995, 55–71.

[FA95b]   Fragopoulou, P., Akl, S.G., Fault tolerant communication algorithms on the star network using disjoint paths, *Proceedings of the Hawaii International Conference on System Sciences* 2, 1995, 5–13.

[FA95c]   Fragopoulou, P., Akl, S.G., A framework for optimal communication on a subclass of Cayley graph based networks, *Proc. of the International Conference on Computers and Communications*, 1995, 241–248.

[FA95d]   Fragopoulou, P., Akl, S.G., Efficient algorithms for global data communication on the multidimensional torus network, *Proc. of the International Parallel Processing Symposium*, 1995, 324–330.

[FA96a]   Fragopoulou, P., Akl, S.G., Edge-disjoint spanning trees on the star network with applications to fault tolerance, *IEEE Transactions on Computers* 45, 1996, 174–185.

[FA96b]   Fragopoulou, P., Akl, S.G., Meijer, H., Optimal communication primitives on the generalized hypercube network, *Journal of Parallel and Distributed Computing* 32, 1996, 173–187.

[GS94]   Gewali, L.P., Stojmenović, I., Computing external watchman routes on PRAM, BSR, and interconnection models of parallel computation, *Parallel Processing Letters* 4, 1994, 83–93.

[Goo97]   Goodrich, M.T., Parallel algorithms in geometry, J.E. Goodman, J. O'Rourke (eds.), *Discrete and Computational Geometry*, CRC Press, New York, 1997, 669–681.

[Gor91]   Gordon, D.M., Parallel sorting on Cayley graphs, *Algorithmica* 6, 1991, 554–564.

[Ham95]   Hamdi, M., Communications in optically interconnected computer systems, D.F. Hsu, A.L. Rosenberg, D. Sotteau (eds.), *Interconnection Networks and Mapping and Scheduling Parallel Computations*, DIMACS Series in *Discrete Mathematics and Theoretical Computer Science* 21, 1995, 181–200.

[Hat91]   Hatcher, P.J., Quinn, M.J., *Data-Parallel Programming on MIMD Computers*, MIT Press, Cambridge, Massachusetts, 1991.

[Hil85]   Hillis, W.D., *The Connection Machine*, MIT Press, Cambridge, Massachusetts, 1985.

[Jaj92]   JáJá, J., *An Introduction to Parallel Algorithms*, Addison-Wesley, Reading, Massachusetts, 1992.

[JLD90]   Jwo, J.S., Lakshmivarahan, S., Dhall, S.K., Embedding of cycles and grids in star graphs, *Proc. of the IEEE Symposium on Parallel and Distributed Processing*, 1990, 540–547.

[KR90]   Karp, R.M., Ramachandran, V., A survey of parallel algorithms for shared memory machines, Vol. A, J. van Leeuwen (ed.) *Handbook of Theoretical Computer Science*, Elsevier, Amsterdam, 1990, 869–941.

[Knu73]   Knuth, D.E., *The Art of Computer Programming* 3, Addison-Wesley, Reading, Massachusetts, 1973.

[KRS85]   Kruskal, C.P., Rudolph, L., Snir, M., The power of parallel prefix, *IEEE Transactions on Computers* **34**, 1985, 965–968.

[KRS90]   Kruskal, C.P., Rudolph, L., Snir, M., Efficient parallel algorithms for graph problems, *Algorithmica* **5**, 1990, 43–64.

[KGG+94]   Kumar, V., Grama, A., Gupta, A., Karypis, G., *Introduction to Parallel Computing*, Benjamin-Cummings, Menlo Park, California, 1994.

[Kun87]   Kunde, M., Optimal sorting on multi-dimensionally mesh-connected computers, *Proc. of the Symposium on Theoretical Aspects of Computer Science*, Lecture Notes in Computer Science No. 247, Springer-Verlag, Berlin, 1987, 408–419.

[LD94]   Lakshmivarahan, S., Dhall, S.K., *Parallel Computing Using the Prefix Problem*, Oxford University Press, New York, 1994.

[Lei92]   Leighton, F.T., *Introduction to Parallel Algorithms and Architectures*, Morgan Kaufmann, San Mateo, California, 1992.

[LO91]   Lin, R., Olariu, S., A simple optimal parallel algorithm to solve the lowest common ancestor problem, *Proc. of the International Conference on Computing and Information*, Lecture Notes in Computer Science, No. 497, Springer-Verlag, Berlin, 1991, 455–461.

[LP92a]   Luccio, F., Pagli, L., The p-shovelers problem (computing with time-varying data), *SIGACT News* **23**, 1992, 72–75.

[LP92b]   Luccio, F., Pagli, L., The p-shovelers problem (computing with time-varying data), *Proc. of the IEEE Symposium on Parallel and Distributed Processing*, 1992, 188–193.

[LPP92]   Luccio, F., Pagli, L., Pucci, G., Three non conventional paradigms of parallel computation, *Proc. of the Heinz Nixdorf Symposium*, Lecture Notes in Computer Science, No. 678, Springer-Verlag, Berlin, 1992, 166–175.

[MG88]   Marberg, J.M., Gafni, E., Sorting in constant number of row and column phases on a mesh, *Algorithmica* **3**, 1988, 561–572.

[MS95]   Melter, R.A., Stojmenović, I., Solving city block metric and digital geometry problems on the BSR model of parallel computation, *Journal of Mathematical Imaging and Vision* **5**, 1995, 119–127.

[MS90]   Menn, A., Somani, A.K., An efficient sorting algorithm for the star graph interconnection network, *Proc. of the International Conference on Parallel Processing* **3**, 1990, 1–8.

[Mul93]   Mulmuley, K., *Computational Geometry: An Introduction through Randomized Algorithms*, Prentice Hall, Englewood Cliffs, New Jersey, 1993.

[NS94]   Nigam, M., Sahni, S., Sorting n numbers on $n \times n$ reconfigurable meshes with buses, *Journal of Parallel and Distributed Computing* **23**, 1994, 37–48.

[NSK90]   Nigam, M., Sahni, S., Krishnamurthy, B., Embedding Hamiltonians and hypercubes in star interconnection graphs, *Proc. of the International Conference on Parallel Processing* **3**, 1990, 340–343.

[ORo94]   O'Rourke, J., *Computational Geometry in C*, Cambridge University Press, Cambridge, England, 1994.

[Pav96]   Pavel, S., *Computation and Communication Aspects of Arrays with Optical Pipelined Buses*, Ph.D. thesis, Department of Computing and Information Science, Queen's University, Kingston, Ontario, 1996.

[PA96a]   Pavel, S., Akl, S.G., Matrix operations using arrays with reconfigurable optical buses, *Journal of Parallel Algorithms and Applications* **8**, 1996, 223–242.

[PA96b]   Pavel, S., Akl, S.G., Area-time trade-offs in arrays with optical pipelined buses, *Applied Optics* **35**, 1996, 1827–1835.

[PA96c]   Pavel, S., Akl, S.G., On the power of arrays with reconfigurable optical buses, *Proc. of the International Conference on Parallel and Distributed Processing Techniques and Applications*, 1996, 1443–1454.

[PA96d]   Pavel, S., Akl, S.G., Efficient algorithms for the Hough transform on arrays with reconfigurable optical buses, *Proc. of the International Parallel Processing Symposium*, 1996, 697–701.

[PA98]   Pavel, S., Akl, S.G., Integer sorting and routing in arrays with reconfigurable optical buses, to appear in *International Journal of Foundations of Computer Science, Special Issue on Interconnection Networks*, 1998.

[PR87]   Prasanna Kumar, V.K., Raghavendra, C.S., Array processor with multiple broadcasting, *Journal of Parallel and Distributed Computing* **4**, 1987, 173–190.

[PS85]   Preparata, F.P., Shamos, M.I., *Computational Geometry: An Introduction*, Springer-Verlag, New York, 1985.

[PV81]   Preparata, F.P., Vuillemin, J.E., The cube-connected cycles: A versatile network for parallel computation, *Communications of the ACM* **24**, 1981, 300–309.

[Qiu92]   Qiu, K., *The Star and Pancake Interconnection Networks: Properties and Algorithms*, Ph.D. Thesis, Department of Computing and Information Science, Queen's University, Kingston, Ontario, 1992.

[QA94a]   Qiu, K., Akl, S.G., Load balancing, selection and sorting on the star and pancake interconnection networks, *Parallel Algorithms and Applications* **2**, 1994, 27–42.

[QA94b]   Qiu, K., Akl, S.G., On some properties of the star graph, *Journal of VLSI Design, Special Issue on Interconnection Networks* **2**, 1994, 389–396.

[QA97]   Qiu, K., Akl, S.G., Parallel point location algorithms on hypercubes, *Proc. of the Tenth International Conference on Parallel and Distributed Computing*, 1997, 27–30.

[QAM94]   Qiu, K., Akl, S.G., Meijer, H., On some properties and algorithms for the star and pancake interconnection networks, *Journal of Parallel and Distributed Computing* **22**, 1994, 16–25.

[QMA91a]   Qiu, K., Meijer, H., Akl, S.G., Parallel routing and sorting on the pancake network, *Proc. of the International Conference on Computing and Information*, Lecture Notes in Computer Science, No. 497, Springer-Verlag, Berlin, 1991, 360–371.

[QMA91b]   Qiu, K., Meijer, H., Akl, S.G., Decomposing a star graph into disjoint cycles, *Information Processing Letters* **39**, 1991, 125–129.

[QMA93]   Qiu, K., Meijer, H., Akl, S.G., On the cycle structure of star graphs, *Congressus Numerantium* **96**, 1993, 123–141.

[RW93]   Rajasekaran, S., Wei, D.S.L., Selection, routing and sorting on the star graph, *Proc. of the International Parallel Processing Symposium*, 1993, 661–665.

[RW97]   Rajasekaran, S., Wei, D.S.L., Selection, routing and sorting on the star graph, *Journal of Parallel and Distributed Computing* **41**, 1997, 225–233.

[RS90]   Ranka, S., Sahni, S., *Hypercube Algorithms*, Springer-Verlag, New York, 1990.

[Rei93]   Reif, J.H. (ed.), *Synthesis of Parallel Algorithms*, Morgan Kaufmann, San Mateo, California, 1993.

[SSS86]   Scherson, I., Sen, S., Shamir, A., Shear-sort: A true two-dimensional sorting technique for VLSI networks, *Proc. of the International Conference on Parallel Processing*, 1986, 903–908.

[Sei84]   Seitz, C.L., Concurrent VLSI architectures, *IEEE Transactions on Computers* **33**, 1984, 1247–1265.

[Sei85]   Seitz, C.L., The cosmic cube, *Communications of the ACM* **28**, 1985, 22–33.

[SM97]   Semé, D., Myoupo, J.-F., A parallel solution of the sequence alignment problem using BSR model, *Proc. of the International Conference on Parallel and Distributed Computing*, 1997, 357–362.

[Sni86]   Snir, M., Depth-size tradeoffs for parallel prefix computation, *Journal of Algorithms* **7**, 1986, 185–201.

[SS89]   Springsteel, F., Stojmenović, I., Parallel general prefix computations with geometric, algebraic and other applications, *International Journal of Parallel Programming* **18**, 1989, 485–503.

[Sto96]   Stojmenović, I., Constant time BSR solutions to parenthesis matching, tree decoding, and tree reconstruction from its traversals, *IEEE Transactions on Parallel and Distributed Systems* **7**, 1996, 218–224.

[Sto83]   Stout, Q.F., Mesh-connected computers with broadcasting, *IEEE Transactions on Computers* **32**, 1983, 826–830.

[SS91]   Sur, S., Srimani, P.K., A fault tolerant routing algorithm in star graphs, *Proc. of the International Conference on Parallel Processing* **3**, 1991, 267–270.

[TV85]   Tarjan, R.E., Vishkin, U., An efficient parallel biconnectivity algorithm, *SIAM Journal of Computing* **14**, 1985, 862–874.

[TW91]   Trew, A., Wilson, G. (eds.), *Past, Present, Parallel*, Springer-Verlag, Berlin, 1991.

[Ull84]   Ullman, J.D., *Computational Aspects of VLSI*, Computer Science Press, Rockville, Maryland, 1984.

[Vis84]   Vishkin, U., A parallel-design distributed implementation (PDDI) general-purpose computer, *Theoretical Computer Science* **32**, 1984, 157–172.

[Vis85]   Vishkin, U., On efficient parallel strong orientation, *Information Processing Letters* **20**, 1985, 235–240.

[WH86]   Wagner, W., Han, Y., Parallel algorithms for bucket sorting and data dependent prefix problems, *Proc. of the International Conference on Parallel Processing*, 1986, 924–930.

[Wyl79]   Wyllie, J.C., *The Complexity of Parallel Computations*, Ph.D. Thesis, Department of Computer Science, Cornell University, Ithaca, New York, 1979.

[XU98]   Xiang, L., Ushijima, K., ANSV problem on BSRs, *Information Processing Letters* **65**, 1998, 135–138.

[XU99]   Xiang, L., Ushijima, K., Decoding and drawing on BSR for a binary tree from its $i - p$ sequence, to appear in *Parallel Processing Letters*, 1999.

III. Languages for Parallel Processing

Ian Foster

Argonne National Laboratory
The University of Chicago, U.S.A.

Summary. This chapter is concerned with programming languages for parallel processing. We first review some basic principles and then use a series of four case studies to illustrate the practical application of these principles. These case studies involve representative systems based on new programming paradigms, explicitly parallel extensions to existing sequential languages, data parallelism, and message-passing libraries, respectively.

1. Motivation for Parallel Languages

Programming languages play an important role in computing, serving variously to simplify the expression of complex algorithms, to increase code portability, to facilitate code reuse, and to reduce the risk of programming errors. A program written in a high-level language is executed by an interpreter or, more commonly, translated by a compiler into appropriate low-level operations; in either case, the programmer is saved the labor of managing low-level resources directly.

Parallel computation further complicates the already challenging task of developing a correct and efficient program. At the root of the additional difficulty is the increased complexity of the underlying hardware. A parallel program must manage not only those concerns that are familiar to us from sequential programming, but also the creation and destruction of multiple concurrent threads of control, the synchronization of thread activities, the communication of information among threads, the distribution of data and threads to processors, and so forth.

Given this additional complexity, we might expect programming languages to play an even more significant role on parallel systems than on sequential computers. And indeed, experience shows that parallel languages can be very effective. For example:

- Data-parallel languages can enable certain programs with sequential semantics to execute efficiently on a parallel computer; hence, a programmer need not write explicit parallel code.
- Parallel functional languages can be used to express highly concurrent algorithms while preventing nondeterministic executions; hence, a programmer need not be concerned with race conditions.
- Message-passing libraries (a very low level form of parallel "language") can be used to write portable programs that nevertheless achieve very high performance on distributed-memory parallel computers; hence, a programmer need not write different programs for different types of computer.

However, the combination of platform complexity, demanding performance requirements, and a specialized user base has prevented any parallel language from acquiring the broad user base of mainstream sequential languages. Instead, we see a variety of languages proposed, some focused on generality and others on high performance but none enabling high-performance execution for a broad range of applications on a variety of parallel platforms.

In the remainder of this section, we categorize these approaches to the design of parallel programming languages. In subsequent sections, we discuss the basic principles of parallel programming paradigms and then use a series of case studies to illustrate the practical application of these principles.

1.1 Types of Parallel Language

Approaches to parallel programming language design can be categorized along a number of axes; we consider six such axes here.

Language extensions vs. new language. The language may be based on extensions to an existing sequential language (e.g., C, Fortran, C++, Java) or may implement a new programming paradigm that is more naturally parallel (e.g., functional [KM77, McL90, Hud89], logic [CM81, Kow79, Sha89], or object-oriented [Agh86, Yon87, Wat88, CGH94, Gri91]). Language extensions can have the advantage of preserving existing expertise, code base, and tools, while new languages can eliminate semantic barriers to the expression of parallelism.

Task parallelism vs. data parallelism. The language may focus on task parallelism, in which the number of threads of control in a program may vary over time or in which different threads may do different things at different times (e.g., occam [TW82], Concert/C [AGG+94], Compositional C++ [CK93], Linda [CG89, CG89a]), or the language may focus on data parallelism, in which parallelism derives from the fact that different processes apply the same operations to different elements of a data structure (e.g., C* [TMC90], Data Parallel C [HQ91], NESL [Ble90], High Performance Fortran [KLS+94]). Typically, task parallelism provides greater flexibility, but data parallelism is more effective for regular problems. Both approaches can also be combined in a single system (e.g., Fx [SSO+93], HPF/MPI [FKK+98]).

Explicit parallelism vs. implicit parallelism. The language may be explicitly or implicitly parallel. In the former case, parallelism is expressed directly by the programmer; in the latter, parallelism is extracted by a compiler. Implicit parallelism is desirable if it allows the programmer to ignore low-level details of parallel algorithms, but explicit parallelism tends to provide greater control and hence can permit higher-performance implementations.

Determinism vs. nondeterminism. The language may guarantee deterministic execution or may allow the programmer to specify nondeterministic executions. Determinism is desirable because it can eliminate an important class of often hard-to-detect errors. However, some algorithms require nondeterminism for efficient execution.

Programming language vs. coordination language. The language may be intended as a complete programming language in its own right or may be designed for use as a coordination language [CG89, Col89, Kel89, LS91, FT90] that provides a parallel superstructure for existing sequential code.

Architecture-specific language vs. architecture-independent language. The language may be specialized for a particular architecture (e.g., shared-memory computers or distributed-memory computers) or even a particular computer (e.g., occam and the Transputer) or may be intended as a general-purpose programming language.

In addition, the subject of "parallel processing languages" can reasonably be extended to embrace sequential languages—if compilation techniques are able to extract parallelism from sequential programs [Wol89, AL93]—and libraries that implement parallel programming paradigms. In this chapter, we consider the latter but not the former. We also explicitly exclude from discussion languages that are primarily intended for the specification of distributed systems and distributed algorithms.

1.2 Classes of Parallel Programming Languages

From our initial discussion, the reader might conclude that the number of parallel languages is large, and this is indeed the case. Fortunately, a number of review articles provide good surveys of this material. The most valuable, and most recent, is certainly that by Skillicorn and Talia [ST98], which considering its moderate length provides an impressively comprehensive and well-structured survey of parallel programming paradigms and languages. More dated surveys include the excellent article by Bal et al. [BST89] and narrower but still useful articles by Shapiro [Sha89], Carriero and Gelertner [CG89], and Karp and Babb [KB88].

Given the wealth of existing survey material, we focus in this chapter not on details of historical development but on the nuts and bolts of parallel programming. To this end, we consider four important classes of parallel programming language and, in each case, use a specific system to illustrate the issues that arise when that parallel language is put to practice.

The four classes of system and representative languages that we consider in this chapter are as follows:

- *New or nontraditional paradigms*, that is, notations that are designed to simplify the expression of highly parallel algorithms. We choose as our representative a concurrent logic programming language, *Strand*. Such languages frequently permit concise and elegant formulations of certain classes of parallel algorithm, but their unfamiliar syntax and semantics can complicate the programming task.
- *Extensions to existing languages*, using *Compositional C++* as our example. This discussion provides useful insights into how sequential language constructs can be extended in interesting ways to address parallelism.
- *Data-parallel languages*, which exploit the parallelism inherent in applying the same operation to all or most elements of large data structures. We use *Fortran 90* and *High Performance Fortran* as our representatives. Data parallel languages have proven extremely effective for certain classes of problem, but their suitability for more general applications remains unproven.
- *library-based approaches* to parallelism, in which a parallel programming paradigm is implemented via function calls rather than by language constructs and a compiler. We use the widely used *Message Passing Interface*

standard as our representative. While language-based approaches do not typically benefit from the advantages of automatic checking and optimization that language-based approaches may enjoy, they provide considerable flexibility.

The material borrows heavily from the book *Designing and Building Parallel Programs* [Fos95], which covers both parallel algorithm design techniques and tutorial presentations of three of the parallel languages considered here.

2. New Programming Paradigms

One view of parallel programming holds that sequential programming languages, being designed explicitly to represent the manipulation of von Neumann computers, are an inappropriate tool for parallel programming. Particularly if the goal is to express (or extract) large amounts of parallelism, new programming paradigms are required in which parallelism is explicitly or implicitly a first-class citizen, rather than an addition to a sequential programming model.

This view has motivated explorations of numerous innovative programming models. For example:

- In *functional programming*, the Church-Rosser property [CR36, McL90] (which holds that the arguments to a pure function can be evaluated in any order or in parallel, without changing the result) is exploited to extract parallelism from programs implemented as pure functions [Hen80, Hud89, HC95, THL+98]. Considerable research has been conducted in functional programming, in the context of both "impure" languages such as LISP [Hal85] and more modern functional languages such as Haskell [Hud89, JH93, THM+96]. SISAL, a functional language incorporating arrays and interactive constructs, is particularly interesting in view of the high performance it has achieved in realistic scientific applications [CFD90].
- In *logic programming*, the parallelism implicit in both conjunctive and disjunctive specifications ("and" and "or" parallelism, respectively) is exploited. Researchers have investigated techniques in Prolog as well as in specialized parallel languages such as Concurrent Prolog [MTS+85, Sha87, Tay89], Guarded Horn Clauses [Ued85], Parlog [CG81, Gre87, Rin88], Strand [FT90, FKT90], and Program Composition Notation[CT91, FOT92].
- In *Actor systems* [Agh86], parallelism is expressed in terms of message passing between entities called actors. An individual actor is activated by the arrival of a message and may then perform some computation and/or send additional messages to other actors. Concurrent Aggregates [PLC95] extends this model to avoid the serialization inherent in the sequential processing of messages by a single actor. *Concurrent object systems* such as

ABCL/1 [Yon87], ABCL/R [Wat88], POOL-T [Ame88], and Concurrent Smalltalk [Yok87] extend sequential object-oriented languages, allowing multiple threads of control to exist.

2.1 Strand: A Concurrent Logic Programming Language

We use as our case study for new programming paradigms the concurrent logic programming language Strand [FT90, FKT90] (see also [Fos96] for more details, and a comparison of Strand with the related Program Composition Notation [CT91, FOT92]). Strand uses a high-level specification of concurrent execution to facilitate the expression of highly parallel computations and an abstract representation of communication and synchronization to simplify the representation of complex communication structures. Its unfamiliar syntax and semantics are a significant obstacle to most programmers, but (as we shall see in the next section) it is possible to map many of its more useful features into more familiar languages.

The Strand language design integrates ideas from earlier work in parallel logic programming [CG81, Gre87, Rin88, Ued85, Sha87], functional programming [KM77, McL90], dataflow computing [Ack82], and imperative programming [Dij75, Hoa78] to provide a simple task-parallel programming language based on four related ideas:

- single-assignment variables,
- a global, shared namespace,
- parallel composition as the only method of program composition, and
- a foreign-language interface.

Single-assignment variables provide a unified mechanism for both synchronization and communication. All variables in Strand follow the single-assignment rule [Ack82]: a variable is set at most once and subsequently cannot change. Any attempt by a program component to read a variable before it has been assigned a value will cause the program component to block. All synchronization operations are implemented by reading and writing these variables. New variables can be introduced by writing recursive procedure definitions.

Strand variables also define a global namespace. A variable can refer to any object in the computation, even another variable. The location of the variable or object being referenced does not matter. Thus, Strand does not require explicit communication operations: processes can communicate simply by reading and writing shared variables.

Traditional sequential programming languages support only the sequential composition of program components: that is, program statements are assumed to be designed one after the other, in sequence. In contrast, Strand—like certain other parallel languages, notably functional languages—supports only parallel composition. A parallel composition of program components executes as a concurrent interleaving of the components, with execution order constrained only by availability of data, as determined by the single-assignment rule. This feature allows Strand programs to provide succinct expressions of many complex parallel algorithms.

The combination of single-assignment variables, a global namespace, and parallel composition means that the behavior of a Strand program is invariant to the placement and scheduling of computations. One consequence of this invariance is that Strand programs are compositional: a program component will function correctly in any environment [CM88, CT91]. Another consequence is that the specification of the location of a computation is orthogonal to the specification of the computation. To exploit these features, Strand provides a mapping operator that allows the programmer to control the placement of a computation on a parallel computer.

By allowing modules written in sequential languages to be integrated into Strand computations, the foreign-language interface supports the use of Strand as a coordination language. Sequential modules that are to be integrated in this way must implement pure functions. The interface supports communication between foreign modules and Strand by providing routines that allow foreign-language modules to access Strand variables passed as arguments.

2.2 Strand Language Constructs

We present here a brief summary of Strand language concepts; details are provided elsewhere [FT90]. The syntax of Strand is similar to that of the logic programming language Prolog. A program consists of a set of procedures, each defined by one or more *rules*. A rule has the general form

$$H \; :- \; G_1, \; G_2, \; ..., \; G_m \; | \; B_1, \; B_2, \; ..., \; B_n. \qquad m, n \geq 0,$$

where the rule head H is a function prototype consisting of a name and zero or more arguments; the G_i are guard tests; "|" is the commit operator; and the B_j are body processes: calls to Strand, C, or Fortran procedures, or to the assignment operator ":=". If $m = 0$, the "|" is omitted. Procedure arguments may be variables (distinguished by an initial capital letter), strings, numbers, or lists. A list is a record structure with a head and a tail and is denoted [*head* | *tail*].

A procedure's rules define the actions that the process executing that procedure can perform. The head and guard of the rule define the conditions under which an action can take place; the body defines the actions that are to be performed. When a procedure executes, the conditions defined by the various heads and guards are evaluated in parallel. Nonvariable terms in a rule head must match corresponding process arguments, and guard tests must succeed. If the conditions specified by a single rule hold, this rule is selected for execution, and new processes are created for the procedures in its body. If two or more rules could apply, one is selected nondeterministically. It suffices to ensure that conditions are mutually exclusive to avoid nondeterministic execution. If no condition holds, an error is signaled. For example, the following procedure defines a consumer process that executes either action1 or action2, depending on the value of variable X.

```
consumer(X) :- X == "msg" | action1(X).
consumer(X) :- X =\= "msg" | action2(X).
```

In this procedure, X is a variable; "msg" is a string; and == and =\= represent equality and inequality tests, respectively. Notice that this procedure is deterministic.

2.2.1 Communication and synchronization.
As noted above, all Strand variables are single-assignment variables. A shared single-assignment variable can be used both to communicate values and to synchronize actions. For example, consider concurrently executing producer and consumer processes that share a variable X:

```
producer(X), consumer(X)
```

The producer may assign a value to X (e.g., "msg") and thus communicate this value to the consumer:

```
producer(X) :- X := "msg"
```

As shown above, the consumer procedure may receive the value and use it in subsequent computation. The concept of synchronization is implicit in this model. The comparisons X == "msg" and X =\= "msg" can be made only if the variable X is defined. Hence, execution of consumer is delayed until producer executes and makes the value available.

The single-assignment variable would have limited utility in parallel programming if it could be used to exchange only a single value. In fact, a single shared variable can be used to communicate a sequence or *stream* of values. This is achieved as follows. A recursively defined producer process incrementally constructs a list structure containing these values. A recursively defined consumer process incrementally reads this same structure. Fig. 2.1 illustrates this technique. The stream_comm procedure creates two processes, stream_producer and stream_consumer, that use the shared variable X to exchange N values. The producer incrementally defines X to be a list comprising N occurrences of the number 10:

$$[10, 10, 10, ..., 10]$$

The statement Out := [10|Out1], which defines the variable Out to be a list with head 10 and tail Out1, can be thought of as sending a message on Out. The new variable Out1 is passed to the recursive call to stream_producer, which either uses it to communicate additional values or, if N==0, defines it to be the empty list [].

The consumer incrementally reads the list S, adding each value received to the accumulator Sum and printing the total when it reaches the end of the list. The match operation [Val|In1] in the head of the first stream_consumer rule determines whether the variable shared with stream_producer is a list and, if so, decomposes it into a head Val and tail In1. This operation can be thought of as receiving the message Val and defining a new variable In1 that can be used to receive additional messages.

```
stream_comm(N) :-
    stream_producer(N, S),          % N is number of messages
    stream_consumer(0, S).          % Accumulator initially 0

stream_producer(N, Out) :-
    N > 0 |                         % More to send (N > 0):
    Out := [10|Out1],               %    Send message "10";
    N1 is N - 1,                    %    Decrement count;
    stream_producer(N1, Out1).      %    Recurse for more.
stream_producer(0, Out) :-          % Done sending (N == 0):
    Out := [].                      %    Terminate output.

stream_consumer(Sum, [Val|In1]) :-  % Receive message:
    Sum1 is Sum + Val,              %    Add to accumulator;
    stream_consumer(Sum1, In1).     %    Recurse for more.
stream_consumer(Sum, []) :-         % End of list (In == []):
    print(Sum).                     %    Print result.
```

Fig. 2.1. Producer/consumer program.

2.2.2 Foreign interface. "Foreign" procedures written in C or Fortran can be called in the body of a rule. A foreign-procedure call suspends until all arguments are defined and then executes atomically, without suspension. This approach achieves a clean separation of concerns between sequential and parallel programming, provides a familiar notation for sequential concepts, and enables existing sequential code to be reused in parallel programs.

2.2.3 Mapping. The Strand compiler does not attempt to map processes to processors automatically. Instead, the Strand language provides constructs that allow the programmer to specify mapping strategies. This approach is possible because the Strand language is designed so that mapping affects only performance, not correctness. Hence, a programmer can first develop a program and then explore alternative mapping strategies by changing annotations. The technique is illustrated below; we shall see similar ideas applied in CC++ and in High Performance Fortran.

2.3 Programming Example

We use a genetic sequence alignment program [BBF+89] to illustrate the use of Strand. The goal is to line up RNA sequences from separate but closely related organisms, with corresponding sections directly above one another and with *indels* (dashes) representing areas in which characters must be inserted or deleted to achieve this alignment. For example, Fig. 2.2 shows (a) a set of four short RNA sequences and (b) an alignment of these sequences.

```
augcgagucuauggcuucggccauggcggacggcucauu
augcgagucuaugguuucggccauggcggacggcucauu
augcgagucuauggacuucggccauggcggacggcucagu
augcgagucaagggggcucccuugggggcaccggcgcacggcucagu
```

(a)

```
augcgagucuauggc----uucg----gccauggcggacggcucauu
augcgagucuauggu----uucg----gccauggcggacggcucauu
augcgagucuauggac---uucg----gccauggcggacggcucagu
augcgaguc-aaggggcucccuugggggcaccggcgcacggcucagu
```

(b)

Fig. 2.2. RNA sequence alignment.

The algorithm uses a divide-and-conquer strategy which works basically as follows. First, "critical points"—short subsequences that are unique within a sequence—are identified for each sequence. Next, "pins"—critical points that are common to several sequences—are identified. The longest pin is used to partition the problem of aligning the sequences into three smaller alignment problems, corresponding to the subsequences to the left of the pin in the pinned sequences, the subsequences to the right of the pin, and the unpinned sequences (Fig. 2.3). These three subproblems then are solved by applying the alignment algorithm in a recursive fashion. Finally, the three subalignments are combined to produce a complete alignment.

This genetic sequence alignment algorithm presents many opportunities for parallel execution. For example, critical points can be computed in parallel for each sequence, and each alignment subproblem produced during the recursive application of the algorithm can be solved concurrently. The challenge is to formulate the algorithm in a way that does not obscure the basic algorithm structure and that allows alternative parallel execution strategies to be explored without substantial changes to the program. The Strand implementation has this property. The procedures in Fig. 2.4 implement the top level of the algorithm. The align_chunk procedure calls pins to compute critical points for each sequence in a set of sequences (a "chunk"), form a set of pins, and select the best pin. If a pin is found (Pin =\= []), divide uses

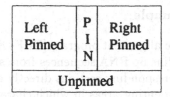

Fig. 2.3. Splitting sequences using a pin.

it to split the chunk into three subchunks. Recursive calls to `align_chunk` align the subchunks. If no pin is found (`Pin == []`), an alternative procedure, `c_basic_align`, is executed.

```
align_chunk(Sequences,Alignment) :-
    pins(Chunks,BestPin),
    divide(Sequences,BestPin,Alignment).

pins(Chunk,BestPin) :-
    cps(Chunk,CpList),
    c_form_pins(CpList,PinList),
    best_pin(Chunk,PinList,BestPin).

cps([Seq|Sequences],CpList) :-
    CpList := [CPs|CpList1],
    c_critical_points(Seq,CPs),
    cps(Sequences,CpList1).
cps([],CpList) :- CpList := [].

divide(Seqs,Pin,Alignment) :-
    Pin =\= [] |
    split(Seqs,Pin,Left,Right,Rest),
    align_chunk(Left,LAlign) @ random,
    align_chunk(Right,RAlign) @ random,
    align_chunk(Rest,RestAlign) @ random,
    combine(LAlign,RAlign,RestAlign,Alignment).
divide(Seqs,[],Alignment) :-
    c_basic_align(Seqs,Alignment).
```

Fig. 2.4. Genetic sequence alignment algorithm.

This example illustrates three important characteristics of the Strand language. First, programs can exploit high-level logic programming features to simplify the specification of complex algorithms. These features include the use of list structures to manage collections of data and a rule-based syntax that provides a declarative reading for program components. Second, programs can call routines written in sequential languages to perform operations that are most naturally expressed in terms of imperative operations on arrays. In the example, three C language procedures (distinguished here by a "c_" prefix) are called in this way. This multilingual programming style permits rapid prototyping of algorithms without compromising performance. (The absence of an array data type means that code for manipulating arrays would be both clumsy and inefficient if written in Strand.) Third, alternative parallel implementation strategies can be explored simply by annotating the program text with different process-mapping directives. For example, in Fig. 2.4 annotations "@ random" are placed on the recursive calls to align to specify that these calls are to execute on randomly selected processors. Alternatively, annotations "@ elsewhere" could be used to specify that these calls are to be scheduled to idle processors by using a load-balancing strategy. Since communication and synchronization are specified in terms of operations on shared single-assignment variables, no other change to the program text is required: the Strand compiler translates these operations into either low-level message-passing or shared-data access operations, as required [CT91].

2.4 New Paradigms Summary

Analysis of application experiences in such areas as computational biology [BBF+89], discrete-event simulation [XT90], telephone exchange control [AV89], automated theorem proving, and weather modeling indicates three particular strengths of the Strand constructs:

- The use of parallel composition and a high-level, uniform communication abstraction simplifies development of task-parallel applications featuring dynamic creation and deletion of threads, complex scheduling algorithms, and dynamic communication patterns. Complex distributed algorithms can often be expressed in a few lines of code by using Strand constructs.
- Parallel composition and single-assignment variables also enforce and expose the benefits of a compositional programming model. This eases program development, testing, debugging, and the reuse of program components.
- The recursively defined data structures and rule-based syntax that Strand borrows from logic programming are useful when implementing symbolic applications, for example in computational biology.

This same analysis also reveals four significant weaknesses that limit the utility of the Strand system, particularly for larger scientific and engineering applications.

- While the use of a separate coordination language for parallel computation is conceptually economical, it is not universally popular. Writing even a simple program requires that a programmer learn a completely new language, and the logic-based syntax is unfamiliar to many.
- The foreign-language interface is often too restrictive for programmers intent on reusing existing sequential code in a parallel framework. In particular, it is difficult to convert sequential code into single-program/multiple-data (SPMD) libraries, since this typically requires the ability to embed

parallel constructs in existing sequential code, something that Strand does not support. As a consequence, combining existing program modules with Strand can require significant restructuring of those modules.

- The Strand abstractions provide little assistance to the programmer applying domain decomposition techniques to regular data structures. In these applications, the principal difficulties facing the programmer are not thread management or scheduling, but translating between local and global addresses, problems that have been addressed in data-parallel languages.
- The use of a new language means that program development tools such as debuggers and execution profilers must be developed from scratch; it also hinders the application of existing sequential development tools to sequential code modules.

Many (but certainly not all) of our observations also apply to other parallel language approaches based on new, explicitly parallel paradigms. We believe that, collectively, these observations explain why such languages have not yet been widely adopted.

3. Language Extensions

Rather than defining a completely new programming language, users may instead choose to incorporate support for parallelism into an existing language by means of appropriately chosen extensions. This approach has in general proven more acceptable than the use of totally new languages. However, the approach introduces its own problems because of the need to work within the constraints of a language that was typically not designed with parallelism in mind. Aspects of a sequential language (e.g., aliasing in Fortran) may make efficient or correct parallel execution difficult. Moreover, extensions that may make sense in one language (e.g., global pointers in a C- or C++-based language) may not be appropriate in another context (e.g., in a Java-based language).

We distinguish here three main classes of language extension:

- *Shared-memory extensions* support a programming model in which multiple concurrent threads operate on a shared address space. Such extensions were studied extensively some years ago (e.g., see [KB88]), saw a decline in interest as distributed-memory computers became widespread, and have become popular again (e.g., OpenMP) with the development of scalable shared-memory computers and software-based distributed shared-memory systems.
- *Distributed memory extensions* support a programming model that exposes the parallel structure of the computation and, hence, allows the programmer to partition it into distinct processes. Examples include Concert/C [AGG+94], which supports both remote procedure call and send/receive communication mechanisms, and Fortran M [FC95], which generalizes

Fortran I/O calls and FOR loops to support channels and parallel loops, respectively.
- *Data-parallel languages* represent a special case, which is discussed in the next section.

Other approaches adopt hybrid models. For example, the Linda [CG89, CG89a] model defines operations for storing and extracting data from a shared associative tuple space; these constructs can be thought of as high-level message-passing operations. (The tuple space concept has seen recent popularity in Java-based systems: e.g., JINI.)

3.1 Compositional C++: An Overview

We choose as our case study for language extensions the language Compositional C++ (CC++), introduced in [CK93] and also described, in a more tutorial fashion, in [Fos95]. CC++ is one of a number of proposals for parallel languages based on C++ (others are described in [WL96]). The language is interesting both in its own right and because of the techniques it uses to incorporate parallelism into a sequential language.

CC++ is a general-purpose parallel programming language comprising all of C++ plus six new keywords. It is a strict superset of the C++ language, in that any valid C or C++ program that does not use a CC++ keyword is also a valid CC++ program. The CC++ extensions implement six basic abstractions:

1. The *processor object* is a mechanism for controlling locality. A computation may comprise one or more processor objects. Within a processor object, sequential C++ code can execute without modification. In particular, it can access local data structures. The keyword **global** identifies a processor object class, and the predefined class **proc_t** controls processor object placement.
2. The *global pointer*, identified by the type modifier **global**, is a mechanism for linking together processor objects. A global pointer is required to access a data structure or to perform computation (using a *remote procedure call*) in another processor object.
3. The *thread* is a mechanism for specifying concurrent execution. Threads are created independently of processor objects, and more than one thread can execute in a processor object. The **par**, **parfor**, and **spawn** statements create threads.
4. The *sync variable*, specified by the type modifier **sync**, is used to synchronize thread execution.
5. The *atomic function*, specified by the keyword **atomic**, is a mechanism used to control the interleaving of threads executing in the same processor object.

6. *Transfer functions*, with predefined type `CCVoid`, allow arbitrary data structures to be transferred between processor objects as arguments to remote procedure calls.

As we describe in the following, these abstractions provide the basic mechanisms required to specify concurrency, locality, communication, and mapping.

3.2 Concurrency in CC++

A CC++ program, like a C++ program, executes initially as a single thread of control (task). However, a CC++ program can use `par`, `parfor`, and `spawn` constructs to create additional threads. A *parallel block* is distinguished from an ordinary C++ block by the keyword `par`.

```
par {
    statement1;
    statement2;
    ...
    statementN;
}
```

The statements inside a parallel block can be any legal CC++ statement except for variable declarations and statements that result in nonlocal changes in the flow of control, such as `goto`.

Statements in a parallel block execute *concurrently*. For example, the following parallel block creates three concurrent threads: two `workers` and a single `master`.

```
par {
    worker();
    worker();
    master();
}
```

A parallel block terminates when all of its constituent statements terminate; execution then proceeds to the next executable statement. Thus, in the preceding parallel block, the thread that executed the parallel block proceeds to the next executable statement after the parallel block only when both the master and the workers have terminated.

A *parallel for-loop* creates multiple threads, all executing the same statements contained in the body of the for-loop. It is identical in form to the do-loop except that the keyword `parfor` is used in place of `for`. For example, the following code creates ten threads of control, each executing the function `myprocess`.

```
parfor(int i=0; i<10; i++) {
    myprocess(i);
}
```

Only the loop body of the **parfor** executes in parallel. Evaluation of the initialization, test, and update components of the statement follows normal sequential ordering. If the initialization section uses a locally declared variable (for example, **int i**), then each instance of the loop body has its own private copy of that variable.

CC++ parallel constructs can be nested arbitrarily. Hence, the following code creates ten **worker** threads and one **master**.

```
par {
    master();
    parfor(int i=0; i<10; i++)
        worker(i);
}
```

Finally, the **spawn** statement can be used to specify unstructured parallelism. This statement can be applied to a function to create a completely independent thread of control. The parent thread does not wait for the new thread to terminate execution, and cannot receive a return value from the called function. One use for the **spawn** statement is as an efficient implementation of remote procedure calls that do not require a return value.

3.3 Locality in CC++

In many parallel languages, the two concepts of locality and concurrency are linked: a task is both a separate address space and a thread of control. In CC++, these two concepts are separated: processor objects are used to represent address spaces, and threads represent threads of control. Processor objects can exist independently of threads, and more than one thread can be mapped to a processor object.

3.3.1 Processor objects. A processor object is defined by a C++ class declaration modified by the keyword **global**. A processor object is identical to a normal C++ class definition in all but two respects:

1. Names of C++ "global" variables and functions (that is, names with file scope) refer to unique objects within different instances of a processor object. Hence, there is no sharing between processor object instances.
2. Private members of a processor object need not be explicitly declared. C++ "global" functions and variables are defined implicitly to be private members of the processor object in which they occur.

Processor object types can be inherited, and the usual C++ protection mechanisms apply, so private functions and data are accessible only from a processor object's member functions or from the member functions of derived objects. Hence, it is the member functions and data declared **public** that represent the processor object's interface.

3.3.2 Global pointers. A processor object is a unit of locality: an address space within which data accesses are regarded as local and hence cheap. A thread executing in a processor object can access data structures defined or allocated within that processor object directly, using ordinary C++ pointers.

Processor objects are linked together by *global pointers*. A global pointer is like an ordinary C++ pointer except that it can refer to other processor objects or to data structures contained within other processor objects. It represents data that are potentially nonlocal and hence more expensive to access than data referenced by ordinary C++ pointers.

A global pointer is distinguished by the keyword **global**, as the following illustrates:

```
float *global gpf;      // GP to a float
char * *global gppc;    // GP to a pointer of type char
C *global gpC;          // GP to an object of type C
```

When the **new** statement is used to create an instance of a processor object, it returns a **global** pointer. For example, the statement

```
MyProcessorObject *global my_pobj = new MyProcessorObject;
```

creates a new processor object of type **MyProcessorObject** and defines **my_pobj** to be a pointer to that object.

3.3.3 Thread placement. By default, a CC++ thread executes in the same processor object as its parent. Computation is placed in another processor object via a *remote procedure call*. A thread needs only a global pointer to another processor object to be able to invoke any of its public member functions. For example, in the following statement, **my_pobj** is a global pointer to a processor object in which a process **consumer** is a public member function:

```
my_pobj->consumer();
```

Remote procedure calls are discussed in more detail below.

3.3.4 CC++ example: tree search. We use a simple example, shown in Fig. 3.1i, to illustrate the CC++ constructs that have been introduced so far. The example uses processor objects and the **par** construct to implement a prototypical tree-structured computation. The program explores a binary tree recursively, creating a task (processor object + thread) for each tree node and returning the total number of leaf nodes that represent solutions. Notice the use of a parallel block to create the threads that search the two subtrees rooted at a nonleaf node. In this simple program, the tree is not represented by an explicit data structure; instead, a process's position in the tree is represented by an integer.

3.4 Communication in CC++

CC++ does not provide low-level primitives for directly sending and receiving data between threads. Instead, threads communicate by operating on shared data structures. For example, one thread may append items to a shared list structure, from which another thread removes items. This process implements a form of channel communication. A wide variety of such communication structures can be specified with CC++ mechanisms.

In this section, we first explain how global pointers are used to communicate data between processor objects. Then, we explain how sync variables and atomic functions are used to provide synchronization and mutual exclusion.

3.4.1 Remote operations. CC++ global pointers are used in the same way as C++ local pointers, with but one exception: CC++ global pointers operate on data or invoke functions that may be located in other processor objects. Hence, the following code fragment first assigns to and then reads from the remote location referenced by the global pointer **gp**, and hence results in communication.

```
global int *gp;
*gp = 5;
a = (*gp) * (*gp);
```

If we invoke a member function of an object referenced by a global pointer, we perform what is called a remote procedure call (RPC). An RPC has the general form

```
<type> *global gp;
result = gp->p(...)
```

where **gp** is a global pointer of an arbitrary **<type>**, p(...) is a call to a function defined in the processor object referenced by that global pointer, and **result** is a variable that will be set to the value returned by p(...). An RPC proceeds in three stages:

```
global class Tree { // Processor object: one member function
public:
    int search(int);
};

int Tree::search(int A) {
    int ls, rs;
    if(leaf(A)) {      // Leaf node: check whether a solution
        if solution(A)
            return(1);
        else
            return(0);
    }
    else {             // Nonleaf node: explore subtrees
        Tree *global lobj = new Tree;
        Tree *global robj = new Tree;
        par {          // Create processes to search subtrees
            ls = lobj->search(left_child(A));
            rs = robj->search(right_child(A));
        }
        delete(lobj); delete(robj);
        return(ls+rs);
    }
}

void main(int argc, char *argv[]) {
    int total;
    // Create new processor object for search
    Tree *global searcher = new Tree;
    // Initiate search
    total = searcher->search(1);
    printf("There were %d solutions\n",total);
}
```

Fig. 3.1. CC++ tree search program. The program uses two parallel constructs. The global keyword declares the processor object Tree, and the par construct defines the parallel block that causes the two recursive calls to search to execute concurrently. Notice how two new processor objects (lobj, robj) are created for the recursive calls and then deleted when these calls complete.

1. The arguments to the function p(...) are packed into a message, communicated to the remote processor object, and unpacked. The calling thread suspends execution.
2. A new thread is created in the remote processor object to execute the called function.
3. Upon termination of the remote function, the function return value is transferred back to the calling thread, which resumes execution.

Basic integer types (char, short, int, long, and the unsigned variants of these), floats, doubles, and global pointers can be transferred as RPC arguments or return values without any user intervention. Structures, regular pointers, and arrays can be transferred with the programmer-supplied transfer functions [CK93, Fos95].

```
int length;          // Global variable: implicitly private

global class Length {
public:
    int read_len()              { return(length); }
    void write_len(int newval) { length = newval; }
};

// Test program: create and operate on datum objects
void test() {
    int len, area;
    // Allocate new processor object
    Length *global lp = new Length;
    // Write the private variable length
    lp->write_len(5);
    // Read the private variable length
    len  = lp->read_len();
    area = (len*len);
}
```

Fig. 3.2. A CC++ implementation of a processor object with member functions supporting read and write operations on a private variable length, and a procedure test that uses these functions.

Fig. 3.2 uses RPCs to access a variable length located in another processor object; contrast this with the code fragment given at the beginning of this section, in which read and write operations were used for the same purpose.

3.4.2 Synchronization. A producer thread can use an RPC to move data to a processor object in which a consumer thread is executing, hence effecting communication. However, we also require a mechanism for synchronizing the execution of these two threads, so that the consumer does not read the data before it is communicated by the producer. The CC++ mechanism used for this purpose is the single assignment or *sync* variable. (This construct is inspired by, and is similar to, the Strand single-assignment variable; but clearly its implementation is quite different.) A sync variable is identified by the type modifier **sync**, which indicates that the variable has the following properties:

- It initially has a special value, "undefined."
- It can be assigned a value at most once, and once assigned is treated as a constant (ANSI C and C++ **const**).
- An attempt to read an undefined variable causes the thread that performs the read to block until the variable is assigned a value.

Any regular C++ type can be declared **sync**, as can a CC++ global pointer. Hence, we can write the following.

```
sync int i;          // i is a sync integer
sync int *j;         // j is a pointer to a sync integer
int *sync k;         // k is a sync pointer to an integer
sync int *sync l;    // l is a sync pointer to a sync integer
```

We use the following code fragment to illustrate the use of **sync** variables. This codes makes two concurrent RPCs to functions defined in Fig. 3.2: one to read the variable **length** and one to write that variable.

```
Length *global lp;
int val;
par {
    val = lp->read_len();
    lp->write_len(42);
}
```

What is the value of the variable **val** at the end of the parallel block? Because the read and write operations are not synchronized, the value is not known. If the read operation executes before the write, **val** will have some arbitrary value. (The **Length** class does not initialize the variable **length**.) If the execution order is reversed, **val** will have the value 42.

This nondeterminism can be avoided by making the variable **length** in Fig. 3.2 a **sync** variable. That is, we change its definition to the following.

```
sync int length;
```

Execution order now does not matter: if **read_len** executes first, it will block until the variable **length** is assigned a value by **write_len**.

3.4.3 Example: channel communication. Global pointers and sync variables can be used to implement a wide variety of communication mechanisms. We illustrate this flexibility by showing how these constructs can be used to implement a simple shared queue class. This class can be used to implement channel communication between two concurrently executing tasks: we simply allocate a queue object and provide both the producer task and the consumer task with pointers to this object. The resulting structure is quite similar to the stream construct used in Strand. However, in CC++, the "stream" is just one of many communication mechanisms that can be defined.

A channel is a message queue to which a sender can append a sequence of messages and from which a receiver can remove messages. The only synchronization constraint is that the receiver blocks when removing a message if the queue is empty. An obvious CC++ representation of a message queue is as a linked list, in which each entry contains a message plus a pointer to the next message. Fig. 3.3 takes this approach, defining a `Queue` class that maintains pointers to the head and tail of a message queue represented as a list of `IntQData` structures, and that provides `enqueue` and `dequeue` functions to add items to the tail of the queue and remove items from the head, respectively.

The data structures manipulated by this program are illustrated in Fig. 3.4. The `sync` variable contained in the `IntQData` structure used to represent a linked list entry ensures synchronization between the `enqueue` and `dequeue` operations. The queue is initialized to be a single list element containing an undefined variable as its message.

The first action performed by `dequeue` is to read the message value associated with the first entry in the queue. If the queue is empty, this read operation will block, providing the necessary synchronization. If the queue is not empty, the `dequeue` function will read the queue value, delete the list element, and advance the `head` pointer to the next list element. Similarly, the `enqueue` function first allocates a new list element and links it into the queue and then sets the `msg` field of the current tail list element. The order in which these two operations are performed is important. If performed in the opposite order,

```
tail->value = msg;
tail->next  = new IntQData;
```

then a `dequeue` function call blocked on the list element `tail->value` and awakened by the assignment `tail->value=msg` could read the pointer `tail->next` before it is set to reference a newly created element.

3.4.4 Mutual exclusion. The `sync` variable allows us to synchronize the transfer of data from a producer to a consumer. In other situations, we may wish to permmit two threads to operate on the same nonsync data structure while ensuring that they do not interfere with each other's execution. For

```
struct IntQData {          // A list element contains:
  sync int value;          //    sync variable (message), &
  struct IntQData *next;   //    pointer to next list element
};

class Queue {
public:
  void enqueue(int);
  int dequeue();
private:
  // Initialize: allocate single element
  void Queue() { head = tail = new IntQData; }
  IntQData *head, *tail;
}

void Queue::enqueue(int msg) {  // Enqueue a value:
  tail->next  = new IntQData;   //    allocate new element,
  tail->value = msg;            //    set message value, &
  tail        = tail->next;     //    advance tail pointer
}

int Queue::dequeue() {              // Dequeue a value:
  int retval = head->value;         //    access message value,
  IntQData *newh = head->next;      //    get next list item,
  delete head;                      //    delete old list head,
  head = newh;                      //    advance head pointer, &
  return retval;                    //    return message value
}
```

Fig. 3.3. The Queue class provides a constructor Queue() that initializes a queue, and enqueue and dequeue functions that add an element to a queue and remove an element from a queue, respectively. The IntQData structure incorporates a sync variable, used to synchronize enqueue and dequeue operations.

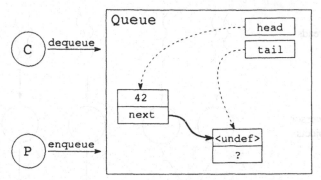

Fig. 3.4. A message queue class, showing the internal representation of a queue as a linked list of IntQData structures (two are shown) with message values represented as sync values that are either defined (42) or undefined (<undef>). Producer and consumer tasks execute enqueue and dequeue operations, respectively.

example, the **enqueue** and **dequeue** operations described above allow a single sender and receiver to communicate by enqueuing to and dequeuing from a shared queue. What if we want multiple senders to be able to append messages to the same queue? We cannot allow two producers to make concurrent calls to **enqueue**, as an arbitrary interleaving of two **enqueue** calls can have bizarre results. What we need is a mechanism to ensure that only one message can be enqueued at a time.

This requirement is satisfied by CC++'s **atomic** keyword. (Java incorporates a similar construct.) Member functions of an object can be declared atomic. This declaration specifies that the execution of such a function will not be interleaved with the execution of any other atomic function of the same object. For example, to allow multiple producers on our channel data type, we would declare the **enqueue** function to be **atomic**, as follows.

```
atomic void Queue::enqueue(int msg) {
    tail->next  = new IntQData;
    tail->value = msg;
    tail        = tail->next;
}
```

This ensures that even if multiple producers attempt to append to the same queue concurrently, the actual **enqueue** operations will occur in some sequential order and a valid queue will be generated.

3.5 Mapping in CC++

A parallel program defined in terms of CC++ constructs can be executed on both uniprocessor and multiprocessor computers. In the latter case, a

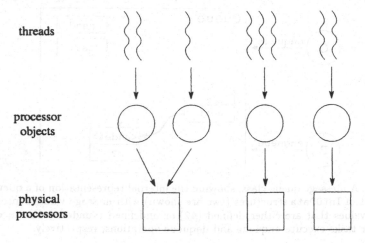

threads

processor
objects

physical
processors

Fig. 3.5. Mapping in CC++. First, threads are mapped to processor objects. Then, processor objects are mapped to physical processors.

complete program must also specify how the processor objects created by a CC++ program are mapped to processors.

Mapping in CC++ is a two-stage process (Fig. 3.5). First, threads are mapped to processor objects, and then processor objects are mapped to processors. The mapping of threads to processor objects can be one-to-one, in which case it is the mapping of processor objects to physical processors that is important. Alternatively, the mapping of processor objects to physical processors may be one-to-one, in which case it is the mapping of threads to processor objects that is important. If both mappings are one-to-one, then the mapping problem is straightforward.

An important aspect of the first mapping stage, processor object placement, is that it *influences performance but not correctness*. Hence, we can develop a program on a uniprocessor and then tune performance on a parallel computer by changing placement decisions. The second mapping stage, thread placement, has this property only if threads do not share data structures.

3.5.1 Processor object placement. By default, a newly created processor object is placed on the same processor as its creator. An alternative placement can be specified by using the placement argument to the **new** operator. In C++, this argument is used to position an object in memory space; in CC++, it can also be used to position a processor object in processor space. The location is specified by an implementation-dependent class named **proc_t**. The public-domain implementation of CC++ provides a constructor function **proc_t** that constructs a placement structure with a specified processor name. Hence, the following code fragment specifies the creation of a new processor object (of type **MyClass**) that will execute on a processor called **mymachine**.

```
MyClass *global G;
proc_t placement("mymachine");
G = new (placement) MyClass;
```

The **new** statement creates a new processor object; the supplied **proc_t** specifies the machine name. To place the new processor object on a different processor, one need change only the second line of this code fragment, for example to the following.

```
proc_t placement("yourmachine");
```

As a further example, the following code creates 32 processor objects, placing each on a different processor of a multicomputer, with nodes named sp#0, sp#1, ..., sp#31. Notice how **parfor** is used to create the different processor objects concurrently.

```
MyClass *global G[32];
parfor(int i=0; i<31; i++) {
    char node_name[256];
    sprintf(node_name,"sp#%d",i);
    proc_t placement(node_name);
    G[i] = new (placement) MyClass;
}
```

This program embeds information about its execution environment. A better approach is to encapsulate mapping decisions in a separate class, for example, the class **Mapping** defined in Fig. 3.6. This class provides an initialization function that allows the programmer to specify the processors on which mapping is to be performed, and two mapping functions **processor** and **random_p** that return a **proc_t** representing the ith of these processors and a randomly selected processor, respectively. Two data transfer functions (omitted for brevity) package and unpackage the node list associated with a mapping object, allowing a mapping to be passed as an argument when creating a new processor object. The use of the **Mapping** class is illustrated in the following example.

Recall that Fig. 3.1 explores a search tree in parallel by creating new threads to explore the subtrees rooted at each nonleaf node. Each thread executes in a new processor object. This program does not specify a mapping strategy for these processor objects. One strategy is to place each newly created processor object/thread pair on a processor selected at random. Fig. 3.7 uses the **Mapping** class of Fig. 3.6 to implement this behavior. There are three significant differences between this program and Fig. 3.1. First, a global **Mapping** object is defined and initialized at the beginning of **main** to contain the names of the processors on which the program is to execute. These names are read from a file. Second, a constructor is provided for the processor object

```
// Mapping class encapsulates a list of processor names
class Mapping {
    friend CCVoid & operator<<(CCVoid &, const Mapping &);
    friend CCVoid & operator>>(CCVoid &, Mapping &);
public:
    proc_t processor(int);    // Access particular node
    proc_t random_p();        // Access random node
    void initmap(char **);    // Supply processor names
private:
    int P;
    char *proc_names[];
};

proc_t Mapping::processor(int i)
{ return(proc_t(proc_names[i%P])); }

proc_t Mapping::random_p()
{ return processor(drand48()*((float) P)); }

// Store list of processor names
void Mapping::initmap(char *plist[]) {
    P = 0;                    // First, count number of processors
    for (char **cPtr=plist; *cPtr!=0; cPtr++)
        P++;
    proc_names = plist;       // Then store processor names
}
```

Fig. 3.6. The class **Mapping** encapsulates information about how to place a processor object on the ith of P processors named in the **initmap** call. The function **processor** returns a **proc_t** structure for a specified processor, while the function **random_p** returns a **proc_t** structure for a random processor. The operators with type **CCVoid** are data transfer functions and are omitted for brevity.

class **Tree** that copies the **Mapping** object to each new processor object as it is created. Third, one of the processor object allocation calls in the **search** function is augmented with a call to **random_p**, which returns a **proc_t** structure on a randomly selected processor.

```
Mapping mapping;                          // Mapping information

global class Tree {
public:
    int search(int);                      // Search function
    Tree(Mapping m) { mapping = m; } // Initialization function
};

int Tree::search(int A) {
    int ls, rs;
    if (leaf(A)) {
        ...
    }
    else {          // Create new processor objects
        Tree *global lobj = new Tree(mapping);
        Tree *global robj =
                  new (mapping.random_p()) Tree(mapping);
        par {       // Create processes to search subtrees
            ls = lobj->search(left_child(A));
            rs = robj->search(right_child(A));
        }
        delete(lobj); delete(robj);
        return(ls+rs);
    }
}

int main(int argc, char *argv[]) {
    char *nodes[] = read_nodes();        // Read node information
    mapping.initmap(nodes);              // Initialize mapping
    Tree *global searcher = new Tree(mapping);
    int total = searcher->search(1);
    printf("There were %d solutions\n",total);
    return(0);

}
```

Fig. 3.7. CC++ tree search program with mapping constructs. The second processor object allocation statement in the **search** function calls **random_p** to create the processor object on a randomly selected processor.

3.5.2 Mapping threads to processor objects. An alternative approach to mapping in CC++ is to create a fixed number of processor objects onto which threads are then placed. This approach is often used in single-program/multiple-data (SPMD) computations, in which case a single thread is mapped to each processor object. Another important application is in situations where a computation creates a large number of lightweight threads that interact only via global pointers. We can map these threads to a static number of processor objects, hence avoiding the overhead of creating a new processor object when creating a new thread of control. Since the threads do not share local data structures, we do not compromise mapping independence.

3.6 Language Extensions Summary

Our examination of CC++ reveals some of the strengths and weaknesses of parallel languages based on extensions to sequential languages. On the positive side, CC++ programs are, in essence, C++ programs. Standard C++ programming techniques can be applied, existing programs can be modified (with varying degrees of difficulty) to produce parallel programs, and in principle standard tools can be used (with some modifications) to analyze, compile, and debug programs. On the negative side, the programmer must learn to appreciate potentially complex interactions between existing sequential and new parallel constructs. CC++ makes this process relatively easy, for example by clearly labeling all "global" pointers; nevertheless, the potential for unexpected interactions exists.

4. Data-Parallel Languages

The term *data parallelism* refers to the concurrency that is obtained when the same operation is applied to some or all elements of a data ensemble. A data-parallel program is a sequence of such operations. A parallel algorithm is obtained from a data-parallel program by applying domain decomposition techniques to the data structures operated on. Typically, the programmer is responsible for specifying the domain decomposition, but the compiler partitions the computation automatically.

The data-parallel programming model is both higher level and more restrictive than the task-parallel models considered in preceding sections. It is *higher level* in that the programmer is not required to specify communication structures explicitly: these are derived by a compiler from the domain decomposition specified by the programmer. It is *more restrictive* because not all algorithms can be specified in data-parallel terms. For these reasons, data parallelism is an important, but not universal, parallel programming paradigm.

Data-parallel programming languages have included Kali [MV91], CM Fortran [TMC93], Fortran D [FHK+90], Vienna Fortran [CMZ92], *Lisp [TMC90], C* [TMC90], pC++[BBG+91], Data-Parallel C [HQ91, HQ91], NESL [Ble90], and DINO [RSW90]. In a rather different approach, several projects have explored the use of C++ class libraries to encapsulate data-parallel operations on data objects such as arrays [DPW93, LQ92].

The compilation of High Performance Fortran (HPF) and related languages requires specialized analysis and optimization techniques. Hiranandani et al. [HKT92] and Zima and Chapman [ZC91] provide a good introduction to these topics; see also papers by Albert, Lukas, and Steele [ALS91], Bozkus et al. [BCF+93], Callahan and Kennedy [CK88], Rogers and Pingali [RP89], and Zima, Bast, and Gerndt [ZBG88] and the monographs by Banerjee [Ban88] and Wolfe [Wol89].

In this section, we introduce the key concepts of data-parallel programming and show how parallel algorithms can be expressed in data-parallel form. We base our presentation on the languages Fortran 90 (F90) and HPF [HPFF93, KLS+94, Lov93]; many of the ideas also apply to other data-parallel languages, such as C* and pC++. F90 provides constructs for specifying concurrent execution but not for domain decomposition. HPF augments F90 with additional parallel constructs and data placement directives, which allow many HPF programs to be compiled with reasonable efficiency for a range of parallel computers [ZC91, Ken99, HKT92].

4.1 Basic Data-Parallel Concepts

We first provide a general introduction to data parallelism and data-parallel languages, focusing on concurrency and locality.

4.1.1 Concurrency. Depending on the programming language used, the data ensembles operated on in a data-parallel program may be regular (e.g., an array) or irregular (e.g., a tree or sparse matrix). In F90 and HPF, the data structures operated on are arrays. In contrast, the data-parallel language pC++ [BBG+91] allows programs to operate not only on arrays but also on trees, sets, and other more complex data structures.

Concurrency may be implicit or may be expressed by using explicit parallel constructs. For example, the F90 array assignment statement is an *explicitly* parallel construct; we write

    A = B*C   ! A, B, C are arrays

to specify that each element of array A is to be assigned the product of the corresponding elements of arrays B and C. This statement also implies *conformality*, meaning that the three arrays have the same size and shape. In contrast, the following do-loop is *implicitly* parallel: a compiler may be able to detect that the various do-loop iterations are independent and hence can be performed in parallel, but this detection requires some analysis.

```
do i = 1,m
  do j = 1,n
    A(i,j) = B(i,j)*C(i,j)
  enddo
enddo
```

A data-parallel program is a sequence of such statements, each specifying operations on all or most elements of large data structures. On a distributed-memory parallel computer, compilation typically generates an SMPD program, in which each processor executes the same code on a subset of the data structures. While different techniques are available, in many cases the compiler can construct this program by first partitioning data structures into disjoint subdomains, one per processor, and then applying the "owner computes" rule to determine which operations should be performed on each processor. This rule states that the computation required to produce a piece of data is performed on the processor on which that data is located.

Compilation also introduces communication operations when computation mapped to one processor requires data mapped to another processor. We illustrate this with the following program.

```
real y, s, X(n)                    ! y, s scalars; X an array

X = X*y                            ! Multiply each X(i) by y
do i = 2,n-1
  X(i) = (X(i-1) + X(i+1)/2        ! Communication required
enddo
s = SUM(X)                         ! Communication required
```

The communication requirements of this program depend on how the three variables X, y, and s are distributed over processors. If X is distributed, while y and s are replicated, then the first assignment can proceed without communication, with each X(i) being computed by the processor that owns X(i). The second assignment (in the do-loop) requires communication: the processor computing X(i) requires the values of X(i-1) and X(i+1), which may be located on different processors. The summation also requires communication.

4.1.2 Locality. Data placement is an essential part of a data-parallel algorithm, since the mapping of data to processors determines the *locality* of data references and hence, to a large extent, the performance of a parallel program. For example, the simple array assignment A = B*C either can proceed without any communication or can require communication for every assignment, depending on whether corresponding elements of the arrays A, B, and C are located on the same or different processors.

Identifying the best distribution of the various data structures operated on by a data-parallel program is a global optimization problem and not generally tractable. Hence, data-parallel languages often provide the programmer with the ability to define how data structures are to be distributed. In HPF, the DISTRIBUTE directive fulfills this function. The statements

```
!HPF$    PROCESSORS pr(16)
         real X(1024)
!HPF$    DISTRIBUTE x(BLOCK) ONTO pr
```

indicate that the array x is to be distributed in a blocked fashion over 16 processors. That is, processor 0 gets the first 1024/16 elements, processor 1 the second 1024/16 elements, and so on.

4.2 Fortran 90

F90 is a data-parallel programming language in its own right: its array assignment statement and array intrinsic functions can be used to specify certain classes of data-parallel computations. Our main interest in F90, however, is that it forms the basis for HPF, which augments it with more flexible parallel constructs and directives for controlling locality.

Fortran 90 (F90) is a complex language; it augments Fortran 77 (F77) with pointers, user-defined datatypes, modules, recursive subroutines, dynamic storage allocation, array operations, new intrinsic functions, and many other features. We focus our attention here on those new features that are most relevant to parallel programming. These are the *array assignment statement* and the *array intrinsic functions*.

4.2.1 Array assignment. F90 allows a variety of *scalar* operations (that is, operations defined on single values) to be applied also to entire arrays. This feature causes the scalar operation to be applied to each element of the array. If an operation involves several values, all must be represented by *conformable* arrays, that is, scalar values or arrays of the same size and shape. The operation is performed on corresponding elements from each array. For example, consider the following scalar operation, which assigns the sum b+c to a.

```
integer a, b, c
a = b + c
```

In F90, we can apply the same operation to arrays A and B and scalar c, as follows. This assigns each element A(i,j) of A the sum B(i,j)+c.

```
integer A(10,10), B(10,10), c
A = B + c
```

In fact, all F90's unary and binary intrinsic operations can be applied to arrays, as in the following examples.

```
real A(10,20), B(10,20)
logical L(10,20)
A = A + 1.0              ! Adds 1.0 to each element of A
A = SQRT(A)              ! Computes square root of each element of A
L = A .EQ. B            ! Sets L(i,j) to .true. if A(i,j)=B(i,j);
                         ! and to .false. otherwise
```

A conformable *array section* (a triplet with the general form *lower-bound* : *upper-bound* : *stride*, with a stride of 1 assumed if "*: stride*" is omitted) can be substituted for an entire array in an array operation. Hence, one can write the following code to compute the sum $A(i)=B(i)+B(i+1)$ for $1 \leq i \leq N-1$:

$$A(1:N-1) = B(1:N-1) + B(2:N)$$

Finally, a masked array assignment uses the WHERE construct to restrict the array elements on which an assignment is performed. For example, the following statement replaces each nonzero element of X with its reciprocal. (The F90 /= operator is equivalent to .NE. in F77.)

$$WHERE(X \mathbin{/=} 0) \; X = 1.0/X$$

4.2.2 Array intrinsics. All F90 intrinsic functions that apply to scalar values can also be applied to arrays, in which case the function is applied to each array element. For example, ABS(A) returns an array containing the absolute values of the elements of array A. In addition, F90 provides a number of *transformational* functions which return a scalar or array result that depends on the values of many elements of an array. For example, MAXVAL, MINVAL, SUM, and PRODUCT perform a reduction operation on an array, returning a scalar value representing the maximum, minimum, sum, or product of the elements of the array, respectively. Hence, the following code sets the scalar variable S to the sum of the elements of the array X.

```
real S, X(100)
S = SUM(X)
```

The CSHIFT function performs a circular shift on an array, returning a new array of the same size and shape but with its elements in a different configuration. A call of the form

$$CSHIFT(A,s,d)$$

performs a circular shift on the elements of the array A, where s is the size (and direction) of the shift (a scalar or array) and the optional argument d indicates the dimension in which the shift is to be applied (Fig. 4.1). This function is often used in expressions involving index expressions. For example, consider the following F77 loop.

```
real X(0:99), B(0:99)
do i = 0,99
   B(i) = ( X(mod(i+99,100) + X(mod(i+1,100)) )/2
enddo
```

(a)

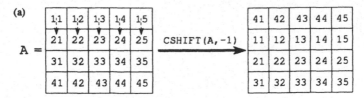

(b)

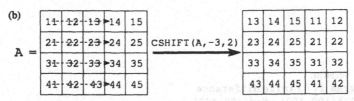

Fig. 4.1. The F90 CSHIFT function. In (a), a negative shift of one element is applied in dimension 1; in (b), a negative shift of three elements is applied in dimension 2.

This can be written in F90 as

```
real X(100), B(100), L(100), R(100)
L = CSHIFT(X,-1,1)
R = CSHIFT(X,+1,1)
B = ( L + R )/2
```

or simply as follows.

```
real X(100), B(100)
B = ( CSHIFT(X,-1,1) + CSHIFT(X,1,1) )/2
```

In both cases, an array assignment sets the array B to the sum of two arrays: X shifted left one element, and X shifted right one element.

Fig. 4.2 illustrates F90's array assignment and array intrinsics. This program, for which both F77 and F90 versions are given, first applies a five-point finite difference stencil to the array X to obtain the array New and then computes the maximum difference between the two arrays. The F90 version uses an array assignment and the intrinsic functions ABS and MAXVAL.

4.2.3 Discussion. F90's array assignment statement and array intrinsics are designed primarily to permit more succinct implementations of array operations. They also reveal opportunities for data-parallel execution, which can be exploited by a compiler on a parallel computer. Nevertheless, F90 has limitations as a data-parallel programming language. First, and most important, F90 lacks mechanisms that would allow the programmer to specify how data should be distributed in order to exploit locality. This limitation hinders efficient implementation on distributed-memory parallel computers. Second, its array operations can be used to implement only a limited class of data-parallel algorithms; in consequence, F90 programs often incorporate

```
C    F77 version:
     program f77_finite_difference
     real X(100,100), New(100,100)
     do i = 2,99
        do j = 2,99
           New(i,j) = (X(i-1, j) + X(i+1, j) +
     $                    X(i, j-1) + X(i, j+1) )/4
        enddo
     enddo
     diffmax = 0.0
     do i = 1,100
        do j = 1,100
           diff = abs(New(i,j)-X(i,j))
           if(diff .gt. diffmax) diffmax = diff
        enddo
     enddo


C    F90 version:
     program f90_finite_difference
     real X(100,100), New(100,100)
     New(2:99,2:99) = ( X(1:98, 2:99) + X(3:100, 2:99) +
     $                    X(2:99, 1:98) + X(2:99, 3:100) )/4
     diffmax = MAXVAL(ABS(New-X))
```

Fig. 4.2. F77 and F90 versions of a two-dimensional finite difference algorithm.

code that, although implicitly parallel, must be executed sequentially if a compiler is unable to detect the implicit parallelism. For example, the following code zeroes the diagonal of an array. Although clearly a parallel operation, this cannot be expressed as such using the F90 array assignment statement.

```
do i = 1,100
    X(i,i) = 0.0
enddo
```

4.3 HPF and Data Distribution

HPF overcomes the limitations of Fortran 90 by augmenting F90's array operations with data distribution directives, a FORALL statement, the INDEPENDENT directive, and new intrinsics. Array assignment, the FORALL statement, and the INDEPENDENT directive are used to identify *concurrency* in an algorithm, while data distribution directives specify how data should be placed on physical processors, and hence provide control over *locality*.

HPF uses array expressions to specify *concurrency*, that is, to identify opportunities for parallel execution. But such expressions do not specify how these opportunities should be exploited on a parallel computer, and hence provide the programmer with control over *locality*. For this latter purpose, HPF introduces three data distribution directives: PROCESSORS, ALIGN, and DISTRIBUTE. The three directives are summarized in Fig. 4.3.

!HPF$ PROCESSORS proc-name(dim1, ..., dimN)
Declare a virtual processor array.
        proc-name   name of virtual processor array
        dim1, ..., dimN   size and shape of array

!HPF$ ALIGN array WITH target
Align array with a target array.
        array   array to be aligned
        target   array name

!HPF$ DISTRIBUTE list-of-arrays [ONTO proc-name]
Distribute array(s) onto processor array.
        list-of-arrays   arrays to be distributed
        proc-name   virtual processor array

Fig. 4.3. HPF data distribution directives.

Fig. 4.4 illustrates the use of ALIGN and DISTRIBUTE. The ALIGN directive is used to align elements of different arrays with each other, indicating that they should be distributed in the same manner. The DISTRIBUTE directive is used to distribute an object (and any other objects that may be aligned with it) onto a virtual processor array. This two-phase mapping strategy

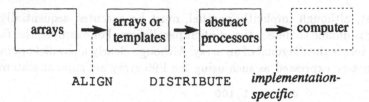

ALIGN   DISTRIBUTE   *implementation-*
                              specific

Fig. 4.4. HPF data allocation model. The mapping of data to abstract processors is performed in two phases: ALIGN is used to create a relationship between objects and DISTRIBUTE is used to partition onto processors both a specified object and any objects that are aligned with it.

reduces the number of changes needed to move from one machine to another. A different machine may necessitate a different partitioning strategy but is less likely to require changes to array alignments.

Data distribution directives can have a major impact on a program's performance but *do not affect the result computed.* This orthogonality makes it possible to experiment with alternative parallel algorithms simply by changing directives. Data distribution directives are *recommendations* to an HPF compiler, not instructions. The compiler does not have to obey them, if for example it believes that performance can be improved by ignoring them.

4.3.1 Processors. A PROCESSORS directive is used to specify the shape and size of an array of virtual processors. For example, both of the following statements declare virtual computers containing 32 virtual processors.

```
!HPF$    PROCESSORS P(32)
!HPF$    PROCESSORS Q(4,8)
```

Normally, one virtual processor is created for each physical processor, although an implementation could in principle use a smaller number of physical processors to implement the virtual processors. The mapping of virtual processors to physical processors is not specified in HPF and can vary according to the implementation.

4.3.2 Alignment. The ALIGN directive is used to specify array elements that should, if possible, be *collocated* (mapped to the same processor). Operations between aligned data objects are likely to be more efficient than operations between objects that are not aligned. An alignment directive has the general form

```
!HPF$    ALIGN array WITH target
```

and indicates that the specified **array** should be aligned with **target**. A list of subscripts associated with the array and target control the alignment, For example, the following code specifies a simple alignment of arrays B and C in which element B(i) is aligned with the corresponding C(i).

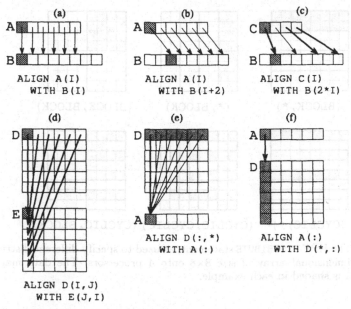

Fig. 4.5. Six examples of the HPF `ALIGN` statement, with arrows and shading used to associate representative aligned components in the two arrays being aligned: (a) a simple alignment of two one-dimensional arrays, (b) alignment with an offset, (c) an alignment of a smaller array onto a larger, (d) alignment with indices inverted (transpose), (e) collapsing a dimension: aligning a two-dimensional array with a one-dimensional array, and (f) replicating data: aligning a one-dimensional array with a two-dimensional array.

```
      real B(50), C(50)
!HPF$  ALIGN C(:) WITH B(:)
```

Dummy arguments can be used in `ALIGN` directives to name dimensions, integer expressions can be used to specify offsets, and * can be used to collapse dimensions. Fig. 4.5 gives examples of the alignments that can be specified using these mechanisms. Notice that an `ALIGN` statement can be used to specify that elements of an array should be replicated over processors. This strategy can improve efficiency if the array is read more often than it is written. For example, assume that the two-dimensional array `Y(N,N)` is to be distributed by columns, so that each processor performs computation on one or more columns. If the computation performed at a single processor requires data from a one-dimensional array `X(N)` that is not updated during a computation, it may be useful to replicate `X`. This is accomplished by the following alignment directive

```
!HPF$   ALIGN X(j) WITH Y(*,j)
```

Care must be taken not to replicate arrays that are frequently updated, since considerable communication or redundant computation can result.

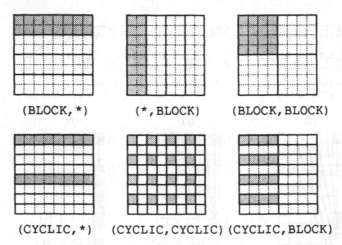

Fig. 4.6. The HPF DISTRIBUTE statement, as used to specify different distributions of a two-dimensional array of size 8×8 onto 4 processors. The data mapped to processor 1 is shaded in each example.

4.3.3 Distribution.

A DISTRIBUTE directive is used to indicate how data is to be partitioned among computer memories. It specifies, for each dimension of an array, a mapping of array indices to virtual processors in a processor arrangement. Each dimension of an array may be distributed in one of three ways.

*	: No distribution
BLOCK(n)	: Block distribution (default: n=N/P)
CYCLIC(n)	: Cyclic distribution (default: n=1)

Let N be the number of elements in an array dimension, and P the number of processors. Then, as illustrated in Fig. 4.6, a BLOCK distribution divides the indices in a dimension into contiguous, equal-sized blocks of size N/P, while a CYCLIC distribution maps every Pth index to the same processor. The optional integer argument to BLOCK and CYCLIC specifies the number of elements in a block.

The ONTO specifier is used to perform a distribution across a particular processor array. If no processor array is specified, one is chosen by the compiler.

A DISTRIBUTE directive applies not only to the named array but also to any arrays that are aligned with it. Hence, a DISTRIBUTE directive cannot be applied to an array that is aligned with another. For example, in the following code fragment the DISTRIBUTE directive specifies a mapping for all three arrays.

```
         !HPF$    PROCESSORS p(20)
                  real A(100,100), B(100,100), C(100,100)
         !HPF$    ALIGN B(:,:) WITH A(:,:)
         !HPF$    ALIGN C(i,j) WITH A(j,i)
         !HPF$    DISTRIBUTE A(BLOCK,*) ONTO p
```

```
         program hpf_finite_difference
!HPF$    PROCESSORS pr(4)                  ! Running on 4 processors
         real X(100,100), New(100,100)     ! Data arrays
!HPF$    ALIGN New(:,:) WITH X(:,:)        ! Arrays decomposed in
!HPF$    DISTRIBUTE X(BLOCK,*) ONTO pr     ! one dimension.

         New(2:99,2:99) = (X(1:98, 2:99) + X(3:100, 2:99) +
     $                     X(2:99, 1:98) + X(2:99, 3:100))/4
         diffmax = MAXVAL(ABS(New-X))
```

Fig. 4.7. HPF implementation of two-dimensional finite difference code.

Fig. 4.7 is an HPF version of Fig. 4.2. Notice that only three statements have been added: **PROCESSORS**, **DISTRIBUTE**, and **ALIGN** directives. These directives partition each of the two arrays by row, hence allocating 25 rows to each of 4 processors.

The following is an alternative set of directives that partitions the two arrays in two dimensions, so that each processor has a block of size 50×50. Notice that only the directives need to be changed to specify this alternative algorithm.

```
         !HPF$    PROCESSORS pr(2,2)
                  real X(100,100), New(100,100)
         !HPF$    ALIGN New(:,:) WITH X(:,:)
         !HPF$    DISTRIBUTE X(BLOCK,BLOCK) ONTO pr
```

The two-dimensional decomposition is typically more efficient than the one-dimensional decomposition because less data is communicated.

4.4 Concurrency

One of the limitations of the F90 array assignment statement is that it is applicable only to a limited set of data-parallel operations. For example, it requires that operands of right-hand side expressions be conformant with (of the same shape as) the left-hand side array.

HPF overcomes this limitation by providing two general mechanisms that allow an explicitly parallel representation of a wider range of data-parallel operations. These mechanisms are the FORALL statement and the INDEPENDENT directive.

4.4.1 The FORALL statement. The FORALL statement allows for more general assignments to sections of an array. A FORALL statement has the general form

FORALL (*triplet*, ..., *triplet*, *mask*) *assignment*

where **assignment** is an arithmetic or pointer assignment and **triplet** has the general form

subscript = *lower-bound* : *upper-bound* : *stride*

(with ": stride" being optional) and specifies a set of indices.

The assignment statement is evaluated for those index values specified by the list of triplets that are not rejected by the optional *mask*. For example, the following statements set each element of X to the sum of its indices, zero the upper right triangle of Y, and zero the diagonal of Z, respectively.

```
FORALL (i=1:m, j=1:n)      X(i,j) = i+j
FORALL (i=1:n, j=1:n, i<j) Y(i,j) = 0.0
FORALL (i=1:n)             Z(i,i) = 0.0
```

A FORALL statement is evaluated as follows. First, the right-hand side expression is evaluated for all index values; these evaluations can be performed in any order. Then, the assignments are performed, again in any order. To ensure determinism, a FORALL statement cannot assign to the same element of an array more than once. A compiler can attempt to detect that this requirement is violated, but is not required to do so. Hence, the following statement is valid only if the array Index does not contain duplicate values.

```
FORALL (i=1:n) A(Index(i)) = B(i)
```

4.4.2 The INDEPENDENT directive and do-loops. An HPF program can reveal additional parallelism by using the INDEPENDENT directive to assert that the iterations of a do-loop can be performed independently — that is, in any order or concurrently — without changing the result computed. In effect, this directive changes a do-loop from an implicitly parallel construct to an explicitly parallel construct.

The INDEPENDENT directive must immediately precede the do-loop to which it applies. In its simplest form, it has no additional argument and asserts simply that no iteration of the do-loop can affect any other iteration. (An iteration *I* affects an iteration *J* if *I* leads to an assignment to a value read by *J*.) For example, in the following code fragment the assertion implies both that the array Index does not contain duplicate indices and that A and B do not share storage.

```
!HPF$    INDEPENDENT
         do i=1,n
           A(Index(i)) = B(i)
         enddo
```

In the following code fragment, the directives indicate that the outer two loops are independent. The inner loop assigns elements of A repeatedly and hence is not independent.

```
!HPF$    INDEPENDENT
         do i=1,n1              ! Loop over i independent
!HPF$    INDEPENDENT
         do j=1,n2              ! Loop over j independent
           do k=1,n3            ! Inner loop not independent
             A(i,j) = A(i,j) + B(i,j,k)*C(i,j)
           enddo
         enddo
         enddo
```

An INDEPENDENT directive can also specify that the assertion would be correct *if* distinct storage were to be used for a specified set of variables for each iteration of the nested do-loop. This is achieved by postfixing a NEW specifier, as in the following example. In this code fragment, interleaved execution of different loop iterations would cause erroneous results if values of tmp1 and tmp2 computed in one iteration were used in another. The NEW specifier ensures that this situation does not arise.

```
!HPF$    INDEPENDENT
         do i=1,n1
!HPF$        INDEPENDENT, NEW(tmp1,tmp2)
             do j=1,n2
               tmp1 = B(i,j) + C(i,j)
               tmp2 = B(i,j) - C(i,j)
               A(i,j) = tmp1*tmp2
             ENDDO
         ENDDO
```

4.4.3 Example: parallel fast fourier transform. A two-dimensional fast Fourier transform (2-D FFT) applies a one-dimensional FFT operation first to each column of a two-dimensional array and then to each row. Since a 1-D FFT involves considerable communication if the array to which it is applied is distributed, it is often efficient to distribute the array by columns (hence allowing the first set of FFTs to proceed without communication) and then to transpose the array before performing the second set of FFTs. The transpose involves considerable communication but is frequently more efficient than an algorithm based on a static decomposition and parallel FFTs. Fig. 4.8

presents an implementation of this algorithm. Notice the initial distribution of A (blocked, by column) and the call to the TRANSPOSE intrinsic. Notice also the use of the INDEPENDENT directive to specify that the fft_1d calls in the do-loop can proceed independently, even though each is passed the entire A array.

```
        subroutine fft_2d(n,A)
!HPF$   PROCESSORS pr(24)
        complex A(n,n)
!HPF$   DISTRIBUTE A(:,BLOCK) ONTO pr
        call fft_1d(n,A)
        A = transpose(A)
        call fft_1d(n,A)
        end

C       One-dimensional FFT on 2-d array
        subroutine fft_1d(n,A)
        complex A(n,n)
!HPF$   PROCESSORS pr(24)
!HPF$   DISTRIBUTE A(:,BLOCK) ONTO pr
!HPF$   INDEPENDENT
        do i = 1,n
          call rowfft(i,n,A)
        enddo
        end

C       One-dimensional FFT on 1 column of 2-d array
        subroutine rowfft(icol,n,A)
        ...
        end
```

Fig. 4.8. Two-dimensional fast Fourier transform using matrix transpose and INDEPENDENT directive.

4.5 Case Study: Gaussian Elimination

To further illustrate the use of HPF, we present a slightly more complex example. The problem that we consider involves the use of Gaussian elimination to solve a system of linear equations

$$Ax = b,$$

where A is a known matrix of size $N \times N$, x is the required solution vector, and b is a known vector of size N. This example is often used in discussions of HPF because it shows the benefits of cyclic distributions. The method proceeds in two stages:

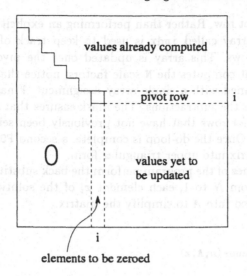

Fig. 4.9. The *i*th step of the Gaussian elimination algorithm, in which nonzero subdiagonal elements in column *i* are eliminated by subtracting appropriate multiples of the pivot row.

1. *Gaussian elimination.* The original system of equations is reduced to an upper triangular form:

$$Ux \ = \ y,$$

where U is a matrix of size $N \times N$ in which all elements below the diagonal are zero, and diagonal elements have the value 1.

2. *Back substitution.* The new system of equations is solved to obtain the values of x.

The Gaussian elimination stage of the algorithm comprises $N - 1$ steps. In the basic algorithm, the *i*th step eliminates nonzero subdiagonal elements in column *i* by subtracting the *i*th row from each row j in the range $[i+1, n]$, in each case scaling the *i*th row by the factor A_{ji}/A_{ii} so as to make the element A_{ji} zero. Hence, the algorithm sweeps down the matrix from the top left corner to the bottom right, leaving zero subdiagonal elements behind it (Fig. 4.9).

For numerical stability, this basic algorithm is modified so that instead of stepping through rows in order, it selects in step i the row in the range $[i, n]$ with the largest element in column i. This row (called the *pivot*) is swapped with row i prior to performing the subtractions.

Fig. 4.10 is an HPF implementation of this algorithm. For efficiency, this program maintains the vector b in the $N + 1$th column of the array A. The first do-loop implements Gaussian elimination. The **MAXLOC** intrinsic is used to identify the pivot row. Rather than performing an explicit swap with row i, an indirection array called indx is used to keep track of the actual indices of selected rows. This array is updated once the pivot is identified. The next statement computes the N scale factors; notice that the computation can be performed with a single array assignment. Finally, the FORALL statement performs the subtractions. The mask ensures that the subtraction is performed only for rows that have not previously been selected as pivots (index(i).EQ.0). Once the do-loop is complete, a second FORALL is used to reorganize the matrix into upper triangular form.

The last four lines of the program perform the back substitution. Working in reverse order from N to 1, each element x_i of the solution is computed and then substituted into A to simplify the matrix.

```
      subroutine gauss(n,A,x)
      integer n
      real A(n,n+1)
      real X(n), Fac(n), Row(n+1)
      integer Indx(n), Itmp(1)
      integer i, j, k, max_indx
      real maxval

      Indx = 0                              ! Initialize mask array
      do k = 1,n                            ! Repeat for each column
C         Find pivot.
      Itmp = MAXLOC(ABS(A(:,k)), MASK=indx .EQ. 0)
      max_indx = Itmp(1)                    ! Extract pivot index
      Indx(max_indx) = k                    ! Update indirection array
      Fac = A(:,k)/A(max_indx,k)            ! Scale factors for column
      Row = A(max_indx,:)                   ! Extract pivot row
C         Row update.
      FORALL (i=1:n, j=k:n+1, Indx(i).EQ.0)
     $                   A(i,j) = A(i,j) - Fac(i) * Row(j)
      enddo

      FORALL (i=1:n) A(Indx(i),:) = A(i,:)   ! Row exchange

      do i = n, 1, -1                       ! Back substitution
      X(i) = A(i,n+1) / A(i,i)
      A(1:i-1, n+1) = A(1:i-1, n+1) - A(1:i-1,i)*X(i)
      enddo
      end
```

Fig. 4.10. HPF implementation of Gaussian elimination.

Before developing data distribution directives for this program, let us determine how much concurrency it exposes and what data dependencies may lead to communication. We can think of the data-parallel program as specifying a fine-grained partition comprising $N \times N$ tasks, each responsible

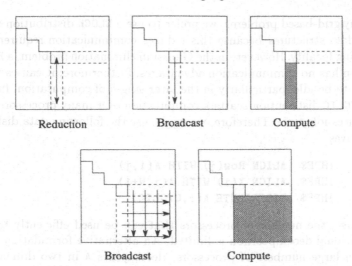

Fig. 4.11. Communication and computation in the various phases of the HPF Gaussian elimination algorithm. Arrows represent communication, and shading indicates tasks involved in computation in each phase. The five phases are described in the text.

for a single element of A. (These tasks characterize the computation that would be associated with data elements by the owner-computes rule.) As illustrated in Fig. 4.11, each of the $N-1$ steps of the elimination algorithm involves five principal steps.

1. The **MAXLOC** statement involves a reduction operation by the N tasks in the kth column.
2. The maximum value identified by the reduction (**max_indx**) must be broadcast within the kth column, since it is required for the computation of scale factors.
3. The computation of scale factors (the array **Fac**) requires N independent operations, one in each task in the kth column.
4. A scale factor (**Fac(i)** and a pivot row value (**Row(j)**) must be broadcast within each column and row, respectively, since they are required for the update.
5. The **FORALL** statement involves $\mathcal{O}(N^2)$ independent operations, one per task.

This algorithm has two interesting attributes. First, there is little locality in communication, beyond the fact that broadcasts and reductions are performed in rows and columns. Second, computation tends to be clustered: in each step, much of the computation is performed by tasks in a single row and column (before the **FORALL**) and in the bottom right-hand corner (the **FORALL**). These attributes can be exploited when developing data distribution directives to complete the parallel algorithm.

In many grid-based problems, we prefer to use a BLOCK distribution of the principal data structures because this reduces communication requirements by enhancing locality. However, in the Gaussian elimination problem, a BLOCK distribution has no communication advantages; furthermore, it causes many processors to be idle, particularly in the later stages of computation. In contrast, a CYCLIC distribution scatters computation over many processors, and hence reduces idle time. Therefore, we might use the following data distribution directives.

```
!HPF$   ALIGN Row(j) WITH A(1,j)
!HPF$   ALIGN X(i) WITH A(i,N+1)
!HPF$   DISTRIBUTE A(:,CYCLIC)
```

Of course, the number of processors that can be used efficiently by this one-dimensional decomposition is limited. An alternative formulation, more efficient on large numbers of processors, decomposes A in two dimensions. This can be specified as follows.

```
!HPF$   ALIGN Row(j) WITH A(1,j)
!HPF$   ALIGN X(i) WITH A(i,N+1)
!HPF$   DISTRIBUTE A(CYCLIC,CYCLIC)
```

4.6 Data Parallelism Summary

We have presented fundamental concepts of data-parallel programming and illustrated the application of these concepts in the programming languages Fortran 90 and High Performance Fortran. F90's array language and HPF's data distribution directives and related constructs provide a powerful notation for data-parallel computations in scientific and engineering computations. Their chief features are as follows:

1. An array language comprising array assignments, array intrinsics, and (in HPF) FORALL and INDEPENDENT constructs is used to reveal the fine-grained concurrency inherent in data-parallel operations on arrays.
2. Data distribution directives are introduced to provide the programmer with control over partitioning, agglomeration, and mapping (and hence locality).
3. An HPF compiler translates this high-level specification into an executable program by generating the communication code implied by a particular set of data-parallel operations and data distribution.

The most attractive feature of the data-parallel approach as exemplified in HPF is that the compiler takes on the job of generating communication code. This has two advantages. First, it allows the programmer to focus on the tasks of identifying opportunities for concurrent execution and determining efficient partition, agglomeration, and mapping strategies. Second, it simplifies the task of exploring alternative parallel algorithms; in principle, only data distribution directives need be changed.

A problematic feature of HPF is the limited range of parallel algorithms that can be expressed in HPF *and* compiled efficiently for large parallel computers. However, algorithms that operate on regular arrays in regular ways can be both expressed naturally and compiled efficiently. The range of problems for which HPF is appropriate is expected to grow as compiler technology improves.

Extensions to the data-parallel programming model that would allow its application to a wider range of problems is an active area of research. For example, Saltz, Berryman, and Wu [SBW91] and Agrawal, Sussman, and Saltz [ASS93] seek to apply it to irregular problems. Subhlok et al. [SSO+93] generate pipeline parallelism automatically from HPF code augmented with additional directives. Foster et al. [FAC+94, FKK+98] introduce explicit parallel constructs into HPF.

5. Library-based Approaches

The final class of parallel programming languages that we consider are not languages at all, but rather parallel programming paradigms that are implemented via calls to library functions. In such approaches, compilers are not available to check for correctness or to perform optimizations, but on the other hand the use of a library can provide considerable flexibility. In practice, most parallel programming today is performed using library-based systems, whether designed for shared-memory systems (e.g., POSIX threads) or distributed-memory systems. We focus our discussion on the latter class of systems and, in particular, on message-passing libraries.

Message-passing functions were incorporated in specialized libraries developed for early distributed-memory computers such as the Cosmic Cube [Sei85], iPSC [Pie88], and NCUBE/1 [nCu90]. Subsequent developments emphasized portability across different computers and explored the functionality required in message-passing systems. Systems such as Express [PC88], p4 [BL94, BBD+87], PICL [GHP+90], PARMACS [Hem91, HHS92], and PVM [Sun90] all run on a variety of homogeneous and heterogeneous systems. Each focuses on a different set of issues, with the commercially supported Express and PARMACS systems providing the most extensive functionality, p4 integrating shared-memory support, PICL incorporating instrumentation, and PVM permitting dynamic process creation. A special issue of *Parallel Computing* includes articles on many of these systems [McB94].

An unfortunate consequence of this exploration was that although various vendor-supplied and portable systems provided similar functionality, syntactic differences and numerous minor incompatibilities made it difficult to port applications from one computer to another. This situation was addressed in 1993 by the Message Passing Interface Forum, a consortium of industrial, academic, and governmental organizations with an interest in standardization [MPI93, MPIF93, GLS95]. The forum produced the MPI design in early 1994. MPI incorporates ideas developed previously in a range of systems, notably p4, Express, PICL, and Parmacs. An important innovation is the use of communicators to support modular design. This feature builds on ideas previously explored in Zipcode [SSD+94], CHIMP [EPCC91, EPCC92], and research systems at IBM Yorktown [BK92, BKR+92]. The more recent MPI-2 extensions to MPI added support for parallel I/O, dynamic process creation, and single-sided operations [GHL+98].

The MPI standard defines a set of functions that implement a message-passing library approach to parallel programming, in which collection of processes execute programs written in a standard sequential language augmented with calls to a library of functions for sending and receiving messages. MPI is a complex system: in its entirety, the initial MPI standard comprises some 129 functions, many of which have numerous parameters or variants; MPI-2 adds more than 100 additional functions. We focus here on a small subset of those functions, ignoring many of the more esoteric features.

5.1 The Message Passing Interface

In the MPI programming model, a computation comprises one or more *processes* that communicate by calling library routines to send and receive messages to other processes. In most MPI implementations, a fixed set of processes is created at program initialization, and one process is created per processor. However, these processes may execute different programs. Hence, the MPI programming model is sometimes referred to as multiple program multiple data (MPMD) to distinguish it from the SPMD model in which every processor executes the same program.

Processes use *point-to-point* communication operations to send a message from one named process to another; these operations can be used to implement local and unstructured communications. A group of processes can call *collective* communication operations to perform commonly used global operations such as summation and broadcast. MPI's ability to *probe* for messages supports asynchronous communication. Probably MPI's most important feature from a software engineering viewpoint is its support for modular programming. The MPI programmer can define modules that encapsulate internal communication structures.

Although MPI is a complex and multifaceted system, just six of its functions are needed to solve a wide range of problems. These functions initiate and terminate a computation, identify processes, and send and receive messages:

MPI_INIT	:	Initiate an MPI computation.
MPI_FINALIZE	:	Terminate a computation.
MPI_COMM_SIZE	:	Determine number of processes.

MPI_COMM_RANK : Determine my process identifier.
MPI_SEND   : Send a message.
MPI_RECV   : Receive a message.

Function parameters are detailed in Fig. 5.1. In this and subsequent figures, the labels IN, OUT, and INOUT indicate whether the function uses but does not modify the parameter (IN), does not use but may update the parameter (OUT), or both uses and updates the parameter (INOUT).

MPI_INIT(int *argc, char ***argv)
Initiate a computation.
  argc, argv are required only in the C language binding,
        where they are the main program's arguments.

MPI_FINALIZE()
Shut down a computation.

MPI_COMM_SIZE(comm, size)
Determine the number of processes in a computation.
  IN   comm   communicator (handle)
  OUT size   number of processes in the group of comm (integer)

MPI_COMM_RANK(comm, pid)
Determine the identifier of the current process.
  IN   comm   communicator (handle)
  OUT pid   process id in the group of comm (integer)

MPI_SEND(buf, count, datatype, dest, tag, comm)
Send a message.
  IN   buf   address of send buffer (choice)
  IN   count   number of elements to send (integer ≥0)
  IN   datatype datatype of send buffer elements (handle)
  IN   dest   process id of destination process (integer)
  IN   tag   message tag (integer)
  IN   comm   communicator (handle)

MPI_RECV(buf, count, datatype, source, tag, comm, status)
Receive a message.
  OUT buf   address of receive buffer (choice)
  IN   count   size of receive buffer, in elements (integer ≥0)
  IN   datatype datatype of receive buffer elements (handle)
  IN   source   process id of source process, or MPI_ANY_SOURCE (integer)
  IN   tag   message tag, or MPI_ANY_TAG (integer)
  IN   comm   communicator (handle)
  OUT status   status object (status)

Fig. 5.1. Basic MPI. These six functions suffice to write a wide range of parallel programs. The arguments are characterized as having mode IN or OUT and having type integer, choice, handle, or status. These terms are explained in the text.

All but the first two calls take a *communicator handle* as an argument. A communicator identifies the *process group* and *context* with respect to which the operation is to be performed. As we shall see later, communicators provide a mechanism for identifying process subsets when we are developing modular programs, and for ensuring that messages intended for different purposes are not confused. For now, it suffices to provide the default value MPI_COMM_WORLD, which identifies *all* processes involved in a computation. Other arguments have type integer, datatype handle, or status. These datatypes are explained in the following.

The functions MPI_INIT and MPI_FINALIZE are used to initiate and shut down an MPI computation, respectively. MPI_INIT must be called before any other MPI function and must be called exactly once per process. No further MPI functions can be called after MPI_FINALIZE.

The functions MPI_COMM_SIZE and MPI_COMM_RANK determine the number of processes in the current computation, and the integer identifier assigned to the current process, respectively. (The processes in a process group are identified with unique, contiguous integers numbered from 0.) For example, consider the following program. This is not written in any particular language: we shall see how to call MPI routines from Fortran and C in the next section.

```
program main
begin
  MPI_INIT()                                 Initiate computation
  MPI_COMM_SIZE(MPI_COMM_WORLD, count)       Find # of processes
  MPI_COMM_RANK(MPI_COMM_WORLD, myid)        Find my id
  print("I am", myid, "of", count)           Print message
  MPI_FINALIZE()                             Shut down
end
```

The MPI standard does not specify how a parallel computation is started. However, a typical mechanism might be a command line argument indicating the number of processes that are to be created: for example, "**myprog -n 4**", where **myprog** is the name of the executable. Additional arguments might be used to specify processor names in a networked environment or executable names in an MPMD computation.

Once a computation is initiated, each of the processes created will normally execute the same program. Hence, execution of the above program gives something like the following output.

```
                    I am 1 of 4
                    I am 3 of 4
                    I am 0 of 4
                    I am 2 of 4
```

The order in which the output from the four processes appears is not defined; we assume here that the output from individual print statements is not interleaved.

Finally, we consider the functions MPI_SEND and MPI_RECV. These are used to send and receive messages, respectively. A call to MPI_SEND has the following general form.

MPI_SEND(buf, count, datatype, dest, tag, comm)

It specifies that a message containing count elements of the specified datatype starting at address buf is to be sent to the process with identifier dest. As will be explained in greater detail subsequently, this message is associated with an *envelope* comprising the specified tag, the source process's identifier, and the specified communicator (comm). A call to MPI_RECV has the following general form.

MPI_RECV(buf, count, datatype, source, tag, comm, status)

It attempts to receive a message with an envelope corresponding to the specified tag, source, and comm, blocking until such a message is available. When the message arrives, elements of the specified datatype are placed into the buffer at address buf. This buffer is guaranteed to be large enough to contain at least count elements. The status variable can be used subsequently to inquire about the size, tag, and source of the message (Section 5.3).

Fig. 5.2 illustrates the use of the six basic calls. The program is designed to be executed by two processes, which call procedures producer and consumer respectively, effectively creating two different tasks. The first process makes a series of MPI_SEND calls to communicate 99 integer messages to the second process.

MPI defines "language bindings" for C, Fortran, and C++ (bindings for other languages can be defined as well). Different language bindings have slightly different syntax, reflecting language peculiarities. Sources of syntactic difference include the function names themselves, the mechanism used for return codes, the representation of the *handles* used to access specialized MPI data structures such as communicators, and the implementation of the status datatype returned by MPI_RECV. (The use of handles hides the internal representation of MPI data structures.)

For example, in the C language binding, function names are as in the MPI definition but with only the MPI prefix and the first letter of the function name capitalized. Status values are returned as integer return codes. The return code for successful completion is MPI_SUCCESS; a set of error codes is also defined. Compile-time constants are all in upper case and are defined in the file "mpi.h", which must be included in any program that makes MPI calls. Handles are represented by special defined types, defined in mpi.h. These will be introduced as needed in the following. Function parameters with type IN are passed by value, while parameters with type OUT and INOUT are passed by

144   Ian Foster

```
program main
begin
  MPI_INIT()                              Initialize
  MPI_COMM_SIZE(MPI_COMM_WORLD, count)
  if(count != 2) exit                     Must be just 2 processes
  MPI_COMM_RANK(MPI_COMM_WORLD, myid)
  if (myid = 0) then                      I am process 0
    producer(99)
  else                                    I am process 1
    consumer()
  endif
  print("Msg is", msg, "on process", myid)
  MPI_FINALIZE()                          Shut down
end

procedure producer(num_messages)          Code for process 0
begin
  for i = 1 to num_messages               Send messages
    MPI_SEND(i, 1, MPI_INT, 1, 0, MPI_COMM_WORLD)
  endfor
  i = -1                                  Send shutdown message
  MPI_SEND(i, 1, MPI_INT, 1, 0, MPI_COMM_WORLD)
end

procedure consumer                        Code for process 1
begin
  MPI_RECV(msg, 1, MPI_INT, 0, 0, MPI_COMM_WORLD)
  while (msg != -1)                       Receive messages
    process_message(msg)                  Use message
    MPI_RECV(msg, 1, MPI_INT, 0, 0, MPI_COMM_WORLD)
  end while
end
```

Fig. 5.2. MPI implementation of a simple producer/consumer problem. This program is designed to be executed by two processes.

reference (that is, as pointers). A status variable has type MPI_Status and is a structure with fields status.MPI_SOURCE and status.MPI_TAG containing source and tag information. Finally, an MPI datatype is defined for each C datatype: MPI_CHAR, MPI_INT, MPI_LONG, MPI_UNSIGNED_CHAR, MPI_UNSIGNED, MPI_UNSIGNED_LONG, MPI_FLOAT, MPI_DOUBLE, MPI_LONG_DOUBLE, and so forth.

5.2 Global Operations

Parallel algorithms often call for coordinated communication operations involving multiple processes. For example, all processes may need to cooperate to transpose a distributed matrix or to sum a set of numbers distributed one per process. Clearly, these global operations can be implemented by a programmer using the send and receive functions introduced previously. For convenience, and to permit optimized implementations, MPI also provides a suite of specialized *collective communication* functions that perform commonly used operations of this type. These functions include the following.

- Barrier: Synchronize all processes.
- Broadcast: Send data from one process to all processes.
- Gather: Gather data from all processes to one process.
- Scatter: Scatter data from one process to all processes.
- Reduction operations: sum, multiply, etc., distributed data.

These operations are summarized in Fig. 5.3. They are all executed in a collective fashion, meaning that each process in a process group calls the communication routine with the same parameters.

5.2.1 Barrier. MPI_BARRIER is used to synchronize execution of a group of processes. No process returns from this function until all processes have called it. A barrier is a simple way of separating two phases of a computation, to ensure that messages generated in the two phases do not intermingle. Of course, in this case as in many others, the need for an explicit barrier can be avoided by appropriate use of tags, source specifiers, or contexts.

5.2.2 Data movement. MPI_BCAST, MPI_GATHER, and MPI_SCATTER are collective *data movement* routines, in which all processes interact with a distinguished root process to broadcast, gather, or scatter data, respectively. The operation of these functions is illustrated in Fig. 5.4. In each case, the first three arguments specify the location (inbuf) and type (intype) of the data to be communicated and the number of elements to be sent to each destination (incnt). Other arguments specify the location and type of the result (outbuf, outtype) and the number of elements to be received from each source (outcnt).

MPI_BCAST implements a one-to-all *broadcast* operation. A single named process (root) sends data to all other processes; each process receives data

MPI_BARRIER(comm)
Global synchronization.
   IN   comm   communicator (handle)

MPI_BCAST(buffer, count, datatype, root, comm)
Broadcast data from root to all processes.

INOUT	inbuf	address of input buffer, or output buffer at root (choice)
IN	incnt	number of elements in input buffer (integer)
IN	intype	datatype of input buffer elements (handle)
IN	root	process id of root process (integer)
IN	comm	communicator (handle)

MPI_GATHER(inbuf, incnt, intype, outbuf, outcnt, outtype, root, comm)
MPI_SCATTER(inbuf, incnt, intype, outbuf, outcnt, outtype, root, comm)
Collective data movement functions.

IN	inbuf	address of input buffer (choice)
IN	incnt	number of elements sent to each (integer)
IN	intype	datatype of input buffer elements (handle)
OUT	outbuf	address of output buffer (choice)
IN	outcnt	number of elements received from each (integer)
IN	outtype	datatype of output buffer elements
IN	root	process id of root process (integer)
IN	comm	communicator (handle)

MPI_REDUCE(inbuf, outbuf, count, type, op, root, comm)
MPI_ALLREDUCE(inbuf, outbuf, count, type, op, comm)
Collective reduction functions.

IN	inbuf	address of input buffer (choice)
OUT	outbuf	address of output buffer (choice)
IN	count	number of elements in input buffer (integer)
IN	type	datatype of input buffer elements (handle)
IN	op	operation; see text for list (handle)
IN	root	process id of root process (integer)
IN	comm	communicator (handle)

Fig. 5.3. MPI global communication functions.

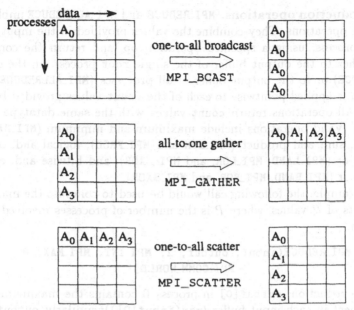

Fig. 5.4. MPI collective data movement functions, illustrated for a group of 4 processors. In each set of 16 boxes, each row represents data locations in a different process. Thus, in the one-to-all broadcast, the data A_0 is initially located just in process 0; after the call, it is replicated in all processes. In each case, both incnt and outcnt are 1, meaning that each message comprises a single data element.

from the root process. At the time of call, the data is located in **inbuf** in process **root** and consists of **incnt** data items of a specified **intype**. After the call, the data is replicated in **inbuf** in all processes. Since the **inbuf** is used for input at the **root** and for output in other processes, it has type **INOUT**.

MPI_GATHER implements an all-to-one *gather* operation. All processes (including the **root** process) send data located in **inbuf** to **root**. This process places the data in contiguous nonoverlapping locations in **outbuf**, with the data from process i preceding that from process $i + 1$. Hence, the **outbuf** in the root process must be P times larger than **inbuf**, where P is the number of processes participating in the operation. The **outbuf** in processes other than the **root** is ignored.

MPI_SCATTER implements a one-to-all *scatter* operation; it is the reverse of **MPI_GATHER**. A specified **root** process sends data to all processes, sending the ith portion of its **inbuf** to process i; each process receives data from **root** in **outbuf**. Hence, the **inbuf** in the root process must be P times larger than **outbuf**. Notice the subtle difference between this function and **MPI_BCAST**: while in **MPI_BCAST** every process receives the *same* value from the root process, in **MPI_SCATTER** every process receives a *different* value.

5.2.3 Reduction operations. MPI_REDUCE and MPI_ALLREDUCE implement reduction operations. They combine the values provided in the input buffer of each process, using a specified operation op, and return the combined value either to the output buffer of the single root process (in the case of MPI_REDUCE) or to the output buffer of all processes (MPI_ALLREDUCE). The operation is applied pointwise to each of the count values provided by each process. All operations return count values with the same datatype as the operands. Valid operations include maximum and minimum (MPI_MAX and MPI_MIN); sum and product (MPI_SUM and MPI_PROD); logical and, or, and exclusive or (MPI_LAND, MPI_LOR, and MPI_LXOR); and bitwise and, or, and exclusive or (MPI_BAND, MPI_BOR, and MPI_BXOR).

For example, the following call would be used to compute the maximum of two sets of P values, where P is the number of processes involved in the reduction.

$$\text{MPI\_REDUCE(inbuf, outbuf, 2, MPI\_INT, MPI\_MAX, 0,}$$
$$\text{MPI\_COMM\_WORLD)}$$

After the reduction, outbuf[0] in process 0 contains the maximum of the first element in each input buffer (max(inbuf[0])); similarly, outbuf([1]) contains max(inbuf[1]).

5.2.4 Example: finite difference. We use a finite difference problem to illustrate the use of global operations. The algorithm that we consider requires both nearest-neighbor communication (to exchange boundary values) and global communication (to detect termination). The MPI implementation given in Fig. 5.5 (expressed in the C language binding) is for a one-dimensional decomposition of a one-dimensional problem, in which each process has two neighbors. It uses MPI_SEND and MPI_RECV for nearest-neighbor communication and four MPI global communication routines, for a total of five distinct communication operations. These are summarized in the following and are illustrated in Fig. 5.6:

1. MPI_BCAST to broadcast the problem size parameter (size) from process 0 to all p processes;
2. MPI_SCATTER to distribute an input array (work) from process 0 to other processes, so that each process receives size/p elements;
3. MPI_SEND and MPI_RECV for exchange of data (a single floating-point number);
4. MPI_ALLREDUCE to determine the maximum of a set of localerr values computed at the different processes and to distribute this maximum value to each process; and
5. MPI_GATHER to accumulate an output array at process 0.

The use of scatter and gather operations to load and store input and output data is particularly simple and convenient. Note, however, that their use in this example is inherently nonscalable. As we solve larger problems,

```
main(int argc, char ***argv) {
  MPI_Init(&argc, &argv);
  com = MPI_COMM_WORLD;
  MPI_Comm_size(com, &p);
  MPI_Comm_rank(com, &me);
  if (me == 0) {                    /* Read problem size at process 0 */
    read_problem_size(&size);
    buff[0] = size;
  }
  /* Global broadcast propagates this data to all processes */
  MPI_Bcast(buff,1,MPI_INT,0,com);
  /* Extract problem size from buff; allocate space for local data */
  size = buff[0]/p;
  local = malloc(size+2);
  /* Read input data at process 0; then distribute to processes */
  if (me == 0) { work = malloc(size*p); read_array(work); }
  MPI_Scatter(work, size, MPI_FLOAT, local+1, size,
              MPI_FLOAT, 0, com);
  leftnbr = (me-1+p)%p;             /* Determine my neighbors in ring */
  rightnbr = (me+1)%p;
  globalerr = 99999.0;
  while (globalerr > 0.1) {         /* Repeat until termination */
    /* Exchange boundary values with neighbors */
    ls = local+size;
    MPI_Send( local+2, 1, MPI_FLOAT, leftnbr, 10, com );
    MPI_Recv( local+1, 1, MPI_FLOAT, rightnbr, 10, com,
              &status );
    MPI_Send( ls-2, 1, MPI_FLOAT, rightnbr, 20, com );
    MPI_Recv( ls-1, 1, MPI_FLOAT, leftnbr, 20, com, &status );
    compute(local);
    localerr = maxerror(local);  /* Determine local error */
    /* Find maximum local error, and replicate in each process */
    MPI_Allreduce(&localerr, &globalerr, 1, MPI_FLOAT,
                  MPI_MAX, com);
  }
  /* Collect results at process 0 */
  MPI_Gather(local, size, MPI_FLOAT, work, size*p,
             MPI_FLOAT, 0, com);
  if (me == 0) write_array(array);
  MPI_Finalize()
}
```

Fig. 5.5. MPI finite difference algorithm. Because of lack of space, variable declarations are not included.

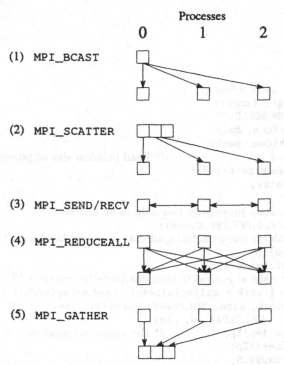

Fig. 5.6. Communication performed in a finite difference program. Each column represents a processor; each subfigure shows data movement in a single phase. The five phases illustrated are (1) broadcast, (2) scatter, (3) nearest-neighbor exchange, (4) reduction, and (5) gather.

storage limitations will eventually prevent us from accumulating all input and output data in a single process. In addition, the associated communication costs may be prohibitive.

5.3 Asynchronous Communication

The need for asynchronous communication can arise when a computation must access elements of a shared data structure in an unstructured manner. Assuming that the shared data is distributed among the computation tasks, individual computation tasks must poll periodically for pending read and write requests. This technique is supported by the MPI_IPROBE function, which we describe in this section along with the related functions MPI_PROBE and MPI_GET_COUNT. The three functions are summarized in Fig. 5.7.

The MPI_IPROBE function checks for the existence of pending messages without receiving them, allowing us to write programs that interleave local computation with the processing of incoming messages. A call to MPI_IPROBE has the following general form.

MPI_IPROBE(source, tag, comm, flag, status)
Poll for a pending message.

IN	source	id of source process, or MPI_ANY_SOURCE (integer)
IN	tag	message tag, or MPI_ANY_TAG (integer)
IN	comm	communicator (handle)
OUT	flag	(logical/Boolean)
OUT	status	status object (status)

MPI_PROBE(source, tag, comm, status)
Return when message is pending.

IN	source	id of source process, or MPI_ANY_SOURCE (integer)
IN	tag	message tag, or MPI_ANY_TAG (integer)
IN	comm	communicator (handle)
OUT	status	status object (status)

MPI_GET_COUNT(status, datatype, count)
Determine size of a message.

IN	status	status variable from receive (status)
IN	datatype	datatype of receive buffer elements (handle)
OUT	count	number of data elements in message (integer)

Fig. 5.7. MPI inquiry and probe operations.

MPI_IPROBE(source, tag, comm, flag, status)

It sets a Boolean argument **flag** to indicate whether a message that matches the specified source, tag, and communicator is available. If an appropriate message is available, then **flag** is set to **true**; otherwise, it is set to **false**. The message can then be received by using MPI_RECV. The receive call must specify the same source, tag, and communicator; otherwise, a different message may be received.

Related to MPI_IPROBE is the function MPI_PROBE, which blocks until a message of the specified source, tag, and communicator is available and then returns, setting its **status** argument. The MPI_PROBE function is used to receive messages for which we have incomplete information.

A successful MPI_IPROBE call constructs a **status** argument that can be used to determine the pending message's source, tag, and size. The inquiry function MPI_GET_COUNT yields the length of a message just received. Its first two (input) parameters are an **status** object set by a previous probe or MPI_RECV call and the **datatype** of the elements to be received, while the third (output) parameter is an integer used to return the number of elements received (Fig. 5.7).

Other information about the received message can be obtained directly from the **status** object. In the C language binding, this object is a structure with fields MPI_SOURCE and MPI_TAG. Thus, status.MPI_SOURCE and status.MPI_TAG contain the source and tag of the message just received. In Fortran, the **status** object is an array of size MPI_STATUS_SIZE, and the constants MPI_SOURCE and MPI_TAG are the indices of the array elements containing the source and tag information. Thus, status(MPI_SOURCE) and status(MPI_TAG) contain the source and tag of the message just received.

The following code fragment use these functions to receive a message containing an unknown number of integers.

```
int count, *buf;
MPI_Probe(source, 0, comm, status);
MPI_Get_count(status, MPI_INT, &count);
if((buf = malloc(count*sizeof(int))) == NULL) exit;
MPI_Recv(buf, count, MPI_INT, source, 0, comm);
```

5.4 Modularity

MPI supports modular programming via its *communicator* mechanism. This provides the information hiding needed when the user is building modular programs, by allowing the specification of program components that encapsulate internal communication operations and provide a local name space for processes. In this section, we show how communicators can be used to implement various forms of sequential and parallel composition. MPI's MPMD programming model means that the full generality of concurrent composition is not available.

An MPI communication operation always specifies a communicator. This identifies the process group that is engaged in the communication operation and the context in which the communication occurs. As we shall see, *process groups* allow a subset of processes to communicate among themselves using local process ids, and perform collective communication operations without involving other processes. The *context* forms part of the envelope associated with a message; a receive operation can receive a message only if it was sent in the same context. Hence, if two routines use different contexts for their internal communication, there can be no danger of their communications being confused.

In preceding sections, all communication operations have used the default communicator MPI_COMM_WORLD. This incorporates all processes involved in an MPI computation and defines a default context. In this section, we describe four functions that allow communicators to be used in more flexible ways. These functions, and their roles in modular design, are as follows.

1. MPI_COMM_DUP. A program may create a new communicator comprising the same process group but a new context, to ensure that communications performed for different purposes are not confused. This mechanism supports sequential composition.
2. MPI_COMM_SPLIT. A program may create a new communicator comprising just a subset of a given group of processes. These processes can then communicate among themselves without fear of conflict with other concurrent computations. This mechanism supports parallel composition.

3. **MPI_INTERCOMM_CREATE**. A program may construct an *intercommunicator* that links processes in two groups. This mechanism supports parallel composition.
4. **MPI_COMM_FREE**. This function can be used to release a communicator created using the preceding three functions.

The four functions are summarized in Fig. 5.8; their arguments and the way they are called are described in the rest of this section.

MPI_COMM_DUP(comm, newcomm)
Create new communicator: same group, new context.
| IN | comm | communicator (handle) |
| OUT | newcomm | communicator (handle) |

MPI_COMM_SPLIT(comm, color, key, newcomm)
Partition group into disjoint subgroups.
IN	comm	communicator (handle)
IN	color	subgroup control (integer)
IN	key	process id control (integer)
OUT	newcomm	communicator (handle)

MPI_INTERCOMM_CREATE(comm, leader, peer, rleader, tag, inter)
Initiate creation of an intercommunicator.
IN	comm	local intracommunicator (handle)
IN	leader	local leader (integer)
IN	peer	peer intracommunicator (handle)
IN	rleader	id of remote leader in peer (integer)
IN	tag	tag for communicator set up (integer)
OUT	inter	new intercommunicator (handle)

MPI_COMM_FREE(comm)
Destroy a communicator.
| IN | comm | communicator (handle) |

Fig. 5.8. MPI communicator functions.

5.4.1 Creating communicators. MPI's message tags provide a mechanism for distinguishing between messages used for different purposes. However, they do not provide a sufficient basis for modular design. For example, consider an application that calls a library routine implementing (for example) an array transpose operation. It is important to ensure that the message tags used in the library are distinct from those used in the rest of the application (Fig. 5.9). Yet the user of a library routine may not know what tags the library uses; indeed, tag values may be computed on the fly.

Communicators provide a solution to this problem. A call of the form

MPI_COMM_DUP(comm, newcomm)

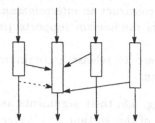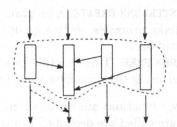

Fig. 5.9. Errors can occur in a sequential composition of two parallel program components (e.g., an application program and a parallel library) if the two components use the same message tags. The figure on the left shows how this situation can occur. Each of the four vertical lines represents a single thread of control (process) in an SPMD program. All call an SPMD library, represented by the boxes. One process finishes sooner than the others, and a message generated during other computation (the dashed arrow) is intercepted by the library. The figure on the right shows how this problem is avoided by using contexts: the library communicates using a distinct tag space, which cannot be penetrated by other messages.

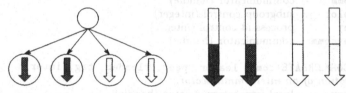

Fig. 5.10. Different views of parallel composition. On the left, we illustrate the task-parallel view, in which new tasks are created dynamically to execute two different program components. Four tasks are created; two perform one computation (dark shading) and two another (light shading). On the right, we show the MPI view. Here, a fixed set of processes (represented by vertical arrows) change character, for example by calling different subroutines.

creates a new communicator `newcomm` comprising the same processes as `comm` but with a new context. This new communicator can be passed as an argument to the library routine (e.g., transpose), as in the following code. The library routine itself will be defined to use the communicator `newcomm` in all communication operations. This ensures that communications performed within the library routine cannot be confused with communications performed outside.

```
    integer comm, newcomm           ! Handles are integers
    ...
    call MPI_COMM_DUP(comm, newcomm)  ! Create new context
    call transpose(newcomm, A)        ! Pass to library
    call MPI_COMM_FREE(newcomm)       ! Free new context
```

5.4.2 Partitioning processes. An application may wish to execute different logic on different processors. As illustrated in Fig. 5.10, this can be achieved by partitioned available processors into disjoint sets, with each set executing the appropriate program. This partitioning is achieved by using the function MPI_COMM_SPLIT. A call of the form

MPI_COMM_SPLIT(comm, color, key, newcomm)

creates one or more new communicators. This function is a collective communication operation, meaning that it must be executed by each process in the process group associated with comm. A new communicator is created for each unique value of color other than the defined constant MPI_UNDEFINED. Each new communicator comprises those processes that specified its value of color in the MPI_COMM_SPLIT call. These processes are assigned identifiers within the new communicator starting from zero, with order determined by the value of key or by the identifier in the old communicator in the event of ties. Thus, a call of the form

MPI_COMM_SPLIT(comm, 0, 0, newcomm)

is equivalent to a call

MPI_COMM_DUP(comm, newcomm)

That is, both calls create a new communicator containing all the processes in the old communicator comm. In contrast, the following code creates three new communicators if comm contains at least three processes (% is a "modulus" operator).

```
MPI_Comm comm, newcomm;
int myid, color;
MPI_Comm_rank(comm, &myid);
color = myid%3;
MPI_Comm_split(comm, color, myid, &newcomm);
```

For example, if comm contains eight processes, then processes 0, 3, and 6 form a new communicator of size three, as do processes 1, 4, and 7; and processes 2 and 5 form a new communicator of size two (Fig. 5.11).

As a final example, the following code fragment creates a new communicator containing at most eight processes. Processes with identifier greater than 8 in communicator comm call MPI_COMM_SPLIT with newid=MPI_UNDEFINED and hence are not part of the new communicator newcomm.

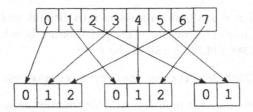

Fig. 5.11. Using MPI_COMM_SPLIT to form new communicators. The first communicator is a group of eight processes; setting color to myid%3 and calling MPI_COMM_SPLIT(comm, color, myid, newcomm) split this into three disjoint process groups.

```
MPI_Comm comm, newcomm;
int myid, color;
MPI_Comm_rank(comm, &myid);
if (myid < 8) {                    /* Select first 8 processes */
  color = 1;
else                               ! Others are not in group
  color = MPI_UNDEFINED;
}
MPI_Comm_split(comm, color, myid, &newcomm);
```

5.4.3 Communicating between groups. A communicator returned by MPI_COMM_SPLIT can be used to communicate within a group of processes. Hence, it is called an *intracommunicator*. (MPI_COMM_WORLD, the default communicator, is an intracommunicator.) It is also possible to create an *intercommunicator* that can be used to communicate between process groups. An intercommunicator that connects two groups A and B containing N_A and N_B processes, respectively, allows processes in group A to communicate with processes $0..N_B - 1$ in group B using MPI send and receive calls (collective operations are not supported); similarly, processes in group B can communicate with processes $0..N_A - 1$ in group A.

An intercommunicator is created by a collective call executed in the two groups that are to be connected. In making this call, the processes in the two groups must each supply a local intracommunicator identifying the processes involved in their group. They must also agree on the identifier of a "leader" process in each group and a parent communicator containing all the processes in both groups, via which the connection can be established. The default communicator MPI_COMM_WORLD can always be used for this purpose. The collective call has the general form

```
MPI_INTERCOMM_CREATE( comm, local_leader, peercomm,
                      remote_leader, tag, intercomm )
```

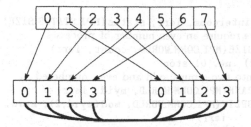

Fig. 5.12. Establishing an intercommunicator between two process groups. At the top is an original group of 8 processes; this is **MPI_COMM_WORLD**. An **MPI_COMM_SPLIT** call creates two process groups, each containing 4 processes; then, an **MPI_INTERCOMM_CREATE** call creates an intercommunicator between the two groups.

where **comm** is an intracommunicator in the local group and **local_leader** is the identifier of the nominated "leader" process within this group. The parent communicator is specified by **peercomm**, while **remote_leader** is the identifier of the other group's leader process *within the parent communicator*. The two other arguments are a unique tag that the two groups' leader processes can use to communicate within the parent communicator's context without confusion with other communications, and the new intercommunicator **intercomm**.

Fig. 5.13 illustrates these ideas. This program first uses **MPI_COMM_SPLIT** to split available processes into two disjoint groups. Processes 0, 2, 4, etc., are in one group; processes 1, 3, 5, etc., are in a second. Calls to **MPI_COMM_RANK** are used to determine the values of the variables **myid** and **mynewid**, which represent each process's identifier in the original communicator and the appropriate new communicator, respectively. In this example, **mynewid=newid/2**. Then, the **MPI_INTERCOMM_CREATE** call defines an intercommunicator linking the two groups (Fig. 5.12). Process 0 within each group is selected as the leader; this corresponds to process 0 and 1 within the original group, respectively. Once the intercommunicator is created, each process in the first group sends a message to the corresponding process in the second group. Finally, the new communicators created by the program are deleted.

5.5 Library-based Approaches Summary

The Message Passing Interface has been a tremendously successful parallel programming system. While very low level, it has provided a standard notation for parallel program design and has permitted the development of high-performance implementations.

Equally important, MPI support for modular program construction has facilitated, almost for the first time, the development of reusable parallel program components. (The Connection Machine's library was one important precursor.) Hence, we see the development of important reusable code bases,

```
      integer comm, intercomm, ierr, status(MPI_STATUS_SIZE)
C  For simplicity, we require an even number of processes
      call MPI_COMM_SIZE(MPI_COMM_WORLD, count, ierr)
      if(mod(count,2) .ne. 0) stop
C  Split processes into two groups: odd and even numbered
      call MPI_COMM_RANK(MPI_COMM_WORLD, myid, ierr)
      call MPI_COMM_SPLIT(MPI_COMM_WORLD, mod(myid,2), myid, comm,
                          ierr)
C  Determine process id in new group
      call MPI_COMM_RANK(comm, mynewid, ierr)
C  Args: 0=local leader; 1=remote leader; 99=tag
      call MPI_INTERCOMM_CREATE(comm, 0, MPI_COMM_WORLD, 1, 99,
                                intercomm, ierr)
      if(mod(myid,2) .eq. 0) then
C     Group 0: send message to corresponding process in group 1.
        call MPI_SEND(msg, 1, type, mynewid, 0, intercomm, ierr)
      else
C     Group 1: receive message from corresponding process in group 0.
        call MPI_RECV(msg, 1, type, mynewid, 0, intercomm,
                      status, ierr)
      endif
C  Free communicators created during this operation
      call MPI_COMM_FREE(intercomm, ierr)
      call MPI_COMM_FREE(comm, ierr)
```

Fig. 5.13. An MPI program illustrating creation and use of an intercommunicator.

such as the PETSc library for scientific computing [BGI+97], which allows application programmers to develop complex parallel programs without writing any explicitly parallel code.

6. Future Directions

Our study of languages for parallel processing has, we hope, provided insight into four distinct approaches to parallel languages and the issues that they raise in actual practice on high-performance computing platforms. We conclude this chapter by noting several areas in which interesting new developments may be expected in the future.

– *Languages for scalable shared-memory systems.* Programming models that emphasize shared memory have seen a recurrence of interest, driven by improvements in the capabilities of both hardware and software implementations of distributed shared memory. One result of this interest is the recent design of OpenMP, which seems likely to become widely adopted as an alternative to the use of threads when programming small shared-memory systems. Unfortunately, this model does not address data distribution issues, which experience suggests are critical to performance on large parallel computers. We can expect to see interesting new proposals for language designs that integrate data distribution information into a shared-memory framework.

- *Languages for deep memory hierarchies.* An increasingly serious obstacle to high performance on parallel computers is the growing complexity of the memory hierarchy. Many researchers believe that the task of managing this hierarchy is too challenging to leave to a compiler and that language constructs are required that will support explicit management of data movement between levels. Neither shared-memory nor distributed-memory models currently provide the required support.

- *Parallel extensions to Java.* The popularity and attractive semantic properties of Java have resulted in a variety of proposals for parallel extensions, including data-parallel constructs, object-based parallel constructs, and Linda-like tuple space extensions (e.g., see the various conferences organized by the Java Grande Forum). However, few users have experience with the use of these extensions, and further evolution is certain to occur.

- *Languages for "grid" environments.* So-called computational grids feature heterogeneous resources with dynamically varying availability [FK99] and are being used to support both traditional applications and novel applications such as collaborative engineering. New language constructs will almost certainly be required to allow programmer management of performance and effective compilation in these environments [GG99, Ken99, FF99].

References

[Ack82]   Ackerman, W. B., Data flow languages, *Computer* **15**, 1982, 15-25.

[Agh86]   Agha, G., *ACTORS: A Model of Concurrent Computation in Distributed Systems*, MIT Press, Cambridge, Massachusetts, 1986.

[ASS93]   Agrawal, G., Sussman, A., Saltz, J., Compiler and runtime support for structured and block structured applications, *Proc. of Supercomputing*, 1993, 578-587.

[ALS91]   Albert, E., Lukas, J., Steele, G., Data parallel computers and the FORALL statement, *Journal of Parallel and Distributed Computing* **13**, 1991, 185-192.

[Ame88]   America, P., POOL-T: A parallel object-oriented language, *Object-Oriented Concurrent Programming*, A. Yonezawa et al. (eds.), MIT Press, Cambridge, MA, 1988, 199-220.

[AL93]   Anderson, J., Lam, M., Global optimizations for parallelism and locality on scalable parallel machines, *Proc. of the SIGPLAN '93 Conference on Program Language Design and Implementation*, Albuquerque, New Mexico, 1993.

[AV89]   Armstrong, J., Virding, S., Programming telephony, *Strand: New Concepts in Parallel Programming*, Prentice-Hall, Englewood Cliffs, New Jersey, 1989.

[AGG+94]   Auerbach, J., Goldberg, A., Goldszmidt, G., Gopal, A., Kennedy, M., Rao, J., Russell, J., Concert/C: A language for distributed programming, *Winter 1994 USENIX Conference*, Usenix Association, 1994.

[BST89]   Bal, H. E., Steiner, J. E., Tanenbaum, A. S., Programming languages for distributed computing systems, *ACM Computing Surveys* 21, 1989, 261-322.

[BK92]   Bala, V., Kipnis, S., Process groups: A mechanism for the coordination of and communication among processes in the Venus collective communication library, Technical report, IBM T.J. Watson Research Center, 1992.

[BKR+92]   Bala, V., Kipnis, S., Rudolph, L., Snir, M., Designing efficient, scalable, and portable collective communication libraries, Technical report, IBM T.J.Watson Research Center, 1992.

[BGI+97]   Balay, S., Gropp, W., McInnes, L., Smith, B., Efficient management of parallelism in object oriented numerical software libraries, E. Arge, A. M. Bruaset, H. P. Langtangen (eds.), *Modern Software Tools in Scientific Computing*, Birkhauser Press, 1997, 163-202.

[Ban88]   Banerjee, U., *Dependence Analysis for Supercomputing*, Kluwer Academic Publishers, Dordrecht, the Netherlands, 1988.

[Ble90]   Blelloch, G., *Vector Models for Data-Parallel Computing*, MIT Press, Cambridge, Massachusetts, 1990.

[BBG+91]   Bodin, F., Beckman, P., Gannon, D. B., Narayana, S., Yang, S., Distributed pC++: Basic ideas for an object parallel language, *Proc. Supercomputing* 1991, 273-282.

[BBD+87]   Boyle, J., Butler, R., Disz, T., Glickfeld, B., Lusk, E., Overbeek, R., Patterson, J., Stevens, R., *Portable Programs for Parallel Processors*, Holt, Rinehart and Winston, Inc., 1987.

[BCF+93]   Bozkus, Z., Choudhary, A., Fox, G., Haupt, T., Ranka, S., Fortran 90D/HPF compiler for distributed memory MIMD computers: Design, implementation, and performance results, *Proc. Supercomputing* IEEE Computer Society Press, 1993.

[BBF+89]   Butler, R., Butler, T., Foster, I., Karonis, N., Olson, R., Overbeek, R., Pfluger, N., Price, M., Tuecke, S., Aligning genetic sequences, *Strand: New Concepts in Parallel Programming*, Prentice-Hall, Englewood Cliffs, New Jersey, 1989.

[BL94]   Butler, R., Lusk, E., Monitors, message, and clusters: The p4 parallel programming system, *Parallel Computing* 20, 1994, 547-564.

[CK88]   Callahan, D., Kennedy, K., Compiling programs for distributed-memory multiprocessors, *J. Supercomputing* 2, 1988, 151-169.

[CFD90]   Cann, D., Feo, J., DeBoni, T., Sisal 1,2: High performance applicative computing, *Proc. of the Symp. Parallel and Distributed Processing*, IEEE Computer Society Press, 1990, 612-616.

[CG89]   Carriero, N., Gelernter, D., How to write parallel programs: A guide to the perplexed, *Computing Surveys* 21, 1989, 323-357.

[CG89a]   Carriero, N., Gelernter, D., Linda in context, *Communications of the ACM* 32, 1989, 444-458.

[CGH94]   Chandra, R., Gupta, A., Hennessy, J., COOL: An object-based language for parallel programming, *Computer* 27, 1994, 14-26.

[CK93]   Chandy, K. M., Kesselman, C., CC++: A declarative concurrent object-oriented programming notation, *Research Directions in Concurrent Object-Oriented Programming*, MIT Press, Cambridge, Massachusetts, 1993.

[CM88]   Chandy, K. M., Misra, J., *Parallel Program Design*, Addison-Wesley, 1988.

[CT91]   Chandy, K. M., Taylor, S., *An Introduction to Parallel Programming*, Jones and Bartlett, 1991.

[CMZ92]   Chapman, B., Mehrotra, P., Zima, H., Programming in Vienna Fortran, *Scientific Programming* 1, 1992, 31-50.

[CR36]   Church, A., Rosser, J. B., Some properties of conversion, *Trans. American Math. Soc.*, **39**, 1936, 472-482.

[CG81]   Clark, K., Gregory, S., A relational language for parallel programming, *Proc. of the 1981 ACM Conf. on Functional Programming Languages and Computer Architectures*, 1981, 171-178.

[CM81]   Clocksin, W., Mellish, C., *Programming in Prolog*, Springer-Verlag, Berlin, 1981.

[Col89]   Cole, M., *Algorithmic Skeletons: Structured Management of Parallel Computation*, MIT Press, Cambridge, Massachusetts, 1989.

[Dij75]   Dijkstra, E., Guarded commands, nondeterminacy and the formal derivation of programs, *Communications of the ACM* **18**, 1975, 453-457.

[DPW93]   Dongarra, J., Pozo, R., Walker, D., ScaLAPACK++: An object-oriented linear algebra library for scalable systems, *Proc. of the Scalable Parallel Libraries Conf.*, IEEE Computer Society Press, 1993, 216-223.

[EPCC91]   Edinburgh Parallel Computing Centre, CHIMP Concepts, University of Edinburgh, 1991.

[EPCC92]   Edinburgh Parallel Computing Centre, CHIMP Version 1.0 Interface, University of Edinburgh, 1992.

[Fos95]   Foster, I., *Designing and Building Parallel Programs*, Addison-Wesley, 1995.

[Fos96]   Foster, I., Compositional parallel programming languages, *ACM Transactions on Programming Languages and Systems* **18**, 1996, 454-476.

[FAC+94]   Foster, I., Avalani, B., Choudhary, R., Xu, M., A compilation system that integrates high performance Fortran and Fortran M, *Proc. of the 1994 Scalable High Performance Computing Conf.*, IEEE Computer Society Press, 1994.

[FC95]   Foster, I., Chandy, K. M., Fortran M: A language for modular parallel programming, *Journal of Parallel and Distributed Computing* **26**, 1995, 24-35.

[FK99]   Foster, I., Kesselman, C., eds., *The Grid: Blueprint for a Future Computing Infrastructure*, Morgan Kaufmann, 1999.

[FKT90]   Foster, I., Kesselman, C., Taylor, S., Concurrency: Simple concepts and powerful tools, *Computer Journal* **33**, 1990, 501-550.

[FKK+98]   Foster, I, Kohr, D. R. Jr., Krishnaiyer, R., Choudhary, A., A library-based approach to task parallelism in a data-parallel language, *Journal of Parallel and Distributed Computing* **45**, 1998, 148-158.

[FOT92]   Foster, I., Olson, R., Tuecke, S., Productive parallel programming: The PCN approach, *Scientific Programming* 1, 1992, 51-66.

[FT90]   Foster, I., Taylor, S., *Strand: New Concepts in Parallel Programming*, Prentice-Hall, Englewood Cliffs, New Jersey, 1989.

[FHK+90]   Fox, G., Hiranandani, S., Kennedy, K., Koelbel, C., Kremer, U., Tseng, C., Wu, M., Fortran D language specification, Technical report TR90-141, Dept. of Computer Science, Rice University, 1990.

162   Ian Foster

[FF99]   Fox, G., Furmanski, W., High-performance commodity computing, I.
            Foster, C. Kesselman (eds.), *The Grid: Blueprint for a Future Com-
            puting Infrastructure*, Morgan Kaufmann, 1999, 237-255.
[GG99]   Gannon, G., Grimshaw, A., Object-based approaches, I. Foster, C.
            Kesselman (eds.), *The Grid: Blueprint for a Future Computing In-
            frastructure*, Morgan Kaufmann, 1999, 205-236.
[GR88]   Gehani, N., Roome, W., *The Concurrent C Programming Language*,
            Silicon Press, 1988.
[GHP+90]   Geist, G. A., Heath, M. T., Peyton, B. W., Worley, P. H., A user's
            guide to PICL: A portable instrumented communication library,
            Technical report TM-11616, Oak Ridge National Laboratory, 1990.
[Gre87]   Gregory, S., *Parallel Logic Programming in PARLOG*, Addison-
            Wesley, 1987.
[Gri91]   Grimshaw, A. S., An introduction to parallel object-oriented pro-
            gramming with Mentat, Technical report 91 07, University of Vir-
            ginia, 1991.
[GHL+98]   Gropp, W., Huss-Lederman, S., Lumsdaine, A., Lusk, E., Nitzberg,
            B., Saphir, W., Snir, M., *MPI—The Complete Reference: Volume 2,
            The MPI-2 Extensions*, MIT Press, 1998.
[GLS95]   Gropp, W., Lusk, E., Skjellum, A., *Using MPI: Portable Parallel
            Programming with the Message Passing Interface*, MIT Press, Cam-
            bridge, Massachusetts, 1995.
[Hal85]   Halstead, R., MULTILISP: A language for concurrent symbolic com-
            putation, *ACM Transactions on Programming Languages and Sys-
            tems* 7, 1985, 501-538.
[HQ91]   Hatcher, P., Quinn, M., *Data-Parallel Programming on MIMD Com-
            puters*, MIT Press, Cambridge, Massachusetts, 1991.
[HQ91]   Hatcher, P., Quinn, M., and others, Data-parallel programming on
            MIMD computers, *IEEE Trans. Parallel and Distributed Syst.* 2,
            1991, 377-383.
[Hem91]   Hempel, R., The ANL/GMD macros (PARMACS) in Fortran for
            portable parallel programming using the message passing program-
            ming model – users' guide and reference manual, GMD, Germany,
            1991.
[HHS92]   Hempel, R., Hoppe,H.-C., Supalov, A., PARMACS 6.0 library inter-
            face specification, GMD, Germany, 1992.
[Hen80]   Henderson, P., Functional Programming, Prentice-Hall, Englewood
            Cliffs, New Jersey, 1980.
[HPFF93]   High Performance Fortran Forum, High Performance Fortran lan-
            guage specification, version 1.0, Technical report CRPC-TR92225,
            Center for Research on Parallel Computation, Rice University, Hous-
            ton, Texas, 1993.
[HC95]   Hilzer, R. C., Crowl, L. A., A Survey of Sequential and Parallel
            Implementation Techniques for Functional Programming Languages,
            Technical report 95-60-05, Department of Computer Science, Oregon
            State University, 1995.
[HKT92]   Hiranandani, S., Kennedy, K., Tseng, C., Compiling Fortran D for
            MIMD distributed-memory machines, *Communications of the ACM*
            35, 1992, 66-80.
[Hoa78]   Hoare, C., Communicating sequential processes, *Communications of
            the ACM* 21, 1978, 666-677.
[Hud89]   Hudak, P., Conception, evolution, and application of functional pro-
            gramming languages, *ACM Computing Surveys* 21, 1989, 359-411.

[JH93]   Jones, M., Hudak, P., Implicit and explicit parallel programming in Haskell, Research Report YALEU/DCS/RR-982, Yale University, 1993.

[KM77]   Kahn, G., MacQueen, D., Coroutines and networks of parallel processes, *Information Processing 77: Proc. of the IFIP Congress*, North-Holland, 1977, 993-998.

[KB88]   Karp, A., Babb, R., A comparison of twelve parallel Fortran dialects, *IEEE Software* 5, 1988, 52-67.

[Kel89]   Kelly, P., *Functional Programming for Loosely-Coupled Multiprocessors*, MIT Press, Cambridge, Massachusetts, 1989.

[Ken99]   Kennedy, K., Compilers, languages, and libraries, I. Foster, C. Kesselman (eds.), *The Grid: Blueprint for a Future Computing Infrastructure*, Morgan Kaufmann, 1999, 181-204.

[KLS+94]   Koelbel, C., Loveman, D., Schreiber, R., Steele, G., Zosel, M., *The High Performance Fortran Handbook*, MIT Press, Cambridge, Massachusetts, 1994.

[Kow79]   Kowalski, R., *Logic for Problem Solving*, North-Holland, 1979.

[LQ92]   Lemke, M., Quinlan, D., P++, a parallel C++ array class library for architecture-independent development of structured grid applications, *Proc. of the Workshop on Languages, Compilers, and Runtime Environments for Distributed Memory Computers*, ACM, 1992.

[Lov93]   Loveman, D., High Performance Fortran, *IEEE Parallel and Distributed Technology* 1, 1993, 25-42.

[LS91]   Lucco, S., Sharp, O., Parallel programming with coordination structures, *Proc. of the Eighteenth Annual ACM Symposium on the Principles of Programming Languages*, Orlando, Florida, 1991.

[McB94]   McBryan, O., An overview of message passing environments, *Parallel Computing* 20, 1994, 417-444.

[McL90]   McLennan, B., *Functional Programming: Practice and Theory*, Addison-Wesley, 1990.

[MV91]   Mehrotra, P., VanRosendale, J., Programming distributed memory architectures using Kali, *Advances in Languages and Compilers for Parallel Computing*, MIT Press, Cambridge, Massachusetts, 1991.

[MPI93]   Message Passing Interface Forum, Document for a Standard Message-Passing Interface, University of Tennessee, Knoxville, Tenn., 1993.

[MPIF93]   Message Passing Interface Forum, MPI: A Message Passing Interface, *Proc. of Supercomputing* IEEE Computer Society Press, 1993, 878-883.

[MTS+85]   Mierowsky, C., Taylor, S., Shapiro, E., Levy, J., Safra, S., Design and implementation of Flat Concurrent Prolog, Technical report CS85-09, Weizmann Institute of Science, Rehovot, Israel, 1985.

[nCu90]   nCUBE Corporation, nCUBE 2 Programmers Guide, r2.0, 1990.

[PLC95]   S.Pakin, M.Lauria, A.Chien, High performance messaging on workstations: Illinois Fast Messages (FM) for Myrinet, *Proc. of Supercomputing*, 1995.

[PC88]   Parasoft Corporation, Express Version 1.0: A communication environment for parallel computers, Parasoft Corp., 1988.

[Pie88]   Pierce, P., The NX/2 operating system, *Proc. of the 3rd Conf. on Hypercube Concurrent Computers and Applications*, ACM Press, 1988, 384-390.

[Rin88]   Ringwood, G., PARLOG86 and the dining logicians, *Communications of the ACM* 31, 1988, 10-25.

164   Ian Foster

[RP89]   Rogers, A., Pingali, K., Process decomposition through locality of reference, *Proc. of the SIGPLAN '89 Conference on Program Language Design and Implementation*, ACM, 1989.

[RSW90]   Rosing, M., Schnabel, R., Weaver, R., The DINO parallel programming language, Technical report CU-CS-501-90, Computer Science Department, University of Colorado at Boulder, Boulder, Colorado, 1990.

[SBW91]   Saltz, J., Berryman, H., Wu, J., Multiprocessors and runtime compilation, *Concurrency: Practice & Experience* 3, 1991, 573-592.

[Sei85]   Seitz, C. L., The cosmic cube, *Communications of the ACM* 28, 1985, 22-33.

[Sha87]   Shapiro, E., *Concurrent Prolog: Collected Papers*, MIT Press, Cambridge, Massachusetts, 1987.

[Sha89]   Shapiro, E., The family of concurrent logic programming languages, *ACM Computing Surveys* 21, 1989, 413-510.

[ST98]   Skillicorn, D. B., Talia, D., Models and languages for parallel computation, *Computing Surveys* 30, 1998, 123-169.

[SSD+94] SKjellum, A., Smith, S., Doss, N., Leung, A., Morari, M., The design and evolution of Zipcode, *Parallel Computing* 20, 1994, 565-596.

[SSO+93] Subhlok, J., Stichnoth, J., O'Halloran, D., Gross, T., Exploiting task and data parallelism on a multicomputer, *Proc. of the 4th ACM SIGPLAN Symposium on Principles and Practice of Parallel Programming*, ACM, 1993.

[Sun90]   Sunderam, V., PVM: A framework for parallel distributed computing, *Concurrency: Practice & Experience* 2, 1990, 315-339.

[TW82]   Taylor, R., Wilson, P., Process-oriented language meets demands of distributed processing, *Electronics*, 1982.

[Tay89]   Taylor, S., *Parallel Logic Programming Techniques*, Prentice-Hall, Englewood Cliffs, New Jersey, 1989.

[TMC90]   Thinking Machines Corporation, The CM-2 Technical Summary, 1990.

[TMC93]   Thinking Machines Corporation, CM Fortran Reference Manual, version 2.1, 1993.

[THL+98] Trinder, P. W., Hammond, K., Loidl, H.-W., Peyton Jones, S. L., Algorithm + strategy = parallelism, *Journal of Functional Programming* 8, 1998, 23-60.

[THM+96] Trinder, P. W., Hammond, K., Mattson, J. S., Partridge, A. S., Peyton Jones, S. L., GUM: A portable implementation of Haskell, *Proc. of Programming Language Design and Implementation*, 1996.

[Ued85]   Ueda, K., Guarded Horn clauses, Technical Raport TR-103, ICOT, 1985.

[Wat88]   Watanabe, T., and others, Reflection in an object-oriented concurrent language *SIGPLAN Notices* 23, 1998, 306-315.

[WL96]   Wilson, G. V., Lu, P., *Parallel Programming Using C++*, MIT Press, 1996.

[Wol89]   Wolfe, M., *Optimizing Supercompilers for Supercomputers*, MIT Press, Cambridge, Massachusetts, 1989.

[XT90]   Xu, M., Turner, S., A multi-level time warp mechanism, *Proc. of the 1990 Summer Computer Simulation Conf.*, Society for Computer Simulation, 1990, 165-170.

[Yok87]   Yokote, Y., and others, Concurrent programming in Concurrent Smalltalk, *Object-Oriented Concurrent Programming*, A. Yonezawa and others (eds.), MIT Press, Cambridge, MA, 1987, 129-158.

[Yon87]   Yonezawa, A., and others, *Object-Oriented Concurrent Programming*, MIT Press, Cambridge, MA., 1987.

[ZBG88]   Zima, H., Bast, H.-J., Gerndt, M., SUPERB: A tool for semi-automatic MIMD/SIMD parallelization, *Parallel Computing* 6, 1988, 1-18.

[ZC91]   Zima, H., Chapman, B., *Supercompilers for Parallel and Vector Computers*, Addison-Wesley, 1991.

IV. Architecture of Parallel and Distributed Systems

D. Litaize, A. Mzoughi, C. Rochange, and P. Sainrat

Institut de Recherche en Informatique de Toulouse, Université Paul Sabatier, Toulouse, France

Summary. Parallelism is nowadays in all levels of computer architectures. The first level is the processor itself, in which we can find enhancements that probably represent the most spectacular breakthroughs of these last ten years. This chapter begins with a detailed description of superscalar processor features which are intended to increase instruction-level parallelism. Mechanisms for tolerating the latency of the memory hierarchy like speculative execution, speculative disambiguation or fine grain multithreading are then presented. A quantitative analysis of the current and future needs in terms of memory bandwidth and latency shows the problems that must be solved in the memory hierarchy and introduces the part dedicated to the memory hierarchy. This part gives the state of the art of available and future memory chips. Multibanked memories are a good introduction to shared-bus multiprocessors, which are the most commercially popular. Physically shared-memory multiprocessors are then analysed, through some classical processor-memory networks. A synthesis of data coherency algorithms is developped and the data consistency problems are shown. Again, a quantitative evaluation of performance needs introduces physically-distributed memory multiprocessors and the analysis of available multiprocessors systems allows us to point out the main advantages and drawbacks of the various possible options, including logically-shared memory systems and message passing systems. Finally, the state of the art of I/O systems is assessed, using a performance analysis of available disk systems and current trends in interconnecting peripherals to processors and memories.

1. Introduction

A multiprocessor is composed of three main parts: processors, memory hierarchies and an interconnection network. Their evolution during the years are quite different and their assembly into a multiprocessor system involves new solutions in order to match their relative performance.

Processors have presented the most spectacular evolution. Today, all of them are superscalar, i.e. they can execute several instructions in parallel each clock cyle. The clock frequency increases regularly mainly because of technological improvements but also because of the heavy use of pipelining. Their development cost is so high and their life time so short that almost all multiprocessor manufacturers use standard processors and not their own. The processor needs are far from being satisfied by the memories. DRAM memories have seen their size growing quickly but the decrease of their access time has been very low. During a 50-ns DRAM access time, a 300-MHz 4-way superscalar processor executes about one hundred instructions. SRAM memories, faster but with lower capacities, are used as caches in order to reduce the dramatic effect of the DRAM access time. However, the gap of performance between the processor and the memory is still increasing and, now, several levels of cache memories are needed: the first level is on the processor chip itself, the second level is external to this chip but may be on a special board and a third-level might be necessary in the near future. Research on the memory hierarchy should be reinforced during the next years.

Considering realisation limits, a printed circuit board of a reasonable size (PC motherboard for example) may interconnect on a shared-bus 2 or 4 (8 soon) processors, each with a second-level cache. Then coherency of cached data is resolved simply and efficiently by using a snooping solution. May be, a multi-chip module will replace the printed board but this will not change the modularity. Considering this board as a cluster, how can we interconnect these clusters to implement a more powerful multiprocessor?

These last years, most solutions implement the "central" memory in the cluster and interconnect these clusters by a network: a Delta for the IBM-SP2, a torus for Cray, and so on. This approach is aimed at scalability and is also due to the bandwidth of the memory which is not high enough to feed all the processors simultaneously. It results in expensive machines that cannot be bought by many. Programming these machines is not easy since processors are communicating by the mean of messages, the efficiency of which might not be controlled. Some of them have additional hardware in order for the physically distributed memory to be considered as logically shared. On such machines, the programmer has only one memory space, the software (compilers or operating systems) being in charge of the best distribution of programs and data. This view of the memory space has been quickly adopted for workstation networks, but implemented in software only. Such networks present a very high level of potential performance that should be exploited.

This approach is certainly attractive for numerous applications where parallelism is coarse-grained, i.e. that show few communications between their parallel processes. However, the physical aspect of the communication media might not be lost of sight by the programmers: if a processor executes one instruction every nanosecond (which corresponds to the most powerful processors today), the electrical or optical wave is only propagated on twenty centimetres during the same time. So, due to the distance between machines, the communication time will become prohibitive with regards to the cycle time of the processor. For example, a round trip time for a single bit over a distance of 100 meters is about 1 microsecond. During this time a processor can execute 1000 instructions. In 5 years, the travel time will remain the same, but the number of instructions executed by a processor will reach 10000: software routines will probably be no more the cause of data transfer latencies.

In order to feed these multiprocessors with data, I/Os should be taken into account: mainly disks and network interfaces. Logically placed at the end of the memory hierarchy, I/Os have their own bus (the I/O bus), linked through a bridge to the memory bus. Most of the time communication is done under DMA mode. I/Os had often been neglected in the past but the performance gap between processors and I/Os has increased so much that, now, they are heavily studied. The evolution of disks is spectacular, but as for DRAM memories, it concerns mainly the capacity and the price and not the performance. While the processor performance has increased by 50% each year, disk access time has been improved only by 7% per year. This has to be taken into account today especially when considering that, with the dramatic increase of the use of internet, new applications appear which have few computing needs but handle gigantic amounts of data. These applications are very different of scientific codes that are up-to-day most of the time taken as a reference for performance evaluation.

2. Superscalar Processors

2.1 Introduction

The major improvement (from a hardware point of view) introduced in RISC processors was the intensive use of pipelining which exploits parallelism in order to approach a rate of one instruction per cycle. Superscalar processors use pipelining but their major feature is their capacity to execute several instructions in parallel.

This possibility is offered by the presence of several functional units (ALUs) and a pipeline that deals with several instructions in the same cycle. The idea of having several functional units is not new. The CDC6600 [Tho61] and the IBM360/91 [AST67] had several functional units but their pipeline was dimensioned for a single instruction per cycle. Thus, the aim of having several functional units was to tolerate their latencies in order to approach the rate of one instruction per cycle.

The aim of superscalar processors is to overcome the rate of one instruction per cycle. The performance of a superscalar processor is defined by the number of instructions per cycle and not by the number of cycles per instruction ! A superscalar processor is designed for a peak rate of d instructions per cycle, d being the degree of the processor i.e. the number of instructions that have completed their execution and can be retired in parallel from the processor each cycle. Of course, the aim of a superscalar processor is to approach a performance which is closest to d.

2.2 Architecture of an Out-Of-Order Superscalar Processor

As RISC processors, superscalar processors use a pipeline in order to fetch, decode and execute instructions but each stage deals with several instructions in parallel. A typical pipeline is composed of several stages: fetch, decode, issue, execute, retire. Usually, the degree of the processor is the number of instructions that can be retired each cycle. Often, it is the same number for the decode stage but it may be different for the other stages in order to compensate for latencies higher than one cycle (in case of a cache miss during the fetch or for an instruction that needs several cycles to be executed). For example, six instructions may be executed in parallel while only four instructions are fetched and decoded in parallel. Thus, buffers are necessary between stages in order to keep instructions that cannot be directed to the next stage.

In most of superscalar processors, the order of execution of the instructions is different of the order of the program. This allows a greater parallelism by a better use of the functional units. Considering a sequence of instructions, the second instruction may be ready to be executed because its operands are known while the first one cannot be executed because the instruction that produces one of its operand has a long execution latency and has not finished its execution yet. The idea of out-of-order execution is that the second instruction should be executed before the first one. A mechanism should be included in the processor to detect if an instruction can be executed i.e. if its operands are ready. This approach looks like a data-flow one except that only those instructions that are fetched and decoded are considered for being executed.

Fig. 2.1 shows a conceptual view of out-of-order execution. To guarantee the correctness of the result of an execution, the program order should be retrieved for retiring the instructions. A usual way to retrieve this order consists in a structure where instructions are enqueued after their decoding and dequeued in the same order once they are executed.

2.2.1 Limits to the exploitation of parallelism. The limits to the exploitation of parallelism are of two types. The first type is inherent to the

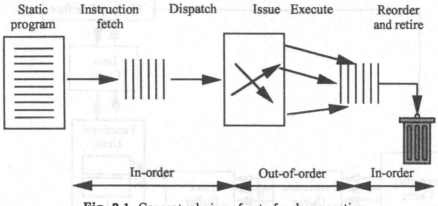

Fig. 2.1. Conceptual view of out-of-order execution.

architecture of the processor. It concerns the degree of the processor, the number and the type of the functional units, the size of the buffers, etc. The second limitation is due to the dependencies in the program. Next section will explain what those dependencies are and how to overcome them.

The architecture of an out-of-order superscalar processor is represented in Fig. 2.2.

The main architectural limitation is the degree followed by the size of the reorder buffer which is tightly related to the degree and contains the instructions the processor is aware of and allows to retrieve the order of the instructions for retiring them.

The issue buffer contains the instructions that are waiting for being executed either because their operands are not yet known or because functional units are busy. This issue buffer may be one large buffer as in the PentiumPro [Pap96] or may be split in sub-buffers according to the type of the instruction as in the MIPS R10000 [Yea96] or in the HP PA-8000 [Hun95] or, finally, it may be distributed among the functional units as in the PowerPC604 [IM94]. In the latter case, each entry of this buffer is usually called a reservation station. Each cycle, each of these entries is looking for its operands. If they are ready, the instruction is candidate for the functional units that can execute it. An arbiter selects the instructions that will be executed according to a policy, which usually gives preference to the oldest instructions.

Of course, the number and type of functional units is also a limitation: they must be carefully chosen [JSL95]. Another limitation is the access to the instructions in the cache. On a mean, d instructions should be fetched each cycle. It is not possible to fetch the same number of instructions each cycle because the required instructions may span 2 cache lines and only one cache line can be accessed each cycle. Thus, a buffer should be introduced to compensate for cycles where less than d instructions are fetched and a mechanism may be implemented to overcome the access to one cache line (see Section 2.5).

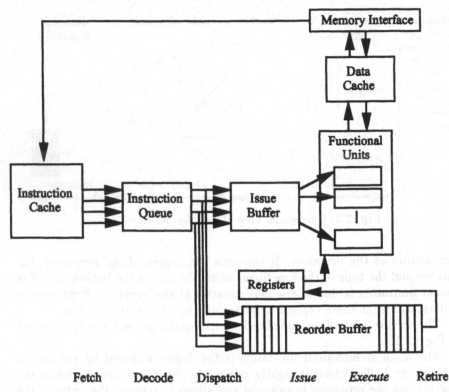

Fetch   Decode   Dispatch   *Issue*   *Execute*   Retire

Fig. 2.2. Macro view of an out-of-order superscalar architecture.

2.3 Overcoming the Limits Due to Dependencies

One constraint to the exploitation of the parallelism is the dependencies which are due either to the programming model (control dependencies and true dependencies) or to the execution model (anti-dependencies, output dependencies).

2.3.1 Definition of the dependencies.

Control Dependencies. Once compiled, a static program is generated. For a given static program, various sequences are executed according to the input data set used. This is due to the presence of conditional branches which control the instructions flow to be executed. Usually, the control consists in executing the next instruction in the static program (the program counter is incremented) except when a control instruction is executed (the program counter is updated). Thus, all instructions following a branch are dependent on this branch because the possibility of being executed depends on the result of the branch.

Data Dependencies. Only the true dependencies are inherent to the programming model. A true dependency exists between two instructions when one of the operands of one of them is the result of the other one.

An output dependency exists between two instructions when the two instructions write their results in the same location (register or memory).

An anti-dependency exists when an instruction reads in a location while the other one writes in it and the instruction that reads is the older one.

Fig. 2.3 shows these dependencies in a program.

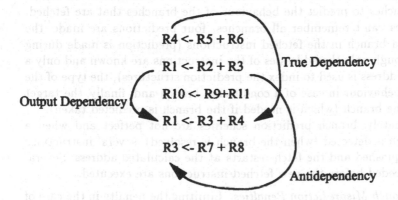

Fig. 2.3. Examples of dependencies.

2.3.2 Overcoming control dependencies. Control dependencies result in a high loss of performance if they are not treated in another way than just calculating the branch. This is due to the fact that the processor has to know the result of a branch in order to fetch the instructions after the branch. It was already the case in scalar processors but it is exacerbated in superscalar processors. The reason is that, at each stage, several (let's say d) instructions are treated. Thus, if there are s stages between the fetch and the execution of the branch, at least $s \times d$ instructions are fetched sequentially and often (if it is a non conditional branch or a taken conditional branch) squashed when the result of the branch is known. This number may be very high as in the PentiumPro [Pap96] the pipeline of which consists of 12 stages, 7 of them being located between the fetch and the execution of the instructions.

Branch Prediction. To overcome this problem, the outcome of branches is predicted as early as possible, i.e. during the fetch. While a set of instructions is fetched, the outcome of the branches in this set is predicted in order to fetch a new set of instructions during the next cycle. These instructions will be executed speculatively until the prediction is confirmed (i.e. when the branch is executed). The instructions being executed speculatively should not modify the state of the processor until the branch is verified, or a way to recover the state of the cycle when the branch was dispatched should be provided. This could be done by saving the value of a register before modifying it or by modifying the registers only when the instructions are retired (i.e. when they have been executed and in the same order as they are fetched). In both cases, additional locations should be implemented to keep the values (old ones or future ones).

Many studies have been made on branch prediction schemes from static ones to 2-level dynamic ones [LS84, YP92, PSR92]. The idea of most branch prediction schemes is to use the information obtained during previous executions of branches to predict the behaviour of the branches that are fetched. As structures can't remember all branches, four predictions are made: the presence of a branch in the fetched instructions (prediction is made during the fetch though only the addresses of the instructions are known and only a part of the address is used to index the prediction structures), the type of the branch, its behaviour in case of a conditional branch and, finally, the target address of the branch (which is needed if the branch is predicted taken).

Unfortunately, branch prediction schemes are not perfect and when a misprediction is detected (when the branch is resolved), several instructions should be squashed and the fetch restarts at the calculated address. Several cycles are needed before the new fetched instructions are executed.

Limiting Branch Misprediction Penalties. Limiting the penalty in the case of branch mispredictions may be resolved by providing a trace cache. The idea behind the trace cache covers more than just limiting the branch penalty. The idea is to construct dynamically instruction traces (sequences of instructions that are executed) and to use these traces instead of fetching again the instructions in the cache memory. Thus a trace cache records traces of decoded instructions. A trace might be several basic blocks long and thus might contain several branches. When the fetch concerns a given address, if there is the corresponding trace in the trace cache, this trace is dispatched (no need to go through fetching and decoding) partially or entirely depending on the prediction of the branches that are in the trace. So, in the case of a branch misprediction, if the good trace is in the trace cache, one cycle after the discovery of the misprediction, the instructions of the good path may be executed. Moreover, if the trace cache is large enough, after the necessary cold-start period to fill it (as well as for the L1 cache), the trace cache might be the main source of instructions instead of the L1 cache.

Trace caches may be implemented in the next generation of processors.

Limits of Branch Prediction. Branch prediction has an accuracy of more than 90% for the best prediction schemes. As there are about one branch every five instructions, if we consider that instruction windows of future processors will be one to several hundreds of instructions large, it means that it could contain dozens of branches, most of them being predicted and not yet executed. Each time a branch is predicted, two paths are possible: the predicted one or the other one.

If we consider 25 predicted but not verified branches, a tree of paths is developed and the probability that the path is the right one decreases at each node. After 25 branches, there is only a probability of 7% that the fetched path is the right one! Thus, other paths in the upper levels of the tree of paths have a higher probability of being useful (See Fig. 2.4). It could be

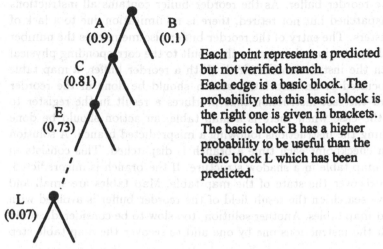

Each point represents a predicted but not verified branch.
Each edge is a basic block. The probability that this basic block is the right one is given in brackets.
The basic block B has a higher probability to be useful than the basic block L which has been predicted.

Fig. 2.4. A tree of paths.

more judicious to execute these paths [US95] but this needs extra hardware to record the tree, choose the paths, etc. that may be too costly with regard to the gain that could be achieved. Several studies are currently carried out on this topic.

2.3.3 Overcoming anti-dependencies and output dependencies: renaming. As seen previously, anti-dependencies and output dependencies are due to the programming model that uses a restricted set of registers. This restriction is due to the heritage of older instruction sets which should be supported. Overcoming these dependencies increases the achieved parallelism.

The compiler may try to move away an instruction from the instruction it depends on. But the compiler only knows the static program with the branches. Moving an instruction beyond a branch is quite difficult so, usually, it moves instructions only between two branches. As branches are very frequent in programs, displacements are highly limited.

Another solution consists in dynamically renaming the locations where the results are stored. The number of physical locations is higher than the number of registers of the programming model. If an instruction is dispatched, and the location of its result is already occupied by another instruction that will produce a result in the same register, the location of the result is mapped to another physical location. If an operand of a following instruction concerns the same register, it is renamed to the corresponding physical location. When an instruction is retired, the result is copied from the physical location to the original register.

There are two ways to implement this. One might be the use of supplementary registers and a map table which indicates the associations between logical and supplementary registers. Otherwise, the locations might be the entries of the reorder buffer. As the reorder buffer contains all instructions which are dispatched but not retired, there is no limitation due to a lack of physical registers. The entry of the reorder buffer also memorises the number of the logical register in order to copy the result to the corresponding physical register when the instruction is retired. With a reorder buffer, a map table may be associated or an associative search should be done in the reorder buffer to find the last instruction that produces a result in the register to rename. In the case when there is a map table, an action should be done when squashing the instructions following a mispredicted branch. A solution is to make a checkpoint each time a branch is dispatched. This consists in copying the map table in a shadow structure. If the branch is mispredicted, it is easy to recover the state of the map table. Map tables are small and an associative search on the result field of the reorder buffer is avoided with checkpointed map tables. Another solution, too slow to be considered, would be to squash the instructions one by one and to recover the map table step by step.

2.3.4 Overcoming true dependencies: value prediction and instruction reuse. While the preceding dependencies are due to the lack of resources and are resolved by adding the missing resources, true dependencies are the essential beings of the programming model as well as control dependencies. Control dependencies are overcome by predicting the behaviour of the branches, executing speculatively the instructions following a predicted branch and recovering a normal state in the case of mispredictions.

The same idea can be applied to predict the results of instructions. Thus, instructions that depend on the result of a predicted instruction may execute in parallel with this instruction. It has been shown that when a static instruction is re-executed, there is 50% chance that the same result is produced and over 60% chance that a result is produced that was already produced during one of the four preceding executions of the instruction. First experiments, based on tables for value predictions, show that instructions are executed early. It increases the parallel execution of instructions and a speedup of, at least, 10% is obtained [LS96].

Moreover, if we can know that the operands of an instruction are the same than during its last execution, the result is already known and the instruction does not need to be executed. This scheme is called instruction reuse and different ways of implementing it are proposed in [SS97].

Limiting Misprediction Penalty. Mispredicted instructions and their dependent instructions should be re-executed. Squashing all instructions after a mispredicted instruction, as for branch prediction, would nullify the gain obtained and is not necessary since only some instructions are dependent on a value-predicted instruction. Thus, a recovery mechanism should be implemented for cancelling the execution of these instructions while limiting the penalty of mispredictions. This is necessary because it seems that value prediction may have a high misprediction rate. Solutions to this problem are examined in [HRS97]. It merely consists in keeping the instructions in the issue buffer and allowing their re-execution if they are dependent on the mispredicted instruction. The processor must keep in mind the dependencies between instructions.

2.3.5 Memory dependencies. Memory dependencies are a bit different of register dependencies. As soon as an instruction is decoded, its registers are known. On the contrary, the address of memory locations should be calculated. Thus, the memory dependencies between memory operations cannot be determined at the dispatch stage as for registers.

The latency of DRAMs is very high compared to the cycle time of processors and this difference increases each year. Thus, several levels of caches have been added (usually two or three). This implies that the latency of loads and stores varies, depending on the level of the memory hierarchy in which the access finds the data, and may be very high (today, up to a few dozens of cycles for the main memory level).

Stores should not deposit their data in the memory when they are speculative or the previous value in memory should be saved before in order to recover it in the case of a mispredicted branch older than the store. The simplest method is to execute stores when they are retired. They are no more speculative since all previous instructions have already been retired and they are executed in-order. This guarantees that no output dependencies are violated, stores are executed as in a usual in-order processor. Moreover, it guarantees a consistent model of the memory (see Section 4.).

The same method could be applied to loads, but loads read data in memory that are useful for other instructions to be executed. As latencies may be very long, this could stall the processor while waiting for this value. Loads can bypass stores provided the addresses are different. Moreover, if a store has the same address as a subsequent load and its data is ready (it just waits to be retired), this data could be forwarded to the load and the load does not need to access the memory.

In most of today processors, the address calculus is decoupled from the memory access. An ordered queue is implemented for load and store instructions where they wait for their access to the memory to be completed. An associative search in this queue is done for each load before (or in parallel with) accessing the memory in order to detect dependencies and eventually benefit of a forward. This queue may also allow the accesses of loads that addresses the same cache block to be combined. Only one access to the cache is made and each load gets its data from the received block of data. The register file contains few registers, and several ports are implemented (enough for all instructions that are dispatched). On the other hand, the cache has many locations and, thus, cannot have many access ports. Usually, the cache blocks are interleaved over two or four banks and one access per bank is allowed. Thus, decreasing the number of accesses to the cache by forwarding and combining is important. Many processors implement this scheme.

However, even with all these features, the presence of stores still delays the execution of loads because their addresses might not be calculated and, consequently, the detection of the dependencies could not be done. A mean to overcome this is to predict the dependencies between loads and stores. In some processors, a blind speculation is made. It is assumed that a load does not depend on previous stores the address of which is not calculated. In the case of mis-speculations, a recovery should be done. In current processors, all the instructions after a mispredicted load are squashed as for a branch misprediction. If the instruction window is small, this could be effective because there are few mispredictions and the number of squashed instructions is small. But, it will not be efficient for large windows. A different recovery mechanism should be adopted in order to cancel only instructions depending on the load and re-execute them without re-fetching them as discussed in the previous section.

A more accurate solution has been proposed in [MBV+97] to predict the dependencies in order to lower the number of mispredictions for large instruction windows.

2.4 Tolerating Memory Latency

As instructions depend on the value produced by loads, loads should be executed as soon as possible because their latency may be long if the access is made in the upper levels of the memory hierarchy. On the contrary, stores just update the memory, no instructions are waiting for this update (except in multiprocessor systems where another processor could need this value). Thus, stores may stay in a queue even if the store is retired, but this queue must be kept coherent in order to detect requests from other processors for locations that should be updated by the stores waiting in this queue. Delaying stores allows loads to be executed early. Stores access the memory only if a port is free.

Three prediction schemes implement a speculative execution of loads.

The first one predicts the address of loads [GG97]. Thus a load may access the memory with the predicted address, it does not wait for the address to be calculated. If the predicted address is right, the access has been made a few cycles (the cycles needed to wait for the operands and to calculate the address) sooner. As the size of the instruction window grows, the time between the fetch of a load and the time where the address is calculated grows too. Thus, address prediction will mask higher latencies.

The second one is value prediction where the results of loads [LS96] are predicted. Value prediction may predict the value of some loads. Thus, instructions dependent of a load are not waiting for the access to be executed.

They use the predicted value. The access is made only to verify the prediction. The latency does not matter as far as predictions are good.

In the two cases, when a prediction is wrong, recovery should be implemented by re-executing the instructions that depend on the mispredicted load. In the case of a misprediction, an access to the memory is made with the correct address. These two schemes still remain academic research.

The third prediction scheme is data prefetching. This has been heavily studied for years. Its aim is to tolerate the latency of the upper levels of the memory hierarchy. It consists in predicting and executing accesses to the memory hierarchy based on previous accesses. Thus, knowing only the addresses of previous accesses, it determines addresses of other accesses that are assumed to be executed in the near future. This is based on the fact that the distance between two accesses is often constant (accesses to an array for example). When two or three accesses are detected at constant-stride locations, the predictor makes an access to the next location. The main drawback is that it needs more memory bandwidth because predictors are not accurate enough. Prefetching may also be done by inserting prefetch instructions either manually or automatically in the program. Software prefetching instructions are implemented in recent instructions sets as in the HP-PA [SGH97].

Finally, multithreading [Hwa93] could be used to tolerate memory latencies. When a miss is encountered in a cache, the processor might change of thread and execute other instructions which do not wait for a cache miss to be resolved. Multithreading may tolerate larger latencies since it executes instructions that are completely independent of the load that miss in the cache. However, it might conduct to frequent conflict misses in the caches.

2.5 Fetching Instructions for High-Degree Processors

The processor cannot execute instructions faster than it fetches them. Even if dozens of functional units could be implemented in a processor, other constraints exist in the instruction-fetch mechanism. In current commercial processors, fetched instructions should belong to the same basic block and they cannot span two cache lines. As most of basic blocks are 5 instructions long, it severely limits the fetch rate. The trace cache, discussed above, memorises traces of decoded instructions and traces may be several basic blocks long and are not related to the cache lines. Another way consists in improving the fetching mechanism. Several basic blocks could be fetched provided they are in the same cache line [CMM+95] or even if they belong to several cache lines [SJS+96]. The major features are a multiple-branch predictor and a dual-ported instruction cache. This needs further studies.

2.6 Another Approach for Extracting ILP

Another approach relies on the compiler for extracting ILP in order to simplify the hardware in the aim of decreasing the cycle time. In VLIW (Very

Large Instruction Word) processors, an instruction is very large and is composed of several operations, always of the same type. For example, a VLIW processor has two integer units, one floating-point unit and two load/store units. An instruction will contain the same operations if they can be detected by the compiler. To be effective, such an approach should contain enough functional units. As the size of basic blocks is small, the compiler should predict their behaviour based on a static prediction or run-time information. So, the detection of several independent operations of the needed type may be grouped together in one VLIW instruction. Of course, if no operation can be found, the field in the instruction is left empty. The corresponding functional unit will not be used. This approach has not yet been implemented in commercial processors except for specialized processors. A variant, called EPIC for Explicit Parallel Instruction Computing, groups several instructions in one but instructions grouped may be of any type and bits are added to the group to provide information on the dependencies between the instructions [Gwe97].

2.7 Integrating Mechanisms for Exploiting a Higher Level of Parallelism

As the number of transistors on a chip drastically grows, one could ask if a superscalar processor will be able to use all these transistors in order to extract enough parallelism from a unique flow of instructions.

Alternative directions are considered in the academic research. One approach is simultaneous multithreading [TEL95] which consists in executing simultaneously instructions from several flows. This approach consists in sharing the resources of the processor (functional units, data cache, etc.) between several different flows of instructions. Only the registers and the program counters are private to the flows in order to keep a coherent state for each flow. Sharing of resources seems attractive. However, it may lead to an increase of the number of misses in the L1 caches due to the presence of the data and instructions of several flows that might map to the same cache block. Thus, L1 caches should be larger and set-associative because, otherwise, the L2 cache will be saturated by the requests due to L1 misses. It seems that, except for subroutine returns that need a special care, branch prediction structures can be shared by the threads and do not suffer of dealing with several different flows provided the size of the tables is large enough. Simultaneous multithreading dynamically chooses the instructions to be executed.

Another approach consists in implementing a shared-memory multiprocessor on a chip [ONH+96]. The architecture of shared-memory multiprocessors will be examined later (see Section 5.). When integrating such multiprocessors on a chip, they share a large L2 cache which should have a high bandwidth. Such multiprocessors are more intended to execute threads, like in the previous case. But, in the case where there is only one thread, they will have a poorer performance compared to simultaneous multithreading because, to incorporate several processors on a chip, each processor should be simpler (i.e. executing at most two instructions per cycle) and only one processor will be used. In simultaneous multithreading, the processor is a wide-issue superscalar processor that can extract most of the ILP even on one thread. As these alternatives are only possible for large chips with numerous transistors, the delays on the lines that interconnect the elements on the chip become long compared to the cycle time. This argues for multiple independent processors rather than simultaneous multithreading in which all elements are closely related. The design of multiprocessors on a chip will probably be simpler than simultaneous multithreaded processors since processors are simpler and they are independent.

In both cases, the performance relies on the capability of the compiler to extract threads of an application. As more and more applications will become multimedia, compilers will be able to extract easily the threads. However, in some cases, it will remain quite difficult. Thus, simultaneous multithreading may be able to extract more ILP. The choice remains open. Perhaps we will be able to implement simultaneous multithreaded processors sooner than multiprocessors on a chip.

3. Uniprocessors vs. Multiprocessors

Apart from very few exceptions, multiprocessors are built using off the shelf processors. Current trends are even to use a complete uniprocessor system as a multiprocessor node. With technology improvements, the node itself becomes gradually a small multiprocessor. ICs have to be placed on some intermediate support, usually a printed board, which in turn has to be ranged in some place, usually a rack. The thrust of integration level leads to a reduced number of ICs to make a system. This naturally conducts to two tendencies. One is to provide simple systems on the smallest possible area, for the purpose of applications where this constraint is important (laptops, mobiles,..). The second one consists in feeding the available surface size with a maximum of logic. Thus, two or more uniprocessor systems are implemented on the same board in such a way that the resulting system is a multiprocessor. In this context, the usual way to build a multiprocessor is to use a shared bus and a shared memory.

Setting a hierarchy of caches on such a close working environment - the board - leads to a good level of performance for this system, as long as the number of processors remains low. Using such a printed board to build a multiprocessor can be done in two ways. Either the on-board uni/multi-processor is built as a closed system, and the only way to make such systems communicate is to use the standard I/O routines and therefore execute a lot of software, or the on-board uni/multi-processor has been designed having in mind some kind of network topology and, in this case, communications between systems are more or less automatically performed by the hardware.

In the first case, off the shelf systems can be used, like PCs or workstations and communication is performed by standard means (Ethernet for example) or specific ones (Myrinet for example), leading to a good level of performance at a low cost.

In the second case, the possible level of performance is higher, but at the expense of a higher cost. Moreover some important choices about main memory have to be made. It can be physically shared with a uniform access time (UMA architectures: Uniform Memory Access, in which the whole memory is located at the same distance of each processor), or physically shared with a non-uniform access time (NUMA architectures, Non UMA, in which each processor is involved in the control of a portion of the shared memory), or physically distributed and logically shared through software routines with more or less hardware assistance (DSM : Distributed Shared Memory).

The choice of the approach depends on the kind of application to be solved. If there are few communications between processes with regards to the computation time, the (relative) high latency of the NUMA/DSM solutions has little impact on the global response time. In the other case, the UMA solution is more appropriate.

Instead of enumerating all kinds of available multiprocessors, this chapter focuses on the particularities of the most currently used. Whatever the solution is, the heart of a node is a hierarchical processor-cache-memory. This leads us of course to study in depth the evolution of uniprocessors, which in fact drives the multiprocessor evolution. PC and workstations are built on the same basic architecture. The PC computer has a shorter renewal cycle, and the mass production leads to lower prices for the ICs involved in the PC design than those used in workstations or other computer systems. As a side effect, these latter try to integrate some of these ICs in their own systems. This is the case for memory ICs, which are consumed up to 70% by the PC market.

3.1 Uniprocessor Architectures

The main memory of a uniprocessor system, based on DRAM chips, is requested to exchange data on one hand with the processor, and on the other hand with the peripheral units, like disks, a network interface or a graphic processor. The classical solution in which these entities were all connected to a time multiplexed shared bus (Fig. 3.1a) has progressively moved to an architecture where the main memory plays a rather central role (Fig. 3.1b). This change is of benefit in two ways: on the performance as the bus arbiter becomes a memory arbiter, and on the normalisation, as interfaces are no more connected to a proprietary shared bus, but to an I/O normalised bus like PCI.

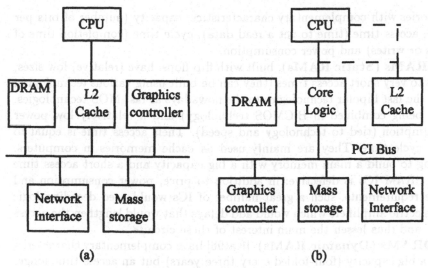

Fig. 3.1. From old architecture (a) to current ones (b).

In an ideal architecture, the main memory provides requested data to the processor in a single processor clock cycle. This means that the memory latency must be ideally equal to the clock period and that the memory bandwidth must fit the requested data quantity i.e. some memory words at each cycle nowadays. Clocks frequencies of current processors are in the range of 200 MHz up to 600 MHz, which involves that the memory should have at least an access time of 5 to 2 nanoseconds. This is far from reality, as current DRAM access time is about 60 nanoseconds, being 10 to 25 times longer than requested. Memory bandwidth is also limited, as linked to the access time. For 25 years, processors performance has roughly been multiplied ten-fold every five years, whereas the main memory access time was roughly divided by ten during the 25 years. This gap of performance has been partially filled by the setting of a hierarchy of cache memories, reducing at the same time the main memory pressure. But this mechanism concerns only the processor side, and the pressure remains of equal importance on the I/O side (disks, network, graphic). As it seems that this evolution will continue at the same rate during at least the next ten years [Yu96], one of the future challenges relies on a great improvement of the main memory performance, while continuing to use DRAM chips, the structure of which is currently evolving, after being built with the same architecture during nearly twenty-five years.

3.2 Memory ICs

In the first RAMs, a bit was recorded in a flip-flop, made up of 6 transistors. In 1968, Dennard proposed an alternative solution based on a capacitor charge guarded by a transistor. These two approaches authorise to produce memories with complementary characteristics: capacity (number of bits per chip), access time (time to get a read data), cycle time (completion time of reads or writes) and power consumption.

SRAMs (Static RAMs), built with flip-flops, have (relative) low sizes, short to very short access times (they can be built using various technologies, from the fast bipolar technologies to the nowadays as fast MOS technologies, both being combined in BiCMOS technology) and a relatively low power consumption (tied to technology and speed). Their access time is equal to their cycle time. They are mainly used as cache memories in computers. Trying to build a main memory with a big capacity and a short access time from SRAM ICs is defective: in addition to price, power consumption and space requirements, such a great number of ICs would need decoding logic and electric amplifiers which would add delays that would lengthen the access time, and thus lessen the main interest of these circuits.

DRAMs (Dynamic RAMs) [Kat96] have complementary characteristics: a big capacity (four-folded every three years) but an access time longer than that of SRAMs and evolving very slowly (7% per year) except for drastic changes in their structure. Only available in MOS technology, DRAMs have cycle times which are approximately twice the read or write access times. This latter point is due to the nature of the record mechanism itself: a bit being represented by the charge of a capacitor, in order to know its value, it is necessary to discharge this capacitor. Thus, the charge must then be restored. As all these capacitors have a natural tendency to lose their charge with the time, a periodical cycle of re-charge must be provided. This explains the internal structure of the chip, build as a matrix of bits, each line of the matrix having to be read ("refreshed ") in a period of some milliseconds, period fixed by the manufacturer. Refresh line reads are generally equally distributed along the refresh cycle. Due to this matrix structure, reading a binary digit is performed in two phases: the line containing the bit is first read, then the bit is selected in the line. The bit address can therefore be split in two parts and passed to the chip in two times, which divide roughly the number of address pins by two. All these functions: address multiplexing, refresh cycles, signals timing, are in fact managed by a DRAM controller, which controls synchronously a set of DRAM ICs in order to access to several bits in parallel. DRAM memory accesses are always done through this controller, giving the illusion to the units accessing the memory that they access a (pseudo-) static memory (see Fig. 3.2). A controller can drive generally up to 4 sets of DRAM chips, each set being in fact a memory bank able to read or write one word at a time, the word size being equal to the data bus width. Using address interleaving techniques, the second part of the cycle time of a read or write access can be hidden by the next memory operation, if it concerns a different bank. This leads to an apparent cycle time equal to the access time. But accesses remain sequential, and even if two or more physical banks are driven by a controller, the whole appears as being a unique logical

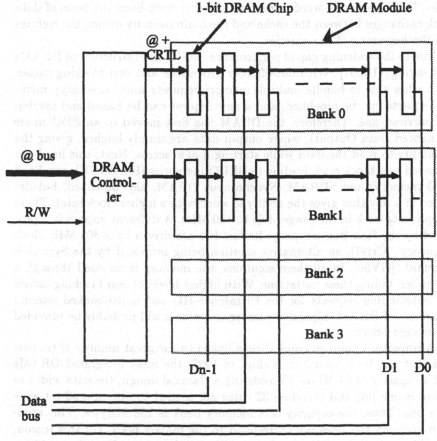

Fig. 3.2. DRAM chips and their controller.

bank with a cycle time equal to the access time in case of successive accesses done on different internal banks.

A bit read in a chip involves a line read. If the line is latched, then the other bits of the line can be read more quickly. In practice, about three bits can be read during the line refresh re-write. This means that during a memory cycle four adjacent bits can be read, instead of one. This "nibble" read leads to a burst mode read of 4 words in a bank in four slots of time of t1, t2, t2, t2 duration. t1 is the time to access the first word, which is the longest, corresponding to the capacitor discharge. t2 is shorter, as we have just to switch to a next bit in the latch register. If the line is kept in the latch and if the next access is located in this same line then the access is done in t2-t2-t2-t2 slots of time. This burst mode is known as FPM (Fast Page Mode). A 4-word block of data can be written in the memory in a same way: the four bits are recorded during the line read, then merged in the line, which is written back to memory: 4 bits have been written during a single memory cycle. This optimum 4-word burst read or write have been the basis of data block exchanges between the cache and the main memory during the eighties and the beginning of the nineties.

Due to the widening gap of performance, the internal structure of DRAMs is changing [Dip97]. With out-of-order processors and non-blocking caches (i.e. caches able to handle multiple memory requests simultaneously), memory requests can be pipelined, and a new request can be issued and overlap the previous one. Therefore, the DRAM has first moved to an EDO mode (Enhanced Data Output), where output data are simply latched, giving the possibility to read the data while starting a new access. Next, this has been extended to a block read, leading to BEDO memories (Burst EDO, pipelined EDO memory) and SDRAM (Synchronous DRAM, also pipelined, but designed in a way that gives the ability to work with a higher clock rate). These components work in the range of 66 to 150 MHz. A different approach is proposed by the RamBus company. Its last ICs are driven by a 800 MHz clock frequency [Cri97], an alternative solution being proposed by the SyncLink standard [GV96]. In all these solutions, the memory is accessed through a controller, hiding these variations. With higher levels of non blocking caches (15 outstanding requests for the Ultrasparc III) and multi-banked internal structures of DRAM chips, new memory interfaces will probably be provided in the near future.

A important point to emphasize is linked to the great number of transistors that can be achieved on a chip. In 1997, the most integrated DRAMs had a capacity of 64 Mbits. Considering a classical design, the data width of a chip is one bit, and therefore 32 chips are needed to obtain a 32-bit wide data bus. Thus, the capacity of a memory bank is 256 MBytes. This minimum memory size does not correspond to the market need. For this reason, DRAMs are built in various packages, with data bus sizes of 1, 4, 8, or 16 bits. Using a unique memory controller, it is then possible to build memories with capacities varying from some megabytes to some gigabytes without complex decoding logic. In the next future, chips will have a capacity between 256-Mbit and 1-Gbit. Data busses will probably be enlarged from current 64 bits to 128 bits. In some sense, this evolution of capacity grows in the opposite direction of the needs, as the only way to increase the bandwidth at constant access time is to set independent memory banks, which would lead to huge capacity far beyond the needs. Most of the time, the memory associated to one processor is composed of a single memory bank accessed through a single controller. Enlarging the bus to a cache block size is often the way chosen to get the maximum bandwidth. But note that the huge internal bandwidth of DRAM chips is not well exploited.

3.3 The Memory Hierarchy

The processor clock frequency raises up continuously. The L1 cache has an access time consistent with the clock period of the processor. This situation will last only if the cache size remains low (8-16K) because an increase of the cache size leads to a higher access time [JW93]. The only way to tolerate this latency is to access the cache in two or more pipelined cycles. The increase of the cache size has also an impact on the virtual to real address translation mechanism. Using a real cache, the directory access can be done in parallel with the TLB access only if the depth of a cache bank is less or equal to a page size. To get a better latency, the external L2 cache is now working synchronously with the processor clock, giving the availability of a tighter timing, but at a lower rate linked to the system bus. The frequency of this system bus increases more slowly than the processor frequency, first because of hard constraints on bus design (power consumption of drivers, voltage swings, signals reflections,...) and also because memory components which are connected to this system bus do not have the performance needed to work at full bandwidth. For example, an L2 cache asynchronous SRAM does a cache block transfer in a 3-2-2-2 cycles at 66 MHz, while a synchronous burst does it in a 2-1-1-1 cycles. At 100 MHz, this transfer takes 3-2-2-2 cycles for the burst DRAM and only the use of a pipelined synchronous SRAM can keep this transfer in a 3-1-1-1 cycles scheme. The system bus frequency is also used to drive transfers between the L2 cache and the main memory, which has also moved to be synchronous, with burst and pipelined data transfers. This explains the reason why the system architecture has moved from a shared bus structure as presented on Fig. 3.1a to a more centralized management of main memory accesses as presented on Fig. 3.1b.

3.4 Virtual Memory

A virtual memory system is needed to hide physical memory space limitation and to provide a mechanism to share and protect data among users. The best way to manage data sharing is to provide a segmented memory. A segment is a piece of information (code or data) of any size which is considered as a whole, from a sharing or protection point of view. Each segment is described by a descriptor. Every user has a table recording the set of segments he can reach. Two or more users share segments through descriptors with different access attributes. Active segments are pointed out through hardware registers. The two main systems can be found in INTEL [AS95] and PowerPC [IM94] (in fact derived from IBM) microprocessors. The first has a 32-bit logical address (with a direct access to 16K segments), and the second a 48-bit logical address (with a direct access to 16 segments). The former size will probably be not enough for future applications, even though segments can be managed per set, as in earlier systems. To overcome the physical memory size limitation, segments are loaded on a fixed page size base in memory. The maximum physical memory size is given by the size of the address bus. As internal registers are becoming 64 bits wide, addresses may have a width of up to 64 bits. Therefore the size of the address bus is in the range of 32 bits (early systems, no more adequate) to 64 bits (far beyond the current need).

The mechanism of address translation from logical to physical is based on page tables. To limit the tables size, two mechanisms are used: the tables are themselves paged, and a search is done through successive page tables accesses, or a hashing function is applied first to the logical address to limit its size, successive searches being also done to find the corresponding right table entry. All these memory accesses for table searches are strongly reduced by caching these tables in the processor, in the so-called TLB (Translation Look-aside Buffer). Very few entries are necessary to get a good hit ratio. For example, 64 entries to 4K pages lead to 256KB of direct information access, corresponding to a measured hit ratio of about 0.99.

3.5 Cache - Virtual Memory Interferences

A processor supplies virtual addresses. The TLB must be sought to find the corresponding physical addresses. This seek can be avoided if the L1 cache is placed in the virtual address space. This solution is of less use nowadays because a user tag must be added at each entry of the directory, as two identical virtual addresses can lead to different physical addresses and also because, in the case of data sharing, all aliasing entries of the directory must be known in order to avoid the load of shared data cache blocks in different cache places. This problem has non trivial solutions [Wu93]. With a cache in the real address space, the TLB must be sought for every access, but this seek can be done in parallel with the cache directory check, as long as address bits are the same in the two spaces, i.e. the page address bits.

4. Memory Consistency and Memory Coherency

4.1 Memory Consistency

When a programmer writes a program for a uniprocessor system, he intuitively assumes a logical memory access model. The memory is for him the only visible place for data, where reading a memory cell will always return the last data written to this memory cell, of course according to the order defined by the program. Moving from a uniprocessor to a multiprocessor system leads naturally to consider the same logical memory access model, i.e. each memory data read returns the last data written into this variable. As much it is easy to define "the last value written" in a uniprocessor system, given by the program order, as much it is difficult to give a precise meaning to this idea in a multiprocessor environment. Processors all compete for main memory, and for several executions of a program the memory access patterns can be different although two sequential accesses issued from the same processor and given by program order occur in this order. A memory consistency model has been defined, which tells to the programmer the way the memory system reacts. Guaranteeing the order of accesses given by the program and for each processor, is quite easy if the memory has only one entry point [AG96]. Memory accesses are automatically queued and processed in FIFO: two successive memory operations in a program are managed in this order by the memory. This also means that a new memory operation is engaged only when the previous one has completed, the temporal observing point being placed at each processor: a memory operation appears as atomic and is seen by all processors at the same time. This principle of access sequence and atomicity of operations cannot guarantee the relative order of accesses between the processors, as from one execution to the other, even with identical sets of data, memory interleaving accesses can be different (due to processors clock skew, program interruptions, memory access arbitration, latency of the memory access network,...). It is therefore mandatory that the parallel program gives correct results in all the interleaving possible schemes, which induce to take care of the validity of some access schemes to variables, as summarised by Lamport [Lam79] in his definition of the memory consistency model, called sequential consistency: "The sequential consistency model requires that the result of any execution is the same as if the operations of all processors were executed in some sequential order, and the operation of each processor were executed in the order specified in the program".

Consider the following example:

	P1	P2
Initial values: A=B=0		
(a)	A = 1	print B
(b)	B = 2	print A

In sequential consistency, if the printing of B gives 2, then the printing of A must give 1. Indeed, if the memory has only one entry point and if writes on A and B have been made in this order by P1, then P2 must necessary find A to be 1 if B has the value 2. If the memory is composed of multiple banks, A and B being not in the same banks, and if the memory access network is able to proceed more than one request at a time, then print B can occur after print A (network collision) and P2 will read the older value of A and the new value of B. To solve this problem and find again the sequential consistency, the print A instruction must appear to all processors as being made before the print B instruction. This means that the order of accesses done by a processor must be seen by all the other processors in that order. This has important consequences and may prohibit some usual uniprocessor optimisations: sequentiality is respected as soon as data and control dependencies are maintained, i.e. the program order in case of execution of two operations on a same memory cell or when one controls the execution of the other. Maintaining theses dependencies leads to the following optimisations:

– at compile time: register allocation, code reordering, loop transformations,
– at execution time: pipelining, multiple instructions initiation, bypass write buffers, overlapping write buffers, non-blocking caches.

This does not mean that these optimisations should no more be used, but that they must be used carefully. Problems are set only when shared data are read and written concurrently by processes executed in parallel on the processors. Relaxed consistency models have been proposed which permit, under some conditions, the use of the above optimisations. These models will be presented later. In the following discussion, only sequential consistency will be considered.

4.2 Memory Coherency

The presence of caches in a multiprocessor environment sets another problem as caches hold duplicated data from main memory.

Let us first consider only one level of cache, each processor having its own cache. When a processor encounters a read miss in its cache, a copy of the block holding the requested data is brought in the cache from the memory. As another processor can access the same block of data, this block will be duplicated in more than one cache. If a processor executes a write and changes the content of that data in its cache, then the other copies (in other caches and in memory) of this data are stale. If the cache implements a write-through strategy, then the data is written in its cache and in the main memory: the cached copies remain stale. It is then necessary either to execute the write in all caches at the same time, or to execute the write locally in the cache and, at the same time, invalidate all copies in all other caches, the main memory update depending on the strategy used: write-through or copy back. The relative performance of each strategy is program dependent, and even though some combining mechanisms have been proposed [EK89] or implemented in commercial machines [SFG+93], the invalidation-based protocol is generally adopted, and we will only consider this option.

Our previous statement "At the same time" needs further explanation. It can effectively be at the same "physical" time, or at the same "logical" time. It is obvious that such an operation as an invalidation in all caches cannot be instantaneous and so a loss of performance can only be avoided by doing it in a logical time.

Observing the different steps to execute a shared data update is enough to be aware of this fact. First, a write request is issued from the processor to its cache. The latter sends an invalidation request to all other caches. This, at the processor scale, lasts some clock cycles. To be informed of the end of this operation, an acknowledge from each cache must be waited for. Then, the write can finally be completed. It must be noticed that an invalidation request can also be issued for this data at the same "physical" time by another cache: it is then necessary to sequencialize these requests, so that the first can effectively do its write and the second and eventually following requests on the same data change their write requests in write miss requests, as this data is no longer present in their caches, being invalidated in the mean time. The way the order is set depends on the kind of architecture. In a shared-bus multiprocessor, requests to the memory are serialised by the bus, and this fact is naturally exploited to order coherency requests and leads to a family of specific algorithms called *snoopy protocols*. In all other cases the serialising mechanism is set at the memory level (this can also be applied to shared-bus architectures). If the latter is composed of independent banks, each of them manages the coherency of its own data. This second class of algorithms are known as *directory protocols*. TLBs are also involved in data coherency. But, as segment and page tables can only be changed by the Operating System, a lighter protocol can be set to keep these specialized caches coherent.

4.3 Memory Coherency vs. Memory Consistency

As previously mentioned, having several caches in a multiprocessor leads to the presence of multiple copies of the same data. These copies are not awkward as long as none of them is modified. In the case of a write, accesses to all of them are locked in order to do, at the same time, either a data update, or a data invalidation. This is a part of the duty of the data coherency algorithm. "At the same time" indicates that the write is seen simultaneously by all the processors and that every following read of this data will return the same value. This means that:

- a write is seen "globally" by all processors,
- two successive writes to a **same** address are seen in this order by all the processors.

These conditions are not sufficient to guarantee the sequential consistency. Coherency guarantees that writes to a **same** address appear to all processors to have occurred in the same order. Consistency guarantees that all writes to **any** address appear to all processors to have occurred in the same order.

4.4 Relaxed Memory Consistency Models

Constraints on memory operation order not only specifies how memory accesses have to be done (in fact have to appear to be done) at execution time, but also how they have to be done at compile time, according to the consistency model. This last point has an important drawback, as it restricts many performance optimisations done by uniprocessor compilers.

For the first point, i.e. at execution time, sequential consistency implies that a processor must wait for an access to complete before issuing the next one. So a processor can execute only non-memory instructions during the time the memory access is being serviced. This conducts to a low overlapping as memory references are on an average done by one instruction out of three [HP96]. As seen in the first paragraph of this chapter, out-of-order execution processors use lookahead buffers. Instructions are inserted in order in this buffer, executed out-of-order from this buffer, and retired in program order from this buffer, the latter point enabling the possibility to make memory operation visible in program order. Speculative execution enables speculative read at a low implementation cost. The read is done prior the knowledge of its validity, and checked further : if not correct, the computation is rolled back. This trick is obviously not possible to implement for write operations, due to the difficulty to recover modified data. Recent processors implement this mechanism (Pentium Pro [Pap96] for example).

For the second point, i.e. at compile time, a *weak consistency model* has been first proposed [DSB86]. It is based on the fact that parallel programs use synchronisation mechanisms to co-ordinate their operations. Between two synchronisation operations, data accesses can be reordered so as to do usual optimisations. At these synchronisation points, special instructions are placed which prevent the execution of a new instruction until all memory reads and writes are completed. The *release consistency model* [Gha90] enhances the weak consistency model by making some distinctions among the synchronisation operations, which are divided in acquire and release operations. Reads and writes which precede the acquire can be overlapped with the memory operations being placed after the acquire but with the condition that the read corresponding to the acquire be first succeeded before doing any following memory operation. A symmetric analysis can be made at the release instruction, the latter corresponding to a write.

5. Bus-Based Shared-Memory Multiprocessors

A uniprocessor as presented on Fig. 3.1 comprises a memory hierarchy nowadays generally built with an internal level 1 cache, an internal or external level 2 cache and lastly with the main memory shared by the processor and the peripherals through an I/O bus. A second processor can be added, in default of being integrated in the chip itself, either at the second level of cache, the latter being external, or at the main memory level. Giving the high performance of current processors, and therefore the high pressure made on the second-level cache, having more than one processor on a second-level cache is unrealistic today. Thus, each processor has its own two levels of caches and the connection of several processors is made at the main memory level. A processor module is then composed of a processor with its two levels of caches, an optional level of main memory, and of optional I/O resources, both being private to the processor. In this context, additional I/O modules must also be provided to be shared by all processors modules. Processor modules and I/O modules are all connected to one or more memory modules through a network. If all these elements are placed on a same printed board, then we get a non-evolutive system and the interconnection network is generally a shared bus. Due to limited area, this kind of inexpensive multiprocessor is limited to two or four processors. Increasing its size needs a different packaging organisation. The shared bus is printed on a board located at the rear of a rack, connecting modules (processors, I/O, memory) plugged in the rack. The shared bus is the simplest network we can think about. Due to its limited and fixed bandwidth, the number of processors can only grow up to a few dozens. However, it is of common use because it exhibits interesting properties (see Section 5.1). To increase further the number of processors, other kinds of networks must be considered.

5.1 Snoopy Protocols

The shared bus can be used to maintain the coherency of data in caches in a simple way. Each read or write request sent by a processor to the main memory goes through the shared bus and can be "seen" by all the other processors: each of them can check its own cache to see if it is concerned by this request and has to engage a coherency action. At first sight, it seems that only a write request can lead to a coherency action as, in this case, all processors, but the one issuing the request, must invalidate the copy of the data residing in their caches, if we consider an invalidation protocol. But, the processor owning the only up-to-date copy of a data must also answer to a read or write request for this data by sending this data from its cache. Last, another special case arises when a processor issues a read miss and, some time after, wants to write this shared data. According to the invalidation protocol, all the other copies must be invalidated before. An invalidation request must be sent through the shared bus, which is the only path between all processors.

We can notice that, if the shared bus has separate address and data busses, a processor requesting a data invalidation may put the data address on the address bus and at the same time place the new data on the data bus, in order to update the main memory while invalidating the copies in the other caches. Following local writes to this data can therefore be performed locally. This mechanism was the first published snoopy protocol [Goo83]. This algorithm is called "write once" because of this double action: invalidation of the copies and main memory updating. However, since the main memory has a cycle time far longer than the cache cycle, the write once memory update is not very efficient. This fact has led to various algorithms, presented in a uniform way for the first time in [AB89].

The most common algorithm currently in use was published by researchers from the University of Illinois [PP84] and is known under the name of Illinois protocol or MESI protocol, the second one being the acronym for the four possible states of a cache block (Modified, Exclusive, Shared, Invalid). This protocol can be found in most current processors (Pentium, PowerPC, MIPS R10000,...).

5.2 The MESI Protocol

Data handled by processors are of various sizes and, obviously, it would be desirable to maintain the coherency for each shared variable. However, the coherency problem is due to the presence of caches and the data transferred between the main memory and caches have a fixed size: a data block or cache line. Thus, it is quite natural (and simpler) to maintain state information at the block level. However, different data modified by different processes can be in a same block. Thus, only a part of the block should be concerned by this coherency action. This problem, known as false sharing, gets harder as block sizes are steadily widening. It can be solved by software, by taking care of data placement, or by hardware, by adding a bit for each word in the block descriptor in order to check coherency at the word level instead of the block level.

In a copy-back uniprocessor cache, each block directory entry has two state bits: the V bit that specifies if the block is valid and the M bit that is set when the block has been locally modified. In a multiprocessor environment, these two bits can be used to code the four following states.

- M (Modified): this block is the only up-to-date copy in the system,
- E (Exclusive): this block is the only cached copy and is identical to the copy of the main memory,
- S (Shared): this block is present in one or more caches,
- I (Invalid): this cache entry is free.

State transitions are described by the state diagram on Fig. 5.1.

This algorithm makes the hypothesis that a shared SHD line exists on the shared bus, connected in a hardwired OR manner to all processors: this line is set if at least one processor drives it. The hardwired OR gives the ability for more than one processor to drive it. So, when a block is loaded in a cache, the state transition is from I to E if the SHD line is not set, and I to S in the opposite case. After an I to E state transition, a later write will involve a state transition from E to M without any coherency action. If a read is observed on the bus for the same block, then a transition from E to S will be fired and the SHD line set. If the block is in the S state, then an invalidation transaction will take place before a write, associated with the S to M transition. When a requested block is present in another cache in the M state, it is possible to make a direct transfer from cache to cache. However, this possibility renders the shared bus implementation more complex and is thus not in use in current multiprocessors. In this case, the shared bus has an additional line (ARTRY: Address ReTRY). The owner of the dirty block (M state) sets this line, which forces the requestor to delay its request and frees the bus. The owner of the block then flushes the dirty block, marked S. If the request is a read, the block is marked S in both caches. If it is a write, the block state becomes I in the previously owning cache and the new copy is marked M. One should notice that the S state does not necessarily mean that a block is shared by at least two processors: for capacity reasons, a block frame may be freed and the block state is locally moved from S to I. This state transition does not need any coherency action and is unnoticed by the other caches. This has obviously no effect on the data coherency.

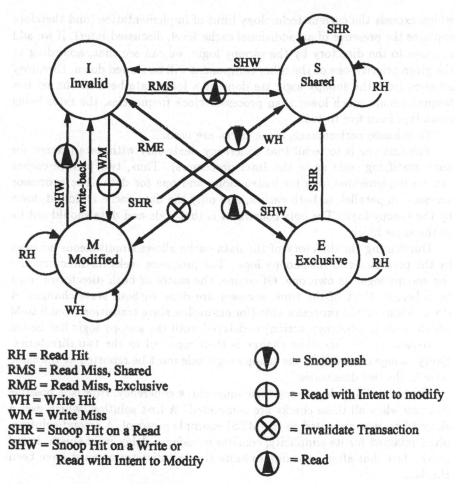

RH = Read Hit
RMS = Read Miss, Shared
RME = Read Miss, Exclusive
WH = Write Hit
WM = Write Miss
SHR = Snoop Hit on a Read
SHW = Snoop Hit on a Write or
      Read with Intent to Modify

= Snoop push

= Read with Intent to modify

= Invalidate Transaction

= Read

Fig. 5.1. MESI diagram represented as a state automata.

5.3 Implementation Constraints

Up to now, we have supposed that each processor was equipped with only one level of cache and that a coherency action was held in the bus cycle. Let us examine implications of these assumptions on the cache and on the shared bus. A cache is located between the processor and the bus. It is accessed on one side by the processor, which seeks the directory and accesses the cache itself, and by the snoopy logic on the other side which only seeks the directory. To set the problem, we will take the example of a current superscalar processor with a 200 MHz clock frequency (quite lower end processor nowadays...), which corresponds to a 5-nanosecond clock period. In each clock cycle, the processor accesses its cache to get instructions and read or write data. So, every 5 nanoseconds, the cache is accessed one or several times by the processor, which exceeds the current technology limit of implementation (and therefore explains the presence of an additional cache level, discussed later). If we add accesses to the directory by the snoopy logic, we can see that, according to the given priority, one or the other component will be slowed down. Directory accesses from the snoopy logic are done at a lower rate because shared bus frequencies are much lower than processor clock frequencies, the ratio being nowadays from five to ten.

To enhance performance, some tricks are used.

The first one is to recall that coherency deals only with data (except for auto-modifying code as in the Intel processors). Thus, two private caches can be implemented, one for instructions and one for data. The processor accesses, in parallel, to both caches, and only the data cache is slowed down by the snoopy logic. The only constraint is that code and data should not be in the same block.

Duplicating the directory of the data cache allows simultaneous accesses by the processor and the snoopy logic. The processor seeks its directory and the snoopy logic its own one. Of course, the states of both directories must be coherent. Most of the time, accesses are done without state changes. A state change on the processor side (for example a state transition from S to M which needs a coherency action) is delayed until the snoopy logic has issued its request on the bus. The change is then reported in the two directories. Every change observed on the snoopy logic side must be reported at the same time in the two directories.

Within a bus cycle, snoopy logic must check coherency. How is it possible to know when all these checks are completed? A first solution, which uses a shared line, was presented in the MESI example protocol. A second solution, often retained for its simplicity, consists in using a delay mechanism, based on the fact that after a maximum finite time all directories must have been checked.

The coherency result must normally be known before each operation: the cache holding the updated copy must provide the data, directly or through the memory. A usual enhancement is to start the main memory read at the beginning of the cycle, and to continue or abort the access depending on the coherency result. This is obviously only possible for reads which, fortunately, are the most frequent.

Is it still possible to enhance the performance of the cache and of the shared bus? The answer for the cache is known and goes through the setting of a hierarchy of caches. For the bus, a well known mechanism is used which consists in separating address and data phases. It was early used to provide concurrent accesses to independent memory banks, and is now necessary to exploit the non blocking caches of current processors. These two points will be developed in the next paragraphs.

Multi-Level Caches. Almost all current processors have a L1 internal cache (the HP-PA8000 is the exception, with a big external cache) and a L2 external cache (internal for the DEC Alpha 21164 [ERP+95], but with an external L3 cache).

We will here only deal with two levels of cache. The L1 cache operates in such a way that its content is always a subset of the contents of the L2 cache, but there is no guarantee that a block has the same value in the two levels, as a write can be done in L1 cache without being immediately reported to L2 cache in case of a copy-back strategy. Nevertheless, the state of the block is the same in the two levels, as the write can only be done if the block is marked E or M in the two levels. This in fact suffices to maintain data coherency which can be maintained by seeking only the L2 directory. Nevertheless, in case of a block state change, the new state must be reported in the two levels. In case of a block flush, modified data from the L1 cache have first to be written back in the L2 cache before doing the flush to memory and the state block is marked as I or S. As the L2 block size can be greater than that of L1 (bigger caches leads to higher block sizes), this write-back can take some cycles. This is avoided if the strategy between the two caches is write-through. In this way, the L1 appears as a subset of L2. This inclusion property is not sufficient to guarantee coherency, but necessary conditions are well known and presented in [BW88]. Moreover, coherency actions can be sent to the various cache levels without precise inclusion respect, at the expense of a higher complexity. Multilevel caches can be maintained coherently provided some rules are respected. But they have a benefit effect on the load of the corresponding directories. Indeed, the L1 directory is used most of the time by the processor and sometimes by the L2 cache, (only when a state change has to be reported), whereas the L2 directory is mainly used by the snoopy logic and sometimes by the L1 cache (in case of a state change request). This looks like the directory duplication mechanism studied above.

As coherency actions deal with the various cache levels, the question now set is to know if bus cycles are not getting longer. Up to now, we have considered atomic transactions on the shared-bus : the bus is busy for the complete memory operation i.e. from address setting up to data sampling. This time can be measured and correspond to a real or "physical" time. We will now see how a "logical" time can enhance the shared bus performance.

Split Bus. A complete transaction (i.e. a block read or write with coherency check) carried out in a single bus cycle permits us to define a strong order on the memory accesses and to define coherent states for the blocks.

A block read is composed first by an arbitration phase, followed by an address transfer phase during which the coherency is checked, then by a data transfer phase which includes waiting time for the main memory. This last phase is the longest in time, and can be slightly reduced by starting the memory access during the address transfer phase.

A block write starts in the same way, but the data transfer phase can start just after the address phase (in the case of an address/data multiplexed bus) or at the same time (with separate address and data busses) as there is no coherency to check: a write is issued by the only node owning the block. In this way, the multi-banked memory is under-used: operations overlapping occurs only in case of a read just followed by a write in a different bank. To get a better use of the banks, it is necessary to dissociate the address transfer phase from the data transfer phase. This supposes that the address bus and the data bus are more or less independent, and gives the ability to have more than one memory access in progress at the same time. To get a good level of performance, it is necessary to place an address queue ahead the main memory, as the arrival frequency of addresses can be greater than the data block transfer frequency, which thus requires a flow control mechanism. This solution is not optimal as two successive addresses can concern the same memory bank and stall the queue: it is therefore better to place a queue in front of each bank. This leads to the possibility of two blocks being returned in the opposite order of their requests. This adds an other level of complexity. How is it now possible to get the coherency maintained in the caches? The important matter is to guarantee an order on the block accesses. Sending addresses sequentially guarantees this order. However, a coherency action can lead to a block state change or to a block flush, which can effectively take place only if the block is in the cache. As a delay now exists between the address transfer and the data return, each cache must record all transactions in progress during these two events. Indeed, a request appearing on the address bus can concern a data block which has just been requested, so the corresponding transaction is already in progress (the data part has not yet been seen on the data bus). It is necessary to get some flow control on requests for the same block. This can be done in the source node, by using state information about the requested block in order to delay the next request on that block until it has reached the new owner. This can also be done in the destination node: the future new owner of the block records the request so as to flush the block to the next owner as soon as possible. In the first case we have to record state information about the recent past and in the second case to record state information about the near future. The length of the time slice concerned is fixed by the lengths of the buffers recording this information. They must be associative as each new request must be compared to all the ones in progress.

Multiple Buses. In a shared-bus architecture, it is possible to handle separately addresses and data. The serialisation property of accesses and the coherency check by snoopy protocols can exclusively be tied to the address bus. Data transfers can be done using various networks, from the simplest bus which can be enlarged up to a cache block size (with strong practical problems: connectors size, current flow on drivers,...), to a crossbar solution as in Bull ESCALA or IBM G30 or SUN Enterprise 10000, where multiple data transfers can occur simultaneously. In this case, the shared address bus becomes again the upper limit that has to be overcome in order to get a higher bandwidth. It is then possible to use two or more address busses for, in the example of two busses, assigning to one of them odd addresses and to the other even addresses, or to use any other address space partition, dedicating for example one bus per memory bank. Taking into account practical bus frequencies and cache directory seek times, the pressure on the cache from snoopy logic remains tolerable for up to few busses. The problem is now data consistency, which can be solved by defining a logic order of accesses over the multiple physical accesses in progress at the same time. This multiple bus solution has been used in Sun SparcCenter 2000 , with two identical XBbus, in the Cray CS6400 with four identical busses, and in the Enterprise 10000 with four address busses (one per memory bank) and a crossbar for data.

5.4 Examples

The rapid evolution of needs can be shown through analysis of the characteristics of the latest shared-bus systems, as presented in Fig. 5.2. We can see that the address bus has been kept shared in order to maintain the data coherency through snoopy protocols, and that the enhancements mainly concerned the data paths, evolving from private busses between processors and the main memory to a crossbar switch playing a central role in the system. This enables blocks to flow directly from one cache to another. A good example of current SMPs is the SGI Challenge.

SGI Challenge. The shared bus, called Powerpath-2, is a sixteen-slot non-multiplexed bus which can be populated with up to nine processor boards (with four R4400 or two R8000 per board), up to four memory boards and I/O boards. The clock frequency of the bus is 47.5 MHz, but an address transaction needs 5 bus cycles: one to start an arbitration phase, one for arbitration resolution, one to send the address, one to check the coherency and finally one for the acknowledgement of this coherency check. When idle, the bus only loops on the two first states. As the address bus size is 40 bits, the address space is 1 Terabyte. A memory board contains two banks of 512-bit-wide DRAM memory. The size of each bank depends on technology, currently of 1 Gigabyte. The data bus is 256 bits wide. As a cache block is 128 bytes wide, it can be read in two memory cycles and sent over the bus in four cycles. So a data transaction occupies the bus also for five cycles, as one bus cycle is used as a turn-around time for a new master to drive the lines. Addresses and data transactions are synchronized. Up to eight reads can be in progress. Each processor records in a buffer the history of these requests. So, an adapted Illinois MESI protocol can be used, as each processor can snoop the address and the data busses. A request related to a block found in the buffer and therefore being in progress is delayed until the data is seen on the bus. So transactions with regard to the same block are serialised giving a "logical" atomicity to a transaction.

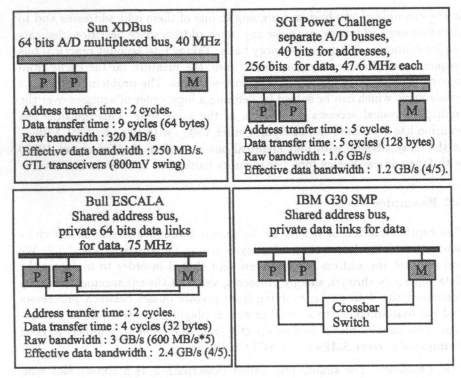

Fig. 5.2. Characteristics of some commercial SMPs.

6. Non Bus-Based Shared-Memory Multiprocessors

As soon as we consider a non-shared bus solution, we are faced with the data coherency problem with a new dimension: if the multiprocessor is composed of hundreds or thousands of processors, how is it possible to maintain data coherency through all caches? On recent multiprocessors, a processor node is generally itself a symmetric multiprocessor, managing a part of the main memory, and is equipped with an interface logic being in charge of the interface between the processors and the main memory on one hand and between the main memory and the network on the other hand, as shown on Fig. 6.1. For the sake of simplicity we will suppose that each node has only one processor. The latter does memory accesses using load and store, some of them being local, other being remote, while the interface logic provides the requested access in a hidden manner. This interface logic must also answer distant requests issued by other nodes in the system while being in operation progress for local requests.

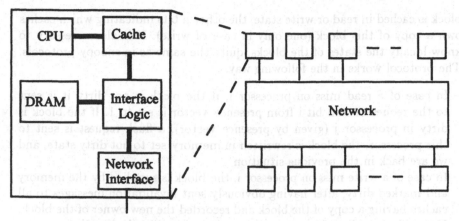

Fig. 6.1. General architecture of NUMA machines.

6.1 Software vs. Hardware Coherence Checking

A first solution to handle the coherency problem is to leave it to the software level. The latter is then faced with a twofold problem: it must distribute data over all the local memories, and try to guess which are private and which are shared. We distinguish four data types: private and local, private and remote, shared and local, shared and remote. Data of the first type can obviously be cached. Data of the second type can also be cached if the interface logic is able to handle cache block transfer. Caching shared data is much more complex as data have to be remain coherent. If the processor instruction set implements single block flush instructions, block flush instructions from the same page, or whole cache flush instructions, then data can be temporally cached. To mark data as cacheable or non cacheable is done in an easy way by the Memory Management Unit (MMU), as each page descriptor has a bit for this purpose. Maintaining data coherency when a read or write is no longer seen by all processors requires a different approach. In snoopy protocols, each processor keeps in real time up to date information about data present in its cache. An initial copy comes always from memory. This observation suggest another solution which is to record and update the state of all blocks dispatched in all caches at the memory level. Various solutions are available, all known under the generic name of "directory protocol".

6.2 Directory-Based Cache Coherence

To each memory block is associated a set of state information. If we still consider an invalidation strategy, as a block may have many copies to be read but only one for writing, the simplest way to record these events is to associate a presence state vector of n+1 bits at each block, n being the number of processors [CF78]. The n+1th bit is the dirty bit indicating whether the block is cached in read or write state, the other n bits indicating which caches own a copy of this block (one only in case of write). It is also necessary to know locally the states of the blocks, quite the same as in snoopy protocols. The protocol works in the following way.

- In case of a read miss on processor i, if the block is not dirty it is sent to the requestor and bit i from presence vector is set to 1. If the block is dirty in processor j (given by presence vector), a flush request is sent to this processor, the block is rewritten in memory, set to not dirty state, and we are back in the previous situation.
- In case of a write miss on processor i, the block is supplied by the memory and marked dirty, after having obviously sent invalidation messages to all caches having a copy of the block and recorded the new owner of the block. If the block is dirty in some cache, a procedure identical to the previous case is followed.
- A write to a clean block in a cache must be preceded by a request to the memory, which permits the write after copies invalidation.

This solution has the drawback that it needs many bits per block and therefore is not scalable. An opposite solution is to record the state of the block by only two bits : no copy dispatch, copy or copies in clean state, copy in dirty state. As block copy locations are no longer known, the ability to broadcast messages must be provided in order to invalidate copies or flush a dirty block. Broadcast of messages can lead quickly to network saturation. A mixed solution is possible as measures have shown that a block is most of the time present in only few caches. p fields of $Log_2 n$ bits can be simply added to the two states bits, the fourth state being now "dispatched in more than p caches". As places of copies of block caches are known up to p, invalidation are done most of the time by at most p individual messages and sometimes by a broadcast message when the number of copies exceed p.

Another interesting approach is to set a linked list for each block, which starts from the memory and goes from cache to cache. For each block, the memory records the name of the last requestor. On a read miss, the block is returned with the name of this last requestor. The memory then updates the corresponding list entry with the name of this new last requestor. An invalidation starts from memory and goes down from cache to cache. A flush request is done immediately. This attractive solution has a shortcoming: if a block belonging to a chain must be flushed for capacity reasons, upstream blocks must be invalidated. A solution to this drawback is to set a double chained list, so as to build the chain over the flushed block. This approach is the basis of the coherency protocol for the IEEE 1596 SCI standard (Scalable Coherent Interface) [Gus92]. A survey of hardware approaches to cache coherence in shared-memory multiprocessors can be found in [TM194, TM294].

7. From Physically-Shared to Logically-Shared Address Space

In the previous sections, we have considered physically-shared memory multiprocessors, where memory is accessed through load and store instructions. Each node must include a specific network interface with buffers to queue messages from remote nodes (requests and answers) and logic to control specific actions, e.g. data coherency management. With this hardware, the whole system can have a unique operating system (OS) which manages all the data structures distributed among the different nodes.

The diametrically opposite solution is to consider a set of workstations interconnected by a standard network, like Ethernet. Only few performance enhancements are possible if standard hardware and software is used. Processes working on different computers can only communicate (data transfers and control messages) through standard I/O routines which drive normalised interfaces. Each system is independent and has a limited knowledge of the exact current state of the whole set of computers. Data exchanged between computers are information blocks, generally of fixed size for control and of variable size for data. The data transfers are controlled through I/O communication routines.

On top of such distributed architectures, both the message-passing and the shared-memory programming models can be implemented.

- Under the message passing model, the programmer is responsible for distributing the data among the nodes and for explicitly controlling the data transfers between the nodes. This typically involves SEND and RECEIVE operations (that respectively send data through the network to a remote node, and accept data coming in from a distant node). Such primitives are available in packages designed for managing sets of computers, like PVM or MPI. When such an operation is invoked, the operating system is in charge of managing the emission onto the network of appropriate messages (request, answer, acknowledgement...) according to the underlying communication protocol.
- If the shared-memory model is supported (this is called DSM: Distributed Shared Memory), the programmer uses simple LOAD/STORE-like operations. The primitives for allocating and accessing memory can be available as library functions (e.g. IVY, Mermaid), as OS calls (e.g. Mirage) or as instructions of a dedicated programming language (e.g. Linda, Orca). Whenever the data is not present in the node local memory, these operations must be converted into messages to remote nodes. The shared-memory model is usually implemented through virtual memory: in case of a page-fault in the local memory, the handler generates the appropriate messages to retrieve the page from a remote memory.

An overview of DSM concepts and systems can be found in [PTM96].

How ever the communication is expressed (SEND/RECEIVE primitives under the message-passing model or LOAD/STORE operations under the shared-memory paradigm), the objective is to transfer a block of data from the user memory space of one system to the user memory space of another system. The sequence of operations is then the following.

- Data are copied from the user space to the system space, both in the local memory, for protection purposes.
- Data are copied from the local memory to the network interface, where a variable size buffer is allocated to keep some words or all the words of the packet to be send.
- The packet is sent over the network.
- The packet is buffered in the network interface at the destination node, and then transferred into the system space in the memory of that node.
- The data is then copied from the system memory space to the user memory space.

Each of these points is critical and must be analysed separately.

7.1 Data Copying from the User Space to the System Space

Whenever a SEND is executed by a process, the operating system verifies the request validity, copies the data to be transferred from the process space to a buffer in the system space (in a buffer queue), and frees the process, for which the SEND seems completed. When a RECEIVE is executed, the OS seeks for an available message in the reception queue of the process. If a message has arrived, it is copied from this system buffer to the user space and the process is freed; otherwise, the process is blocked until the the message arrives. Non-blocking mechanisms can be implemented using receive queue checking primitives.

7.2 Data Copying from the System Space to the Network Interface

The OS is supposed to keep sufficient free memory space to be able to receive messages permanently. Two communication modes can be defined: either a message is simply sent (asynchronous mode), which assumes that the receiver is always ready to receive messages, or a preliminary negotiation is initiated to prepare the transfer (synchronous mode) and to make sure that the receiver is ready. This negotiation is transparent to the network interface, which only executes DMA transfers. There must be at least one DMA channel for each transfer direction, each executing a sequence of commands. These commands represent global transfers or successive partial transfers, depending on the possibility for the interface to work in the virtual space. Even in a uniprocessor system, data coherency is maintained between the I/O interface and the processor. If the interface is not able to manage data coherency, then the OS has to flush all the cache lines containing the data to be transferred before the effective transfer (it must also set a lock to prevent the data to come back into the cache before the end of the transfer). For each received message, an interrupt is raised and the OS eventually signals a blocked process and frees the message buffer.

7.3 Network Interface

The network interface sends data according to the network protocol. In case of workstations, this protocol can be, for example, Ethernet or ATM. In case of a more specific design, the interface can be involved in message routing and/or flow control, in a relatively simple way as in SCI or in a more complex one like in the nCUBE/2 systems.

7.4 Examples

The three points just slightly developed can lead to a more or less sophisticated design. As interactions between levels are overlapped, there exists a great number of possible implementations, and the overview of some current representative systems will show the trends.

Myrinet. Myrinet [BCF+95] is probably the most currently used system to interconnect workstations or PCs. Each computer system must be equipped with a Network Interface Card (NIC) plugged on a PCI bus (or S-bus for Sparc systems, but is less efficient). This card permits to connect the system to a switch using an 18-wire cable with a working frequency of 100 MHz, leading to a bi-directional link of about 160 MB/s (8 bits plus parity in each direction). A switch can have 2, 4 or 8 ports, and a message goes from the source to the destination through a set of switches using a wormhole routing strategy, the header of the message containing the address of the successive switches of the path. The NIC card contains its own processor for an intelligent flow control of messages between the system and the network, a local memory and three DMA engines, one for data transfers between the main memory of the node and the local memory, and one for each direction for data transfers between the local memory and the network. Message queues in each direction are managed by the processor on the NIC card, allowing user processes, under kernel control, to read and write messages directly in the NIC card.

MPC. MPC (for MultiPC) [MPC98] uses high speed serial links to connect PCs together, through a dedicated PCI board. These links are conform to the IEEE 1355 standard: point to point connection, bi-directional and full-duplex 1Gbits per second link. The length of the cable must be under 5 meters, using coaxial cable technology. The PCI board comprises two specific VLSI chips. The first one is a router chip called Rcube, which implements a complete 8*8 cross-bar switch and is automatically in charge of the message routing in a wormhole strategy. Seven out of the eight ports are used to connect the PC to other PCs. The 8th port is available also as a parallel port and is used to connect the router to a second VLSI chip which manages the communication protocol and the PCI interface. It allows copying data directly from the memory of the source node to the memory of the destination without any local temporary copy.

8. Inputs/Outputs in Parallel and Distributed Systems

8.1 Introduction

In the last few years, Inputs/Outputs (I/Os) for parallel and distributed computer systems has attracted strongly attention of both designers and users of computer systems. Indeed, it has become clear that I/O performance may be the limiting factor, rather than CPU performance. To reduce the effect of this limiting factor in future systems, many studies of the I/O bottleneck in parallel and distributed systems have started.

The main question is: on what grounds the I/O subsystem becomes a bottleneck and an increasingly important component of overall system performance?

- First of all, in the few past decades the speeds of CPU have been increasing at a much more rate than the speed of I/O devices which is limited by the speed of mechanical components like disks or tapes. Indeed CPU speeds have been increasing at 50-100% per year, while disk access time has decreased by only about one third in ten years [HP96], and these tendencies will probably remain quantitatively at the same level.
- Second, this speed mismatch is specially accentuated in parallel and distributed computers where the combination of multiple CPUs are used simultaneously. Indeed, this increases computational performance, leaving the I/O as a serial bottleneck that limits scalability [Amd67].
- Finally, many new scientific and commercial application domains like multimedia, graphics, and grand challenge problems such as seismic processing or climate modelling are creating huge volumes of I/O requirements.

8.2 Applications and Requirements of I/Os

Scientific computing with huge sets of data, as can be found in climate modelling, seismic processing [DC94] and databases [BD83], [BDL+85], have been considered as two major application domains where I/O in parallel computer systems has generally been found to be a bottleneck. But for scientific computing, particularly grand challenge problems, the I/O bottleneck effect continues to increase to such an extent that it is now commonly recognized as a serious obstacle [Sha95]. Many scientific applications produce 1GB of I/O per run [CHK+93], and even today some applications perform an order of magnitude more of I/Os per run. A work, developed by Acharya et al [AUB+96], describes an earth-science program (called pathfinder) which performs a total I/O of 28GB per run; other areas of applications such as physics and fluid dynamics are estimated to generate total I/O on the order of 1TB per run [DC94]. It becomes obviously clear that these total I/O requirements will continue to increase more and more and as many as the phenomena will be studied at larger scales and finer resolutions respectively of space and time. The I/O rates required will also continue to increase, since the response time required to obtain computational results must decrease in order to be tolerated by humans. Thus while current applications require I/O rates of tens of MBps for secondary storage, in the near future they will require about 1 GBps [DC94].

In the domain of databases, a similar trend can be seen, particularly for applications such as data mining [DG92]. Today new applications imply large-scale database searches on gigabytes and eventually terabytes of data such as mapping the human genome.

Many new classes of applications, such as image visualisation [Kau94] and multimedia information processing [RR95], are rapidly becoming omnipresent. For example today multimedia information is to be found in nearly, if not all, computing environments [IEE93]. However, throughput requirements needed by multimedia information systems are much higher than traditional computer applications. Furthermore other constraints not found in the traditional applications, such as real-time and synchronized data transfers [AOG93, GVK+95], are also introduced by multimedia information systems. Thus, parallel-I/O architectures must be provided to support the parallel computational architecture.

In the following sections, we will briefly give at first a review of the I/O architecture fundamentals and terminology in the case of a typical uniprocessor architecture, and then an outline of the fundamental issues in parallel-I/O architecture design. Our discussion will be focused on major questions raised by the I/O bottleneck and architectural responses proposed these last few years.

8.3 Review of I/O Architecture Fundamentals and Terminology

Fig. 8.1 shows a typical uniprocessor architecture. The *processor-memory* buses are often proprietary designs (design-specific). They are short, generally high speed and tuned to match the memory system so as to maximize processor-memory bandwidth. On the other hand *I/O buses* are typically based on standard buses such as SCSI or PCI. They can be lengthy and can have different types of devices connected to them such as disks, networks or printers.

Also they have a wide range of data bandwidths related to the devices connected to them. I/O buses do not typically connect directly to the memory, but use a *bus adapter* to bridge the proprietary processor-memory bus and the I/O bus. The connections between specific I/O devices (disk, network, or graphics) to the standard buses are accomplished by *controllers*. The management of the devices at the low-level by interpreting standard I/O commands from the bus are also performed by these controllers. During the design phase, the designer of the CPU board needs only to take into account the availability of an adapter to a standard I/O bus whereas the designer of the device needs only to take into account the availability of a controller to connect to the standard I/O bus. In this way, CPU board vendors need to provide adapters, and device vendors need to provide controllers. Sometimes, devices provide directly a standard I/O interface (such as SCSI bus) by including the controller in their package, for example a SCSI disk.

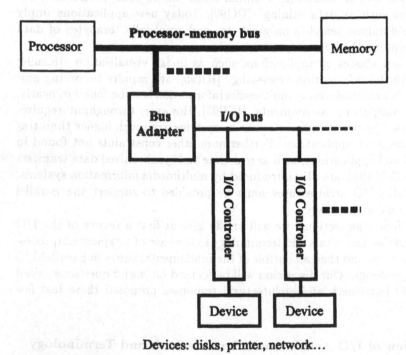

Fig. 8.1. A typical uniprocessor architecture, showing the main components and their interconnections.

If a data transfer from the disk(s) to the memory is needed, the path taken by the data is : from the disk(s) data must flow across the I/O bus, through the bus adapter, across the processor-memory bus, and into the memory. If the same data should then be sent to another processor, the data must flow back out of the memory, across the processor-memory bus, through the bus adapter, across the I/O bus, through the network interface, and across the network. In addition, an in-memory copy may be necessary to restore the data, thus, it may flow through to processor and its cache. Any of these components crossed by data during their transfer from their sources to their destinations may be a bottleneck. In [FCH+96], Feitelson et al. note that the peak I/O bandwidth, in any architecture, is limited by the slowest component. Note also that, because memory and processor-memory bus are used more than once, their bandwidth must be 2 or 4 times the total disk or network bandwidth.

The architectural systems discussed below are based on SIMD (Single Instruction stream, Multiple Data stream) and MIMD (Multiple Instruction stream, Multiple Data stream) machines, such as Maspar MP-2. In the case of the MIMD machines, we distinguish between parallel distributed-memory computers and parallel shared-memory computers. In parallel distributed-memory systems such as nCube/ten or CM-5, a multiple-address-space is used. Indeed each processor (node) has its own private physical address space and the memory is physically distributed. Communication between processors is expressed explicitly by passing messages over an interconnection network. As stated in the previous sections, communication between processors in shared-memory systems (such as SGI Challenge or DEC AlphaServer 2100 for UMAs or KSR 2 for NUMAs) is implicit, because accesses to remote addresses are translated by hardware into messages on the interconnection network. Furthermore, either architecture can support several programming paradigms including shared-memory and message-passing.

In parallel computers we can find up to three node types dedicated and optimized to perform some specialized tasks (functions).

- *Computation nodes:* perform numeric and floating-point calculations, and generally have no local disk except perhaps for paging, booting, and operating-system software,
- *I/O nodes:* contain the system's secondary storage, and provide the parallel file-system services,
- *Gateway nodes:* provide connectivity to external data servers and mass-storage systems.

Sometimes, one node can serve more than one function. For example, a node often handles I/O and gateway functions. A typical architecture of a multiprocessor with its I/O systems is given in Fig. 8.2.

8.4 Fundamental Issues in Parallel-I/O Architecture Design

Today most parallel computers have an internal parallel-I/O subsystem based on multiple I/O nodes because it performs data transfers in parallel between computation nodes and I/O nodes. Furthermore, most of these multiprocessors are also connected to an external mass-storage system. An internal parallel-I/O subsystem has many interesting properties and character-

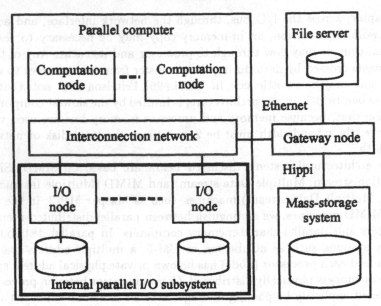

Fig. 8.2. A typical multiprocessor architecture, showing the I/O subsystems.

istics compared to an external mass-storage system. Consequently, we choose to focus our discussion on internal parallel-I/O subsystems rather than on network-attached file servers, and we lay emphasis on disks only.

An internal parallel-I/O uses the same multiprocessor's internal high performance network rather than an external network. Then, the computation nodes and I/O nodes communicate through a shared memory, if applicable, or use a reliable low-latency, message-passing protocol. Therefore, an internal parallel-I/O provides more effective performance: low latency and high bandwidth. It can efficiently handle the small, fragmented requests generated by parallel programs. So, it allows data to be shared and reused by storing them with more effectiveness. The internal parallel-I/O subsystem's bandwidth and capacity are scalable by adding I/O nodes or disks in order to

- maintain a well-balanced performance with the computation nodes when their number or speed is increased,
- support out-of-core applications [FCB+95].

Fitting out a multiprocessor with a high-performance parallel-I/O hardware seems to be very expensive. In reality, it is of no outcome in the end on the effective cost of the multiprocessor because an internal parallel-I/O can greatly reduce

- the requirements placed on external file servers, since it allows an optimal use of the multiprocessor,

- the development cost by using the same architecture for I/O nodes and computation nodes.

In the following subsections, we will focus our discussion on six fundamental issues in an internal parallel-I/O architecture design: disk arrays, architecture of an internal parallel-I/O subsystem, I/O-nodes interconnection, I/O-nodes placement, I/O buffering and caching, and finally availability and reliability.

8.4.1 Disk arrays and RAID. One of the important concepts implemented in the recent years to improve the capacity and bandwidth of the disk subsystem is to set several disks into a disk array, and distribute data across all the disks in the set. This represents a fundamental form of parallel I/O. There are two ways to distribute data across among disks of the disk array, called striping and declustering. There is no consistent definition of these terms in the literature, but common usage seems are the followings.

- Disk striping: distributes data across all disks in round-robin fashion at a constant level of granularity (the stripping unit) such as bytes or blocks. Multiple disks are viewed as a single large fast disk by the user. Disk arrays such as RAIDs [Gib92, PCG+88], have used disk striping to provide data redundancy and high throughput.
- Disk declustering: sometimes used as a synonym of disk striping, but generally defines an arbitrary distribution of file data across multiple disks.

In 1988 Patterson, Gibson, and Katz, at the Berkeley University, presented a case of disk array called Redundant Array of Inexpensive Disks (RAID) [PCG+88]. The idea of the RAID design is that multiple low-cost disks can be used to provide an equivalent single reliable mainframe disk.

The original notion as presented in [Gib89] is that a reliable disk array can be implemented using several unreliable disks with appropriate error correction schemes. For example, 10 small disks with an independent time between failures of 20,000 hours each would yield one failure every 2000 hours. Implementations based on the RAID concept employ disks that are reliable to start with, and use the RAID concepts to provide a higher reliability than previously possible with a single mainframe disk.

The redundancy in a RAID system can be provided in many different ways. We summarize here the RAID level 0 to 5 definitions as provided in [Gib89].

- **RAID level 0: array disk with no redundancy.**
  Simple disk striping based on block size with no redundancy (Fig. 8.3).
- **RAID level 1: mirrored disks.**
  The array is organized in paired disks (Fig. 8.4), all data writes are sent to both disks. This organization provides a highly reliable system, but it is very expensive since only 50% of the disk capacity is available for data. Disk failure can be detected through errors from the disk or controller. The

Fig. 8.3. RAID level 0.

White: Data disks   Black: Mirror disks

Fig. 8.4. RAID level 1 uses block-sized striping.

striping unit is still based on block. Mirrored disks are implemented in the IBM 3990 Model 3 and in the Symmetrix subsystem.

- **RAID level 2: Hamming code for error detection.**
  Hamming code for error detection and correcting has been employed for a long time with RAM chips which are more vulnerable to single and multi-bit errors. A few check bits are added to each RAM word to detect and correct failures. As an example, assume data striped across 4 disks, in this case three check disks are required to detect and correct an error (Fig. 8.5). Although the 42% overhead for level 2 is better than the 100% overhead for RAID level 1, it is very difficult to justify the costs of implementation for any application.
  The drawback of RAID level 2 is that at all data must be spread over all data disks, since the striping unit at RAID level 2 is typically one bit. For example, assume data striped across 4 disks and the physical sector size on disk is 512 bytes, this implies a minimum of 2-Kbyte transfers. Consequently, smaller write transfers will need always a long read-modify-write cycle of 2-Kbyte. Even reads require that all disks are read to verify the error correction codes. The Thinking Machines DataVault [TMC90] was one successful RAID level 2 product.

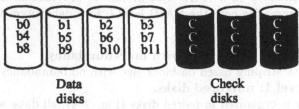

Data
disks

Check
disks

Fig. 8.5. RAID level 2 uses bit-sized striping (C stands for ECC-like check bits).

– RAID level 3: parity disk.

The Hamming code is designed so that it can identify failing components as well as errors. Its use in the RAM chips case is essential, since a failing RAM chip will not identify itself. However, when a disk fails, it is known to have failed, and its identity is also known (the failing disk is detected during the read operation since each disk sector is written with its own checksum). Therefore, it is sufficient to employ a single parity-bit for each N-bit data word to recover the lost bit in that word. Parity is implemented by writing an extra bit for each N-bit data word. If one disk fails, the parity can be used to determine whether the failing bit was a zero or one. Thus, RAID level 3 uses only one *parity disk* for any set of size N (Fig. 8.6). The overhead for a group of 4 disks is 25% of the configuration's capacity. The problems with read-modify-write cycles for small records remain just as for RAID level 2 disks. Here also, the bit-sized striping unit is used.

Data disks   **Parity disk**

Fig. 8.6. RAID level 3 uses bit-sized (sometimes byte-sized) striping (Pi for parity bits).

– RAID level 4: independent read and writes.

As described obove in RAID levels 2 and 3, the data is stripped, in a bit-sized (sometimes a byte-sized) unit, over all data disks which are synchronized to be accessed simultaneously. Therefore, the size of transfers is a minimum of the physical sector size times the number of data disks, this leads to large sizes of transfers. It is clear that RAID levels 2 and 3 are effective only for large reads and writes. But some workloads, such as transaction processing, often make read or write requests to single and small data records. Level 4 RAID attempts to improve performance for small reads and writes by using blocks instead of bits as the striping unit, although parity is computed in the same way (Fig. 8.7). Thus, small records are written to individual disks, and can now be read from a single disk. However, it is still necessary to read all disks in a group if an error must be corrected. Any write requires that the parity is recomputed. Computing the new parity requires two read (old data and old parity) and two write (new data and new parity) I/O operations.

While this implementation improves the performance of reads for small records, it introduces a new problem for writes. The parity disk is used for every write request and can easily become a bottleneck for write performance.

Data disks   **Parity disk**

Fig. 8.7. RAID level 4 uses block-sized striping.

- **RAID Level 5: spreading data and parity.**
  To overcome the parity disk bottleneck in RAID level 4, RAID Level 5 solves this problem by spreading parity blocks over all disks (Fig. 8.8) instead of having a dedicated parity disk. Each stripe still contains N data blocks and one parity block, but their positions are different on each stripe. The advantage of this organization is that the parity disk will no longer tend to become a bottleneck as the I/O rate increases.

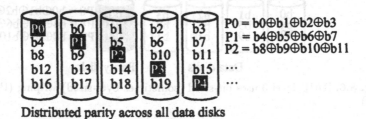

Distributed parity across all data disks

Fig. 8.8. RAID level 5 uses block-sized striping, and distribute parity all data disk.

Although all RAID levels as mentioned above provide a higher reliability through redundancy, they also share some drawbacks:

- It is much more efficient to write a 32-kbyte block to disk in a single I/O, than to write a 32-kbyte stripe of nine (eight plus parity) 4-kbyte blocks to a RAID of eight data disks plus one parity disk. Indeed, since data are distributed across multiple disks, more I/O actions are required. A data write operation in the RAID approach, needs a read-modify-write cycle in order to compute and to update the parity, this leads to four I/O operations: two read (old data and old parity) and two write (new data and new parity).
- Write operations will be slower for large blocks that update an entire stripe (all blocks). But they are yet about three times slower for writes that update a partial stripe (some blocks) in level 4 or 5 systems.
- In the I/O service time (response time) in current systems, the seek and latency times represent the largest terms. Unfortunately, the RAID architecture is not able to reduce these terms, since they are inherent to the mechanical parts of the disk. Indeed, the seek and latency delays will be

larger since RAID systems are based on the use of lower performance disks and for each write operation multiple physical I/Os are required.

In practice, the most used RAIDs are of level 0 (if no reliability is needed), of level 1 (when reliability is a most important issue, for example critical database applications), of level 3 (for applications needing high bandwidth large-read and large-write), and of level 5 (for applications generating small I/O requests).

8.4.2 Internal parallel-I/O subsystem architectures. There are three fundamental architectures for an internal parallel-I/O subsystem (disk system):

Disk-attached computation node architectures. It probably represents the simplest architecture of parallel I/O disk systems, particularly if the computation nodes are fairly standard CPU boards (Fig. 8.9). This approach uses local disks directly connected through an I/O-bus adapter (such as a SCSI-bus adapter) to processors as for uniprocessor architectures (Fig. 8.1). When local disks are used to store persistent files, this approach would set some problems. The difficulty to collocate applications and their required data on the same local disk (the same computation node) leads either to load imbalance, or to internode communication for I/O. Furthermore, these two factors are very antagonistic. For example, to run an application that uses some file located on the disk attached to a specific computation node, the execution should take place on that node. If that node is already running another application, an overloading of the node may occur if that new application is executed on it. The overloading could spread over all computation nodes leading to a strong degradation of the multiprocessor's performance. Avoiding this load imbalance by running the new application elsewhere would result in bulky communications between computation nodes for the I/O operations. In addition, these communications for I/O operations could interfere with the executions of others applications.

As each computation node must manage its attached disk(s), the time normally available for computation is reduced by that required to serve I/O requests. Unpredictable interrupt requests produced by these I/O requests may interfere with any application even those that do not perform any I/O operation.

Variants of this architecture are used in the KSR 1 and IBM SP1 machines. But the IBM SP1 uses the local disks as paging and scratch space disks.

Disk-attached network architectures. In this architecture, disks are attached to the network through a specific-built custom adapter instead of being directly attached to specific computation nodes (Fig. 8.10). Like the previous architecture, applications cannot collocate with their required data. But this is not necessary since, any disk can be equally accessed by any computation node. However, the interference between nodes is still existing and continues

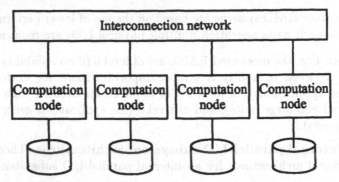

Fig. 8.9. An internal parallel-I/O disk systems attaching disks to computation nodes.

to generate conflict accesses. To avoid this internode interference, blocks allocation on a disk must be synchronized over nodes. Solutions such as shared data structures with locks and an access protocol for their updating, as used in shared-memory systems, may be applied here. Although this architecture avoids an extra copy through the computation node memory, the access disk management is still more complicated. An alternative used by many systems is to add a local I/O processor in order to manage accesses to the disk.

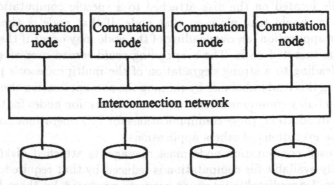

Fig. 8.10. An internal parallel-I/O disk systems attaching disks to network.

Dedicated I/O nodes architectures. This solution is used in many commercial supercomputers such as nCube/ten, KSR 2, CM-5, and IBM SP2. Each I/O node includes a processor, memory, and disks (Fig. 8.11). By uniformly declustering a parallel file across the I/O nodes, each I/O node maintains shares of different parallel files. Thus, each I/O node is responsible for managing buffering and block allocation of only the shares stored on its disks. In addition, data movements between the compute nodes and I/O nodes, produced by different applications, may occur simultaneously without direct coordination among the computation nodes.

Dedicated I/O nodes give a parallel computer much more flexibility. Indeed, the I/O nodes may be configured with a given I/O bandwidth and capacity, so as to balance performances of computation and I/O nodes. Also, with dedicated I/O nodes, the parallelism can be configured at the I/O subsystem interface and at the disk level by respectively changing the number of I/O nodes and the disks [FCB+95].

A parallel-I/O disk system designed with dedicated I/O nodes avoids drawbacks existing in the two previous architectures. However, dedicated I/O nodes introduce again two new, other drawback types:

- I/O access latency will increase in comparison with that of a local disk. Feitelson et al [FCB+95] show that I/O access latency is the sum of the latencies introduced by the interconnection network (typically tens of micro-seconds), the communication and file-system software (milliseconds in the case of large requests and if data is copied between software layers), and the disk access (typically tens of milliseconds). It seems obvious that the dominant part of I/O access latency is due to that of disk-access latency. It will be shown below (see 8.4.5) that buffering and caching reduce I/O access times below the disk-access time.
- Parallel computer cost will increase when additional dedicated I/O nodes are added to it. The cost increases relatively to the disk-attached computation nodes, since no additional processors and network ports are required. But as we have shown above, this has a negative impact on the available computation time, since computation nodes must also serve I/O requests. In addition it also impacts negatively on the execution performance of an application, because unpredictable hardware interrupts generated by I/O demands to computation nodes may occur even if no I/O is performed by that application. That would be worse if more than one application is running.

The choice between dedicated I/O nodes architecture and disk-attached computation node or disk-attached network architecture becomes the everlasting balancing problem between performance and cost.

8.4.3 I/O-nodes interconnection. Any of the previous internal parallel-I/O architectures needs data movements between several I/O-nodes (or disks) and several memories, consequently an interconnection network is needed. Three fundamental issues may be used to interconnect I/O nodes to computation nodes:

- The cheapest uses the primary network.
- The most expensive uses a dedicated I/O network.
- The intermediate solution is to connect each I/O node to some points in the primary network by using an extra link. Thus, the communications between I/O-nodes and computation nodes may be routed through the network and the extra links.

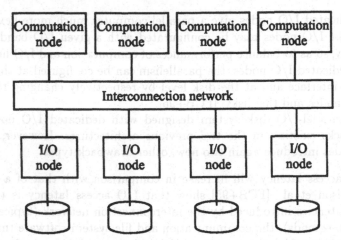

Fig. 8.11. An internal parallel-I/O disk systems using dedicated I/O nodes.

Until now, we assumed that the I/O-nodes are directly connected to the primary interconnection network. However, two types of traffic having different characteristics occur on that primary interconnection network: I/O-related network traffic and internode (computation nodes) network traffic. Any congestion generated by each traffic type leads to a strongly reduced performance of the other [BBH96], [BBH95]. For example in KSR 2, I/O nodes are connected directly to the primary network. Besides, the network interface supports a specialized shared-memory protocol. In the CM-5 computer some computation nodes, equipped with I/O-device controllers, are specialized to play the role of dedicated I/O-nodes. Therefore, they are connected to the main network.

It is very important to distinguish between the two traffic types, because I/O messages often are typically large and burst-like. In contrast, internode messages are small. In addition throughput is usually the goal for I/O-related communication, whereas latency is typically important for internode messages.

Although the approach using dedicated I/O network is expensive, it separates the two forms of traffic, and also gives a parallel computer much more flexibility of choosing the I/O network connectivity and bandwidth. In the nCUBE/ten computer, the dedicated I/O nodes are interconnected by a dedicated network, and are connected to selected computation nodes. The network wires are connected directly to the computation node itself, but are not accessible from the user level [Kot96].

8.4.4 I/O-nodes placement. An interconnection network is a compulsory component required by all parallel computers. Each interconnection network is characterized by its topology. Topologies may be simple such as buses and rings, or complex such as meshes, torus, and hypercubes. The physical distance between any couple of nodes in the network makes great impacts on the communication latency, the bandwidth, and network contention. So, the location of I/O-nodes in the network, if badly chosen, can have a negative consequence on the performance of the I/O subsystem. However, there are two typical placement options:

- All I/O-nodes are concentrated in the same region of the network.
- I/O-nodes are placed with a careful distribution in the network.

The distance overhead between internode (computation nodes) messages is typically less important than the message-startup, whereas the distance is usually important for I/O messages, since I/O messages often are larger and burst-like than other internode messages. Thus, distributing the I/O-nodes can potentially reduce network contention compared to clustering I/O-nodes in the same area. Otherwise, contention can become very important. Indeed, if all I/O-nodes are concentrated in one area of the network, then the I/O traffic with its large I/O-messages may be forced to circulate in only this area, that may lead to congestion in the network. However, if I/O-nodes are distributed in the network, I/O-related network traffic and internode (computation nodes) network traffic may interfere together. This is the case in the nCube/ten, where I/O-nodes are connected together to a dedicated network and then some I/O-nodes are connected to some spaced out computation nodes. On the other hand, clustering the I/O nodes in one region in the network can possibly reduce interference between programs. This is the case in the CM-5, where dedicated computation nodes are specialized to perform I/O tasks and are clustered in a particular partition of the fat tree network. Because the tree network is based on hierarchical switching, if several programs run in their own partition, then I/O traffic avoids interference with the traffic of other partitions. Indeed, I/O-related traffic between the computation nodes and the I/O-nodes moves through the top-level network switching elements rather than through the uninvolved partitions [FH88, GGD93, BBH95]. The Maspar MP-2 has only one I/O controller connected to all processors through a global router.

8.4.5 I/O Buffering and caching. Buffering and caching play important roles at different levels of any I/O subsystem. They may be placed at several hardware levels of the I/O subsystem, in order to reduce existing latencies due to the ill-matched speeds of its different components. For example, small speed-matching buffers placed in the interconnection network, and/or in disk controllers, and/or inside the disk drive itself, lead often to hide a dominant portion of the disk response time (rotational latency and seek time), and to avoid network congestion.

Also a buffer cache, holding recently used blocks, and placed in the I/O node itself can avoid I/O operations entirely. A buffer cache takes another advantage of interprocessor locality, that can reduce I/O access latency below a local disk latency. That reduced latency occurs when multiple computation nodes request different parts of the same block [KN95]. The first requests of certain computation nodes seems to be an initiate prefetch for the other computation nodes. The nCube/ten computer has 4MB on each I/O board, 128KB is dedicated for each I/O node (4 nodes per board), and the remaining is used for the host processor. Some of this memory is used by the system software for I/O buffering. In CM-5, each I/O node has 8MB of RAM dedicated to buffering. In Maspar MP-2, the I/O controller has 8MB of memory, augmented by up to 1GB of I/O RAM. The memory is dedicated to I/O as buffer space and managed by the file system as a buffer cache.

8.4.6 Availability and reliability. Any multiprocessor involves several computation nodes interconnected by a given network having a certain topology. Assume an I/O system, for that multiprocessor, based on either disk-attached or dedicated I/O-nodes connected to either the primary network or a dedicated network. All these components are used in parallel to improve computational performance. The best way to use storage devices in parallel is distribute data across them. Unfortunately, the price of that performance improvement is payed by the decrease of the multiprocessor Mean Time Between Failures (MTBF). A study by Horst shows that a thousand-node multiprocessor may probably average one failure per day [Hor94].

Thus, any component of the multiprocessor has some likelihood to fail, that leads to decrease multiprocessor's availability. For maximum fault tolerance, components must be considered to warrant the reliability (data and functioning), by providing a redundant copy of each [WGS+95]. Regardless computation nodes and interconnection network failures, since methods for handling them are well-established, we distinguish two sources of failure at the I/O subsystem level:

- *Disk failure*, that can be hidden by redundant disk arrays (RAIDs). As shown (in 8.4.1), RAIDs guarantee data availability and reliability in case of one disk failure.
- *I/O-node failure*, which is more complicated Feitelson et al. suggest an astute solution to handle this failure type. This solution is described in the paper referenced [FCB+95].

For reliability and availability, RAIDs are becoming widely used in most supercomputers. For example, in the KSR 2 computer, each I/O-node is fitted out with RAID 1 or RAID 3 to support disk failure. The operating system provides software support for RAID across I/O-nodes. The nCube/ten computer also uses RAIDs at disk level to insure reliability. But there is no hardware to support availability. Reconfiguring procedures are implemented in the system allowing messages to be re-routed when failure happens at I/O-node level. In the CM-5 machine the security is obtained at disk level by managing all disks as a software RAID 3. CM-5 includes a dedicated diagnostic network for detecting and diagnosing failures. The Maspar MP-2 uses a hardware RAID 3 disk array.

9. Conclusions

Computer architecture is a topic which is particularly exciting, mainly because it is in permanent and quick change. It is very difficult to guess how things will evolve, the only certainty being the fact that changes will continue at a rate probably growing. We can nevertheless observe some cycles in this evolution: many concepts important nowadays have been studied earlier in a different technological context.

A first example is given by the cache memory. The birth of the cache memory concept, whose first performances measurement were published by Mattson [MGS+70], was due to the growing gap between the processor speed, built in electronic components, and the memory speed, built with magnetic core. In general use around the seventies, the arrival of electronic memory has cut this gap and removed the necessity of using a cache memory during a few years. Due again to the differential evolution of processor speed and memory performance, the cache has reappeared in the eighties, and is used more and more intensively through a hierarchy of cache memories. We don't see at present time any reason for a change in the general use of a hierarchy of caches, but the possibility in a near future to put on the same chip the processor and whole or a part of its memory will probably make some changes in the way this hierarchy is designed. Bringing the memory nearer to the processor can also lead to put some logic in the memory. These two approaches are currently hot research topics (PIM : Processor In Memory [GHI95], IRAM : Intelligent RAM [PAC+97, KPP+95].

A second example is given by dynamic scheduling found in out-of-order execution processors. These mechanisms were intensively used at the end of the sixties, then discarded during the microprogramming period and the first RISC period. These mechanisms are of a great complexity to implement, and it is not sure that they will be pushed on their extreme possibilities. A mix of VLIW, Dataflow and software assist will probably be the receipt of the next processor generations, the key word being processor parallelism.

A third example is given by multiprocessor machines themselves. The MPP machine, popular at the end of the eighties, seems to be the object of few researches nowadays, the M in the acronym having progressively evolved from Massively to Moderate. This can be explained first by the huge advances done in the structure of the processor itself, on which main efforts have been put and results obtained, and second by the existence of important sets of standard PCs and workstations which are very often idle and linked together through some network, thus being able to work together. So, parallel processing is more viewed today either at a very fine grain level in the processor itself or at a coarse grain level where processors are connected by a more or less powerful network. The possibility to integrate in a near future a lot of functional units on the same chip will probably cast again this topic. The only novelty of these last years in this MPP world is supported by the TERA computer, in which no caches are present in order to avoid the coherency problem and therefore where long memory latency is tolerated by multithreading facilities. It is too early to perceive what will be the impact of such an approach, which seems limited to important scientific applications, good candidates for providing a great number of threads.

How things will evolve is hard to predict: will there be an enforcement of the concept of "a processor for each engineer", or will there be a return in the opposite direction to light terminals connected through high speed networks to powerful multiprocessors? According to the principle of cycles, this second tendency should be enforced. In fact, there is probably room for a mix of the two approaches, due to the low cost of systems and also from the force of habit. Nevertheless, technical reasons can be set forth in favour of the second solution.

A first one comes from the fact that for 25 years we have got into the habit of a regular increase of clock frequency, but it seems that some threshold will soon be reached. The clock period corresponding to 1 GHz is 1 nanosecond, time during which an electrical wave propagates 20 centimetres in copper medium (we get the same value considering optical fibre transmission. Even if transmission speed in copper is 2/3 of that of optic, the optical wave does not travel in a straight line and, thus gives almost the same travel time). In a few years, the clock frequency of the processor will reach 4 GHz, and the number of instructions executed in parallel will be at least 8 (effective): a processor will execute an instruction, on average, each 1/32th of a nanosecond. If two processors are 100 meters apart, the time corresponding to a return trip for a bit of information is then 1000 nanoseconds, and during this time a processor can, in theory, execute 32000 instructions; this value is no more consistent with fine grain parallelism.

A second reason is related to network enhancements. A one Gbits per second network corresponds to a 125 MB/s bandwidth. Such a bandwidth is much higher than current disks bandwidth but is consistent with RAID arrays. Thus, disks located at the server can be accessed through such high speed networks as quick as if they were close to the processors, as the time needed to go from the server to the terminal adds only microseconds to the access time, measured in milliseconds.

But these arguments can also be in favour of the first solution: as a processor will execute the same program ten times quicker in five years, the software gap of message passing systems will be reduced by approximately the same amount of time, shifting the gap to another place, and a high speed network is more likely to smooth the peaks of data requests.

These arguments will stress more and more the gap between fine grain and coarse grain multiprocessors systems. The only main point is that the physical distance will have to be taken into account wherever it will be.

References

[AUB+96]   Acharya, A., Uysal, M., Bennett, R., Mendelson, A., Beynon, M., Hollingsworth, J., Saltz, J., Sussman, A., Tuning the performance of I/O-intensive applications, *Proc. Workshop on I/O in Parallel and Distributed Systems (IOPADS)*, 1996, 15-27.

[AG96]   Adve, S.V., Gharacholoo, K., Shared memory consistency models: A tutorial, *IEEE Computer* **29**, 1996, 66-76.

[Amd67]   Amdahl, G., Validity of the single processor approach to achieving large scale computing capabilities, *Proc. of AFIPS Conference* **30**, 1967, 483-485.

[AOG93]   Anderson, D., Osawa, Y., Govindan, R., A File System for Continuous Media, *ACM Transactions on Computer Systems* **10**, 1992, 311-337.

[AS95]   Anderson, D., Shanley, T., *Pentium Processor System Architecture, 2nd edition*, Addison Wesley, 1995.

[AST67]   Anderson, D.W., Sparacio, F.J., Tomasulo, R.M., The IBM System 360 Model 91: Machine philosophy and instruction-handling, *IBM Journal of Research and Development* **11**, 1967, 8-24.

[AB89]   Archibald, J., Baer, J.L., Cache coherence protocols: Evaluation using a multiprocessor simulation model, *ACM Transactions on Computer Systems* **4**, 1989, 273-298.

[BW88]   Baer, J.L., Wang, W.H., On the inclusion properties for multi-level cache hierarchies, *Proc. 15th Annual International Symposium on Computer Architecture*, 1988, 73-80.

[BBH95]   Baylor, S., Benveniste, C., Hsu, Y., Performance evaluation of a parallel I/O architecture, *Proc. 9th International Conference on Supercomputing*, 1995, 404-413.

[BBH96]   Baylor, S., Benveniste, C., Hsu, Y., Performance evaluation of a massively parallel I/O subsystem, in: Jain, R., Werth, J., Browne J., (eds.) *Input/Output in Parallel and Distributed Computer Systems*, Kluwer Academic Publishers, Dordrecht, 1996, 293-310.

[BCF+95]   Boden, N.J., Cohen, D., Felderman, R.E., Kulawik, A.E., Seitz, C.L., Seizovic, J.N., Su, W.K., Myrinet: A gigabit per second local area network, *IEEE Micro* **15**, 1995, 29-36, (See http://www.myri.com/).

[BD83]   Boral, H., DeWitt, D., Database machines: An idea whose time has passed? A critique of the future of database machines, *Proc. 3rd Int'l. Workshop on Database Machines*, 1983, 166-187.

[BDL+85]   Browne, J., Dale, A., Leung, C., Jenevein, R., A parallel multi-stage I/O architecture with self-managing disk cache for database management applications, *Proc. 4th Int'l. Workshop on Database Machines*, Springer-Verlag, 1985.

[CF78]   Censier, L., Feautrier, P., A new solution to cache coherence problems in multiprocessor systems, *IEEE Transactions On Computer Systems* **C-27**, 1978, 1112-1118.

[CMM+95]   Conte, T.M., Menezes, K.N., Mills, P.M., Patel, B.A., Optimization of instruction fetch mechanisms for high issue rates, *Proc. 22nd Annual International Symposium on Computer Architecture*, 1995, 333-344.

[Cri97]   Crisp, R., Direct Rambus technology: the new main memory standard, *IEEE Micro* **17**, 1997, 18-28.

[CHK+93]   Cypher, R., Ho, A., Konstantinidou, S., Messina, P., Architectural requirements of parallel scientific applications with explicit communication, *Proc. 20th Annual International Symposium on Computer Architecture*, 1993, 2-13.

[DC94]   Del Rosario, J.M., Choudhary, A., High-performance I/O for massively parallel computers: Problems and prospects, *IEEE Computer* **27**, 1994, 59-68.

[DG92]   DeWitt, D., Gray, J., Parallel database systems: The future of high performance database systems, *Communications of the ACM* **35**, 1992, 85-98.

[Dip97]   Dipert, B., Advanced DRAM puts you in the fast lane, *EDN*, 1997, 52-80.

[DSB86]   Dubois, M., Scheurich, C., Briggs, F., Memory access buffering in multiprocessors, *Proc. 13th Annual International Symposium on Computer Architecture*, 1986, 434-442.

[ERP+95]   Edmonson, J.H., Rubinfeld, P., Preston, R., Rajagopalan, V., Superscalar instruction execution in the 21164 Alpha microprocessor, *IEEE Micro* **15**, 1995, 33-43.

[EK89]   Eggers, S., Katz, R., The effect of sharing on the cache and bus performance of parallel programs, *Proc. 3rd International Conference on Architectural Support for Programming Languages and Operating Systems*, 1989, 257-270.

[FCB+95]   Feitelson, D., Corbett, P., Baylor, S., Hsu, Y., Parallel I/O subsystems in massively parallel supercomputers, *IEEE Parallel and Distributed Technology* **3**, 1995, 33-47.

[FCH+96]   Feitelson, D., Corbett, P., Hsu, Y., Prost, J., *Parallel I/O Systems and Interfaces for Parallel Computers*, World Scientific, 1996.

[FH88]   Flynn, R., Hadimioglu, H., A distributed hypercube file system, *Proc. 3rd Conference on Hypercube Concurrent Computers and Applications*, 1988, 1375-1381.

[GVK+95]   Gemmell, D., Vin, H., Kandlur, D., Venkat Rangan, P., Rowe, L., Multimedia storage servers: A tutorial, *IEEE Computer* **28**, 1995, 40-49.

[Gha90]   Gharachorloo, K., Memory consistency and event ordering in scalable shared-memory multiprocessors, *Proc. 17th Annual International Symposium on Computer Architecture*, 1990, 15-26.

[GGD93]   Ghosh, J., Goveas, K., Draper, J., Performance evaluation of a parallel I/O subsystem for hypercube multiprocessors, *Journal of Parallel and Distributed Computing* **17**, 1993, 115-121.

[Gib89]   Gibson, G., Performance and reliability in redundant arrays of inexpensive disks, *Proc. International Conference on Management of Data*, 1989, 381-391.

[Gib92]   Gibson, G., *Redundant Disk Arrays: Reliable, Parallel Secondary Storage*, ACM Distinguished Dissertations, MIT Press, 1992.

[GV96]   Gillingham, P., Vogley, B., SLDRAM: High-performance, open standard memory, *IEEE Micro* **17**, 1996, 29-39.

[GHI95]   Gokhale, M., Homes, B., Iobst, K., Processing in memory: The terasys massively parallel PIM array computer, *IEEE Computer* **28**, 1995, 23-31.

[GG97]   Gonzales, J., Gonzales, A., Memory address prediction for data speculation, *Proc. Europar'97*, 1997, 1084-1091.

[Goo83]   Goodman, J.R., Using cache memory to reduce processor-memory traffic, *Proc. 10th Annual International Symposium on Computer Architecture*, 1983, 124-131.

[Gus92]   Gustavson, D., The scalable coherent interface and related standards projects, *IEEE Micro* **12**, 1992, 10-22.

[Gwe97]   Gwennap, L., Intel, HP make EPIC disclosure, *Microprocessor Report* **11**, 1997, 1-9.

[HRS97]   Hai, P.T., Rochange, C., Sainrat, P., An evaluation of misprediction recovery strategies for load speculation schemes, Technical Report IRIT 97-27-R, Institut de Recherche en Informatique de Toulouse, 1997.

[HP96]   Hennessy, J., Patterson, D., *Computer Architecture: A Quantitative Approach - Second Edition*, Morgan Kaufmann Publishers, 1996.

[Hor94]   Horst, R., Massively parallel systems you can trust, *Proc. IEEE Computer Society International Conference (COMPCON)*, 1994, 236-241.

[Hun95]   Hunt, D., Advanced performance features of the 64-bit PA-8000, *Proc. IEEE Computer Society International Conference (COMPCON)*, 1995, 123-128.

[Hwa93]   Hwang, K., *Advanced Computer Architecture: Parallelism, Scalability, Programmability*, McGraw-Hill, 1993.

[IM94]   IBM, Motorola. *PowerPC 604 RIC Microprocessor User's Manual*, 1994, (See http://www.chips.ibm.com/products/powerpc/chips-/604e/604eUM_book.pdf).

[IEE93]   *IEEE Spectrum, Special Issue on Interactive Multimedia*, 1993.

[JW93]   Jouppi, N.P., Wilton, S.J.E., Tradeoffs in two-level on-chip caching, Technical Report WRL Research Report 93/3, Digital Western Research Laboratory Palo Alto, 1993.

[JSL95]   Jourdan, S., Sainrat, P., Litaize, D., Exploring configurations of functional units in an out-of-order superscalar processor, *Proc. 22nd Annual International Symposium on Computer Architecture*, 1995, 117-125.

[Kat96]   Katayama, Y., Trends in semiconductor memories, *IEEE Micro* **17**, 1996, 10-17.

[KN95]   Kotz, D., Nieuwejaar, N., File-system workload on a scientific multiprocessor, *IEEE Parallel and Distributed Technology* **3**, 1995, 51-60.

[Kau94]   Kaufman, A. (ed.), *IEEE Computer* **27**, Computer Special Issue on Visualisation, 1994.

[Kot96]   Kotz, D., Introduction to multiprocessor I/O architecture, in: Jain, R., Werth, J., Browne, J. (eds), *Input/Output in Parallel and Distributed Computer Systems*, Kluwer Academic Publishers, 1996, 97-124.

[KPP+95]   Kozyrakis, C., Perissakis, S., Patterson, D., Anderson, T., Asanovic, K., Cardwell, N., Fromm, R., Golbus, J., Gribstad, B., Keeton, K., Thomas, R., Treuhaft, N., Yelick, K., Scalable processors in the billion-transistor era :IRAM, *IEEE Computer* **30**, 1995, 75-78.

[Lam79]   Lamport, L., How to make a multiprocessor computer that correctly executes multiprocess programs, *IEEE Transactions On Computer* **C-28**, 1979, 690-691.

[LS84]   Lee, J.K., Smith, A.J., Branch prediction strategies and branch target buffer design, *IEEE Computer* **17**, 1984, 6-22.

[LS96]   Lipasti, M.H., Shen, J.P., Exceeding the dataflow limit via value prediction, *Proc. 29th Annual International Symposium on Microarchitecture*, 1996, 226-237.

[MGS+70]   Mattson, R.L., Gecsei, J., Slutz, D.R., Traiger, I.L., Evaluation techniques for storage hierarchies, *IBM Systems Journal* **9**, 1970, 78-117.

[MBV+97]   Moshovos, A., Breach, S.E., Vijaykumar, T.N., Sohi, G.S., Dynamic speculation and synchronization of data dependencies, *Proc. 24th Annual International Symposium on Computer Architecture*, 1997, 181-193.

[MPC98]   MPC: A low-cost parallel multiprocessor using a 1 Gbit/s communication network, 1998, (See http://www-asim.lip6.fr/mpc/).

[ONH+96]   Olukotun, K., Nayfeh, B.A., Hammond, L., Wilson, K., Chang, K., The case for a single-chip multiprocessor, *Proc. 7th International Conference on Architectural Support for Programming Languages and Operating Systems*, 1996, 2-11.

[PSR92]   Pan, S.-T., So, K., Rameh, J.T., Improving the accuracy of dynamic branch prediction using branch correlation, *Proc. 5th International Conference on Architectural Support for Programming Languages and Operating Systems*, 1992, 76-84.

[PP84]   Papamarcos, M., Patel, J., A low overhead coherence solution for multiprocessors with private cache memories, *Proc. 11th Annual International Symposium on Computer Architecture*, 1984, 348-354.

[Pap96]   Papworth, D.B., Tuning the Pentium Pro microarchitecture, *IEEE Micro* **16**, 1996, 8-15.

[PAC+97]   Patterson, D., Anderson, T., Cardwell, N., Fromm, R., Keeton, K., Kozyrakis, C., Thomas, R., Yelick, K., A case for intelligent RAM, *IEEE Micro* **17**, 1997, 34-44.

[PCG+88]   Patterson, D., Chen, P., Gibson, G., Katz, R., A case for redundant arrays of inexpensive disks (RAIDS), *Proc. ACM-SIGMOD International Conference on Management of Data*, 1988, 109-116.

[PTM96]   Protic, J., Tomasevic, M., Milutinovic, V., Distributed shared memory: Concepts and systems, *IEEE Parallel and Distributed Technology* **4**, 1996, 63-79.

[RR95]   Rodriguez, A., Rowe, L., (eds.), *IEEE Computer* **28**, *Special Issue on Multimedia Systems and Applications*, 1995.

[SGH97]   Santhanam, V., Gornish, E.H., Hsu, W.C., Data prefetching on the HP PA-8000, *Proc. 24th Annual International Symposium on Computer Architecture*, 1997, 264-273.

[SJS+96]   Seznec, A., Jourdan, S., Sainrat, P., Michaud, P., Multiple-block ahead branch predictors, *Proc. 7th International Conference on Architectural Support for Programming Languages and Operating Systems*, 1996, 116-127.

[Sha95]   Sharp, O., The grand challenges, *Byte*, 1995, 65-72.

[SFG+93]   Sindhu, P., Frailong, J.M., Gastinel, J., Cekleov, M., Yuan, L., Gunning, B., Curry, D., XDBus: A high-performance, consistent, packet-switched VLSI bus, *Proc. IEEE Computer Society International Conference (COMPCON)*, 1993, 338-344.

[SS97]   Sodani, A., Sohi, G.S, Dynamic instruction reuse, *Proc. 22nd Annual International Symposium on Computer Architecture*, 1997, 194-205.

[TMC90]   Thinking machines corporation, *Programming The CM I/O System*, 1990.

[Tho61]   Thornton, J.E., Parallel operation in the Control Data 6600, *Proc. Fall Joint Computers Conference* **26**, 1961, 33-40.

[TM194]   Tomasevic, M., Milutinovic, V., Hardware approaches to cache coherence in shared-memory multiprocessors, Part 1, *IEEE Micro* **14**, 1994, 52-59.

[TM294]   Tomasevic, M., Milutinovic, V., Hardware approaches to cache coherence in shared-memory multiprocessors, Part 2, *IEEE Micro* 14, 1994, 61-66.

[TEL95]   Tullsen, D.M., Eggers, S.J., Levy, H.M., Simultaneous multithreading: Maximizing on-chip parallelism, *Proc. 22nd Annual International Symposium on Computer Architecture*, IEEE/ACM, 1995, 392-403.

[US95]   Uht, A.K., Sindagi, V., Disjoint eager execution: An optimal form of speculative execution, *Proc. 28th Annual International Symposium on Microarchitecture*, 1995, 313-325.

[WGS+95]   Wilkes, J., Golding, R., Staelin, C., Sullivan, T., The HP AutoRAID hierarchical storage system, *Proc. 5th ACM Symposium on Operating Systems Principles*, ACM, 1995, 96-108.

[Wu93]   Wu, C.E., A quantitative evaluation of cache types for high-performance computer systems, *IEEE Transactions On Computers* 42, 1993, 1154-1161.

[Yea96]   Yeager, K.C., The MIPS R10000 superscalar microarchitecture, *IEEE Micro* 16, 1996, 28-41.

[YP92]   Yeh, T.Y., Patt, Y.N., Alternative implementations of two-level adaptive training branch prediction, *Proc. 19th Annual International Symposium on Computer Architecture*, 1992, 124-134.

[Yu96]   Yu, A., The future of microprocessors, *IEEE Micro* 17, 1996, 46-53.

V. Parallel Operating Systems

João Garcia, Paulo Ferreira, and Paulo Guedes

IST/INESC, Lisbon, Portugal

Summary. Parallel operating systems are the interface between parallel computers (or computer systems) and the applications (parallel or not) that are executed on them. They translate the hardware's capabilities into concepts usable by programming languages.

Great diversity marked the beginning of parallel architectures and their operating systems. This diversity has since been reduced to a small set of dominating configurations: symmetric multiprocessors running commodity applications and operating systems (UNIX and Windows NT) and multicomputers running custom kernels and parallel applications. Additionally, there is some (mostly experimental) work done towards the exploitation of the shared memory paradigm on top of networks of workstations or personal computers.

In this chapter, we discuss the operating system components that are essential to support parallel systems and the central concepts surrounding their operation: scheduling, synchronization, multi-threading, inter-process communication, memory management and fault tolerance.

Currently, SMP computers are the most widely used multiprocessors. Users find it a very interesting model to have a computer, which, although it derives its processing power from a set of processors, does not require any changes to applications and only minor changes to the operating system. Furthermore, the most popular parallel programming languages have been ported to SMP architectures enabling also the execution of demanding parallel applications on these machines.

However, users who want to exploit parallel processing to the fullest use those same parallel programming languages on top of NORMA computers. These multicomputers with fast interconnects are the ideal hardware support for message passing parallel applications. The surviving commercial models with NORMA architectures are very expensive machines, which one will find running calculus intensive applications, such as weather forecasting or fluid dynamics modelling.

We also discuss some of the experiments that have been made both in hardware (DASH, Alewife) and in software systems (TreadMarks, Shasta) to deal with the scalability issues of maintaining consistency in shared-memory systems and to prove their applicability on a large-scale.

1. Introduction

Parallel operating systems are primarily concerned with managing the resources of parallel machines. This task faces many challenges: application programmers demand all the performance possible, many hardware configurations exist and change very rapidly, yet the operating system must increasingly be compatible with the mainstream versions used in personal computers and workstations due both to user pressure and to the limited resources available for developing new versions of these system.

In this chapter, we describe the major trends in parallel operating systems. Since the architecture of a parallel operating system is closely influenced by the hardware architecture of the machines it runs on, we have divided our presentation in three major groups: operating systems for small scale symmetric multiprocessors (SMP), operating system support for large scale distributed memory machines and scalable distributed shared memory machines.

The first group includes the current versions of Unix and Windows NT where a single operating system centrally manages all the resources. The second group comprehends both large scale machines connected by special purpose interconnections and networks of personal computers or workstations, where the operating system of each node locally manages its resources and collaborates with its peers via message passing to globally manage the machine. The third group is composed of non-uniform memory access (NUMA) machines where each node's operating system manages the local resources and interacts at a very fine grain level with its peers to manage and share global resources.

We address the major architectural issues in these operating systems, with a greater emphasis on the basic mechanisms that constitute their core: process management, file system, memory management and communications. For each component of the operating system, the presentation covers its architecture, describes some of the interfaces included in these systems to provide programmers with a greater level of flexibility and power in exploiting the hardware, and addresses the implementation efforts to modify the operating system in order to explore the parallelism of the hardware. These topics include support for multi-threading, internal parallelism of the operating system components, distributed process management, parallel file systems, inter-process communication, low-level resource sharing and fault isolation. These features are illustrated with examples from both commercial operating systems and research proposals from industry and academia.

2. Classification of Parallel Computer Systems

2.1 Parallel Computer Architectures

Operating systems were created to present users and programmers with a view of computers that allows the use of computers abstracting away from the details of the machine's hardware and the way it operates. *Parallel operating systems* in particular enable user interaction with computers with parallel architectures. The physical architecture of a computer system is therefore an important starting point for understanding the operating system that controls it. There are two famous classifications of parallel computer architectures: Flynn's [Fly72] and Johnson's [Joh88].

2.1.1 Flynn's classification of parallel architectures. Flynn divides computer architectures along two axes according to the number of data sources and the number of instruction sources that a computer can process simultaneously. This leads to four categories of computer architectures:

SISD - Single Instruction Single Data. This is the most widespread architecture where a single processor executes a sequence of instructions that operate on a single stream of data. Examples of this architecture are the majority of computers in use nowadays such as personal computers (with some exceptions such as Intel Dual Pentium machines), workstations and low-end servers. These computers typically run either a version of the Microsoft Windows operating system or one of the many variants of the UNIX operating system (Sun Microsystems' Solaris, IBM's AIX, Linux...) although these operating systems include support for multiprocessor architectures and are therefore not strictly operating systems for SISD machines.

MISD - Multiple Instruction Single Data. No existing computer corresponds to the MISD model, which was included in this description mostly for the sake of completeness. However, we could envisage special purpose machines that could use this model. For example, a "cracker computer" with a set of processors where all are fed the same stream of ciphered data which each tries to crack using a different algorithm.

SIMD - Single Instruction Multiple Data. The SIMD architecture is used mostly for supercomputer vector processing and calculus. The programming model of SIMD computers is based on distributing sets of homogeneous data among an array of processors. Each processor executes the same operation on a fraction of a data element. SIMD machines can be further divided into pipelined and parallel SIMD. Pipelined SIMD machines execute the same instruction for an array of data elements by fetching the instruction from memory only once and then executing it in an overloaded way on a pipelined high performance processor (e.g. Cray 1). In this case, each fraction of a data element (vector) is in a different stage of the pipeline. In contrast to pipelined SIMD, parallel SIMD machines are made from dedicated processing elements connected by high-speed links. The processing elements are special purpose processors with narrow data paths (some as narrow as one bit) and which execute a restricted set of operations. Although there is a design effort to keep processing elements as cheap as possible, SIMD machines are quite rare due to their high cost, limited applicability and to the fact that they are virtually impossible to upgrade, thereby representing a "once in a lifetime" investment for many companies or institutions that buy one.

An example of a SIMD machine is the Connection Machine (e.g. CM-2) [TMC90a], built by the Thinking Machines Corporation. It has up to 64k processing elements where each of them operates on a single bit and is only able to perform very simple logical and mathematical operations. For each set of 32 processing cells there are four memory chips, a numerical processor for floating point operations and a router connected to the cell interconnection. The cells are arranged in a 12-dimensional hyper-cube topology. The concept of having a vast amount of very simple processing units served three purposes: to eliminate the classical memory access bottleneck by having processors distributed all over the memory, to experiment with the scalability limits of parallelism and to approximate the brain model of computation.

The MasPar MP-2 [Bla90] by the MasPar Computer Corporation is another example of a SIMD machine. This computer is based on a 2 dimensional lattice of up to 16k processing elements driven by a VAX computer that serves as a front end to the processing elements. Each processing element is connected to its eight neighbours on the 2D mesh to form a torus. The user processes are executed on the front-end machine that passes the parallel portions of the code to another processor called the Data Parallel Unit (DPU). The DPU is responsible for executing operations on singular data and for distributing the operations on parallel data among the processing elements that constitute the lattice.

MIMD - Multiple Instruction Multiple Data. These machines constitute the core of the parallel computers in use today. The MIMD design is a more general one where machines are composed of a set of processors that execute different programs which access their corresponding datasets[1]. These architectures have been a success because they are typically cheaper than special purpose SIMD machines since they can be built with off-the-shelf components. To further detail the presentation of MIMD machines it is now useful to introduce Johnson's classification of computer architectures.

2.1.2 Johnson's classification of parallel architectures. *Johnson's classification* [Joh88] is oriented towards the different memory access methods. This is a much more practical approach since, as we saw above, all but the MIMD class of Flynn are either virtually extinct or never existed. We take the opportunity of presenting Johnson's categories of parallel architectures to give some examples of MIMD machines in each of those categories. Johnson divides computer architectures into:

UMA - Uniform Memory Access. UMA machines guarantee that all processors use the same mechanism to access all memory positions and that those accesses are performed with similar performance. This is achieved with a shared memory architecture where all processors access a central memory unit. In a UMA machine, processors are the only parallel element (apart from caches which we discuss below). The remaining architecture components

---

[1] although not necessary in mutual exclusion.

(main memory, file system, networking...) are shared among the processors. Each processor has a local cache where it stores recently accessed memory positions. Most major hardware vendors sell UMA machines in the form of symmetric multiprocessors with write-through caches. This means that writes to cache are immediately written to main memory. In the alternative policy of write-back caching, writes to the cache are only written to main memory when the cache line containing the write is evicted from the processor's cache.

In order to keep these processor caches coherent and thereby give each processor a consistent view of the main memory a hardware coherence protocol is implemented. There are two techniques for maintaining cache coherence: directory based and bus snooping protocols. Bus snooping is possible only when the machine's processors are connected by a common bus. In this case, every processor can see all memory accesses requested on the common bus and update its own cache accordingly. When snooping is not possible, a directory-based protocol is used. These protocols require that processor keeps a map of how memory locations are distributed among all processors in order to be able find it among the machine's processors when requested. Typically, bus snooping is used in shared memory SMPs and directory-based protocols are used in distributed memory architectures such as the SGI Origin 2000.

The Alpha Server family [Her97], developed by the Digital Equipment Corporation (now owned by Compaq), together with Digital UNIX has been one of the most commercially successful server and operating system solutions. Alpha Servers are symmetric multiprocessor based on Alpha processors, up to 4 of them, connected by a snoopy bus to a motherboard with up to 4 GByte of memory. The Alpha Server has separate address and data buses and uses a cache write-back protocol. When a processor writes to its cache, the operation is not immediately passed on to main memory but only when that data element has to be used by another memory block. Therefore, processors have to snoop the bus in order to reply to other processors that might request data whose more recent version is in their cache and not in main memory.

A more recent example of a UMA multiprocessor is the Enterprise 10000 Server [Cha98], which is Sun Microsystems' latest high-end server. It is configured with 16 interconnected system boards. Each board can have up to 4 UltraSPARC 336MHz processors, up to 4GB of memory and 2 I/O connections. All boards are connected to four address buses and to a 16x16 connection Gigaplane-XB interconnection matrix. This architecture, called Starfire, is a mixture between a point- to-point processor/memory topology and a snoopy bus. The system board's memory addresses are interleaved among the four address buses, which are used to send packets with memory requests from the processors to the memory. The requests are snooped by all processors connected to the bus, which allows them to implement a snooping coherency protocol. Since all processors snoop all requests and update their caches, the replies from the memory with the data requested by the processors do not have to be seen and are sent on a dedicated high-throughput

Gigaplane connection between the memory bank and the processor thereby optimising memory throughput. Hence, the architecture's bottleneck is at the address bus, which can't handle as many requests as the memory and the Gigaplane interconnection. The Enterprise 10000 runs Sun's Solaris operating system.

NUMA – Non-Uniform Memory Access. NUMA computers are machines where each processor has its own memory. However, the processor interconnection allows processors to access another processor's local memory. Naturally, an access to local memory has a much better performance than a read or write of a remote memory on another processor. The NUMA category includes replicated memory clusters, massively parallel processors, cache coherent NUMA (CC-NUMA such as the SGI Origin 2000) and cache only memory architecture. Two recent examples of NUMA machines are the SGI Origin 2000 and Cray Research's T3E. Although NUMA machines give programmers a global memory view of the processors aggregate memory, performance conscious programmers still tend to try to locate their data on the local memory portion and avoid remote memory accesses. This is one of the arguments used in favour of MIMD shared memory architectures.

The SGI Origin 2000 [LL94] is a cache coherent NUMA multiprocessor designed to scale up to 512 nodes. Each node has one or two R10000 195MHz processors with up to 4GB of coherent memory and a memory coherence controller called the hub. The nodes are connected via a SGI SPIDER router chip which routes traffic between six Craylink network connections. These connections are used to create a cube topology were each cube vertex has a SPIDER router with two nodes appended to it and additional three SPIDER connections are used to link the vertex to its neighbours. This is called a bristle cube. The remaining SPIDER connection is used to extend these 32 processors (4 processor x 8 vertices) by connecting it to other cubes. The Origin 2000 uses a directory-based cache coherence protocol similar to the Stanford DASH protocol [LLT+93]. The Origin 2000 is one of the most innovative architectures and is the setting of many recent research papers (e.g. [JS98] [BW97]).

The Cray T3E is a NUMA massively parallel multicomputer and one of the most recent machines by the Cray Research Corporation (now owned by SGI). The Cray T3E has from 6 to 2048 Alpha processors (some configurations use 600MHz processors) connected in a 3D cube interconnection topology. It has a 64-bit architecture with a maximum distributed globally addressable memory of 4 TBytes where remote memory access messages are automatically generated by the memory controller. Although remote memory can be addressed, this is not transparent to the programmer. Since there is no hardware mechanism to keep the Cray's processor caches consistent, they contain only local data. Each processor runs a copy of Cray's UNICOS microkernel on top of which language specific message-passing libraries support parallel processing. The I/O system is distributed over a set of nodes on the surface of the cube.

NORMA – No Remote Memory Access. In a *NORMA machine* a processor is not able to access the memory of another processor. Consequently, all inter-processor communication has to be done by the explicit exchange of messages between processors and there is no global memory view. NORMA architectures are more cost-effective since they don't need all the hardware infrastructure associated with allowing multiple processor to access the same memory unit and therefore provide more raw processing power for a lower price at the expense of the system's programming model's friendliness.

The CM-5 [TMC90b] by the Thinking Machine Corporation is a MIMD machine, which contrasts with the earlier SIMD CM-1 and CM-2, a further sign of the general tendency of vendors to concentrate on MIMD architectures. The CM-5 is a private memory NORMA machine with a special type of processor interconnection called a fat tree. In a fat tree architecture, processors are the leaves of an interconnection tree where the bandwidth is bigger at the branches placed higher on the tree. This special interconnection reduces the bandwidth degradation implied by an increase of the distance between processors and it also enables bandwidth to remain constant as the number of processors grows. Each node in a CM-5 has a SPARC processor, a 64k cache and up to 32MB of local 64 bit-word memory. The CM-5 processors, which run a microkernel, are controlled by a control processor running UNIX, which serves as the user front end.

The Intel Paragon Supercomputer [Div95] is a 2D rectangular mesh of up to 4096 Intel i860 XP processors. This supercomputer with its 50Mhz 42 MIPS processors connected point-to-point at 200MByte/sec full duplex competed for a while with the CM-2 for the title of the "world's fastest supercomputer". The processor mesh is supported by I/O processors connected to hard disks and other I/O devices. The Intel Paragon runs the OSF/1 operating system, which is based on Mach.

In conclusion, it should be said that, after a period when very varied designs coexisted, parallel architectures are converging towards a generalized use of shared memory MIMD machines. There are calculus intensive domains were NORMA machines, such as the CRAY T3-E, are used but the advantages offered by the SMP architecture, such as the ease of programming, standard operating systems, use of standard hardware components and software portability, have overwhelmed the parallel computing market.

2.2 Parallel Operating Systems

There are several components in an operating system that can be parallelized. Most operating systems do not approach all of them and do not support parallel applications directly. Rather, parallelism is frequently exploited by some additional software layer such as a distributed file system, distributed shared memory support or libraries and services that support particular parallel programming languages while the operating system manages concurrent task execution.

The convergence in parallel computer architectures has been accompanied by a reduction in the diversity of operating systems running on them. The current situation is that most commercially available machines run a flavour of the UNIX OS (Digital UNIX, IBM AIX, HP UX, Sun Solaris, Linux). Others run a UNIX based microkernel with reduced functionality to optimise the use of the CPU, such as Cray Research's UNICOS. Finally, a number of shared memory MIMD machines run Microsoft Windows NT (soon to be superseded by the high end variant of Windows 2000).

There are a number of core aspects to the characterization of a parallel computer operating system: general features such as the degrees of coordination, coupling and transparency; and more particular aspects such as the type of process management, inter-process communication, parallelism and synchronization and the programming model.

2.2.1 Coordination. The type of coordination among processors in parallel operating systems is a distinguishing characteristic, which conditions how applications can exploit the available computational nodes. Furthermore, application parallelism and operating system parallelism are two distinct issues: While application concurrency can be obtained through operating system mechanisms or by a higher layer of software, concurrency in the execution of the operating system is highly dependant on the type of processor coordination imposed by the operating system and the machine's architecture. There are three basic approaches to coordinating processors:

– Separate supervisor - In a *separate supervisor parallel machine* each node runs its own copy of the operating system. Parallel processing is achieved via a common process management mechanism allowing a processor to create processes and/or threads on remote machines. For example, in a multicomputer like the Cray T3E, each node runs its own independent copy of the operating system. Parallel processing is enabled by a concurrent programming infrastructure such as an MPI library (see Section 4.) whereas I/O is performed by explicit requests to dedicated nodes. Having a front-end that manages I/O and that dispatches jobs to a back-end set of processors is the main motivation for separate supervisor operating system.

– Master-slave - A *master-slave parallel operating system* architecture assumes that the operating system will always be executed on the same processor and that this processor will control all shared resources and in particular process management. A case of master-slave operating system, as we saw above, is the CM-5. This type of coordination is particularly adapted to single purpose machines running applications that can be broken into similar concurrent tasks. In these scenarios, central control may be maintained without any penalty to the other processors' performance since all processors tend to be beginning and ending tasks simultaneously.

– Symmetric - Symmetric OSs are the most common configuration currently. In a *symmetric parallel OS*, any processor can execute the operating system kernel. This leads to concurrent accesses to operating system components and requires careful synchronization. In Section 3. we will discuss the reasons for the popularity of this type of coordination.

2.2.2 Coupling and transparency. Another important characteristic in parallel operating systems is the system's degree of coupling. Just as in the case of hardware where we can speak of loosely coupled (e.g. network of workstations) and highly coupled (e.g. vector parallel multiprocessors) architectures, parallel OS can be meaningfully separated into loosely coupled and tightly coupled operating systems.

Many current distributed operating systems have a highly modular architecture. There is therefore a wide spectrum of distribution and parallelism in different operating systems. To see how influential coupling is in forming the abstraction presented by a system, consider the following extreme examples: on the highly coupled end a special purpose vector computer dedicated to one parallel application, e.g. weather forecasting, with master-slave coordination and a parallel file system, and on the loosely coupled end a network of workstations with shared resources (printer, file server) running each their own application and maybe sharing some client-server applications.

Within the spectrum of operating system coupling there are three landmark types:

– *Network Operating Systems* - These are implementations of a loosely coupled operating systems on top of loosely coupled hardware. Network operating systems are the software that supports the use of a network of machines and provide users that are aware of using a set of computers, with facilities designed to ease the use of remote resources located over the network. These resources are made available as services and might be printers, processors, file systems or other devices. Some resources, of which dedicated hardware devices such as printers, tape drives, etc... are the classical example, are connected to and managed by a particular machine and are made available to other machines in the network via a service or daemon. Other resources, such as disks and memory, can be organized into true distributed systems, which are seamlessly used by all machines. Examples of basic services available on a network operating system are starting a shell session on a remote computer (remote login), running a program on a remote machine (remote execution) and transferring files to and from remote machines (remote file transfer).

– *Distributed Operating Systems* - True distributed operating systems correspond to the concept of highly coupled software using loosely coupled hardware. Distributed operating systems aim at giving the user the possibility of transparently using a virtual uniprocessor. This requires having an adequate distribution of all the layers of the operating system and providing a global unified view over process management, file system and inter-process communication, thereby allowing applications to perform transparent migration of data, computations and/or processes. Distributed file systems (e.g. AFS, NFS) and distributed shared memories (e.g. TreadMarks [KDC+94], Midway[BZ91], DiSoM [GC93]) are the most common supports for migrating data. Remote procedure call (e.g. Sun RPC, Java RMI, Corba) mechanisms are used for migration of computations. Process migration is a less common feature. However, some experimental platforms have supported it [Nut94], e.g. Sprite, Emerald.

- *Multiprocessor Timesharing OS* - This case represents the most common configuration of highly coupled software on top of highly coupled software. A multiprocessor is seen by the user as a powerful uniprocessor since it hides away the presence of multiple processor and an interconnection network. We will discuss some design issues of SMP operating systems in the following section.

2.2.3 HW vs. SW. As we mentioned a parallel operating system provides users with an abstract computational model over the computer architecture. It is worthwhile showing that this view can be achieved by the computer's parallel hardware architecture or by a software layer that unifies a network of processors or computers. In fact, there are implementations of every computational model both in hardware or software systems:

- The hardware version of the shared memory model is represented by symmetric multiprocessors whereas the software version is achieved by unifying the memory of a set of machines by means of a distributed shared memory layer.
- In the case of the distributed memory model there are multicomputer architectures where accesses to local and remote data are explicitly different and, as we saw, have different costs. The equivalent software abstractions are explicit message-passing inter-process communication mechanisms and programming languages.
- Finally, the SIMD computation model of massively parallel computers is mimicked by software through data parallel programming. Data parallelism is a style of programming geared towards applying parallelism to large data sets, by distributing data over the available processors in a "divide and conquer" mode. An example of a data parallel programming language is HPF (High Performance Fortran).

2.2.4 Protection. Parallel computers, being multi-processing environments, require that the operating system provide protection among processes and between processes and the operating system so that erroneous or malicious programs are not able to access resources belonging to other processes. Protection is the access control barrier, which all programs must pass before accessing operating system resources. Dual mode operation is the most common protection mechanism in operating systems. It requires that all operations that interfere with the computer's resources and their management is performed under operating system control in what is called protected or kernel mode (in opposition to unprotected or user mode). The operations that must be performed in kernel mode are made available to applications as an operating system API. A program wishing to enter kernel mode calls one of these system functions via an interruption mechanism, whose hardware implementation varies among different processors. This allows the operating system to verify the validity and authorization of the request and to execute it safely and correctly using kernel functions, which are trusted and well-behaved.

3. Operating Systems for Symmetric Multiprocessors

Symmetric Multiprocessors (SMP) are currently the predominant type of parallel computers. The root of their popularity is the ease with which both operating systems and applications can be ported onto them. Applications programmed for uniprocessors can be run on an SMP unchanged, while porting a multitasking operating system onto an SMP requires minor changes. Therefore, no other parallel architecture is so flexible running both parallel and commodity applications on top of generalist operating systems (UNIX, NT). The existence of several processors raises scalability and concurrency issues, e.g. hardware support for cache coherence (see Section 2.), for the initialisation of multiple processors and the optimisation of processor interconnection. However, regarding the operating system, the specific aspects to be considered in a SMP are process synchronization and scheduling.

3.1 Process Management

A process is a program's execution context. It is a set of data structures that specify all the information needed to execute a program: its execution state (global variables), the resources it is using (files, processes, synchronization variables), its security identity and accounting information.

There has been an evolution in the type of tasks executed by computers. The state description of a traditional process contains much more information than what is needed to describe a simple flow of execution and therefore commuting between processes can be a considerably costly operation. Hence, most operating systems have extended processes with lightweight processes (or threads) that represent multiple flows of execution within the process addressing space. A thread needs to maintain much less state information than a process, typically it is described by its stack, CPU state and a pointer to the function it is executing, since it shares process resources and parts of the context with other threads within the same address space. The advantage of threads is that due to their low creation and context switch performance penalties they become a very interesting way to structure computer programs and to exploit parallelism.

There are operating systems, which provide kernel threads (Mach, Sun Solaris), while others implement threads as a user level library. In particular, user threads, i.e. threads implemented as a user level library on top of a single process, have very low commuting costs. The major disadvantage of user-level threads is the fact that the assignment of tasks to threads at a user-level is not seen by the operating system which continues to schedule processes. Hence, if a thread in a process is blocked on a system call (as is the case in many UNIX calls), all other threads in the same process become blocked too.

Therefore, support for kernel threads has gradually appeared in conventional computer operating systems. Kernel threads overcame the above disadvantages of user level threads and increased the performance of the system.

A crucial aspect of thread performance is the locking policy within the thread creation and switching functions. Naive implementations of these features, guarantee their execution as critical sections, by protecting the thread package with a single lock. More efficient implementations use finer and more careful locking implementations.

3.2 Scheduling

Scheduling is the activity of assigning processor time to the active tasks (processes or threads) in a computer and of commuting them. Although sophisticated schedulers implement complex process state machines there is a basic set of process (or thread) states that can be found in any operating system: A process can be running, ready or blocked. A running process is currently executing on one of the machine's processor whereas a ready process is able to be executed but has no available processor. A blocked process is unable to run because it is waiting for some event, typically the completion of an I/O operation or the occurrence of a synchronization event.

The run queue of an operating systems is a data structure in the kernel that contains all processes that are ready to be executed and await an available processor. Typically processes are enqueued in a run queue and are scheduled to the earliest available processor. The scheduler executes an algorithm, which places the running task in the run queue, selects a ready task from the run queue and starts its execution. At operating system level, what unites the processors in an SMP is the existence of a single run queue. Whenever a process is to be removed from a processor, this processor runs the scheduling algorithm to select a new running process. Since the scheduler can be executed by any processor, it must be run as a critical section, to avoid the simultaneous choice of a process by two separate executions of the scheduler. Additionally, most SMP provide methods to allow a process to run only on a given processor.

The simplest scheduling algorithm is first-come first-served. In this case, processes are ordered according to their creation order and are scheduled in that order typically by means of first-in first-out (FIFO) queue. A slight improvement in overall performance can be achieved by scheduling jobs according to their expected duration. Estimating this duration can be a tricky issue.

Priority scheduling is the approach taken in most modern operating system. Each job is assigned a priority and scheduled according to that value. Jobs with equal priorities are scheduled in FIFO order.

Scheduling can be preemptive or non-preemptive. In preemptive scheduling, a running job can be removed from the processor if another job with a higher priority becomes active. The advantage of non-preemption is simplicity: by avoiding to preempt a job, the operating system knows that the process has left the processor correctly without leaving its data structures or the resources it uses corrupted. The disadvantage of non-preemption is the slowness of reaction to hardware events, which cannot be handled until the running process has relinquished the processor.

There are a number of measures of the quality of an OS' scheduling algorithm. The first is CPU utilization. We would like to optimise the amount of time that the machine's processors are busy. CPU utilization is not however a user oriented metric. Users are more interested in other measures, notably the amount of time a job needs to run and, in an interactive system, how responsive the machine is, i.e. whether a user-initiated request yields results quickly or not. A measure that translates all these concerns well is the average waiting time of a process, i.e. the amount of time a process spends in the waiting queue.

The interested reader may find more about scheduling strategies in Chapter VI.

3.3 Process Synchronization

In an operating system with multiple threads of execution, accesses to shared data structures require synchronization in order to guarantee that these are used as critical sections. Gaining permission to enter a critical section, which involves testing whether another process has already an exclusive access to this section, and if not, locking all other processes out of it, has to be performed atomically. This requires hardware mechanisms to guarantee that this sequence of actions is not preempted. Mutual exclusion in critical sections is achieved by requiring that a lock is taken before entering the critical section and by releasing it after exiting the section.

The two most common techniques for manipulating locks are the test-and-set and swap operations. Test-and-set atomically sets a lock to its locked state and returns the previous state of that lock to the caller process. If the lock was not set, it is set by the test and set call. If it was locked, the calling process will have to wait until it is unlocked.

The swap operation exchanges the contents of two memory locations. Swapping the location of a lock with a memory location containing the value corresponding to its locked state is equivalent to a test-and-set operation.

Synchronizing processes or threads on a multiprocessor poses an additional requirement. Having a busy-waiting synchronization mechanism, also known as a spin lock, in which a process is constantly consuming bandwidth on the computer's interconnection to test whether the lock is available or not, as in the case of test-and-set and swap, is inefficient. Nevertheless, this is how synchronization is implemented at the hardware level in most SMP, e.g. those using Intel processors. An alternative to busy-waiting is suspending processes which fail to obtain a lock and sending interrupt calls to all suspended processes when the lock is available again. Another synchronization primitive which avoids spin a lock are semaphores. Semaphores consist of a lock and a queue, which is manipulated in mutual exclusion, containing all the processes that failed to acquire the lock. When the lock is freed, it is given to one of the enqueued processes, which is sent an interrupt call. There are other variations of synchronization primitives such as monitors [Hoa74], eventcount and sequencers [RK79], guarded commands [Dij75] and others but the examples above illustrate clearly the issues involved in SMP process synchronization.

3.4 Examples of SMP Operating Systems

Currently, the most important examples of operating systems for parallel machines are UNIX and Windows NT running on top of the most ubiquitous multi-processor machines, which are symmetric multiprocessors.

3.4.1 UNIX. UNIX is one the most popular and certainly the most influential operating system ever built. Its development began in 1969 and from then on countless versions of UNIX have been created by most major computer companies (AT&T, IBM, Sun, Microsoft, DEC, HP). It runs on almost all types of computers from personal computers to supercomputers and will continue to be a major player in operating system practice and research. There are currently around 20 different flavours of UNIX being released. This diversity led to various efforts to standardize UNIX and so there is an ongoing effort by the Open Group, supported by all major UNIX vendors, to create a unified interface for all UNIX flavours.

Architecture. UNIX was designed as a time-sharing operating system where simplicity and portability are fundamental. UNIX allows for multiple processes that can be created asynchronously and that are scheduled according to a simple priority algorithm. Input and output in UNIX is as similar as possible among files, devices and inter-process communication mechanisms. The file system has a hierarchical structure and includes the use of demountable volumes. UNIX was initially a very compact operating system. As technology progressed, there have been several additions to it such as support for graphical interfaces, networking and SMP that have increased its size considerably, but UNIX has always retained its basic design traits.

UNIX is a dual mode operating system: the kernel is composed of a set of components that are placed between the system call interface provided to the user and the kernel's interface to the computer's hardware. The UNIX kernel is composed of:

- Scheduler - The scheduler is the algorithm which decides which process is run next (see *Process management* below). The scheduling algorithm is executed by the process occupying the processor when it is about to relinquish it. The context switch between processes is performed by the *swapper* process, which is one of the two processes constantly running (the other one is the *init* process which is the parent process of all other processes on the machine).

- File system - A file in UNIX is a sequence of bytes, and the operating system does not recognize any additional structure in it. UNIX organizes files in a hierarchical structure that is captured in a metadata structure called the *inode* table. Each entry in the *inode* table represents a file. Hardware devices are represented in the UNIX file system in the */dev* directory which contributes to the interface standardization of UNIX kernel components. This way, devices can be read and written just like files. Files can be known in one or more directories by several names, which are called links. Links can point directly to a file within the same file system (hard links) or simply refer to the name of another file (symbolic links). UNIX supports mount points, i.e. any file can be a reference to another physical file system. *inodes* have a bit for indicating whether they are mount points or not. If a file that is a mount point is accessed, a table with the equivalence between filenames and mounted file system, the mount table, is scanned to find the corresponding file system. UNIX filenames are sequences of filenames separated by '/' characters. Since UNIX supports mount points and symbolic links, filename parsing has to be done on a name by name basis. This is required because any filename along the path to the file being ultimately referred to can be a mount point or symbolic link and indirect the path to the wanted file.

- Inter-process communication (IPC) mechanisms - Pipes, sockets and, in more recent versions of UNIX, shared memory are the mechanisms that allow processes to exchange data (see below).

- Signals - Signals are a mechanism for handling exceptional conditions. There are 20 different signals that inform a process of events such as arithmetical overflow, invalid system calls, process termination, terminal interrupts and others. A process checks for signals sent to it when it leaves the kernel mode after ending the execution of a system call or when it is interrupted. With the exception of signals to stop or kill a process, a process can react to signals as it wishes by defining a function, called a signal handler, which is executed the next time it receives a particular signal.

- Memory management - Initially, memory management in UNIX was based on a swapping mechanism. Current versions of UNIX resort also to paging to manage memory. In non-paged UNIX, processes were kept in a contiguous address space. To decide where to create room for a process to be brought from disk into memory (swapped-in), the swapper process used a criterion based on the amount of idle time or the age of processes in memory to choose which one to send to disk (swap-out). Conversely, the amount of time a process has been swapped out was the criterion to consider it for swap-in.

Paging has two great advantages: it eliminates external memory fragmentation and it eliminates the need to have complete processes in memory, since a process can request additional pages as it goes along. When a process requests a page and there isn't a page frame in memory to place the page, another page will have to be removed from the memory and written to disk.

The target of any page replacement algorithm is to replace the page that will not be used for the longest time. This ideal criterion cannot be applied because it requires knowledge of the future. An approximation to this algorithm is the least-recently-used (LRU) algorithm which removes from memory the page that hasn't been accessed for the longest time. However, LRU requires hardware support to be efficiently implemented. Since most systems provide a reference bit on each page that is set every time the page is accessed, this can be used to implement a related page replacement algorithm, one which can be found in some implementations of UNIX, e.g. 4.3BSD, the second chance algorithm. It is a modified FIFO algorithm. When a page is selected for replacement its reference bit is first checked. If this is set, it is then unset but the page gets a second chance. If that page is later found with its reference bit unset it will be replaced.

Several times per second, there is a check to see if it is necessary to run the page replacement algorithm. If the number of free page frames falls beneath a threshold, the *pagedaemon* runs the page replacement algorithm. In conclusion, it should be mentioned that there is an interaction between swapping, paging and scheduling: as a process looses priority, accesses to its pages become more infrequent, pages are more likely to be paged out and the process risks being swapped out to disk.

Process management. In the initial versions of UNIX, the only execution context that existed were processes. Later several thread libraries were developed (e.g. POSIX threads). Currently, there are UNIX releases that include kernel threads (e.g. Sun's Solaris 2) and the corresponding kernel interfaces to manipulate them.

In UNIX, a process is created using the *fork* system call, which generates a process identifier (or *pid*). A process that executes the *fork* system call receives a return value, which is the *pid* of the new process, i.e. its child process, whereas the child process itself receives a return code equal to zero. As a consequence of this process creation mechanism, processes in UNIX are organized as a process tree. A process can also replace the program it is executing with another one by means of the *execve* system call. Parent and children processes can be synchronized by using the *exit* and *wait* calls. A child process can terminate its execution when it calls the *exit* function and the parent process can synchronize itself with the child process by calling *wait*, thereby blocking its execution until the child process terminates.

Scheduling in UNIX is performed using a simple dynamic priority algorithm, which benefits interactive programs and where larger numbers indicate a lower priority. Process priority is calculated using:

$Priority = Processor\_time + Base\_priority[+nice]$

The nice factor is available for a processor to give other processes a higher priority. For each quantum that a process isn't executed, it's priority improves via:

$Processor\_time = Processor\_time/2$

Processes are assigned a CPU slot, called a quantum, which expires by means of a kernel timeout calling the scheduler. Processes cannot be preempted while executing within a kernel. They relinquish the processor either because they blocked waiting for I/O or because their quantum has expired.

Inter-process communication. The main inter-process communication mechanism in UNIX are pipes. A pipe is created by the *pipe* system call, which establishes a reliable unidirectional byte stream between two processes. A pipe has a fixed size and therefore blocks writer processes trying to exceed their size. Pipes are usually implemented as files, although they do not have a name. However, since pipes tend to be quite small, they are seldom written to disk. Instead, they are manipulated in the block cache, thereby remaining quite efficient. Pipes are frequently used in UNIX as a powerful tool for concatenating the execution of UNIX utilities. UNIX shell languages use a vertical bar to indicate that a program's output should be used as another program's input, e.g. listing a directory and then printing it (*ls | lpr*).

Another UNIX IPC mechanism are sockets. A socket is a communication endpoint that provides a generic interface to pipes and to networking facilities. A socket has a domain (UNIX, Internet or Xerox Network Services), which determines its address format. A UNIX socket address is a file name while an Internet socket uses an Internet address. There are several types of sockets. Datagram sockets, supported on the Internet UDP protocol, exchange packets without guarantees of delivery, duplication or ordering. Reliable delivered message sockets should implement reliable datagram communication but they are not currently supported. Stream sockets establish a data stream between two sockets, which is duplex, reliable and sequenced. Raw sockets allow direct access to the protocols that support other socket types, e.g. to access the IP or Ethernet protocols in the Internet domain. Sequenced packet sockets are used in the Xerox AF_NS protocol and are equivalent to stream sockets with the addition of record boundaries.

A socket is created with a call to *socket*, which returns a socket descriptor. If the socket is a server socket, it must be bound to a name (*bind* system call) so that client sockets can refer to it. Then, the socket informs the kernel that it is ready to accept connections (*listen*) and waits for incoming connections (*accept*). A client socket that wishes to connect to a server socket is also created with a *socket* call and establishes a connection to a server socket. Its name is known after performing a *connect* call. Once the connection is established, data can be exchanged using ordinary *read* and *write* calls.

A system call complementary to UNIX IPC mechanisms is the *select* call. It is used by a process that wishes to multiplex communication on several files or socket descriptors. A process passes a group of descriptors into the select call that returns the first on which activity is detected.

Shared memory support has been introduced in several recent UNIX versions, e.g. Solaris 2. Shared memory mechanisms allow processes to declare shared memory regions (*shmget* system call) that can then be referred to via an identifier. This identifier allows processes to attach (*shmat*) and detach (*shmdt*) a shared memory region to and from its addressing space. Alternatively, shared memory can be achieved via memory-mapped files. A user can choose to map a file (*mmap/munmap*) onto a memory region and, if the file is mapped in a shared mode, other processes can write to that memory region thereby communicating among them.

Internal parallelism. In a symmetric multiprocessor system, all processors may execute the operating system kernel. This leads to synchronization problems in the access to the kernel data structures. The granularity at which these data structures are locked is highly implementation dependent. If an operating system has a high locking cost it might prefer to lock at a higher granularity but lock less often. Other systems with a lower locking cost might prefer to have complex fine-grained locking algorithms thereby reducing the probability of having processes blocked on kernel locks to a minimum. Another necessary adaptation besides locking of kernel data structures is to modify the kernel data structures to reflect the fact that there is a set of processors.

3.4.2 Microsoft Windows NT. *Windows NT* [Cus93] is the high end of Microsoft Corporation's operating systems range. It can be executed on several different architectures (Intel x86, MIPS, Alpha AXP, PowerPC) with up to 32 processors. Windows NT can also emulate several OS environments (Win32, OS/2 or POSIX) although the primary environment is Win32. NT is a 32-bit operating system with separate per-process address spaces. Scheduling is thread based and uses a preemptive multiqueue algorithm. NT has an asynchronous I/O subsystem and supports several file systems: FAT, high-performance file system and the native NT file system (NTFS). It has integrated networking capabilities which support 5 different transport protocols: NetBeui, TCP/IP, IPX/SPX, AppleTalk and DLC.

Architecture. Windows NT is a dual mode operating system with user-level and kernel components. It should be noted that not the whole kernel is executed in kernel mode. The Windows NT components that are executed in kernel mode are:

- Executive - The executive is the upper layer of the operating system and provides generic operating system services for managing processes, threads and memory, performing I/O, IPC and ensuring security.
- Device Drivers - Device drivers provide the executive with a uniform interface to access devices independently of the hardware architecture the manufacturer uses for the device.
- Kernel - The kernel implements processor dependent functions and related functions such as thread scheduling and context switching, exception and interrupt dispatching and OS synchronization primitives
- Hardware Abstraction Layer (HAL) - All these components are layered on top of a hardware abstraction layer. This layer hides hardware specific details, such as I/O interfaces and interrupt controllers, from the NT executive thereby enhancing its portability. For example, all cache coherency and flushing in a SMP is hidden beneath this level.

The modules that are executed in user mode are:

- System & Service Processes - These operating system processes provide several services such as session control, logon management, RPC and event logging.
- User Applications
- Environment Subsystems - The environment subsystems use the generic operating system services provided by the executive to give applications the interface of a particular operating system. NT includes environment subsystems for MS-DOS, 16 bit Windows, POSIX, OS/2 and for its main environment, the Win32 API.

In NT, operating system resources are represented by objects. Kernel objects include processes and threads, file system components (file handles, logs), concurrency control mechanisms (semaphores, mutexes, waitable timers) and inter-process communication resources (pipes, mailboxes, communication devices). In fact, most of the objects just mentioned are NT executive interfaces to low-level kernel objects. The other two types of Windows NT OS objects are the user and graphical interface objects which compose the graphical user interface and are private to the Win32 environment.

Calls to the kernel are made via a protected mechanism that causes an exception or interrupt. Once the system call is done, execution returns to user-level by dismissing the interrupt. These are calls to the environment subsystems libraries. The real calls to the kernel libraries are not visible at user-level.

Security in NT is based on two mechanisms: processes, files, printers and other resources have an access control list and active OS objects (processes and threads) have security tokens. These tokens identify the user on behalf of which the process is executing, what privileges that user possesses and can therefore be used to check access control when an application tries to access a resource.

Process management. A Windows NT process is a data structure where the resources held by an execution of a program are managed and accounted for. This means that a process keeps track of the virtual addressing space and the corresponding working set its program is using. Furthermore an NT process includes a security token identifying its permissions, a table containing the kernel objects it is using and a list of threads. A process' handle table is placed in the system's address space and therefore protected from user-level "tampering".

In NT, a process does not represent a flow of execution. Program execution is always performed by a thread. In order to trace an execution a thread is composed of a unique identifier, a set of registers containing processor state, a stack for use in kernel mode and a stack for use in user mode, a pointer to the function it is executing, a security access token and its current access mode.

The Windows NT kernel has a multi-queue scheduler. It has 32 different priority levels. The upper 15 are reserved for real time tasks. Scheduling is preemptive and strictly priority driven. There is no guaranteed execution period before preemption and threads can be preempted in kernel mode. Within a priority level, scheduling is time-sliced and round robin. If a thread is preempted it goes back to the head of its priority level queue. If it exhausts its CPU quantum, it goes back to the tail of that queue.

Regarding multiprocessor scheduling, each task has an ideal processor, which is assigned, at the thread's creation, in a round-robin fashion among all processors. When a thread is ready, and more than one processor is available, the ideal processor is chosen. Otherwise, the last processor where the thread ran is used. Finally, if the thread has not been waiting for too long, the scheduler checks to see if the next thread in the ready state can run on its ideal processor. If it can, this second thread is chosen. A thread can run on any processor unless an affinity mask is defined. An affinity mask is a sequence of bits where each represents a processor and which can be set to restrict the processors where a thread is allowed to execute. However, this this forced thread placement, called hard affinity, may lead to a reduced execution of the thread.

Inter-process communication. Windows NT provides several different inter-process communication (IPC) mechanisms:

Windows sockets. The Windows Sockets API provides a standard Windows interface to several communication protocols with different addressing schemes, such as TCP/IP and IPX. The Windows Sockets API was developed to accomplish two things. One was to migrate the sockets interface, developed for UNIX BSD in the early 1980s, into the Windows NT environments, and the other was to establish a new standard interface capable of supporting emerging network capabilities such as real time communications and QoS (quality of service) guarantees. The Windows Sockets, currently in their version 2, are an interface for networking, not a protocol. As they do not implement a particular protocol, the Windows Sockets do not affect the data being transferred through them. The underlying transport protocol can be of any type. Besides the usual datagram and stream sockets, it can, for example, use a protocol designed for multimedia communications. The transport protocol and name providers are placed beneath the Windows Socket layer.

Local Procedure Calls. LPC is a message-passing facility provided by the NT executive. The LPC interface is similar to the standard RPC but it is optimised for communication between two processes on the same machine. LPC communication is based on ports. A port is a kernel object that can have two types: connection port and communication port. Connections are established by sending a connect request to another process' connection port. If the connection is accepted, communication is then established via two newly created ports, one on each process. LPC can be used to pass messages directly through the communication ports or to exchange pointers into memory regions shared by both communicating processes.

Remote Procedure Calls (RPC). Apart from the conventional inter-computer invocation procedure, the Windows NT RPC facility can use other IPC mechanisms to establish communications between the computers on which the client and the server portions of the application exist. If the client and server are on the same computer, the Local Procedure Call (LPC) mechanism can be used to transfer information between processes and subsystems. This makes RPC the most flexible and portable IPC choice in Windows NT.

Named pipes and mailslots. Named pipes provide connection-oriented messaging that allows applications to share memory over the network. Windows NT provides a special application programming interface (API) that increases security when using named pipes.

The mailslot implementation in Windows NT is a subset of the Microsoft OS/2 LAN Manager implementation. Windows NT implements only second-class mailslots. Second class mailslots provide connectionless messaging for broadcast messages. Delivery of the message is not guaranteed, though the delivery rate on most networks is high. It is most useful for identifying other computers or services on a network. The Computer Browser service under Windows NT uses mailslots. Named pipes and mailslots are actually implemented as file systems. As file systems, they share common functionality, such as security, with the other file systems. Local processes can use named pipes and mailslots without going through the networking components.

NetBIOS. NetBIOS is a standard programming interface in the PC environment for developing client-server applications. NetBIOS has been used as an IPC mechanism since the early 1980s. From a programming aspect, higher level interfaces such as named pipes and RPCs are superior in their flexibility and portability. A NetBIOS client-server application can communicate over various protocols: NetBEUI protocol (NBF), NWLink NetBIOS (NWNBLink), and NetBIOS over TCP/IP (NetBT).

Synchronization. In Windows NT, the concept of having entities through which threads can synchronize their activities is integrated in the kernel object architecture. The synchronization objects, objects on which a thread can wait and be signalled, in the NT executive are: process, thread, file, event, event pair, semaphore, timer and mutant (seen at Win32 level as a mutex). Synchronization on these objects differs in the conditions needed for the object to signal the threads that are waiting on it. The circumstances in which synchronization objects signal waiting threads are: processes when their last thread terminates, threads when they terminate, files when an I/O operation finishes, events when a thread sets them, semaphores when their counter drops to zero, mutants when holding threads release them, timers when their set time expires. Synchronization is made visible to Win32 applications via a generic wait interface (*WaitForSingleObject* or *WaitForMultipleObjects*).

4. Operating Systems for NORMA environments

In Section 2. we showed that parallel architectures have been restricted mainly to symmetric multiprocessors, multicomputers, computer clusters and networks of workstations. There are some examples of true NORMA machines, notably the Cray T3E. However since networks of workstations and/or personal computers are the most challenging NORMA environments today, we chose to approach the problem of system level support for NORMA parallel programming to raise some of the problems that arise in the network of workstations environment. Naturally, most of those problems are also highly prominent in NORMA multiprocessors.

While in a multiprocessor every processor is exactly like every other in capability, resources, software and communication speed, in a computer network that is not the case. As a matter of fact, the computers in a network are most probably heterogeneous, i.e. they have different hardware and/or operating systems. More precisely, the heterogeneity aspects that must be considered, when exploiting a set of computers in a network, are the following: architecture, data format, computational speed, machine and network load.

Heterogeneity of architecture means that the computers in the network can be Intel personal computers, workstations, shared-memory multiprocessors, etc... which poses the problems of incompatible binary formats and different programming methodologies.

Data format heterogeneity is an important obstacle to parallel computing because it prevents computers from correctly interpreting the data exchanged among them.

The heterogeneity of computational speed may result in unused processing power because the same task can be accomplished much faster in a multiprocessor than in a personal computer, for example. Thus, the programmer must be careful at splitting the tasks among the computers in the network so that no computer sits idle.

The computers in the network have different usage patterns, which lead to different loads. The same reasoning applies to network load. This may lead to a situation in which a computer takes a lot of time to execute a simple task, because it is too loaded, or stays idle, because it is waiting for some message.

All these problems must be solved in order to take advantage of the benefits of parallel computing on networks of computers, which can be summarized as follows:

- low price given that the computers already exist;
- optimised performance by assigning the right task to the most appropriate computer (taking into account its architecture, operating system and load);
- the resources available can easily grow by simply connecting more computers to the network (possibly with more advanced technologies);
- programmers still use familiar tools such as in a single computer (editors, compilers, etc.)

4.1 Architectural Overview

Currently, stand-alone workstations and personal computers are very ubiquitous and almost always connected by means of a network. Each machine provides a reasonable amount of processing power and memory which remains unused for long periods of time. The challenge is to provide a platform that allows programmers to take advantage of such resources easily. Thus, the computational power of such computers can be applied to solve a variety of computationally intensive applications. In other words, this network-based approach can be effective in coupling several computers, resulting in a configuration that might be economically and technically difficult to achieve with supercomputer hardware.

On the other extreme of the spectrum of NORMA systems are of course multicomputers generally running separate supervisor microkernels. These machines derive their performance from high performance interconnection and from very compact and therefore very fast operating system. The parallelism is exploited not directly by the operating system but by some language level functionality. Since each node is a complete processor and not a simplified processing node as in SIMD supercomputers, the tasks it performs can be reasonably complex.

System level support for NORMA architectures involves providing mechanism to overcome the physical processor separation and to coordinate activities on processors running independent operating systems. This section discusses some of these basic mechanisms: distributed process management, parallel file systems and distributed recovery.

4.2 Distributed Process Management

In contrast with the SMP discussed in the previous section that are generally used as glorified uniprocessor in the sense that they execute an assorted set of applications, NORMA systems are targeted at parallel applications. *Load balancing* is an important feature to increase the performance of many parallel applications. However, efficient load balancing, in particular receiver initiated load balancing protocols, where processors request tasks from others, requires an underlying support for process migration.

4.2.1 Process migration. *Process migration* [Nut94] is the ability to move an executing process from one processor to another. It is a very useful functionality although it is costly to execute and challenging to implement. Basically, migration consists of halting a process in a consistent state in the current processor, packing a complete description of its state, choosing a new processor for the process, shipping the state description to the destination processor and restarting it there. Process migration is most frequently motivated by the need to balance the load of a parallel application. However, it is also useful for reducing inter-process communication (processes communicating with increasing frequency should be moved to the same processor), reconfiguring a system for administrative reasons or exploiting a special capability specific of a particular processor. There are several systems that implemented process migration such as Sprite[Dou91], Condor [BLL92] or Accent [Zay87]. More recently, as migration capabilities where introduced in object oriented distributed and parallel systems, the interest in migration has shifted into object migration, or mobile objects as in Emerald[MV93] or COOL[Lea93]. However, the core difficulties remain the same: ensuring that the migrating entity's state is completely described and capturing, redirecting and replaying all interactions that would have taken place during the migration procedure.

4.2.2 Distributed recovery. Recovery of a computation in spite of node failures is achieved via checkpointing, which is the procedure of saving the state of an ongoing distributed computation so that it can be recovered from that intermediate state in case of failure. It should be noted that checkpointing allows a computation to recover from a system failure. However, if an execution fails due to an error induced by the process' execution itself, the error will repeat itself after recovery. Another type of failures not addressed by checkpointing are secondary storage failures. Hard disk failures have to be addressed by replication using mirrored disks or RAID (cf. Section 8.4 of Chapter V).

Checkpointing and process migration require very similar abilities from the system point of view since the complete state of a process must be saved so that the processor (the current one in the case of checkpointing or another in the case of process migration) can be correctly loaded and restarted with the process' saved state. There are four basic approaches for checkpointing [EJW96]:

- Coordinated checkpointing - In coordinated checkpointing, the processes involved in a parallel execution execute their checkpoints simultaneously in order to guarantee that the saved system state is consistent. Thus, the processes must periodically cooperate in computing a consistent global checkpoint. Coordinated checkpoints were devised because simplistic protocols with lack of coordination tend to create a so-called domino effect. The domino effect is due to the existence of orphan messages. An orphan message appears when a process, after sending messages to other processes, needs to rollback to a previous checkpoint. In that case, there will be processes that have received messages, which, from the point of view of the failed process that has rolled back, haven't been sent. Suppose that in a group of processes each saves its state independently. Then, if a failure occurs and a checkpoint has to be chosen in order to rollback to it, it is difficult to find a checkpoint where no process has orphan messages. As a result the system will regress indefinitely trying to find one checkpoint that is consistent for all processors. Coordinated checkpointing basically eliminates the domino effect, given that processes always restart from the most recent global checkpointing. This coordination even allows for processes to have non-deterministic behaviours. Since all processors are restarted from the same moment in the computation, the new computation could take a different execution path. The main problem with this approach is that it requires the coordination of all the processes, i.e. process autonomy is sacrificed and there is a performance penalty to be paid when all processes have to be stopped in order to save a globally consistent state.
- Uncoordinated checkpointing - With this technique, processes create checkpoints asynchronously and independently of each other. Thus, this approach allows each process to decide independently when to take checkpoints. Given that there is no synchronization among computation, communication and checkpointing, this optimistic recovery technique can tolerate the failure of an arbitrary number of processors. For this reason, when failures are very rare, this technique yields better throughput and response time than other general recovery techniques.
  When a processor fails, processes have to find a set of previous checkpoints representing a consistent system state. The main problem with this approach is the domino effect, which may force processes to undo a large amount of work. In order to avoid the domino effect, all the messages received since the last checkpoint was created would have to be logged.
- Communication-induced checkpointing - This technique complements uncoordinated checkpoints and avoids the domino effect by ensuring that all processes verify a system-wide constraint before they accept a message

from the outside world. A number of such constraints that guarantee the avoidance of a domino effect have been identified and this method requires that any incoming message is accompanied by the necessary information to verify the constraint. If the constraint is not verified, then a checkpoint must be taken before passing the message on to the parallel application. An example of a constraint for communication induced logging is the one proposed in Programmer Transparent Coordination (PTC) [KYA96] which requires that each process take a checkpoint if the incoming message makes it depend on a checkpoint that it did not previously depend upon.

– Log-based rollback recovery - This approach requires that processes save their state when they perform a checkpoint and additionally save all data regarding interactions with the outside world, i.e. emission and reception of messages. This stops the domino effect because the message log bridges the gap between the checkpoint to which the failed process rolled back and the current state of the other processes. This technique can even include non-deterministic events in the process' execution if these are logged too. A common way to perform logging is to save each message that a process receives before passing it on to the application code.

During recovery the logged events are replayed exactly as they occurred before the failure.

The difference of this approach with respect to to the previous ones is that in both, coordinated and uncoordinated checkpointing, the system restarts the failed processes by restoring a consistent state. The recovery of a failed process is not necessarily identical to its pre-failure execution which complicates the interaction with the outside world. On the contrary, log-based rollback recovery does not have this problem since it recorded all its previous interactions with the outside world.

There are three variants of this approach: pessimistic logging, optimistic logging, and causal logging.

In pessimistic logging, the system logs information regarding each non-deterministic event before it can affect the computation, e.g. a message is not delivered until it is logged.

Optimistic logging takes a more relaxed but more risky approach. Non-deterministic events are not written to stable storage but saved in a faster volatile log and only periodically written in an asynchronous way to a stable storage. This is a more efficient approach since it avoids constantly waiting for costly writes to a stable storage. However, should a process fail, the volatile log will be lost and there is the possibility of thereby creating orphan messages and inducing a domino effect.

Causal logging uses the Lamport *happened-before* relation [Lam78], to establish which events caused a process' current state, and guarantee that all those events are either logged or available locally to the process.

4.3 Parallel File Systems

Parallel file systems address the performance problem faced by current network *client-server file systems*: the read and write bandwidth for a single file is limited by the performance of a single server (memory bandwidth, processor speed, etc.). Parallel applications suffer from the above-mentioned performance problem because they present I/O loads equivalent to traditional supercomputers, which are not handled by current file servers. If users resort to parallel computers in search of fast execution, the file systems of parallel computers must also aim at serving I/O request rapidly.

4.3.1 Striped file systems.
Dividing a file among several disks enables an application to access that file quicker by issuing simultaneous requests to several disks [CK93]. This technique is called declustering. In particular, if the file blocks are divided in a round-robin way among the available disks it is called striping. In a striped file system, either individual files are striped across the servers (per-file striping), or all the data is striped, independently of the files to which they belong, across the servers (per-client striping). In the first case, only large files benefit from the striping. In the second case, given that each client forms its new data for all files into a sequential log, even small files benefit from the striping.

With per-client striping, servers are used efficiently, regardless of file sizes. Striping a large amount of writes allows them to be done in parallel. On the other hand, small writes will be batched.

4.3.2 Examples of parallel file systems.
CFS (Concurrent File System) [Pie89] is one of the first commercial multiprocessor file systems. It was developed for the Intel iPSC and Touchstone Delta multiprocessors. The basic idea of CFS is to decluster files across several I/O processors, each one with one or more disks. Caching and prefetching are completely under the control of the file system; thus, the programmer has no way to influence it. The same happens with the clustering of a file across disks, i.e. it is not predictable by the programmer.

CFS constitutes the secondary storage of the Intel Paragon. The nodes use the CFS for high-speed simultaneous access to secondary storage. Files are manipulated using the standard UNIX system calls in either C or FORTRAN and can be accessed by using a file pointer common to all applications, which can be used in four sharing modes:

- Mode 0: Each node process has its own file pointer. It is useful for large files to be shared among the nodes.
- Mode 1: The computer nodes share a common file pointer, and I/O requests are serviced on a first-come-first-serve basis.
- Mode 2: Reads and writes are treated as global operations and a global synchronization is performed.
- Mode 3: A synchronous ordered mode is provided, but all write operations have to be of the same size.

The PFS (Parallel File System) [Roy93] is a striped file system which stripes files (but not directories or links) across the UNIX file systems that were assembled to create the file system. The size of each stripe, the stripe unit is determined by the system administrator.

Contrary to the previous two file systems, the file system for the nCUBE multiprocessor [PFD+89] allows the programmer to control many of its features. In particular, the nCUBE file system, which also uses file striping, allows the programmer to manipulate the striping unit size and distribution pattern.

IBM's Vesta file system [CFP+93], a striped file system for the SP-1 and SP-2 multiprocessors, allows the programmer to control the declustering of a file when it is created. It is possible to specify the number of disks, the record size, and the stripe-unit size. Vesta provides users with a single name space. Users can dynamically partition files into subfiles, by breaking a file into rows, columns, blocks, or more complex cyclic partitioning. Once partitioned, a file can be accessed in parallel from a number of different processes of a parallel application.

4.4 Popular Message-Passing Environments

4.4.1 PVM. *PVM* [GBD94] supports parallel computing on current computers by providing the abstraction of a parallel virtual machine which comprehends all the computers in a network. For this purpose, PVM handles message routing, data conversion and task scheduling among the participating computers.

The programmer develops his programs as a collection of cooperating tasks. Each task interacts with PVM by means of a library of standard interface routines that provide support for initiating and finishing tasks on remote computers, sending and receiving messages and synchronizing tasks.

To cope with heterogeneity, the PVM message-passing primitives are strongly typed, i.e. they require type information for buffering and transmission.

PVM allows the programmer to start or stop any task, or to add or delete any computer in the network from the parallel virtual machine. In addition, any process may communicate or synchronize with any other. PVM is structured around the following notions:

- The user with an application running on top of PVM can decide which computers will be used. This set of computers, a user-configured host pool, can change during the execution of an application, by simply adding or deleting computers from the pool. This dynamic behaviour is very useful for fault-tolerance and load-balancing.
- Application programmers can specify which tasks are to be run on which computers. This allows the explicit exploitation of special hardware or operating system capabilities.

- In PVM, the unit of parallelism is a task that often, but not necessarily, is a UNIX process. There is no process-to-processor mapping implied or enforced by PVM.
- Heterogeneity: Varied networks and applications are supported. In particular, PVM allows messages containing more than one data type to be exchanged by machines with different data representations.
- PVM uses native message-passing support on those computers in which the hardware provides optimised message primitives.

4.4.2 MPI. *MPI* [MPI95] stands for Message Passing Interface. The goal of MPI is to become a widely used standard for writing message-passing programs. It is a standard that defines both the syntax and semantics, of a message-passing library that can efficiently be implemented on a wide range of computers. The defined interface attempts to establish a practical, portable, efficient, and flexible standard for message-passing. The MPI standard provides MPI vendors with a clearly defined base set of routines that they can implement efficiently or, in some cases, provide hardware support for, thereby enhancing scalability.

MPI has been strongly influenced by work at the IBM T. J. Watson Research Center, Intel's NX/2, Express, nCUBE's Vertex, and p4.

Blocking communication is the standard communication mode in MPI. By default, a sender of a message is blocked until the receiver calls the appropriate function to receive the message. However, MPI does support non-blocking communication. Although MPI is a complex standard, six basic calls are enough to create an application:

- **MPI_Init** - initiate a MPI computation
- **MPI_Finalize** - terminate a computation
- **MPI_Comm_size** - determine the number of processes
- **MPI_Comm_rank** - determine the current process' identifier
- **MPI_Send** - send a message
- **MPI_Recv** - receive a message

MPI is not a complete software infrastructure that supports distributed computing. In particular, MPI provides neither process management, i.e. the ability to create remote tasks, nor support for I/O. So, MPI is a communications interface layer that will be built upon native facilities of the underlying hardware platform. (Certain data transfer operations may be implemented at a level close to hardware.) For example, MPI could be implemented on top of PVM.

5. Scalable Shared Memory Systems

Traditionally parallel computing has been based on the message-passing model. However there are a number of experiences with distributed shared memory that have shown that there is not necessarily a great performance penalty to pay for this more amenable programming model. The great advantage of shared memory is that it hides the details of interprocessor communication from the programmer. Furthermore, this transparency allows for a number of performance-enhancing techniques, such as caching and data migration and replication, to be used without changes to application code.

Of course, the main advantage of shared memory, transparency, is also the major flaw, as pointed out by the advocates of message-passing: a programmer with application specific knowledge can better control the placement and exchange of data than an underlying system can do it in an implicit, automatic way. In this section, we present some of the most successful scalable shared memory systems.

5.1 Shared Memory MIMD Computers

5.1.1 DASH.
The goal of the Stanford DASH [LLT+93] project was to explore large-scale shared-memory architecture with hardware directory-based cache coherency. DASH consists of a two dimensional mesh of clusters. Each cluster contains four processors (MIPS R3000 with two levels of cache), up to 28 MB of main memory, a directory controller, which manages the memory metadata, and a reply controller, which is a board that handles all requests issued by the cluster. Within each cluster cache consistency is maintained with a snoopy bus protocol. Between clusters, cache consistency is guaranteed by a directory-based protocol. To enforce this protocol a full-map scheme is implemented. Each cluster has a complete map of the memory indicating whether a memory location is valid on the local memory or if the most recent value is held at a remote cluster. Requests for memory locations that are locally invalid are sent to the remote cluster, which replies to the requesting cluster. The DASH prototype is composed of 16 clusters with a total of 64 processors. Due to the various caching levels, locality is a relevant factor for the performance of DASH whose performance degrades as application working sets increase.

5.1.2 MIT Alewife.
The MIT Alewife's architecture [ACJ+91] is similar to that of the Stanford DASH. It is composed by a 2D mesh of nodes, each with a processor (a modified SPARC called Sparcle), memory and a communication switch. However, the Alewife uses some interesting techniques to improve performance. The Sparcle processor is able to switch quickly context between threads. So when a thread accesses data that is not available locally, the processor, using independent register sets, quickly switches to another thread. Another interesting feature of the Alewife is its LimitLESS cache coherence technique. LimitLESS emulates a directory scheme similar to that of the DASH but it uses a very small map of cache line descriptors. Whenever a cache line is requested that is outside that limited set, the request is handled by a software trap. The leads to a much smaller performance degradation

than should be expected and has the obvious advantage of reducing memory occupation.

5.2 Distributed Shared Memory

Software distributed shared memory (DSM) systems aim at capturing the growing computational power of workstations and personal computers and the improvements in the networking infrastructure to create a parallel programming environment on top of them. We present two particularly successful implementations of software DSM: TreadMarks and Shasta.

5.2.1 TreadMarks. TreadMarks [KDC+94] is a DSM platform developed by Rice University, which uses lazy release consistency as its memory consistency model. A memory consistency model defines under which circumstances memory is updated in a DSM system. The release consistency model depends on the existence of synchronization variables whose accesses are divided into *acquire* and *release*. The release consistency model requires that accesses to regular variables are followed by the *release* of a synchronization variable which must be *acquired* by any other process before accessing the regular variables again. In particular, the lazy release consistency model postpones the propagation of memory updates performed by a process until another process acquires the corresponding synchronization variable.

Another fundamental option in DSM is deciding how to detect that applications are attempting to access memory. If the DSM layer wants to do the detection automatically by using memory page faults then the unit of consistency, i.e., the smallest amount of memory that can be updated in a consistency operation will be a memory page. Alternatively, smaller consistency units can be used but in this case the system can no longer rely on page faults and changes have to be made to the application code to indicate where data accesses are going to occur.

The problem with big consistency units is false sharing. False sharing happens when two processes are accessing different regions of a common consistency unit. In this case, they will be communicating frequently to exchange updates of that unit although in fact they are not sharing data at all.

The designers of TreadMarks chose the page-based approach. However they use a technique called lazy diff creation for reducing the amount of data exchanged to update a memory page. When an application first accesses a page TreadMarks creates a copy of the page (a twin). When another process requests an update of the page, a record of the modifications made to the page (a diff) is created by comparing the two twin pages, the initial and the current one. It is this diff that is sent to update the requesting processes page. TreadMarks has been used for several applications, such as genetic research where it was particularly successful.

5.2.2 Shasta. Shasta [SG97] is a software DSM system that runs on AlphaServer SMPs connected by a Memory Channel interconnection. The Memory Channel is a memory-mapped network that allows a process to transmit data to a remote process without any operating system overhead via a simple store into a mapped page. Processes check for incoming memory transfers by polling a variable.

Shasta uses variable sized memory units, which are multiples of 64 bytes. Memory units are managed using a per-processor table where the state of each block is kept. Additionally, each processor knows for each of its local memory units, the ones initially placed in its memory, which processors are holding those memory units.

Shasta implements its memory consistency protocol by instrumenting the application code, i.e. altering the binary code of the compiled applications. Each access to application data is bracketed in code that enforces memory consistency. The added code doubles the size of applications. However using a set of optimisations, such as instrumenting sequences of contiguous memory accesses as a single access, this overhead drops to an average of 20 %. Shasta is a paradigmatic example of a non-intrusive transition of a uniprocessor application to a shared memory platform: the designers of Shasta were able to execute the Oracle database transparently on top of Shasta.

References

[ACJ+91]   Agarwal, A., Chaiken, D., Johnson, K., Kranz, D., Kubiatowicz, J., Kurihara, K., Lim, B., Maa, G., Nussbaum, D., *The MIT Alewife Machine: A Large-Scale Distributed-Memory Multiprocessor, Scalable Shared Memory Multiprocessors*, Kluwer Academic Publishers, 1991.

[Bac93]   Bacon, J., *Concurrent Systems, An Integrated Approach to Operating Systems, Database, and Distributed System*, Addison-Wesley, 1993.

[BZ91]   Bershad, B.N., Zekauskas, M., Midway, J., Shared memory parallel programming with entry consistency for distributed memory multiprocessors, Technical Report CMU-CS-91-170, School of Computer Science, Carnegie-Mellon University, 1991.

[Bla90]   Blank, T., The MasPar MP-1 architecture, *Proc. 35th IEEE Computer Society International Conference (COMPCON)*, 1990, 20-24.

[BLL92]   Bricker, A., Litzkow, M., Livny, M., Condor technical summary, Technical Report, Computer Sciences Department, University of Wisconsin-Madison, 1992.

[BW97]   Brooks III, E.D., Warren, K.H., A study of performance on SMP and distributed memory architectures using a shared memory programming model, *SC97: High Performance Networking and Computing*, San Jose, 1997.

[Cha98]   Charlesworth, A., Starfire: Extending the SMP envelope, *IEEE Micro* 18, 1998.

[CFP+93]   Corbett, P.F., Feitelson, D.G., Prost, J.P., Johnson-Baylor, S.B., Parallel access to files in the vesta file system, *Proc. Supercomputing '93*, 1993, 472-481.

[CK93]   Cormen, T.H., Kotz, D., Integrating theory and practice in parallel file systems, *Proc. the 1993 DAGS/PC Symposium*, 1993, 64-74.

[Cus93]   Custer, H., *Inside Windows NT*, Microsoft Press, Washington, 1993.

[Dij75]   Dijkstra, E.W., Guarded commands, nondeterminancy and the formal derivation of programs, *Communications of the ACM* 18, 1975, 453-457.

[Dou91]   Douglis, F., Transparent process migration: Design alternatives and the Sprite implementation, *Software Practice and Experience* 21, 1991, 757-785.

[EJW96]   Elnozahy, E.N., Johnson, D.B., Wang, Y.M., A survey of rollback-recovery protocols in message-passing systems, Technical Report, School of Computer Science, Carnegie Mellon University, 1996.

[Fly72]   Flynn, M.J., Some computer organizations and their effectiveness, *IEEE Transactions on Computers* 21, 1972, 948-960.

[GBD94]   Geist, A., Beguelin, A., Dongarra, J., *PVM: Parallel Virtual Machine: A Users' Guide and Tutorial for Networked Parallel Computing*, MIT Press, Cambridge, 1994.

[GC93]   Guedes, P., Castro, M., Distributed shared object memory, *Proc. Fourth Workshop on Workstation Operating Systems (WWOS-IV)*, Napa, 1993, 142-149.

[GST+93]   Gupta, A., Singh, J.P., Truman, J., Hennessy, J.L., An empirical comparison of the Kendall Square Research KSR-1 and Stanford DASH multiprocessors, *Proc. Supercomputing'93*, 1993, 214-225.

[Her97]   Herdeg, G.A., Design and implementation of the Alpha Server 4100 CPU and memory architecture, *Digital Technical Journal* 8, 1997, 48-60.

[Hoa74]   Hoare, C.A.R., Monitors: An operating system structuring concept, *Communications of the ACM* 17, 1974, 549-557.

[Div95]   Intel Corporation Supercomputer Systems Division, *Paragon System User's Guide*, 1995.

[JS98]   Jiang, D., Singh, J.P., A methodology and an evaluation of the SGI Origin2000, *Proc. SIGMETRICS Conference on Measurement and Modeling of Computer Systems*, 1998, 171-181.

[Joh88]   Johnson, E.E., Completing an MIMD multiprocessor taxonomy, *Computer Architecture News* 16, 1988, 44-47.

[KDC+94]   Keleher, P., Dwarkadas, S., Cox, A.L., Zwaenepoel, W., TreadMarks: Distributed shared memory on standard workstations and operating systems, *Proc. the Winter 94 Usenix Conference*, 1994, 115-131.

[KYA96]   Kim, K.H., You, J.H., Abouelnaga, A., A scheme for coordinated independent execution of independently designed recoverable distributed processes, *Proc. IEEE Fault-Tolerant Computing Symposium*, 1996, 130-135.

[Lam78]   Lamport, L., Time, clocks and the ordering of events in a distributed system, *Communications of the ACM* 21, 1978, 558-565.

[LL94]   Laudon, J., Lenoski, D., The SGI Origin: A ccNUMA highly scalable server, Technical Report, Silicon Graphics, Inc., 1994.

[Lea93]   Lea, R., Cool: System support for distributed programming, *Communications of the ACM* 36, 1993, 37-46.

[LLT+93]   Lenoski, D., Laudon, J., Truman, J., Nakahira, D., Stevens, L., Gupta, A., Hennessy, J., The DASH prototype: Login overhead and performance, *IEEE Transactions on Parallel and Distributed Systems* 4, 1993, 41-61.

[MPI95]   Message Passing Interface Forum, MPI: A message-passing interface standard - version 1.1, 1995.

[MV93]   Moos, H., Verbaeten, P., Object migration in a heterogeneous world - a multi-dimensional affair, *Proc. Third International Workshop on Object Orientation in Operating Systems*, Asheville, 1993, 62-72.

[Nut94]   Nuttall, M., A brief survey of systems providing process or object migration facilities, *ACM SIGOPS Operating Systems Review* **28**, 1994, 64-80.

[Pie89]   Pierce, P., A concurrent file system for a highly parallel mass storage system, *Proc. the Fourth Conference on Hypercube Concurrent Computers and Applications*, 1989, 155-160.

[PFD+89]   Pratt, T.W., French, J.C., Dickens, P.M., Janet, S.A., Jr., A comparison of the architecture and performance of two parallel file systems, *Proc. Fourth Conference on Hypercube Concurrent Computers and Applications*, 1989, 161-166.

[RK79]   Reed, D.P., Kanodia, R.K., Synchronization with eventcounts and sequencers, *Communications of the ACM* **22**, 1979, 115-123.

[Roy93]   Roy, P.J., Unix file access and caching in a multicomputer environment, *Proc. the Usenix Mach III Symposium*, 1993, 21-37.

[SG97]   Scales, D.J., Gharachorloo, K., Towards transparent and efficient software distributed shared memory, *Proc. 16th ACM Symposium on Operating Systems Principles (SIGOPS'97)*, *ACM SIGOPS Operating Systems Review* **31**, 1997, 157-169.

[SG94]   Silberschatz, A., Galvin, P.B., *Operating System Concepts*, Addison-Wesley, 1994.

[SS94]   Singhal, M., Shivaratri, N.G., *Advanced Concepts in Operating Systems*, McGraw Hill, Inc., New York, 1994.

[SH97]   Smith, P., Hutchinson, N.C., Heterogeneous process migration: The Tui system, Technical Report, Department of Computer Science, University of British Columbia, 1997.

[TMC90a]   Thinking Machines Corporation, *Connection Machine Model CM-2 Technical Summary*, 1990.

[TMC90b]   Thinking Machines Corporation, *Connection Machine Model CM-5 Technical Summary*, 1990.

[Zay87]   Zayas, E.R., Attacking the process migration bottleneck, *Proc. Symposium on Operating Systems Principles*, Austin, 1987, 13-22.

VI. Management of Resources in Parallel Systems

Jacek Błażewicz[1], Maciej Drozdowski[1], and Klaus Ecker[2]

[1] Institute of Computing Science, Poznań University of Technology, Poznań, Poland
[2] Institut für Informatik, Technische Universität Clausthal, Clausthal-Zellerfeld, Germany

Summary. In this chapter we discuss the parallel processing context of scheduling in computer systems. Only *deterministic model* of scheduling will be examined. This does not mean that only static problems in which all parameters are known in advance and the solutions are in all ways fixed, are discussed. Also dynamic problems are possible in which some characteristics are not known in advance. In the following, basic classical scheduling approaches will be recalled and then a special attention will be paid to three new models of scheduling in parallel systems: scheduling multiprocessor tasks, scheduling with communication delays and scheduling divisible tasks.

1. Introduction

Parallel processing is believed to bring computers' power to a new and yet unprecedented levels. However, raw processing speed of parallel processors may remain only an unexploited potential if it is not wisely harnessed by software systems. This means, for example, that parts of parallel applications should not wait for execution longer than necessary. In other words, resources of parallel systems and parallel programs must be properly managed. This kind of managing resources is termed *scheduling*. Scheduling [BEP+96] can be understood broadly as allocating resources over time to perform tasks being parts of some processes. As *processors* are the source of the processing power, which is the reason for parallelism, we concentrate on managing them as the *most important resource*. In contemporary parallel architectures processors are spatially distributed and communicate via various kinds of interconnections. Therefore, we will consider *communication medium* as another important resource. From the above description it can be inferred that scheduling is particularly related to the construction of operating systems (Chap.V), compilers (Chap.III), and libraries (Chap.VII).

Comprehensive description of scheduling problems is beyond the size and scope of this work. Scheduling is tightly related to the field of operations research. More information on scheduling in general can be found e.g. in [BEP+96, Bru98, CCL+95, Cof76, LLR+93, Pin95].

The deterministic formulation imposes tight connection with discrete mathematics. We assume that the reader has a basic knowledge of discrete mathematics. However, we do not refrain from introducing important notions and methods of the latter that are useful in analyzing deterministic scheduling problems. They will be presented in the following paragraphs of this section together with the formulation of the basic scheduling problem. Section 2 will be devoted to the classical scheduling approaches. In the following sections we examine in more detail three new models devised for scheduling parallel applications. In Section 3 a model of multiprocessor tasks will be considered, while in Section 4 scheduling single processor tasks with communication delays will be presented. Finally, Section 5 will analyze divisible task scheduling problem.

1.1 Basic Notions and Methods

1.1.1 Basic structures. In this paragraph we introduce, in an informal way, some basic notions from discrete mathematics used throughout this chapter. We intend to give the reader some intuition rather than strict mathematical definitions. An extensive treatment of this subject can be found e.g. in [GKP94, RW92].

A *set* can be described as a collection of distinguishable objects. If, for instance, element a belongs to set A we will denote it by $a \in A$. Examples of sets are the set of natural numbers which will be denoted Z^+, the set of real numbers, sets of programs running on a computer, $\{a, b, c\}$ which is a set of elements $a, b,$ and c. A *subset* of some set is a selection of its elements, e.g. $A = \{a, b\}$ is a subset of $B = \{a, b, c, d\}$ and this fact can be denoted as $A \subset B$. When the inclusion is not strict, i.e. set A may be included in B or be identical with B we will denote such a case by $A \subseteq B$. In simple words, *cardinality* $| A |$ of set A can be understood as the number of elements included in A.

Cartesian product $A_1 \times A_2 \times \ldots \times A_k$ of sets $A_1, A_2, \ldots, A_k$ is the set of all tuples $(a_1, a_2, \ldots, a_k)$ where $a_i \in A_i$, $i = 1, \ldots, k$. *Relation* over sets $A_1, \ldots, A_k$ is a subset of $A_1 \times \ldots \times A_k$. If $k = 2$ then the relation is called *binary*. *Function* f from A to B (which is denoted $f : A \to B$) is a relation f over A and B such that for any $a \in A$ there exists exactly one $b \in B$ such that tuple $(a, b) \in f$. This can be also denoted $f(a) = b$. A is a *domain*, and B is a *range* of function B.

A *graph* is a pair $G = (V, E)$, where V is the set of *vertices* or *nodes*, E is the set of *edges* or *arcs*. An example graph is depicted in Fig.4.1a. A realistic example of a graph is the set of cities and communication links: cities are nodes, communication links are edges. Also projects and computations can be presented as graphs. For example, nodes can represent stages in performing of a project and arcs represent activities, or calculations, undertaken to make a transition from one state to another. Note a difference between the last two examples. In the first example, an edge usually can be traversed in both directions. In the second, the arcs are unidirectional, because in real world it is rather difficult to revert completely the results of some operation. Thus, we distinguish two classes of graphs: undirected graphs (or just graphs) and *directed graphs* or *digraphs*. In the former case set E of edges consists of two-element subsets of V. In the latter case E is a relation over $V \times V$, and $(i, j) \in E$ denotes that arc (i, j) can be traversed from node i to node j only.

Graph $G' = (V', E')$ is a *subgraph* of $G = (V, E)$, which we denote $G' \subseteq G$, if $V' \subseteq V$, and $E' \subseteq E$ is the set of edges adjacent to the nodes of V' (both ends of the edge are in V').

A *path* in an undirected graph $G = (V, E)$ is a sequence $i_1, \ldots, i_k$ of distinct nodes of V such that for each pair i_r and i_{r+1} we have $\{i_r, i_{r+1}\} \in E$ for $r = 1, \ldots, k - 1$. In the case of directed graphs a *directed path* is again defined as a sequence of vertices $i_1, \ldots, i_k$ for which $(i_r, i_{r+1}) \in E$ for $r = 1, \ldots, k-1$. An undirected *cycle* is defined as a path but additionally $\{i_k, i_1\} \in E$. A directed cycle is a directed path together with $(i_k, i_1) \in E$. A graph without cycles is called *acyclic*. Two vertices are *connected* if there is an undirected path between them. A graph is *connected* when all pairs of vertices are connected by a path. A *vertex degree* is the number of edges adjacent to the vertex.

Consider now directed graphs only. If there is a directed path from vertex u to v then we say that u is a *predecessor* of v, and v is a *successor* of u. When $(u, v) \in E$ then u is an *immediate* or *direct predecessor* and v is an *immediate (direct) successor.* An *out-degree* of vertex $v \in V$ is the number of arcs beginning in v, i.e. $out\text{-}degree(v) =| \{(v, u) : (v, u) \in E\} |$. Analogously, an *in-degree* of v is the number of arcs finishing at v. We can distinguish special classes among directed graphs. *Directed acyclic graphs* (DAGs) (i.e. digraphs without a directed cycle) are important as they can represent many computational processes. A *chain* is a DAG in which all arcs form a directed path. In other words, for any pair of vertices $u, v \in V$, u is either a successor or a predecessor of v. An *in-tree* is a connected DAG with exactly one vertex of out-degree 0, and all other vertices have out-degree 1. An *out-tree* is a connected DAG with exactly one vertex with in-degree 0 and all other vertices with in-degree 1. An *out-forest* (resp. *in-forest*) is a set of not connected out-trees (in-trees).

Let V be a nonempty set and $\mathcal{E}$ a collection of subsets of V. A pair $H = (V, \mathcal{E})$ is called a *hypergraph*. A hypergraph is a generalization of the graph concept allowing the hyperedges to link more than two vertices.

In the following, $\forall_a b$ denotes an abbreviation of the sentence: for all objects satisfying a, b is true.

1.1.2 Complexity issues. Here we present basic concepts of a computational complexity analysis for combinatorial problems (i.e. for problems characterized by a finite set of parameters), such as deterministic scheduling problems. Our description is only a rough outline of the theory. A comprehensive treatment can be found in [GJ79]. The idea behind the computational complexity (precise definitions are given in the following parahraphs) can be understood intuitively as follows: Many combinatorial problems expose combinatorial explosion, i.e. exponential (or faster) growth of possible cases that must be analyzed in order to find a desired one. This phenomenon is unwanted, because it prevents from building usable algorithms. Can one avoid combinatorial explosion? Sometimes it is possible. Yet, according to the current state of the knowledge, the answer is negative for many practical problems. The complexity analysis enables to determine the computational complexity class of the considered problem (cf. Fig.1.2). Then, it gives directions for dealing with problems in certain classes. A problem is computationally easy when an algorithm exists that solves this problem in time bounded from above by some polynomial in the size of the problem. In the opposite case the problem is computationally hard (strictly, its decision version is NP-complete) and cannot be solved both to optimality and in time polynomially bounded. In the latter case there are two ways of dealing with the problem: either strive for optimality but sacrifice time, or minimize solution time without guarantees of optimality. The rest of this section gives detailed definitions of the above notions.

Before going into further details let us note the difference between problem π and its instance I. As an example problem π consider the well-known TRAVELLING SALESMAN PROBLEM (TSP). It consists in finding in some graph the shortest cycle such that each vertex is visited exactly once. When we are

given a particular graph, and want to find the shortest cycle connecting e.g.
the 100 biggest cities in the world we deal with an instance I of problem π.
Therefore, instance I of problem π can be understood as a particular case of
π for which all variables have been set to specific values.

Among the combinatorial problems one can distinguish decision problems
and optimization ones. Decision problems consist in answering "yes" or "no"
to some question. Optimization problems require extremization of some objective function. Each optimization problem has its decision version which
consists in answering whether a solution with an acceptable value of the objective function exists. An algorithm solving the optimization version can be
also used to solve the decision version. Therefore, the decision version is not
computationally harder than the original optimization version. Hence, it is
possible to analyze computational hardness of optimization problems, e.g.
scheduling problems, by considering only their decision counterparts. When
the decision version is computationally hard, then the optimization version is
also hard. For the above reasons computational complexity classes are defined
on the basis of decision problems.

We are going to classify inherent computational complexity of various
problems basing on dependence between the solution time and the size of the
instance of the problem. A versatile theory needs to be problem and computer
independent. Consequently, two reliable measures are necessary: a measure of
the problem instance size, and a measure of the execution time. As a measure
of the size of the problem instance I, the length $N(I)$ of a string encoding its
data is used. All encoding schemes are equivalent for purposes of complexity
analysis provided that numbers are encoded using counting system with base
greater than 1, encoding is not redundant, and the encoded string can be
decoded. A measure of the execution time for algorithm A and problem size
n, is the maximum number of elementary steps taken by a computer for any
instance $I \in D_\pi$, where D_π is the domain of problem π and $n = N(I)$. Such
a measure of execution time is called algorithm computational complexity
function (in short: *complexity*). We will say that algorithm A has complexity
$O(f(n))$ when its complexity function $g_A(n)$ satisfies: there is a constant C
such that for almost all $I \in D_\pi : g_A(N(I)) \leq Cf(N(I))$. When the number of
steps $g_A(n)$ can be bounded from above by a polynomial in the problem size
$f(n)$ we say that the algorithm is *polynomial time* (or *polynomial* in short).
Otherwise, when the complexity function cannot be bounded in this way the
algorithm is called *exponential time* (*exponential* in short). Still, the execution time cannot be reliably measured without establishing a model of the
computer system. We distinguish realistic and unrealistic computer system
models. The class of *realistic models* comprise such models of real computers
as the Deterministic Turing Machine (DTM), the k-tape Deterministic Turing Machine, and the Random Access Machine [GJ79]. All the above models
are equivalent for the task of classifying complexity of considered problems
because algorithms polynomial on one of the three models remain polynomial

on any other realistic machine. The class of unrealistic models includes e.g. the Nondeterministic Turing Machine (NDTM), and the Oracle Turing Machine (OTM). Unrealistic models can be interpreted as capable of executing an unbounded number of computations per unit of time.

A key point of computational complexity analysis is establishing the complexity class the considered problem belongs to. In this presentation we use four basic classes of computational complexity for decision problems: **P**, **NP**, the class of NP-complete problems (NPc in short), and the class of problems NP-complete in the strong sense (sNPc).

Definition 1.1. *Class **P** includes all problems solvable in polynomial time on DTM.*

This means that a problem in class **P** can be solved in polynomial time on any really existing computer. We introduce additional notions to define the remaining classes.

Definition 1.2. *Class **NP** includes all problems solvable in polynomial time on NDTM.*

From these definitions and definitions of DTM, NDTM [GJ79] it is known that $P \subseteq NP$. Yet, neither has it been proved that $P \neq NP$ nor that $P = NP$. It is only known that in the worst-case DTM can simulate NDTM in exponential time.

Definition 1.3. *A polynomial transformation of problem π_2 to problem π_1 (which is denoted by $\pi_2 \propto \pi_1$) is a function $f : D_{\pi_2} \to D_{\pi_1}$ which:*
(i) $\forall_{I_2 \in D_{\pi_2}}$ the answer is "yes" if and only if it is "yes" for $I_1 = f(I_2)$,
(ii) $\forall_{I_2 \in D_{\pi_2}}$ function f can be calculated in time polynomial in $N(I_2)$.

Definition 1.4. *Decision problem π_1 is NP-complete (NPc for short) if $\pi_1 \in NP$ and $\forall_{\pi_2 \in NP} \pi_2 \propto \pi_1$.*

Hence, if there existed a polynomial algorithm for any NP-complete problem then any problem in **NP** would be solvable in polynomial time. Furthermore, $P \neq NP$ would imply that no polynomial algorithm exists for any NPc problem. On the other hand, $P = NP$ would imply that all problems in **NP** (and hence also all NPc problems) can be solved in polynomial time. Though it has not been shown that $P \neq NP$ for years, no polynomial time algorithm has been found for any NPc problem. This class includes many difficult (decision) combinatorial problems such as TRAVELLING SALESMAN PROBLEM, INTEGER LINEAR PROGRAMMING, GRAPH COLORING, PARTITION. By Definition 1.4, to prove NP-completeness of some problem it is enough to show that some NPc problem polynomially transforms to the analyzed problem. The first problem that has been proved to be NPc is SATISFIABILITY. It is known that class NPc includes thousands of problems and subproblems from many fields of combinatorial optimization.

Though no polynomial algorithms are known for problems in NPc, for some of them e.g. dynamic programming algorithms have been found with complexity bounded by polynomial in the instance size $N(I)$ and the maximum numerical value $Max(I)$ occuring in the instance I. Such algorithms are called *pseudopolynomial*. Mind that these are not polynomial algorithms because the numerical value $Max(I)$ cannot be bounded from above by any polynomial in $N(I)$ for all instances of the problem. Therefore, conditions of Definition 1.1 are not satisfied. On the other hand, for some problems pseudopolynomial time algorithms were hard to be found. Strongly NP-complete problems are the ones for which no pseudopolynomial algorithms exist unless **P=NP**. This class is defined as follows.

Definition 1.5. *Let π_p for problem π and some polynomial p denote the subproblem of π obtained by restricting D_π to instances such that $Max(I) \leq p(N(I))$. Problem π is strongly NP-complete if $\pi \in$ **NP** and $\pi_p \in NPc$.*

The relations between the defined classes are presented in Fig. 1.1.

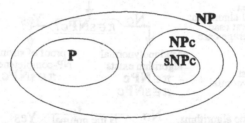

Fig. 1.1. Relations between complexity classes provided that **P≠NP**.

An optimization problem which decision counterpart is NP-complete is called NP-hard (NPh in short), and strongly NP-hard (sNPh in short) when the decision version is strongly NP-complete.

As mentioned at the beginning of this section there are practical consequences of determining the complexity class for the considered problem. When the problem belongs to class **P** (in the decision version) then it is solvable in polynomial time which generally means in acceptable time. On the contrary, NP-hardness of some problem (or NP-completeness of its decision version) results in the combinatorial explosion when the optimal solution is searched for. Thus, only exponential *optimization* (i.e. finding the optimal solutions) algorithms have been proposed for NPh problems. For NPh problems which are not sNPh, pseudopolynomial algorithms, like dynamic programming, can be proposed. When the optimality of the solution is not as important as the time in which a feasible solution is obtained, heuristics can be used. A *heuristic* is an algorithm which finds a feasible solution of the problem, however, there is no guarantee of optimality. A prerequisite of using some method as a heuristic is its low-order polynomial execution time. Heuristics which give solutions close to the optimum (on average, in the worst case) are obviously preferred. To evaluate the worst-case quality of some heuristic H we will use the *worst-case performance ratio*: $S_H = \inf\{r \geq 1 : \forall_{I \in D} \frac{H(I)}{OPT(I)} \leq r\}$, where I is some instance of the problem, D the problem domain, $H(I)$ the value of solution generated by H on instance I, and $OPT(I)$ is the optimal value of the criterion for I. Heuristics with known performance ratio are called *approximation algorithms*. The way of analyzing problem complexity and the resulting solution methods are summarized in Fig. 1.2. The solid lines show ways of establishing the complexity class of the problem, while dashed lines indicate possible algorithmic approaches to the problem.

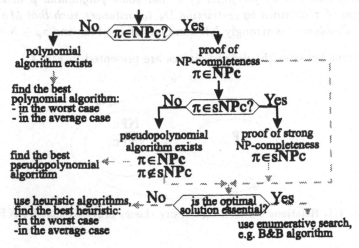

Fig. 1.2. An outline of the complexity analysis procedure. π denotes a decision version of some optimization problem.

1.1.3 Algorithmic approaches. In the sequel we will describe typical algorithmic approaches to solving computationally hard, i.e. NP-hard, scheduling problems. Since a full description of algorithmic methods applicable in such cases is not possible here we only describe the most important methods. As mentioned in the previous section, after establishing NP-hardness of some problem we have two options in general: apply some fast algorithm but optimality of the result may not be guaranteed, or try to find an optimal solution which may take exponential time in the worst case. Let us start with a short description of the first approach which has heuristics as a base.

Among various kinds of scheduling heuristics *list scheduling algorithms* are common and practical. List algorithms order tasks on a certain list. Whenever a processor becomes idle the first task from the list eligible for execution is scheduled on the available processor. The tasks can be ordered on the list according to their processing times, deadlines, some way defined urgencies or weights.

Another class of general purpose heuristics are *metaheuristics* also called *local search heuristics*. Metaheuristics were successfully applied in a very diverse class of combinatorial optimization problems [AL97, GL97]. The notion metaheuristic characterizes the fact that algorithms of this class were designed as universal global optimization tools operating on a highly abstract solution space. These methods guide low level heuristics tailored to a particular combinatorial problem. Consider a problem of minimizing an objective function f over set S of all admissible solutions, called a solution space. A natural approach to such a problem is to start from some feasible solution $x \in S$ and try reaching a better solution y from the neighborhood $N(x) \subset S$ of x. $y \in N(x)$ is obtained by a local modification or perturbation of x. In other words, the new solution y is in some sense 'close' to x. Hence such strategies are called local search heuristics. The classical *hill climbing* method works according to this scheme by always selecting the best $y \in N(x)$. However, this method stops as soon as a local optimum is found. Metaheuristics are global optimization methods and are able to exit from the local optima. They differ in the way of searching the solution space S, methods of constructing neighborhood $N(x)$, selecting new solution y, etc. Below we shortly describe some standard metaheuristics.

Tabu search [HW90, GL97] works similarly to hill climbing algorithm, i.e. the best neighbor $y \in N(x)$ is preferred as the next solution. However, a local optimum z would trap the search because z is better than any of its neighbors. Thus, the search would be returning to z cyclicly. To avoid this situation a *tabu list* is applied, which is a queue used to prohibit reverting some number of just performed perturbations.

Simulated annealing [Cer85, KGV83, LA87] is based on simulating slow cooling of a solid [MRR+53]. In the case of an optimization problem a neighbor $y \in N(x)$ is accepted as a new solution if it reduces the value of the optimization function f (in the case of minimization). If the perturbation increases value of the objective function by $\Delta f > 0$, then the new solution is accepted with probability $e^{-\frac{\Delta f}{c_k}}$ where c_k is a control parameter equivalent to temperature. The method of gradual decreasing c_k and changing other parameters of the algorithm is called *cooling schedule*. The probability of accepting worse solutions decreases as the control parameter c_k decreases. Therefore, escaping local minima is easy at the beginning of the algorithm execution when c_k is high. As the iteration number k increases, improving perturbations are more likely to be accepted which eventually may terminate the search in the global minimum. Simulated annealing can be understood as a random walk guided roughly in the direction improving the objective function.

Genetic search tries to imitate the genetic nature of the evolution [Gol89, Mic92]. In a simple version of the algorithm each solution is represented by a string equivalent to a gene. Good solutions from the initial population are combined to obtain a new population. The measure of a solution quality is called *fitness function* (the objective function is a good candidate for the fitness function, but not the only possible). There are three classical operators used to obtain new 'individuals'. *Reproduction* copies a solution to the new population. *Crossover* is a binary operator exchanging tails of the strings in two genes starting in a randomly selected place. The effect of the crossover is that certain properties of the initial solutions can be implicitly identified and combined. *Mutation* makes random changes in the individuals and diversifies in the population. In this way new populations are obtained iteratively from the old ones until some stopping criterion is reached.

When optimality of the solution is essential then an optimization algorithm must be applied. This may result in the enumeration of a potentially exponential number of possible points in the search space S. Hence, optimization algorithms are often called *enumerative methods*.

The *branch-and-bound* (B&B) algorithm is a classical enumerative method [Cof76, LW66]. It resembles divide and conquer method in programming. Instead of attacking a difficult problem detail by detail one may divide it into easier subproblems and try solving them separately. Similarly, in B&B solution space S is divided into mutually exclusive subsets $S_1, \ldots, S_k$. The subsets can be further divided until obtaining a single solution. The search in S can be viewed as a search in a tree in which some branch or node i represents a subset S_i of solutions while subsets of S_i are successors of i in such a tree. The idea of B&B is to eliminate subsets (nodes in the search tree) from further consideration as soon as possible. Some subset S_i can be eliminated for the reasons that: (i) S_i includes no better solution than some currently known solution x, (ii) S_i has no feasible solutions, (iii) all solutions in S_i are dominated by some other subset $S_j \subset S$, i.e. solutions in S_j are known to be at least as good as solutions in S_i therefore only S_j needs to be analyzed. The basic mechanism used in B&B is (i). To be able to apply it, some estimate or bound of the objective function for the solutions in S_i must be implemented. The known solution x can be obtained by some heuristic or it can be the best solution obtained during the execution of the B&B. Hence, to construct a B&B algorithm one must decide about *branching* strategy which is the method of dividing and searching in S, and about *bounding* strategy that estimates the objective function and eliminates nodes in the search tree.

As mentioned in Section 1.1.2, in some cases pseudopolynomial algorithms based on *dynamic programming* can be proposed. These are also enumerative methods, because all possible solutions can be visited in the worst case. Foundations of dynamic programming can be traced back to Bellman's principle of optimality [Bel57, BD62]. This approach can be applied when the problem can be solved by a sequence of decisions in a number of stages. In the context of combinatorial optimization problems Bellman's principle can be formulated as follows: Starting at any current state, the optimal policy for the subsequent stages is independent of the policies adopted in the previous stages. In other words, for the given stage subsequent (later) decisions must be optimal. Consequently, recursive equations can be derived which describe the value of the objective function at some (subsequent) stage on the basis of the results at the previous stages.

1.2 General Formulation of the Scheduling Problem

In this section we introduce basic notions of deterministic scheduling theory. Necessary extensions will be introduced in the following sections.

Deterministic scheduling problems are described by three elements: the computing environment comprising processor set $\mathcal{P}$ other resources $\mathcal{R}$, task system $\mathcal{T}$, and the optimality criterion.

Let $\mathcal{P}=\{P_1, \ldots, P_m\}$ denote the set of processors. Two classes of processors can be distinguished. *Dedicated processors* and *parallel processors*. Dedicated processors are specialized devices performing different functions. For example, we often say that specialized processors such as I/O, arithmetic, vector, graphic, signal processors are dedicated. In certain situations even identical processors can behave like dedicated ones. For instance, certain mapping of parts of a parallel application to processors can be advantageous due to the communication pattern of the parallel application. Changing the assignment may increase the communication overhead, and should be avoided. In production systems machines are regarded as dedicated rather than parallel. In the classical setting of the scheduling theory [BEP+96, CCL+95, Cof76, LLR+93, Pin95] tasks may consist of operations executed by dedicated processors. In such a case three types of dedicated processor systems are distinguished: *flow-shop*, *open-shop*, and *job-shop*. In the flow-shop all tasks have the same number of operations which are performed in the same order by all the processors. In the open-shop the order among the operations is immaterial. For the job-shop, the sequence of operations and the required processors are determined for each task separately.

In the case of parallel processors each processor can execute any task. Parallel processors are divided into three classes: *identical* processors where all processors execute all tasks with the same speed, *uniform* processors which have different processing speeds b_i $(i = 1, \ldots, m)$ independent of the tasks, and *unrelated* processors for which execution speed depends both on the processor and on the task.

Apart from the processors there can be also a set $\mathcal{R} = \{R_1, \ldots, R_k\}$ of additional resources, each available in $\mid R_i \mid$ units $(i = 1, ..., k)$. Computer memory, shared variables, I/O devices are examples of the resources. Tasks may acquire resources, and thus exclude concurrent execution of other tasks.

The second constituent of scheduling problems is the task system. First, we explain the relation between certain concepts in parallel processing and operating systems, and the notions used in scheduling models. An *application* (or a program) can be executed (at least potentially) by many processors working concurrently. A *thread* is the basic unit of processor utilization [Hwa93, SPG91, Tan95]. Thus, any thread is executed by a single processor. A thread is equivalent to a program stream with its own instruction counter running within the environment of an application. Memory spaces of the threads within the application are not isolated from each other. Here, any activity inherently running on a single processor will be considered as equivalent, from the scheduling viewpoint, to a thread. Analogously, activities which can be performed on many processors in parallel (even only potentially) will be considered as applications. A *task* is the basic unit in scheduling theory. The relation between the task, application and thread depends on the scheduling model. In classical scheduling models the application consists of some (potentially) concurrent threads which are subject to scheduling. In this case tasks correspond to threads. In the case of multiprocessor task model, where the application is considered without its internal structure, the task corresponds to the application.

We consider task set $\mathcal{T} = \{T_1, \ldots, T_n\}$ for which it is possible to determine such features as preemptability (or nonpreemptability) of tasks and existence (or non-existence) of precedence constraints [BEP+96, Cof76] among the tasks. Tasks are *preemptable* when each task can be interrupted and restarted later, possibly on a different processor, without incurring additional costs. In such a case the schedule is called *preemptive*. Otherwise, tasks are *nonpreemptable* and the schedule is called *nonpreemptive*. Two tasks T_i and T_j are *dependent* if T_i must be completed before starting task T_j. The dependency relation between T_i and T_j is denoted by $T_i \prec T_j$. Dependencies are represented as a directed acyclic graph (DAG, see 1.1.1) and are called *precedence constraint graph* or *task graph*. If there is no dependency relation between any pair of tasks then tasks are called *independent*.

Each task T_j $(j = 1, \ldots, n)$ is described by a number of parameters. In the following we describe the most important ones.

1. *Processing time* p_{ij} $(i = 1, \ldots, m)$ is the time needed to execute task T_j on processor P_i. When processors are identical, $\forall_i p_{ij} = p_j$. In the case of uniform processors, $p_{ij} = \frac{p_j}{b_i}$, where p_j is processing time of task T_j on some standard processor and b_i is the speed of processor P_i.

2. *Ready time* or *arrival time* r_j. A task can be executed at r_j or after .

3. *Due-date* or *deadline* d_j. A task should be finished not later than by d_j. If the task must be finished not later than d_j (which is a critical limit), then d_j is called a *deadline*.

4. *Weight* or priority w_j which can be interpreted as the cost per time unit of T_j residing in the computer system.

5. *Resource requirements* R_{ji}. Task T_j may require R_{ji} units of resource R_i.

Before describing optimality criteria, i.e. the third element of a scheduling problem formulation, we define a schedule.

Definition 1.6. *A schedule is an assignment of tasks to processors and resources in time satisfying the following requirements:*

- *Each task is assigned to one processor at a time.*
- *Each processor executes at most one task at a time.*
- *Task T_j is not executed before time r_j $(j = 1, \ldots, n)$.*
- *For each pair $T_i \prec T_j$, task T_i is completed before T_j starts.*
- *All tasks are completed.*
- *Nonpreemptable tasks are not interrupted, and preemptable tasks are interrupted a limited number of times.*
- *Additional resource requirements (if any) are satisfied.*

A schedule satisfying the above definition is called *feasible*. A *Gantt chart* is a convenient method of presenting schedules graphically. In these charts time is represented on the horizontal axis while the processors are placed along the vertical axis. Examples of Gantt charts can be found in Fig.3.1, Fig.3.5, Fig.4.4. In a given schedule one can determine for task T_j:

  - *completion time c_j,*
  - *flow time $f_j = c_j - r_j$,*
  - *lateness $l_j = c_j - d_j$,*
  - *tardiness $\tau_j = \max\{0, c_j - d_j\}$*
  - *whether it is late: $U_j = 1$ if $c_j > d_j$, $U_j = 0$ otherwise.*

The third element of a scheduling problem specification is the optimality criterion. Several criteria are of interest: :

  Schedule length (makespan) $C_{max} = \max_{1 \le j \le n}\{c_j\}$.

  Maximum lateness $L_{max} = \max_{1 \le j \le n}\{l_j\}$.

  Mean flow time $\overline{F} = \frac{1}{n}\sum_{j=1}^{n} f_j$. Note that this is equivalent to the *sum of completion times* $\sum_{j=1}^{n} c_j$. The mean flow time criterion could be named equivalently as mean response time.

  Mean weighted flow time $\overline{F_w} = \frac{\sum_{j=1}^{n} w_j f_j}{\sum_{j=1}^{n} w_j}$, which is equivalent to the *total weighted completion time* $\sum_{j=1}^{n} w_j c_j$.

  Number of late tasks $U = |\{T_j : U_j = 1\}|$.

  Weighted number of late tasks $\sum_{j=1}^{n} w_j U_j$.

  Mean tardiness $\frac{1}{n}\sum_{j=1}^{n} \tau_j$, which is equivalent to $\sum_{j=1}^{n} \tau_j$.

In the most obvious case a solution of a deterministic scheduling problem can be thought of as a static schedule in which the tasks are fixed in time and on processors. Note that problems defined in the deterministic way not always have static schedules as their solutions. There exist situations in which position of the task in space and time is not a priori fixed. It is not unthinkable to imagine an algorithm building schedules dynamically according to the current state of the computer system. Such an algorithm can work equally well basing on the deterministic description of the task and computer systems. Dynamic algorithms building schedules using only the information about the tasks present in the system are called *on-line*.

2. Classical Approaches

2.1 Classical Deterministic Scheduling Theory Model

We give here a rough outline of the classical deterministic scheduling results and picture limits of their applicability (for details see e.g. [BEP+96, Bru98, CCL+95, Cof76, LLR+93, Pin95]).

Many problems of scheduling on parallel processors are computationally hard. For example, when schedule length is the optimality criterion, tasks are nonpreemptable and have arbitrary processing times, the problem is NP-complete (in its decision version) even for two processors ($m = 2$)[Kar72]. This observation guided the research in several directions. Firstly, heuristics were analyzed for scheduling problems. Secondly, the most complicated (but still) polynomially solvable problems were sought for. List algorithms are easy to implement. Therefore, these are the tools commonly used to solve scheduling problems. It has been shown [Gra66] that the worst case performance ratio of an arbitrary list scheduling algorithm LS for C_{max} criterion is $S_{LS} = 2 - \frac{1}{m}$, where m is the number of processors.

Longest Processing Time (LPT) is an algorithm which orders tasks such that $p_1 \geq p_2 \ldots \geq p_n$, i.e. from the longest to the shortest. The tasks are assigned to free processors in the same order. When there are no precedence constraints among tasks the worst case performance ratio of LPT is $S_{LPT} = \frac{4}{3} - \frac{1}{3m}$ [Gra66]. In this case the relative distance of a solution from the optimum is approximately 33.3%.

Shortest Processing Time (SPT) is a list scheduling algorithm which orders the tasks in the opposite order, i.e. according to nonincreasing processing times $p_1 \leq p_2 \leq \ldots \leq p_n$. SPT builds optimal schedules for the mean flow time criterion when no precedence constraints exist among the tasks.

On the other hand, the most involved problems solvable to optimality in polynomial time were surveyed to delineate the border between the hard and the easy cases. Thus, when tasks are nonpreemptable, but have equal processing times ($\forall_j p_j = 1$) the problem of building the shortest schedule on *two processors* can be solved in polynomial time, e.g.:

− for in- or out-tree precedence constraints [Hu61] (even for arbitrary number of processors),
− for arbitrary precedence constraints [CG72],
− for due-dates, release times and arbitrary precedence constraints [GJ77] (even for L_{max} criteron).

However, for an arbitrary number of processors and if we have both precedences of the out-tree form and due-dates the problem is already NPh [BGJ77]. It turned out that preemptable scheduling problems are often easier than nonpreemptable ones. For example, shortest schedules can be found in polynomial time for the following problems:

- arbitrary number of processors, no precedence constraints, no due-dates, no release times [McN59];
- arbitrary number of processors, in- or out-tree precedences, no due-dates, no release times [MC69, MC70];
- two processors, arbitrary precedences, no due-dates, no release times [MC69, MC70].

Yet, when the number of processors is arbitrary and the precedence constraints are arbitrary, then the problem is sNPh even for preemptable tasks [Ull76].

The classical scheduling theory originated in the times when multiprocessor systems with few tightly coupled processors dominated. In such systems processors could be considered as fully connected and the communication overheads were negligible. Nowadays, parallel systems are often multicomputers comprising many processing elements connected via some kind of network, and communication time may not be ignored. A great variety of interconnection characteristics influences this time. For example, each processing element may be able (or unable) to communicate and compute simultaneously, to communicate over several ports simultaneously, messages can be transferred according to store-&-forward, circuit-switched and other methods of routing. Thus, the communication system is an important element of the multiprocessor computer system which should be included in modern scheduling algorithms.

2.2 Allocation

Scheduling can be viewed as allocation and sequencing. In some situations sequencing is not as important as allocation. For example, an application for image processing may consist of several modules that simultaneously coexist in the multiprocessor computer system. The stream of consecutive frames flows through modules and processors. A good allocation of the modules is necessary so that communication paths are not long and computationally intensive modules are executed by fast processors. Since the actual sequencing of the activities is not taken into account, the precedence constraint graph is reduced to an undirected graph representing interactions among the tasks "accumulated" over run-time. Such a graph is called a *task graph*.

Now, we describe the allocation problem more precisely. Consider a parallel application which modules (tasks) are communicating with each other. The application is to be executed on a set of processors connected by some network. Define:

$x_{ik} = 1$ when task i is executed on processor k, otherwise $x_{ik} = 0$ (the matrix of binary variables x_{ik} defines an allocation of tasks to processors, it is to be determined);

α_{ij} - the number of data units transferred from task i to task j;

C_{kl} - is an interconnection-related communication cost of moving one unit of data between processors k and l;

t_{ik} - cost of executing task i on processor k.

The problem is to minimize:

$$\sum_{k=1}^{m}\sum_{i=1}^{n}(t_{ik}x_{ik} + \sum_{l=1}^{m}\sum_{j=1}^{n}\alpha_{ij}C_{kl}x_{ik}x_{jl}) \tag{2.1}$$

subject to

$$\sum_{k=1}^{m} x_{ik} = 1 \quad \text{for} \quad i = 1, \dots, n$$

The formula (2.1) is an objective function. Its first part $(\sum_{k=1}^{m}\sum_{i=1}^{n}t_{ik}x_{ik})$ represents the total cost of computation. The other part represents the total cost of communication. The second equation guarantees that each task is executed on exactly one processor. The above objective function (2.1) is reasonable for unrelated processors. However, for identical and uniform processors its minimum is achieved when all the work is performed on the fastest processor. Thus, instead of function (2.1) the working time of the most loaded processor can be the objective function and one has to minimize:

$$\max_{k}\{\sum_{i=1}^{n}(t_{ik}x_{ik} + \sum_{l=1}^{m}\sum_{j=1}^{n}\alpha_{ij}C_{kl}x_{ik}x_{jl})\}$$

The allocation problem usually was solved by enumerative search (e.g. branch- and-bound), heuristics tailored to the problem, and metaheuristics (see 1.1.3).

2.3 Embedding

Mapping of tasks to the processors and the interconnection network is also called *embedding*. However, in the literature a different problem is considered as embedding than the allocation problem defined above. Let $G = (V, E)$ be a task graph and let $H = (\mathcal{P}, N)$ be a graph consisting of nodes $\mathcal{P}$ representing processors, and a set of edges N representing the interconnection network. More precisely the embedding $< f, b >$ of G into H consists of mapping f of the nodes from G to processors of H and mapping b of each edge $e = (u, v) \in E$ to some path $b(e)$ connecting $f(u)$ and $f(v)$. The cost function of an embedding can be: the *dilatation* defined as the maximum length of any $b(e)$, the *expansion* equal to $\frac{|\mathcal{P}|}{|V|}$, or the *congestion* which is the maximum over $e' \in N$ of $| \{e \in E : e' \in b(e)\} |$ (i.e. the maximum number of different paths $b(e)$ assigned to some edge e'). Embedding is computationally hard in general. For example, embedding a cycle graph G (a ring) into a graph H with $| V | = | \mathcal{P} |$ and congestion 1 is equivalent to HAMILTONIAN CIRCUIT [GJ79].

2.4 Load Balancing

The term load balancing is often considered as equivalent with scheduling. It is not the case here. *Load balancing* is an approach which attempts to minimize the application execution time by distributing the computations evenly among the processors. A task created during the computations produces additional load which must be distributed to the processors. Thus, load balancing almost inherently considers on-line scheduling problems in which a full knowledge about the incoming tasks cannot be assumed. A first step towards load balancing is *load sharing* whose goal is supplying each processor with at least some load.

Before implementing any load balancing method, several problem areas must be addressed. A measure of the processor load is required. It can be the number of threads per processor, the number of data units assigned for processing, processor or memory utilization, or average response time. In a parallel branch-and-bound algorithm, for example, load can be expressed by the number of search tree nodes assigned to a processor, or by some estimate of the expected number of nodes emerging from the nodes already assigned to the processor [LM92]. On the other hand, it was demonstrated in [Kun91] that sophisticated load measures are not more effective than the simple ones. Another problem are data dependencies. When there are no dependencies between load elements it is possible to move them in an arbitrary fashion. However, in many practical applications dependencies exist, and provisions must be made to avoid widely scattering related (e.g. mutually communicating) load elements.

Load balancing methods differ by the initiator of load balancing [Gos91, GKR92]. The procedure can be initiated by a processor which ran out of work or it can be initiated by a processor on which a new load appeared. Next, the decision about moving the load can be done globally using information about the whole system status [XH93], or this decision can be done in a distributed manner based on the information available locally [LM92]. The global approach has bad scalability and the central "load balancer" can easily become a bottleneck. On the other hand, due to the lack of information distributed approaches can result in imbalance. Finally, the amount of load to be transferred must be determined. Two distributed methods of calculating this value are the most common: *nearest neighbor averaging* and *diffusion*. Let λ_i denote a load of processor P_i before load balancing, λ_i' after load balancing, and Δ_i the set of P_i's neighbors. The nearest neighbor averaging intends to change the load such that it is equal to the mean load of the processor and its neighbors, i.e. $\lambda_i' = (\lambda_i + \sum_{j \in \Delta_i} \lambda_j)/(|\Delta_i| + 1)$. To achieve this goal processor P_i transfers to processor P_j the amount of data equal to $(\lambda_i - \lambda_i')q_j/(\sum_{j \in \Delta_i} q_j)$, where $q_j = \max\{0, \lambda_i' - \lambda_j\}$. In the diffusion approach processor P_i sends to P_j the amount $\alpha(\lambda_i - \lambda_j)$ of data units, where $\alpha \in (0,1)$. Thus, after a load balancing step processor P_i has $\lambda_i' = \lambda_i + \alpha \sum_{j \in \Delta_i}(\lambda_i - \lambda_j)$ data units.

2.5 Loop Scheduling

Loops are considered a natural source of parallelism in many applications. The key scheduling problem is to determine the *chunk* size, i.e. the number of loops assigned to a processor in one iteration of loop distribution. Two important factors must be taken into account: unpredictability of the actual loop execution time, and the overhead related to the access to the work "distributor" (the loop index is a critical section). In the following let t denote the total number of loops and m the number of processors. Below we present the most widely known ways of loop scheduling [LSL94, ML94].

Static Chunk. Each processor is assigned t/m loops to execute. This results in low overhead in accessing the loop scheduler but in bad load-balance among processors.

Self-Scheduling. Each processor is assigned one loop at a time and fetches a new iteration to perform when it becomes idle. This results in good load balance, but the overhead due to accessing the scheduler is significant (proportional to the number of loops). A variant of self-scheduling is *chunk self-scheduling* in which a processor is assigned k loops at a time.

Guided Self-Scheduling. A processor requesting for work is assigned $1/m$ of the remaining unassigned loops. This results in good balance and low overhead if the loops are uniform. When the loops are not uniform, assigning t/m loops to the first requesting processors may result in load imbalance. Furthermore, at the end of the computation processors are assigned one loop at a time which may result in contention while accessing the scheduler.

Trapezoid Self-Scheduling. The first assigned chunk of work has size N_s. The following chunks are decreased linearly by some step d until some final size N_f. Example values of N_s and N_f can be $N/(2m)$ and 1, respectively. A disadvantage of this method is, that the difference between the chunks assigned to the processors at the first round is md, which for big m results in load imbalance.

Factoring. Here, at each successive loop allocation the algorithm evenly distributes half of the remaining iterations among the processors. Thus, $\alpha_i = \lceil B_i/(2m) \rceil$ iterations are assigned to each processor in step i, where $B_1 = t$ and $B_{i+1} = B_i - m\alpha_i$.

Affinity scheduling. [ML94] Affinity scheduling tries to take an advantage of using local memory or cache. In contrast to the previous methods each processor has its own work queue. Thus, the need for synchronization is minimized. Initially, loops are divided into chunks of size $\lceil t/m \rceil$ and appended to each processor's queue. A processor performs work in batches of $1/k$ of the loops from its queue (where k is a parameter of the algorithm). When the queue becomes empty, the processor finds the most loaded processor (i.e. the one with the longest queue) removes $1/k$ of the iterations from that processor's queue and executes them.

Safe Self-Scheduling. [LSL94] This scheme assigns statically the main portion of the loops and then balances the load by assigning the so-called smallest critical chores. More precisely, the processors are assigned statically $\alpha t/m$ loops in the first batch. The value $\alpha t/m$ is computed at the compile time. At the runtime, the ith processor fetching some load is assigned $\max\{k, (1-\alpha)^{\lceil i/m \rceil} t\alpha/m\}$ loops. It was proposed to calculate α from the equation: $\alpha = \frac{1}{2}(1 + PR(E_{max}) + PR(E_{min})E_{min}/E_{max})$ where E_{min} is the minimum execution time of a loop, E_{max} is the maximum execution time of a loop, and $PR(x)$ is the probability of executing a loop with time x. Thus, to use this method effectively, the probability distribution of the loop execution time must be known.

3. Scheduling Multiprocessor Tasks

As we discussed in Section 2. there are several approaches dealing with scheduling tasks on processors in parallel computing systems. One of these assumes tasks to require more than one processor at a time. In this section the model of *multiprocessor tasks* will be considered. Paragraphs 3.1 through 3.3 deal with parallel processors, dedicated processors and refinement scheduling, respectively. If not stated otherwise, schedule length will be the optimality criterion. Before presenting results we will discuss basic assumptions of the model.

As far as processor systems are concerned, they may be divided (as in the classical model) into two classes: parallel and dedicated. Usually each processor has its *local memory. Parallel processors* are functionally identical, but may differ from each other by their speeds. On the other hand, *dedicated processors* are usually specialized to perform specific computations (functions). Several models of processing task sets on dedicated processors are distinguished; flow shop, open shop and job shop being the most representative [BEP+96]. However, in the context of the considered multiprocessor computer systems, dedication of processors may also denote a preallocation feature of certain tasks to functionally identical processors. As will be discussed later a task can be preallocated to a single processor or to several processors at a time.

In the model of task processing that is considered in this section, the communication times are already included in the task processing times. Usually, a task requires then more than one processor at a time. Thus, we may call it a *multiprocessor task*. Multiprocessor tasks may specify their processor requirements either in terms of the number of simultaneously required processors or in terms of an explicit processor subset. In the first case we will speak about *parallel processor requirements*, whereas in the second we will speak about *dedicated processor requirements*.

The case when a unique number of simultaneously required processors is specified for the tasks will be called *size* processor requirements, and the number of processors needed by task T_j will be denoted $size_j$. A special sub-case denoted *cube* processor requirements is when tasks require numbers of processors being powers of 2. In a generalization of model *size* a task can be processed on various numbers of processors. However, for each possible number, the processing time is specified.

On the other hand, dedicated processor requirements can be either a unique (fixed) set of processors defined for each task or can be a family of alternative processor sets that can execute the task. The first case is called *fix* processor requirements, and fix_j denotes the unique set of processors required by task T_j. In the second case set_j denotes the family of alternative processor sets that can execute T_j.

An interesting question concerns the specification of task processing times. In case of parallel processors there are manyways to define the dependency of this time on the size of the processor system required by a task. In the following we will assume that the task processing time is inversely proportional to the processor set size, i.e. $p_j^k = p_j^1/k_j$, where $k_j = size_j$. We refer the interested reader to [Dro97] where more complicated models are analyzed. In case of dedicated processors each task processing time must be explicitly associated with the processor set required, i.e. with each processor set $\mathcal{D}$ which can be assigned to task T_j, processing time $p_j^{\mathcal{D}}$ is associated. As in the classical scheduling theory a preemptable task is completed if all its parts processed on different sets of processors sum up to 1 in the terms of normalized fractions of a unit.

3.1 Parallel Processors

3.1.1 *Size* processor requirements.
We start a discussion with an analysis of the simplest problems in which each task requires a *fixed number* of parallel processors during execution. Following Błażewicz et al.[BDW84, BDW86] we will set up the subject more precisely. Tasks are to be processed on a set of identical processors. The set of tasks is divided into k subsets $\mathcal{T}^1 = \{T_1^1, T_1^2, \ldots, T_{n_1}^1\}$, $\mathcal{T}^2 = \{T_1^2, T_2^2, \ldots, T_{n_2}^2\}, \ldots, \mathcal{T}^k = \{T_1^k, T_2^k, \ldots, T_{n_k}^k\}$ where $n = n_1 + n_2 +, \ldots, +n_k$. Each task T_i^1, $i = 1, \ldots, n$, requires exactly one of the processors for its processing and its processing time is equal to p_i^1. Similarly, each task T_i^s, where $1 < s \leq k$, requires l arbitrary processors simultaneously for its processing during a period of time which length is equal to p_i^s. We will call the tasks from $\mathcal{T}^s$ *width-l tasks* or $\mathcal{T}^s$-*tasks*. For the time being tasks are assumed to be *independent*, i.e. there are no precedence constraints among them. A schedule will be called feasible if, besides the usual conditions, each $\mathcal{T}^s$-task is processed by l processors at a time, $s = 1, \ldots, k$. Minimizing the schedule length is taken as an optimality criterion.

Independent tasks, nonpreemptive scheduling. We start our considerations with non-preemptive scheduling. The general problem is NP-hard (cf. Section 2.1), and starts to be strongly NP-hard for $m = 5$ processors [DL89]. Thus, we may concentrate on unit-length tasks. Let us start with the problem of scheduling tasks which belong to two sets only: $\mathcal{T}^1$ and $\mathcal{T}^k$, for arbitrary $k > 1$. This problem can be solved optimally by the following algorithm.

Algorithm 3.1 *Scheduling unit tasks from sets $\mathcal{T}^1$ and $\mathcal{T}^k$ to minimize C_{max}* [BDW86].
begin
Calculate the length of the optimal schedule according to the formula

$$C^*_{max} = max\{\lceil \frac{n_1 + kn_k}{m} \rceil, \lceil n_k / \lfloor \frac{m}{k} \rfloor \rceil\}; \qquad (3.1)$$

Schedule $\mathcal{T}^k$ -tasks in time interval $[0, C^*_{max}]$ using *first-fit algorithm*, i.e. assigning task T_i^k to the first time slot into which it fits;
Assign $\mathcal{T}^1$ -tasks to the remaining free processors;
end;

It should be clear that (3.1) gives a lower bound on the schedule length of an optimal schedule and this bound is always met by a schedule constructed by Algorithm 3.1.

If tasks belong to sets $\mathcal{T}^1, \mathcal{T}^2, \ldots, \mathcal{T}^k$ where k is a fixed integer, the problem can be solved by an approach, based on integer linear programming, similar to that for the problem of nonpreemptive scheduling of unit processing time tasks under fixed resource constraints [BE83].

Independent tasks, preemptive scheduling. Now, we will pass to preemptive scheduling. First, let us consider the problem of scheduling arbitrary length tasks from sets $\mathcal{T}^1$ and $\mathcal{T}^k$ in order to minimize schedule length. Processors are assumed to be *identical*. In [BDW84, BDW86] it has been proved that among minimum-length schedules for the problem there always exists a feasible *normalized schedule*, i.e. one in which first all $\mathcal{T}^k$-tasks are assigned in time interval $[0, C^*_{max}]$ using McNaughton's rule [McN59] (that is one by one on consecutive processors, preempting a task if necessary at moment C^*_{max} and assigning the rest of it to next processor at time 0), and then all $\mathcal{T}^1$-tasks are assigned, using the same rule, in the remaining part of the schedule (cf. Fig. 3.1). Following the above result, we will concentrate on finding an optimal schedule among the normalized ones. A lower bound on the optimal schedule length C^*_{max} can be obtained as follows. Define

$$X = \sum_{i=1}^{n_1} p_i^1, \quad Y = \sum_{i=1}^{n_k} p_i^k, \quad Z = X + kY,$$

$$p_{max}^1 = max_{T_i \in \mathcal{T}^1}\{p_i^1\}, \quad p_{max}^k = max_{T_i \in \mathcal{T}^k}\{p_i^k\}.$$

Then,

$$C^*_{max} \geq C = max\{Z/m, Y/\lfloor m/k \rfloor, p_{max}^1, p_{max}^k\}. \qquad (3.2)$$

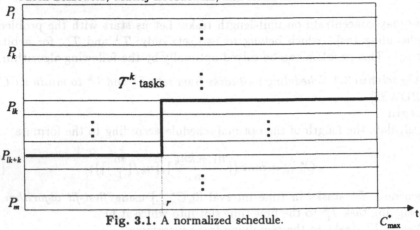

Fig. 3.1. A normalized schedule.

It is clear that no feasible schedule can be shorter than the maximum of the above values, i.e. mean processing requirement on one processor, mean processing requirement of $\mathcal{T}^k$-tasks on a set of existing k-tuples, the maximum processing time among $\mathcal{T}^1$-tasks, and the maximum processing time among $\mathcal{T}^k$-tasks. If $mC > Z$, then in any schedule there will be an idle time of minimum length $IT = mC - Z$. On the basis of bound (3.2) and the reasoning preceding it one can try to construct a preemptive schedule of minimum length equal to C. However, this will not always be possible and one has to lengthen the schedule. Below we present the reasoning that allows one to find the optimal schedule length. Let $l = \lfloor Y/C \rfloor$. It is quite clear that if $l > 0$, then the optimal schedule length C^*_{max} must obey the inequality

$$C \leq C^*_{max} \leq Y/l.$$

We know that there exists an optimal normalized schedule where tasks are arranged in such a way that kl processors are devoted entirely to $\mathcal{T}^k$-tasks, k processors are devoted to $\mathcal{T}^k$-tasks in time interval $[0, r]$, and $\mathcal{T}^1$-tasks are scheduled in the remaining time (cf. Fig. 3.1). Let m_1 be the number of processors that can process $\mathcal{T}^1$-tasks during time interval $[0, r]$, i.e. $m_1 = m - (l + 1)k$. In a normalized schedule which completes all tasks by some time B, where $C \leq B \leq Y/l$, we will have $r = Y - Bl$. Thus, the optimum value C^*_{max} will be the smallest value of $B(B \geq C)$ such that the $\mathcal{T}^1$-tasks can be scheduled on m_1 processors available during the interval $[0, B]$ and on $m_1 + k$ processors available in the interval $[r, B]$. Below we give necessary and sufficient conditions for the unit width tasks to be scheduled. To do this, let us assume that these tasks are ordered in such a way that $p_1^1 \geq p_2^1 \geq, \ldots, \geq p_{n_1}^1$. For a given pair B, r, with $r = Y - Bl$, let $p_1^1, p_2^1, \ldots, p_j^1$ be the only processing times greater than $B - r$. Consider now two cases.

Case 1: $j \leq m_1 + k$. Then $\mathcal{T}^1$-tasks can be scheduled if and only if

$$\sum_{i=1}^{j} [p_i^1 - (B - r)] \leq m_1 r. \tag{3.3}$$

To prove that this condition is indeed necessary and sufficient, let us first observe that if (3.3) is violated the T^1-tasks cannot be scheduled. Suppose now that (3.3) holds. Then one should schedule the excesses (exceeding $B-r$) of "long" tasks $T_1^1, T_2^1, \ldots, T_j^1$, and (if (3.3) holds without equality) some other tasks on m_1 processors in time interval $[0, r]$ using McNaughton's rule. After this operation the interval is completely filled with unit width tasks on m_1 processors.

Case 2: $j > m_1 + k$. In that case T^1-tasks can be scheduled if and only if

$$\sum_{i=1}^{m_1+k} [p_i^1 - (B - r)] \leq m_1 r. \tag{3.4}$$

Other long tasks will have enough space on the left-hand side of the schedule because condition (3.2) is obeyed.

Next we describe how the optimum value of schedule length (C_{max}^*) can be found. Let $W_j = \sum_{i=1}^{j} p_i^1$. Inequality (3.3) may then be rewritten as

$$W_j - j(B - r) \leq m_1(Y - Bl).$$

Solving it for B we get

$$B \geq \frac{(j - m_1)Y + W_j}{(j - m_1)l + j}.$$

Define

$$H_j = \frac{(j - m_1)Y + W_j}{(j - m_1)l + j}.$$

Thus, we may write

$$C_{max}^* = max\{C, H_{m_1+1}, H_{m_2+1}, \ldots, H_{n_1}\}.$$

Let us observe that we do not need to consider values $H_1, H_2, \ldots, H_{m_1}$ since the m_1 longest T^1-tasks will certainly fit into the schedule of length C (cf. (3.2)). Finding the above maximum can clearly be done in $O(n_1 \log n_1)$ time by sorting the unit width tasks by p_i^1. But one can do better by taking into account the following facts.

1. $H_i \leq C$ for $i \geq m_1 + k$
2. H_i has no local maximum for $i = m_1 + 1, \ldots, m_1 + k - 1$

Thus, to find a maximum over $H_{m_1+1}, \ldots, H_{m_1+k-1}$ and C we only need to apply a linear time median finding algorithm [AHU74] and a binary search. This will result in an $O(n_1)$ algorithm that calculates C^*_{max}. (Finding the medians takes $O(n_1)$ the first time, $O(n_1/2)$ the second time, $O(n_1/4)$ the third time etc. Thus the total time to find the medians is $O(n_1)$).

Now we are in the position to present an optimization algorithm for scheduling width-1 and width-k tasks.

Algorithm 3.2 *Scheduling preemptable tasks from sets* $\mathcal{T}^1$ *and* $\mathcal{T}^k$ *to minimize* C_{max} [BDW86].

begin
Calculate the minimum schedule length C^*_{max};
Schedule $\mathcal{T}^k$-tasks in interval $[0, C^*_{max}]$ using McNaughton's rule;

$$l := \lfloor Y/C^*_{max} \rfloor; \quad m_1 := m - (l+1)k; \quad r := Y - C^*_{max}l;$$

Calculate the number j of long $\mathcal{T}^1$-tasks that exceed $C^*_{max} - r$;
if $j \le m_1 + k$ **then**
    begin
    Schedule the excesses of the long tasks and possibly some other parts
    of tasks on m_1 processors using McNaughton's rule to fill interval
    $[0, r]$ completely;
    Schedule the remaining processing requirement in interval
    $[r, C^*_{max}]$ on $m_1 + k$ processors using McNaughton's algorithm;
    end
else
    begin
    Schedule part $((m_1 + k)(C^*_{max} - r)/ \sum_{i=1}^{j} p_i^1)p_h^1$ of each
    long task (plus possibly parts of smaller tasks T_z^1 with
    processing times $p_z^1, r < p_z^1 \le C^*_{max} - r$) in interval $[r, C^*_{max}]$
    on $m_1 + k$ processors using McNaughton's rule;
    -- if among smaller tasks not exceeding $(C^*_{max} - r)$ there are some
    -- tasks longer than r, then this excess must be taken into account in
    -- denominator of the above rate
    Schedule the rest of the task set in interval $[0, r]$ on m_1 processors
    using McNaughton's algorithm;
    end;
end;

The optimality of the above algorithm follows from the preceding discussion. Its time complexity is $O(n_1 + n_k)$, thus we get $O(n)$.

Considering the general case of preemptively scheduling tasks from sets $\mathcal{T}^1, \mathcal{T}^2, \ldots, \mathcal{T}^k$, we can use a linear programming approach [BEP+96]. We will describe it below. This approach has come from project scheduling [WBC+77]. Its basic concept is that of *a processor feasible set*, i.e. such a

subset of the set of all tasks $\mathcal{T}$ for which a total requirement of the tasks
constituting it is less than or equal to m. Let us number these sets from 1
to some K. Now, let Q_j denote the set of indices of processor feasible sets in
which task $T_j \in \mathcal{T}$ may be performed, and let x_i denote the duration of the
i'th feasible set.

Then, a linear programming problem can be formulated in the following way
[WBC+77, BCS+76]:

$$\text{Minimize } C_{max} = \sum_{i=1}^{k} x_i \tag{3.5}$$

$$\text{subject to } \sum_{i \in Q_j} x_i = p_j, \quad j = 1, 2, \dots, n \tag{3.6}$$

$$x_i \geq 0, \quad i = 1, 2, \dots, K \tag{3.7}$$

An optimal solution of the above LP problem gives optimal values of
x_i^*, $i = 1, 2, \dots, K$, which denote the lengths of subintervals of the optimal
schedule. The number of variables in this LP problem depends polynomially
on the input length, when the number of processors m is fixed. We may then
use a nonsimplex algorithm (e.g. from [Kha79] or [Kar84]) which solves any
LP problem in time polynomial in the number of variables and constraints.
Hence, we may conclude that for fixed m the above procedure solves our
scheduling problem in polynomial time as well.

Now let us consider the case of *uniform processors*.
In [BDS+94] a scheduling problem has been considered for a multiprocessor system built up of uniform k-tuples of identical parallel processors.
The processing time of task T_i is the ratio p_i/b_i, where b_i is the speed
of the slowest processor that executes T_i. It is shown that this problem
is solvable in $O(nm + n \log n)$ time if the sizes required are such that
$size_j \in \{1, k\}, j = 1, 2, \dots, n$. For a fixed number of processors, a linear
programming formulation is proposed for solving this problem in polynomial
time for sizes belonging to $\{1, 2, \dots, k\}$ (cf. LP formulation (3.5)-(3.7)).

Minimization of other criteria has not been considered yet, except for
maximum lateness and identical processors. In this context problem with a
fixed number of processors has been formulated as a modified linear programming problem (3.5)-(3.7). Thus, it can be solved in polynomial time for fixed
m [BDW+96].

Dependent tasks. Let us now consider the case of non-empty precedence constraints. Arbitrary processing times result in the strong NP-hardness of the
problem, even for chains and two processors [DL89]. In case of unit processing
times the last problem can be solved for arbitrary precedence constraints using basically the same approach as in the Coffman-Graham algorithm, where
a priority of a task depends on its level and a number of its successors in
a precedence graph [Llo81]. On the other hand, three processors result in a

computational hardness of the problem even for chains and unit processing times [BL96]. However, if task requirements of processors are either uniform or monotone decreasing (or increasing) in each chain then the problem can be solved in $O(n \log n)$ time even for an arbitrary number m of processors ($m < 2size_j$ for the case of monotone chains) [BL96].

3.1.2 Cube processor requirements. Let us consider now a variant of the above problem in which each task requires a fixed *number* of processors being a power of 2, thus requiring a cube of a certain dimension. Because of the complexity of the problem we will only consider the preemptive case.

In [CL88b] an $O(n^2)$ algorithm is proposed for building the schedule (if any exists) for tasks with a common deadline C. This algorithm builds so-called stair-like schedules. A schedule is said to be *stair-like* if there is a function $f(i)$, $i = 1, \ldots, m$, such that processor P_i is busy before time moment $f(i)$ and idle after, and f is nonincreasing. Function f is called a *profile* of the schedule. Tasks are scheduled in the order of nonincreasing number of required processors. A task is scheduled in time interval $[C - p_j, C]$, utilizing the first of the subcubes of the task's size on each "stair" of the stair-like partial schedule. Using a binary search, the C_{max}^* is calculated in time $O(n^2(\log n + \log(max\{p_j\})))$. The number of preemptions is at most $n(n-1)/2$.

In [Hoe89], a feasibility-testing algorithm of time complexity $O(n \log n)$ is given. To calculate C_{max}^* with this algorithm $O(n \log n (\log n + \log(max\{p_j\})))$ time is needed. This algorithm uses a different method for scheduling, it builds so-called *pseudo-stair-like* schedules. In this case $f(i) < f(j) < C$, for $i, j = 1, \ldots, m$, implies that $i > j$. Each task is feasibly scheduled on at most two subcubes. Thus the number of generated preemptions is at most $n - 1$. A similar result is presented in [AZ90], but the number of preemptions is reduced to $n - 2$ because the last job is scheduled on one subcube, without preemption. This work was the basis for the paper [SR91] in which a new feasibility testing algorithm is proposed, with running time $O(mn)$. The key idea is to schedule tasks in the order of nonincreasing execution times, in sets of tasks of the same size (number of required processors). Based on the observation that there exists some task in each optimal schedule utilizing all the remaining processing time on one of the processors in the schedule profile, an $O(n^2 m^2)$ algorithm is proposed to calculate C_{max}^*.

Minimization of L_{max} can be solved via linear programming formulation (cf. (3.5)-(3.7)) [BDW+96]

3.1.3 Arbitrary processor requirements. Let us consider now the most complicated case of parallel processor requirements specified by numbers of processors required, where task processing times depend arbitrarily on numbers of processors assigned.

Nonpreemptive scheduling. A *dynamic programming* approach leads to the observation that two-processor and three-processor cases are solvable in pseudopolynomial time [DL89]. Arbitrary schedules for instances of these problems can be transformed into so called *canonical schedules*. A canonical schedule on two processors is one that first processes the tasks using both processors. It is completely determined by three numbers: the total execution times of single-processor tasks on processor P_1 and P_2, respectively, and the total execution time of biprocessor tasks. For the case of three processors, similar observations are made. These characterizations are the basis for the development of the pseudopolynomial algorithms. The problem with four processors remains open; no pseudopolynomial algorithm is given.

Preemptive scheduling. Surprisingly preemptions do not result in polynomial time algorithms [DL89]. The case with an arbitrary number of identical processors is proved to be strongly NP-hard by a reduction from 3-PARTITION [DL89]. With a restriction to two processors the problem is still NP-hard, as is shown by a reduction from PARTITION. Using Algorithm 3.2 [BDW86], Du and Leung [DL89] show that for any fixed number of processors the problem is also solvable in pseudopolynomial time. The basic idea of the algorithm is as follows. For each schedule S of the problem with arbitrary processor requirements, there is a corresponding instance of the problem with size processor requirements and with sizes belonging to $\{1, \ldots, k\}$, in which task T_i is an l-processor task if it uses l processors with respect to S. An optimal schedule for the latter problem can be found in polynomial time by Algorithm 3.2. What remains to be done is to generate optimal schedules for all instances of the problem with *size* processor requirements that correspond to schedules of the problem with arbitrary processor requirements, and choose the shortest among all. It is shown by a dynamic programming approach that the number of schedules generated can be bounded from above by a pseudopolynomial function of the input size of the problem considered.

If in the above problem one assumes a linear model of dependency of task processing times on a number of processors assigned, the problem starts to be solvable in polynomial time. That is the problem with equal ready times for all the tasks is solvable in $O(n)$ time [DK95] and the problem with arbitrary ready times is solvable in $O(n^2)$ time [Dro96].

3.2 Dedicated Processors

In this section we will consider the dedicated processor case. Following the remarks at the beginning of Section 3., we will denote here by $\mathcal{T}^{\mathcal{D}}$ the set of tasks each of which requires set $\mathcal{D}$ of processors simultaneously. Task $T_i \in \mathcal{T}^{\mathcal{D}}$ has processing time $p_i^{\mathcal{D}}$. For the sake of simplicity we define by $p^{\mathcal{D}} = \sum_{T_i \in \mathcal{T}^{\mathcal{D}}} p_i^{\mathcal{D}}$ the total time required by all tasks which use set of processors $\mathcal{D}$. Thus, e.g. $p^{1,2,3}$ is the total processing time of tasks each of which requires processors P_1, P_2, and P_3 at the same time (for simplicity reasons we write $p^{1,2,3}$ instead of $p^{\{P_1,P_2,P_3\}}$). We will start with task requirements concerning only one subset of processors for each task. Again, if not stated otherwise, schedule length will be the optimality criterion.

3.2.1 Fixed set processor requirements. Nonpreemptive scheduling.
The problem with *unit processing times* can be proved to be strongly NP-hard for an arbitrary number of processors [KK85]. Moreover, in [HVV94] it has been proved that even the problem of deciding whether an instance of the problem has a schedule of length at most 3 is strongly NP-hard. As a result there is no polynomial time algorithm with worst case performance ratio smaller than $4/3$ unless $\mathbf{P} = \mathbf{NP}$. On the other hand, if the number of processors is fixed, then again an approach for nonpreemptive scheduling of unit length tasks under fixed resource constraints [BE83] can be used to solve the problem in polynomial time.

If the task processing times are arbitrary, it is trivial to observe that the problem of nonpreemptive scheduling tasks on two processors under fixed processor requirements is solvable in polynomial time. On the other hand, if the number of processors is increased to three, the problem starts to be strongly NP-hard [BDO+92]. Despite the fact that the general problem is hard we will show below that there exist polynomially solvable cases of three-processor scheduling problem [BDO+92]. Let us denote the latter problem by π. R^i denotes the total time processor P_i processes tasks. For instance, $R^1 = p^1 + p^2 + p^{1,3}$. Moreover, let us denote by RR the total time during which two processors must be used simultaneously, i.e. $RR = p^{1,2} + p^{1,3} + p^{2,3}$. We have the following:

Lemma 3.1. *[BDO+92] In case of problem π, $C_{max} \geq max\{max_i\{R^i\}, RR\}$.*
□

Now we consider the case for which $p^1 \leq p^{2,3}$. The result given below also covers cases $p^2 \leq p^{1,3}$ and $p^3 \leq p^{1,2}$ if we take into account renumbering of processors.

Theorem 3.1. *[BDO+92] If $p^1 \leq p^{2,3}$, then problem π can be solved in polynomial time. The minimum makespan is then*

$$C_{max} = max\{max_i\{R^i\}, RR\}.$$

Proof. The proof is constructive in nature and we consider four different subcases.

Case a: $p^2 \leq p^{1,3}$ and $p^3 \leq p^{1,2}$. In Fig. 3.2 a schedule is shown which can always be obtained in polynomial time for this case. The schedule is such that $C_{max} = RR$, and thus, by Lemma 3.1, it is optimal.

Case b: $p^2 \leq p^{1,3}$ and $p^3 > p^{1,2}$. Observe that in this case $R^3 = max_i\{R^i\}$, and thus this schedule is optimal (cf. Lemma 3.1)

Case c: $p^2 \geq p^{1,3}$ and $p^3 \geq p^{1,2}$. Observe that $R^1 \leq R^2$ and $R^1 \leq R^3$. Two subcases have to be considered here.

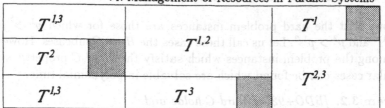

Fig. 3.2. Case a of Theorem 3.1.

Case c': $R^2 \leq R^3$. The schedule which can be obtained in this case in polynomial time is shown in Fig. 3.4(a). Its length is $C_{max} = R^3 = max_i\{R^i\}$.

Case c": $R^2 > R^3$. The schedule which can be obtained in this case in polynomial time is shown in Fig. 3.4(b). Its length is $C_{max} = R^2 = max_i\{R^i\}$.

Fig. 3.3. Case b of Theorem 3.1.

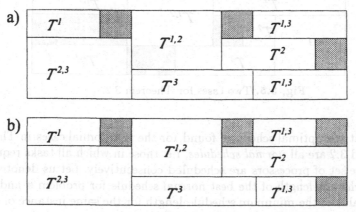

Fig. 3.4. Case c of Theorem 3.1.

Case d: $p^2 \geq p^{1,3}$ and $p^3 \leq p^{1,2}$. Note that the optimal schedule would be the same as in Case b if we renumbered the processors. $\square$

It follows that the hard problem instances are those for which $p^1 > p^{2,3}$, $p^2 > p^{1,3}$ and $p^3 > p^{1,2}$. Let us call these cases the *Hard-C* subcases. However, also among the problem instances which satisfy the *Hard-C* property, some particular cases can be found which are solvable in polynomial time.

Theorem 3.2. *[BDO+92] If Hard-C holds and*

$$R^1 \geq p^2 + p^3 + p^{2,3} \text{ or } p^1 \geq p^2 + p^{2,3}$$

then problem π can be solved in polynomial time, and $C_{max} = max_i\{R^i\}$.

Proof. Observe that if $R^1 \geq p^2 + p^3 + p^{2,3}$ then $R^1 \geq R^2$ and $R^1 \geq R^3$. The schedule which can be immediately obtained in this case, is shown in Fig. 3.4a. As $C_{max} = R^1$, the schedule is optimal by Lemma 3.1.

If $p^1 \geq p^2 + p^{2,3}$, the optimal schedule is as shown in Fig. 3.4b. In this case $C_{max} = max\{R^1, R^3\}$. □

a)
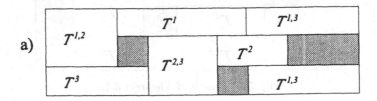

b)
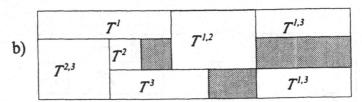

Fig. 3.5. Two cases for Theorem 3.2.

Observe that the optimal schedules found for the polynomial cases in Theorems 3.1 and 3.2 are all *normal schedules*, i.e. those in which all tasks requiring the same set of processors are scheduled consecutively. Let us denote by C^S_{max} the schedule length of the best normal schedule for problem π and by C^*_{max} the value of the minimum schedule length for the same instance of the problem. Then [BDO+92]

$$\frac{C^S_{max}}{C^*_{max}} < \frac{4}{3}$$

Since the best normal schedule can be found in polynomial time [BDO+92], we have defined a polynomial time approximation algorithms with the worst case behavior not worse than 4/3. Recently this bound has been improved. In [OST93] and in [Goe95] new approximation algorithms have been proposed with bounds equal to 5/4 and 7/6, respectively.

A constrained version of the problem is considered in [HVV94]. It is assumed that in problem π all biprocessor tasks that require the same processors are scheduled consecutively. Under this assumption this problem is solvable in pseudopolynomial time.

An interesting approach to the solution of the problem of scheduling tasks requiring several dedicated processors simultaneously is concerned with graph theoretic methods. The computational complexity when $| fix_j |= 2$ is analyzed in [CGJ+85]. The problem is modeled by the use of the so-called *file transfer graph*. In such a graph, nodes correspond to processors and edges correspond to tasks. A weight equal to the execution time is assigned to each edge. A range of computational complexity results have been established. For example, the problem with unit processing times is easy when the file transfer graph is one of the following types of graphs: bipartite, tree, unicyclic, star, caterpillar, cycle, path; but, in general, the problem is NP-hard. It is proved that the makespan C_{max}^{LS} of the schedule obtained with any list-scheduling algorithm satisfies $C_{max}^{LS} \leq 2C_{max}^* + max\{0, max\{p_j\}(1 - 2/d)\}$, where d is the maximum degree of any vertex in the graph.

In [Kub87], the problem is modeled by means of weighted edge coloring. The graph model is extended in such a way that a task requiring one processor is represented as a loop which starts and ends in the same node. When $| fix_j |\in \{1, 2\}$ the problem is NP-hard for a graph, which is either a star with a loop at each noncentral vertex or a caterpillar with only one loop. In [BOS94] problem π is also analyzed with the use of the graph theoretic approach. This time, however, the graph reflecting the instance of the problem, called a *constraint graph*, has nodes corresponding to tasks, and edges join two tasks which cannot be executed in parallel. An execution time is associated with each node. It is shown that problem with unit processing times is NP-hard but can be solved polynomially for $m = 2, 3, 4, 5$ processors. Next, when the constraint graph is a comparability graph, the transitive orientation of such a graph gives an optimal solution. In this case, C_{max} is equal to the weight of the maximum weight clique. The transitive orientation (if any exists) can be found in time $O(dn^2)$. For the general case, when the constraint graph is not a comparability graph, a branch and bound algorithm is proposed. In this case, the problem consists in adding (artificial) edges such that the new graph is a comparability graph. The search is directed by the weight of the heaviest clique in the new graph. Results of computational experiments are reported.

If we consider *precedence constrained* task sets, the problem immediately starts to be computationally hard, since even the problem with 2 processors and chains precedence graphs is strongly NP-hard [HVV94] (cf.[BLR+83]).

Let us consider now minimization of the mean flow time criterion. The general version of the problem has been considered in [HVV94]. The main result is establishing NP-hardness in the ordinary sense for 2 processors and strong NP-hardness for three processors and arbitrary processing times. The problem with unit processing times is solvable in polynomial time when the numbers of processors and task types are fixed [Bru98]. The weighted version, however, is shown to be NP-hard in the strong sense. The problem with unit processing times is NP-hard in the strong sense if the number of processors is a part of the problem instance, but is solvable in polynomial time in the case of fixed numbers of processors and task types [Bru98]. As could be expected, introduction of precedence constraints does not reduce the computational complexity. It was shown that even the problem with two processors, unit processing times, and chain-type precedence constraints, is NP-hard in the strong sense [HVV94].

Preemptive scheduling. Let us consider now preemptive case. In general, the problem with an arbitrary number of processors is strongly NP-hard [Kub96]. For simpler cases of the problem, however, linear time algorithms have been proposed [BBD+94]. An optimal schedule for the problem with 2 processors does not differ from a schedule for the nonpreemptive case. For three processors an optimal schedule has the following form: biprocessor tasks of the same type are scheduled consecutively (without gaps and preemptions) and uniprocessor tasks are scheduled in the free processing capacity, in parallel with appropriate biprocessor tasks. The excess of the processing time of uniprocessor tasks is scheduled at the end of the schedule. The complexity of the algorithm is $O(n)$. In a similar way, optimal schedules can be found for 4 processors. When m is limited, the problem can be solved in polynomial time using feasible sets concept and a linear programming approach [BBD+94].

Since the nonpreemptive scheduling problem with the L_{max} criterion is already strongly NP-hard for two processors [HVV94], more attention has been paid to preemptive case. In [BBD+97a] linear time algorithms have been proposed for the two-processor case and for some special subcases of three and four processor scheduling. More general cases can be solved by a linear programming approach [BBD+97b] even for different ready times for tasks.

3.2.2 Set processor requirements.

Nonpreemptive scheduling. Let us consider now the case of *set* processor requirements. In [CL88b] this problem is restricted to single-processor tasks of unit length. In the paper matching technique is used to construct optimal solutions in $O(n^2 m^2)$ time. In [CC89] the same problem is solved in $O(min\{\sqrt{n}, m\}nm \log n)$ time by the use of network flow approach. More general cases have been considered in [BBD+95].

The problem with arbitrary processing times is NP-hard, but for two processors can be solved in pseudopolynomial time by a dynamic programming procedure. In this case, the schedule length depends on three numbers: total execution time of tasks requiring $P_1(p^1)$, tasks requiring $P_2(p^2)$, and tasks requiring P_1 and $P_2(p^{1,2})$. In an optimal schedule, $\mathcal{T}^{1,2}$ tasks are executed first, the uniprocessor tasks are processed in any order without gaps. A similar procedure is proposed for a restricted version of three-processor scheduling in which one type of dual-processor task is absent (e.g., $\mathcal{T}^{1,3}$). On the other hand, for the general problem, the shortest processing time (SPT) heuristic is proposed. Thus, tasks are scheduled in any order, in their shortest-time processing configuration. A tight performance bound for this algorithm is m. Some other cases, mostly restricted to uniprocessor tasks, are analyzed in [Bru98].

Preemptive scheduling. In case of preemptions again the modified linear programming approach (3.5)-(3.7) can be used to solve the problem in polynomial time for fixed m [BBD+95]. Following the results for *fix* model of processor requirements, most of the other cases for *set* requirements are computationally hard. One of the few exceptions is problem with L_{max} criterion which can be solved by a linear programming formulation [BBD+97b].

3.3 Refinement Scheduling

Usually deterministic scheduling problems are formulated on a single level of abstraction. In this case all information about the processor system and the tasks is known in advance and can thus be taken into account during the scheduling process. We also know that generating a schedule that is optimal under a given optimization criterion is usually very time consuming in case of large task systems, due to the inherent computational complexity of the problem.

On the other hand, in many applications it turns out that detailed information about the task system is not available at the beginning of the scheduling process. One example is the construction of complex real-time systems that is only possible if the dependability aspects are taken into account from the very beginning. Adding non-functional constraints at a later stage does not work. Another example are large projects that run over long periods; in order to settle the contract, reasonable estimates must be made in an early stage when probably only the coarse structure of the project and rough estimates of the necessary resources are known. A similar situation occurs in many manufacturing situations; the delivery time must be estimated as a part of the order although the detailed shop floor and machine planning is not yet known.

A rather coarse grained knowledge of the task system in the beginning is refined during later planning stages. This leads to a stepwise refinement technique where intermediate results during the scheduling process allow to recognize trends in

- processing times of global steps,
- total execution time,

- resource requirements,
- feasibility of the task system.

In more detail, we first generate a schedule for the coarse grained (global) tasks. For these we assume that estimates of processing times and resource requirements are known. Next we go into details and analyze the structure of the global tasks (refinement of tasks). Each global task is considered as a task system by itself consisting of a set of sub-tasks, each having a certain (maybe estimated) processing time and resource requirement. For each such sub-task a schedule is generated which then replaces the corresponding global task. Proceeding this way from larger to smaller tasks we are able to correct the task completion times from earlier planning stages by more accurate values, and get more reliable information about the feasibility of the task system.

Algorithm 3.3 *Refinement scheduling* [EH94].

begin
Define the task set in terms of its structure (precedence relations), its estimated resource consumption (processing times) and its deadlines;
　　-- Note that the deadlines are initially defined at the highest level
　　-- (level 0) as part of the external requirements. During the refinement
　　-- process it might be convenient to refine these deadlines too; i.e. to
　　-- assign deadlines to lower level tasks. Depending on the type of problem,
　　-- it might, however, be sufficient to prove that an implementation at a
　　-- particular level of refinement obeys the deadlines at some higher level.

Schedule the given task set according to some discipline, e.g. earliest deadline first;
repeat
Refine the task set, again in terms of its structure, its resource consumption and possibly also its deadlines;
Try to schedule the refinement of each task within the frame that is defined by the higher level schedule;
　　-- Essentially this boils down to introducing a virtual deadline as
　　-- the finishing time of the higher level task under consideration.
　　-- Note that the refined schedule might use more resources (processors)
　　-- than the initial one.
　　-- If no feasible schedule can be found, backtracking must take place.
　　-- In our case this means, that the designer has to find another task
　　-- structure, e.g. by redefining the functionality of the tasks or by
　　-- exploiting additional parallelism [VWH+95] (introduction of
　　-- additional processors, cloning of resources and replacement of
　　-- synchronous by asynchronous procedure calls).
Optimize the resulting refined schedule by shifting tasks forward or backward;
　　-- This step aims at restructuring (compacting) the resulting schedule

- - in such a way that the number of resources (processors) is as small
- - as possible.

until the finest level is reached;
end;

The algorithm essentially defines a first schedule from the initial task set and refines it recursively. At each refinement step a preliminary schedule is developed that is refined (detailed) in the next step. This way, we will finally end up with a schedule at the lowest level. The tasks are now the elementary actions that have to be sequenced such that all the initially given global tasks are realized.

4. Scheduling Uni-Processor Tasks with Communication Delays

This section deals with deterministic task scheduling in a distributed or parallel computer system. The task themselves are thought of being computational activities with known (or at least estimated upper bounds of) processing-times. For the problem of deterministic task scheduling under the simplifying assumption that communication delays can be neglected, many results dealing with algorithms for scheduling sets of tasks optimally had been published in the last decades. The more important results in this area can be found in [BEP+96]. Considering processes in a parallel or distributed system however, it will happen that data or code has to be communicated between processors occasionally and under defined conditions. Rather recently, consideration of delays due to interprocessor communication developed to a topic of growing interest. Not only in real-time applications estimates about the communication delays are crucial for the correct behavior of the system, but also in other, e. g. commercial applications, one is guided to optimize system performance by minimizing delays due to communication overhead and schedule tasks optimally.

4.1 Motivation and Introduction

Scheduling with consideration of communication delays has become a wide research area, primarily because of the various possible technical preconditions under which communication takes place. The transmission technique used in the network, the chosen communication protocol, and the performance of network components are examples of factors that influence the speed and performance of the network. Knowledge of these communication properties is of course essential in the attempt to process the tasks in some optimal manner.

In this section we give an overview of distributed and parallel task execution with communication delays. The problem considered here is that of scheduling set $\mathcal{T}$ of tasks on a network of identical processors in minimal time. In the static scheduling paradigm considered here each task T_j of the given set $\mathcal{T}$ has a known processing time p_j. Precedence constraints between pairs of tasks, denoted by $T_i \prec T_j$, may also be given. In particular, as in the preceding sections, we are interested in algorithms that find schedules of *minimum makespan*. This problem will be discussed under different technical conditions such as circuit or packet switched transmissions, packet buffering at intermediate nodes, and others.

In the following we present a simple scheduling example with no communication delays in the first place. Communication delays will be introduced in the following sections, and the example will be adjusted to the changing transmission properties of the network.

Example. A set of tasks $\mathcal{T}$ as given in Table 4.1 should be processed on a system of four identical processors P_1, P_2, P_3, P_4. An interconnection network is not specified at the moment, but will be given later. Precedence constraints among the tasks are as in Fig. 4.1 (a). A schedule of minimum makespan is presented in Fig. 4.1 (b).

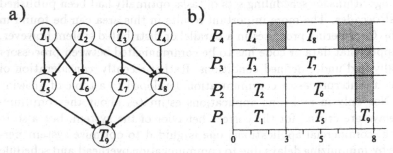

Fig. 4.1. (a) Tasks with precedence constraints (b) A Gantt chart for the task system of Fig. 4.1(a) without considering communication delays.

Table 4.1. Processing times.

T_j	T_1	T_2	T_3	T_4	T_5	T_6	T_7	T_8	T_9
p_j	3	3	2	2	4	4	5	3	1

In this (simplest) example we deal only with the tasks, without considering any processor interconnection network. One can justify this simplification by the argument that the network structure is of no concern as long as communication times can be neglected. The same model can also be applied in systems where communication runs over a common memory. If a task needs to access some data (e.g. computed by a preceding task) the access time can be included in the task processing time. The model we are faced with in these simplest cases is the classical version of scheduling problems, that has already been discussed in earliest papers on task scheduling (cf. [BEP+96] or [Bru94] as surveys).

4.1.1 Representation of schedules. As long as problem instances are small, i.e. there are not too many tasks, Gantt charts as in Fig. 4.1 are a useful mean to visualize schedules. But for several reasons we need a formal description of schedules: for describing the output of a scheduling algorithm, and for presenting schedules to the schedule dispatcher in an operating system. Moreover, there are algorithms that work directly on the set of feasible schedules, the "solution space" (cf. Section 1.1.3). Hence we need a formalism that allows to represent any *feasible* schedule for a given problem instance, and to specify the total solution space. The question is which mathematical terms should be used.

Whereas this question seems to be trivial (everybody has an idea how a schedule looks like), we want to make clear that just the opposite is true in general. First of all, whatever (non-trivial) instance is given, there is an infinite number of feasible schedules. To reduce the solution space one usually restricts to *greedy schedules* where no processor is kept intentionally idle as long as tasks are waiting to be processed. In fact it turns out that most optimization criteria of practical relevance (such as the here considered criterion of minimizing makespan) have greedy optimal schedules.

We discuss the question of schedule representation by starting from the non-communication case and proceeding in the course of the following sections to the more complex ones. For scheduling problems with m identical processors and no communication delays it suffices to specify a task sequence (or task list) $(T_{\alpha_1}, \ldots, T_{\alpha_n})$, combined with the rule that each time a processor becomes idle, it "grabs" the first task from the list, i.e. the processor starts the first task as soon as its preceding tasks are completed. Since processors are identical, it would not matter which processor grabs first in case that two or more processors become idle at the same time. But if necessary, we can also arrive at a unique assignment by giving the processors priorities, and control the order of grabbing by means of processor priorities. As we see, the solution space consists of all tasks sequences that are in accordance with the given precedence relation (so-called *linear extensions* of $\prec$). This set contains all possible greedy schedules; of course they are not necessarily optimal.

If communication delays are involved, the list representation has at least to be extended by information about the processors the tasks are processed on. As we shall see, in simpler situations a schedule can indeed be described by a sequence of (task,processor)-pairs where the order of tasks still has the linear extension property. In general, however, to specify schedules we need to include in addition information about the order in which communications are performed. Before we go into these details we need to say more about data transmission in processor networks.

4.1.2 Communication delays. We turn now to more general situations where processors have local memories, and data transfers take place over links connecting the processors. We may assume that data dependencies between tasks are the original reason for the occurrence of precedence constraints between tasks. The time required for transmitting a data packet from one processor to another consists of several components.

- *Communication processing time*: for local management of a communication, i. e. for creating the data packet (framing, addressing, etc.), and for unpacking.
- *Path selection time*: choosing and activating a path from the sender to the target node.
- *Transmission time*: sending the bits of the packet.
- *Queueing time*: possible delays at intermediate nodes between the sender and the target processor, due to buffering and waiting times in queues.
- *Additional delays* such as acknowledging messages, due to the underlying transmission protocol.

Some of these parameters are difficult or even impossible to evaluate in advance. The queueing time, for example, depends on the communication load in the network. Hence the above model appears to be inappropriate for deterministic task scheduling. Rather, a communication model should combine both, simplicity and expressive power, and should be as realistic as possible, with regard to the actual applications running on the particular processor network. For example, the *logP* model described by Culler et al. [CKP93], was developed under these guidelines. The main parameters of the model are:

- P, the number of processor/memory modules.
- l, the *latency*, or maximum delay, associated with delivering a message.
- o, the *overhead*, representing the length of time for which a processor is busy during the transmission or reception of a message; in this interval the processor cannot perform other operations.
- g, the *gap*, a lower bound on the time between the transmission of successive messages, or the reception of successive messages, at the same processor.

Simplifying the situation, we shall assume that the overhead and the gap are 0. Both assumptions can be justified by assuming that at each node there is an I/O-processor that handles transmission and reception. As for the latency, we consider here two cases: unit time communication, where the data transmission takes constant time measured in a properly chosen time unit, and an arbitrary (but fixed for each pair of dependent tasks) amount of time. The first is justified for cases where packets have fixed sizes, and there is exactly one data packet between a pair of dependent tasks. In the second we allow different packet sizes. Delays due to packet framing etc. and possibly acknowledging messages are assumed as being already included in the transmission time.

Generally, if $T_i \prec T_j$, and T_i, T_j are processed on respective processors P_k, P_l, we assume that data packet C_{ij} has to be transmitted to processor P_l before task T_j can start. If there is a link λ_{kl} connecting the processors then the action of sending C_{ij} along λ_{kl} is referred to as a *communication task* (C_{ij}, λ_{kl}). More generally, if π is a path connecting processors P_k and P_l then the corresponding communication task is denoted by (C_{ij}, π). If the particular path is of no concern we write $(C_{ij}, (k, l))$; this means that C_{ij} has to be sent from P_k to P_l along an arbitrary path. The communication time can often be specified in a table that gives the delay for each pair of dependent tasks and each pair of processors these tasks are assigned to. Such a table entry is then denoted by $c(T_i, P_k; T_j, P_l)$. We want to emphasize the fact that in this table we are only able to present fixed times, independent of the transmission path, and without considering buffering of packets at intermediate nodes or other workload- dependent factors. Such delays must be considered separately. In some special cases we can use an even simpler notation: c_{ij} if the transmission time for C_{ij} does not depend on the processors, and c, if all communication times are the same.

In order to reduce or even avoid communication delays, it might be profitable to allow *task duplication*, which means that copies of the same task are processed on different processors. The then required careful decision between the two options of task duplication vs. acceptance of communication delay makes the problem much more difficult.

4.1.3 Modes of communication. In the following, the scheduling of tasks is considered under several different assumptions concerning the amount of transmitted data, the communication capacities of the processors and the links between them, and the general transmission properties of the processor network. The following issues being relevant for the network performance are discussed in greater detail:

(i) *Transmission by circuit switching versus packet switching.* In *circuit switching*, a communication path from the sender to the target processor is activated, and the transmission duration is independent of the distance (i.e. the number of nodes) between the sending and the receiving processor. In *packet switching*, a transmission to a remote target node is performed in a *store-and-forward* manner, and the packet may be buffered at the intermediate nodes. In this case, the transmission duration increases with the path length.

(*ii*) *Contention*: The transmission capacity of a link is usually limited in the way that only a certain number of packets can be transmitted simultaneously. If more packets are due to be transmitted, traffic contention occurs, and some of the packets have to wait.

Generally, we assume that processors can start the next task while simultaneously transmitting the data of the previously completed task. Moreover, in case of no contention the processor may send several packets at the same time to different destinations.

The problem cases considered in following are circuit switching without contention (Section 4.2), packet switching without contention (Section 4.3), circuit switching with contention (Section 4.4), and packet switching with contention (Section 4.5). We consider these problems separately because they all require more or less different approaches. In particular, as soon as contention is involved, we end up with a new type of a non-trivial problem: that of scheduling *communication tasks* in addition to normal tasks.

4.1.4 Synchronous vs. asynchronous task execution.

Another important question is how the execution of computations and communications is organized in a parallel system. In principle there are two possibilities:

- In *synchronous* execution, there are alternatively processed phases of computations and communications.
- In *asynchronous* execution, there is no clear separation between computation and communication phases. In other words, the phases are processed in an interleaved way, and both types of activities are allowed at the same time.

Compared to asynchronous execution, synchronous execution has the advantage of being easier to organize. Also, the division in phases allows us to solve scheduling and communication problems separately, and thus simplifies the problem. But on the other hand, the price to be paid is that the overall makespan will be longer than in an asynchronous execution. In this monograph we shall consider mainly asynchronous task execution. Only at the end of Section 4.5 we shall come back to synchronous execution.

4.2 Circuit Switching, Communication without Contention

Considering a pair $T_i \prec T_j$ of dependent tasks, T_j can only start if it has access to data packet C_{ij} that may contain some results of T_i. If both tasks are processed on the same processor there will be no delay because T_j has direct access to the data stored at the same location. Otherwise, if the tasks are processed on different processors, T_j has to wait for the data to arrive. The time for transmitting C_{ij}, which of course depends on the packet size, is assumed to be a fixed amount and independent of the (different) processors where tasks T_i and T_j are located. Hence, the communication delays considered here do not depend on the structure of the processor network at all, and in particular do not depend on the distance between sender and target node. These assumptions are justified in the circuit switching communication mode. Furthermore we assume that contention is of no concern. This will be true as long as data streams between different pairs of processors do not interfere, and they can be transmitted independently and simultaneously through the network. This, however, is only justified as long as the transmission capacities of the links and the nodes are sufficiently high. Though such an assumption would work only in low traffic situations, we may accept it as an approximation.

Example. Fig. 4.2 shows how the schedule of Fig. 4.1(b) changes if communication delays are introduced, while tasks are still processed on the same processors.

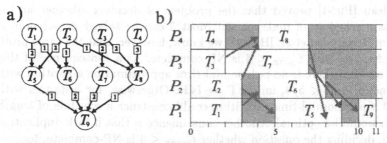

Fig. 4.2. (a) Introducing individual communication delays between pairs of dependent tasks from Fig. 4.1(a) (b) A schedule for non-unit time communication delays for the task set given in Fig. 4.2(a).

4.2.1 Representation of schedules. If communication is considered, but link and node capacities are unlimited, it suffices to describe schedules by sequences of pairs (T_i, P_k), where each pair specifies the processor on which the corresponding task (given in the first component) is to be processed. Idle processor P_k would then grab T_i as soon as the conditions to start T_i are true. Obviously the sequence of tasks, as defined from the sequence of (*task, processor*)-pairs, must be a linear extension of the precedence relation.

We mention that for (non-preemptive) schedules on non-identical processors, without or with communication, the same representation can be used.

4.2.2 Theoretical results. There are many theoretical results available about this type of scheduling problems. Most of these investigations deal with NP-completeness questions under various restrictions, such as concerning the precedence relation or the number of processors, and various assumptions about communication time.

Unit communication time c = 1. We start our discussion assuming unit time communication. The problem of scheduling unit processing time tasks with arbitrary precedence constraints appears to be somewhat simpler if the number of processors is unbounded, or equivalently, if the number n of tasks, does not exceed the number m of processors. In this case, deciding whether $C_{max} < l$ can be done in polynomial time for $l \leq 5$, but is NP-complete for $l \geq 6$. As a consequence there is no polynomial-time approximation algorithm with performance bound $< 7/6$, unless $\mathbf{P} = \mathbf{NP}$ [HLV92]. Munier and König [MK96] presented a list scheduling algorithm with relative performance $4/3$. Restricting to tree precedences, the problem can be solved in $O(n)$ time [Chr89a].

Let us next turn to problems with a limited number of processors m. That means, an instance may have any (finite) number of processors. One of the first results was presented by Rayward-Smith in [Ray87a] who established the NP-hardness for the problem of scheduling unit time tasks with arbitrary precedence constraints, under the objective of minimizing schedule length.

Picouleau [Pic91] proved that the problem of deciding whether an instance has a schedule of makespan at most 3 can be solved in polynomial time. From Hoogeveen et al. [HLV92] we know, however, that the same problem for schedules with $C_{max} \leq 4$ is NP-complete. As a consequence of this result we see that there is no polynomial-time approximation algorithm with performance bound $< 5/4$, unless $\mathbf{P} = \mathbf{NP}$. Otherwise, for instances with $C_{max} = 4$ a polynomial-time algorithm could construct a schedule of length < 5 which would be optimal. Another consequence is that if task duplication is allowed, deciding the question whether $C_{max} \leq 4$ is NP-complete, too.

Rayward-Smith [Ray87a] also discussed the performance of list schedules. The ratio of the makespan C^L_{max} of a list schedule to an optimal schedule, C^*_{max} can be proved to be $\frac{C^L_{max}}{C^*_{max}} \leq 3 - \frac{2}{m}$.

A polynomial time approximation algorithm using a special labeling technique has been designed in [HM94]. The asymptotic performance of this algorithm is $3 - 6/(m+1)$ for $m \geq 3$ processors, and $4/3$ in the case of $m = 2$ processors. Munier and Hanen [MH95] discussed a list mechanism that uses information given by a solution on an unlimited number of processors during the construction phase of a schedule on m processors. They proved that if a schedule for an unlimited number of processors has performance ρ, the list algorithm for m processors has the performance bound $1 + \rho - \rho/m$. Using the $4/3$ result of [MK96] for an unlimited number of processors, this list algorithm has a relative performance bound of $7/3 - 4/(3m)$.

A list scheduling algorithm that includes task duplicates, and whose performance ratio is $2 - 1/m$, can be found in [MH97].

Restricting the precedence relation to special classes allows often to simplify the problem. For example, if the width of the precedence graph, i.e. the cardinality of the largest subset of incomparable tasks in $(\mathcal{T}, \prec)$, is bounded, then the problem of scheduling unit time tasks on a bounded number of processors can be solved in polynomial time [Moh89, Vel93]. On the other hand, for tree-like precedences, it has been proved in [LVV96] that the above problem is still NP-hard. Another example sometimes considered in literature is concerned with interval order precedences; for these the problem can be solved in polynomial time [Pic92].

If the number of processors is fixed, the question if the problem with unit time tasks remains NP-hard, is still open in general. For tree-like precedences and a fixed number m of processors, however, an optimization linear programming algorithm of time complexity $O(n^{2(m-1)})$ is known [VRK93], and an $O(n)$ approximation algorithm computing a schedule whose length exceeds the optimum by no more than $m - 2$ units is presented in [Law93]. Also, for a special class of series-parallel graphs. Finta provides a quadratic algorithm to compute an optimal schedule for two processors.

In [BBG+96], the problem with two uniform processors of speeds 2 and 1, respectively, is considered, where the execution of a task takes two units of time on the slower processor (P_1) and one unit of time on the faster processor (P_2). The precedence relation is assumed to be a complete in-tree. If two tasks being in relation $\prec$ are processed on different processors the communication delay is one unit of time. An $O(h)$ time algorithm is presented for this problem for trees of height h.

Uniform communication time c. Let us now turn to problems where communication times not necessarily require unit time, but are uniform, i.e. they are the same for all packet transmissions. This situation occurs, for example, if the task processing times define the length of the time unit.

Assume first that the number of processors is unbounded. If all task processing times are the same (chosen 1), an algorithm based on dynamic programming which time complexity grows polynomially with the number of tasks, but exponentially with the communication delay c, $O(n^{c+2})$, is presented by Jung et al. [JKS89]. Here, arbitrary precedence constraints between tasks are allowed. For the same problem but where the precedence relation is a complete k-ary tree, Jakoby and Reischuk [JR92] presented an $O(n^2 \log n)$-time algorithm. If completeness of the tree is not guaranteed, the problem is NP-hard even for in-trees where each task has in-degree at most 2 [JR92]. If task duplication is allowed, Papadimitriou and Yannakakis [PY90] showed that the problem with unit processing times, arbitrary precedence constraints and an unbounded number of processors is NP-hard.

For the case of arbitrary processing times p_j, assuming that they are at least as large as the constant communication delay c, with $c \leq 1$, and again for an unlimited number of processors, we know from [Pic91] and [Vel93] that the problem to decide whether an instance has a schedule of length $C_{max} \leq 5 + 3c$ or $C_{max} \leq 6c$, respectively, is NP-complete. The condition $p_j \geq c$ is a special case of the coarse grained scheduling problems discussed below.

On the other hand, if the communication delay is large compared to the processing time, it can be useful to get information about how far the makespan is influenced by the largest communication delay. From [BGK96] it is known that for a bounded number of processors, deciding whether the makespan of a given instance does not exceed $c + 2$ can be solved in polynomial time, whereas the decision problem with $C_{max} \leq c + 3$ is NP-complete, even for bipartite[1] precedences. Furthermore, there is a lower bound on the performance of approximation algorithms: there exists no polynomial-time algorithm with performance bound smaller than $1 + 1/(c + 3)$, unless $\mathbf{P} = \mathbf{NP}$. This result also holds in the special case of bipartite precedence relations.

General communication times. We finally assume that each pair of dependent tasks $T_i \prec T_j$ needs an individually specified amount of time c_{ij} to transmit the data.

Only for the very restricted problem where trees are of depth 1, and again under the assumptions of an unbounded number of processors and unit processing times, Picouleau [Pic92] was able to present an $O(n \log n)$ time algorithm. While scheduling an out-tree is NP-hard, the same problem becomes simple if task duplication is allowed, even for arbitrary processing times [Chr94]. An approximation algorithm proposed in [PY90] for the similar problem but with arbitrary precedence constraints brings out quite interesting ideas on the way to design heuristics. The algorithm proposed has time complexity $O(n^2(e + n \log n))$ where e denotes the number of precedence constrained task pairs.

Several other investigations on general communication delay problems make assumptions on the relationship between the sizes of processing times and communication times: The granularity g of an instance can be defined as $g := \min_i\{p_i\}/\max_{ij}\{c_{ij}\}$. An instance is said to be *coarse* if $g \geq 1$. Another also useful definition is that of the *grain* of a task: The *grain* g_j of task T_j is defined by $g = \min_{i \in ipred(T_j)}\{p_i\}/\max_{i \in ipred(T_j)}\{c_{ij}\}$, where $ipred(T_j)$ denotes the set of tasks immediately preceding T_j. Based on this notion, Chretienne and Picouleau [CP91] use a less restrictive definition of instance granularity: An instance is of *coarse-grained type* if $g_j \geq 1$ for all $j = 1, \ldots, n$. We distinguish between these two definitions by writing "$g \geq 1$" in the first and "$g_j \geq 1$" in the second case.

Coarse grained problems with $g \geq 1$ and an unlimited number of processors were first independently studied by Gerasoulis and Yang [GY92] and Picouleau [Pic91]. Both papers presented approximation algorithms based on critical paths with the worst case bound $1 + 1/g$, under the assumptions of general precedence constraints, arbitrary task processing times, and task-dependent communication times. This result has been improved in [HM95] where a polynomial time approximation algorithm with the worst case bound $1 + 1/(2g + 1)$ is presented. Restricting the problem to special precedence re-

---

[1] A precedence relation is *bipartite* if the longest path in the corresponding precedence graph has length 2.

lations, for tree-like precedences this problem can be solved in $O(n)$ time [Chr89a, AHC90]. A similar problem with $g_j \geq 1$ and bipartite or series-parallel precedence constraints is solvable in polynomial time [CP91].

For scheduling out-trees on m processors, Munier [Mun96] discusses the performance of arbitrary list algorithms in terms of the granularity ratio g, and proves that their worst case bound is $1 + (1 - 1/m)(2 + g)/(1 + g)$.

4.3 Packet Switching, Communication without Contention

Accepting the same restrictions as in 4.2, we now discuss the case where data transmission time depends linearly on the distance between sender and target node. The following motivation for this case is somewhat artificial: we might think of the packets being transmitted in a store-and-forward manner from node to node. The transmission time along each link is the same, and there is no queueing delay at the nodes, which is in fact a consequence of the no-contention assumption. Moreover, since different data streams do not interfere, the data can be transmitted independently and simultaneously through the network along shortest paths. These assumptions are indeed unrealistic in general, but they will be a good approximation if an application has not too many communications.

Suppose that pairs of dependent tasks have individually specified sizes of data packets to transmit, and s_{ij} is the time needed to transmit the data of task T_i to task T_j along a single link. Assuming that all links have the same technical specification, it follows immediately that, if the tasks are on the respective processors P_k and P_l, and a shortest path connecting them has $d_{kl} \geq 1$ links (distance between P_k and P_l), the transmission time will be $d_{kl}s_{ij}$. Hence, the model we end up with is such that the data transmission times $c(T_i, P_k; T_j, P_l)$ depend not only on the tasks themselves but also on the processors the tasks are running on.

Example. Adjusting the example to this situation, we assume a linear array of four processors (see Fig. 4.3).

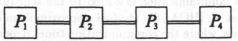

Fig. 4.3. A four processor linear array.

For the task system of Fig. 4.2, assuming that the tasks are assigned to exactly the same processors as before we get the following communication times $d_{kl}s_{ij}$ in the linear array, as summarized in Table 4.2. The corresponding schedule is presented in Fig. 4.4.

4.3.1 Representation of schedules. As in Section 4.2, schedules can obviously be represented by sequences of (*task, processor*)-pairs. If we have,

Table 4.2. Communication times $d_{kl}s_{ij}$ in the linear array of Fig. 4.3.

T_i	P_k	T_j	P_l	s_{ij}	d_{kl}	communication time
T_1	P_1	T_6	P_2	1	1	1
T_2	P_2	T_5	P_1	2	1	2
T_2	P_2	T_8	P_4	1	2	2
T_3	P_3	T_8	P_4	2	1	2
T_6	P_2	T_9	P_1	2	1	2
T_7	P_3	T_9	P_1	2	2	4
T_8	P_4	T_9	P_1	1	3	3

Fig. 4.4. A schedule for the linear array of Fig. 4.3, with packet switching.

for instance, two pairs (T_i, P_k) and (T_j, P_l) with $T_i \prec T_j$ and $P_k \neq P_l$, i.e. where a data packet C_{ij} has to be transmitted before T_j can be started, the transmission time is fixed and is determined by the shortest distance between P_k and P_l. Hence, the set of all possible schedules is given by the set of all feasible task sequences (linear extensions), together with information about the processors the tasks are assigned to.

4.3.2 Algorithmic approaches. There is a general and very simple way describing how schedules with included communication delays can be constructed. This strategy is called *extended list scheduling*, ELS, and is a straight-forward extension of list scheduling. The ELS method adopts a two-step strategy. First tasks are allocated to processors by applying list scheduling as if the underlying system were free of communication overhead. Second, the necessary communication is added to the schedule obtained in the first step. Hwang et al. [HCA+89] studied approximation list algorithms for scheduling problems, where the communication times depend both on the involved tasks and on the processors which execute the tasks. The underlying communication system model allows to cover all types of network topologies such as fully connected systems, hypercubes, or bus systems, but the communication is assumed to be contention free. Denoting by C_{ELS} the makespan of a schedule derived by applying extended list scheduling, and by C^*_{nocomm} the makespan of an optimal schedule for the same instance where communication delays are not considered, Hwang et al. proved the following bound

$$C_{ELS} \leq (2 - \frac{1}{m})C_{nocomm}^* + \sum_{T_i \prec T_j} c_{ij}.$$

It is also shown that this bound cannot be improved in general.

Since the performance of ELS is unsatisfactory, an improved strategy called the *earliest task first* (ETF) was proposed in [HCA+89]. This algorithm uses a greedy strategy where the earliest ready task is scheduled first. The strategy is improved by the ability to postpone a scheduling decision to the next decision moment if a task completion between two decision points may make a more urgent task schedulable. The performance ratio obtained from a detailed analysis is

$$C_{ETF} \leq (2 - \frac{1}{m})C_{nocomm}^* + c_{max}$$

where c_{max} is the maximum communication requirement along all chains of $\mathcal{T}$, that is

$$c_{max} = \max\{\sum_{i=1}^{l-1} c_{\alpha_i \alpha_{i+1}} | (T_{\alpha_1}, \ldots, T_{\alpha_l}) \text{ is a chain in } \mathcal{T}\}.$$

4.3.3 Theoretical results. Picouleau [Pic92] studied a problem where the communication time is distance-dependent: For each pair of processors, P_k, P_l, their distance d_{kl} is defined by $d_{kl} = |k - l|$. The communication time $c(T_i, P_k; T_j, P_l)$ is assumed to be $s_{ij} d_{kl}$, provided that $T_i \prec T_j$. This distance function can be motivated as being appropriate for a linear array network of infinite length. If precedences are trees of depth one, and the number of processors is unbounded, the problem is NP-hard. This can be shown by a transformation from PARTITION.

There are more papers available that consider problems of the kind discussed in this section. Most of them consider special network topologies such as rings or mesh connected processors, or discuss the problem of mapping a task precedence graph on a special processor network.

4.4 Circuit Switching, Communication with Contention

The cases discussed below differ from those considered so far in the more realistic assumption that links and processor nodes have *limited transmission capacities*. Due to this limitation data streams can block each other from simultaneous transmission. As a consequence, transmission times are no longer independent of each other, and hence it is not possible to specify communication times by a table with fixed entries $c(T_i, P_k; T_j, P_l)$.

In contrast to the discussion of Section 4.2, a connecting path from the sender to the target processor can only be activated if there is sufficient capacity available along the links and nodes of the path. A link in which a certain number of available channels are set up, may simply be busy with transmissions, without free capacity; a node being able to receive and transmit a certain maximum number of packets at a time, may also be not available for an additional packet. On the other hand, a packet can be transmitted as soon as there is sufficient capacity on both, links and nodes along some path. Transmission time will then be independent of the path length.

What can happen is that while one path is not available, another path connecting the same pair of processors, could offer the required capacity. To perform a given set of tasks, we need to have the knowledge about all possible paths between each pair of processor nodes, in order to check availability of paths. Consequently, the time at which some communication will take place depends on two factors: the topology of the underlying network, and the present workload.

We see that in fact we end up with a task scheduling problem, where a second type of tasks has to be carefully planned. For $T_i \prec T_j$ let again C_{ij} denote the packet of data to be transmitted from T_i to T_j before T_j can start. If some path π is selected for transmission, we refer to the pair (C_{ij}, π) as a *communication task*. So we distinguish two types of tasks:

- *Computation tasks:* These are the "real" tasks given originally in the problem. Since we deal with parallel or distributed systems for computations, the tasks are some given computation activities. These tasks need processors and - maybe - other resources during their execution, but not the resources offered by the network.
- *Communication tasks:* These are tasks equivalent to a transmission of data between processor nodes. These activities need network resources like links, I/O processors, network interfaces, buffers, but not the resources required by the "real" tasks.

Another essential difference between computation tasks and communication tasks is that the first ones are fixed and well known (at least in the deterministic scheduling paradigm), whereas the occurrence of the latter depends on several factors, for example on the chosen assignment of the computation tasks to the processors, on the overall system workload (assuming greedy task execution), and on the structure and the transmission properties of the network.

4.4.1 Representation of schedules. To characterize feasible schedules formally appears much more difficult than in the case of contention-free communication: As before, one may use pairs (T_i, P_k) do describe task-to-processor assignments. In addition, if $T_i \prec T_j$, with T_j assigned to $P_l(\neq P_k)$, and π_{kl} is a path from P_k to P_l , then the communication task (C_{ij}, π_{kl}) has to be placed between the pairs (T_i, P_k) and (T_j, P_l). The problem in fact is that the solution space not only consists of all feasible sequences of task-to-processor pairs, but in each such sequence one must also consider the communication task for each possible path between processors P_k and P_l that process two dependent tasks.

Example. To illustrate this situation consider again the linear array of four processors. For simplicity reasons we assume that each link can transmit and each node can accept/receive/transmit one packet at a time. An example schedule with the communication delays of Fig. 4.2(a) is given in Fig. 4.5.

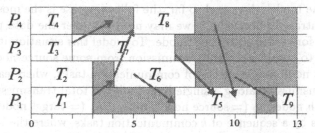

Fig. 4.5. The schedule for the problem in Fig. 4.2(a) under the assumption of node and link capacity equal to 1.

In this schedule a possible task sequence (without communication tasks) is

$$(T_1, P_1), (T_2, P_2), (T_3, P_3), (T_4, P_4), (T_7, P_3), (T_6, P_2), (T_8, P_4), (T_5, P_1), (T_9, P_1).$$

Next, between each pair (T_i, P_k) and (T_j, P_l) with $T_i \prec T_j$ and $P_k \neq P_l$ we have to include some communication task (C_{ij}, π_{kl}). Notice that we assumed a linear array network, hence π_{kl} is uniquely determined by P_k and P_l. For example, the sequence[2]

$$(T_1, P_1), (T_2, P_2), (T_3, P_3), (T_4, P_4), (C_{38}, \pi_{34}), (T_7, P_3), (C_{16}, \pi_{12}), (T_6, P_2),$$

$$(C_{28}, \pi_{24}), (T_8, P_4), (C_{25}, \pi_{21}), (T_5, P_1), (C_{79}, \pi_{31}), (C_{89}, \pi_{41}), (C_{69}, \pi_{21}), (T_9, P_1)$$

is a possible description of the schedule in Fig. 4.5. Notice that the packet transmissions that use a common link (such as (C_{38}, π_{34}) and (C_{28}, π_{24}), or (C_{28}, π_{24}) and (C_{25}, π_{21})) must be sequenced because of the transmission limitations of the network links.

4.4.2 Theoretical results. Of course, the order in which concurrent transmissions are resolved will in general be of essential influence for the optimality of the final result - it thus adds a new dimension to the task scheduling problem. Most of the available results consider special types of processor networks, such as the multistage interconnection networks (viz. e.g. [SH86]), or mapping of precedence graphs on a processor network (embedding problem, e.g. [MT93]), or analyze contention situations as in the so-called hot spot problem (e.g. [LK90]). We do not go into details here because of their rather special character, as compared to the general approach followed here (cf. also Section 2.3).

---

[2] If links allow transmission in either direction then $\pi_{kl} = \pi_{lk}$

312   Jacek Błażewicz, Maciej Drozdowski, and Klaus Ecker

In Section 4.5, when we discuss the problem in a more general form, we shall introduce the notion of a network hypergraph that could serve as a general basis for scheduling algorithms with communication delays.

4.5 Packet Switching, Communication with Contention

Compared to the models discussed so far, the following case is the most complex one. In contrast to Section 4.3, we may need to buffer the data packets before they are forwarded to the next node. To model this situation it would be appropriate to consider a data transmission from some source node to a (remote) target node as a sequence of communication tasks, where each one handles the transmission along a single link. So if the total transmission follows a path with nodes n_0 (= source node), $n_1, \ldots, n_k$ (= target node), then we describe this by a sequence of k communication tasks, where the i-th one is for the transmission from node n_{i-1} to n_i $(i = 1, \ldots, k)$.

Example. Again we consider scheduling on the linear array of four processors, and assume for simplicity reasons that each link can transmit, and each node can accept/receive/transmit at most one packet at a time. An example schedule is shown in Fig. 4.6.

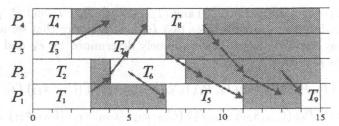

Fig. 4.6. Packet switching with contention.

4.5.1 Representation of schedules. As in Section 4.4, the problem is that the solution space not only consists of all possible sequences of task-processor pairs, but between those pairs all possibilities for communication paths between P_k and P_l have to be considered. The situation is now even more complex because each communication path is replaced by a sequence of single communication steps; in addition, since usually there will be a set of communication paths overlapping in time, the condition of maximum buffer sizes has to be observed.

A possible description of a solution schedule would therefore have the form

$$\ldots (T_i, P_k), \ldots, (C_{ij}, \lambda_{rs}), \ldots, (T_j, P_l), \ldots$$

where (C_{ij}, λ_{rs}) denotes the communication task for transmitting C_{ij} along the link λ_{rs} from processor P_r to P_s. For a feasible sequence (i.e. one which represents a schedule), we can formulate the following conditions:

- The subsequence of pairs of kind (T, P) is a linear extension of the given precedence relation.
- For $T_i \prec T_j$, consider the pairs (T_i, P_k) and (T_j, P_l) with $(P_k \neq P_l)$: there is a subsequence of pairs (C_{ij}, λ_{rs}) between them, where the sequence defined by the links λ_{rs} is a path from P_k to P_l.
- If buffers at the nodes are of limited sizes then additional restrictions have to be considered. We do not go into details here and assume simply unlimited buffer sizes.

Example. To illustrate this description, the following sequence defines the schedule of Fig. 4.6:

$$(T_1, P_1), (T_2, P_2), (T_3, P_3), (T_4, P_4), (T_7, P_3), (C_{38}, \lambda_{34}), (C_{16}, \lambda_{12}), (T_6, P_2),$$

$$(C_{28}, \lambda_{23}), (C_{28}, \lambda_{34}), (C_{25}, \lambda_{21}), (T_8, P_4), (T_5, P_1), (C_{79}, \lambda_{32}), (C_{79}, \lambda_{21}),$$

$$(C_{69}, \lambda_{21}), (C_{89}, \lambda_{43}), (C_{89}, \lambda_{32}), (C_{89}, \lambda_{21}), (T_9, P_1)$$

Notice that, besides the precedences between computation tasks, there are now also precedences between communication tasks, e.g. $(C_{28}, \lambda_{23}) \prec (C_{28}, \lambda_{34})$.

4.5.2 Algorithmic aspects. If contention occurs, there are several possibilities to deal with the packets waiting in a node buffer:

a) Forward them in first-in-first-out mode.
b) If the receiving tasks have different priorities, as for example in scheduling problems where tasks have different weights, packets of higher priority can be chosen first.
c) Looking at the packets waiting in all the nodes, and considering the total set of all communication tasks, we could try to sequence these in an optimal manner, for example in such a way that the overall goal of minimizing the maximum makespan is met. This is especially interesting in synchronous executions where computation and communication phases alternate.
d) Apply re-routing, i.e. consider alternative paths for some of the packets. This concerns rather the dynamic task scheduling paradigm where tasks arrive at unforeseen points of time. However, in static scheduling rerouting could make sense in heuristic strategies in the attempt to improve the so far obtained solution by changing communication paths.

An optimization algorithm should perform the following three steps more or less interleaved:

(i) choosing a task assignment to processors,
(ii) dealing with communication tasks in buffers: find an optimal sequencing for these,
(iii) routing: if alternative paths are available, choose an optimal route, under consideration of alternative routes in case of traffic contention.

For finding the best solution we have to optimize in these three directions, and it should be clear that there is a strong relationship which does not allow us to optimize (i), (ii), and (iii) independently. Indeed, the occurrence of communication tasks depends highly on the chosen assignment of the (real) tasks to processors, and the chosen communication paths in the network.

Unfortunately, there is no optimal algorithm known so far that solves the problem in its most general form. In the following we describe some basics for a possible general algorithmic approach to the problem.

4.5.3 Network hypergraph.
We finally present a formal model for communication networks that allows one to describe the structure and communication properties in a uniform way. This so-called *network hypergraph* was first presented in [EH93] and is very general in the sense that it can be applied to different kinds of networks under various assumptions about the transmission capabilities of links and nodes.

Essentially, the network hypergraph informs about maximal sets of simultaneous communications in the network. To define the hypergraph, one has to analyze first different types of communication. A *communication type* is defined as a processor pair (P_k, P_l) where a data packet can be sent directly and without intermediate delay from P_k to P_l. Especially in packet switching networks, a communication type represents the link between two processors (a further distinction can be made between bi-directional and unidirectional communication types). Let C be the set of all possible communication types. In the second step, we check which subsets of communication types are conflict-free: A subset $\{\gamma_1, \ldots, \gamma_k\} \subseteq \Gamma$ is called *non-conflicting* if communication tasks $(C_1, \gamma_{\alpha_1}), \ldots, (C_k, \gamma_{\alpha_k})$ (for arbitrary packets $C_1, \ldots C_k$) can be transmitted simultaneously in the network. To be more precise, we are interested in *maximal subsets* $H \subseteq \Gamma$ of *non-conflicting communication types*, because if H is *non-conflicting* then each subset of H is *non-conflicting*, too. Let $\mathcal{H}$ be the set of all possible maximal subsets H. Then the *hypergraph* for the network is defined as the pair $(C, \mathcal{H})$ with node set C and set of hyperedges $\mathcal{H}$.

The hypergraph obviously depends highly on the communication properties of the network, such as the capacities of the links and nodes, or packet or circuit switching networks. The practical implication of this notion is that $\mathcal{H}$ informs about maximal possible simultaneous transmissions.

If a set of communication tasks has to be performed in minimum time, this means in terms of the hypergraph that we have to select a sequence of hyperedges of minimum length. We mention that limited buffer sizes impose additional conditions on the optimal sequence, because the hypergraph by itself does not consider this restriction.

Example. In the linear array network of Fig. 4.3 we consider packet switching and assume that the communication capabilities are as follows:

- links are bi-directional and of capacity one,
- a node can send one packet to one of its neighbors,
- a node can receive a packet from one of its neighbors,
- a node can simultaneously send to one neighbor and receive from another neighbor.

Under these assumptions the hypergraph has four hyperedges, each represented by a row in Table 4.3 (• means that the corresponding communication type is in the hyperedge):

Table 4.3. A hypergraph for the linear array network of Fig. 4.3.

Communication type ▷ Hyperedge↓	(P_1,P_2)	(P_2,P_1)	(P_2,P_3)	(P_3,P_2)	(P_3,P_4)	(P_4,P_3)
H_1	•		•		•	
H_2		•		•		•
H_3	•					•
H_4			•		•	

When applying the network hypergraph, we should differentiate between synchronous and asynchronous task execution (see 4.1.4). In synchronous execution we can solve the computation phases by any algorithm that solves the communication-free scheduling problem (cf. Section 1.1.3). For scheduling the communication phases we make use of the network hypergraph. Since we can assume that we have exact knowledge about the set of communication tasks we can try to schedule them optimally, i.e. to determine a sequence of minimum length. This means that we have to select hyperedges, and each hyperedge takes care of some communication tasks.

If task execution is organized asynchronously, the hypergraph approach can also be applied, but then the communication tasks arrive at different times for being communicated, that is at times where computation tasks are completed. We may interpret these times as *release times* for communication tasks (relative to the completion time of the originating task), and end up this way with an even more general scheduling problem. No algorithms are known so far for this case.

To define the phases in case of synchronous execution, the end of a *computation* phase may be defined by the condition that all possible tasks are processed, i.e. at the end of the phase there are only tasks waiting for some data to be sent over the network. For the end of a *communication* phase we may establish the condition that all packets have arrived at their destination, i.e. there are no more pending communication tasks.

In the following we discuss the synchronous execution in more detail. Before we turn to algorithms we present an example.

Example. Separating computation and communication phases in Fig. 4.6 we get the following computation and communication phases:

1. Computation phase:
   $(T_1, P_1), (T_2, P_2), (T_3, P_3), (T_4, P_4), (T_7, P_3)$
2. Communication phase:
   $(C_{38}, \lambda_{34}), (C_{16}, \lambda_{12}), (C_{28}, \lambda_{23}) \prec (C_{28}, \lambda_{34}), (C_{25}, \lambda_{21}),$
   $(C_{79}, \lambda_{32}) \prec (C_{79}, \lambda_{21})$
3. Computation phase:
   $(T_6, P_2), (T_8, P_4), (T_5, P_1)$
4. Communication phase:
   $(C_{69}, \lambda_{21}), (C_{89}, \lambda_{43}) \prec (C_{89}, \lambda_{32}) \prec (C_{89}, \lambda_{21})$
5. Computation phase:
   (T_9, P_1)

Packet lengths are as in Fig. 4.2(a). An optimal schedule for the first communication phase needs five time units (buffers at the nodes are assumed to be sufficiently large). Notice that communication tasks of length > 1 must be processed non-preemptively, i.e. continued in the next time slot. This fact imposes restrictions on the choise of the next hyperedge.

Selected hyperedge → Communication type (link) ↓	H_2	H_2	H_1	H_4	H_4
(P_1, P_2)			C_{16}		
(P_2, P_1)	C_{25}	C_{25}		C_{79}	C_{79}
(P_2, P_3)			C_{28}		
(P_3, P_2)	C_{79}	C_{79}			
(P_3, P_4)				C_{38}	C_{38}	C_{28}
(P_4, P_3)						*time*

Fig. 4.7. A schedule for the first communication phase.

Generally, we can find an optimal schedule for these tasks by applying, for instance, a branch and bound technique in the following way: The root represents the total communication problem (of a communication phase). Each inner node represents the problem that remains when one or more hyperedges have been selected. To proceed from a node N of the tree to a successor node by using hyperedge H, for each communication type in the hyperedge we have to remove one task of that type from the set of communication tasks of N. The leaves of the tree are those nodes where no communication tasks are left. An optimal solution is defined by the hyperedges along a shortest path from the root to the leaves.

A more detailed formulation of the optimization problem can easily be given under the special assumptions of *(i)* unit time communications and *(ii)* independent communication tasks. Let $K = \{(C_1, \gamma_{\alpha_1}), \ldots, (C_k, \gamma_{\alpha_k})\}$ be the set of communication tasks in a communication phase. Recall that each C_i represents a packet of data, and each γ_{α_i} is a link (or path) along which the packet can be transmitted in a single operation of unit time duration. The optimization problem can then be formulated in the following way: Find a sequence $(H_1, \ldots, H_l)$ of hyperedges of minimum length such that

- each communication task (C_i, γ_{α_i}) is assigned to a hyperedge H_h with $\gamma_{\alpha_i} \in H_h$,
- each two tasks (C_i, γ_{α_i}) and (C_j, γ_{α_j}) with $\gamma_{\alpha_i} = \gamma_{\alpha_j}$ are assigned to different hyperedges.

This can be formalized in terms of a linear integer programming problem. Describe each hyperedge H_j, $j = 1, 2, \ldots, |\mathcal{H}|$ by a vector h_j of dimension L (= number of communication types), where, in the i-th position, 0 means absence, and 1 means an existence of the i-th communication type γ_i in H_j. The input sequence K is represented as a vector k of dimension L, where the i-th component gives the number of communication tasks of type γ_i. Then find coefficients $a_1, \ldots, a_{|\mathcal{H}|} \in N_0$ such that

$$\sum_{j=1}^{|\mathcal{H}|} a_j h_j \geq k \text{ (component-wise } \geq \text{), and } \sum_{j=1}^{|\mathcal{H}|} a_j \text{ is minimal.}$$

The schedule corresponding to the solution has a_j time slots with hyperedge H_j, $j = 1, 2, \ldots, L$, and the length of the schedule is given by $\sum a_j$.

5. Scheduling Divisible Tasks

5.1 The Concept of a Divisible Task

A new scheduling model applicable in many parallel architectures is presented in this section. We analyze scheduling divisible tasks, i.e. tasks that can be divided into parts of arbitrary size. These parts can be processed in parallel and independently of each other. In other words, divisible tasks are parallel applications which include no data dependencies (precedence constraints) and whose granularity of parallelism is fine.

Before going into details we give some motivation of the model and introduce basic concepts. Consider, as an example, searching for a record in a huge database with thousands (or more) records. This can be done by cooperating processors. The database file can be divided into parts with granularity of one record. Note that the granularity of the division is fine compared the total size of a database. The search can be conducted in each part independently of the other parts. Thus, the two assumptions of the divisible task model are fulfilled. Finally, the results are reported to a master processor. This approach can be applied while searching for a pattern in a text, graphical, audio, etc. file. A similar situation takes place when sorting a database file in a distributed way. Further examples of divisible tasks are related to data parallelism: processing big measurement data files [CR88], image and signal processing [BGM+96], simulations of molecular dynamics [ADK+93], some problems of linear algebra on big matrices [BT90], solving partial differential equations by the finite element method [Wi91] and many other engineering and scientific problems. Observe that similar assumptions on divisibility of the work are made in loop scheduling [LSL94, ML94] and load balancing [Gos91, GKR92, LM92, XH93] models of parallel applications (see Sections 2.4 and 2.5).

Now, we outline the process of data dissemination and processing. A parallel computer consists of m processing elements (PEs), each of which comprises a processor, local memory, and is capable of communicating over the interconnection network (either by an independent network processor, or by the use of software run on the processor). The notions of a processor from the scheduling theory and the processing element are equivalent here. Only when a PE has a network processor is it capable of simultaneously computing and communicating. Initially, the whole volume V of data (or work) to be processed resides in one processor called originator. The originator processes locally α_1 data units and sends the rest (i.e. $V - \alpha_1$) to its idle neighbors. Each processing element intercepts for local computing some data from the received volume and sends the rest to the idle neighbors. Thus, PE number i (denoted by P_i) intercepts and processes locally α_i data units which lasts $\alpha_i A_i$ units of time. A_i represents the processing rate, i.e. the reciprocal of the speed, for P_i, $i = 1, \ldots, m$. The transmission time of x data units over communication link i joining two processors is $S_i + xC_i$. S_i is the startup time that is spent to initiate the communication, and C_i is the transmission rate. Our goal is to find such a distribution of task parts (i.e. α_i's) that the communications and computations are finished in the shortest time. For simplicity of the presentation we assume that the processing time depends linearly on the volume of processed data. It will be demonstrated that this assumption can be relaxed.

The above description still leaves space for details including, e.g. a communication algorithm tailored to the interconnection network. In the following sections we present solutions for different network topologies. Observe that when no results are returned to the originator, all the processors must stop working at the same moment of time. It can be explained intuitively: when P_i finishes earlier, then it is possible to off-load other PEs by moving some part of the load to P_i. Thus, the whole schedule would be shortened. This observation has been proved both for particular interconnections [CR88, SR93] and for a general type of interconnection [BD97]. Assuming that the results are not returned simplifies the presentation. However, we show in the following sections that also the case where results are returned to the originator can be included in our model. Unless stated otherwise we assume that the number of divisible tasks is equal to one. The process of distributing workload which is a distribution of information in which each PE receives different data is called *scattering*.

This part of the book is organized as follows. In Section 5.2 we present results of applying the idea of divisible task in various distributed systems. We concentrate on basic models, and then show the way of expanding them to cover more complex cases. Performance evaluation is one of divisible task model applications. Examples of such an evaluation are presented in Section 5.3. Section 5.4 describes some results of verifying divisible task model experimentally.

5.2 Scheduling Divisible Task in Processor Networks

5.2.1 Linear array of processors.
To our knowledge, the first work analyzing divisible tasks was [CR88]. It considered the method of finding an optimal balance between parallelism and necessary communication in a linear array (i.e. a chain) of intelligent sensors. Such sensors can process their data locally or send some part of work to the neighbors for remote processing. The key question was how much data should be computed locally and how much in a distributed way.

Basic model. We will describe now a basic model for the linear array network. A Gantt chart of communications and computations is depicted in Fig. 5.1.

For simplicity of the presentation we assume first that no results are returned to the originator, the PEs have network processors and the originator is located at the end of the chain. The part of the load which is not processed by the originator is sent to the nearest neighbor. The neighbor divides the received data into a part processed locally and forwards the rest to the next idle processor. This procedure is repeated until the last processor is activated. Since there is no returning of data all the processors must stop computing at the same moment of time [BD97, CR88]. As can be observed in Fig.5.1,

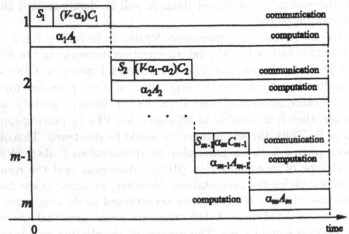

Fig. 5.1. Communication and computation in a linear array of processors.

processing on a sending PE lasts as long as communication to the receiver and processing on the receiver. Thus, we can find a distribution of the load from the following set of equations [BD97, CR88]:

$$\alpha_i A_i = S_i + (\alpha_{i+1} + \ldots + \alpha_m)C_i + \alpha_{i+1}A_{i+1}, \quad i = 1, \ldots, m-1$$
$$V = \alpha_1 + \alpha_2 + \ldots + \alpha_m \tag{5.1}$$
$$\alpha_1, \alpha_2, \ldots, \alpha_m \geq 0$$

where S_i, C_i are startup time and transmission rate of a link joining P_i and P_{i+1}, and A_i is processing rate of P_i. The above equation set can be solved in $O(m)$ time by a reduction of α_i to a linear function of α_m: $\alpha_i = k_i \alpha_m + l_i$, where $k_m = 1, l_m = 0, k_i = \frac{C_i}{A_i} \sum_{j=i+1}^{m} k_j + \frac{A_{i+1}}{A_i} k_{i+1}, l_i = \frac{C_i}{A_i} \sum_{j=i+1}^{m} l_j + \frac{A_{i+1}}{A_i} l_{i+1} + \frac{S_i}{A_i}$ for $i = 1, \ldots, m-1$. From the last equation of formulation (5.1) we obtain $\alpha_m = (V - \sum_{i=1}^{m} l_i)(\sum_{i=1}^{m} k_i)$. It may happen that a feasible solution of equations (5.1) does not exist. Practically spoken, it means that data can be processed by less than m processors in a shorter time than required to activate all m PEs. Then, the maximum number of usable processors and the optimal distribution of the load can be found by a binary search over m in time $O(m \log m)$.

Including data return. Note that results are returned in the inverted order of data distribution. After finishing the computations the last processor returns the results to the penultimate processor. This one may still keep finishing its computations while obtaining results from the last processor. On receipt of these results processor $m - 1$ starts returning its own results and the results of processor m. Hence, while P_i computes, the spare data is sent to P_{i+1}, processed on $P_{i+1}, \ldots, P_m$ and results are returned to P_i. Thus, the first line in equations (5.1) has the form:

$$\alpha_i A_i = 2S_i + (\alpha_{i+1} + \ldots + \alpha_m)C_i + \alpha_{i+1}A_{i+1} + \beta(\alpha_{i+1} + \ldots + \alpha_m)C_i \quad i = 1, \ldots, m-1$$

$$(5.2)$$

where $\beta(x)$ is the amount of results returned for x units of data. In simple cases $\beta(x)$ can be constant (when a simple answer is required e.g. "yes/no", "found at address/not found") or a linear function of x (e.g. distributed FFT, sorting, etc.).

Lack of network processors. Without network processors PEs cannot compute and communicate simultaneously. Therefore, a processor starts processing its share of data after having sent the unneeded load to its idle neighbors. Hence, equations (5.1) should be modified in the following way:

$$\alpha_i A_i = S_{i+1} + (\alpha_{i+2} + \ldots + \alpha_m)C_{i+1} + \alpha_{i+1}A_{i+1}, \quad i = 1, \ldots, m-2$$
$$\alpha_{m-1}A_{m-1} = \alpha_m A_m \qquad\qquad\qquad\qquad (5.3)$$

Circuit switching routing. In the previous cases we assumed that PEs receive data in full for itself and all its successors. Then, the part of the load is sent to the idle neighbors. This is a feature of the so-called store and forward routing (cf. Section 4.) There exists a different routing strategy called circuit switching. In circuit switching a direct (electrical) connection between the sender and the receiver is established. Consequently, the communication delay does not depend significantly on the covered distance. Hence, it can be advantageous to send some data far ahead and then redistribute it from two (or more) points. A similar situation takes place for some packet-switching communication methods (e.g. wormhole routing) [NMK93]. In the following we assume that the originator is located in the center of the linear array network, results are not returned, all PEs have network processors and can simultaneously transmit over both ports. The originator sends data simultaneously to two distant PEs. In the next step both the originator and the two previously activated PEs send data to two new processors (cf. Fig.5.2). The process is repeated activating in each step twice as many processors as were active at the beginning of the step. We will call by a *layer* the set of PEs activated in the same distribution step. Thus, all processors are working after $h = \lceil \log_3 m \rceil$ steps. Distributing data and a diagram of communication and computing is depicted in Fig. 5.2. We denote by A the processing rate of all (identical) processors, by C the communication rate of all links, by S the startup time of all links, by h the number of steps in data distribution algorithm, and by α_i the load of each PE in layer i. Since no results are returned, all the PEs must finish their computations simultaneously. Note that the time of computing on the PEs of the sending layer is equal to the time of communicating to and computing on the PEs of the receiving layer (cf. Fig. 5.2). Thus, equations (5.1) have now the form:

$$\alpha_{h-i}A = S + (\alpha_{h-i+1} + 2\sum_{j=2}^{i} 3^{j-2}\alpha_{h-i+j})C + \alpha_{h-i+1}A, \quad i = 1, \ldots, h-1$$

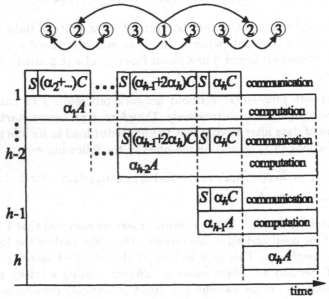

Fig. 5.2. Communication and computation in a linear array with circuit-switching routing.

$$V = \alpha_1 + 2\sum_{j=2}^{h} 3^{j-2}\alpha_j \qquad (5.4)$$

The above set of equations can be solved in $O(h) = O(\log m)$ time by a method analogous to the one proposed to solve equations (5.1).

Other extensions of the model. We reduced the above problems to sets of linear equations which we solved by rather procedural methods. This approach can be inconvenient in some situations. For that reason closed-form expressions were proposed in [MG94] to solve the basic model of the chain architecture. It was also shown that in the linear arrays of identical processors with the originator located in the network interior, the whole load processing time is independent of the direction the originator sends the data first. The case of the originator located inside the chain was analyzed in [BD97, MG94], and the case of rings of PEs in [BD97]. In [BR92, Rob93] a concept of the equivalent processor was proposed, by which a single-processor equivalent of the original multiprocessor system was understood. The ultimate performance limits were calculated. In [GM94] closed-form formulae expressing the limit of the performance enhancement obtained by using additional processors are presented. [BGM95b] examines a chain network in which PEs are equipped with 1-port network processors. This means that a PE can communicate only over one link at a time. By the use of the intermediate PEs' network processors the originator sends the shares of data directly to a particular PE. Thus, any PE can start computing right after receiving its data, without waiting for the load being forwarded to the following PEs. In the previous discussion we assumed that the originator sent the data to its neighbors in one chunk. This may result in long communication delays and idle period on PEs before computing can be started. In [Dro97] a different data distribution method based on pipelining and circuit-switched routing was proposed, i.e. rather than in one big chunk the data are sent to the PEs in many smaller ones.

5.2.2 Star, bus and trees. Star topology (or single-level tree [BGM+96], or a hub) is a convenient model not only from the hardware point of view, but can also represent a master-slave paradigm of parallel applications. We assume that the originator is located in the center of the star (or in the root of the single-level tree) which is P_1. All the communications are performed by the originator which distributes data to the PEs consecutively, and then collects the results (if any). P_i is connected with the originator via link i with parameters S_i, C_i. In the (single) bus interconnection the bus is a resource which cannot be shared by the communications, and must be accessed sequentially. Hence, the originator activates other PEs one by one as in the case of the star topology. Therefore, the bus and the star can be analyzed in the same way. Below we refer to the star terminology.

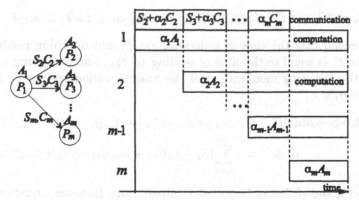

Fig. 5.3. Communication and computation in a star interconnection.

Basic model. The process of data distribution and computations for a star of PEs with network processors, without returning the results is depicted in Fig.5.3. It can be observed that the time of computing on P_i equals to the sum of the time required for sending the load to P_{i+1} and computing on P_{i+1}. Thus, distribution of the load can be found from formulae (5.1) where the first line is replaced by:

$$\alpha_i A_i = S_{i+1} + \alpha_{i+1}(C_{i+1} + A_{i+1}), \quad i = 1, \ldots, m-1 \qquad (5.5)$$

This set of equations can be solved analogously to (5.1).

Including data return. There are at least two ways of returning results in a
star network. Firstly, results can be returned in the inverted order of activating PEs (Fig.5.4(a)). Secondly, they can be returned in the order of activating
the PEs (Fig.5.4(b)). In the first case computing on P_i lasts as long as sending

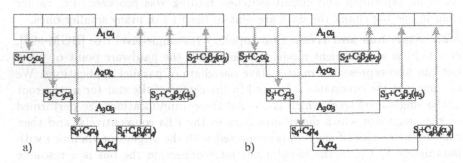

Fig. 5.4. Returning results in the star architecture. (a) in the inverted order of
activating the PEs, (b) in the order of activating the PEs.

data to P_{i+1}, processing on it and returning the results from P_{i+1}. Therefore,
distribution of the load can be found by (5.1) with modified first line:

$$\alpha_i A_i = 2S_{i+1} + C_{i+1}(\alpha_{i+1} + \beta(\alpha_{i+1})) + A_{i+1}\alpha_{i+1} \quad i=1,\ldots,m-1 \qquad (5.6)$$

In the second case the time of processing on P_i and returning results from
processor P_i is equal to the time of sending to P_{i+1} and processing on P_{i+1}.
Hence, the following modification of the basic equation set can be used to
calculate α_i's:

$$\alpha_i A_i + S_i + \beta(\alpha_i)C_i = S_{i+1} + \alpha_{i+1}(C_{i+1} + A_{i+1}), \quad i=2,\ldots,m-1 \qquad (5.7)$$

$$\alpha_1 A_1 = \sum_{i=2}^{m}(S_i + \alpha_i C_i) + \alpha_m A_m + S_m + C_m\beta(\alpha_m)$$

Both (5.6), and (5.7) can be solved in $O(m)$ time. However, equations (5.7)
have a solution even if V is so small that no schedule of the exact form
presented in Fig.5.4b exists. To avoid such a case one should verify whether a
non-negative idle time on the network processor of P_1 exists, i.e. whether the
following condition holds: $\alpha_1 A_1 > \sum_{i=2}^{m}(2S_i + C_i(\alpha_i + \beta(\alpha_i)))$. Otherwise, a
shorter schedule using fewer processors may be possible.

Lack of network processors. In this variant of the basic star model it can be
observed that the originator cannot start computing until all communications
are completed. Thus, formulae (5.5) must be changed only for $i = 1$ to the
following equation:

$$\alpha_1 A_1 = \alpha_m A_m \qquad (5.8)$$

Trees. Now, consider a tree of PEs with network processors. When the results are not to be returned all PEs must stop computing simultaneously. We assume that the order of processor activation is given, data is distributed to a receiver in one chunk, and then redistributed to its descendants. P_1 is the originator and the root of the tree. Each node of data distribution tree (except leaves) becomes an originator for its descendants. Let $succ(i)$ denote the set of the successors of P_i (not necessarily immediate). Let $pred(i)$ denote a PE activated immediately before P_i by the same node P_j as P_i (i.e. both P_i and $pred(i)$ received their data from P_j). When P_i was the first PE activated by P_j then $pred(i) = P_j$. For each pair of PEs activated one after another we can formulate a modified version of equations (5.5):

$$\alpha_{pred(i)} A_{pred(i)} = S_i + (\alpha_i + \sum_{j \in succ(i)} \alpha_j) C_i + \alpha_i A_i \quad i = 2, \ldots, m \quad (5.9)$$

Extensions and generalizations. In the above models we assumed that the order of activating processors is known. Determining the optimal order (i.e. giving the shortest total processing time) is not obvious. In the case of multiple busses the problem is NP-hard in the strong sense [BD97]. A solution based on mixed integer linear programming was proposed in [Dro97]. When communication links are identical the optimal activation order is the order of decreasing PE speeds [BD97]. When $\forall_{2 \leq i \leq m} S_i = 0$ then the optimal order coincides with decreasing speed of communication links [BD97, BGM94], but the speeds of PEs are irrelevant. Closed-form solutions for finding distribution of the load in bus and tree networks were proposed in [BHR94]. Star and trees of PEs which can communicate over all their ports were considered in [BD97]. [SR94] studies the problem of scheduling multiple divisible applications according to FIFO scheme. The problem of scheduling a divisible task on a bus system in the presence of background activities which affect communication and processing rates is investigated in [SR95]. A new data distribution pattern based on pipelining (i.e. rather a greater number of small chunks is sent to each processor than one big) is proposed in [BGM95a]. In [Dro97] the idea of divisible tasks was applied in the context of distributed batch systems, and on-line scattering heuristics.

5.2.3 Meshes. In a regular non-toroidal d-dimensional mesh each PE is directly coupled up to $2d$ neighbors (cf. Fig.5.5). In the toroidal mesh PEs at the mesh opposite 'sides' are connected, and each PE is connected with exactly $2d$ neighbors. We assume here that communication links and processors are identical, PEs are equipped with network processors, results are not returned to the originator located in the center of the network. Each PE is capable of simultaneous communication over $p \in \{1, \ldots, 2d\}$ links (ports). We will call by a layer the set of PEs activated in the same stage of data distribution.

Two-dimensional rectangular mesh networks with store-and-forward communication mode were considered in [BD96]. A scattering method based on routing messages only between the nearest neighbors was presented. Thus, the layers of PEs form squares around the originator. In [BDG+99] a more efficient method based on circuit-switched routing was proposed for a two-dimensional mesh. Scattering methods were further extended in [Dro97] to the case of a 3-dimensional mesh with $p = 1, \ldots, 6$. Due to space limitations we describe only the case of $p = 1, 2, 3$ in 3-dimensional mesh (the following discussion and formulae apply also in the case of $p = 4, 5, 6$). The methods of scattering in 3-dimensional mesh for PEs using $p = 1, 2, 3$ ports simultaneously are depicted in Fig.5.5.

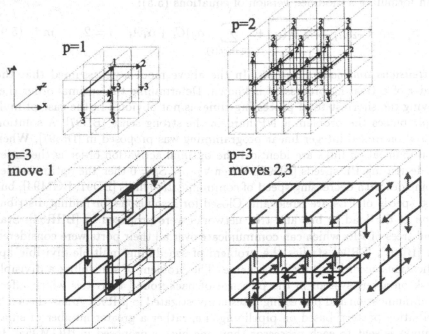

Fig. 5.5. Scattering in 3-dimensional regular mesh, for $p = 1, 2, 3$

The algorithms are based on recursive division of the mesh into sub-meshes of smaller size. In each step of scattering $(p+1)^3$ PEs are activated. These PEs become originators for scattering in the next step. Thus, in each step the initial mesh is divided into $(p+1)^3$ submeshes of $p+1$ times smaller size. Each of the steps consists, in turn, of three moves. The same moves are performed simultaneously by all the active PEs. Each move increases the number of active PEs p times, which is maximum because only p ports can be used simultaneously. Hence, after k moves the number of working PEs is $(p+1)^k$. For $p = 1$ and $p = 2$, each move of a step activates p PEs neighboring along a different dimension. In a 3-port system the originator activates three PEs located in the same two-dimensional cross-section of the initial mesh (say, along the plane $y0z$). Next, the four active PEs send data along the third dimension (x dimension). In the third move each active processor sends data to the neighbors along the hull of the initial mesh and to one neighbor inside the mesh.

Let us denote by α_i the amount of data to be processed by a PE activated in move i, and by $k = \log_{p+1} m$ the number of moves. The diagram of communication and computation is given in Fig.5.2, but here the number of ports involved simultaneously can be greater. Similarly, computing on the sending layer of PEs lasts as long as communicating to and computing on the PEs of the receiving layer. The distribution of data can be found from the following set of equations ($p \in \{1, \ldots, 6\}$):

$$A\alpha_{k-i} = S + C(\alpha_{k-i+1} + p\sum_{j=2}^{i}\alpha_{k-i+j}(p+1)^{i-2}) + A\alpha_{k-i+1}$$

$$\text{for } i = 1, \ldots, k \quad (5.10)$$

$$V = \alpha_0 + p\sum_{i=1}^{k}(p+1)^{i-1}\alpha_i$$

A broadcasting method for d-dimensional toroidal mesh with $2d$-port PEs and edge size $(2d+1)^k$ ($k \in Z^+$) has been proposed in [PC96]. This method activates $(2d+1)^{kd}$ PEs in kd moves. Thus, the methods proposed here can be extended to toroidal meshes of arbitrary dimension when $p = 2d+1$. Observe that also scattering methods for $p = 1$ and $p = 2$ can be applied in meshes of higher dimension. The proposed scattering algorithms are optimal in the sense that the number of activated processors in the allowed number of steps is the biggest possible. Equations (5.10) can be applied in any architecture in which PEs can be activated in the same way as above, i.e. each active PE in each move starts p new processors. One of such architectures can be multistage interconnection [Dro97].

5.2.4 Hypercube. A d-dimensional hypercube network consists of 2^d PEs. Each of the PEs can be labeled by a unique d-bit binary word such that directly connected processors have their labels differing in exactly one bit. The idea of divisible task was applied to hypercubes in [BD95, BD97]. The scattering method was based on consecutively activating the nearest neighbors of the active processors. Thus, the originator P_0 (labeled $(0, \ldots, 0)$) activated d PEs with exactly one 1 in the label. Those PEs, in turn, activated PEs with exactly two 1's in the label etc. Let us call by a layer the set of PEs activated in the same step of scattering, i.e. the set of PEs with the same number of 1's in their labels. Note that each PE in layer i can be reached by i links (the number of 1's in the label), and has $d-i$ inactive neighbors in layer $i+1$. The number of PEs in layer i is $\binom{d}{i}$. We assume that PEs are identical, each PE has a network processor and the time of returning the results is negligible. Then, the diagram of computing and communication is the same as the one in Fig.5.1, and processors of the layer activated earlier compute as long as it is required to send data to the next layer and compute on the next layer. Thus, distribution of the load can be found from the following equations:

$$\alpha_i A = S + \frac{\left(V - \sum_{j=0}^{i} \binom{d}{j} \alpha_j\right) C}{\binom{d}{i}(d-i)} + \alpha_{i+1} A \quad i = 0, \ldots, d-1 \quad (5.11)$$

$$V = \sum_{i=0}^{d} \binom{d}{i} \alpha_i$$

where α_i is the load computed by one processor of layer i; S, C are parameters of the communication links in the homogeneous hypercube network; A is the processing rate of all PEs. Different scattering methods were proposed in [Dro97]. In one of them the PEs started working on their share of data as soon as it was received instead of waiting for the whole message including data for the following layers. Network processors were re-routing the rest of data to the next layer. In two other algorithms data were first sent from P_0 to P_{2^d-1} on the opposite 'end' of the hypercube. Then the hypercube was activated from the directions of the two antipodes. The above three algorithms were advantageous only for hypercubes of dimension 8 and bigger. Other scattering algorithms considered in [Dro97] turned out to be less efficient.

5.3 Performance Prediction Based on the Divisible Task Model

In this section we give some examples of applying the divisible task method. First let us consider a numerical example.

Example. Consider a computer system consisting of four identical PEs connected by identical communication links. Each PE has a network processor, and is capable of simultaneous computing and communicating. The amount of the returned results is constant and equal to 1024 bytes. The order of data return is the order of activating PEs (cf. Fig.5.4(b)). We use equations (5.7) to find the distribution of the load. From the solution one can compute the total processing time, which is $A\alpha_1$. In the following table results of solving equations (5.7) for $m = 4, V = 10^6$ bytes, are presented.

	system A	system B	system C
A[s/byte]	0.0002324	0.000692	0.000596
C[s/byte]	1E-11	1.25E-08	1.7485E-06
S[s]	1.08E-07	3.9E-05	0.0011377
processing time [s]	581	1730	1497

In the above table parameters A, S, C were not intended to represent any particular computer system. Still, system A may represent a shared memory supercomputer from the 80-ties, system B is a representative of massively parallel message passing computer from the beginning of the 90-ties, while system C is a cluster of contemporary (1997) PC-compatible computers with Linux operating system and PVM. The conclusion that can be derived from the above table is that contemporary PCs are as good as leading computers 6-7 years ago. Thus, time beats any machine.

As we are able to compute the processing time for the whole load both on a single machine, and on the given number of PEs, we are also able to compute speedup, utilization etc. for the considered computer system and communication algorithm. In the following example we will analyze a 3-dimensional mesh with PEs using 1 port at a time ($p = 1$) and circuit switched routing. Since speedup can be an ambiguous performance measure, we will concentrate on the processing time. In Figs.5.6 and 5.7 we present a relation between the processing time and the volume of work V for 1-, 4-, 16-, 64-, 256-, 1024-processor systems. In both figures the communication parameters are $C = 10^{-9}\frac{s}{byte}$, and $S = 10^{-5}s$. In Fig.5.6 processors have $A = 10^{-6}\frac{s}{byte}$, and in Fig.5.7 processing rate is better and equal to $A = 10^{-8}\frac{s}{byte}$. As it

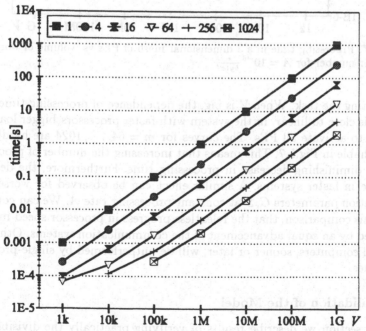

Fig. 5.6. Processing time in a 3-dimensional mesh of PEs vs. volume of work, and processor number for $A = 10^{-6}\frac{s}{byte}$.

can be seen in both figures not all volumes can be processed by any number of processors. Communication time dominates in the processing time when the volume is small. Therefore, only few processors can be activated before

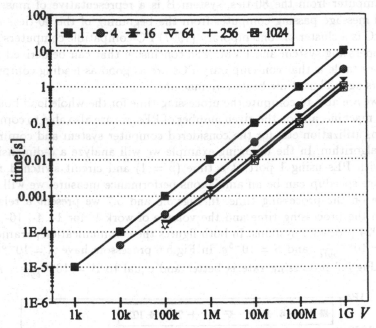

Fig. 5.7. Processing time in a 3-dimensional mesh of PEs vs. volume of work, and processor number for $A = 10^{-8} \frac{s}{byte}$.

completing the task. When V is big, the dependence of processing time on m and V is close to linear. In the system with faster processors bigger loads are needed to activate all PEs. The curves for $m = 64, \ldots, 1024$ are hardly distinguishable in Fig.5.7. This means that increasing the number of processors gives a diminishing decrease in processing time. Furthermore, the decrease is worse in faster systems. A similar effect can be observed for worse communication parameters C, S at constant processing rate A. We can conclude from this comparison, that the relentless progress in processor speed must be matched by an equal advancement of the communication systems. Otherwise parallel computers, sooner or later, will be outperformed by single-processor machines.

5.4 Validation of the Model

In this section we describe results of verifying practically the divisible task concept in a star architecture.

5.4.1 Transputer system. The star model depicted in Fig.5.4a and described by equations (5.6) has been tested in T805 transputer system. We outline here only the results of the experiments, more technical details can be found in [BDM99]. The application tested was a distributed search for a pattern in a text file. The experiments were organized such that computations and communications did not overlap. Processing rates (A_i) were measured for each PE as an average rate of 100 experiments in searching a given 300000-byte file. Communication rates and startup-times (C_i, S_i) were measured in a set of experiments in which the originator sent to PEs messages of changing size. In all experiments the size of returned data was constant. In Fig. 5.8 we present the difference between the expected and measured execution time. The difference is in the range $[-1.5\%, 1.5\%]$.

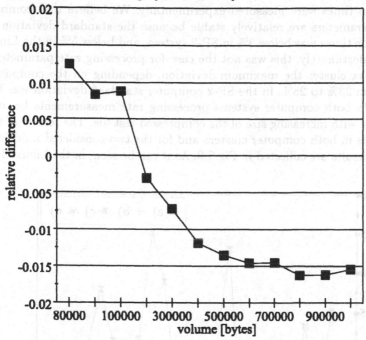

Fig. 5.8. Relative difference between the expected and measured execution time for eight transputers vs size V of the searched file.

5.4.2 Workstation cluster and PVM. Another set of experiments were conducted in two kinds of workstation clusters. The first one was a cluster of six heterogeneous PC's with the Linux operating system. The background load of computers was 'light' but hardly controllable. The second computer system was dedicated (i.e. 'single user') pool of six IBM SP-2 processors. A Parallel Virtual Machine (PVM) was used as a software environment for experiments. We present the final results of the experiments only. A detailed description is given in [DD97]. The star architecture was chosen, and communication models depicted in Fig.5.4(a) (equations (5.6)), which we will call Model 1, and Fig.5.4(b) (equations (5.7)), which will be called Model 2, were assumed. The application analyzed was distributed file compression using the LZW method [Wel84, ZL78]. It is typical of the application that the compression ratio depends on the size and contents of the compressed file. The bigger the file the better was the compression obtained. Hence, in further experiments PEs received data in chunks of at least 10kB, which was enough to make the compression ratio relatively stable. Therefore, it was justified to assume in equations (5.6) and (5.7) that function $\beta(x)$ of the amount of returned results for x units of data was $\beta(x) = cx$. The coefficient $c = 0.55$ was measured experimentally (with standard deviation 9%). Similarly to the previous experiments, computer processing rates, communication transfer rates and startup times were measured experimentally. We believe that communication parameters are relatively stable because the standard deviation of transmission times was below 3% in SP-2 system, and below 5% in the Linux cluster. Unfortunately, this was not the case for processing rate parameters. In the Linux cluster the maximum deviation, depending on the computer, ranged from 23% to 28%. In the SP-2 computer standard deviation was below 23%. In both computer systems processing rate measurements became more stable with increasing size of the compressed test file. The results of the experiments in both computer clusters and for the two considered models of returning results are collected in Fig.5.9. As it can be seen, in the Linux clus-

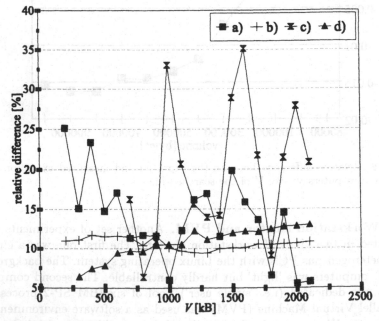

Fig. 5.9. Relative difference between the expected and measured execution time vs size V of the compressed file in Model 1: a)Linux, b)IBM SP-2, and Model 2: c)Linux, d)IBM SP-2.

ter the difference is below 25% in Model 1, and below 35% in Model 2. In the dedicated pool of SP-2 processors the difference is more stable and remains between 5% and 15%. The sources of the difference between the theoretical model and the reality can be imprecision in the parameters A_i, C_i, S_i and function $\beta(x)$.

We infer that the divisible task concept can be a useful model for distributed applications. Though the model is crude and neglects many details of actual computer systems, a practical verification proved viability of its principles.

5.5 Conclusions

In this section we considered divisible tasks, i.e. parallel applications that can be arbitrarily divided and executed in parallel. The analysis usually included two steps: devising a scattering algorithm and solving a set of linear equations. The former covered the underlying hardware/software architecture. The latter included solving two types of equations: equations linking processing time and communication time of the sender and the receiver, and an equation expressing that all the load must be processed. This method has been applied successfully to analyze many different types of computer architectures.

We assumed a linear relation between the processing time and the volume of data. Yet, even distributed sorting has a nonlinear dependence between the processing time and the size of processed data. Such nonlinear dependencies can be included in our equations (e.g. (5.1), (5.5), (5.10), etc.) as a nonlinear processing time function of the amount of assigned load. However, in this case the equations would be more difficult to solve.

Let us also mention that the divisible task approach can be applied in production - transportation systems. In such systems the transportation system is equivalent of the computer interconnection network, while production facilities represent processors.

Acknowledgement. The research of J.Błażewicz and M.Drozdowski was partially supported by KBN grant No 8T11C04012, and by Project CRIT-2. Computational experiments were partially supported by Poznań Supercomputing and Networking Center.

References

[AL97]   Aarts, E., Lenstra, J.K., *Local Search in Combinatorial Optimization*, J.Wiley, New York, 1997.

[AHU74]   Aho, A.V., Hopcroft, J.E., Ullman, J.D., *The Design and Analysis of Computer Algorithms*, Addison-Wesley, Reading, Mass., 1974.

[AZ90]   Ahuja, M., Zhu, Y., An O(logn) feasibility algorithm for preemptive scheduling of n independent jobs on a hypercube, *Information Processing Letters* **35**, 1990, 7-11.

[ADK+93] Alda, W., Dzwinel, W., Kitowski, J., Mościński, J., Yuen, D.A., Penetration mechanics via molecular dynamics. Research Report UMSI 93/58, University of Minessota Supercomputing Institute, 1993.

[AHC90]   Anger, F.D., Hwang, J., Chow, Y., Scheduling with sufficiently loosely coupled processors, J. Parallel Distributed Comput. 9, 1990, 87-92.

[BGK96]   Bampis, E., Giannokos, A., König, J.-C., On the complexity of scheduling with large communication delays, European Journal of Operational Research 94, 1996, 252-260.

[BHR94]   Bataineh, S., Hsiung, T.-Y., Robertazzi, T.G., Closed form solutions for bus and tree networks of processors load sharing a divisible job, IEEE Transactions on Computers 43, 1994, 1184-1196.

[Bel57]   Bellman, R., Dynamic Programming, Princeton University Press, Princeton, N.J., 1957.

[BD62]   Bellman, R., Dreyfus, S.E., Applied Dynamic Programming, Princeton University Press, Princeton, N.J., 1962.

[BGM94]   Bharadwaj, V., Ghose, D., Mani, V., Optimal sequencing and arrangement in distributed single-level tree networks with communication delays, IEEE Transactions on Parallel and Distributed Systems 5, 1994, 968-976.

[BGM95a] Bharadwaj, V., Ghose, D., Mani, V., Multi-installment load distribution in tree networks with delays, IEEE Transactions on Aerospace and Electronic Systems 31, 1995, 555-567.

[BGM95b] Bharadwaj, V., Ghose, D., Mani, V., An efficient load distribution strategy for a distributed linear network of processors with communication delays, Computers and Matheamtics with Applications 29, 1995, 95-112.

[BGM+96] Bharadwaj, V., Ghose, D., Mani, V., Robertazzi, T., Scheduling Divisible Loads in Parallel and Distributed Systems, IEEE Computer Society Press, Los Alamitos CA, 1996.

[BR92]   Bataineh, S., Robertazzi, T.G., Ultimate performance limits for networks of load sharing processors, CEAS Technical Report 623, State University of New York at Stony Brook, 1992.

[BBD+94] Bianco, L., Błażewicz, J., Drozdowski, M., Dell'Olmo, P., Scheduling preemptive multiprocessor tasks on dedicated processors, Performance Evaluation 20, 1994, 361-371.

[BBD+95] Bianco, L., Błażewicz, J., Drozdowski, M., Dell'Olmo, P., Scheduling multiprocessor tasks on a dynamic configuration of dedicated processors, Annals of Operations Research 58, 1995, 493-517.

[BBD+97a] Bianco, L., Błażewicz, J., Drozdowski, M., Dell'Olmo, P., Linear algorithms for preemptive scheduling of multiprocessor tasks subject to minimal lateness, Discrete Applied Mathematics 72, 1997, 25-46.

[BBD+97b] Bianco, L., Błażewicz, J., Drozdowski, M., Dell'Olmo, P., Preemptive multiprocessor task scheduling with release times and time windows, Annals of Operations Research 70, 1997, 43-55.

[BOS94]   Bianco, L., Dell'Olmo, P., Speranza, M.G., Nonpreemptive scheduling of independent tasks with prespecified processor allocations, Naval Research Logistics Quarterly 41, 1994, 939-971.

[BT90]   Blanc, J.-Y., Trystram, D., Implementation of parallel numerical routines using broadcast communication schemes, E.Burkhart (ed.), Lecture Notes in Computer Science 457, CONPAR 90-VAPP IV, Joint International Conference on Vector and Parallel Processing, Springer-Verlag, Berlin, 1990, 467-478.

[BBG+96]   Błażewicz, J., Bouvry, P., Guinand, F., Trystram, D., Scheduling complete in-trees on two uniform processors with communication delays, *Information Processing Letters* 58, 1996, 255-263.

[BCS+76]   Błażewicz, J., Cellary, W., Węglarz, J., Deterministyczne problemy szeregowania zadań na równoległych procesorach, Cz. II, Zbiory zadań zależnych, *Podstawy Sterowania*, 1976, 297-320.

[BD95]   Błażewicz, J., Drozdowski, M., Scheduling divisible jobs on hypercubes, *Parallel Computing* 21, 1995, 1945-1956.

[BD96]   Błażewicz, J., Drozdowski, M., Performance limits of two-dimensional network of load-sharing processors, *Foundations of Computing and Decision Sciences* 21, 1996, 3-15.

[BD97]   Błażewicz, J., Drozdowski, M., Scheduling divisible jobs with communication startup costs, *Discrete Applied Mathematics* 76, 1997, 21-41.

[BDG+99]   Błażewicz, J., Drozdowski, M., Guinand, F., Trystram, D., Scheduling under architectural constraints, *Discrete Applied Mathematics* 94, 1999, 35-50.

[BDM99]   Błażewicz, J., Drozdowski, M., Markiewicz, M., Divisible task scheduling - concept and verification, *Parallel Computing* 25, 1999, 87-98.

[BDO+92]   Błażewicz, J., Drozdowski, M., Dell'Olmo, P., Speranza, M.G., Scheduling multiprocessor tasks on three dedicated processors, *Information Processing Letters* 41, 1992, 275-280. Corrigendum: *Information Processing Letters* 49, 1994, 269-270.

[BDS+94]   Błażewicz, J., Drozdowski, M., Schmidt, G., de Werra, D., Scheduling independent multiprocessor tasks on a uniform k-processor system, *Parallel Computing* 20, 1994, 15-28.

[BDW84]   Błażewicz, J., Drabowski, M., Węglarz, J., Scheduling independent 2-processor tasks to minimize schedule length, *Information Processing Letters* 18, 1984, 267-273.

[BDW86]   Błażewicz, J., Drabowski, M., Węglarz, J., Scheduling multiprocessor tasks to minimize schedule length, *IEEE Transactions on Computers* C-35, 1986, 389-393.

[BDW+96]   Błażewicz, J., Drozdowski, M., de Werra, D., Węglarz, J., Deadline scheduling of multiprocessor tasks, *Discrete Applied Mathematics* 65, 1996, 81-96.

[BE83]   Błażewicz, J., Ecker, K., A linear time algorithm for restricted bin packing and scheduling problems, *Operations Research Letters* 2, 1983, 80-83.

[BEP+96]   Błażewicz, J., Ecker, K., Pesch, E., Schmidt, G., Węglarz, J., *Scheduling Computer and Manufacturing Processes*, Springer Verlag, Heidelberg, New York, 1996.

[BLR+83]   Błażewicz, J., Lenstra, J.K., Rinnoy Kan, A.H.G., Scheduling subject to resource constraints: classification and complexity, *Discrete Applied Mathematics* 5, 1983, 11-24.

[BL96]   Błażewicz, J., Liu, Z., Scheduling multiprocessor tasks with chain constraints, *European Journal of Operational Research* 94, 1996, 231-241.

[Bru94]   Brucker, P., A polynomial algorithm for the two machine job-shop scheduling problem with a fixed number of jobs, *OR Spektrum* 16, 1994, 5-7.

[Bru98]   Brucker, P., *Scheduling Algorithms*, Springer, Berlin, 1998.

[BGJ77]   Brucker, P.J., Garey, M.R., Johnson, D.S., Scheduling equal-length tasks under treelike precedence constraints to minimize maximum lateness, *Mathematics of Operations Research* 2, 1977, 275-284.

[Cer85]   Cerny, V., Thermodynamical approach to the trvaling salesman problem; an efficient simulation algorithm, *J. Optimization Theory and Applications* **45**, 1985, 41-51.

[CL88b]   Chang, R.S., Lee, R.C.T., On a scheduling problem where a job can be executed only by a limited number of processors, *Computers and Operations Research* **15**, 1988, 471-478.

[CC89]   Chen, Y.L., Chin, Y.H., Scheduling unit-time job on processors with different capabilities, *Computers and Operations Research* **16**, 1989, 409-417.

[CR88]   Cheng, Y.-C., Robertazzi, T.G., Distributed computation with communication delay, *IEEE Transactions on Aerospace and Electronic Systems* **24**, 1988, 700-712.

[Chr89a]   Chretienne, P., A polynomial algorithm to optimally schedule tasks over an ideal distributed system under tree-like precedence constraints, *European Journal of Operational Research* **2**, 1981, 225-230.

[Chr94]   Chretienne, P., Tree scheduling with communication delays, *Discrete Applied Mathematics* **49**, 1994, 129-141.

[CCL+95]   Chretienne, P., Coffman Jr., E.G., Lenstra, J.K., Liu, Z., (eds), *Scheduling Theory and its Applications*, New York, 1995.

[CP91]   Chretienne, P., Picouleau, C., The basic scheduling problem with interprocessor communication delays, MASI Report 91/6, Institut Blaise Pascal, Paris, 1991.

[Cof76]   Coffman Jr., E.G., (ed.), *Computer and Job-Shop Scheduling Theory*, New York, 1976.

[CGJ+85]   Coffman Jr., E.G., Garey, M.R., Johnson, D.S., La Paugh, A.S., Scheduling file transfers, *SIAM J. on Computing* **14**, 1985, 744-780.

[CG72]   Coffman Jr., E.G., Graham, R.J., Optimal scheduling for two-processor systems, *Acta Informatica* **1**, 1972, 200-213.

[CC91]   Colin, I.Y., Chretienne, P., C.P.M. scheduling with small communication delays and task duplication, *Operations Research* **39**, 1991, 680-684.

[CKP93]   Culler, D.E., Karp, R.M., Patterson, D.A., Sahay,A., Schauser, K.E., Santos, E., Subramonian, R., von Eicken, T., LogP: Towards a realistic model of parallel computation, In Fourth ACM SIGPLAN Symposium on Principles and Practice of Parallel Programming, 1993.

[Dro96]   Drozdowski, M., Real-time scheduling of linear speedup parallel tasks, *Information Processing Letters* **57**, 1996, 35-40.

[Dro97]   Drozdowski, M., *Selected Problems of Scheduling Tasks in Multiprocessor Computer Systems*, Poznań University of Technology Press, Poznań, 1997.

[DK95]   Drozdowski, M., Kubiak, W., Scheduling parallel tasks with sequential heads and tails, Working paper, Memorial University of Newfoundland, St. John's, 1995.

[DD97]   Drzewiecki, D., Drozdowski, M., Rozdział obciążeń w rozproszonym systemie komputerowym metodą zadania jednorodnego, Technical Report RB-008/97, Institute of Computing Science, Poznań University of Technology, 1997.

[DL89]   Du, J., Leung, J.Y-T., Complexity of scheduling parallel tasks systems, *SIAM J. on Discrete Mathematics* **2**, 1989, 473-487.

[EH94]   Ecker, K., Hammer, D., Integrated scheduling for CIM systems, *Proc. TIMS XXXII*, Anchorage, 1994.

[EH93]   Ecker, K.H., Hirschberg, R., Scheduling communication demands in networks, *Proc. of the Workshop on Parallel and Distributed Real-Time Systems*, Newport Beach, 1993.

[GJ77]   Garey, M.R., Johnson, D.S., Two-processor scheduling with start-times and deadlines, *SIAM J. on Computing* **6**, 1977, 416-426.

[GJ79]   Garey, M.R., Johnson, D.S., *Computers and Intractability: A Guide to the Theory of NP-Completeness*, Freeman, San Francisco, 1979.

[GY92]   Gerasoulis, A., Yang, T., On the granularity and clustering of directed acyclic task graphs, Report TR-153, Dept. Comput. Sci., Rutgers University, 1992.

[GM94]   Ghose, D., Mani, V., Distributed computation with communication delays: Asymptotic performance analysis, *Journal of Parallel and Distributed Computing* **23**, 1994, 293-305.

[GL97]   Glover, F., Laguna, M., *Tabu Search*, Kluwer Academic Pubishers, London, 1997.

[Goe95]   Goemans, M., An approximation algorithm for scheduling on three dedicated processors, *Discrete Applied Mathematics* **61**, 1995, 49-60.

[Gol89]   Goldberg, D.E., *Genetic Algorithms in Search, Optimization and Machine Learning*, Addison-Wesley, Reading, Mass., 1989.

[Gos91]   Goscinski, A., *Distributed Operating Systems*, Addison-Wesley, Sydney, 1991.

[Gra66]   Graham, R.L., Bounds for certain multiprocessing anomalies, *Bell System Technical Journal* **45**, 1966, 1563-1581.

[Gra69]   Graham, R.L., Bounds on multiprocessing timing anomalies, *SIAM J. on Applied Mathematics* **17**, 1969, 263-269.

[GKP94]   Graham, R.L., Knuth, D.E., Patashnik, O., *Concrete Mathematics. A Foundation for Computer Science*, Addison-Wesley, Reading, Mass., 1994.

[GKR92]   Grama, A.Y., Kumar, V., Rao, V.N., Experimental evaluation of load balancing techniques for hypercube, D.J.Evans, G.R.Joubert, H.Liddell, (eds), *Parallel Computing '91*, Elsevier Science, New York, 1992, 497-514.

[HM94]   Hanen, C., Munier, A., Performance of Coffman-Graham schedules in presence of unit communication delays, Technical Report 12, Laboratoire LITP, Paris, 1994.

[HM95]   Hanen, C., Munier, A., An approximation algorithm for scheduling dependent tasks on m processors with small communication delays, in *Proc. of IEEE Symposium on Emerging Technologies and Factory Automation*, Paris, 1995.

[HW90]   Hertz, A., de Werra, D., The tabu search metaheuristic: How we use it, *Annals of Mathematics and Artificial Intelligence* **1**, 1990, 111-121.

[Hoe89]   van Hoesel, C.P.M., Preemptive scheduling on a hypercube, Report 8963/A Econometric Institute, Erasmus University, Rotterdam, 1989.

[HLV92]   Hoogeveen, J.A., Lenstra, J.K., Veltman, B., Three, four, five, six or the complexity of scheduling with communication delays, Report BS-R9229, CWI, Amsterdam, 1992.

[HVV94]   Hoogeven, J.A., van de Velde, S.L., Veltman, B., Complexity of scheduling multiprocessor tasks with prespecified processor allocation, *Discrete Applied Mathematics* **55**, 1994, 259-272.

[Hu61]   Hu, T.C., Parallel sequencing and assembly line problems, *Operations Research* **96**, 1961, 841-848.

[Hwa93]   Hwang, K., *Advanced Computer Architecture: Parallelism, Scalability, Programmability*, MCGraw-Hill, New York, 1993.

338   Jacek Błażewicz, Maciej Drozdowski, and Klaus Ecker

[HCA+89] Hwang, J.-J., Chow, Y.-C., Anger, F.D., Lee, C.-Y., Scheduling prece-
          dence graphs in systems with interprocessor communication times,
          SIAM J. on Computing **18**, 1989, 244-257.
[JR92]   Jakoby, A., Reischuk, R., The complexity of scheduling problems with
          communication delays for trees, *Proc. Scandinavian Workshop on Al-
          gorithmic Theory* **3**, 1992, 165-177.
[JKS89]   Jung, H., Kirousis, L., Spirakis, P., Lower bounds and efficient al-
          gorithms for multiprocessor scheduling of DAGs with communication
          delays, *Proc. ACM Symp. Parallel Algorithms and Architectures*, 1989,
          254-264.
[Kar84]   Karmarkar, N., A new polynomial-time algorithm for linear program-
          ming, *Combinatorica* **4**, 1984, 373-395.
[Kar72]   Karp, R.M., Reducibility among combinatorial problems, R.E.Miller,
          J.W.Thatcher (eds.), *Complexity of Computer Computations*, Plenum
          Press, New York, 1972, 85-104.
[Kha79]   Khachiyan, L.G., A polynomial algorithm for linear programming (in
          Russian), *Dokl. Akad. Nauk SSSR* **244**, 1979, 1093-1096.
[KGV83]   Kirkpatrick, S., Gelatt Jr., C.D., Vecchi, M.P., Optimization by sim-
          ulated annealing, *Science* **220**, 1983, 671-680.
[KK85]   Krawczyk, H., Kubale, M., An approximation algorithm for diagnos-
          tic test scheduling in multicomputer systems, *IEEE Transactions on
          Computers* **C-34**, 1985, 869-872.
[Kub87]   Kubale, M., The complexity of scheduling independent two-processor
          tasks on dedicated processors, *Information Processing Letters* **24**,
          1987, 141-147.
[Kub96]   Kubale, M., Preemptive versus nonpreemptive scheduling of biproces-
          sor tasks on dedicated processors, *European Journal of Operational
          Research* **94**, 1996, 242-251.
[Kun91]   Kunz, T., The influence of different workload descriptions on a heuris-
          tic load balancing scheme, *IEEE Transactions on Software Engineer-
          ing* , **17**, 1991, 725-730.
[LA87]   van Laarhoven, P.J.M., Aarts, E.H.L., *Simulated Annealing: Theory
          and Applications*, Reider, Dordrecht, 1987.
[LK90]   Lang, T., Kurisaki, L., Nonuniform traffic spots (NUTS) in multistage
          interconnection networks, *J. Parallel and Distributed Computing* **10**,
          1990, 55-67.
[Law93]   Lawler, E.L., Scheduling trees on multiprocessors with unit communi-
          cation delays, *Proc. Workshop on Models and Algorithms for Planning
          and Scheduling Problems*, Villa Vigoni, Italy, 1993.
[LLR+93] Lawler, E.L., Lenstra, J.K., Rinnoy Kan, A.H.G., Shmoys, D.B., Se-
          quencing and scheduling: Algorithms and complexity, Graves, S.C.,
          Rinnoy Kan, A.H.G., Zipkin, P.H., (eds.), *Handbook in Oprations Re-
          search and Management Science, Vol. 4: Logistics of Production and
          Inventory*, Elsevier, Amsterdam, 1993.
[LW66]   Lawler, E.L., Wood, D.E., Branch and bound methods: A survey, *Op-
          erations Research* **14**, 1966, 699-719.
[LVV96]   Lenstra, J.K., Veldhorst, M., Veltman, B., The complexity of schedul-
          ing trees with communication delays, *Journal of Algorithms* **20**, 1996,
          157-173.
[LSL94]   Liu, J., Saletore, V.A., Lewis, T.G., Safe Self-Scheduling: A parallel
          loop scheduling scheme for shared-memory multiprocessors, *Interna-
          tional Journal of Parallel Programming* **22**, 1994, 589-616.

[Llo81]   Lloyd, E.L., Concurrent task systems, *Operations Research* **29**, 189-201.

[LM92]   Lüling, R., Monien, B., Load balancing for distributed branch & bound, *Proc. of 6th International Parallel Processing Symposium*, 1992, 543-548.

[MT93]   Ma, E., Tao, L., Embeddings among meshes and tori, *J. Parallel and Distributed Computing* **18**, 1993, 44-55.

[MG94]   Mani, V., Ghose, D., Distributed computation in linear networks: Closed-form solutions. *IEEE Transactions on Aerospace and Electronic Systems* **30**, 1994, 471-483.

[ML94]   Markatos, E.P., LeBlanc, T.J., Using processor affinity in loop scheduling on shared-memory multiprocessors, *IEEE Transactions on Parallel and Distributed Systems* , **5**, 1994, 379-400.

[McN59]   McNaughton, R., Scheduling with deadlines and loss functions, *Management Science* **12**, 1959, 1-12.

[MRR+53]   Metropolis, M., Rosenbluth, A., Rosenbluth, M., Teller, A., Teller, E., Equation of state calculations by fast computing machines, *J. Chemical Physics* **21**, 1953, 1087-1092.

[Mic92]   Michalewicz, Z., *Genetic Algorithms + Data Structures = Evolution Programs*, Springer, Berlin, 1992.

[Moh89]   Möhring, R.H., Computationally tractable classes of ordered sets, I. Rival (ed.), *Algorithms and Order*, Kluwer, Dordrecht, 1989, 105-193.

[Mun96]   Munier, A., Approximation algorithms for scheduling trees with general communication delays, Technical report, Laboratoire LITP, Paris, 1996.

[MH95]   Munier, A., Hanen, C., An approximation algorithm for scheduling unitary tasks on m processors with unitary communication delays, Technical Report 12, Laboratoire LITP, Paris, 1995.

[MH97]   Munier, A., Hanen, C., Using duplication for scheduling unitary tasks on m processors with communication delays, *Theoretical Computer Science*, 1997, to appear.

[MK96]   Munier, A., König, J.-C., A heuristic for a scheduling problem with communication delays, *Operations Research*, 1996, to appear.

[MC69]   Muntz, R.R., Coffman Jr., E.G., Optimal preemptive scheduling on two-processor systems, *IEEE Transactions on Computers* **18**, 1969, 1014-1020.

[MC70]   Muntz, R.R., Coffman Jr., E.G., Preemptive scheduling of real-time tasks on multiprocessor systems, *Journal of the ACM* **17**, 1970, 324-338.

[NMK93]   Ni, L.M., McKinley, P.K., A survey of warmhole routing techniques in direct networks, *Computer* **26**, 1993, 62-76.

[OST93]   Dell'Olmo, P., Speranza, M.G., Tuza, Z.S., Easy and hard cases of a scheduling problem on 3 dedicated processors, Report, IASI, Roma, 1995.

[PY90]   Papadimitriou, C.H., Yannakakis, M., Towards an architecture-independent analysis of parallel algorithms, *SIAM J. on Computing* **19**, 1990, 322-328.

[PC96]   Park, J.L., Choi, H., Circuit-switched broadcasting in torus mesh networks, *IEEE Transactions on Parallel and Distributed Systems* **7**, 1996, 184-190.

[Pic91]   Picouleau, C., Two new NP-complete scheduling problems with communication delays and unlimited number of processors, Report

RP91/24, MASI, Institut Blaise Pascal, Universite Paris VI, 1991, to appear in *Discrete Applied Mathematics*

[Pic92]   Picouleau, C., Etude de problèmes d'optimization dans les systèmes distributés, Ph.D. Thesis, Université Paris VI, 1992.

[Pin95]   Pinedo, M., *Scheduling: Theory, Algoritms, and Systems*, Prentice-Hall, Enlewood Cliffs, N.J., 1995.

[Ray87a]   Rayward-Smith, V.J., UET scheduling with unit interprocessor communication delays, *Discrete Applied Mathematics* **18**, 1987, 55-71.

[Rob93]   Robertazzi, T.G., Processor equivalence for a linear daisy chain of load sharing processors, *IEEE Trans. on Aerospace and Electronic Systems* **29**, 1993, 1216-1221.

[RW92]   Ross, K.A., Wright, C.R.B., *Discrete Mathematics*, Prentice-Hall Inc., Enlewood Cliffs, N.J., 1992.

[SR91]   Shen, X., Reingold, E.M., Scheduling on a hypercube, *Information Processing Letters* **40**, 1991, 323-328.

[SPG91]   Silberschatz, A., Peterson, J.L., Galvin, P.B., *Operating Systems Concepts*, Addison-Wesley, 1991.

[SR93]   Sohn, J., Robertazzi, T.G., Optimal load sharing for a divisible job on a bus network, In *Proc. of the 1993 Conference on Information Sciences and Systems*, The John Hopkins University, Baltimore, MD, 1993, 835-840.

[SR94]   Sohn, J., Robertazzi, T.G., A muli-job load sharing strategy for divisible jobs on bus networks, Technical Report 697, Department of Electrical Engineering, SUNY at Stony Brook, Stony Brook, New York, 1994.

[SR95]   Sohn, J., Robertazzi, T.G., An optimum load sharing strategy for divisible jobs with time-varying processor speed and channel speed, Technical Report 706, Department of Electrical Engineering, SUNY at Stony Brook, Stony Brook, New York, 1995.

[SRL95]   Sohn, J., Robertazzi, T.G., Luryi, S., Optimizing computing costs using divisible load analysis, Technical Report 719, Department of Electrical Engineering, SUNY at Stony Brook, Stony Brook, New York, 1995.

[SH86]   Szymanski, T.H., Hamacher, V.C., On the universality of multipath multistage interconnection networks, *J. Parallel and Distributed Computing* **7**, 1989, 541-569.

[Tan95]   Tanenbaum, A.S., *Distributed Operating Systems*, Prentice-Hall, Enlewood Cliffs, N.J., 1995.

[Ull76]   Ullman, J.D., Complexity of sequencing problems, Coffman Jr., E.G., (ed.), *Scheduling in Computer and Job Shop Systems*, New York, 1976.

[VRK93]   Varvarigou, T., Roychowdhury, V.P., Kailath, T., Scheduling in and out forests in the presence of communication delays, *Proc. Intern. Parallel Processing Symposium*, Newport Beach, 1993, 222-229.

[Vel93]   Veltman, B., *Multiprocessor Scheduling with Communication Delays*, Ph.D. Thesis, CWI-Amsterdam, 1993.

[VWH+95]   Verhoosel, J.P.C., Welch, L.R., Hammer, D.K., Stayenko, A.D., A model for scheduling of object-based, distributed real-time systems, *J. Real-Time Systems* **8**, 1995.

[Wel84]   Welch, T.A., A technique for high-performace data compression, *IEEE Computer* **17**, 1984, 8-19.

[WBC+77]   Węglarz, J., Błażewicz, J., Cellary, W., Słowiński, R., An automatic revised simplex method for constrained resource network scheduling, *ACM Transactions on Mathematical Software* **3**, 1977, 295-300.

[Wi91]   Williams, R.D., Performance of dynamic load balancing algorithms for
            unstructured mesh calculations, *Concurrency: Practice and Experience*
            3, 1991, 457-481.
[XH93]   Xu, J., Hwang, K., Heuristic methods for dynamic load balancing in
            a message-passing multicomputer, *Journal of Parallel and Distributed
            Computing* **18**, 1993, 1-13.
[ZL78]   Ziv, J., Lempel, A., Compression of individual sequences via variable-
            rate coding, *IEEE Transactions on Information Theory* **24**, 1978, 530-
            536.

VII. Tools for Parallel Computing: A Performance Evaluation Perspective

Allen D. Malony

Department of Computer and Information Science
University of Oregon, U.S.A.

Summary. To make effective use of parallel computing environments, users have come to expect a broad set of tools that augment parallel programming and execution infrastructure with capabilities such as performance evaluation, debugging, runtime program control, and program interaction. The rich history of parallel tool research and development reflects both fundamental issues in concurrent processing and a progressive evolution of tool implementations, targeting current and future parallel computing goals. The state of tools for parallel computing is discussed from a perspective of performance evaluation. Many of the challenges that arise in parallel performance tools are common to other tool areas. I look at four such challenges: modeling, observability, diagnosis, and perturbation. The need for tools will always be present in parallel and distributed systems, but the emphasis on tool support may change. The discussion given is intentionally high-level, so as not to exclude the many important ideas that have come from parallel tool projects. Rather, I attempt to present viewpoints on the challenges that I think would be of concern in any performance tool design.

1. Introduction

Computer systems are arguably the most complex machines ever invented, and parallel computers and distributed computers are the most complex computer systems. In simple terms, parallel and distributed systems are designed to support concurrent computer operations. Although concurrent actions are a common phenomenon in the natural world, encoding concurrency in a computer system such that the computation is "correct" is not a simple task, even for seemingly trivial problems. Parallel systems also have a more specific aim to support the simultaneous execution of concurrent operations for achieving high performance. Maintaining high efficiency in parallel execution further complicates how parallel systems are programmed and used.

Parallel systems are important as computing platforms because they offer the potential to solve problems requiring multiple computing resources and high-end performance. However, this potential cannot be actualized without the support of *tools*, particularly tools for *performance analysis* and *debugging*. Designing and developing tools for parallel systems is intrinsically difficult due to the complexity, both architecturally and operationally, of the computing space represented. In general, a tool should

- Incorporate a *model* of the system and its operation in order to reduce problem complexity;
- Be sensitive to *observability* constraints that limit the scope of what is knowable of and about the system;
- *Diagnose* important system states so as to aid the user in analysis; and
- Account for possible *perturbation* of the system caused by instrumentation intrusion or perturbation of the model results cause by model abstractions.

A tool's utility is determined partly by the sophistication of the system model on which it is based, and this sophistication requires knowledge of system operation and behavior. Given the complexity of parallel platforms, this knowledge may be difficult to obtain. Utility is also affected by the ability to capture the requisite information about the system under certain access, accuracy, and granularity constraints. Certain information may be unobtainable and, hence, unavailable to the tool. Perhaps the most important aspect of a tool is its benefit to problem solving. A tool can be a tremendous aid in discovering and avoiding parallel computing problems if it supported the ability to diagnose system states. However, tools can also influence the system when making measurements for purposes of analysis. In the worst case, system behavior can be perturbed to the point that observations are unreliable and the models that use the data lead to misleading conclusions.

There is a rich research history in the field of parallel and distributed tools. Many important contributions have been made to understand concurrency, control program behavior, debug program correctness, evaluate performance, and present results to users. Rather than attempt a comprehensive summary of these contributions, the reader is directed to the conference proceedings, journals, and bibliographic databases given in the references for the extensive background in the field. In particular, the reader can find excellent recent research surveys of the field in [HM98, RB98, RWM+98, HML95, RC98]. This chapter instead presents a higher-level view of parallel tools than what might be appear in tool surveys. Out of respect for the many important tools that have been developed, only a few will be cited as examples of more general themes. The perspective presented is based on a consideration of the four challenging problems for tools listed above — modeling, observability, diagnosis, and perturbation — specifically as they concern tools for parallel performance evaluation. It is my hope that this more abstract discussion of parallel performance evaluation tools will provide some insight into the parallel tools field as a whole.

In the remainder of the chapter, I first introduce (Section 2) the general problem of parallel performance evaluation as a motivation for tools. In Section 3, a performance environment is advocated as a general guiding framework for tool development. Section 4 discusses the use of models in tool design and how, given a model, performance measurement and analysis techniques are implemented. The problem of performance observability is discussed in Section 5. In Section 6, the concept of a performance diagnosis system is introduced. Parallel performance can be perturbed by several factors. The challenge of performance perturbation analysis is considered in Section 7. Finally, concluding remarks are given in Section 8.

2. Motivation

Two years after Scherr's classic Ph.D. dissertation [Sch65], considered by some to be the seminal work in computer systems performance evaluation [Fer78], Amdahl published his now famous paper on the limits of parallel performance speedup [Amd67]. Although there have been significant advancements in performance evaluation techniques since Scherr's thesis (particularly in the areas of monitoring, simulation, analytic modeling, and bottleneck analysis), "Amdahl's Law"[1] has arguably remained the most fundamental (and the most controversial) result in parallel systems performance evaluation:

> "For over a decade prophets have voiced the contention that the organization of a single computer has reached its limits and that truly significant advances can be made only by interconnection of a

---

[1] Amdahl's Law states that if s is the fraction of a computation that must be executed serially, then the speedup of the computation is bounded above by $\frac{1}{s+(1-s)/n}$, where n is the number of processors used. Note, $\lim_{n\to\infty} \frac{1}{s+(1-s)/n} = \frac{1}{s}$.

multiplicity of computers in such a manner as to permit cooperative solution. ... Demonstration is made of the continued validity of
the single processor approach. ... A fairly obvious conclusion which
can be drawn at this point is that the effort expended on achieving
high parallel processing rates is wasted unless it is accompanied by
achievements in sequential processing rates of very nearly the same
magnitude. ... At any point in time it is difficult to foresee how the
previous bottlenecks in a sequential computer will be effectively overcome." [Amd67]

Amdahl's Law is fundamental in its simplicity and its generality: it defines
an upper bound on the performance of a parallel computation, relative to
its sequential execution time, in terms of a single software parameter (the
fraction of sequential computation) and a single hardware parameter (the
number of processors). Amdahl's Law is controversial because this speedup
bound places severe limits on the performance benefits of parallel computer
systems; in general, it implies that achieving good parallel performance will
be exceedingly difficult.

The last thirty years attest to the veracity of Amdahl's arguments. Several
studies have extended his simple speedup model to further quantify parallel
execution overheads, effects of execution partitioning strategies, and tradeoffs
in speedup versus efficiency. The principal issue is one of *parallel performance
scalability*: how does the performance of a parallel system change relative to
the hardware and software effects of increasing the number of processors used
to execute a program and/or increasing the size of a program's input? Various
scalability metrics have been defined to evaluate whether parallel computers
can deliver their performance potential. The most recognized of these, "scaled
speedup," has even been used to refute the suitability of Amdahl's Law for
evaluating the performance of large-scale parallel systems [Gus88]. However,
regardless of the metric used, the critical performance question remains: how
is the performance potential offered by parallel computer systems achieved
by general-purpose parallel applications?

Ferrari characterized a *performance evaluator* as one that tries to solve
computer systems problems and uses the most appropriate techniques and
tools at hand (a process Ferrari calls *applied performance evaluation*) [Fer78].
In the context of parallel computer systems, two questions are of importance:

– What is the role of the performance evaluator (and, in general, performance
  evaluation)?
– What are the performance problems and the appropriate techniques and
  tools used to solve them?

The discussion of Amdahl's Law gives us a point of reference for addressing
these questions in parallel computing.

First, delivered performance is the *raison d'être* of parallel computer systems: if the purpose of a sequential computer system is to execute a program

to perform a computation, the purpose of a parallel computer system is to execute a program faster than a sequential computer system. Amdahl presents this purpose in the form of a single performance metric, *speedup*, which can be use to evaluate the effectiveness of a parallel program's execution on a parallel machine. Although Amdahl's Law was used to downplay the importance of parallel systems, it equally represents a challenge: good performance is possible, but it will be difficult to obtain. In this respect, the role of performance evaluation in parallel systems is to understand the causes of actual performance behavior for purposes of performance optimization.

Second, parallel performance is an inherently complex metric. Although the limits of parallel performance (both offered potential and speedup bounds) are relatively simple to define (e.g., Amdahl's Law), the *performance space* is large, ranging from the performance achieved on one processor to the peak performance on all processors. Furthermore, the difference between potential and delivered performance on a parallel machine can be significant. Amdahl's Law describes these variations in terms of a single parameter, but, in general, many factors can contribute to performance variability. These factors are interdependent, and seemingly minor changes in their relationship can often induce large changes in the performance achieved. Hence, the performance space is multi-dimensional and can be highly irregular.

Third, parallel performance is difficult to measure, characterize, and understand. It is known that Amdahl's Law is an oversimplification of the cause of parallel performance degradation (i.e., sequential execution); clearly, other overheads limit performance. Even so, determining the amount of time a parallel computation spends in sequential execution can be nontrivial. In general, parallel performance factors are dynamic in time, distributed in location and state, and parallel in occurrence. Although a parallel system is a deterministic automaton, and, in principle, one could envision having full knowledge of system activities, the complexity of hardware and software restricts performance observation: any measurement will be incomplete and any characterization will be an abstraction of true performance behavior. Moreover, performance behavior (the interaction and importance of performance factors) can be highly sensitive to changes in execution context.

Finally, parallel performance is the product of a specific combination of parallel system (hardware and system software) and application program. The performance evaluation requirements are therefore dictated by the specific needs of the problem context and the user. In contrast to sequential computers, the performance evaluation of parallel systems is more specialized in its role and more personalized in its application; in fact, the "performance evaluator" is most often the parallel program developer, because intimate knowledge of the program is usually required to hunt down "performance bugs." Although the advances in performance evaluation technology for sequential systems can be leveraged in the parallel domain, the individuality and complexity of the parallel performance problem mandates that the techniques be uniquely and carefully applied. New parallel performance evaluation techniques must also be developed, with an orientation towards performance optimization.

Since Amdahl's paper was published, there has been a growing crisis in parallel performance evaluation: the technological advances in parallel computer systems (hardware and software) are increasing the complexity of the computational environment, progressively diminishing the general user's ability to operate these systems near the high-end of their performance range. Presently, the crisis is acute. There are scalable parallel machines being introduced today whose performance characteristics are reported only as unachievable peak performance numbers. Furthermore, the system support for obtaining performance data and the integration of this data into the overall system environment are woefully inadequate. Although the growing acceptance of massively parallel computing and the arguments for performance scalability continue to uphold the promise of parallelism, the intellectual challenge to achieve good parallel performance, as originally articulated by Amdahl over thirty years ago, remains.

The development of performance evaluation environments for parallel computer systems is one approach to overcoming this crisis. The idea is to develop an environment for solving performance problems based on a methodology of applied parallel performance evaluation and an integrated set of tools for performance modeling, measurement, analysis, presentation, and prediction. The goal is to relieve the user of the manual effort of performance investigation while reducing the intellectual burden of understanding complex performance behavior. The above discussion supports the need for environments for parallel performance evaluation as a way to reduce the complexities of the performance problem for the user. However, to be effective, performance evaluation environments must be carefully developed to be an integral component of a parallel system's design and use.

3. Environment Design

The *scientific method* — the systematic testing of hypotheses through controlled measurement of observable phenomena, analysis of collected data, and modeling of empirical results — has been advocated as the working definition of "experimental (computer) science" [Den80] and as the basis of the "quantitative philosophy of performance evaluation" [Fer78]. Denning remarked that "science classifies knowledge", and that "experimental science classifies knowledge derived from observations" [Den80]. The advancement of computer science knowledge will increasingly require an experimental approach — the building of experimental apparatus to understand new ideas and to validate their usefulness in practice. Denning commented that the experimental apparatus is not usually the subject of such research and that unless the apparatus is used to obtain significant new knowledge, the research is not substantive.

However, in any field (and performance evaluation, in particular), progress in experimental science is inextricably coupled with advances in observational technology; the ability to test hypotheses that predict the existence of heretofore undetected phenomena intimately depends on the requisite tools to more accurately measure and analyze known phenomena. In performance evaluation, the new "scientific" knowledge sought is the understanding of and solution to computer systems problems. The quantitative tools used are the experimental apparatuses of applied performance evaluation. Better tools to observe and model performance will lead to better solutions to performance problems.

Although the scientific method's systematic measurement and hypothesis testing is both necessary and desirable for parallel performance evaluation, the limited understanding of parallel execution and the complexities of performance observation make the construction of parallel performance environments based on the scientific approach especially difficult. In general, the environment design must meet two basic requirements:

- The need to specify new parallel performance problems in terms of the characteristics of the parallel system, the structure and parameters of the application program, the stored *performance knowledge*, and the current, empirical performance data (*performance hypothesis formulation*).
- The need to conduct performance experiments (including measurement, analysis, presentation, and modeling) to assess performance behavior (*performance observation*).

The first requirement reflects the notion that effective parallel performance evaluation will involve the application of a cyclic (scientific) methodology of designing new performance experiments based on cumulative system and performance information. This includes the initial targeting of performance hypotheses from experiences with other performance problems and the progressive refinement of the hypotheses as a result of performance experiments. The second requirement focuses on the issues concerned with building and applying tools to test performance hypotheses. In particular, the need for performance data to validate a hypothesis must be balanced against the observational capabilities of the performance tools as constrained by the parallel system hardware and software.

Fig. 3.1 shows a general design framework for a parallel performance evaluation environment based on the scientific approach. This framework is more a reflection of an idealized environment than one that might be realized in practice, due to the design complexities and implementation tradeoffs involved. However, our belief is that this design view serves as a useful basis to discuss some of the challenges that arise when attempting to develop parallel performance tools. Because the development of any set of performance tools will involve tradeoffs between feasibility, functionality, accuracy, and cost, considering these issues in a general context will provide us with a founda-

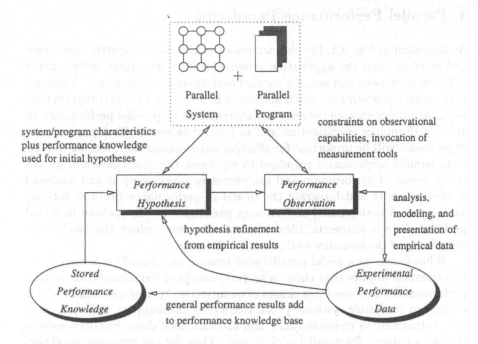

system/program characteristics
plus performance knowledge
used for initial hypotheses

constraints on observational
capabilities, invocation of
measurement tools

hypothesis refinement
from empirical results

analysis,
modeling, and
presentation of
empirical data

general performance results add
to performance knowledge base

Fig. 3.1. Parallel Performance Evaluation Environment Design.

tion to evaluate the capabilities of present environments and to describe the requirements of parallel performance environments of the future.

The Pablo[2] project [RAN+93] best exemplifies our environment design model as a methodological and experimental framework for developing a suite of parallel performance tools driven by the evolving requirements for performance analysis in parallel systems and by the types of performance problems these systems present. The Pablo research has explored all aspects of the model throughout the last ten years, demonstrating a range of techniques for modeling, measurement, analysis, and visualization. Its current use in the Delphi system [RPF99] demonstrates the logical extension of a performance evaluation model into an integrated environment that includes knowledge of the parallel computing platform for modeling at multiple system levels, parallelizing compiler technology for language-level performance instrumentation, mapping, and prediction, and distributed computing support for tool interoperation.

---

[2] The Pablo project homepage is *http://www-pablo.cs.uiuc.edu.*

4. Parallel Performance Paradigms

As suggested in Fig. 3.1, the characteristics of the parallel system (hardware and software) and the application program will be important determinants in the development and use of a parallel performance environment. Although performance problems are often addressed in a specific system/program context, the ability to apply conceptual abstractions of parallel performance to guide performance investigation and to generalize results from performance experiments will be important for effective environment use. Here we use the term *parallel performance paradigm* to represent the combination of an abstract model of performance and the processes (measurement and analysis) needed to apply and integrate the model in performance problem solving. To the extent that parallel performance paradigms can be realized in actual performance environments, they will serve to help reduce the intellectual complexity of performance evaluation for the user.

What counts as a useful parallel performance paradigm? On a basic level, this question implies that there is an (are) accepted definition(s) of parallel performance. There are three classes of quantitative "performance indices" for evaluating computer systems: *productivity* (i.e., throughput), *responsiveness* (i.e., turnaround or response time), and *utilization*. Of these, responsiveness is the index of merit for parallel performance. Thus, for our purposes, good parallel performance paradigms will be those that can express, in some general manner, the influence of the most important parallel system and application factors on response time performance.

The execution time speedup model, represented in Amdahl's Law, is an example of a simple, universal parallel performance paradigm. It is simple because the number of processors and sequential execution time are the only performance factors that matter in the model. It is universal because the paradigm can be used for any parallel environment or program both for performance experimentation — the measurement of speedup as function of the number of processors — and for performance prediction — the estimation of the performance on n processors based on the sequential execution time measurements on m processors. However, execution speedup is a poor paradigm for investigating performance problems (i.e., performance diagnosis), serving only as an indicator of good or bad parallel performance. The performance scalability extensions to the basic speedup models help to quantify the influence of additional performance factors, but are still too general to explain performance behavior.

The power of a parallel performance paradigm comes from both its ability to represent performance abstractly, for comparative and predictive purpose, and its ability to characterize performance specifically, for reasons of diagnosis and tuning. The generality of the underlying model can be at odds with the specificity needed in performance measurement and execution analysis. Paradigms can either be extended to add performance metrics while keeping the analysis models simple, or be made more specific with greater model detail and analysis resolution, but at the risk of less general application.

A paradigm based on the parallel execution profile of a particular performance metric (e.g., execution time or degree of parallelism) is important because it expresses a procedure for evaluating performance limiting behavior. The profile might be coarse-grained, describing parallel performance by a set of summary statistics, or fine-grained, representing parallel performance as a time sequence of metric values. For instance, the common execution time profile orders code segments according to their impact on total execution time; code segments representing a higher percentage of the total time might be candidates for performance optimization. A parallelism profile, on the other hand, reflects a history of parallelism behavior and highlights regions where there is the potential for parallelism improvement. However, parallel performance paradigms based on profiles alone are insufficient as a basis for formulating performance hypotheses because they offer no explanation as to why the performance behavior occurred.

Alternatively, parallel performance paradigms based on the properties of the parallel execution environment and the program's computation have a greater potential for investigating performance problems. For instance, performance models can be defined with respect to computational structures for parallel workflow (e.g., *pipelined*, *master-slave*, or *work queue*), or with respect to parallel work synchronization mechanisms (e.g., *fork-join*, *barrier*, or *message passing*) or scheduling algorithms (e.g., *task level* or *loop level*; *self scheduling* or *block scheduling*). A parallel performance paradigm based on such models will specify the required measurements for the type of structures, mechanisms, and scheduling algorithms used and will designate the associated types of analysis to be undertaken. Higher level performance models are based on computational abstractions (e.g., *control flow* versus *data flow*; *control parallel* versus *data parallel*; or *single program, multiple data* versus *bulk synchronous parallel*), which can be used to refine and to prioritize lower level measurements to performance problems in the computational domain. The important point here is that the performance paradigm is founded on the characteristics of the parallel execution of interest, thereby providing a means for expressing and evaluating observed performance behavior.

Parallel performance paradigms provide a framework for defining performance measurements, aiding in performance diagnosis, and supporting performance prediction. During the performance evaluation process the paradigms should be modified and refined as new performance knowledge is gained through observation. For this reason, multi-paradigm approaches are common. A paradigm might employ *resource usage models* to identify performance anomalies and then *event models* to identify computational states that lead to the anomalies. The *program activity graph* is a well-known multi-paradigm representation that uses nodes in the graph to signify significant events in the program's execution and arcs to show the ordering of events within a process or the synchronization dependencies between processes. By overlaying parallel program performance metrics one can see how the inter-event, inter-process dependencies in a parallel program influence which procedures are important to a program's execution time.

Many parallel tool researchers have naturally applied paradigms in their work. In their paper "Analyzing Parallel Program Execution Using Multiple Views" [LMF90], LeBlanc, Mellor-Crummey, and Fowler emphasize the need to develop a (general) unified approach to parallel program analysis that supports the creation and integration of multiple views of an execution and allows the user to tailor views to specific analysis. The Paradyn[3] project [MCC95] is an excellent example of this approach in practice. Paradyn is based on a flexible model of performance instrumentation and a well-defined notion of performance bottlenecks and program structure, so that measurements can be made for investigating bottlenecks associated with specific causes and specific parts of a program. Measurements are possible at different levels of the parallel system and open interfaces for performance analysis and visualization are provided for constructing alternative performance tools.

5. Performance Observability

In order to evaluate the performance of a parallel application executing on a parallel computer system, certain aspects of application and system behavior must be made observable. Whereas a performance paradigm provides a conceptual foundation for investigating and understanding performance problems, an environment must also support a means for performance experimentation — the measurement, analysis, and presentation of parallel performance phenomena. *Parallel performance observability* is the ability to accurately capture, analyze, and present (collectively, to *observe*) information about the performance of a parallel computer system [Mal90]. Tools for performance observability must balance the *need* for performance data against the *cost* of obtaining it (environment complexity and performance intrusion). Too little performance data makes performance evaluation difficult; too much data can be complex to analyze and might perturb the measured system. What combination of tools for performance observation is appropriate for parallel computer systems? How do the architecture, hardware, and system software affect how performance data is collected? What performance events can and cannot be observed? How do the performance evaluation tools affect the performance being measured? How should performance information be conveyed to the performance analyst? Unfortunately, there is no formal approach to determine, given a parallel performance evaluation problem, how to accurately "observe" parallel execution in order to produce the required performance results. Furthermore, any parallel performance experiment will ultimately be

---

[3] The Paradyn project homepage is *http://www.cs.wisc.edu/ paradyn*.

constrained by the capabilities of the available tools for performance observation.

Performance measurement is the foundation of performance observability. If an experiment cannot be constructed, even in principle, to measure a phenomenon, it cannot operationally be said to exist. If a phenomenon cannot be measured in practice, it cannot be observed. The complexity of parallel computer systems makes *a priori* performance prediction difficult and experimental performance measurement crucial. A complete characterization of software and hardware dynamics is needed to understand the performance of parallel execution and requires efficient techniques for runtime performance instrumentation and data collection. Although performance measurement is a necessary component of parallel performance environments, the degree and type of performance measurement support depends on its intended purpose, and the nature of the performance experiments to be conducted defines the needed capabilities of the performance monitoring system, its observational detail, and acceptable cost.

The diversity of parallel performance problems makes it difficult to develop a single set of performance monitoring techniques. For every performance experiment, there nonetheless exists a minimal set of required events that must be captured. In general, a parallel execution can be regarded as a sequence of *actions* representing the computational activities one wishes to observe. The execution of an action generates an *event*, an encoded instance of the action. A "performance measurement" can be viewed as the collection of a (possibly infinite) set of events. Indeed, event-based models have been widely used to describe program behavior and to define techniques for performance measurement. A system can be represented in terms of the observable effects and interactions of system components as represented by a stream of characteristic atomic behaviors (i.e., events), giving an abstract view of program behavior in terms of a sequence of hierarchically defined events. In general, the more detailed the measurement, the more data can be provided to a performance model, allowing for more detailed analysis.

However, before events can be analyzed, they must be detected and captured by a monitoring system. The selection of instrumentation and data collection tools defines both the granularity and detail of performance data that can be measured. Events of interest can occur at different observation points (hardware and software), which may or may not be accessible. Furthermore, depending on the type of measurement desired, the amount of performance data that must be collected and stored can vary. In practice, the need to observe time-dependent parallel performance behavior and the problems associated with the specification of complex performance events and their detection often necessitates measurement solutions that capture a large volume of time-based event data (e.g., tracing) for later analysis.

The design and development of tools for detailed performance instrumentation and data capture on parallel machines is non-trivial, often requiring significant engineering effort for their implementation. Monitoring solutions based on tracing must solve several implementation problems, including event timestamp consistency (both in accuracy and synchronization), trace buffer allocation, tracing overhead, and trace I/O. Although software recording of performance data suffices for low frequency events, capture of detailed, high-frequency performance data ultimately requires hardware support if the performance instrumentation is to remain efficient and unobtrusive. Alternatively, techniques to control monitoring overhead dynamically by changing instrumentation during execution have been successful in reducing significantly the amount of performance data captured.

The lesson of measurement detail versus accuracy is that because parallel programs are composed of multiple threads of control, the accuracy of performance characterization depends on some global knowledge of program state. Although behavioral models of parallel program execution allow events to be measured independently for each thread of execution and then combined to determine global states, certain measurements must additionally be made to preserve global performance data integrity (e.g., "global" time measurement). That is, parallel program measurement must not only capture thread actions that reflect logical, operational behavior, but also data that will be used to establish an accurate reference for performance analysis (e.g., global time reference).

There have been many research studies on the different aspects of the performance observability problem discussed above, particularly in respect to the problem of instrumentation and monitoring. Modeling and evaluating design alternatives for performance observability will always remain a challenge. Rover, Waheed, and Hollingsworth [RWH98] took on that challenge in their study of design alternatives for on-line instrumentation systems based on different criteria for effectiveness, intrusion, and complexity of implementation. Their results establish models based on metrics derived from these criteria as they applied in different system architecture contexts: network of workstations (NOW), symmetric multiprocessors (SMP), and massively parallel processing (MPP) systems. These models are intended to be used to provide early feedback to tool developers regarding instrumentation overhead and performance.

6. Performance Diagnosis

Given a foundation for performance modeling and a means for performance measurement, a parallel performance environment can support an process commonly known as *performance debugging*. When a performance problem (i.e., a *performance bug*) is present, tools in the environment can be used to investigate the problem, identify its source, and provide data for performance improvement. Performance debugging is the process of applying these tools. How performance bugs are identified and how they are explained is the problem of *performance diagnosis* [MH99]. Expert parallel programmers often improve program performance enormously by experimenting with their programs on a parallel computer, then interpreting the results of these experiments to suggest changes. This expertise has had difficulty finding its way into performance environments for two reasons. First, researchers lack a theory of what diagnosis methods work, and why. There is no formal way to describe or compare how expert programmers solve their performance diagnosis problems in particular contexts. There is no standard theory for understanding diagnosis system features and fitting them to the programmer's particular needs. As a result, researchers cannot easily compare and evaluate the performance debugging tools they produce, and many potential users do not find systems that are applicable to their performance diagnosis problems. Second, performance debugging tools are not easily adaptable to new requirements. Highly automated systems, while providing considerable help to the programmer, are hard to change, hard to extend, and hard to combine with other systems.

In simple terms, performance diagnosis guides the programmer in identifying poor decisions made in parallel programming or in configuring parallel execution. By finding and explaining the chief performance problems of the program, diagnosis helps the programmer determine which decisions had the worst performance effects and how those effects might be repaired. During performance diagnosis, the programmer decides which performance data to collect, which features to judge significant, which hypotheses to pursue, and what confirmation to seek. A *performance diagnosis method* can be defined as the policies used to make such decisions, and a *performance diagnosis system* as a suite of programs that supports some diagnosis method, ideally in an automatic way. The research problem is to define a theory of performance diagnosis methods and to use that theory to create more automated, adaptable performance diagnosis systems.

To attack the first obstacle to performance diagnosis systems, lack of theoretical justification, a "knowledge-level" theory of performance diagnosis must be developed. In particular, a knowledge-level theory must answer the question, What knowledge does a programmer use to choose actions to meet performance diagnosis objectives? The theory breaks the question down into two parts: What methods do expert programmers use?, and How can we rationalize the programmer's choice of methods? Underlying the challenge of developing a knowledge base is the fact that different performance metrics provide useful information for different types of performance bottlenecks (bugs). This is one reason for the emphasis on an underlying parallel performance paradigm: it provides a context for performance data interpretation. The use of multiple paradigms help to address different performance issues. Since every parallel application may have a different set of possible performance problems, the user is often left to select the appropriate application; a comprehensive pre-enumeration of possible performance diagnoses (hypotheses) is difficult. However, recent research has tried first to provide better guidance to the user by treating the problem of finding a performance bottleneck as a search problem, and second to define this space by describing "fault taxonomies" for the performance problems that commonly arise [MH99].

The forgoing discussion suggests one reason why performance diagnosis systems are not widely used: they are not adaptable to a wide variety of contexts. To help arrive at an initial diagnosis, performance diagnosis systems define a limited fault taxonomy, a finite set of performance problems to look for. To date, systems have derived this set from the workings of the programming language and runtime system they support. It follows that the diagnosis systems are limited to a particular class of target machines and environments (more abstractly, parallel performance paradigms). However, if we could find methods and rationales that cut across a substantial number of diagnosis systems, then we might be able to identify general methods, and differences among systems could then be studied to extract rationale.

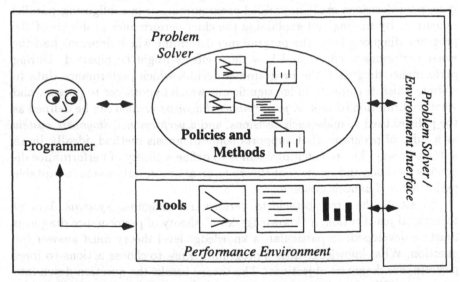

Fig. 6.1. Framework of a Parallel Performance Diagnosis System.

The second obstacle to the acceptance of diagnosis systems — poor automation and adaptability — can be addressed by a new diagnosis system framework (Fig. 6.1). Here, policies would be interpreted by a goal-oriented problem solver to choose methods to pursue. The methods would in turn interface with the programming environment to apply tools to carry out experiments. The problem solver is based on knowledge-level theory of expert performance diagnosis and is able to perform actions to accomplish a method's diagnostic goal, often instructing a tool to perform some measurement or analysis experiment that will add new information to the performance database. The purpose of the environment interface is to support adaptable diagnosis by separating diagnosis methods from the software tools that support those methods. It specifies diagnosis actions in terms of their effects on a high-level performance database. Methods can thus execute these actions and track their effects without knowing what commands are sent to tools, or how data and programs are stored in files. As a result, general methods can be adapted unchanged to new tools. One can reuse knowledge about which steps to take in performance diagnosis in contexts where the manner in which those steps are taken differs significantly.

The ideas above have been captured in our Poirot performance diagnosis research [MH99]. One of the unique aspects of this work is that we have reconstructed or "reverse engineered" some answers to the above questions (i.e., the knowledge-level theory) from a survey of research papers on performance diagnosis systems, and from the case studies that appeared in those papers. The goal was to find methods and rationale that cut across a substantial number of diagnosis systems. Each performance diagnosis system was viewed as a collection of methods for heuristic classification. Similarities among systems were analyzed to identify general methods, and differences among systems were studied to extract rationale. The result of the survey is a rationalized classification of performance diagnosis systems, a systematic description of what methods performance diagnosis systems use, and why they use them. These results can be found in [MH99].

Hollingsworth's W3 search model [HML95] is an excellent representative of a diagnosis fault taxonomy that has been actualized in a working tool, the Paradyn Performance Consultant [MCC95]. The W3 search model looks for performance problems through an iterative process of refining the answers to three questions: *why* is the application performing poorly, *where* is the bottleneck, and *when* does the problem occur. To answer the why question, tests are conducted to identify the type of bottleneck (e.g., synchronization, I/O, computation). Answering the where question isolates a performance bottleneck to a specific resource used by the program (e.g., a disk system, a synchronization variable, or a procedure). Answering when a problem occurs, tries to isolate a bottleneck to a specific phase of the program's execution. The Performance Consultant uses the W3 search model to automatically guide it in instrumentation and analysis as the program is executing.

7. Performance Perturbation

Computer system performance evaluation is subject to the same instrumentation pitfalls facing any experimental science; notably, uncertainty and instrumentation perturbation. Instrumentation, no matter how unobtrusive, introduces performance perturbations, and the degree of perturbation is proportional to the fraction of the system state that is captured: excessive instrumentation perturbs the measured system, but limited instrumentation reduces measurement detail. Simply put, performance instrumentation manifests an *Instrumentation Uncertainty Principle* [Mal90]:

- Instrumentation perturbs the system state.
- Execution phenomena and instrumentation are coupled logically.
- Volume and accuracy are antithetical.

The terms "Heisenberg Uncertainty" and "probe effect" have been used to describe the error introduced in the performance measurement due to a monitor's intrusion on computer system behavior. The primary source of instrumentation perturbations is the execution of additional instructions. However, ancillary perturbations can result from disabled compiler optimizations and additional operating system overhead. These perturbations manifest themselves in several ways: execution slowdown, changes in memory reference patterns, event reordering, and even register interlock stalls. Perturbation due to instrumentation has two effects on the events occurring during parallel execution: temporal effects and resource assignment effects. In addition to the slowdown caused by instrumentation overhead, temporal effects include possible event re-orderings as the measurement changes the likelihood of different partial order executions. Resource assignment effects occur because the instrumentation changes the dynamic resource demands. In instances where the computation dynamically adapts to resource availability, instrumentation can perturb resource allocation and utilization.

Performance measurements can differ significantly from actual execution (where measurements are disabled) unless the perturbation effects are taken into account by the performance environment during performance analysis. The goal of *performance perturbation analysis* is the recovery of actual runtime performance behavior from perturbed performance measurements. Formal models of performance perturbation are needed that permit quantitative evaluation of perturbations given instrumentation costs, measured event frequency, and desired instrumentation detail. Techniques based on timing and event models have been applied with positive results [Mal90]. Because actual performance behavior is inferred (approximated) by these models from the performance measurements, however, no absolute means for testing the accuracy of perturbation analysis is available. Rather, performance approximations were empirically validated with respect to two measures: total program execution time and selected even timings.

It is not uncommon that execution time is degraded many-fold when a program is measured. If total program execution time is accurately approximated after perturbation analysis is applied, the implication is that perturbation analysis errors are not accumulating. On the other hand, the reason detail performance measurements are made is to observe events of finer granularity. Perturbation analysis must also accurately resolve individual event timings. To determine the accuracy of trace events, one needs a standard of reference.

No such standard exists, because the actual event trace is unknown. Instead, a sequence of event traces, each with successively smaller subsets of the detailed trace measurement, must be produced and the approximated event timings of correlated events compared. From the measurement uncertainty principle, as the number of trace events decreases, the presumed accuracy of the event timing approximations increases. If the approximated times of events correlated across the traces correspond, then it follows that the timing of other events in the detailed trace should also be accurate.

However, this validation approach is not wholly satisfying, because it lacks a theoretical basis. In general, concurrent execution involves data dependent behavior. The states of parallel programs inherently form a partial order that must be followed during execution. If dependency control is spread across threads of execution, instrumentation can perturb the timing relationships of events and, thus, their actual execution ordering. If performance instrumentation is designed correctly, an un-instrumented parallel execution that satisfies Lamport's *sequential consistency* criterion[4] [Lam79] implies that the performance measurement will be *non-interfering* and *safe*. If the performance measurements involve only the detection and recording of event occurrence (i.e., tracing), the partial order relationships will be unaffected and the set of *feasible* executions[5] will remain unchanged. Beginning with a total ordering of measured events consistent with the *happened before* relation [Lam78] defined by the original partial order execution, time-based and event-based perturbation analysis can be applied to thread events that occurred either during independent execution to remove the instrumentation overhead or in dependent execution to enforce the semantics of operations that implement inter-thread synchronization. As long as the total ordering of dependent events present in the measured execution is maintained during this analysis, the final approximated execution will also be a feasible execution.

But is the final approximated execution a "likely" execution? That is, would the approximated execution ever actually occur, and with what expectancy would it occur? Any perturbation analysis approximation must be safe (i.e., must not violate partial ordering relationships) and, therefore, must be provided sufficient measurements that capture the operations that enforce ordering during execution. However, the accuracy of perturbation analysis depends not only on more precise synchronization measurements, but also on additional knowledge of actual (likely) execution behavior, which is unattainable from measurements alone. The set of *likely* executions is the subset of the *feasible executions* that are most probable. In many cases, the complete range of feasible executions will be restricted to a smaller set of likely executions due to the computational environment. If instrumentation is added, the set of

---

[4] A parallel execution is sequentially consistent if the result is the same as if the operations were executed in some sequential order obtained by arbitrarily interleaving the thread execution streams.

[5] The set of program executions that could result from the partial order of program events is known as the *partially ordered set* of (feasible) executions.

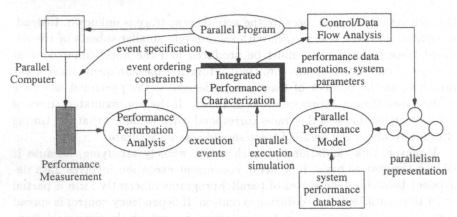

Fig. 7.1. Unifying Framework for Measurement-Based Experimental Performance Analysis.

likely executions can change. Computing the likelihood distribution of feasible executions is an extremely difficult problem, requiring an execution time model of concurrent operation. Thus, the inability to predict likely executions makes it difficult to bound the error of measurement-only perturbation analysis.

Simply put, performance measurement alone is insufficient to solve the perturbation analysis problem. If additional information were provided to the perturbation analysis process that describes certain behavioral properties and resource allocation and usage of the parallel computation (e.g., data dependency information, loop scheduling algorithms, processor allocation, memory usage), the perturbation analysis could use this information to make more accurate approximations by modeling the effects of nondeterministic execution in the presence of instrumentation.

This observation suggests a strong relationship between parallel performance paradigms which are used to define methodologies for performance measurement and diagnosis, and performance perturbation analysis.

- The accuracy of parallel performance models depend on the validity of the performance data used.
- Performance perturbation analysis depends on knowledge of context-dependent execution control and system performance information, which is provided in the parallel performance models, to resolve perturbation errors.

This relationship can be captured in a framework for measurement-based experimental performance analysis, unifying performance perturbation analysis and parallel performance modeling research; see Figure 7.1. The interesting parts of the framework concern the feedback paths:

- to event specification and program analysis, for changing the granularity of performance observation;

- to perturbation analysis, for preventing execution ordering violations; and
- to parallel performance modeling, for annotating the representational form of the parallel program with measured performance data and system parameters.

One can consider performance perturbation more generally as a change to "real", unperturbed performance of a parallel computation as a result of some change to the parallel execution environment. This change could be the result of performance measurement, as we have discussed here, or the result of performance analysis abstraction. Because we are trying to discover the "real" performance by an analysis process, whether it is based on measurement, simulation, or analytical modeling, there is always a question about the accuracy of the performance approximation. That accuracy can be perturbed not only by instrumentation intrusion, but also by inaccurate or incorrect modeling assumptions. The important insight is that perturbation analysis can be more fully regarded as a general performance prediction problem. The goal is to estimate (predict) performance based on stored performance knowledge coupled with abstractions of parallel program and system behavior. Only by understanding the interplay of performance knowledge with parallel models (actual or abstract) can high confidence approximations be achieved. The natural tension between the complexity of measurement and modeling makes this an interesting challenge.

Our work on perturbation analysis [MR91, MRW92] demonstrates the effectiveness of perturbation models in approximating aggregate performance data from traces gathered using intrusive monitoring, even in cases of behavioral changes due to event ordering influences. We show that even in cases of very high intrusion, accurate analysis is possible. The effect of perturbation of an execution environment is considered in our work on performance extrapolation [SM95]. Here we use measurements of a multithreaded program running on a single processor to estimate the performance of the program on a target parallel machine, substituting performance models for architectural and system components (e.g., network and scheduling) that are being varied (i.e., perturbed).

The trace recovery research of Gannon et al. [GWA+94] combines perturbation analysis with software modeling. They develop a tool that generates timed Petri net (TPN) models of intrusively monitored software; reinstruments the software as needed; and then uses the TPN model to recover, from the corrupted trace, the approximate trace that would have been observed had monitoring-induced timing and event order changes not been present. The amount and type of trace information provided by this approach is often sufficient to resimulate a system accurately to some known point. This allows the user to not only determine when behavioral changes occur due to intrusion, but also determine the sensitivity of program behavior to intrusion (i.e.. program robustness). The correct trace can also be fed to a deterministic TPN simulator to visualize the process, which may allow the programmer to determine and alleviate bottlenecks that limit program performance.

8. Summary

The changing nature of the parallel computing platform extends the bounds of how these systems are programmed and used, further increasing computational and performance complexity. Tools must adapt to this change. Designing and building tools for parallel performance evaluation is one of the most challenging research areas in computer science. Not only are there fundamental issues associated with modeling and observing concurrent, parallel operations, but the self-referential and self-diagnostic notions of computer-based tools trying to understand computational behavior are extraordinary. This chapter has presented a performance evaluation perspective on the general research area of parallel tools. The views presented on modeling, observability, diagnosis, and perturbation are applicable to the more general field as a whole. They are also useful as guideposts for understanding how tools should evolve to meet the requirements of next-generation systems.

References

[Amd67]   Amdahl, D., Validity of the single-processor approach to achieving large-scale computer capabilities, *Proc. of the AFIPS Conference*, 1967, 483-485.

[Den80]   Denning, P., What is experimental computer sciene, *Communications of the ACM* **23**, 1980, 543-544.

[Fer78]   Ferrari, D., *Computer Systems Performance Evaluation*, Prentice-Hall, Englewood Cliffs, 1978.

[GWA+94]   Gannon, J., Williams, K., Andersland, M., Casavant, T., Lump, J., Trace recovery in multiprocessing systems: Architectural considerations, *Proc. of the 1994 International Conference on Parallel Processing*, 1994, 97-101.
            this item is not referred to

[Gus88]   Gustafson, J., Reevaluating Amdahl's law, *Communications of the ACM* **31**, 1988, 532-533.

[HM98]   Hollingsworth, J., Miller, B., Instrumentation and measurement, in Foster, I., Kesselman, C., (eds.), *The GRID: Blueprint for a New Computing Infrastructure*, Morgan Kaufman Publishers, San Francisco, 1998, 339-366.

[HML95]   Hollingsworth, J., Miller, B., Lumpp, J., Techniques for performance measurement of parallel programs, in Casavant, T., Tvrdik, P., Plasil, F., (eds.), *Parallel Computers: Theory and Practice*, IEEE Computer Society Press, 1995.

[Lam78]   Lamport, L., Time, clocks, and the ordering of events in a distributed system, *Communications of the ACM* **21**, 1978, 558-565.

[Lam79]   Lamport, L., How to make a multiprocessor computer that correctly
            executes multiprocess programs, *IEEE Transactions on Computers* 28,
            1979, 690-691.
[LMF90]   LeBlanc, T., Mellor-Crummey, J., Fowler, R., Analyzing parallel pro-
            gram executions using multiple views, *Journal of Parallel and Dis-
            tributed Computing* 9, 1990, 203-217.
[Mal90]   Malony, A., *Performance Observability*, PhD thesis, University of Illi-
            nois, Urbana-Champaign, 1990.
[MH99]   Malony, A., Helm, R., A theory and architecture for automating per-
            formance diagnosis, *Fifth Generation Computing Systems, (Special Is-
            sue on Performance Data-mining in Parallel and Distributed Comput-
            ing)*, 1999.
[MR91]   Malony, A., Reed, D., Models for performance perturbation analysis,
            Proc. of the Workshop on Parallel and Distributed Debugging, 1991,
            1-12.
[MRW92]   Malony, A., Reed, D., Wijshoff, H., Performance measurement intru-
            sion and perturbation analysis, *IEEE Transactions on Parallel and
            Distributed Computing* 3, 1992, 433-450.
[MCC95]   Miller, B., Callaghan, B., Cargille, J., Hollingsworth, J., Irvin, R., Kar-
            avanic, K., Kunchitkapadam, K., Newhall, T., The paradyn parallel
            performance measurement tools, *IEEE Computer* 28, *(Special Issue on
            Performance Evaluation Tools for Parallel and Distributed Computer
            Systems)*, 1995, 37-46.
[RC98]   Rajamony, R., Cox, A., Parallel programming tools, Technical Report,
            Rice University, 1998,
[RAN+93]   Reed, D., Aydt, R., Noe, R., Roth, P., Shields, K., Schwartz, B.,
            Tavera, L., Scalable performance analysis: The pablo performance
            analysis environment, in Skjellum, A., (ed.), *Proc. of the Scalable Par-
            allel Libraries Conference*, 1993, 104-113.
[RPF99]   Reed, D., Padua, D., Foster, I., Gannon, D., Miller, B., Delphi: An
            integrated, language-directed performance prediction, measurement,
            and analysis environment, *Frontiers '99: The 9th Symposium on the
            Frontiers of Massively Parallel Computation*, 1999, (See http://www.
            computer.org/conferen/proceed/frontiers/0087/0087toc.htm).
[RB98]   Reed, D., Ribler, R., Performance analysis and visualization, in Foster,
            I., Kesselman, C., (eds.), *The GRID: Blueprint for a New Computing
            Infrastructure*, Morgan Kaufman Publishers, San Francisco, 1998, 367-
            394.
[RWH98]   Rover, D., Waheed, A., Hollingsworth, J., Modeling and evaluating de-
            sign alternatives for an on-line instrumentation system: A case study,
            IEEE Transactions on Software Engineering 24, 1998, 451-470.
[RWM+98]   Rover, D., Waheed, A., Mutka, M., Bakic, A., Software tools for com-
            plex distributed systems: Toward integrated tool environments, *IEEE
            Concurrency* 6, *(Special Issue on Engineering of Complex Distributed
            Computing Systems)*, 1998, 40-54.
[Sch65]   Scherr, A., *An Analysis of Time Shared Computer Systems*, PhD the-
            sis, Massachusetts Institute of Technology, Cambridge, 1965.
[SM95]   Shanmugam, K., Malony, A., Performance extrapolation of parallel
            programs, *Proc. of the International Conference on Parallel Process-
            ing*, 1995, 117-120.

VIII. Parallel Database Systems and Multimedia Object Servers

Leana Golubchik and Richard R. Muntz

University of Maryland at College Park
University of California at Los Angeles

Summary. The mainstay of persistent storage has been the magnetic disk for the past four decades. Based on recent trends soon there will be 100 GB disks on the market with peak transfer rates of 20 to 40 MBps. Not only will each home have at least one PC, but more than likely each will have a terabyte store to go with the computational power. What do we do with all that storage? There is an ever widening number of exciting application areas that are becoming economically viable due to technological advances in storage. One that is emerging rapidly is decision support in database management systems. Multimedia is another fast growing area with applications in entertainment, education, the sciences, manufacturing, etc. Storage plays an important role in these applications since the size of multimedia objects can be prodigious. It may seem that storage technology has been advancing quite strongly. However, communications and processing speeds have increased even more rapidly and I/O is often a bottleneck in data intensive applications. The resource demands on disk storage have three dimensions: storage capacity, bandwidth, an access frequency. Depending on the application demands, any one of these can necessitate multiple disks be utilized to meet requirements. This chapter presents a summary of the state of the art in the use of parallel I/O mainly in two areas: database systems and multimedia storage servers.

1. Introduction

The mainstay of persistent storage has been the magnetic disk for the past four decades. The recent trends are that the cost per megabyte decreases at a rate of 60% per year, the areal capacity is increasing at 60% per year, and bandwidth is increasing at 40% per year. Soon there will be 100 GB disks on the market with peak transfer rates of 20 to 40 MBps (megabytes per second). Not only will each home have at least one PC, but more than likely each will have a terabyte store to go with the computational power. (At the current rate of decrease in prices a terabyte of disk storage will cost $2000 in 2005.)

What do we do with all that storage? There is an ever widening number of exciting application areas that are becoming economically viable due to technological advances in storage. One that is emerging rapidly is decision support in database management systems. Particularly in the past decade the ability to have more data online for analysis and decision support has spurred much research on how to use this data for business advantage and a great deal of industry and academic activity in data warehousing and data mining has resulted. Multimedia is another fast growing area with applications in entertainment, education, the sciences, manufacturing, etc. Storage plays an important role in these applications since the size of multimedia objects can be prodigious. For example one hour of MPEG-2 encoded video will require more than 2 GB of storage. The UCLA film library contains about 25,000 hours of newsreel film from the first half of the 20-th century. It is desirable to store a higher resolution version, but even at MPEG-2 compression rates, the total would be over 50 terabytes. In fact, it has been estimated [GVW96] that in another six years more than half of all storage will be devoted to multimedia (as opposed to conventional file system and business database storage). In addition to these applications there are many others that will emerge as requiring extensive storage and processing. Scientific, environmental and medical applications come to mind. For example, the multinational Earth Observing System is expected to produce on the order of one terabyte of data per day in a few years. As an example from medicine, a single x-ray image requires about 50 megabytes of storage for adequate resolution.

It may seem that storage technology has been advancing quite strongly; particularly in cost and capacity this is true. However, communications and processing speeds have increased even more rapidly and I/O is often a bottleneck in data intensive applications. Not only are multiple disks required for their storage capacity but the bandwidth and latency requirements also often necessitate multiple disks to meet performance requirements. In fact, since disk capacity is increasing faster than disk bandwidth (and significantly faster than the decrease in seek times and rotational latency), more and more applications will dictate the number of disks to meet bandwidth requirements rather than storage capacity requirements.

This chapter presents a summary of the state of the art in the use of parallel I/O mainly in two areas: database systems and multimedia storage servers. Due to space limitations we do not discuss scientific, medical or geographic information systems in any detail. We first give a brief introduction to disk operation, performance metrics and some general principles that cut across many application areas and follow this with a discussion of parallel database systems and multimedia object servers.

1.1 Parallelism in Disk Subsystems

Disks are a particularly interesting resource for a number of reasons. Although many basic principles of parallelism do apply, such as the tradeoff between overheads of parallelism versus the benefits of reduced response times, some characteristics are unique to disk subsystems. Whereas in the case of resources such as CPUs, one could consider a pool of interchangeable resources whose use can be determined at runtime (at least when dynamic scheduling is used), all disk resources are not equivalent since a disk's utility is determined by the data stored on it. Moreover, the placement of the data is typically determined a priori. Of course, data can be dynamically redistributed but with concomitant overhead.

This "partitioning" of resources (based on data placement) contributes to some of the difficulties in designing cost-effective parallel I/O systems. Solutions to this problem, through data layout and scheduling techniques, are often application dependent (as will be illustrated in the context of the database and multimedia applications later in this chapter).

Finally, it is important to remember that disks can be viewed as a "multidimensional" resource; the dimensions being storage capacity, bandwidth capacity, and access rate. Depending on the application one or the other resource can be the bottleneck or constraining aspect. For example, an online transaction processing (OLTP) database application is one in which there is a high volume of transactions but each accesses only a few records. In this type of application it is often the access rate that determines the transaction throughput/response time performance of the system. A decision support database application or a video server will, conversely, often require a "full scan" of very large data objects and the major performance aspect of the disk subsystem is the bandwidth. In either case, the data layout maps logical accesses to physical accesses. It is therefore possible that a logical access pattern which balances the load over data objects can be mapped to a skewed physical access pattern and produce an imbalance in the physical access pattern. Of course, the opposite is also true. Further complicating this issue is that the logical access pattern often varies with time. Therefore an "optimal" mapping at one point in time may be a poor mapping at another time. Dynamically redistributing data is one option but, of course, has the disadvantage of the overhead in moving data. As we shall see later, there are methods of data allocation that tend to "decouple" the storage layout from the other two disk resources in the sense that the system becomes relatively insensitive to the logical access pattern. How this can be done and the degree to which it is successful are often application dependent, as we will illustrate later in the chapter.

1.2 Performance and Reliability Metrics

1.2.1 Basic disk performance characteristics. [1] Disks are highly *non work conserving*. which means that the amount of time it takes to serve a request is not independent of the scheduling order of requests. This is mainly due to the seek time and rotational latency of an I/O request. Maximum seek times are currently in the range of 10 to 20 milliseconds; average seek times for randomly ordered requests will be approximately one third of the maximum. Maximum rotational delays depend on rotational speed; the current 10,000 rpm disks have maximum rotational delays of 6 milliseconds and an average of 3 milliseconds.

Transfer speed from or to a disk is a function the rotational speed and the linear recording density on a track. Recent increases in rotational speed have resulted in much of the improvement in transfer rates; increases in linear bit density on a track have contributed also but quite a bit less. Another oddity of magnetic disks is that the linear bit density is the same on all tracks and the rotational speed is constant. Therefore the total capacity of an outer track is larger than that of an inner track and also, the transmission rate for an outer track is faster than that of an inner track. For disks today the ratio of capacity (and transmission rate) between an outer and an inner track can be a factor of 2 or 3 and therefore can not be ignored for many applications. Since the capacity of a track will vary, cylinders are typically partitioned into *zones* in which the capacity of each track is the same. The number of zones varies with the disk model but is typically in the range of five to twenty.

The trends in disk performance are that capacity and transfer rates are increasing at 60% per year. Rotational latency has recently decreased significantly but it is unclear if this will continue at the same rate. Seek times have decreased much more slowly and therefore will, over time, become a more significant percentage of the total time to serve a request. However, the effect of seek and rotational latency overheads are less significant as the number of bytes read (or written) increases. For general purpose file systems using, for example, an 8K byte page size, seek and rotational latencies can be significant since typical timings are: (1) approx. 8 msec seek, (2) approx. 3 msec rotational delay, and (3) approx. 0.8 msec. transfer time (at 10 MBps). However, for multimedia applications like video, where a 128KB read is reasonable, the transfer time grows to about 12.5 msec. and overhead latencies are a much

---

[1] We assume the reader has a basic understanding of disks and computer architecture. Thus, for example, we assume that terms such as disk cylinder, seek, disk controller, etc. are familiar to the reader (see [RW94] for details).

smaller fraction of the time; thus the effective utilization of the disk is much higher. However due to disk zones, larger transfers will have a much larger variance. In multimedia applications worst case performance must be considered in order to provide quality of service guarantees. In this case the slowest rate may have to be assumed and again significant performance is sacrificed.

Performance of disks is also closely tied to the disk controllers, the physical connections (e.g., SCSI or IDE), and the operating system drivers. For example, disk controllers are able to prefetch data and to cache data in anticipation of future requests. For example, when an 8K byte file page is read, the disk controller can read additional bytes and cache them. If the next 8K byte page is physically contiguous (which the file system data allocation policy can make more probable), the next read can be satisfied from the cache rather than requiring a physical read from the disk. Of course the page may have already been replaced from the cache also. For the most part we will not discuss the details of disk controllers. For multimedia systems the prefetching and caching that is useful for many general purpose applications are not effective; due to the lack of locality in most multimedia applications (see Section 3.1 for details). For a more detailed discussion of disks and disk controllers, we refer the reader to [RW94].

1.2.2 Disk reliability. Disk reliability has increased dramatically in the past decade. Often the mean time to failure of a single disk is on the order of 500, 000 hours or more. (Of course this varies with the disk model.) To give a little better perspective, one year is approximately 8, 000 hours so the mean time to failure is a little over 60 years. If we assume that all disks fail independently and at a constant rate (or equivalently that the time to failure is exponentially distributed) then a 100 disk system will have a mean time between some disk failing of 0.6 years or about every 7 months. However, it should be mentioned that it is not completely clear how the mean time to failure is estimated by manufacturers. One conjecture is that the aggregate time of all sold units is divided by the number of reported failures. This would then not account accurately for the degree of activity on the disks or for disks that failed but were not reported back to the manufacturer. Thus, for example, if disks are heavily used in a particular application, they could experience a higher failure rate.

1.2.3 The role of redundancy. Redundancy serves two purposes: reliability and load balancing. Reliability because if a device fails and makes one copy of some data unavailable, the other copy may be accessible. Performance can be enhanced if, when one device is heavily loaded, another copy of the data can be read from a less busy device. Sometimes one purpose is emphasized to the extent that the other is ignored completely but most often, they can both be served. Furthermore, if one considers not only performance under nominal conditions when all disks are operational, but also degraded mode operation with one or more disks failed, then load balancing can be a major consideration as we shall demonstrate later.

It is convenient to partition the consideration of data redundancy in disk based systems into two main categories: parity based and mirroring. Here mirroring is not limited to disk mirroring in which the contents of two disks are kept identical; we just mean that there is a complete, "in the clear" copy of every data block on two distinct disks. RAID (Level 5) [PGK88] is perhaps the best known example of parity based redundancy in disk storage. Due to space limitations we are not able to discuss all the variations of RAID technology in detail. (We refer the reader to an extensive survey in [CLG+94].) The original motivation for RAID was that smaller, slower disks were much more economical than large, fast disks. So, following the theme of making a large, powerful resource by combining a number of smaller, more cost effective resources, the RAID goal was to use a number of disks in parallel to get the effect of a larger, faster disk. Redundancy in the form of parity was motivated solely for reliability. An example of data layout in a RAID level 5 array is shown in Fig. 1.2. Data is meant to be striped across all the disks. The parity is precessed across the disks to balance the write load (a parity block has to be written whenever a data block is changed in the associated parity group). One of the interesting performance characteristics of RAID is that when a disk has failed, then the read load can double for each surviving disk in the array in Fig.1.2. This occurs under the following scenario. Assume that the reads are "small reads" in which some portion of a single block is read in each request. Then when a disk fails, consider a read request to a data block B on the failed disk which is in a parity group G. When a read request accesses block B, then all of the other blocks in parity group G have to be read in order to construct the contents of the unavailable block B (by exclusive OR of the other blocks in G). When the number of blocks in each parity group is the same as the number of disks in the array, then it is easy to see that every access to a data block on a failed disk can result in a request to read a block on each of the surviving disks. Assuming that the read requests were evenly distributed over the disks originally, it is easy to see that the rate of read requests will double on the surviving disks. If the maximum throughput of the surviving disks will not sustain a doubling of the read rate, the disks become the bottleneck and throttle the rate at which applications execute. In a real-time system such as a video server, this might mean lowering the quality of the video streams being served or even dropping some streams when a disk fails. (These issues will be discussed much more fully later in the context of particular types of systems.)

As already mentioned, in the case of RAID with parity, the redundancy is used solely for reliability[2]. In mirroring, there are several copies of the same

---

[2] One exception is the work reported in [BMW96, Bir97] which reports on the potential use of parity based redundancy for load balancing in video-on-demand systems.

data and either one can be read. So read requests can be thought of as directed to a logical block and the system can choose which copy to read. (Of course on a write, all copies have to be updated.) In the classic case of mirrored disks as illustrated in Fig. 1.1(a) pairs of disks contain identical content. In this case reads can be sent to disks according to which can provide the most efficient access, e.g., shortest seek [BG88]. Fig. 1.1(b) shows an alternative method of replication in which half of each disk is replicated on a neighboring disk (modulo the number of disks). This again allows a request to be directed to either of the disks containing a copy of the requested block. This form of data distribution is called Chained Declustering [HD90]. Comparing this to mirrored disks we observe that there is intuitively a bit more flexibility in load balancing in Chained Declustering since load on disk can be "shed" to either of the neighboring disks (assuming that not all of the requests are to the same half of the disk). Note that in either case, all data is accessible when only one disk is down. However, some combinations of two disks failing can cause some data to become inaccessible. To a first approximation the mean time until data is inaccessible is proportional to the number of combinations of two disks that cause data to be inaccessible. (All other things being equal such as mean time to repair the failed disk.) For mirrored disks the number of combinations of two disk causing data inaccessibility is $N/2$; for Chained Declustering it is N. So Chained Declustering is a less reliable but more flexible in load balancing in the no failure case. Even more to the credit of Chained Declustering is that when a disk has failed, it is much better able to spread the load among all of the surviving disks [HD90]. Theoretically at least it is possible to evenly spread the load among all the surviving disks while with mirrored disks the single survivor disk of a pair must handle the entire read load of the failed disk; thus doubling the read load on that disk. The ideal redistribution of load when a failure occurs in a Chained Declustering based system is illustrated in Fig. 1.1(b) and (c).

2. Parallel Database Systems

Database systems have been a target of parallelism for more than three decades. The application of parallelism to relational database systems in particular has been a tremendous success story [DG92]. Today commercial database systems with tens of terabytes of online storage and consisting of hundreds of processing nodes are in routine operation. To a large extent this success has been due to the declarative, set oriented nature of the relational model and relational languages (e.g., SQL). Using a declarative language separates the execution strategy from the statement of the query and permits optimizations and implementations to change without change to applications. Parallelization for example, can be realized transparently to the user or application program since any existing applications are oblivious to the changes

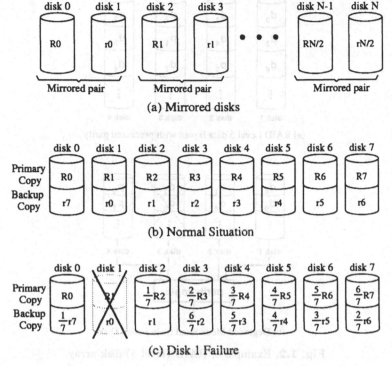

Fig. 1.1. Mirroring and Chained Declustering.

that may occur on the database side of the interface. In addition the relational model is set oriented and the basic relational operators are set oriented which leads to simple, natural parallelization for most operators. As a simple example, consider the SELECT operator that applies a predicate to each tuple in a table (set of tuples). In SQL this would be expressed as:

```
SELECT    *
FROM      T
WHERE     T.A = v
```

where T is a table and A is an attribute of tuples in T.

This query returns all tuples for which the value of attribute A equals v. For convenience in exposition we can express this query more succinctly as:

$SELECT_{A=v}(T)$

Then if $T = \bigcup_i T_i$ we can clearly rewrite the query as:

$SELECT_{A=v}(T) = \bigcup_i SELECT_{A=v}(T_i)$

which clearly expresses the parallelism available by doing the select operation on each subset of T and then merging (or unioning) the result. This is an example of *data parallelism*.

In the following sections we will consider the major issues in the design and implementation of parallel database systems. We first discuss advan-

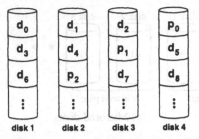

(a) RAID Level 5 data layout with precessed parity

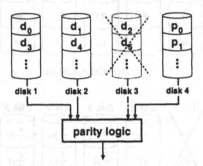

(b) Degraded Mode Read from Failed Disk

Fig. 1.2. Example of RAID (level 5) disk array.

tages and disadvantages of the three major types of organizations for such systems which are commonly known as: Shared Nothing, Shared Disk, and Shared Everything. Then we will concentrate on data layout strategies and indexing strategies for enhancing parallelism in query processing. Finally, fault-tolerance and other systems issues are discussed.

2.1 Database Architectures

There are three main architectures that have been identified for parallel database systems [Sto86]. These are illustrated in Figure 2.1. In a shared everything architecture all processors have access to all of memory as well as to all disks. The main advantages of this architecture are simplicity in the software design and flexibility in sharing resources. For example any degree of processor parallelism is easily supported since the processors form a resource pool of anonymous, identical resources [3] The main disadvantage of this architecture compared to the others, is lack of scalability and fault-tolerance. In a shared disk system each processor has its own private memory

---

[3] Affinity based processor scheduling complicates the situation a bit. This recognizes the benefit of rescheduling a task on the same processor if possible to minimize the degree to which the cache has to be reinitialized.

but all have access to all the disks. In this case, a query, or subquery, can be processed by any processor since all of the database is directly accessible to each processor. Advantages of this architecture include flexibility in assigning processors (since all are equally capable, including access to any part of the database) and some degree of fault tolerance is easily provided, since a failed processor module does not render any data inaccessible. The largest disadvantage of this architecture is that parts of the database can be cached in any processor's private memory and maintaining consistency of the database becomes a major issue. The final architecture is the shared nothing architecture in which disks and memory are accessible by a single processor. This is the most popular architecture for large systems. It scales well for set oriented databases and can be configured to provide a high degree of fault-tolerance by providing data redundancy and multiple access paths to data (e.g., dual ported disks with more than one processor able to access a disk).

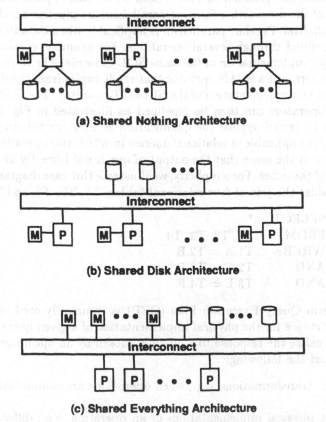

Fig. 2.1. Three basic types of parallel architectures for database systems.

We note that there are a large number of variations to these three basic architecture types. For example, a single node of a shared nothing architecture could be a "shared everything" symmetric multiprocessor. In addition, the physical system architecture should be distinguished from the software architecture. For example, a shared disk physical configuration may be organized as a shared nothing database implementation. In this case the database is partitioned logically and each processor, by design of the software, accesses only the data in one partition. In such a system the ability for any processor to access any disk is useful for a reconfiguration of responsibilities when a processor module has failed but is not used in normal operation.

2.2 Parallel Query Processing

The SQL example given above illustrated *partition parallelism* or *data parallelism* in which an operation on a set of data is executed in parallel on different partitions of the data. Other forms of parallelism are pipeline parallelism and *bushy parallelism*. Pipeline parallelism is applicable when data items in a set can be pipelined through several operations. For example, consider a possible physical implementation of the same SQL example. The implementation could be in terms of a SCAN operator that reads tuples from the disk storage system and an implementation of the SELECT operator. The SCAN and the SELECT operators can then be pipelined as illustrated in Fig. 2.3 so that tuples can be tested against the qualification as they are being read. *Bushy parallelism* is applicable in relational queries in which two operations have no dependency in the sense that the output of one is not (directly or indirectly) the input of the other. For simplicity, we illustrate this case diagrammatically only. Consider the join of four relational tables, T1, T2, T3, and T4.

```
SELECT    *
FROM      T1, T2, T3, T4
WHERE     T1.A = T2.B
AND       T2.C = T3.D
AND       T3.E = T4.F
```

The term Query Execution Plan (QEP) is commonly used to refer to a particular choice for the physical implementation of a given query. The QEP to use to realize the response to a query is chosen by an optimizer that takes into account the following:

- algebraic transformations, e.g., when operations are commutative or transitive.
- different physical implementations of an operation, e.g., different join algorithms, or use of an index versus a full scan of a table.
- statistics of the data, e.g., the selectivity of a qualification
- cost of operations, e.g., processor cycles, I/O operations, main memory

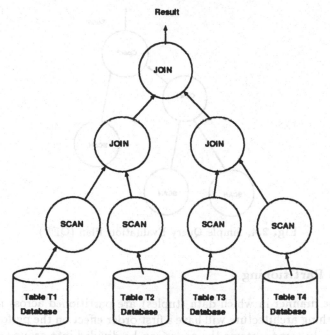

Fig. 2.2. Example of bushy parallelism.

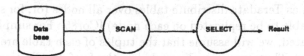

Fig. 2.3. Pipeline parallelism.

- interrelationship of operations, e.g., the output of one operation if it result in tuples in a certain order, can enable a more efficient implementation of the next operation.

From this point on we use an abstract representation of a QEP as a directed tree structure in which each node of the tree is the physical implementation of an operator. Such a QEP is illustrated in Fig. 2.4. The leaves of the QEP tree are generally SCAN operators which read from stored tables (or table segments) on disk. In general one should think of the arcs from an operator node to it's parent operator node as representing a flow of tuples. (There are cases where the complete output of an operator has to be accumulated before the parent operator can start. This occurs, for example, when the parent operator requires the tuples to be in some order and that order can only be guaranteed by collecting all the output and explicitly sorting the tuples. We will not cover this case explicitly for lack of space. In essence, one can partition the QEP into components based on where these *blocking operators* occur, such that each partition has simple data flow between operators.)

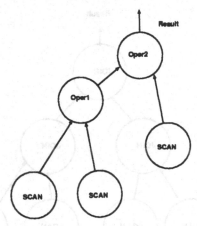

Fig. 2.4. Simple Query Evaluation Plan (QEP).

2.3 Data Partitioning

Clearly the manner in which data (tuples) are partitioned across nodes of a shared-nothing architecture will have a first order effect on the performance of the system. In some systems the nodes can be divided into groups and tables can be distributed over members of a particular group [BFG+95]. Other systems such as Teradata distribute tables over all nodes (or, for small tables, permit the table to be replicated on each node) [Cor85]. For simplicity, unless otherwise stated, we will assume that the tuples of each table are distributed over all nodes. There are several popular methods of distribution:

- hashing: here, if there are N nodes, a (set of) attributes of each tuple are hashed to a node number and the tuple is stored on that node. Most systems use one, system wide hash function. As we will see when we cover some specific query processing strategies, it is convenient that the same hash function is used for all tables.
- value based partitioning: here a user may specify a partition range for some attribute such that all tuples with attribute value in subrange i will be stored on node i.
- round robin: here each new tuple is stored on the next sequential node, modulo the number of nodes.

2.3.1 Prime key accesses. While round-robin is a simple method and results in an even distribution of tuples over the nodes, one strong disadvantage is that the distribution scheme gives no clue as to how to find a tuple based on any attribute value. Thus any simple key based access, e.g.:

    SELECT   balance
    FROM   Accounts
    WHERE   acct-num = 1234 ;

would require a subquery to be executed on each node (in the absence of an index on the attribute). On the other hand, assuming that the tuples are hashed on the acct-num attribute, the query manager can immediately direct the query to precisely the node that contains the record (assuming that the account number is a valid one). The same observation holds for the value partitioned data distribution method. Particularly for simple queries such as this example it is very important that the system can direct the query immediately to a particular node. Consider what happens with the round-robin scheme (again, assuming no appropriate index is available). Either nodes are accessed sequentially or all in parallel. In either case the number of nodes that must be sent a message is linear in the total number of nodes. For simplicity assume that all nodes are sent the query concurrently. Even if the processing of the query was insignificant on each node, if just receiving the message and responding to it took 1 msec. Then the entire system (independent of N) would have a maximum throughput of 1000 such queries per second. On the other hand, if only one node is sent the query, the total throughput is 1000xN.

Hashing is more popular than value based partitioning because it tends to balance the load automatically. However hashing has some obvious drawbacks for range searches. Let A be the attribute in a range query. If tuples have been value partitioned on the basis of attribute A, then only a subset of nodes, those with storage ranges that overlap the query range, have to be sent the query. Each searches its local segment of the table and the answer is the union of these responses. If rows are distributed based on some attribute other than A, then the query has to be sent to all storage nodes. At this point it is worthwhile to note that the distribution of data can be considered a *two-level* decision. The top level determines how data is partitioned among storage nodes. The second level determines how local data is organized (clustered, indexed, etc.) on a given storage node.

2.3.2 Join operations and data partitioning. We will consider only equi-joins where the condition is "T1.A = T2.B". Let A be the attribute on which $T1$ was hashed and B be the attribute on which $T2$ was hash. Further, let $T1_i$ be the portion of table $T1$ that resides on node i. A similar definition holds for the partitions of $T2$. Then, assuming that the same hash function is used for $T1$ and $T2$, it is clear that

$$T1 \; JOIN \; T2 \; = \; \bigcup_{i=1}^{N} \; T1_i \; JOIN \; T2_i$$

and the local joins can be carried out in parallel with a merge step at the end.

There are a number of obvious variations of this scheme. For example, if T2 was hash partitioned on attribute B but T1 was distributed in some other manner, then a possible strategy would be to "redistribute" the tuples of T1 based on attribute A, e.g., each node, in parallel, reads the local segment of $T1$, hashes each tuple adn sends it to the appropriate node based on the hash value. When distribution is complete, the local joins can be carried out and the results merged.

An alternative occurs when one table is very small (or there is a selection condition that few tuples satisfy). In this case, the small number of tuples can be replicated on all nodes and joined with the local partition of the second relation. This approach is captured in the following expression:

$$T1 \ JOIN \ T2 \ = \ \bigcup_{i=1}^{N} T1 \ JOIN \ T2_i$$

where $T1$ plays the role of the smaller set of tuples that is replicated on all nodes and $T2$ is partitioned over the nodes.

2.3.3 Indexing. Indicies are also tables. An index on attribute A of table T can be viewed as a table with entries of the form $[row - ID, A - value]$ with row-ID being the key. Viewed as tables we can consider the distribution of index entry tuples using the same methods as for base tables; round-robin, value partitioning and hashing. If we were to distribute index entries this way, the tuples should be distributed on the basis of the A-value, not the row-ID since we will want to look up row-IDs based on the A-value rather than the other way around. For example, consider a query to find the account balance based on the account holder's name. (This example is illustrated in Fig. 2.5(b).) Assume that the table key attribute and the basis for account tuple distribution is the account number. A secondary index based on the account holder's name could then be hash partitioned in the account holder's name. The query can then be efficiently answered by the following steps:

1. Hash the account holder's name to determine the node, j that contains the index entry for this name.
2. Send a message to node j to look up the index entry for the specified name (we assume that there is only one account with this holder's name).
3. Use the row-ID (which has the node number embedded) to forward the message to node i where the account tuple resides.
4. Nodes i processing task receives the message, uses the row-ID to look up the tuple and returns the tuple.

Note that only two nodes had to receive and process messages. Again, this allows the system to scale with the number of nodes.

Of course the efficiency of the scheme just outlined depends on there being one or just a small number of row-IDs for a given attribute value. As this number grows the cost will grow and at some point becomes a suboptimal strategy. A very different alternative for indexing is to store, on node i the index (sub)table for the rows of the base table that reside on node i. This type of index is illustrated in Fig. 2.5(a). For example. suppose there is an account type based on commercial, personal, public, trust, etc. and we wanted an index on this attribute. Assume, as is likely, that there would be a fair number of accounts of each type and that account tuples are hashed on account number. Then on each node we would have a mixture of account

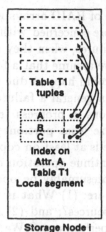

Storage Node i

(a) Indexing a Local Segment on a Storage Node

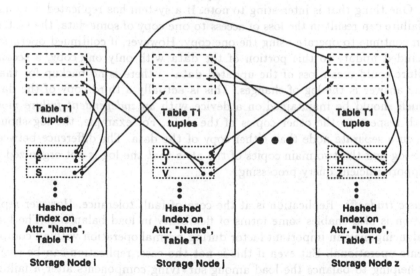

(b) Hashed Index: Index table entries are hashed to storage nodes.

Fig. 2.5. Options for organizing indexes.

types and we could have an index on account type just for the rows on node i, $1 \leq i \leq N$. To find all the tuples for a given type of account, the query is broadcast to all of the nodes and each node can use the index to efficiently locate the local tuples for accounts of the requested type.

2.4 Fault Tolerance

Fault tolerance is a strength of the shared-nothing architecture. Individual components or subsystems can be made fault tolerant independently of the database application, e.g., use of RAID arrays will make the disk subsystem more reliable. Here we are more concerned with the database systems issues associated with component failures, when they do happen ... as they will.

Within a parallel system we assume that a failure can occur which makes some data inaccessible. This could happen due to a connection network failure, a processor failure, etc. In general a failure will cause a system restart with an abort of all transactions in progress (not yet committed). In addition the system must recognize what portions of the system are no longer operational and whether there is at least on copy of all data accessible. If so, a decision can be made to continue operation once recovery procedures are completed. The system will presumably be operating in a degraded mode. Among the important issues are: (1) What is the performance hit due the loss of part of the system resources?; and (2) How quickly can the system be brought back to nominal performance? We will discuss these issues at a relatively high level rather than attempt to cover all of the details.

One thing that is interesting to note. If a system has replicated data and a failure can result in the loss of access to one copy of some data, the system can continue to operate using the one copy. However, if continued operation included update to this portion of the data with only one copy, a second failure could mean loss of the updated data ... there is no backup for that. One answer is the log of changes. This is actually a third copy of the data which should be maintained on a device with an *independent failure mode* with respect to the other copies of the data. For example, the log should be on a separate node than either copy of the data. The difference between the log and the two main copies of the at is that the log is not organized to support efficient query processing.

Basic tradeoffs. Replication is at the core of fault tolerance. However replication is also enables some forms of flexibility in load balancing. The load balancing may an important factor during normal operation with all components operational. But even if this is not the case, replication can be useful in helping to balance the load among surviving components after a failure. This can be very important since if one portion of the system that is slow the whole system can be slowed down due to dependencies between the throughput of the different components. Assuming a workload in which each job splits into a task for each node and then the job is done when all tasks have completed. Clearly if the work is evenly divided but one node is slower than the others, then this "slow node" will pace the entire system and reduce the overall throughput. A node being asked to handle a disproportionate share of the workload has the same effect as the node being slower; it does not complete tasks at the same average rate as the other nodes and slows the entire systems down. Note that if one node in a ten node system loses one tenth of its capacity, or gets one tenth more load than the other nodes, the whole system will go at only about 9o% of capacity ... each of the other nodes can only operate at 90% capacity. If there are 1000 nodes in the system, the same is true; the whole system only operates at about 90% capacity.

3. Multimedia Object Servers

As multimedia applications are relatively novel, we begin by describing their characteristics before proceeding to the discussion of the design of parallel multimedia storage servers. The main characteristics of multimedia applications that lead to difficulties in storage systems design are that they have very large bandwidth and storage requirements, often coupled with real-time constraints. Furthermore, different media types have vastly different storage, performance, and reliability requirements. For instance, text does not have large storage and bandwidth requirements ($\approx$ 12KB per page [DN91]) and is not delay sensitive, in a sense that it is still meaningful with arbitrary delays during the delivery. However, text is very sensitive to "integrity of data" issues. Images have large storage and bandwidth requirements (anywhere from $\approx$ 400 KB per bit mapped page [DN91] to $\approx$ 125 MB per radiology image such as an Xray [BGM+93]), but like text images are not (usually) sensitive to delays. Depending on the application, image data can be more or less sensitive to reliability issues; for instance, compression techniques used in medical imaging applications must be lossless, or at least preserve the integrity of the "critical" portions of the image. Video and audio are both examples of continuous media and are very sensitive to delay (or jitter) in data delivery. Video has very large storage and bandwidth requirements (e.g., color, full-screen, full-motion video requires $\approx$ 30 MB/sec [DN91]); relatively speaking, audio does not consume very much storage and bandwidth (e.g., digitized voice data only requires $\approx$ 8 KB/sec [DN91]). Neither video nor audio is as sensitive to reliability issues as numeric data since there is some redundancy inherently present (with respect to human perception) in these types of media.

Thus, one challenging task in designing multimedia storage systems is satisfying the real-time requirement of continuously transmitting a multimedia object (e.g., a video) with specific bandwidth requirements; for instance, if this object is a movie, then, once it begins, it must be displayed continuously for the duration of the film at a specified bandwidth. Another challenging aspects of designing multimedia storage systems is providing *on-demand* (or near on-demand) service to multiple clients simultaneously, and thus realizing economies of scale; that is, users expect to access objects, e.g., movies, within a small and "reasonable" latency, upon request, where latency can be attributed to deficiency of resources at any level of the storage hierarchy (e.g., disk bandwidth, buffer space, and so on), at the time the request is made.

Another significant challenge is that designs of storage systems that succeed for "small" versions of multimedia applications often simply do not scale-up. Therefore (although "small" versions currently exist) without properly architectured storage systems, we will not be able to build "large" versions of these applications. For instance, consider two applications, Application-1, which is a Video-on-Demand (VOD) system that delivers popular movies (e.g., top 10 movies for that week) and Application-2, also a VOD system *but* one that delivers all possible movies, T.V. programs, documentaries, and so on that were ever made. A storage architecture that was designed to support the first application (for instance, one approach is to use a reasonable size RAID system), will not not simply scale-up to support the second application, i.e., we will not be able to support the second application by increasing the number of disks in the RAID system, and furthermore, we will not be able to cost-effectively scale it up by "stringing together" a collection of RAID systems. This is due to the differences in user access patters and storage and retrieval costs between the two applications. In other words, not only does Application-2 have to store significantly larger amounts of data, but it must also service requests for very popular and therefore cheaper to deliver movies as well as movies that are rarely accessed and whose storage and delivery costs are therefore difficult to amortize over multiple requests. Moreover, because it is difficult to make such a grand scale system cost-effective, there is a need for economy of scale, i.e., support of concurrent access by a several orders of magnitude larger "audience".

Thus, a whole new storage architecture is needed to make an economical transition from Application-1 to Application-2. For instance, one step in the right direction would be to use a *multilevel* storage hierarchy with proper *migration* of data through the hierarchy, where less frequently accessed objects are stored at lower levels *with* proper schemes in place for migrating them up the hierarchy in a timely manner that satisfies real-time or other constraints of the media involved, e.g., video. Note that involving a different level of a storage hierarchy in one's design (for instance, using a disk-based system when we can no longer guarantee that the data for our application will fit in main memory) necessarily requires a whole different set of data storage and retrieval techniques. This is due to the significant architectural differences between various types of storage devices which result in vastly different performance and reliability characteristics.

Real-time or continuity constraints, large bandwidth, large storage, and concurrent access by multiple users — these are "old" (although not necessarily solved) challenges, found in the context of VOD servers. Although a lot of important aspects of multimedia information servers have been illustrated in the context of such systems, this is only the tip of the iceberg, in the sense that video-on-demand is a relatively simple application. There exists a multitude of interesting and important applications, and they all require support of an efficient storage system. Below, we describe a few of the more challenging new applications.

As wireless and mobile communication matures, mechanisms for effective mobile access to multimedia information are becoming increasingly important. One challenging problem is the delivery of multimedia data, including continuous media, such as video, over relatively low bandwidth channels to devices with relatively little memory. Furthermore, as we overcome the technological difficulties in graphics and image processing fields, another challenging problem that begins to emerge is the (real-time) delivery of multimedia data to 3D display or virtual/augmented reality applications. These applications exhibit similar (to VOD servers) real-time requirements but are far more interactive. For instance, these include architectural walk-throughs, various scientific visualization problems, distributed multimedia warfare simulations, medical imaging applications, and many more. Most current state-of-the-art systems can only handle 3D or virtual worlds that can fit in main memory. Current needs call for worlds that will not even fit on disk-based systems.

Thus the new applications result in new challenges, namely having to deal with interactive, mobile, and wireless environments. Interactivity means that we must deal with unpredictable changes in workloads. Mobility combined with more traditional problems of component failures, such as disk and communication link failure, means that we must deal with an "unstable" and constantly changing topology of (both storage and communication) systems. Note that one challenge is that availability of resources in the communication and delivery mechanism must affect the behavior of the storage system. Another challenge is that wireless communication combined with large bandwidth and storage requirements of multimedia data necessarily means that (at least in wireless/mobile environments) we have to deliver information using *relatively* small amounts of resources, for instance small "pipes" for delivery over wireless networks, small amounts of memory in mobile units, as compared to the size required by the entire application, and so on.

In summary, in designing and building large high performance multimedia storage systems, one must consider a whole spectrum of applications, from relatively low bandwidth, high throughput, and "just-in-time" delivery of video-on-demand servers to very high bandwidth, relatively low volume, and "ASAP" delivery of supercomputing/scientific applications. Such systems must be able to accommodate the various storage, performance, and reliability requirements of the different types of media and applications.

3.1 Resources and Performance Metrics

The resources that are considered in the context of multimedia applications in this chapter, for the most part, include:

- *I/O bandwidth:* including, disk and tertiary device bandwidth
- *storage space:* including, buffer space, disk space, and tertiary storage space

The issues that arise in management of these resource when delivering multimedia data are as follows:

- *data layout:* placement of objects (or portions of objects) on either secondary or tertiary storage
- *scheduling*[4] *:* allocation of (either disk or tertiary store) bandwidth as well
  as buffer space to requests for either reading or writing of objects
- *access (or admission) control:* admission of new requests into the system,
  in such a way as to still guarantee timely delivery of existing requests
- *fault tolerance:* recovery from failure of various hardware components of
  the storage server, (possibly in real-time)
- *management of the storage hierarchy:* at which level of the storage hierarchy
  does an object belong, and when should it be moved (fully or partially) to
  a higher or lower level of the hierarchy

where there is a multitude of criteria for choosing a particular resource management scheme which include: load balancing, increasing throughput, avoiding storage and bandwidth fragmentation problems, and so on.

The amount of each resource (as described above) plus the data layout, scheduling, access control, fault tolerance, and hierarchy management
schemes that are used, determine the *quality of service* (QoS) that can be
provided by a particular system. Although quality of service is a somewhat
vague term, for the purposes of this chapter we will discuss it in terms of:

- *latency (or response time):* for continuous media, the amount of time that
  elapses between the moment a request enters the system and the time
  when we can start streaming the required bits off the disks; for the non-
  continuous media, the amount of time that elapses between the moment a
  request enters the system and the time the data block is retrieved from the
  storage subsystem (network communication issues will not be considered
  here)
- *throughput:* number of requests that can be supported simultaneously
- *jitter:* variation in delay bounds (i.e., the difference between maximum and
  minimum delay in receiving a block of data)
- *reliability:* behavior under hardware failure

In addition to considering a particular metric to describe the quality of service
provided by a storage server, we also make a distinction between *deterministic*
and *stochastic* QoS guarantees. Deterministic guarantees correspond to striv-
ing for no jitter (i.e., probability of missing a deadline equal to zero) which
usually results in making worst-case assumptions about the demands of the
system workload, when designing data layout, scheduling, admission control,
etc. techniques. In contrast, stochastic guarantees imply some amount of jitter in the system (i.e., probability of missing a deadline is greater than zero).

---

[4] There are also *synchronization* issues which arise in delivery of multimedia objects; for instance, in multimedia conferencing applications where voice and
video data can be transmitted from different servers and jitter in network delivery can cause the two streams to lose synchronization [RR93]. However, we
do not discuss synchronization issues here.

Thus, deterministic guarantees result in better QoS provisions but in poorer resource utilization, whereas stochastic guarantees result in more efficient use of resources, but at the cost of some amount of QoS — in many cases, in designing the data layout, scheduling, admission control, etc. schemes, we can tradeoff QoS for efficient use of resources, i.e., there is a continuum of choices here and we can control the degradation in the QoS based on user/application requirements. We come back to this issue and discuss it in more detail later in the chapter.

3.1.1 Storage and retrieval of continuous media. We begin with the delivery of continuous media, such as video and audio. As already mentioned, one difficulty in the delivery of continuous (or delay sensitive) media is the satisfaction of the real-time constraint, where the constraint is not real-time in the sense of a deadline for starting the delivery, but rather in the sense of providing continuity, once the delivery begins. In other words, once we start delivering a video or an audio object, we must maintain the specified bandwidth for that object, for the entire duration of that object's display. Below, we briefly describe basic principles and tradeoffs in delivery of continuous media from the disk subsystem.

Consider the transmission of data, from the disks to the display stations, as illustrated in Fig. 3.1. The object transmission begins on the disk subsys-

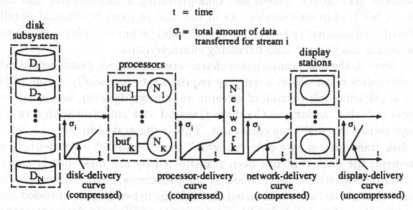

Fig. 3.1. Transmission of Data .

tem, in its compressed form, and continues through the processors and the network (again, in its compressed form). The "display-delivery" curve depicts the true bandwidth requirements or continuity requirements of a continuous media object (e.g., in it's uncompressed form a video objects displayed on television in U.S. requires a frame rate of 30 frames per second).

Given the current magnetic disk technology, in many cases, a single disk can service multiple continuous streams simultaneously; for instance, given an effective disk bandwidth of 5 MB/s and MPEG-2 streams which might require, for example, a 0.5 MB/s playout rate, a single disk should be able to service on the order of 10 MPEG-2 streams simultaneously. Here lies part of the difficulty in designing cost effective continuous media servers, i.e., a cost-effective server design must efficiently *multiplex* a single disk's bandwidth between multiple streams.

Another difficulty in designing continuous media storage servers is the need to provide for potentially *variable* bit rate requirements of a compressed continuous media stream. That is, depending on the compression algorithm used, the resulting continuous media stream might exhibit either variable bit rate (VBR) or constant bit rate (CBR) transmission requirements (see [MPE90]). One advantage of using VBR encoding (as opposed to CBR) is the constant *quality* of video that can be provided throughout the duration of an object's display. However, VBR video can exhibits significant variability in required video display rates. This variability can affect resource utilization in the system and complicate scheduling of both transmission of objects over a communication network as well as their retrieval from the storage subsystem.

Given the storage and bandwidth requirements of multimedia objects, yet another difficulty is the need, in large scale systems, to deal with parallel or distributed architectures of such servers. Such architectures necessarily imply a *partitioning* of system resources, at least to a certain degree, which, under possibilities of skews in data access, becomes a critical issue in maintaining a balanced load on the system and thus providing a cost-effective and high performance multimedia service. As in the case of more traditional parallel or distributed database systems, data placement techniques play a major role in achieving the desired load balancing characteristics.

In general, the disk transmission characteristics can not match exactly the characteristics of an object's delivery requirements (especially, if one of the goals is efficient multiplexing of streams on storage devices), but a delivery scheme is "valid" as long as the disks transmit at a sufficiently high rate to always satisfy the real-time constraint. This is illustrated in Fig. 3.1, where the disk transmission rate only "roughly" matches the object's delivery requirement; the data that has been transmitted by the disks but is not yet due at a display station, is buffered at the processors. In this discussion, we assume that the data is transmitted through the network in compressed form to reduce the network bandwidth requirements and is only decompressed at a display station; in addition, we assume that a display station performs the decompression, and that it is not capable of buffering more than a few frames, i.e., any buffering required by the scheduling schemes must be provided by the video server.

In order for the storage server to insure the satisfaction of the real-time constraint, it is necessary for the "disk-delivery" curve (see Fig. 3.1) to either coincide with or stay above the "transmission-requirement" curve (see Fig. 3.2(a)). We define two basic categories of schemes for delivery of compressed data: (1) *constant-bit-rate* (CBR) schemes, which transmit the data from the disks at a constant rate for each object, as illustrated in Fig. 3.2(a) and

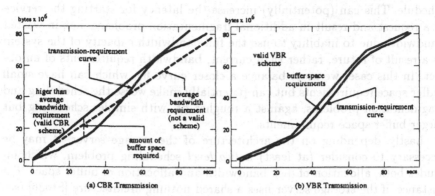

(a) CBR Transmission   (b) VBR Transmission

Fig. 3.2. Disk Transmission.

(2) *variable-bit-rate* (VBR) schemes, which adjust the transmission rate to more closely match an object's requirements, as illustrated in Fig. 3.2(b). To *guarantee*[5] satisfaction of the real-time constraint with a constant-bit-rate scheme, we would have to pick a higher than average transmission rate for each object, i.e., in Fig. 3.2(a), the line representing a "valid" constant-bit-rate scheme would have to always stay above the "transmission-requirement" curve, where the space between the line and the curve represents the buffering requirements. An advantage of using a constant-bit-rate scheme is that we can take advantage of *simple* scheduling and data layout techniques (e.g., as in [BGM+94]). A disadvantage of such a scheme is that it can result in large buffer space requirements, if the highest transmission rate required by an object is not representative of the rest of the transmission-requirement curve. Large buffer space requirements could result in a restriction on the number of requests that can be serviced simultaneously, even when the bandwidth needed to service these requests is available, i.e., the buffer limitations, rather than the maximum bandwidth of the system, might prove to be the bottleneck.

A variable-bit-rate scheme (whose "disk-delivery" curve must still stay above the "trans-mission-requirement" curve) would help remedy the buffer space problem, since it gives more control over the buffer usage; this is shown in Fig. 3.2(b) where a piecewise-linear curve is constructed to better fit the bandwidth requirements of the object. However, such a scheme could result in significant complications in the scheduling algorithms (e.g., as in [LL95, NMH95]). In order to schedule a new request with a variable-bit-rate scheme, it is not sufficient to consider the current bandwidth availability of the system; instead, the availability of the necessary bandwidth for the entire

---

[5] For simplicity of exposition, here we assume *deterministic* QoS guarantees; later we discuss *statistical* QoS guarantees.

duration of an object's display must be taken into consideration (at admission control time) in order to decide where a new request "fits" into the current schedule. This can (potentially) increase the latency for starting the service of a request and result in additional fragmentation problems, i.e., in wasted bandwidth due to inability to use the full bandwidth capacity of the system as a result of future, rather than current, bandwidth requirements of an object. In this case, we must balance a closer curve fit, which can have small buffer space requirements but can potentially make worse the scheduling and fragmentation problems, against a rougher fit, with simpler scheduling but larger buffer space requirements.

Lastly, depending on the architecture of the storage server, it may be necessary to consider (at least) a *two level* scheduling problem, which includes both, allocation of disk bandwidth and allocation of buffer space. For instance, if the storage server uses a shared-nothing architecture [Sto86] (see Fig. 2.1(a)), then the buffer pool would have to be distributed among all its nodes. In this case, when scheduling a request, it is necessary to consider not only the total amount of buffer space that it will require, but also which node(s) of the storage server will need to allocate that buffer space. In general, in a large scale server, multi-level scheduling of system resources is needed.

3.1.2 Storage and retrieval of non-continuous media. Although the storage and retrieval of text and image data are not constrained by continuity requirements, there are still some difficult issues that must be addressed in the context of storage and delivery of these non-continuous types of media. More specifically, even without the continuity requirements, applications using such media exhibit very large storage and very large (aggregate) bandwidth requirements. For example, a simple bit mapped page requires on the order of 400KB of storage [DN91]. Or, consider medical imaging applications such as radiology [SK94], where centers like UCLA's produce several terabytes of radiology images annually. Furthermore, for certain types of applications, there could still be real-time constraints, but in the more traditional sense of having a deadline rather than providing continuity; for instance, emergency medical care applications.

Other data and storage intensive applications include scientific applications, e.g., a 3-D perspective rendering system [CKH+92], which computes a perspective view of a planet's surface by integrating satellite image data (where each image is on the order of 850MB) with surface elevation data, where each resulting image or frame is on the order of 8MB and the resulting animation runs at 30 frames per second.

Since these applications require significant amounts of storage, bandwidth, as well as computation, high performance parallel or distributed mass storage systems play an important role in the successful design of multimedia information systems [GH94, LSP94]. By mass storage servers [CHC+93, CKH+92] we mean integrated systems consisting of a multitude of network attached storage devices whose function it is to provide cheap and rapid access to vast amounts of data. Although thus far in this section we have given examples of non-continuous media applications, mass storage systems can also be considered for use as archives for continuous media data, for applications such as video-on-demand. Consider Fig. 3.3 where the mass storage system serves as an archive of videos to a collection of (local) VOD servers, each one serving a different neighborhood, for instance.

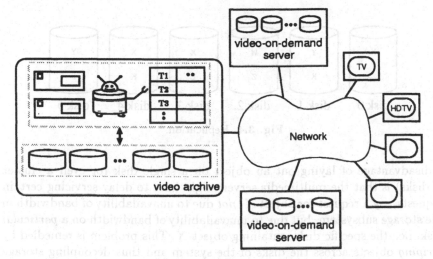

Fig. 3.3. Video Archive.

3.1.3 Combining continuous and non-continuous media.

One challenging issue that must be addressed when combining continuous media and non-continuous media in one information system is the issue of scheduling [And93]. This is not a trivial issues due to the differences in delay sensitivity of the different media types. For instance, when scheduling continuous media, such as video or audio, we must be careful to provide continuity in its delivery; however, as long as we manage to stay on schedule with respect to continuity, we can use any access capacity to service other types of media, i.e., there is nothing to be gained[6] from being ahead of schedule on delivery of continuous data.

3.2 Data Layout

As already mentioned, depending on the architecture of the system, proper data placement can be a central issue in insuring efficient use of disk bandwidth in a multimedia server, especially under skews in data access. In many

---

[6] In fact, there is something to be lost, namely, buffer space.

cases, data placement also has a direct effect on the scheduling techniques that can be used for data retrieval. Below, we describe the basic issues that need to be considered in designing a data placement scheme in a parallel I/O environment.

One approach would be to place an entire video object on a single disk, e.g., as in [RV93, BMC94, OLW95, GKS95], where skews in data access can be addressed through replication of popular objects (the number of copies of each object would be proportional to its popularity), as in Fig. 3.4. However,

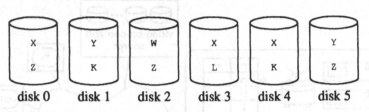

Fig. 3.4. Replication.

a disadvantage of laying out an object on a single disk (or even a cluster of disks) is that the multimedia server might have to delay servicing certain requests, say a request for object X, *not* due to unavailability of bandwidth in the storage subsystem, but due to unavailability of bandwidth on a *particular* disk, i.e., the specific disk containing object X. This problem is remedied by *striping* objects across the disks of the system and thus decoupling storage allocation from bandwidth allocation (as in [BGM+94]).

The basic idea behind striping is that all objects are striped across all the disks in the system. Each object is divided into subobjects, which corresponds to the amount of data to be read from a single disk (refer to Fig. 3.5) in a single *time interval*, where a time interval is the amount of time a disk needs to position its head and read the subobject. The size of a subobject is chosen

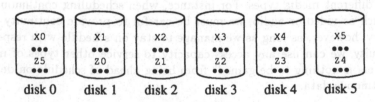

Fig. 3.5. Striping.

to be sufficiently large to amortize the seek and rotational latency over a large enough number of bytes to obtain most of the available disk bandwidth. If subobject X_i of object X is placed on disk k then subobject X_{i+1} is placed on disk $k + 1$ (modulo the number of disks).

Scheduling transmission of object X works as follows. We first find the time interval in which the disk corresponding to X's first subobject, namely disk 0 in our example, is idle. This is the time slot, time t, in which we can begin transmitting X, i.e., at time t we can transmit X_0 from disk 0, then at time $t + 1$ we can transmit X_1 from disk 1, etc. Note that, because the subobjects of X are *striped* across all the clusters in the system, after transmitting X_0 at time t, disk 0 is free to satisfy other requests at time $t + 1$, e.g., requests for object Z. In other words, the latency for starting the transmission of object Z, in this case, would be a single time interval (something on the order of a third of a second [BGM+94]). Thus, given a large disk subsystem (on the order of 100's of disks) the maximum latency experienced by a request (when there is bandwidth available in the system) would be on the order of a few minutes; compare this to (possibly) a 2 hour delay when storing an entire object on a single disk.

As already mentioned, an advantage of striping is that it decouples *data layout* from *bandwidth allocation*. Simply stated, it enables the storage server to continue servicing incoming requests as long as there is bandwidth available in the disk subsystem which is done by avoiding bottleneck formation by distributing each object across all the disks in the system, thus balancing the system's load without resorting to replication of data. In a multimedia system, such as an on-demand video server, disk space is limited, in the sense that only a fairly small fraction of the objects can reside on secondary storage. Eliminating the need for replication increases the number of disk-resident objects and therefore reduces the probability of having to satisfy a request by fetching an object from tertiary storage. Increasing the number of simultaneously serviced requests without resorting to replication of data results in a significant improvement in the response time of requests.

However, the approach of striping each object across all the disks in the system suffers from the several shortcomings. A processing node can only be attached to a limited number of disks, therefore, a multi-node system must be considered which results in additional complexity, e.g., some form of synchronization in delivery of a single object from multiple nodes would have to be addressed. In addition, it is not practical to assume that a system can be constructed from homogeneous disks, i.e., as the system grows[7] we would be forced to use disks with different transfer and storage capacity characteristics — having to stripe objects across heterogeneous disks would lead to further complications. Finally, an increase in the size of the disk subsystem will result in (potential) "restriping" of all objects. To address these shortcomings, one could consider a "hybrid" approach, that is: (a) divide the disk subsystem into clusters, (b) only stripe a particular object *within* a cluster (but not between clusters), and (c) replicate popular objects on different clusters. The replication of popular objects will aid in dealing with load imbalance under

---

[7] The need to purchase additional disks can be due either to a growth in user demand or to disk failures and the need to replace those disks.

skewed data access (see Section 3.3 for details), and limiting of striping to a cluster will aid in dealing with the heterogeneity problem (i.e., only disks within a cluster need be homogeneous).

Lastly, there are also various issues that arise in the context of data layout of subobjects on a single disk, e.g., as in the following works [RV93, BMC94, OLW95, GKS95]. However, for the sake of brevity and because these considerations are not directly related to parallel I/O issues, we omit these here.

3.3 Scheduling

Although, scheduling techniques are partly determined by the data layout schemes, there are still issues to be considered in proper bandwidth allocation to existing requests in a manner that would insure (at least to some degree) that quality of service constrains are satisfied. In the remainder of this section we use the notation given in Fig. 3.6.

$\tau_{seek} = $ maximum seek time (from inner to outer cylinder)

$\tau_{trk} = $ max. time attributable to reading a track as well as the speedup & slowdown fraction of the seek time

$B = $ number of bytes per track

$D = $ number of disks in the system

$T_t(r) = $ maximum time to read r tracks $T_t(r) = \tau_{seek} + r * \tau_{trk}$

$T_{cyc} = $ cycle time (sec)

$N = $ (max) total number of active streams in a system

$k_r = $ number of tracks read in a "read cycle" per stream

$k_t = $ number of tracks trasmitted per stream per cycle; assume that it's an integer multiple of k_t where k_r / k_t is the num. of cycles between "read cycles" for a stream

$b_0 = $ object bw req. (MB/s)

Fig. 3.6. Parameters.

A simple approach to data retrieval of N streams from the disk subsystem is to schedule each stream independently. Such a scheme is illustrated in Fig. 3.7, where the schedule, in each time interval of length T, consists of first retrieving a block of data for object A, then a block for object B, and so on. The buffer space requirements, for all N streams in this case are $(N + 1) * B$, and the proper value of T or conversely N is determined as follows (the time interval and corresponding disk efficiency in these scheduling schemes can be controlled by choices of both, N and B).

The amount of time needed to playout B bytes of data is $T = \frac{k_t * B}{b_0}$. Given a system of D disks, we must also insure that there is sufficient time to

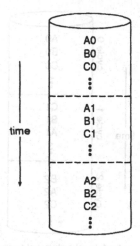

AO
BO
CO
⋮

A1
B1
C1
⋮

A2
B2
C2
⋮

time

schedule, not physical layout
(for one logical disk)

Fig. 3.7. Independent Data Retrieval.

retrieve data for all N streams during this time interval T, i.e., $\frac{N}{D} * T_t(k_r) \leq T$ which implies that $\frac{N}{D}(\tau_s eek + k_r * \tau_{trk}) \leq \frac{k_1 * B}{b_0}$. Thus, the maximum number of streams that we can admit, per disk, in such a parallel disk system is $\frac{N}{D} = \left[\frac{B * k_1}{b_0}\right] / [\tau_{seek} + k_r * \tau_{trk}]$.

Since response time of a magnetic disk is composed of seek time, rotational latency, and transfer time, one approach to improving the system's performance, and more specifically its throughput, is to reduce the amount of time that is spent on performing disk seeks and thus increase the effective disk bandwidth, e.g., as in cycle-based scheduling [TPB+93]. As is clear from the above equations, in treating each stream independently we are potentially paying a full seek for each stream access.

In cycle-based scheduling algorithms, the retrieval of data from the disk sub-system, for servicing continuous requests, is performed on a cyclic basis where each cycle is of length T and in each cycle, the system retrieves data for N streams, as illustrated in Fig. 3.8. Note that in cycle-based scheduling algorithms, the transmission of data retrieved in the ith cycle does not start until the beginning of the $(i+1)^{st}$ cycle[8]. As already stated, this is motivated by the increased opportunities for performing seek optimization (i.e., data blocks needed for service are retrieved using a SCAN-type algorithm). The cost of this optimization is that the system needs additional buffer space to hold the retrieved data until the beginning of the next cycle. This cycle-based

---

[8] That is, here we assume that the server is responsible for maintaining the continuity in data delivery, where the clients have relatively little buffer space. Thus, if the data delivery is not "offset" by one cycle from data retrieval, jitter may occur (due to seek optimization).

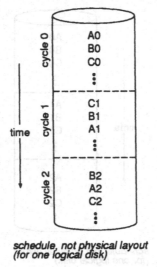

schedule, not physical layout
(for one logical disk)

Fig. 3.8. Cycle Based Scheduling on a Single Logical Disk.

or (group-based) approach to servicing continuous streams is, for instance, suggested in [CKY93, TPB+93, YCK92], and the tradeoff between improved utilization of the disk bandwidth (due to seek optimization) and the need for additional buffer space is analyzed in several works[9], e.g., [CKY93, BGM95, YCK92]. One important consequence of the schemes in [TPB+93] is that a high degree of system reliability and continued data delivery can be assured in the event of disk failure (e.g., as in [BGM95]). We discuss this in more detail in Section 3.5.

A generalization of cycle-based scheduling to multiple parallel disk clusters is illustrated in Fig. 3.9. (Other improvements are possible, but we omit these due to lack of space.) In this case, the cycle time is determined as follows, $T_{cyc} = \frac{k_t*B}{b_0}$. In order to insure that there is sufficient time in a cycle to read data for all N streams we must have that $T_t\left(\frac{N*k_r}{D}\right) \le T_{cyc}$ which implies that $\tau_{seek} + \frac{N*k_r}{D}*\tau_{trk} \le \frac{k_t*B}{b_0}$. Thus, the maximum simultaneous number of streams that we could service under this scheme, per disk in a parallel disk system with D disks, is $\frac{N}{D} \le \left[\frac{B*k_r}{b_0} - \tau_{seek}\right]/[k_r * \tau_{trk}]$. Compare this to the maximum number of streams that can be serviced under the independent retrieval scheme above. Of course, the tradeoff is the increase in buffer space needed to support this scheme; in this case, assuming double buffering, it is $2 * N * B$.

Improvements in system throughput can also be achieved through replication of popular objects (as suggested in the previous section). An interesting approach, using replicated data, is considered in [WSY95], where techniques

---

[9] In general, larger values of N_c afford better seek optimization opportunities, but they also result in larger buffer space requirement.

schedule,
not physical
layout

	Cluster 0				Cluster 1				Cluster 2			
	disk0	disk1	disk2	disk3	disk4	disk5	disk6	disk7	disk8	disk9	disk10	disk11
cycle 0	A0 B0 C0 ⋮	A1 B1 C1 ⋮	A2 B2 C2 ⋮	A3 B3 C3 ⋮	X0 Y0 Z0 ⋮	X1 Y1 Z1 ⋮	X2 Y2 Z2 ⋮	X3 Y3 Z3 ⋮	J0 K0 L0 ⋮	J1 K1 L1 ⋮	J2 K2 L2 ⋮	J3 K3 L3 ⋮
cycle 1					A3 B3 C3 ⋮	A4 B4 C4 ⋮	A5 B5 C5 ⋮	A6 B6 C6 ⋮	X3 Y3 Z3 ⋮	X4 Y4 Z4 ⋮	X5 Y5 Z5 ⋮	X6 Y6 Z6 ⋮
cycle 2									A6 B6 C6 ⋮	A7 B7 C7 ⋮	A8 B8 C8 ⋮	A9 B9 C9 ⋮

time

Fig. 3.9. Cycle Based Scheduling on Multiple Parallel Clusters.

from resource allocation theory [IK88] are used to determine how many copies of each disk resident video should be stored and then the so-called "DASD Dancing" algorithm is used to shift the load *dynamically*, between copies of *currently* displayed streams, to accommodate changes in the workload and improve performance through better load balancing. An example of the distribution of objects on 9 disk clusters, under this scheme, is illustrated in Fig. 3.10, where each node of the graph corresponds to a disk cluster. The

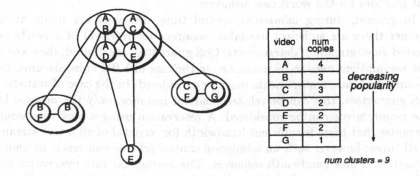

video	num copies	
A	4	
B	3	*decreasing popularity*
C	3	
D	2	
E	2	
F	2	
G	1	

num clusters = 9

Fig. 3.10. DASD Dancing.

number of copies of each object is determined by its popularity. Short-term fluctuations in workload and the resulting load imbalance on the disk clusters is addressed by dynamically shifting streams, while they are being played out, from one cluster to another; the potential shifts of streams are depicted by edges between nodes in the example of Fig. 3.10. One important advantage of this technique is that it easily allows for use of heterogeneous disks and thus can make system expansions significantly simpler.

Lastly, another scheduling technique that can be used to improve the system throughput is sharing of data between requests for popular objects. As this is not directly related to parallel I/O consideration, we omit data sharing issues from this chapter.

3.4 Admission Control

Unlike traditional database systems, multimedia storage servers must exercise some form of admission control due to the real time constraints of continuous media retrievals, i.e., some form of guarantee on future availability of bandwidth capacity must be made in order to satisfy the real time constraints. In the previous section we illustrated this concept in the context of specific scheduling techniques. Below, we give a more general treatment of this topic.

Many different approaches to allocating (or reserving) bandwidth, at admission control time, for servicing video streams are possible. For instance, one can either admit new requests only when *deterministic* guarantees can be made (e.g., as in [BGM+94]) that there are sufficient resource available in the system to service this new request, or one can provide *statistical* guarantees at admission control time (e.g., as in [SZK+96]). For instance, in [VGG+94], the authors investigate the benefits of a *statistical* admission control algorithm by considering distributions of access times and playback rates. In other words, they use an aggressive admission control policy which improves system utilization (at the cost of QoS) as compared to a deterministic policy that provides for the worst case behavior.

In general, during *admission control* time, decisions are made about whether there are sufficient available resources for retrieval of a newly requested video stream. If deterministic QoS guarantees are desired, then worst-case assumptions need to be made, i.e., in the case of VBR video streams, the stream's *peak* rate requirements must be considered. In the case of statistical QoS guarantees, this can be relaxed, and for instance, only the *average* bit rate requirements can be considered. A reservation using a *peak* rate would guarantee that there is sufficient bandwidth for retrieval of all active streams at all times; however such an admission control scheme can result in under-utilization of disk bandwidth resources. The average bit rate reservation can utilize resources more efficiently, but leads to potential congestions (due to the variability of the stream bandwidth demand); this congestion would either have to be resolved through a scheduling scheme or a user will experience a degradation in QoS. Below, we illustrate this concept in more detail, in the context of cycle based scheduling.

Stochastic vs. deterministic QoS guarantees. One important design parameter in cycle-based scheduling is the actual value of the cycle length T. In general, the value of T is a function of the *maximum* number of continuous requests, N_c, that can be service by the system within a cycle and the degree of QoS that the system can provide. For instance, when insuring jitter-free retrieval/delivery of data, i.e., providing *deterministic (or worst-case) guarantees* [TPB+93, BGM95], T can determined by considering the maximum time needed to retrieve N_c data blocks by scanning a disk. Formally, T can be expressed as:

$$T = \tau_{seek}^{max}(N_c) + N_c * \left(\tau_{rot}^{max} + \tau_{tfr}^{max}\right) \tag{3.1}$$

where $\tau_{seek}^{max}(N_c)$ refers to the worst case seek time for servicing N_c requests, i.e., when these N_c requests are uniformly distributed across the disk surface [GM98], τ_{rot}^{max} refers to the worst case rotational latency (i.e., a full rotation if we assume that the disk cannot support zero latency reads [RW94]), and τ_{tfr}^{max} refers to the worst case transfer time. Given a variable bit rate (VBR) stream (e.g, an MPEG-2 stream), the worst case transfer time can be determined by the peak display rate. Based on the above assumptions, the value of T will provide deterministic guarantee (e.g., all requests will receive service before the end of the cycle). However, the undesirable effect is that it can result in poor disk bandwidth utilization when there is a large deviation between the peak and the mean display rate.

Another approach to determining the value of T is to provide *statistical guarantees*. That is, let τ_{N_c} be the random variable representing the service time of N_c continuous requests. Then, the system guarantees that the probability of the event where τ_{N_c} is greater than T is less than some predefined system parameter, e.g., p. Mathematically, we have:

$$\text{Prob}[\tau_{N_c} \geq T] \leq p \tag{3.2}$$

One can rely, for instance, on the Chernoff's bound[10] [Kle75] to determine the value of T so as to service N_c requests under the probability constraint p. Let $F_{N_c}^*(s)$ be the Laplace transform for the random variable τ_{N_c} and let $F_{rot}^*(s)$ and $F_{tfr}^*(s)$ be the Laplace transforms for the random variables of rotational latency time and data transfer time, respectively. Since a cycle-based algorithm employs seek optimization (e.g., some form of a SCAN-type algorithm) and since the worst case seek time occurs when these N_c requests are equally spaced out on the disk surface [GM98], we have:

$$F_{N_c}^*(s) = e^{(-s\ \tau_{seek}^{max}(N_c))} \left[F_{rot}^*(s)F_{tfr}^*(s)\right]^{N_c} \tag{3.3}$$

Let $M_{N_c}(s)$ be the moment generating function for the random variable τ_{N_c}. Since $M_{N_c}(s)$ is equal to $F_{N_c}^*(-s)$, applying Chernoff's theorem to bound the tail of the random variable τ_{N_c}, gives us the following:

---

[10] Other approaches to bounding the tail of a sum of random variables exist; see [Kle75] for details.

$$\text{Prob}[\tau_{N_c} \geq T] = p \ \leq \ \inf_{\theta \geq 0} \left\{ \frac{M_{N_c}(\theta)}{e^{\theta T}} \right\} \tag{3.4}$$

Note that the infimum (inf) operator applies to Equation (3.4), since, based on the Markov's inequality [Kle75], that inequality holds for all $\theta \geq 0$. Therefore, the tightest bound is obtained by using the *best* θ. Using standard numerical solution techniques, we can obtain the optimal θ^* which gives the tightest upper bound and thereby obtain the value of T. If τ_{N_c} is larger than T, then an *overflow* event occurs. In general, there are several approaches to handling the overflow situation. For example, the system can allow overflowing into the next cycle (i.e., finish servicing the requests in cycle i where, as a consequence, the N_c requests in cycle $i+1$ will have less than T time units to meet their deadlines). Or, the system can stop servicing the requests in the (overflowing) cycle i and proceed to service the next N_c continuous requests in cycle $i + 1$. In either case, overflow causes jitter in the delivery of data to clients, and thus p is an important system parameter whose value can be determined at system design time.

3.5 Fault Tolerance

Challenging tasks in designing large-scale multimedia information systems include not only satisfying the real-time constraints of continuous delivery of objects at specified rates, which has been addressed in the following works [BGM+94, CKY93, GS94, OBR+94, RV93, RV91, TPB+93] (to name a few) in the form of various data layout, scheduling, and access control algorithms, but also providing a high degree of reliability and availability. To exhibit reasonable economies of scale, the VOD server should contain a large number of disks; something on the order of 1000 drives would not be uncommon[11]. Although a single disk can be fairly reliable, with a mean time to failure (MTTF) on the order of 300,000 hours, given such a large disk subsystem, the probability that some disk fails can be fairly high, e.g., in a 1000 disk system the MTTF of some disk would be on the order of 300 hours (or 12.5 days). Due to the real-time constraints, the reliability and availability requirements of VOD systems are even more stringent than those of traditional information systems. Several works on fault tolerance schemes for VOD servers have appeared in the last few years, including [BGM95, CB95, GM95, ORS+96, TPB+93, VSR95]. Issues and tradeoffs involved in providing fault tolerance in VOD servers *in a cost-effective manner* is the focus of this section.

---

[11] For example, a storage subsystem of 1000 (1 GByte) disks would provide enough storage for $\approx$ 222 (100 min) MPEG-2 movies (at $\approx$ 6 Mbits/sec) or $\approx$ 888 MPEG-1 movies [Gal91] (at $\approx$ 1.5 Mbits/sec) or some combination of the two. Similarly, assuming a bandwidth of 4 MBytes/sec/drive, 1000 disk drives would provide enough bandwidth to support $\approx$ 5333 concurrent MPEG-2 users or $\approx$ 21,333 concurrent MPEG-1 users.

A large-scale VOD server employs a *multi-level* storage hierarchy, where an object's location in the hierarchy can be based on its "popularity". Given such an architecture, a disk failure does not result in data loss, since a copy of each object is stored on tertiary storage. However, a disk failure can result in interruption of requests in progress. If some of the data for an object currently being displayed is on a disk that fails, then a discontinuity in delivery, or a *hiccup*, occurs. Since objects are typically striped over multiple disks, a single disk failure can cause multiple hiccups in the display of many objects. Without some provisions for fault tolerance, these hiccups will occur on each access to the failed disk and will continue until the missing information can be reconstructed and placed on an operational disk (which can then replace the failed disk). Rebuilding a failed disk from tertiary storage can be a slow process. Loading the missing data onto a spare disk requires portions of many objects to be loaded from a tertiary store; many tapes may need to be referenced, which is a significantly time consuming task. Given the size of the disk subsystem, duration of videos, and the real-time constraints, it would be unacceptable for a system not to recover from disk failure *in real time*. Thus, some mechanism for continuing delivery of video objects under failure is essential, i.e., schemes are needed for real-time reconstruction and timely delivery of data missing due to failure, until the failed disk can be rebuild and the system can return to normal operation. To build a cost-effective VOD server, fault tolerance issues must be considered when designing data layout and retrieval techniques.

3.5.1 Issues and tradeoffs. A fundamental problem that makes fault tolerant design of VOD servers different from traditional information systems, is the existence of real-time constraints in the delivery of video data, that is, the fact that recovery from failure and continuation of service of all (or as many as possible) active requests must occur in real time. Existing approaches to fault tolerant design of VOD servers can be divided into two categories: redundancy-based techniques (e.g. [BGM95, TPB+93]) and non-redundancy-based techniques (e.g. [VSR95]). That is, redundancy-based techniques, such as parity-based or replication-based schemes, are those that store redundant information which, under failure, is used to *reconstruct* the missing data. Whereas non-redundancy-based techniques exploit the redundancy that is "inherently" present in video data in order to *approximate* the missing data without storing redundant information. In this section, we focus our discussion on redundancy-based techniques, partly because the loss of image quality in non-redundancy-based schemes is somewhat difficult to evaluate objectively. (A detailed *quantitative* comparison of the redundancy-based schemes can be found in [GLP98].)

If redundancy-based techniques are used to provide fault tolerant behavior, then data layout and scheduling of data retrieval in VOD servers must be "planned" in such a manner as to be able to access the information needed for reconstructing the missing data in *real-time*. Furthermore, the "goodness"

of a fault tolerance scheme can be assessed based on: (1) reliability considerations, (2) number of simultaneous display streams it can support, and
(3) penalties or costs associated with storing and retrieving redundant information. These penalties fall into one of three categories[12]: (a) disk storage,
i.e., the amount of disk storage that must be dedicated to storing redundant
information (e.g., parity) and cannot be used to store actual data; (b) bandwidth, i.e., the amount of bandwidth that must be dedicated to retrieving
redundant information (e.g., parity) and cannot be used for retrieving actual
data; and (c) buffer space, i.e., the amount of memory needed to support a
redundancy scheme (e.g., for storing some portion of a parity group, used
in reconstruing missing data, until it can be delivered to display stations).
In general, these penalties are not independent of each other, and it is often
possible to tradeoff one for the other.

Redundancy-based techniques can further be subdivided into two categories: (1) those that exploit sequentiality of video data delivery, e.g.,
[BGM95] and (2) those that disregard sequentiality of video data delivery,
e.g., [CB95]. That is, a fault tolerance scheme can either exploit the fact that
video display can be "pre-planned" and utilize the information retrieved for
reconstruction of missing data for normal display. Or it can disregard the
fact that this information can be utilized for normal display (and not just
reconstruction of missing data), and thus discard the data blocks retrieved
for reconstruction, i.e., the reading of data blocks for normal display would
be scheduled separately from the reading of the same data blocks for the
purpose of reconstructing (and displaying) data missing due to failure.

This means that a fundamental tradeoff in choosing one or the other
type of an approach is between I/O bandwidth and buffer space. That is, by
using a sequential-type scheme, we can utilize the I/O bandwidth better by
retrieving each data block only once, and using it for both normal display and
reconstruction purposes; however, this efficiency in I/O bandwidth utilization
is achieved at the cost of additional buffer space, since the blocks retrieved for
reconstruction of missing information must be buffered until they are needed
for normal display. In contrast, when using a non-sequential-type scheme, we
can discard data as soon as reconstruction of missing information is complete,
and hence there is no need for additional buffer space; however, this efficiency
in buffer space utilization is achieved at the cost of inefficient bandwidth
usage, since, even under normal operation, we must reserve sufficient I/O
bandwidth during scheduling of data retrieval so as to be able to access all
the information needed for reconstruction of missing data, in real time, when
a failure does occur — this includes both parity information *and* the surviving
data blocks in the same parity group.

Since it is not immediately clear how to compare savings in I/O bandwidth with savings in buffer space, one approach is to assess this trade-

---

[12] More qualitative considerations can also be explored, but we do not discuss
these here due to lack of space.

off through cost considerations. Thus, a meaningful performance measure is $/stream, i.e., one can compare alternative fault tolerance schemes by considering: (a) the overall cost of the system based on system requirements, e.g., in terms of the cost of disks plus main memory, which are dictated by I/O bandwidth, buffer space, and storage for fault tolerance needs, and (b) the maximum number of streams that can be simultaneously supported by the corresponding VOD architecture. It is worth noting that different schemes have their optimum operating points at different architectural configurations; thus it is not the case that one fault tolerance scheme is absolutely better than another, but rather that one must understand the system requirements and constraints (e.g., minimum number of simultaneously supported streams) and then choose a fault tolerance scheme accordingly. Finally, it must also be noted that the reliability characteristics (such as MTTF) of a particular fault tolerance scheme should not be neglected, since that is the initial motivation for this work; however, it is reasonable to compare schemes which are above an "acceptable" reliability threshold based on the $/stream metric. Below we further illustrate the above mentioned tradeoff using RAID-based techniques, since RAID technology is likely to be more familiar to the reader[13].

RAID-based sequential-type scheme. An example of a sequential-type fault tolerance scheme is the *Streaming RAID* (SR) approach [TPB+93], where a traditional RAID3 (or RAID4 or RAID5) [PGK88] system can be used. Given C disks per cluster, parity groups are constructed from $C - 1$ logically *sequential* data blocks of a *particular video object* and a corresponding parity block (of course, each of the C blocks is placed on a different disk of the cluster). For each active stream that is being delivered by the VOD server, an entire parity group is retrieved simultaneously and then delivered to the network according to the display rate of the video object. Since an entire parity group is read for each active stream before delivery of any data block in that group begins, in the even of a disk failure the missing data that would have been read from the failed disk can be reconstructed on-the-fly, and without hiccups, from the other data blocks and the partity block in the same parity group[14]. This scheme can withstand up to one disk failure per cluster before some data is lost from the disk subsystem or before there are insufficient resources to continue servicing all requests that were active before the failure.

The main advantage of using this approach is its high reliability. The SR scheme exhibits the same performance characteristics under failure as it does under normal operation. This is partly due to the fact that it exploits the

---

[13] We do not discuss replication-based techniques here due to lack of space; however, in many cases, replication can be treated as a degenerate case of a parity-based scheme.

[14] Some scheduling adjustments might be necessary to account for the computation of the XOR, but this is a relatively minor complication which is not discussed any further here.

sequential nature of video data delivery and thus, under failure, utilizes the information retrieved for reconstruction of missing data for normal display, i.e., no additional bandwidth is needed under failure. The tradeoff here is the amount of buffer space required to store data, needed for reconstruction of missing information, which might be retrieved significantly earlier than is required by the display rate of the video[15]. Thus, the high reliability of this scheme is gained at the cost of buffer space. Note that, there is also a bandwidth penalty associated with this scheme, since a fraction, $\frac{1}{C}$, of the disk bandwidth must be reserved for retrieving parity information (although not as much as in the case of non-sequential schemes, as described below). Thus, there is an incentive for large parity groups which will facilitate more efficient use of disk bandwidth and disk storage space (i.e., proportionately less redundant information will have to be stored and retrieved); however, this must be balanced against the cost of additional buffer space, which grows with the size of the parity group.

RAID-based non-sequential-type scheme. An alternative to the SR scheme would be to still use a RAID-based system, but disregard the sequentiality of video data delivery. That is, we could use a traditional RAID5 (R5) system, with a (basically) *arbitrary* assignment of data blocks to parity groups. Data retrieval can proceed according to the rate required by the display (rather than be dictated by fault tolerance considerations) and thus obviate the need for large amounts of buffer space[16]. Hence, this scheme precludes the possibility that, under failure, information retrieved for reconstruction of missing data can also be utilized for normal display. This means that, to be able to recover from failure in *real time*, we would have to reserve disk bandwidth in the system to insure that when a failure does occur, there will be sufficient bandwidth to retrieve enough information to reconstruct the missing data and to continue service of all requests that were active before the failure. Of course, some additional buffer space would also be needed under failure, for storage of data required for reconstruction of missing information (this is a relatively small amount, since all data from the same parity group can be XORed into the same buffer).

The R5 scheme is just as reliable as the SR scheme. Furthermore, it exhibits better buffer space utilization characteristics. However, its bandwidth utilization characteristics are quite a bit poorer than those of the SR scheme. In a (basically) read-only system, like a VOD server, under the R5 scheme a

---

[15] We could achieve a small improvement in buffer space requirements by not reading the parity information during normal operation; however, that could result in hiccups in data delivery at the time the failure occurs.

[16] There is almost no advantage to reading full parity groups in this case; since most of the blocks in the parity group (except for the one immediately needed for transmission), would be discarded, the only advantage of reading the whole parity group at once would be to prevent hiccups in data delivery at the time the failure occurs.

failure of one disk in a cluster will result in double the load on all other disks in that cluster. Thus, in the R5 scheme we would have to reserve *half* of the system's bandwidth to insure real-time recovery under disk failure. In other words, we would obtain a large reduction in buffer space requirements at the cost of significant bandwidth loss.

3.5.2 Improvements in resource utilization. Whether the sequential-type or the non-sequential-type approach is used, measures can be taken to improve resource usage and lower costs. Such approaches have been explored in previous works, including [BGM95, CB95, GM95, ORS+96, TPB+93, VSR95]. We briefly outline a couple of basic techniques below; a more detailed survey of these approaches with analysis and comparison of techniques, based on the metrics described earlier, can be found in [GLP98].

Sequential-type schemes. Improvements in buffer space requirements, as compared to a sequential-type RAID-based scheme, can be achieved by constructing data layouts and retrieval schedules that allow alternative behavior during normal and failed modes of operation. Such schemes achieve improvements in buffer space requirements by (under normal operation) retrieving data at rates closer to the required display rates, rather than retrieving entire parity groups at once (as was done in the case of the SR scheme above) as well as have provisions for modifying the retrieval schedule to access the needed information (i.e., entire parity groups) once a failure occurs. Of course, in the event of a failure, additional buffer space is required to store information used for reconstruction of missing data, until it can be utilized for normal display. In fact, a system can continue operating with multiple failures, as long as there is no more than one failure per cluster, and thus buffer space is needed to support each one of those failed clusters. The savings in buffer space can be achieved by *not* providing sufficient buffer space for *all* clusters in the system to be able to operate under failure, but only for a *sufficiently large number*, such that the probability that a *larger* number of clusters will be operating under failure is acceptably low. Thus, some amount of system reliability is sacrificed. However, as long as it is still above an acceptable threshold, significant improvements in buffer space requirements and therefore cost can be achieved. Similarly, this approach can be applied to reducing additional bandwidth requirements of a sequential-type scheme (i.e., those needed for reading parity information). Variations on this approach as well as other techniques are explored in [BGM95, GM95, ORS+96].

Non-sequential-type schemes. Improvements in bandwidth utilization, as compared to a RAID-based non-sequential-type scheme, can be achieved by exloiting the idea that the size of parity groups can be smaller than the corresponding size of the disk cluster over which the parity groups are laid out, i.e., ideas similar to the Clustered RAID approach [ML90] used in traditional information systems. With smaller parity groups, less bandwidth must be reserved on a disk cluster to retrieve data needed for reconstruction of missing information (i.e., parity plus the surviving data blocks in the same parity group). These saving in bandwidth requirements are achieved at the cost of additional storage space (with smaller parity groups, the overhead for storing redundant information is higher). Variations on this approach are explored in [CB95, ORS+96].

In summary, fault tolerance issues in multimedia storage systems are complicated by the necessity to recover from failure in real time. In this section, we discussed some of the fundamental issues associated with providing fault tolerance in multidisk VOD servers. In conclusion, we would like to impress upon the reader that the main point of this paper is the exposition of trade-offs and issues associated with designing fault tolerant VOD servers rather than a description of specific schemes. It is not the case that one fault tolerance scheme is absolutely better than another, but rather that one must understand the tradeoffs as well as one's system constraints and then choose a fault tolerance scheme accordingly.

3.6 Mixed Workload Servers

Many modern applications can benefit (cost-wise) from sharing resources such as network bandwidth, disk bandwidth, etc. In addition, information systems would like to store data that can be of use to multiple classes of applications, e.g., digital libraries type systems. Part of the difficulty in efficient resource management in such systems can then occur when these applications have vastly different performance and quality-of-service (QoS) requirements as well as resource demand characteristics.

One approach to dealing with this problem would be to simply share the resources among the different classes of requests with a best-effort attempt to meet the performance or quality-of-service (QoS) requirements of each. Another approach would be to partition the available resource between the different classes of workloads/requests, i.e., essentially maintain separate and independent servers. However, in general, this is not a good idea, since one set of resources might remain idle while another set is overloaded. Furthermore, if copies of the same data are of use to multiple classes of applications, we may have to, in addition, incur a "penalty" for having to maintain consistency between multiple copies of the data. Thus, a more sensible approach would be to consider techniques which can share the resources among the different types of workloads while satisfying (to some degree) their performance requirements and QoS constraints.

Here, we consider such as system, namely, a multimedia storage server which, in general, can service a variety of applications, requesting video, image, audio, and text data. For instance, the storage system can service two types of workloads: (1) continuous (or real-time), and (2) non-continuous (or non-real-time)[17], where the real-time (with continuity-type requirements)

---

[17] We will use the terms "real-time" and "continuous" interchangeably throughout the paper; likewise for the terms "non-real-time" and "non-continuous".

workload can correspond to requests for video streams whereas the non-real-time workload can correspond, for instance, to billing inquiries about the videos, thumbnails of images corresponding to particular scenes in a video, etc.

Clearly, the two types of workloads have different performance and QoS requirements. Specifically, the real-time workload requirements can be low latency for starting a video display and delivery of data at a particular rate (e.g., at 1.5 Mbps for an MPEG-I stream) with little jitter, once the video display has been started[18]. On the other hand, the non-real-time workload, although it does not have jitter-type requirements, still requires reasonable response time — by *reasonable* we mean that it meets a user-specified requirement, e.g., database applications, such a billing service, might require that $X\%$ of all transactions complete in under Y minutes.

Below we describe a prototype multimedia storage system designed for mixed workloads with real-time, non-real-time, and highly interactive quality of service requirements.

Random I/O. New multimedia applications, such as 3D interactive virtual worlds, have I/O patterns much less predictable than video or audio. In a 3D interactive virtual world application the user navigates through large 3D graphic models at variable speed and along user controlled paths. In order for the display engine to show the current world view, the graphical models of nearby 3D objects need to be continuously retrieved from disk as the user moves. The access pattern to storage objects thus depends on the speeds and paths selected by the user, which makes prediction imperfect at best. 3D virtual world models have been used for different applications such as architectural building design, urban city models, scientific visualization, etc.; and will be increasingly common in the future.

Because of the difficulties in predicting the I/O pattern of multimedia data access, in [MSB98] the authors state that multimedia data servers will move towards solutions that do not rely on a careful data layout designed to match a predicted pattern of access. Their approach to the problem is to use a random allocation scheme for laying out data on disks that results in a uniformly random access pattern at the physical level regardless of any reference pattern at the logical level[19].

---

[18] The low latency can also be viewed as high throughput, i.e., being able to sustain as many simultaneous video streams as possible, given a particular server architecture.

[19] As discussed in Section 3.2, there are a number of proposals for layout of video data on parallel disks. The most common method being to stripe each object across the parallel disks using a fixed size stripe granule (i.e., disk block). While allocation of a disk block on a disk is often random, logically consecutive blocks are typically allocated in strictly round-robin order to disks. In [MSB98] the authors randomly select the disk to hold each data block as well as randomly select the location of the block on the disk.

This approach has the advantage of mapping all workloads and all access patterns of different multimedia applications into the same workload at the physical disk access level. Thus a single problem remains to be solved: for a stream of independent I/O requests which are uniformly distributed over the parallel disks, design the scheduling algorithm to support the largest possible throughput for a given maximum delay and a given probability of exceeding the delay bound. If one can satisfactorily solve this problem the same storage system can be used for any multimedia application. The RIO multimedia object server [MSB98] is one solution and it is offered as a generic multimedia storage system capable of efficient, concurrent retrieval of many types of media objects.

RIO is the storage subsystem for a multimedia information system under development at UCLA called the Virtual World Data Server (VWDS). The VWDS addresses many different issues including data storage, memory management, network communication, admission control, traffic policing and shaping, and also specific issues of 3D model virtual worlds, such as spatial indexing, adaptive quality of service, user motion and perception modeling, etc. The prototype is implemented on a SUN E4000 machine, having 10 Ultrasparc processors, 1.25 Gbytes of shared memory, fourteen 4 Gbyte disks dedicated to multimedia data storage, with ATM and Ethernet connections to client machines. The first prototype is operational and has been used to simultaneously support delivery of MPEG encoded videos, and 3D urban simulation city models. Other applications for realtime scientific visualization and medical VR are also under development.

References

[And93]   Anderson, D. P., Metascheduling for continuous media, *ACM Transactions on Computer Systems* 11, 1993, 226–252.

[BFG+95]   Baru, C., Fecteau, G., Goyal, A., Hsiao, H., Jhingran, A., Padmanabhan, S., Wilson, W., An overview of DB2 parallel edition, *Proc. of the ACM International Conference on Management of Data (SIGMOD)*, 1995, 460-462.

[BGM+93]   Berra, P. B., Golshani, F., Mehrotra, R., Liu Sheng, O. R., (eds.), Introduction multimedia information systems, *IEEE Transactions on Knowledge and Data Engineering*, 1993, 545-550.

[BGM+94]   Berson, S., Ghandeharizadeh, S., Muntz, R. R., Ju, X., Staggered striping in multimedia information systems, *Proc. of the ACM International Conference on Management of Data (SIGMOD)*, 1994, 79-90.

[BGM95]   Berson, S., Golubchik, L., Muntz, R. R., Fault tolerant design of multimedia servers, *Proc. of the ACM International Conference on Management of Data (SIGMOD)*, San Jose, CA, 1995, 364-375.

[BMW96]   Berson, S., Muntz, R., Wong, W.R., Randomized data allocation for real-time disk IO, *IEEE Computer Society International Conference (COMPCON'96)*, February, 1996, 286-290.

[Bir97]   Birk, Y., Random RAIDs with selective exploitation of redundancy for high performance video servers, *Proc. of the International Conference on Network and Operating System Support for Digital Audio and Video (NOSSDAV'97)*, 1997.

[BG88]   Bitton, D., Gray, G., Disk shadowing, *International Conference on Very Large Databases VLDB*, 1988, 331-338.

[BMC94]   Bocheck, P., Meadows, H., Chang, S.-F., A disk partitioning technique for reducing multimedia acess delay, *Proc. of the International Conference on Distributed Multimedia Systems and Applications*, 1994.

[BBD+96]   Bolosky, W.J., Barrera, J.S., Draves, R.P., Fitzgerald, R.P., Gibson, G.A., Jones, M.B., Levi, S.P., Myhrvold, N.P., Rashid, R.F., The Tiger video fileserver, Technical Report MSR-TR-96-09, Microsoft Research, 1996.

[CKY93]   Chen, M., Kandlur, D., Yu, P., Optimization of the grouped sweeping scheduling (GSS) with heterogeneous multimedia streams, *ACM Multimedia '93*, 1993, 235-242.

[CLG+94]   Chen, P., Lee, E., Gibson, G., Katz, R., Patterson, D., RAID: high-performance, reliable secondary storage, *ACM Computing Surveys*, 1994, 145-186.

[CB95]   Cohen, A., Burkhard, W. A., Storage architectures for continuous digital video retrieval, *Proc. of SPIE, Photonics East*, 1995, 58-69.

[CHC+93]   Coyne, R. A., Hulen, H., Coleman, S., Watson, R., The emerging new storage management paradigm, *Proc. of the 12th IEEE Symposium on Mass Storage Systems*, Monterey, California, 1993.

[CKH+92]   Cypher, R., Konstantinidou, S., Ho, A., Messina, P., Architectural requirements of parallel scientific applications with explicit communications, Technical Report RJ 9079 (80892), IBM, Almaden Research Center, 1992.

[Cor85]   Teradata Corp. DBC1012 database computer system manual release 2.0, *Document No. C10-0001-02*, 1985.

[DN91]   Davies, N. A., Nicol, J. R., Technological perspective on multimedia computing, *Computer Communications* 14, 1991, 260-272.

[DG92]   DeWitt, D., Gray, J., Parallel database systems: the future of high performance database systems, *Communications of the ACM*, 1992, 85-98.

[Gal91]   Le Gall, D., MPEG: a video compression standard for sultimedia applications, *Communications of the ACM*, 1991, 46-58.

[GH94]   Gennart, B. A., Hersch, R. D., Multimedia performance behavior of the gigaview parallel image server, *Proc. of the 13th IEEE Symposium on Mass Storage Systems*, 1994, 90-98.

[GKS95]   Ghandeharizadeh, S., Kim, S. H., Shahabi, C., On configuring a single disk continuous media server, *Proc. of the ACM International Conference on Measurement and Modeling of Computer Systems (SIGMETRICS)*, 1995, 37-46.

[GM98]   Ghandeharizadeh, S., Muntz, R. R., Design and implementation of scalable continuous media servers, *Parallel Computing Journal* 24, special issue on Parallel Data Servers and Applications, 1998, 91-122.

[GS94]   Ghandeharizadeh, S., Shahabi, C., On multimedia repositories, personal computers, and hierarchical storage, *Proc. of the Second ACM International Conference on Multimedia*, 1994, 407-416.

[GVW96]   Gibson, G., Vitter, J.S., Wilkes, J., Strategic directions in storage IO issues in large scale computing, *ACM Computing Surveys*, 1996, 209-209.

[GLM95]   Golubchik, L., Lui, J. C.S., Muntz, R. R., I/O stream sharing for continuous media systems, *Bulletin of the Technical Committee on Data Engineering*, 1995, 17-26.

[GLP98]   Golubchik, L., Lui, J. C.S., Papadopouli, M., Designing efficient fault tolerant VOD storage servers: techniques, analysis, and comparison, *the special issue of Parallel Computing Journal on Parallel Data Servers and Applications*, 1998, 123-155.

[GM95]   Golubchik, L., Muntz, R. R., Fault tolerance issues in multidisk video-on-demand storage servers, *Proc. of SPIE, Photonics East*, 1995, 70-87.

[GR98]   Golubchik, L., Rajendran, R. K., A study on the use of tertiary storage in multimedia systems, *Proc. of the Joint NASA and IEEE Mass Storage Conference*, 1998, 91-122.

[HD90]   Hsiao, H.-I., DeWitt, D., A new availability strategy for multiprocessor database machines, *Proc. of the Int'l. Conf. on Data Engineering (ICDE'90)*, 1990, 456-465.

[IK88]   Ibaraki, T., Katoh, N., *Resource Allocation Problems*, The MIT Press, 1988.

[Kle75]   Kleinrock, L., *Queueing Systems, Volume I*, Wiley-Interscience, 1975.

[LL95]   Lau, S. W., Lui, J. C. S., A novel video-on-demand storage architecture for supporting constant frame rate with variable bit rate retrieval, *Proc. of the 5th Intl. Conf. on Network and Operating System Support for Digital Audio and Video (NOSSDAV '95)*, 1995, 294-305.

[LSP94]   Lougher, P., Shepherd, D., Pegler, D., The impact of digital audio and video on high-speed storage, *Proc. of the 13th IEEE Symposium on Mass Storage Systems*, 1994, 84-89.

[ML90]   Muntz, R. R., Lui, J. C.S., Performance analysis of disk arrays under failure, *VLDB Conference*, 1990, 162-173.

[MPE90]   Motion Picture Expert Group, *Coding of moving pictures and associated audio*, Committee Draft of Standard IS011172: ISO/MPEG 90/176, 1990.

[MSB98]   Muntz, R. R., Santos, J. R., Berson, S., A parallel storage system for realtime multimedia applications, *International Journal of Intelligent Systems* 13, *special issue on Multimedia Computing Systems*, 1998.

[NMH95]   Neufeld, G., Makaroff, D., Hutchinson, N., The design of a variable bit rate continuous media server, *Proc. of the Fifth International Conference on Network and Operating System Support for Digital Audio and Video (NOSSDAV '95)*, 1995, 354-357.

[OLW95]   Oyang, Y.-J., Lee, M.-H., Wen, C.-H., A video storage system for on-demand playback, *Proc. of Data Engineering Conference*, 1995, 457-465.

[OBR+94]   Ozden, B., Biliris, A., Rastogi, R., Silberschatz, A., A low-cost storage server for movie on demand databases, *Proc. of the 20th Intl. Conf. on Very Large Data Bases*, 1994, 594-605.

[ORS+96]   Ozden, B., Rastogi, R., Shenoy, P., Silberschatz, A., Fault-tolerant architectures for continuous media servers, *Proc. of the ACM International Conference on Management of Data (SIGMOD)*, Montreal, Canada, 1996, 79-90.

[PGK88]   Patterson, D. A., Gibson, G., Katz, R. H., A case for redundant arrays of inexpensive disks (RAID), *Proc. of the ACM International Conference on Management of Data (SIGMOD)*, 1988, 109-116.

[RR93]   Ramanathan, S., Rangan, P. V., Adaptive feedback techniques for syn-
            chronized multimedia retrieval over integrated networks, *IEEE/ACM
            Transaction on Networking* 1, 1993, 246–260.
[RV91]   Rangan, P. V., Vin, H. M., Designing file systems for digital video
            and aduio, *Proc. of the 13th ACM Symposium on Operating Systems
            Principles*, 1991, 81–94.
[RV93]   Rangan, P. V., Vin, H. M., Efficient storage techniques for digital con-
            tinuous multimedia, *IEEE Transactions on Knowledge and Data En-
            gineering*, 1993, 564–573.
[RW94]   Ruemmler, C., Wilkes, J., An introduction to disk drive modeling,
            IEEE Computer Magazine, 1994, 17–28.
[SZK+96]   Salehi, J., Zhang, Z., Kurose, J. F., Towsley, D., Supporting stored
            video: Reducing rate variability and end-to-end resource requirements
            through optimal smoothing, *Proc. of the ACM International Confer-
            ence on Measurement and Modeling of Computer Systems (SIGMET-
            RICS)*, 1996, 222–231.
[SK94]   Sauer, F., Kabuka, M., Multimedia technology in the radiology depart-
            ment, *Proc. of the Second ACM International Conference on Multime-
            dia*, 1994, 263–269.
[Sto86]   Stonebraker, M., The case for shared nothing, *Database Engineering
            Bulletin* 9, 1986, 4–9.
[TPB+93]   Tobagi, F. A., Pang, J., Baird, R., Gang, M., Streaming RAID - a disk
            array management system for video files, *ACM Multimedia Conference*,
            1993, 393–399.
[VGG+94]   Vin, H. M., Goayl, P., Goyal, A., Goyal, A., A statistical admission
            control algorithm for multimedia servers, *Proc. of the Second ACM
            International Conference on Multimedia*, 1994, 33–40.
[VSR95]   Vin, H. M., Shenoy, P. J., Rao, S. S., Efficient failure recovery in mul-
            tidisk mulltimedia servers, *Proc. of SPIE, Photonics East*, 1995, 12–21.
[WSY95]   Wolf, J., Shachnai, H., Yu, P., DASD dancing: a disk load balancing
            optimization scheme for video-on-demand computer systems, *Proc. of
            the ACM International Conference on Measurement and Modeling of
            Computer Systems (SIGMETRICS)* , 1995, 157–166.
[YCK92]   Yu, P. S., Chen, M.-S., Kandlur, D. D., Design and analysis of a
            grouped sweeping scheme for multimedia storage management, *Third
            International Workshop on Network and Operating System Support for
            Digital Audio and Video*, 1992, 44–55.

IX. Networking Aspects of Distributed and Parallel Computing

Jarek Nabrzyski, Maciej Stroiński, and Jan Węglarz

Poznań Supercomputing and Networking Center, Poznań, Poland

Summary. This chapter is aimed at those who are interested in getting the highest available communication performance for their parallel and distributed applications and at those who are interested in the communication aspects of distributed and parallel computing. The chapter is focused on high-speed communication networks such as: Fast Ethernet, Gigabit Ethernet, FDDI, Fibre Channel, ATM and HIPPI. The performance aspects of the networks and of the I/O subsystems of supercomputers are presented. Some classes of services for ATM, (e.g. VBR, UBR, CBR) are described and the level of QoS fulfilled by these classes is discussed. The chapter should also be interesting for users who would like to write their own programs using different vendor native APIs, such as Fore ATM API and Iris HIPPI API.

1. Introduction

The rapid development of information technologies in the last decade as well as the enormous success of computer networks and the Internet resulted in the formation of new concepts collectively known and summarized in the notion of the information society. The realization of this idea could be compared to the beginning of an intellectual and social revolution which continuously change the way we think and solve problems. But the revolution still needs more and more modern services and applications for the fundamental changes to prosper. The vision, that if computational scientists and engineers from various specific disciplines could be brought together, thereby creating many benefits for society in general, has motivated and driven the nations of the world to act. The give and take between the two communities (computer scientists and application researchers) has only worked well in isolated cases in the past; the next stage is to reap the benefits of a much closer collaboration. Day to day work has proved that our primary goal should be to provide desktop access to the most powerful computational science and engineering infrastructure ever assembled   [McR97, Sma97]. Of course, this can only be achieved with high levels of parallelism, high performance computing and high performance networking. One of the most important factors that these activities are sensitive to is communication performance.

Different disciplines of life and their supporting new applications have various requirements concerning communication performance. For example, such disciplines as: basic science, crisis management, education, environment, government information services, health care, manufacturing etc., use different applications and different technologies for solving their problems. From among these we can list the most important:

Collaborative technologies. Applications based on video-conferencing, shared documents and databases, remote access to shared documents and research facilities.

Distributed computing. Applications requiring access to remote computers, storage systems, databases, scientific instruments, advanced display devices. Applications of this group need to be able to locate the resources and computations, determine properties of resources, configure resources and computations, support diverse communications mechanisms including RPC, message passing, streaming video, multicast, monitor and manage computations etc.

Digital libraries. Applications requiring distributed mass storage systems, high performance access for users to the content, which often takes the form of multiple multimedia objects and high performance computing to manipulate the data.

Remote operations. Applications that give a remote user the ability to impose changes and be able to monitor them.

Obviously network is a significant factor for these applications. Of course, different applications will require different quality of service (QoS) parameters of underlying networks. Thus, it is very important to discover the design features of the applications in order to provide them with the optimal performance networks. The applications can send messages very often or very rarely, they can write or read data remotely, they can send short or long messages etc. Also the content of the information being sent can differ from application to application. The following are the characteristic features of various applications [CHK+93]:

Message frequency. The more communication intensive the application, the more we would expect its performance to be affected by the machine's communication performance. For applications that use short messages the most important factor is the message frequency, or equivalently the average interval between messages. However, the behavior may be influenced by the burstiness of communication and the balance of traffic between processors.

Write or read based. Applications which read remote data and wait for the results are likely to be more sensitive to latency (delay incurred in communicating a message from its source processor/memory module to its target) than applications which mostly write remote data. The latter are likely to be more sensitive to bandwidth. However, dependencies that cause delays can appear in applications in many forms.

Short or long messages. Application which use bulk messages may have high data bandwidth requirements, even though message initiations are infrequent.

Synchronization. Applications can be bulk synchronous or task queue based. Tightly synchronized applications are likely to be dependent on network round trip times, and thus may be very sensitive to latency. Task queuing applications may tolerate latency, but may be sensitive to overhead (lenght of time that a processor is engaged in the transmission or reception of each message). A task queue based application attempts to overlap message operations with local computations from a task queue. An increase in overhead decreases the available overlap between the communication and local computation/communication balance: Balance is simply the ratio of the maximum number of messages sent per processor to the average number of messages sent per processor. It is difficult to predict the influence of network performance on applications with a relatively large communication imbalance since the parameters described above may exacerbate or may alleviate the imbalance.

Real time control. For real time control the maximum delivery time must be guaranteed. So, the communication priorities must be supported.

Multimedia transmission. Multimedia requires the specified QoS (low latency, high bandwidth, isochronism).

The features also show which network parameters are important for different types of applications. Such parameters as network bandwidth, latency and their isochronism, performance of the host-network interface, the availability of transmission priorities, the possibility for multicasting and broadcasting, as well as network behavior during burst traffic are important for the distributed applications programmer. Now the question arises of how the programmers can optimally use networks and their protocols to get the specified QoS parameters? They have several options to realize this. Fig. 1.1 shows the general communication architecture from the application point of view.

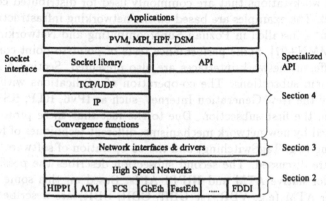

Fig. 1.1. General communication architecture from the applications point of view.

Programmers can invoke various system primitives to send messages between processes executing on different nodes, resulting in a message passing program. They can use a traditional socket interface based on TCP/IP protocols or specialized APIs based on direct access to native network protocols supported by different vendors. It is obvious that the first model doesn't support the QoS specification and has to be modified by additional protocols which will make the reservation of resources, QoS support etc., possible. They can also use communication libraries (e.g. MPI, PVM) [GBD94, GLS97], which provide a common interface across different computer architectures. However, at this level the specialization of communication is also possible [FGK+97]. In order to further simplify the programmer's task and to improve code portability, the programmer may use data parallel languages, such as High Performance Fortran (HPF) [Lov93], and leave it to the compiler to translate high level data parallel constructs into appropriate communication primitives. Another possibility is to use the distributed-shared memory (DSM) model in which processes are allowed to directly address memory located at other nodes [NL]. Whichever programming paradigm is used, efficient communication is critical to the performance of distributed parallel applications.

This chapter is aimed at those who are interested in getting the highest available communication performance for their applications and at those who are interested in the communication aspects of distributed parallel computing. We intend to use this chapter as an introductory handbook for distributed applications developers who want to use networks efficiently. The content of the chapter is organized according to the communication architecture presented in Fig. 1.1. Each section describes different layers of the architecture. In Section 2 such high speed networks as Fast Ethernet, Gigabit Ethernet, FDDI, Fibre Channel, ATM and HIPPI are described. In Section 3 the performance evaluation of sample I/O subsystems of supercomputers and workstations that are commonly used for distributed computing is presented. The examples are based on the networking infrastructure of the metacomputer installed in Poznan Supercomputing and Networking Center [NSW96, MMN+97], Some performance tests of point-to-point communication for different network interfaces are also presented. Section 4 is divided into two main subsections. The co-operation of applications with different protocols of the New Generation Internet, such as IPv6, RTP, RSVP etc. is discussed in the first subsection. Due to the fact that these protocols must be supported by new network mechanisms, different techniques of high speed IP switching (e.g. TagSwitching) and the co-operation of software with such networks are discussed. The second subsection describes the possibilities of using vendor native ATM and HIPPI APIs. Based on this some classes of services for ATM (e.g. VBR, rst UBR, CBR, UBR) are described and the level of QoS fulfilled by these classes is discussed. The way in which the performance of distributed parallel systems can be improved by such aspects as communication specialization, parallel communication etc. is finally explored in Section 5.

2. Computer Networks for Distributed Computing

Computer networks are a key factor of distributed systems. workstations are connected to high-speed local area networks such as Fast Ethernet (100 Mbps (mega bits per second)), 100 VG Any LAN (100 Mbps), FDDI (100 Mbps) and ATM (155 Mbps). The servers and supercomputers are connected via 622 Mbps ATM, 800/1600 Mbps HIPPI, 1 Gbps (giga bits per second) Fibre Channel, 1 Gbps Gigabit Ethernet and 1 Gbps GigaRing. The connections between these networks should be at least faster by an order of magnitude, e.g. Gigabit Ethernet (1 Gbps), ATM (2.4 Gbps). Soon residential users will be able to gain access to a high speed global network either through twisted pair and xDSL (Digital Subscriber Line) modems or cable TV and cable modems with a bandwidth up to 30 Mbps. In the immediate future a significant acceleration of network performance is planned. The current research and development programs [NGI98] are progressing towards networks with speeds of up to 100 times faster. An example of the required growth of computer networks bandwidth is presented in Fig. 2.1 [Sma97]. As can be seen the bandwidth of LANs will increase from 0.8 Gbps (HIPPI-8) to 51.6 Gbps (HIPPI-64, 8 channel) and for WANs up to 38.4 Gbps (4 x OC-192). While the network bandwidth grows, new network technologies such as: IP over SONET, wavelength division multiplexing networks (WDM) and optical networks will be introduced. These new technologies will be able to implement the terabit networks.

Alliance Partner WAN/LAN Network Bandwidth Requirements					
	FY 1998	FY 1999	FY 2000	FY 2001	FY 2002
LAN	0.8 Gbps (HIPPI-8)	6.4 Gbps (HIPPI-64)	21.8 Gbps (HIPPI-64, 2 channel)	35.6 Gbps (HIPPI-64, 4 channel)	51.6 Gbps (HIPPI-64, 8 channel)
WAN development testbeds	622 Mbps OC12	2.4 Gbps OC-48	9.6 Gbps OC-192	19.2 Gbps 2xOC-192	38.4 Gbps 4xOC-192
WAN advanced hardware partners	155 Mbps OC-3	622 Mbps OC-12	2.4 Gbps OC-48	9.6 Gbps OC-192	19.2 Gbps 2xOC-192
WAN mid-level partners	45 Mbps T3	155 Mbps OC-3	310 Mbps 2xOC3	622 MBps OC-12	2.4 Gbps 2.5 OC-48

Fig. 2.1. Expected network bandwidths.

We will now describe what we feel are the most important networks available today for new generation distributed applications.

2.1 Fast Ethernet, Gigabit Ethernet

The access methods as well as the frame formats for Fast Ethernet (100 Mbps) and Gigabit Ethernet (1 Gbps) are the same as for the well known Ethernet (10 Mbps). Fast Ethernet and Gigabit Ethernet are defined by IEEE 802.3.u and IEEE 802.3.z respectively. For this reason the networks will react in a similar way to the transferred traffic. They are still sensitive to the characteristics of the traffic and they are more efficient while transferring long frames than short frames. Both networks can be shared or switching. With the shared networks, the diameter of the collision domain cannot be greater than 2.56 ms for Fast Ethernet and 0.256 ms for Gigabit Ethernet. In practice this causes some topology constraints for the size of the network (up to 200m) and in consequence extends the possible shortest frame to the size of 512 bytes for Gigabit Ethernet in comparison with Ethernet. This feature, called Carrier Extension, is transparent to the user. The extension of the minimal size of the frame causes a decrease of the network bandwidth while transmitting a large number of very short frames. To solve this problem the Packet Bursting mode of transmission has been introduced. In this mode only the first frame is extended, and the rest are transferred with minimal inter-packet gaps. This procedure is repeated until the value of the burst timer will equal the value zero. It means that 1500 bytes of information has been sent. Switches make it possible to construct bigger networks for which the full bandwidth on the port is guaranteed. However, the latency is also growing.

Additional functionality of switches provides the separation of collision domains within one broadcast domain (logical subnet IP). It is performed on the second level of the network architecture and is called bridge function. Moreover, the administrator can define such subnets, i.e. virtual LANs (VLAN), for a group of workstations within one or several logical segments of the network (e.g. connection ports of the switch) [Smi97]. The vendor implementations of VLANs are now becoming the standard (e.g. IEEE 802.1Q - the standard for Virtual Bridged Local Area Network). In effect one can use the traffic engineering in the network by its segmentation and further one can improve its efficiency. VLANs are also very important for improving the security of networks. All the functions described above are realized in switches without any effort from the user workstations. Bridge operations in the switches can be extended by frame priority functions and the filtering of multicast frames (IEEE 802.1p - Traffic Class and Dynamic Multicast Filtering Services in Bridged Local Area Network). The first of these functions allows some traffic classes to be defined. The user can apply these functions to adjust the application requirements for end-to-end transmissions to network characteristics.

2.2 Fiber-Distributed Data Interface (FDDI)

FDDI is a 100 Mbps local area network standard developed by ANSI (ANSI X3T9.5). The standard allows up to 500 stations to communicate via fiber optic cables using a time-token access protocol. Normal data traffic as well as time constrained traffic such as voice, video, and real-time applications are supported. The FDDI network supports error detection and correction. It is done by a specific network topology which most often is based on a dual ring with some tree-like branches. The total length of the network cannot exceed 200km which is equivalent to a cable length of 100km. The maximum frame size is 4500 bytes. Unlike the token access protocol of IEEE 802.5, FDDI uses a timed-token access protocol that allows both synchronous and asynchronous traffic simultaneously. Synchronous traffic consists of delay sensitive traffic such as voice packets, which need to be transmitted within a certain time interval. The asynchronous traffic consists of data packets produced by various applications such as mail or data transfer. The maximum access delay - the time between successive transmission opportunities - is bounded for both synchronous and asynchronous traffic. Although the maximum access delay for the synchronous traffic is short, it can be long for asynchronous traffic depending upon the network configuration and load. Unless care is taken, the access delay may be as long as 165 seconds. This means that a station wanting to transmit asynchronous traffic may not get a usable token for 165 seconds. Such long access delays are clearly not desirable and can be avoided by proper settings of the network parameters and configurations.

The standard allows for up to eight priority levels for asynchronous traffic. The selection of the number of levels depends on the designers and users of the network. A unique scheme based on token rotation time ensures that only higher priority frames are transmitted if the load is high. The performance of FDDI network depends on fixed and user settable parameters. Examples of fixed parameters are cable length and the number of stations. The settable parameters which can be set by the network manager or the individual station manager, include various timer values. Most of these timers affect the reliability of the ring and the malfunction detection time. The key parameters that affect performance are synchronous time allocations. The workload also has a significant impact on FDDI performance. The most important parameters for the workload are: the number of active stations and the load per station. The active stations include those that have frames to transmit and are waiting for the right to access, that is, for a usable token to arrive along with the currently transmitting station, if any. The number of active stations is particularly important for synchronous traffic. While transmitting multimedia over FDDI the number of active stations should not exceed a maximum number of 30. The quality of service provided by the network is measured by its productivity (throughput) and responsiveness (response time and access delay). At loads near or above capacity, the response time reaches infinity. With these loads, the access delay is more meaningful. The productivity metric that the network manager may be concerned with is the total throughput of the ring in Mbps. Over any reasonable interval, the throughput is equal to the load. That is, if the load on the ring is 40 Mbps, the throughput is also 40 Mbps. This, of course, does not hold if the load is high. For example, if there are three stations on the ring, each with a 100 Mbps load, the total arrival rate is 300 Mbps and the throughput is obviously much less. Thus, the key metric is not the throughput under low load but the maximum obtainable throughput under high load. This latter quantity is also called the usable bandwidth of the network. The ratio of the usable bandwidth to nominal bandwidth (100 Mbps for FDDI) is defined as the efficiency . Thus, if for a given set of network and workload parameters, the usable bandwidth on FDDI is never more than 90 Mbps, the efficiency is 90 percent for that set of parameters. Another metric that is of interest for a shared resource, such as

FDDI, is the fairness with which the resource is allocated. Fairness is particularly important under heavy load. However, the FDDI protocols have been shown to be fair provided that priority levels are not implemented. Given a heavy load, the asynchronous bandwidth is equally allocated to all active stations. Low-priority stations closer to high-priority stations may get better service than those further ones. A single priority implementation is assumed here to keep the analysis simple.

2.3 Asynchronous Transfer Mode (ATM)

ATM [Bou92] is a standard developed by the networking standards communities: ITU and ATM Forum. It resides above the physical layer and directly below the ATM Adaptation Layer (AAL). It specifies the switching and multiplexing mechanisms for fixed-size cells or packets. Cells consist of 53 bytes - a 5 byte header and a 48 byte information payload. ATM provides a virtual connection for any two physically dislocated processes which wish to communicate. All cells from the same call traverse the same physical path, or virtual connection. Virtual connections are specified by a virtual circuit identifier (VCI) and virtual path identifier (VPI), found in each cell header. The VPI and VCI are used for multiplexing, demultiplexing, and switching the cells through the network. The ATM connection-oriented service has the potential to provide low-latency. ATM is independent of any particular physical layer, but is most commonly associated with Synchronous Optical Network (SONET). SONET defines a standard set of optical interfaces for network transport. It is a hierarchy of optical signals that are integer multiples of a basic signal rate of 51.84 Mbps called OC-1 (Optical Carrier Level 1). OC-3 (155.52 Mbps) and OC-12 (622.08 Mbps) have been designated as customer access rates in B-ISDN. OC-3, 155 Mbps, is the rate currently supported by the first generation ATM networks. Recall, that the aggregate throughput of the current available high-speed shared-medium networks, such as FDDI, is 100 Mbits/sec. Since ATM is a switch-based network architecture, the aggregate throughput is usually several gigabits. For example each host on an OC-3 ATM network has access to a link speed of 155 Mbits/sec. ATM was intended for the support of multiple classes of service, i.e., classes of traffic with varying quality of service parameters such as cell loss, delay, cell inter-arrival times, and data transfer rates. These parameters reflect the varying types of traffic ATM was intended to support, such as connection-oriented traffic types (e.g., audio, video), connectionless traffic types (e.g., file transfers), etc. The purpose of the ATM adaptation layer (AAL) is to provide a link between the services required by higher network layers and the generic ATM cells used by the ATM layer. It allows to adapt and transfer different kinds of traffic, such as audio, video, text, data etc. Five service classes are being standardized to provide these services. The recommendation for ATM specifies five AAL protocols which are listed as follows:

- AAL Type 1 - supports constant bit rate services, such as traditional voice transmission.
- AAL Type 2 - supports variable bit rate video and audio information. Maintains the timing relation between the source and destination pair.
- AAL Type 3 - supports connection-oriented data service and signaling.
- AAL Type 4 - supports connectionless data services. Currently Type 4 is combined with AAL Type 3.
- AAL Type 5 - provides a simple and efficient ATM adaptation layer that can be used for bridged and routed Protocol Data Units (PDU).

Some special service categories have been defined and implemented in the ATM switches. These ATM service categories are described by QoS descriptors i.e. parameters that specify the characteristics of the delivery of cells by the network. The following five classes of services are defined below [ATM]:

- CBR (Constant Bit Rate) : Describes a service where the source is expected to send cells at an essentially constant rate specified by the peak cell rate (PCR) and where the network guarantees a maximum delay, delay jitter (delay variation), and cell loss ratio. This service is appropriate for audio and constant rate video.
- rt-VBR and nrt-VBR (Variable Bit Rate) : Service where the source sends a traffic constrained by its PCR, burst tolerance (BT), and sustained information rate (SIR) and where the network guarantees the cell transfer delay (maximum and variation for real- time, average for non-real-time) and the cell loss ratio.
- ABR (Available Bit Rate) : A service in asynchronous transfer mode that attempts to use its spare resources fairly and efficiently.
- UBR (Unspecified Bit Rate) : Best effort service.

The services mentioned above were originally defined to satisfy various typical applications. However, an application is not constrained by its requirements and it may select any service categories consistent with its needs among those made available by a network. The table (Fig. 2.2) gives some proposals for the possibly optimal mapping of the services to applications: The overriding factor which distinguishes ATM from other network architectures lies in its flexibility. It is based upon a high-speed medium and thus provides the basic infrastructure for supporting high-speed transport. It also provides a network architecture based upon fast packet switching which is suitable for a wide range of applications. From the application viewpoint some problems occur when using the requirements concerning the QoS. The traditional networking applications support the co-operation with the connectionless networks (based on IP, IPX), while ATM offers connection-based services. To support the co-operation of both types of networks specialized convergence functions have been designed, e.g. classical IP over ATM (RFC 2225) or LAN Emulation for multi-protocol transmission. Another possibility of using the advantages of ATM networks is a direct access to the native net-

Application Area	CBR	rt-VBR	nrt-VBR	ABR	UBR
Critical Data	**	*	***	*	n/s
LAN Interconnect LAN Emulation	*	*	**	***	***
Data transport/ Internetworking	*	*	**	***	***
Circuit emulation PABX	***	**	n/s	n/s	n/s
POTS/ISDN Video conference	***			n/s	n/s
Compressed audio	*	***	**	**	**
Video distribution	***	**	*	n/s	n/s
Interactive multimedia	***	***	**	**	**

Scores indicate:the "advantage": optimum (***), good (**), fair (*)
n/s means: not suitable;   not quoted are presently not applicable

Fig. 2.2. Applications and adequate services.

work protocols from the applications. Vendors support this model with some specialized Application Programming Interfaces (APIs). Some APIs will be described in Section 4.

2.4 Fibre Channel

Fibre Channel (1 Gbps) [ANS93] is the data transfer interface technology that maps several common transport protocols including IP and SCSI allowing to merge high-speed I/O and networking functionality in a single connectivity technology. Fibre Channel is an open standard as defined by ANSI and OSI standards and operates over copper and fiber optic cabling at distances of up to 10 km. It is unique in its support of multiple inter- operable topologies including point-to-point, arbitrated-loop, switching and offers several qualities of service for network optimization. With its large packet sizes, Fibre Channel is ideal for storage, video, graphic and mass data transfer applications. Physically, the Fibre Channel can be an interconnection of multiple communication points, called NPorts, interconnected by a switching network, called a Fabric, or a point-to-point link.

Fibre Channel is quickly becoming the de facto connectivity standard for high-speed storage access and server clustering, and is a natural solution for gigabit enterprise backbones, and gigabit LANs for high speed storage, image, video and mass data transfer applications. Fibre Channel Arbitrated Loop was developed with peripheral connectivity in mind. It natively maps SCSI (as SCSI FCP), making it an ideal technology for high-speed I/O connectivity. Native Fibre Channel Arbitrated Loop (FC-AL) disk drives will allow storage applications to take full advantage of Fibre Channel's Gbps bandwidth, passing SCSI data directly onto the channel with access to multiple servers or nodes. FC-AL supports a 127 node address ability and a 10 km cabling range between nodes. Its Gigabit bandwidth and functionality also make the technology an attractive solution for server clustering. The peak transfer rate [LHD+94b] of a Fibre Channel port is 1.062 Gbps, or 100 MBps, which is the link rate of the full-speed interface. A Fibre Channel adapter can burst a 2048 bytes frame at the link rate. The ability to sustain peak flow is limited by design trade-offs, such as frame processing overhead, and system constraints, such as burst capabilities of the host PCI Bus Interface, system configuration, traffic characterization, and interconnect (fabric/loop) model.

Another measure of performance is latency. In high-performance clustering environments, one of the critical performance parameters is buffer-to-buffer latency. The actual time elapsed in passing a message from one node to another bounds the minimum time for distributed lock management algorithms to establish resource ownership. The tight coupling between a host DMA and hardware protocol processing results in extremely low latencies for Fibre Channel. In TCP/IP environments, if an unmodified protocol stack is used with the host system, the protocol stack overhead may become the limit of sustainable performance. The protocol assist in Fibre Channel ASICs provide considerable offload for host drivers, however this assist is not transparent if frames are small. In other words, maximum performance, as measured in Mbps, increases as the frame size increases. Transfers should always be blocked in the largest possible sequences to achieve maximum performance. Host bus issues can also limit performance if not understood and corrected. Fibre Channel is currently specified at 133 Mbps, 266 Mbps, 532 Mbps, and 1.0625 Gbps bandwidths. Accounting for overhead, at the Gigabit speed Fibre Channel the maximum data rate is 100 MBps (200 MBps duplex). Work is being done to develop 4 Gbps Fibre Channel specifications and products. With the support for 16 million switched port connections, Fibre Channel's switched topology is as much a network as ATM is. Fibre Channel consists of point-to-point links which are configured into a loop or Fabric topology which provides the management control. The FC-FG (Fabric Generic) and FC-SW (Switch) and FC-AL (Arbitrated Loop) [AC92] documents specify the networking characteristics. Specification for all three Fibre Channel topologies, point-to-point, loop, and switch are completed. One might look on traditional networks as taking a single transport medium and optimizing it to obtain the best performance out of it. Fibre Channel takes a different approach, choosing switch technology as the basis for providing bandwidth as needed in a simple and cost-effective manner. Interestingly, Fibre Channel supports the ATM protocol, meaning it can map ATM over its physical layer, another level of flexibility in Fibre Channel topology. Therefore, Fibre

Channel is compatible with ATM and can co-exist with it.

Three classes of service are defined in Fiber Channel specyfiction. These classes of service are distinguished primarily by the methodology with which the communication circuit is allocated and retained between the communicating NPorts and the level of delivery integrity required for an application. Classes of service are topology independent. If the Fabric is not present, the service is provided as a special case of a point-to-point link. Fabrics and NPorts are not required to support all classes of service.

- Class 1 service - Dedicated Connection Class 1 is a service which establishes Dedicated Connections. Once established, a dedicated connection is retained and guaranteed by the Fabric. This service guarantees maximum bandwidth available between two NPorts across the established connection. In Class 1, frames are delivered to the destination NPort by the Fabric in the same order as they are transmitted by the source NPort. If the Fabric is not present, this service becomes a special case of point-to-point.
- Class 2 service - Multiplex Class 2 is a Connectionless service with the Fabric multiplexing frames at frame boundaries. If a Fabric is not present, this service becomes a special case of point-to-point. The transmitter transmits Class 2 Data frames in a sequential order within a given sequence. However, the Fabric may not guarantee the order of delivery and frames may be delivered out of order. The Fabric guarantees notification of delivery or failure to deliver in the absence of link errors. In case of link errors, notification is not guaranteed since the `Source_Identifier` (SID) may not be error free.
- Class 3 service - Datagram Class 3 is a Connectionless service with the Fabric multiplexing frames at frame boundaries, if a Fabric is present. If a Fabric is not present, this service becomes a special case of point-to-point. Class 3 supports only unacknowledged delivery where the destination NPort does not send any confirmation LinkControl frames on receipt of valid data frames. Any acknowledgement of Class 3 service is up to and determined by ULPs (Upper Level Protocols). The transmitter transmits Class 3 Data frames in sequential order within a given Sequence. However, the Fabric may not guarantee the order of delivery and frames may be delivered out of order. In Class 3, the Fabric is expected to make a best effort to deliver the frame to the intended destination and does not issue a busy or reject frame to the source NPort if unable to deliver the frame. When a Class 3 frame is received in error, any error recovery or notification is performed at the ULP level.

2.5 High Performance Parallel Interface (HIPPI)

The HIPPI [ANS91, AFP92], is one of the high-speed network or channel solutions commercially available. It is a simple point-to-point interface for transferring data at peak rates of 800 or 1600 Mbps over distances of up to

25 meters. A related standard defines the usage of a crossbar switch to support multiple interconnections between HIPPI interfaces on different hosts [ASC92]. Standards [RN92] were also defined to support popular network protocols such as TCP/IP and UDP/IP over HIPPI. To extend HIPPI's connectivity, an implementor's agreement (the Serial-HIPPI [SHI91]) specifies how the HIPPI packets are to be carried over a pair of fiber optical cables. The HIPPI can be extended up to 10 km on a single-mode fiber [HF94]. HIPPI supports transmission and reception as separate channels. Because of this design, it is possible for a system to have applications that only receive, applications that only send, and/or applications that do both. In addition, each channel can be accessed with a different method.

A connection can be single-packet or many-packet. A single-packet connection is when one packet is sent and then the HIPPI subsystem automatically closes the connection. A many-packet connection is a connection that is kept open as long as the application wants. In the latter case, the application must indicate when it wants the connection closed. A packet can be single-write or multiple-write. A single-write packet is a HIPPI packet that is created by the HIPPI subsystem from an application's single write() call. A multiple-write packet is created from two or more write() calls. In the latter case, the application must indicate the start of each packet. The HIPPI connection rules are designed to permit the best utilization of the available bandwidth under the constraint that each destination must be made available frequently to receive packets from different sources. This discipline asks both sources and destinations to minimize connection setup overhead to deliver high performance. Low connection setup times are easily achieved by hardware implementations but overhead may be too high if software is required to execute between the initial request of a connection and the beginning of data transfer. Hardware implementations in which the connection setup and the data transfer proceed from a single software action are very desirable.

HIPPI connections are controlled by HIPPI sources; a destination, being unable to initiate a disconnect without the possibility of data loss, is a slave to the source once it has accepted a connection. Optimizations of connection strategy are therefore the province of the HIPPI source, and several optimizations are permitted. If the rate of available message traffic is less than the available HIPPI bandwidth and destinations are seldom busy when a connection is requested, connection optimizations do not pay off and the simplest strategy of waiting indefinitely for each connection to be made and sending messages strictly in the order queued cannot be improved upon. However if some nodes are slow, or network applications can send or receive messages at a higher aggregate rate than the available HIPPI bandwidth, sources may frequently encounter a busy destination. In these cases, certain host output queuing strategies may enhance channel utilization. Sources may maintain separate output queues for different HIPPI destinations, and abandon one destination in favor of another if a connection attempt without Camp-on (when several sources contend for a single destination, the Camp-on feature allows the HIPPI switch to arbitrate and ensure that all sources have fair access) is rejected or a connection request with Camp-on is not accepted within a predetermined interval. Such a strategy results in aborted connection sequences (defined in HIPPI-PH (PHysical layer): REQUEST is de- asserted before any data is sent). Destinations must treat these as normal events, perhaps counting them but otherwise ignoring them.

Two components of the connection setup time are beyond the control of both source and destination. One is the time required for the switch to connect source to destination, currently less than four microseconds in the largest commercially available (32 port) switch. The second component is the round trip propagation time of the REQUEST and CONNECT signals, negligible on a standard 25 meter copper HIPPI cable, but contributing a total of about 10 microseconds per kilometer on fiber optic links. HIPPI-SC LANs spanning more than a few kilometers will have a reduced throughput. Limited span networks with buffered gateways or bridges between them may perform better than long serial HIPPI links. A Source is required to drop its connection after the transmission of 68 HIPPI bursts. This number was chosen to allow the transmission of one maximum sized packet or a reasonable number of smaller sized packets. The following table lists some possibilities with calculated maximum burst and bandwidth rates in MBps:

Table 2.1. Maximum HIPPI bandwidth rates.

User data	Number of packets	Hold time (μsec)	Burst Rate (MBps)	Max throughput (MBPs)					
				Connection Setup Overhead (μsec)					
				10	30	60	90	120	150
63K	1	654	98.7	97.2	94.4	90.4	86.8	83.4	80.3
32K	2	665	98.6	97.1	94.3	90.4	86.8	83.5	80.4
16K	4	667	98.3	96.8	94.1	90.2	86.6	83.3	80.2
8K	7	587	97.8	96.1	93.0	88.7	84.8	81.2	77.8
4K	13	551	96.7	95.0	91.7	87.2	83.1	79.4	76.0
2K	22	476	94.6	92.7	89.0	84.0	79.6	75.6	72.0
1K	34	384	90.8	88.5	84.2	78.5	73.5	75.8	65.3

These calculations are based on 259 clock periods of length 40 ns to transmit a full burst and 23 clock periods for short burst. (HIPPI-PH specifies three clock periods of overhead per burst.) A packet of "n" kB of user data consists of "n" full bursts and one short burst equal in length to the number of bytes in the HIPPI, LLC, IP and TCP headers. The "Hold Time" is the minimum connection duration needed to send the packets. The "Burst Rate" is the effective transfer rate for the duration of the connection, not counting connection switching time. Throughput rates are in megabytes/second, accounting for connection switching times of 10, 30, 60, 90, 120 and 150 micro seconds. These calculations ignore any limit on the rate at which a source or destination can process small packets; such limits may further reduce the

available throughput if small packets are used. Below the main features of
the HIPPI network are summarized:

- Speeds: 800 Mbps and 1.6 Gbps
- Cabling: 50-pair STP, singlemode and multimode fiber
- Distance: 50 meters point-to-point over copper. Cascaded switches can be
  extended up to 200 meters over copper; 300 meters over multimode fiber;
  10 kilometers over single-mode fiber
- Connection time: Less than 1 microsecond for dedicated connection
- Latency: 160 nanoseconds on average

3. Performance Evaluation of Network Interfaces

From the viewpoint of communication performance the host-network interface connection is very important. The Network Interface Card (NIC) structure and the way in which it is connected to the I/O should not constrain the
available bandwidth of the network. Thus, some analysis of the system technical parameters have to be done while designing the network infrastructure.

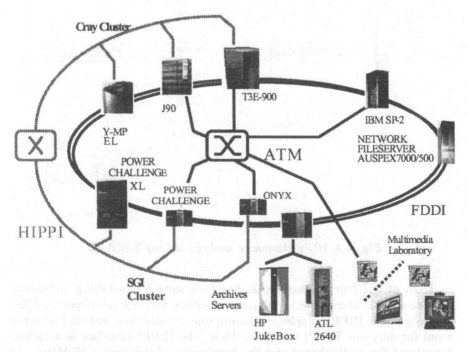

Fig. 3.1. Exemplary networking infrastructure of a metacomputer.

To present the methodology we take as an example the network infrastructure of the metacomputer installed at the Poznan Supercomputing and

Networking Center (PSNC) (Fig. 3.1), for which positive and negative aspects will be identified. In this section some tests for ATM and HIPPI networks are also described.

3.1 I/O Performance Evaluation

In this subsection we present the methodology of I/O performance analysis based on the systems Cray Y-MP EL, Cray J916, IBM SP2 and SGI PowerChallenge. In the Cray Y-MP EL supercomputer the maximal bandwidth between processor and I/O devices is 4.2 GBps (giga bytes per second). This is the result of the fact that each of the four processors has four memory ports with a bandwidth of 264 MBps each. To one of the ports (port D) just two I/O subsystems can be attached (VME I/O) with a bandwidth of 40 MBps each (which makes 160 MBps per processor and 640 MBps per maximal configuration). Y-MP EL installed at PSNC has two such subsystems installed. Thus, the maximum bandwidth of I/O equals 80 MBps. Fig. 3.2 below presents the I/O performance analysis of the Cray Y-MP EL.

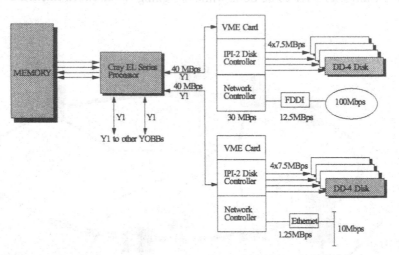

Fig. 3.2. I/O performance analysis of Cray Y-MP EL.

Each of the four motherboards has four slots for installing additional interfaces. This allows the installation of either four Y1 interfaces to IOSs or two pairs of HIPPI interfaces. Having one Y1 interface installed we have room for only one HIPPI interface. Thus, the HIPPI interface is attached directly to the motherboard and the bandwidth of this link is 80 MBps. As can be seen, there is a limitation compared to the available bandwidth of the HIPPI network. Connections to the Ethernet and FDDI of the system will not cause any bottlenecks. However, if we connect some additional devices, the situation may change. Thus it is necessary to make a proper configuration of the system based on such an analysis.

Fig. 3.3 presents the I/O performance analysis of the Cray J916 system. In this case the maximum bandwidth between processor and I/O devices equals 25.6 GBps. All of the 16 processors can operate with two memory ports with a bandwidth of 800 MBps each. The maximum number of I/O subsystems that can be attached is 16. In our configuration there are only 4 such subsystems available with 100 MBps each. The bandwidth that is needed by all the devices to be serviced without bottlenecks is about 164 MBps. The maximum available bandwidth is 4x100 MBps, which makes a total of 400 MBps. HIPPI connections are made directly to the motherboard with a bandwidth of 100 MBps. The IBM SP2 I/O is presented in Fig. 3.4.

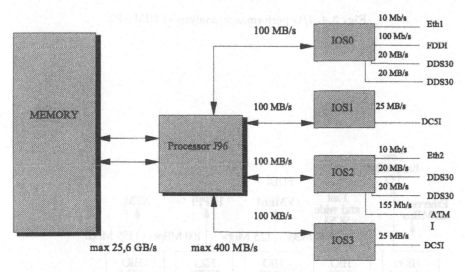

Fig. 3.3. I/O Performance analysis of Cray J916.

When we look at the communication interfaces the connections of Ethernet, HPS (High Performance Switch - 45 MBps), FDDI and ATM take about 66 MBps. Thus, we have some free bandwidth left as the maximum for the port is 80 MBps and the maximum for the node 160 MBps.

The POWER CHALLENGE I/O subsystem consists of one to four POWER-channel-2 boards (one in our configuration) together with associated HIO (High-Speed I/O) modules various I/O adapters are attached. POWERchannel-2 board contains I/O adapters to connect a basic I/O complement consisting of an Ethernet transceiver, two 16-bit SCSI-2 channels, three serial ports, and a parallel port. Each POWERchannel-2 provides connection slots for two HIO modules, allowing up to 12 HIO modules in a maximally configured system. The only constraint in that I/O architecture is its HiPPI interface limited to only 90 MBps. In modern architectures of computer systems (e.g. ORIGIN 2000, Sun Ultra Enterprise) vendors provide

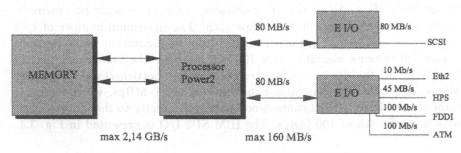

Fig. 3.4. I/O performance analysis of IBM SP2.

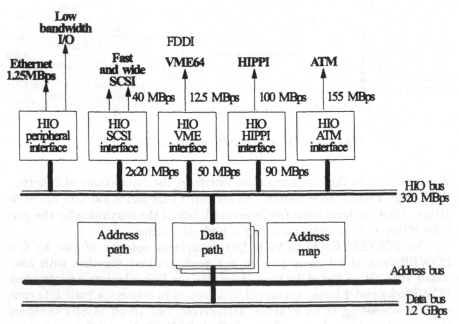

Fig. 3.5. I/O performance analysis of SGI PowerChallenge.

a PCI interface. PCI is a robust interconnection mechanism designed specifically to accommodate multiple high performance peripherals for graphics, full motion video, SCSI, LAN, etc. It is a very interesting idea for connecting hosts to various networks. Below we present the solutions which came from Silicon Graphics ORIGIN2000 and Sun Ultra Enterprise. PCI within

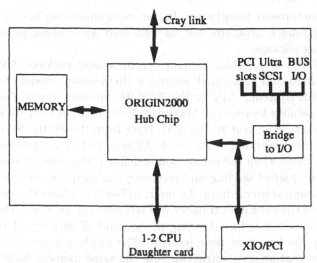

Fig. 3.6. PCI within ORIGIN 2000.

the Silicon Graphics ORIGIN2000 (Fig. 3.6) system is supported as an option through the internal PCI card cage. One has to remember that there is only a single PCI expansion box supported per deskside or rack module. Each PCI expansion cage provides support for two 64-bit PCI full size cards. The 64-bit PCI bus has a peak bandwidth of 267 MBps, which allows connecting even full duplex Fibre Channel interface without any bottlenecks. The PCI I/O board in Enterprise 3000-6000 servers has dual 528 MBps PCI-66 (66MHz, 64-bit) channels. Each channel leads to a PCI slot. There are also two 264 MBps standard PCI channels. One channel leads to an on-board 10/100 Mbps Ethernet and other The I/O Board to the Gigaplane. Thus, the PCI I/O Board throughput is 668 MBps. The throughput of the above described PCI interfaces enables Gigabit Ethernet (full duplex), Fibre Channel and other network interface cards to be supported.

3.2 Performance Evaluation of ATM and HIPPI

ATM, HIPPI and Fibre Channel are emerging as the leaders of high performance networks. As mentioned above, large data applications like distance learning, video conferencing, scientific visualization etc. require high throughput whereas distributed network computing environments like MPI require low latencies. In this subsection we compare the throughput and latencies provided by ATM and HIPPI. For Fibre Channel performance tests we refer to [LHD+94a].

3.2.1 Hardware test environment. The experiments described were performed on a cluster of CrayT3E and CrayJ90 systems connected via the network topology presented in Fig. 3.1.

3.2.2 Measurement programs. In our experiments we have developed a network benchmark program, but as well used an existing public domain benchmarking package.

NetPerf [HP94] is a public domain benchmarking package developed by Hewlett-Packard and structured around a client-server model. NetPerf can use the FORE Systems' API or the TCP/IP protocol suites. NetPerf provides the capability to vary the Maximum Transmission Unit (MTU) size of the data packet being sent to the AAL layer from the FORE Systems' API. The link protocol selection of Ethernet, ATM or HIPPI is passed as an argument to the client when the connection is defined. One metric available from NetPerf is the pair of sending and receiving throughputs over an ATM and HIPPI communication medium. An input to NetPerf allows the user to select the amount of time the data transfer will last over the network. The resulting throughput is calculated by dividing the amount of data transferred during this time by the length of time interval. The implementation of NetPerf is simplified by continuously retransmitting the same memory buffer until the specified time interval expires. Another input allows the buffer size to be defined by the user.

A simple echo program was used to test both throughput (for large messages) and latency (for small messages). The general concept of the programs is presented in the Fig. 3.7. The client sends N-byte messages to the server and waits for the response of the server with the same amount of the data being sent back. The client starts to count the round trip time of the message when it sends the whole message to the server and ends counting when it receives the whole message back. Additional time duration is added (0.5 sec) between every iteration to avoid any possible effects of pipelining in the interface cards or the switches. It is obvious that the total round trip time depends on the protocol stack, device driver, the host interface, signal propagation and switch routing. The communication latency can be estimated as half of the total round-trip time. The throughput is calculated as $2*N/time$. After the last iteration the minimum, maximum and average time is calculated from the collected timing data.

3.2.3 Test results. The following graphs present the latency and bandwidth of ATM and HIPPI measured by the echo program outlined above. Fig. 3.8 and Fig. 3.9 show the latency of ATM and HIPPI networks, respectively. For very small messages (16 bytes to 16 kB) HIPPI is faster with an average minimum latency of 140 ns. ATM has an average minimum latency of 1.8 ms. Having noticed that minimum times are close to the average ones

CLIENT SIDE	SERVER SIDE

begin
    N:=16 bytes
    for i:=1 to n do
        begin
            Start Timer;
            Send N;
            Receive N;
            Stop Timer;
            Sleep(0.5 sec)
            Increment(N);
        end;
end;
	begin
	    for i:=1 to n do
	        begin
	            Receive N;
	            Send N;
	        end;
	end;

Fig. 3.7. Echo server program.

we conclude that delays from the operating system happen infrequently thus allowing the interfaces to work at peak efficiency. Fig. 3.10 and Fig. 3.11 show the bandwidth of ATM and HIPPI networks respectively. As the message size increases both of the network bandwidths also increase and reach a maximum rate of 12.6 MBps for ATM and 87.2 MBps for HIPPI. The test results clearly show that HIPPI offers lower end-to-end latency than the ATM network. Lower latency and greater available bandwidth show that the HIPPI network is very efficient for distributed applications on a local area basis (up to 25m). For that reason HIPPI is used in such solutions as PowerChallenge Array, where it connects all the PowerChallenge systems of the cluster. Of course these tests are not an absolute measure that could be repeated in other environments, however the relations between the tests will remain the same or similar. In each case the dotted line is the trend line for particular test data.

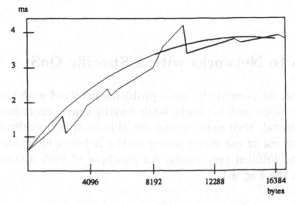

Fig. 3.8. ATM latency.

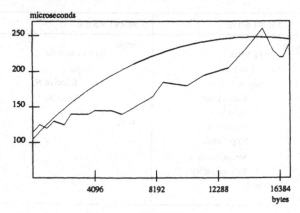

Fig. 3.9. HIPPI latency.

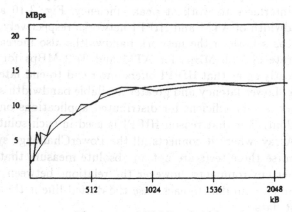

Fig. 3.10. ATM bandwidth.

4. Access to Networks with a Specific QoS

In this section we present the main problems involved with the co-operation of the applications with networks while having some communication requirements. In general, such applications are able to apply communication based on some protocol or use direct access to the network in which their requirements can be fulfilled very easily. An example of such a communication is presented in the Fig. 4.1.

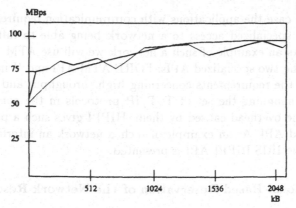

Fig. 3.11. HIPPI bandwidth.

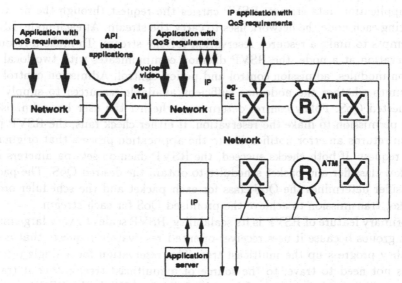

Fig. 4.1. IP application with QoS requirements.

In the first case the traditional set of TCP/IP protocols has to be enriched with some specialized protocols and a procedure of the reservation of some specific resources on the network end-to-end path, i.e. starting from the end application, through NICs, switches and routers, up to the remote end application (e.g. server). For this purpose one can use the specific functions of the switches as well as dedicated access software or specialized protocols which allow devices to interact on the transmission path, e.g. RSVP, NHRP (see Section 4.1 for explanation). The presentation of these protocols, as well as problems relating to the application-protocol interaction, are one of the main parts of this section.

In the second case the applications with communication requirements make use of direct, specialized access to a network being able to fulfill these requirements. As an example of such a network we will use ATM. Based on it we will describe two specialized APIs: FORE ATM API and Winsock-2. The realization of the requirements concerning high throughput and low latency also leads to spanning the set of TCP/IP protocols in the communication to decrease the overhead caused by them. HIPPI gives such a possibility by the specialized API. As an example of such a network an interface with the application the IRIS HIPPI API is presented.

4.1 IP Protocol-Based Reservation of the Network Resources

4.1.1 Resource reservation protocol (RSVP).
A host uses RSVP to request a specific Quality of Service (QoS) from the network, on behalf of an application data stream. RSVP carries the request through the network, visiting each node the network uses to carry the stream. At each node, RSVP attempts to make a resource reservation for the stream. To make a resource reservation at a node, the RSVP daemon communicates with two local decision modules, admission control and policy control. Admission control determines whether the node has sufficient available resources to supply the requested QoS. Policy control determines whether the user has administrative permission to make the reservation. If either check fails, the RSVP program returns an error notification to the application process that originated the request. If both checks succeed, the RSVP daemon sets parameters in a packet classifier and packet scheduler to obtain the desired QoS. The packet classifier determines the QoS class for each packet and the scheduler orders packet transmission to achieve the promised QoS for each stream.

A primary feature of RSVP is its scalability. RSVP scales to very large multicast groups because it uses receiver-oriented reservation requests that merge as they progress up the multicast tree. The reservation for a single receiver does not need to travel to the source of a multicast tree; rather it travels only until it reaches a reserved branch of the tree. While the RSVP protocol is designed specifically for multicast applications, it may also make unicast reservations. RSVP is also designed to utilize the robustness of current Internet routing algorithms. RSVP does not perform its own routing; instead it uses underlying routing protocols to determine where it should carry reservation requests. As routing changes paths to adapt to topology changes, RSVP adapts its reservation to the new paths wherever reservations are in place. This modularity does not rule out RSVP from using other routing services. Current research within the RSVP project is focusing on designing RSVP to use routing services that provide alternate paths and fixed paths. RSVP runs over IP, both IPv4 and IPv6. Among RSVP's other features, it provides non-transparent transport of traffic control and policy control messages, and provides transparent operation through un-supporting regions.

Architecture. RSVP requests resources for simplex flows, i.e., it requests resources in only one direction. Therefore, RSVP treats a sender as logically distinct from a receiver, although the same application process may act as both a sender and a receiver at the same time. RSVP operates on top of IPv4 or IPv6, occupying the place of the transport protocol in the protocol stack. However, RSVP does not transport application data but is rather an Internet control protocol, like ICMP, IGMP, or routing protocols. Like the implementations of routing and management protocols, an implementation of RSVP will typically execute in the background, not on the data forwarding path (see Fig. 4.2). In order to efficiently accommodate large groups, dynamic

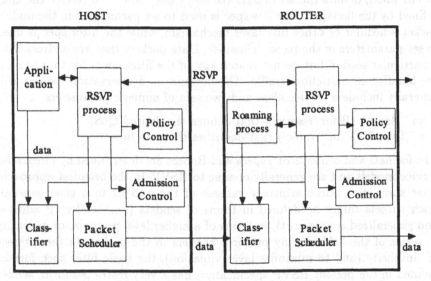

Fig. 4.2. RSVP in Hosts and Routers.

group membership, and heterogeneous receiver requirements, RSVP makes receivers responsible for requesting a specific QoS. A QoS request from a receiver host application is passed to the local RSVP process. The RSVP protocol then carries the request to all the nodes (routers and hosts) along the reverse data path(s) to the data source(s). As a result, RSVP's reservation overhead is in general logarithmic rather than linear in the number of receivers. Quality of service is implemented for a particular data flow by mechanisms collectively called "traffic control". These mechanisms include (1) a packet classifier, (2) admission control, and (3) a packet scheduler or some other link-layer-dependent mechanism to determine when particular packets are forwarded. The packet classifier determines the QoS class (and perhaps the route) for each packet. For each outgoing interface, the packet scheduler or other link-layer-dependent mechanism achieves the promised QoS. Traffic control implements QoS service models defined by the Integrated Services

Working Group. Since the membership of a large multicast group and the resulting multicast tree topology are likely to change with time, the RSVP design assumes that state of RSVP and the traffic control state are to be built and destroyed incrementally in routers and hosts. For this purpose, RSVP establishes a "soft" state; that is, RSVP sends periodic refresh messages to maintain the state along the reserved path(s). In the absence of refresh messages, the state automatically times out and is deleted.

Reservation Model. An elementary RSVP reservation request consists of a "flowspec" together with a filterspec"; this pair is called a "flow descriptor". The flowspec specifies the desired QoS. The filter spec, together with a session specification, defines the set of data packets - the "flow" - to receive the QoS defined by the flowspec. The flowspec is used to set parameters in the node's packet scheduler or other link layer mechanism, while the filter spec is used to set parameters in the packet classifier. Data packets that are addressed to a particular session but do not match any of the filter specs for that session are handled as best-effort traffic. The flowspec in a reservation request will generally include a service class and two sets of numeric parameters:

– an "Rspec" (R for 'reserve') that defines the desired QoS,
– a "Tspec" (T for 'traffic') that describes the data flow.

The formats and contents of Tspecs and Rspecs are determined by integrated service models and are generally opaque to RSVP. In the broadest approach, filter specs may select arbitrary subsets of the packets in a given session. Such subsets might be defined in terms of senders (i.e., sender IP address and generalized source port), in terms of a higher level protocol, or generally in terms of the fields in any protocol headers in the packet. In the interest of simplicity (and to minimize layer violation), the basic filter spec format defined in the present RSVP specification has a very restricted form: sender IP address and optionally the UDP/TCP port number SrcPort. Because the UDP/TCP port numbers are used for packet classification, each router must be able to examine these fields. The basic RSVP reservation model is "one pass": a receiver sends a reservation request upstream (in the sender direction), and each node on the path either accepts or rejects the request. This scheme provides no easy way for a receiver to discover the resulting end-to-end service. Therefore, RSVP supports an enhancement to one-pass service known as "One Pass With Advertising" (OPWA). With OPWA, RSVP control packets are sent downstream (in the receiver direction), following the data paths, to gather information that may be used to predict the end-to-end QoS. The results ("advertisements") are delivered by RSVP to the receiver hosts and perhaps to the receiver applications. The advertisements may then be used by the receiver to construct, or to dynamically adjust an appropriate reservation request.

Reservation Styles. A reservation request includes a set of options that are collectively called the reservation "style". One reservation option concerns the treatment of reservations for different senders within the same session: either establish a distinct reservation for each upstream sender, or else make a single reservation that is "shared" among all packets of selected senders. Another reservation option controls the selection of senders; it may be an "explicit" list of all selected senders, or a "wildcard" that implicitly selects all the senders to the session. In an explicit sender-selection reservation, each filter spec must exactly match one sender, while in a wildcard sender-selection no filter spec is needed. The following styles are currently defined (see Fig. 4.3):

Sender Selection	RESERVATIONS	
	Distinct	Shared
Explicit	Fixed-Filter (FF) Style	Shared-Explicit (SE) Style
Wildcard	(None defined)	Wildcard-Filter (WF) Style

Fig. 4.3. Reservation Attributes and Styles.

− Wildcard-Filter (WF) Style
  The WF style implies the following options: shared reservation and wild-card sender selection. Thus, a WF style reservation creates a single reservation shared by flows among upstream senders. This reservation may be thought of as a shared pipe, whose size is that of the largest resource request from all receivers, independent of the number of senders using the reservation. A WF style reservation is propagated upstream towards all sender hosts, and it automatically extends to new senders as they appear.
− Fixed-Filter (FF) Style
  The FF style implies the following options: distinct reservations and explicit sender selection. Thus, an elementary FF style reservation request creates a distinct reservation for data packets from a particular sender, not sharing them with other senders' packets for the same session.
− Shared Explicit (SE) Style
  The SE style implies the following options: shared reservation and explicit sender selection. Thus, an SE style reservation creates a single reservation shared by selected upstream senders. Unlike the WF style, the SE style allows a receiver to explicitly specify the set of senders to be included.

Each data flow arrives from a previous hop through a corresponding incoming interface and departs through one or more outgoing interface(s) (Fig. 4.4). The same interface may act in both incoming and outgoing roles for different data flows in the same session. Multiple previous hops and/or next hops may be reached through a given physical interface; for example, the figure implies that D and D' are connected to (d) via a broadcast LAN. There are two

fundamental RSVP message types: Resv and Path. Each receiver host sends
RSVP reservation request (Resv) messages upstream towards the senders.
These messages must follow exactly the reverse of the path(s) the data packets
will use, upstream to all the sender hosts included in the sender selection.
They create and maintain "reservation state" in each node along the path(s).
Resv messages must finally be delivered to the sender hosts themselves, so
that the hosts can set up appropriate traffic control parameters for the first
hop. Each RSVP sender host transmits RSVP "Path" messages downstream

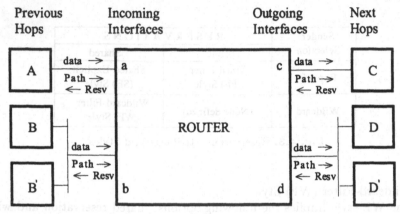

Fig. 4.4. Router Using RSVP.

along the uni/multicast routes provided by the routing protocol(s), following
the paths of the data. These Path messages store "path state" in each node
along the way. This path state includes at least the unicast IP address of the
previous hop node, which is used to route the Resv messages hop-by-hop in
the reverse direction.

4.1.2 RSVP over ATM. One of the important features of ATM technology is the ability to request a point-to-point Virtual Circuit (VC) with a
specified Quality of Service (QoS). Point-to-multipoint VCs allow leaf nodes
to be added and removed from the VC dynamically and so provide a mechanism for supporting IP multicast. It is only natural that RSVP and the
Internet Integrated Services (IIS) model would like to utilize the QoS properties of any underlying link layer, including ATM. Classical IP over ATM is
based on a Logical IP Subnetwork (LIS), which is a separately administered
IP subnetwork. Hosts within an LIS communicate using the ATM network,
while hosts from different subnets communicate only by going through an
IP router (even though it may be possible to open a direct VC between the
two hosts over the ATM network). Classical IP over ATM provides an Address Resolution Protocol (ATMARP) for ATM edge devices to resolve IP
addresses to native ATM addresses. For any pair of IP/ATM edge devices
(i.e. hosts or routers), a single VC is created on demand and shared for all

traffic between the two devices. A second part of the RSVP and IIS over ATM problem, IP multicast, is being solved with MARS , the Multicast Address Resolution Server. A key remaining issue for IP in an ATM environment is the integration of RSVP signaling and ATM signaling in support of the Internet Integrated Services (IIS) model. There are two main areas involved in supporting the IIS model, QoS translation and VC management. QoS translation concerns mapping a QoS from the IIS model to a proper ATM QoS, while VC management concentrates on how many VCs are needed and which traffic flows are routed over which VCs.

Permanent Virtual Circuits (PVCs). PVCs emulate dedicated point-to-point lines in a network, so the operation of RSVP can be identical to the operation over any point-to-point network. The QoS of the PVC must be consistent and equivalent to the type of traffic and service model used. The devices on either end of the PVC have to provide traffic control services in order to multiplex multiple flows over the same PVC. With PVCs, there is no issue of when or how long it takes to set up VCs, since they are made in advance but the resources of the PVC are limited to what has been pre-allocated. PVCs that are not fully utilized can tie up ATM network resources that could be used for SVCs. An additional issue for using PVCs is one of network engineering. Frequently, multiple PVCs are set up such that if all the PVCs were running at full capacity, the link would be over-subscribed. This frequently used "statistical multiplexing gain" makes providing IIS over PVCs very difficult and unreliable. Any application of IIS over PVCs has to be assured that the PVCs are able to receive all the requested QoS.

Switched Virtual Circuits (SVCs). SVCs allow paths in the ATM network to be set up "on demand". This gives a flexibility in the use of RSVP over ATM along with some complexity. Parallel VCs can be set up to allow best effort and better service class paths through the network, as shown in Fig. 4.5. The cost and time to set up SVCs can impact their use. For example, it may be better to initially route QoS traffic over existing VCs until a SVC with the desired QoS can be set up for the flow. Scaling issues can come into play if a single RSVP flow is used per VC. Assuming one flow per VC, the number of VCs in any ATM device may also be limited, so the number of RSVP flows that can be supported by a device can be strictly limited to the number of available VCs. While RSVP is receiver oriented, ATM is sender oriented. This might seem like a problem but the sender receives RSVP RESV messages and can determine whether a new VC has to be set up to the destination.

Point-to-MultiPoint. In order to provide QoS for IP multicast, an important feature of RSVP, data flows must be distributed to multiple destinations from a given source. Point-to-multipoint VCs provide such a mechanism. It is important to map the actions of IP multicasting and RSVP (e.g. IGMP JOIN/LEAVE and RSVP RESV/RESV TEAR) to add party and drop party functions for ATM. Point-to-multipoint VCs have a single service class for all destinations. This is contrary to the RSVP "heterogeneous receiver" concept.

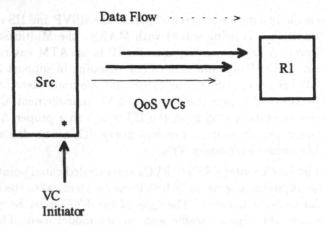

Fig. 4.5. Data Flow VC Initiation.

It is possible to set up a different VC to each receiver requesting a different QoS, as shown in Fig. 4.6. This again can run into scaling and resource problems when multiple VCs on the same interface to different destinations are to be managed. RSVP sends messages both up and down the multicast distribution tree. In the case of a large ATM network, this could result in a RSVP message implosion at an ATM ingress point with many receivers. UNI 4.0 expands on the point-to-multipoint VCs by adding the Leaf Initiated Join (LIJ) capability. LIJ allows an ATM end point to join onto an existing point-to-multipoint VC without necessarily contacting the source of the VC. This can reduce the burden on the ATM source point for setting up new branches and more closely matches the receiver-based model of RSVP and IP multicast. However, many of the same scaling issues exist and the new branches added to a point-to-multipoint VC must use the same QoS as the existing branches.

Dynamic QoS. RSVP provides dynamic quality of service (QoS) in that the requested resources may change at any time. There are several common reasons for a change of QoS reservation which are listed below.

1. An existing receiver can request a new larger (or smaller) QoS.
2. A sender may change its traffic specification (TSpec), which can trigger a change in the reservation requests of the receivers.
3. A new sender can start sending to a multicast group with larger traffic specification than existing senders, thus triggering larger reservations.
4. A new receiver can make a reservation that is larger than existing reservations.

If a limited heterogeneity model is used and the merge node for the larger reservation is an ATM edge device, a new larger reservation must be set up across the ATM network. Since the ATM service, as currently defined in UNI

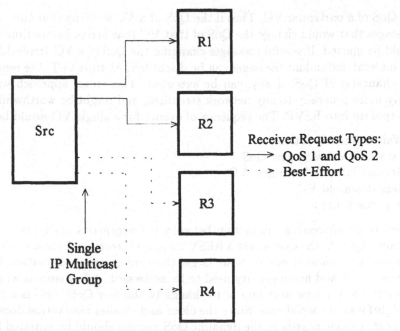

Fig. 4.6. Types of Multicast Receivers.

3.x and UNI 4.0, does not allow for renegotiating the QoS of a VC, dynamically changing the reservation means creating a new VC with a new QoS, and tearing down an established VC. Tearing down a VC and setting up a new VC in ATM are complex operations that involve a great amount of processing time, and may have a substantial latency. There are several options for dealing with this mismatch in service. The default method for supporting changes in RSVP reservations is to attempt to replace an existing VC with a new appropriately sized VC. During setup of the replacement VC, the old VC must be left in place unmodified. The old VC is left unmodified to minimize the interruption of QoS data delivery. Once the replacement VC is established, data transmission is shifted to the new VC, and the old VC is then closed. If the setup of the replacement VC fails, then the old QoS VC should continue to be used.

One additional issue is that only one QoS change can be processed at one time per reservation. If the requested QoS is changed while the first replacement VC is still being setup, then the replacement VC is released and the whole VC replacement process is restarted. To limit the number of changes and to avoid excessive signaling load, implementations may limit the number of changes that will be processed in a given period.

One implementation approach could have each ATM edge device configured with a time parameter T (which can change over time) that gives the minimum amount of time the edge device will wait between successive changes of the QoS of a particular VC. Thus if the QoS of a VC is changed at time t, all messages that would change the QoS of that VC that arrive before time t+T would be queued. If several messages changing the QoS of a VC arrive during the interval, redundant messages can be discarded. At time t+T, the remaining change(s) of QoS, if any, can be executed. This timer approach would apply more generally to any network structure, and might be worthwhile to incorporate into RSVP. The sequence of events for a single VC would be:

- Wait if timer is active
- Establish VC with new QoS
- Remap data traffic to new VC
- Tear down old VC
- Activate timer.

There is an interesting interaction between heterogeneous reservations and dynamic QoS. In the case where a RESV message is received from a new next-hop and the requested resources are larger than any existing reservation, both dynamic QoS and heterogeneity need to be addressed. A key issue is what to do first: add the new next-hop or to change to the new QoS. This is a fairly straightforward special case. Since the older and smaller reservation does not support the new next-hop, the dynamic QoS process should be initiated first. Since the new QoS is only needed by the new next-hop, it should be the first end-point of the new VC. This way signaling is minimized when the setup to the new next-hop fails.

4.2 IP Switching

IP switching is a modern technology for packet routing. Contrary to classical routing technology in which the node of the network has to read the IP address of every packet, analyze it and then transmit it to the desired port, IP switching is based on sophisticated hardware and software solutions (e.g. ATM switches) which enable to switch packets. One of the important technologies which gains more and more support from various vendors is MPOA (Multiprotocol over ATM). MPOA is not only an IP switching technology as it is able to serve the files generated by any communication protocol operating in the third layer of the OSI network architecture (IP, IPX etc.). Other standards and protocols for IP switching are MPLS (Multiprotocol Label Switching) and NHRP (Next-Hop Resolution Protocol). All these technologies will be described in this subsection.

4.2.1 MultiProtocol label switching (MPLS). MPLS is a method for hosts and routers which support both label switching and RSVP to associate labels with RSVP flows. The goal is to provide a routing technology for label switching routers (LSRs) to be able to identify the appropriate reservation state for a packet based on its label value. The association between RSVP flows and labels involves the allocation of a label to a flow. The receiver of data allocates labels for best effort traffic. The label stacking mechanism can be useful in some scenarios independent of a routing hierarchy. The basic concept of stacking is to provide a mechanism to segregate streams within a switched path. Under normal operation, when packets are encapsulated into a single L2 (Layer 2) header, if multiple streams are forwarded into a switched path, it will require L3 (Layer 3) processing to segregate a certain stream at the end of the switched path. The stacking mechanism provides an easy way to maintain the identity of various streams which are merged into a single switched path. An interesting use can be in conjunction with RSVP flows. In RSVP, sender's flows can be logically merged under a single resource reservation using the Shared and the Wildcard filters. The stacking mechanism can be used to merge flows into a single label, and the shared QoS can be applied to a single label on top of the stack. Since sender flows within the merged switched path maintain their identity, it is easy to de-merge at a downstream node without requiring L3 processing of the packets. Another similar application can be merging of several premium service flows with similar QoS into a single switched path. This helps in conserving labels in the backbone of large networks.

4.2.2 NBMA next hop resolution protocol (NHRP). The Non-Broad-cast, Multi-Access (NBMA) Next Hop Resolution Protocol (NHRP) allows a source station (a host or router), wishing to communicate over a NBMA subnetwork, to determine the internetworking layer addresses and NBMA addresses of suitable "NBMA next hops" toward a destination station. If the destination is connected to the NBMA subnetwork, then the NBMA next hop is the destination station itself. Otherwise, the NBMA next hop is the egress router from the NBMA subnetwork that is "nearest" to the destination station. One way to model an NBMA network is by using the notion of logically independent IP subnets (LISs). LISs have the following properties:

- All members of the LIS have the same IP network/subnet number and address mask.
- All members of the LIS are directly connected to the same NBMA subnet-work.
- All hosts and routers outside of the LIS are accessed via a router.
- All members of the LIS access each other directly (without routers).

Address resolution only resolves the next hop address if the destination station is a member of the same LIS as the source station; otherwise, the source station must forward packets to a router that is a member of multiple LIS's. In multi-LIS configurations, hop-by-hop address resolution may not be sufficient to resolve the "NBMA next hop" toward the destination station, and IP packets may have multiple IP hops through the NBMA subnetwork. Another way to model NBMA is by using the notion of Local Address Groups (LAG's). The essential difference between the LIS and the LAG models is that while with the LIS model the outcome of the "local/remote" forwarding decision is driven purely by addressing information, with the LAG model the outcome of this decision is decoupled from the addressing information and is coupled with the Quality of Service and/or traffic characteristics. With the LAG model any two entities on a common NBMA network could establish a direct communication with each other, irrespective of the entities' addresses. Support for the LAG model assumes existence of a mechanism that allows any entity (i.e., host or router) connected to an NBMA network to resolve an internetworking layer address to an NBMA address for any other entity connected to the same NBMA network. This resolution would take place regardless of the address assignments to these entities. For example, when the internetworking layer address is of type IP, once the NBMA next hop has been resolved, the source may either start sending IP packets to the destination or may first establish a connection to the destination with the desired bandwidth.

The most prominent feature of NHRP is that it avoids extra router hops in an NBMA with multiple LISs. To reach this goal, NHRP provides the source with the NBMA address of the destination, only if the destination is directly attached to the NBMA. If the destination station is not attached to the NBMA, then NHRP provides the source with the NBMA address of an exit router that has connectivity to the destination. In general, there may be multiple exit routers that have connectivity to the destination. If NHRP uses the services of a dynamic routing algorithm in fulfilling its function, which is necessary for robust and scalable operation, then the exit router identified by NHRP reflects the selection made by the network layer dynamic routing protocol. In general, the selection made by the routing protocol would often reflect a desirable attribute, such as identifying the exit router that induces the least number of hops in the original routed path. When routing IP packets over an NBMA network where there is potentially a direct Source to Destination connectivity with QoS options, the decision on local vs. remote is no longer as fundamentally important. Thus, in an NBMA network with QoS options, the basic decision becomes the one of short-cut vs. hop-by-hop network layer routing. In this case, the relevant criterion becomes applications' QoS requirements. NHRP is particularly applicable for environments in which the decision on local vs. remote is superseded by the decision on short-cut vs. hop-by-hop network layer routing.

Let us assume that the trade-off is in favor of a short-cut NBMA route. Generally, an NHRP request can be issued by a variety of NHRP aware entities, including hosts and routers with NBMA interfaces. If an IP packet traverses multiple hops before a short-cut path has been established, then there is a chance that multiple short-cut paths could be formed. In order to avoid such an undesirable situation, a useful operation rule is to authorize only the following entities to issue an NHRP request and to perform short-cut routing:

– The host that originates the IP packet, if the host has an NBMA interface.

- The first router along the routing path of the IP packet such that the next hop is reachable through the NBMA interface of that particular router.
- A policy router within an NBMA network through which the IP packet has to traverse.

4.2.3 MultiProtocol over ATM (MPOA). The ATM Forum's Multiprotocol Over ATM (MPOA) subworking group is developing an approach to support seamless transport of layer 3 protocols across ATM networks (IP and IPX). MPOA, operating at layer 2 and 3, will use the ATM Forum LAN Emulation (LANE) for its layer 2 forwarding. As such, MPOA can be seen as an evolution beyond LANE. LANE basically connects together a single legacy LAN subnet across ATM. MPOA goes one step further by allowing direct ATM connectivity between hosts in different subnets. The proposed architecture consists of edge devices and route servers. An edge device (not necessarily user equipment) would forward packets between the LAN and ATM networks, establishing ATM connections when needed, but would not be involved directly in routing. Edge devices would query a Route Server when an unknown host address is encountered. Route Servers would be able to map a host address into the information needed by the edge device to establish a connection across the ATM network. This would be the layer 3 address of the optimal exit point from the ATM network as well as the ATM address of that exit point. Route servers would also be able to forward packets on to the exit point on behalf of the edge device while they are establishing their own ATM virtual circuits.

5. Networking APIs

Even experienced application developers don't like to go deep into the network interfaces using low level programming techniques. That is what Application Programming Interface (API) is all about - hiding the complexity of the network from the application layer. The APIs can be found at any of the different layer boundaries in the network stack. End-user applications and application development tools typically access only the API at the top of the stack, but middleware, operating systems, network protocols, and other network layers also use the APIs to insulate themselves from the layers below.

5.1 ATM APIs

Such APIs like BSD sockets or Microsoft WINSOCK were not designed with ATM's signaling and quality of service in mind. That's why the developers accustomed to working with those APIs would rather not contend with these ATM-specific issues when coding new applications. There were some concepts to construct an API which would eliminate the need for a network-layer protocol. It would directly access ATM at the data link layer, where

Signalling & Control	User Aplications (Data, Voice, Video)
Signalling AAL	ATM Adaptation
ATM Layer	
Physical Layer	

Fig. 5.1. ATM layers.

all addressing and signaling functions are performed (see Fig. 5.1). The two existing examples of such APIs are the FORE API and WINSOCK 2 API.

5.1.1 FORE Systems API. FORE Systems' user-level ATM library routines provide a portable interface to the ATM data link layer. It is an ATM adaptation layer based programming interface, allowing software designers to create applications without the TCP/IP protocol stack and the socket layer buffering mechanisms. The library routines for SunOS and IRIX platforms are STREAMS-based. The ATM library provides a connection-oriented client and server model. Before data can be transferred a connection has to be established between the client and the server. Once the connection is established, the network makes a "best effort" to deliver the ATM cells to the destination. The cells may be dropped depending on the network resources remaining. End-to- end flow control and retransmission are left to the application. Applications first open a file descriptor with atm_open() and then bind a local ASAP to the file descriptor with atm_bind(). The local NSAP is also implicitly bound to the same file descriptor. The remote ASAP and NSAP are associated with the file descriptor when a connect indication or a connect confirmation is received. Connections are established using atm_connect() in combination with atm_accept(). These operations allow the data transfer to be simplex, duplex, or multicast. ATM Virtual Path Identifiers (VPI) and Virtual Channel Identifiers are assigned by the network during connection establishment. The ATM device driver associates the VPI/VCI with an ASAP which is in turn associated with a file descriptor. When a connection is duplex, both an incoming and an outgoing VPI/VCI are associated with the ASAP; the two need not to be the same. It provides guaranteed bandwidth reservation for each connection. The network uses the bandwidth information, and will refuse connection if the requested bandwidth is not available. Applications can also select the kind of ATM Adaptation Layer (AAL) to be used for data exchange. In the current implementation of FORE, AAL type 1 and 2 are not supported, and types 3 and 4 are treated identically. The main difference between AAL 3/4 and AAL 5 lies in their multiplexing and error detection capabilities as well as in the amount of overhead generated by each of them and the reduction of the effective available bandwidth. The functions `atm_send()` and `atm_recv()` are used to transfer user messages. One Protocol Data Unit (PDU) is transferred on each call. The maximum size of the PDU depends on the AAL chosen for the connection and the constraints of the underlying socket-based or stream-based device driver implementation. The ATM library can be used to establish connections between two endsystems in a point-to-point configuration (i.e. in the absence of a switch). Below the most important functions of the FORE Systems ATM API are presented:

- `atm_open()` - open an ATM connection endpoint and get ATM connection information
- `atm_bind()` - bind an ASAP to an ATM end-point
- `atm_connect()` - establish a connection with another ATM end-point
- `atm_accept()` - accept a pending connection request
- `atm_listen()` - listen for an ATM connection request
- `atm_close()` - close a connection with an ATM endpoint
- `atm_gethostbyname()` - get the ATM address for a hostname
- `atm_recv()`, `atm_recvfrom()`, `atm_recv_null()` - receive data from an established ATM connection
- `atm_send()`, `atm_sendto()`, `atm_send_null()` - send data over an established ATM connection

5.1.2 Example program for FORE Systems ATM API. The program source codes presented below are simple echo service server and client, respectively. They use all the above mentioned FORE ATM API functions. The server waits for the connection request, gives the specified QoS parameters to a client and receives and sends back the text written by the client. By simple modifications of these short programs, it is possible to write different advanced programs with a specified QoS.

```
-----------------------------------------------------------
Program 1. Echo service server
-----------------------------------------------------------
#include <stdio.h>
#include <sys/file.h>
#include <sys/fcntl.h>
#include <fore/types.h>
#include <fore_atm/fore_atm_user.h>
#define SERVER_SAP  4096
main(argc, argv)
    int     argc;
    char    *argv[];
{
    int fd, i, mtu, qlen, conn_id;
```

```
        u_int switchid, portid;
        Atm_info info;
        Atm_endpoint calling;
        Atm_qos qos;
        Atm_sap ssap;
        Aal_type aal;
        Atm_dataflow dataflow = duplex;
        char *device_name;
        char *tbuf, *rbuf;
        if (argc < 2) {
            fprintf(stderr, "Usage: %s device [server-sap]\n",
                    argv[0]);
            exit(1);
        }
        device_name = (char *) malloc(strlen("/dev/") +
        strlen(argv[1]) + 1);
        sprintf(device_name, "/dev/%s", argv[1]);
        if ((fd = atm_open(device_name, O_RDWR, &info)) < 0) {
            perror("atm_open");
            exit(1);
        }
        mtu = info.mtu; /* Max packet size */
        rbuf = (char *) malloc(mtu);
/*
 * Bind to a well known sap and set
pending connect request queue
length.
*/
        ssap = (argc == 3) ? atoi(argv[2]) : SERVER_SAP;
        qlen = 1; /* non zero value for server */
        if (atm_bind(fd, ssap, &ssap, qlen) < 0) {
            atm_error("atm_bind");
            exit(1);
        }
        printf("SAP assigned=%d\n", ssap);
/*
 * Wait for a connection request.
*/
        if (atm_listen(fd,&conn_id,&calling,&qos,&aal) < 0) {
            atm_error("atm_connect");
            exit(1);
        }
/*
 * Extract the switch id and port id from the NSAP.
```

```
*/
    GET_SWITCH(switchid, calling.nsap);
    GET_PORT(portid, calling.nsap);
    printf("calling switch=%x, port=%d, sap=%d, aal=%d\n",
        switchid, portid, calling.asap, aal);
    printf("qos target peak=%d, mean=%d, burst=%d\n",
        qos.peak_bandwidth.target,
        qos.mean_bandwidth.target,
        qos.mean_burst.target);
    printf("qos minimum peak=%d, mean=%d, burst=%d\n",
        qos.peak_bandwidth.minimum,
        qos.mean_bandwidth.minimum,
        qos.mean_burst.minimum);
    printf("connect conn_id=%d\n", conn_id);
/*
* Request some quality of service.
*/
    qos.peak_bandwidth.target = 0; /* kbit/sec */
    qos.peak_bandwidth.minimum = 0; /* kbit/sec */
    qos.mean_bandwidth.target = 128; /* kbit/sec */
    qos.mean_bandwidth.minimum = 64; /* kbit/sec */
    qos.mean_burst.target = 2;  /* 2 kbit packet length */
    qos.mean_burst.minimum = 1; /* 1 kbit packet length */
/*
* Accept the connection request.
*/
    if (atm_accept(fd, fd, conn_id, &qos, dataflow) < 0) {
        atm_error("atm_accept");
        exit(1);
    }
    i = 0;
    while (1) {
        if (atm_recv(fd, rbuf, mtu) < 0) {
            atm_error("atm_recv");
            break;
        }
  i += (strlen (rbuf) + 1);
        printf("RECIVED: %s\n", rbuf);
        if  (dataflow == duplex) {
            if (atm_send(fd, rbuf, strlen(rbuf)+1) < 0) {
                atm_error("atm_send");
                break;
            }
            printf("SENT: %s\n", rbuf);
```

```
            break;
        }
    };
    printf ("Recived %d bytes of data.\n", i);
    sleep(1);
    return(0);
}
```

Program 2. Echo client service

```
#include <stdio.h>
#include <sys/file.h>
#include <sys/fcntl.h>
#include <fore/types.h>
#include <fore_atm/fore_atm_user.h>
#include <sys/signal.h>
#define SERVER_SAP    4096
int fd, /* file descriptor */
    i; /* number of sent bytes */
void terminate(void) {
    printf ("\nSent %d bytes of data.\n", i);
    sleep (1);
    close (fd);
    signal (SIGINT, SIG_DFL);
    exit (0);
}
main(argc, argv)
    int      argc;
    char     *argv[];
{
    int j, mtu, qlen;
    Atm_info info;
    Atm_endpoint dst;
    Atm_qos qos;
    Atm_qos_sel qos_selected;
    Atm_sap ssap;
    Aal_type aal = aal_type_4;
    Atm_dataflow dataflow = duplex;
    char *device_name;
    char *tbuf, *rbuf;
    if (argc < 3) {
        fprintf(stderr,
        "Usage: %s device server-hostname [server-sap]\n",
 argv[0]);
```

```
        exit(1);
    }
    device_name = (char *) malloc(strlen("/dev/") +
    strlen(argv[1]) + 1);
    sprintf(device_name, "/dev/%s", argv[1]);
    if ((fd = atm_open(device_name, O_RDWR, &info)) < 0) {
        perror("atm_open");
        exit(1);
    }
    mtu = info.mtu; /* Max packet size */
    tbuf = (char *) malloc(mtu);
    rbuf = (char *) malloc(mtu);

/* Let ATM driver assign a source SAP by specifying
 * sap of zero. Set incoming connect request length to
 * zero since we're the client. Servers set queue length
 * to non zero.
 */
    ssap = 0;
    qlen = 0;
    if (atm_bind(fd, ssap, &ssap, qlen) < 0) {
        atm_error("atm_bind");
        exit(1);
    }
    printf("SAP assigned=%d\n", ssap);
/*
 * Initialize the server's data link address.
 */
    if (atm_gethostbyname(argv[2], &dst.nsap) < 0) {
        fprintf(stderr, "atm_gethostbyname failed\n");
        exit(1);
    }
    dst.asap = (argc == 4) ? atoi(argv[3]) : SERVER_SAP;
/*
 * Request some quality of service.
 */
    qos.peak_bandwidth.target = 0;  /* kbit/sec */
    qos.peak_bandwidth.minimum = 0; /* kbit/sec */
    qos.mean_bandwidth.target = 128;/* kbit/sec */
    qos.mean_bandwidth.minimum = 64;/* kbit/sec */
    qos.mean_burst.target =2;       /* 2 kbit packet length*/
    qos.mean_burst.minimum =1;      /* 1 kbit packet length*/
    if (atm_connect(fd, &dst, &qos, &qos_selected,
        aal, dataflow) < 0) {
```

```
        atm_error("atm_connect");
        exit(1);
    }
    printf("selected qos peak=%d, mean=%d, burst=%d\n",
        qos_selected.peak_bandwidth,
        qos_selected.mean_bandwidth,
        qos_selected.mean_burst);
    signal(SIGINT, terminate);
    i = 0;
    while (1) {
        printf("Enter data: ");
        gets(tbuf);
        tbuf[strlen(tbuf)] = 0;
        if (atm_send(fd, tbuf, strlen(tbuf)+1) < 0) {
            atm_error("atm_send");
            exit(1);
        }
        printf("\"%s\" sent\n", tbuf);
        if (dataflow == duplex) {
            if (atm_recv(fd, rbuf, j) < 0) {
                atm_error("atm_recv");
                exit(1);
            }
            printf("ECHO: %s\n", rbuf);
            break;
        }
    };
}
```

5.1.3 WINSOCK 2 API.

Windows Sockets Version 2.0 is the successor to Version 1.1, which has been the standard since its release in January of 1993. WINSOCK Version 1.1 has met, if not exceeded, its authors' original intent to provide a powerful and flexible API for creating universal TCP/IP applications. One can create any type of client or server TCP/IP application with an implementation of Windows Sockets based on the Version 1.1 Windows Sockets specification. One can port Berkeley Sockets applications and take advantage of the message-based Microsoft Windows programming environment and paradigm.

The authors of Windows Sockets Version 1.1 intentionally limited its scope to expedite the process and ensure its success. WINSOCK 1.1 deals primarily with TCP/IP because the involved software vendors sold TCP/IP network software, but it also conveniently allowed them to ignore the difficult issue of how to provide a single API for multiple vendors simultaneously. This focus on TCP/IP did not preclude the possibility that WINSOCK like its Berkeley Sockets Model could support other protocol suites at some point in the future. The future is now. Windows Sockets version 2.0 (WINSOCK 2) formalizes the API for a number of other protocol suites - ATM, IPX/SPX, and DECnet - and allows them to co-exist simultaneously. WINSOCK 2 also adds substantial new functionality. Most importantly, it does all this and still retains full backward compatibility with the existing 1.1 some of which are clarified further - so all existing WINSOCK applications can continue to run without modification (the only exception are WINSOCK 1.1 applications that use blocking hooks, in which case they need to be rewritten to work without them).

WINSOCK 2 goes beyond simply allowing the coexistence of multiple protocol stacks; it also allows the creation of applications that are network protocol independent. A WINSOCK 2 application can transparently select a protocol based on its service needs. The application can adapt to differences in network names and addresses using the mechanisms WINSOCK 2 provides. Here is a list of the new features that WINSOCK 2 provides:

- Multiple Protocol support: Windows Open System Architecture (WOSA) lets service providers "plug-in" and "pile-on".
- Transport Protocol Independence: Choose protocol by the services the service providers give.
- Multiple Namespaces: Select the protocol you want to resolve hostnames, or locate services.
- Scatter and Gather: Receive and send, to and from multiple buffers.
- Overlapped I/O and Event Objects: Utilize Win32 paradigms for enhanced throughput.
- Quality of Service: Negotiate and keep track of bandwidth per socket or socket group.
- Socket Groups: Group sockets within an application, and prioritize them.
- Multipoint and Multicast: Protocol independent APIs and protocol specific APIs.
- Conditional Acceptance: Ability to reject or defer a connect request before it occurs.
- Connect and Disconnect data: For transport protocols that support it.
- Socket Sharing: Two or more processes can share a socket handle.
- Vendor IDs and a mechanism for vendor extensions: Vendor specific APIs can be added.
- Layered Service Providers: The ability to add services to existing transport providers.

WINSOCK2 also clarifies existing ambiguities in the Version1.1 of WINSOCK specification and adds new extensions that take advantage of operating system features and enhance application performance and efficiency. Finally, WINSOCK 2 includes a number of new protocol-specific extensions. These extensions - such as multicast socket options - are relegated to a separate annex, since the main WINSOCK 2 protocol specification is protocol- independent. As we mentioned earlier, the authors of WINSOCK version 1.1 deliberately limited its scope in the name of expediency. One result of this is the simple architecture of WINSOCK 1.1. A single WINSOCK.DLL (or WSOCK32.DLL) provides the WINSOCK API, and this DLL "talks" to the underlying protocol stack via a proprietary programming interface. This works fairly well since Version 1.1 of WINSOCK only supports one protocol suite - TCP/IP - and most computers running Windows have only a single network interface. However, this WINSOCK Version 1.1 architecture limits a system to only one WINSOCK DLL active in the system path at a time. As a result, it is not easy to have more than one WINSOCK implementation on a machine at one time. There are legitimate reasons to want multiple WINSOCK implementations. For example, one might want a protocol stack from one vendor over the Ethernet connection and a different vendor's stack over the Serial Line. WINSOCK 2 has an all new architecture that provides much more flexibility. This architecture allows for simultaneous support of multiple protocol stacks, interfaces, and service providers. There is still one DLL on top, but there is another layer below, and a standard service provider interface, both of which add flexibility. WINSOCK 2 adopts the WOSA model, which separates the API from the protocol service provider. In this model the WINSOCK DLL provides the standard API, and each vendor installs its own service provider layer underneath. The API layer "talks" to a service provider via a standardized Service Provider Interface (SPI), and it is capable of multiplexing between multiple service providers simultaneously. The Fig. 5.2 illustrates the WINSOCK 2 architecture. Note that the WINSOCK 2 specification has

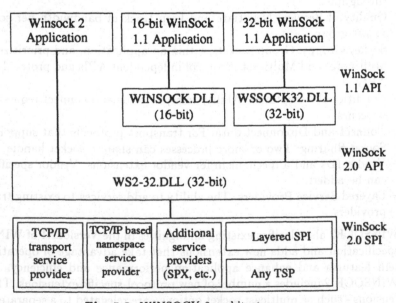

Fig. 5.2. WINSOCK 2 architecture.

two distinct parts: the API for application developers, and the SPI for protocol stack and namespace service providers. Notice also that the intermediate DLL layers are independent of both the application developers and service providers. These DLLs are provided and maintained by Microsoft and Intel. And lastly, notice that the Layered Service Providers would appear in this illustration one or more boxes on top of the transport service provider.

5.2 HIPPI API

The IRIS HIPPI product includes an API that allows customer-developed applications to change the information in their Upper Layer Protocol Object (ULPO) and File Descriptor Objects (FDO) and to control the HIPPI subsystem. There are two access methods possible for HIPPI, namely HIPPI-FP (Framing Protocol) and HIPPI-PH (PHysical Layer)(see Fig. 5.3). In general there is only one access method possible for each single application. By invoking different IRIS HIPPI API commands, customer-developed programs define their access method, data flow (packet) control, connection control, and HIPPI protocol processing. In the following section only the program-

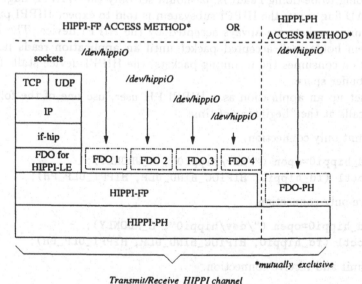

Transmit/Receive HIPPI channel

Fig. 5.3. HIPPI interface.

ming for the HIPPI-PH access method will be described. For programming for the HIPPI-FP access method please refer to IRIS HIPPI API Programmer's Guide.

5.2.1 Programming for the HIPPI-PH access method. This section describes how to program a module that accesses the HIPPI subsystem at the physical layer (that is, it does not use the HIPPI Framing Protocol). For maximum throughput, DMA between the HIPPI board and the host application occurs directly to or from a user's application space. Because of this, and due to the fact that the DMA component (ASIC) has a 64-bit interface, all application read() and write() functions must specify buffers that are 8-byte word aligned, and the data byte count must be a multiple of 8.

Opening and binding to the device. At the beginning of each program the line

```
#include <sys/hippi.h>
```

must be attached. An application can open a HIPPI device (for example, hippi0 or hippi1) for read-only, write- only, or read-and-write access. The acronym fd_hippi0 in the examples below refers to the file descriptor for the opened HIPPI device.

```
fd_hippi0 = open("/dev/hippi0", ACCESS_FLAG);
```

It is important to note that the application opens the HIPPI device with only the read/write flag settings that it needs. For example, if an application is not going to be doing read()s, it should set only the WRITE flag. When the READ flag is set, the HIPPI subsystem is told to expect HIPPI packets, so incoming packets are always accepted by the HIPPI device. The HIPPI subsystem holds each accepted packet until an application reads it. If no application consumes the incoming packets, the HIPPI device stalls for the lack of buffer space.

To set up an application as a HIPPI-PH user, use one of the following sets of calls at the "beginning of time":

– transmit-only connection,

```
fd_hippi0=open ("/dev/hippi0", O_WRONLY);
ioctl (fd_hippi0, HIPIOC_BIND_ULP, HIPPI_ULP_PH);
```

– receive-only connection,

```
fd_hippi0=open ("/dev/hippi0", O_RDONLY);
ioctl (fd_hippi0, HIPIOC_BIND_ULP, HIPPI_ULP_PH);
```

– transmit and receive connection.

```
fd_hippi0=open ("/dev/hippi0", O_RDWR);
ioctl (fd_hippi0, HIPIOC_BIND_ULP, HIPPI_ULP_PH);
```

Transmitting. For an application to transmit over its HIPPI-PH connection, one of the following sets (scenarios) of calls must be made. The order of the calls is immaterial except for the initial write() call, which actually starts sending the data. Many of the ioctl() calls write or set a value for a stored ULPO or FDO parameter. These values are not cleared when a transmission completes, so prior settings can be reused with subsequent write() calls without resetting. All the calls should be made for the first transmission (since the device was opened) in order to initialize them to non-default values. Programmers must take notice of the following:

- When the HIPIOCW_CONNECT call is used, the HIPPI subsystem sets up a "permanent" connection. In contrast, when the HIPIOCW_CONNECT call is not used, the connection is disconnected as soon as the packet has been sent.
- When the HIPIOCW_START_PKT call is used, many write()s may make up one packet. In contrast, when the HIPIOCW_START_PKT call is not used, one write() is a single packet.

Four functionality scenarios are supported.

- Functionality scenario 1 This scenario describes transmissions of small packets (under 2 megabytes) that use one write() for each packet. The connection disconnects when the packet has been completely sent. The application makes an ioctl() call to specify the I-field, then makes the write() call. The maximum packet size with this method is 2 megabytes. The packet and connection are both terminated when the data from the single write() call has completed.

```
ioctl (fd_hippi0, HIPIOCW_I, I-fieldValue);
write (fd_hippi0, buffer, size);
```

In the example the I-field does not need to be reset for each packet. The PACKET line goes low (false) after one write. Connection is dropped after one write.

- Functionality scenario 2 This scenario describes transmission of large packets that require many write() calls and where the connection disconnects when the packet has been completely sent. The application makes an ioctl() call to specify the I-field, and one to define the size (byte count) of the packet. It then makes the first write() call; subsequent write() calls are treated as part of the same packet until the byte count is reached. The PACKET and CONNECTION signals are automatically dropped after the specified number of bytes have been sent. This scheme allows an application to send very large packets as well as some data gathering on output.

```
ioctl (fd_hippi0, HIPIOCW_I, I-fieldValue);
ioctl (fd_hippi0, HIPIOCW_SHBURST, firstburstsize);
/* only if size is changing */
ioctl (fd_hippi0, HIPIOCW_START_PKT, byte count);
write (fd_hippi0, buffer, size);
/* buffer can point to FPheader + D1 data */
write (fd_hippi0, buffer, size);
/* size=only a part of the complete pkt*/
write (fd_hippi0, buffer, size);
```

```
/* max size for each write is 2 MB*/
write (fd_hippi0, buffer, size);
```

Here the connection is dropped when packet is completely sent.

- Functionality scenario 3 This scenario describes the transmission of small packets (under 2 megabytes) that use only one write() for each packet. The connection is kept open. The application makes an ioctl() call to specify the I-field for its "permanent" connection, then makes a write() call to send the first packet. The maximum-sized packet with this method is 2 megabytes. The PACKET signal is dropped when the write() call completes. The connection, however, is not terminated, so the next packet can be another single-write, or a multiple-write.

```
ioctl (fd_hippi0, HIPIOCW_CONNECT, I-fieldValue);
write (fd_hippi0, buffer, size);
./* first packet*/
write (fd_hippi0, buffer, size);
/* second packet*/
```

The PACKET line goes low after one write. The connection is not dropped. When the application wants the connection to be torn down, it tells the HIPPI subsystem to disconnect:

```
ioctl (fd_hippi0, HIPIOCW_DISCONN);
```

- Functionality scenario 4 This scenario describes the transmission of large packets that require many write() calls and where the connection is kept open. The application makes an ioctl() call to specify the I-field for its "permanent" connection and one to specify the size (byte count) of the packet. Each write() is treated as part of the same packet, until the byte count is satisfied, at which time the packet is ended. When the application wants to terminate the connection, it makes an ioctl() call to disconnect.

```
ioctl (fd_hippi0, HIPIOCW_CONNECT, I-fieldValue);
ioctl (fd_hippi0, HIPIOCW_SHBURST, firstburstsize);
/* only if size is changing */
ioctl (fd_hippi0, HIPIOCW_START_PKT, byte count);
write (fd_hippi0, buffer, size);
/* buffer can point to FPheader + D1 data */
write (fd_hippi0, buffer, size);
/* size=only a part of the complete pkt*/
write (fd_hippi0, buffer, size);
/* max size for each write is 2 MB */
```

Here again when pkt's byte count is complete, PKT line goes low and the connection is not dropped. Optionally, if the application wishes to start another packet, it proceeds as follows:

```
ioctl (fd_hippi0, HIPIOCW_SHBURST, firstburstsize);
/* only if size is changing */
ioctl (fd_hippi0, HIPIOCW_START_PKT, byte count);
```

When the application wants the connection to be torn down, it tells the HIPPI subsystem to disconnect:

```
ioctl (fd_hippi0, HIPIOCW_DISCONN)
```

Special use of functionality scenario 4

This scenario is used for an infinite-sized packet on a long-term ("permanent") connection. The application makes an ioctl() call to specify the I-field for its "permanent" connection and one to specify the byte count of the packet. The byte count is specified as HIPPI_D2SIZE_INFINITY. All write() calls are then treated as one "infinite-sized" packet (that is, the PACKET signal is not deasserted), until the packet is specifically terminated by the application with a special ioctl() call. The connection is not dropped until the application disconnects it.

```
ioctl (fd_hippi0,HIPIOCW_CONNECT,I-fieldValue);
ioctl (fd_hippi0,HIPIOCW_SHBURST,firstburstsize);
/* only if size is changing */
ioctl (fd_hippi0,HIPIOCW_START_PKT,HIPPI_D2SIZE_INFINITY);
/*infinity=0xFFFFFFFF) */
write(fd_hippi0,buffer,size);
/*max size for each write is 2 MB*/
write(fd_hippi0,buffer,size);
```

Optionally, if the application wishes to terminate this packet, it has to perform the following operation:

```
ioctl (fd_hippi0,HIPIOCW_END_PKT);
```

If the application wishes to start another packet, it does one of the following:

```
ioctl (fd_hippi0,HIPIOCW_START_PKT,HIPPI_D2SIZE_INFINITY);
```

or

```
ioctl (fd_hippi0,HIPIOCW_START_PKT,byte count);
```

When the application wishes to tear down the connection, it does one of the following:

```
ioctl (fd_hippi0,HIPIOCW_END_PKT);
ioctl (fd_hippi0,HIPIOCW_DISCONN);
```

or

```
ioctl (fd_hippi0,HIPIOCW_DISCONN);
```

Receiving. In HIPPI-PH mode, all incoming data is accepted when the device file is opened for reading. The HIPPI subsystem does not reject any connection requests. To retrieve its data, the application uses the calls below. All read()s retrieve sequentially received data. If a packet contained an FP header and D1 data, the HIPPI subsystem does not interpret them and does not separate them from the D2 data, so the first read() may contain FP header, D1 data, and/or D2 data. To determine packet boundaries, the application can use an ioctl() call to retrieve the current offset (received byte count) for the packet. When the returned value is 0, the next read() retrieves the first bytes from a new packet. All application read()s must specify buffers that are 8-byte word aligned and the data byte count must be a multiple of 8.

```
offset = ioctl (fd_hippi0, HIPIOCR_PKT_OFFSET);
/*when 0, nxt read is new pkt*/
read (fd_hippi0, buffer, size);
offset = ioctl (fd_hippi0, HIPIOCR_PKT_OFFSET);
/*when 0, nxt read is new pkt*/
read (fd_hippi0, buffer, size);
```

When the application wishes to stop receiving data, it closes the file descriptor using the call: close (fd_hippi0)

5.2.2 Example of program code. The program listed below is a simple "HelloWorld" program. It uses the HIPPI-PH access method for connecting to the destination host and sending the data from the buffer:

```
---------------------------------------------------------
Program 3. Example HIPPI program.
---------------------------------------------------------
#include <sys/types.h>
#include <sys/stat.h>
#include <sys/hippi.h>
#include <fcntl.h>
#include <string.h>
#include <stdio.h>
#define I_TULIP 0x01000001
#define I_ELDER 0x01000002
#define HIPPIDEV "/dev/hippi0"
/* hippi device */
#define HIPPIDST I_ELDER
/* I-field value of the destination host*/
int n;
int pktsize, npkts;
int hip; /* file descriptor */
char *buf; /* buffer */
main(int argc, char *argv[]) {
```

```
    pktsize = 2000;
    npkts = 10;
    buf = memalign(8, pktsize);
/* set the buffer size equal to 8 bytes */
    int nread;
    hip = open(HIPPIDEV, O_RDONLY);
/* open hippi device */
    ioctl(hip, HIPIOC_BIND_ULP, HIPPI_ULP_PH)
/* access method HIPPI-PH */
    read(hip, buf, pktsize);
/* wait for the first packet */
    for (n = 0; n < npkts; n++) {
      nread = read(hip, buf, pktsize);
/* receive the rest of the packets */
      close(hip);
/* close hippi device*/
    hip = open(HIPPIDEV, O_WRONLY);
/* open hippi device */
    ioctl(hip, HIPIOC_BIND_ULP, HIPPI_ULP_PH);
/* access method HIPPI-PH */
    ioctl(hip, HIPIOCW_CONNECT, HIPPIDST);
/* connect to destination host*/
    strcpy(buf, "Hello world!");
    write(hip, buf, pktsize);
/* send the first packet */
    for (n = 0; n < npkts; n++) {
      write(hip, buf, pktsize);
/* send the rest of the packets */
      }
    ioctl(hip, HIPIOCW_DISCONN);
/* disconnect */
    close(hip);
/* close the device */
    }
  }
```

6. Future of the Networks for HPC

The vision of communication systems development can be precisely defined if some important facts concerning the current applications of communication can be observed and brought together. Today fiber optic is the main transmission medium for communication systems. However, its utilization does not achieve even 10 percent of the theoretical capacity. The computing power of single processors achieves the level of 1000 MIPS or 1Gflops. I/O subsystems of supercomputers are able to process the transmission up to several Gbps. The traffic on the internet is growing with a factor of 10 every year. Residential users have broadband access to network services.

Thus, the transformation from Gigabits to Terabits per second is a natural step in this development. Such a transformation for networks means that there must be a move towards solutions based on the optic technology. The WDM or DWDM networks are already in very advanced stages of implementation. For computers such a transformation may produce the first photon computers. But the question whether the applications are able to make use of these transformations remains open [Par93].

There are some ideas of how to improve communication within the applications. The first idea is based on parallel I/O, especially for the computer network. Another possibility is to design lighter protocols by simplifying the protocol stack. Having this done it would be necessary to bring the applications closer to the networks. For this purpose such solutions as IP over SONET, IP over WDM etc. are now being developed. Some advanced intelligent systems, based on local processing, expert system technologies, will probably be used for management of this terabit world of communication and computing.

According to the predictions concerning the development of telecommunication services in the year 2005 about 80 percent of the traditional telecommunication traffic (e.g. telephones) will be realized by IP protocol. That is why application developers need to think of optimizing the communication functions in applications and adjusting them to still evolving communication technologies.

References

[AC92]   Andersen, T.M., Cornelius, R.S., High performance switching with fiber channel, *IEEE Proc. of CompCon*, 1992, 261-264.

[ANS91]   ANSI X3.183-1991, High-performance parallel interface: Mechanical, electrical, and signalling protocol specification, *HIPPI-PH*, American National Standard Institute, Inc., 1991.

[AFP92]   ANSI X3.210-199x, *High-Performance Parallel Interface: Framing Protocol (HIPPI-FP)*, American National Standard Institute, Inc., 1992.

[ASC92]   ANSI X3.222-199x, High-performance parallel interface: Physical switch control, *HIPPI-SC*, American National Standard Institute, Inc., 1992.

[ANS93]   ANSI X3T9.3, Fiber channel - physical and signalling interface, *FC-PH*, 4.2 edition, 1993.

[ATM]   ATM Forum White Paper, ATM services categories: The benefits to the user.

[Bou92]   Boudec, J., The asynchronous transfer mode: A tutorial, *Computer Networks and ISDN Systems* **24**, 1992, 279-309.

[CHK+93]   Cypher, R., Ho, A., Konstantinidou, S., Messina, P., Architectural
            requirements of parallel scientific applications with explicit communi-
            cation, *Proc. of the 20th International Symposium on Computer Ar-
            chitecture*, 1993, 2-13.
[FGK+97]   Foster, I., Geisler, J., Kesselman, C., Tuecke, S., Managing multiple
            communication methods in high-performance networked computing
            systems, *Parallel and Distributed Computing* **40**, 1997, 35-48.
[GBD94]   Geist, A., Beguelin, A., Dongarra, J., *PVM: Parallel Virtual Machine*,
            A users' guide and tutorial for networked parallel computing, MIT
            Press, 1994.
[GLS97]   Gropp, W., Lusk, E., Skjellum, A., *Using MPI*, MIT Press.
[HP94]   Hewlett Packard, NetPerf: A network performance benchmark, Infor-
            mation Networks Division, HP, 1994.
[HF94]   Hughes, J., P., Franta, W., R., Geographical extension of HIPPI chan-
            nels via high speed SONET, *IEEE Network*, 1994, 42-53.
[LHD+94a] Lin, M., Hsieh, J., David, H., C., Du and James A. MacDonald, Per-
            formance of high-speed network I/O subsystems: Case study of a fibre
            channel network, *Proc. of Supercomputing '94*, Washington D.C., 1994.
[LHD+94b] Lin, M., Hsieh, J., Du, D., MacDonald, J., Performance of high-speed
            network I/O subsystems: Case study of a fibre channel network, *IEEE
            Proc. of Supercomputing*, 1994.
[Lov93]   Loveman, D., B., High performance fortran, *IEEE Parallel and Dis-
            tributed Technology* **1**, 1993, 25-42.
[MMN+97]   Mazurek, C., Meyer, N., Nabrzyski, J., Stroiński, M., High perfor-
            mance networking infrastructure for metacomputing, *Proc. of the
            PPAM97*, Zakopane, 1997.
[NSW96]   Nabrzyski, J., Stroiński, M., Węglarz, J., Metacomputing at Poznan
            Supercomputing and Networking Center, *Proc. of European School on
            Parallel Programming Environment*, Grenoble, 1996, 27-35.
[NGI98]   NGI Implementation Plan, Next generation internet initiative, 1998,
            (See: http://www.ngi.gov/ngi/implementation/).
[NL]   Nitzberg B., Lo, V., DSM: A survey of issues and algorithms, *IEEE
            Computer* **24**, 52-60.
[McR97]   McRae, G., J., How application domains define requirements for the
            grid, *Communication of the ACM* **40**, 1997, 75-83.
[Par93]   Partridge, C., Gigabit Networking, A-W Professional Computing Se-
            ries, 1993.
[RN92]   Renwick J., Nicholson, A., IP and ARP on HIPPI, RFC 1374, 1992.
[SHI91]   Serial HIPPI Implementors Group, Serial HIPPI specification, Revi-
            sion 1.0, 1991.
[Sma97]   Smarr, L., Toward the 21st century, *Communication of the ACM* **40**,
            1997, 29-32.
[Smi97]   Smith, M., *Virtual LANs*, McGraw-Hill series on Computer Commu-
            nications, 1997.

X. Parallel and Distributed Scientific Computing

A Numerical Linear Algebra Problem Solving Environment Designer's Perspective

A. Petitet[2], H. Casanova[2], J. Dongarra[1,2], Y. Robert[3] and R. C. Whaley[2]

[1] Oak Ridge National Laboratory, Oak Ridge, TN 37831, USA
[2] University of Tennessee, Knoxville, TN 37996, USA
[3] Ecole Normale Supérieure de Lyon, 69364 Lyon Cedex 07, France

Summary. This chapter discusses the design of modern numerical linear algebra problem solving environments. Particular emphasis is placed on three essential components out of which such environments are constructed, namely well-designed numerical software libraries, software tools that generate optimized versions of a collection of numerical kernels for various processor architectures, and software systems that transform disparate, loosely-connected computers and software libraries into a unified, easy-to-access computational service.

A brief description of the "pioneers", namely the EISPACK and LINPACK software libraries as well as their successor, the Linear Algebra PACKage (LA-PACK), illustrates the essential importance of block-partitioned algorithms for shared-memory, vector, and parallel processors. Indeed, these algorithms reduce the frequency of data movement between different levels of hierarchical memory. A key idea in this approach is the use of the Basic Linear Algebra Subprograms (BLAS) as computational building blocks. An outline of the ScaLAPACK software library, which is a distributed-memory version of LAPACK, highlights the equal importance of the above design principles to the development of scalable algorithms for MIMD distributed-memory concurrent computers. The impact of the architecture of high performance computers on the design of such libraries is stressed.

Producing hand-optimized implementations of even a reduced set of well designed software components such as the BLAS for a wide range of architectures is an expensive and tedious proposition. For any given architecture, customizing a numerical kernel's source code to optimize performance requires a comprehensive understanding of the exploitable hardware resources of that architecture. Since this time-consuming customization process must be repeated whenever a slightly different target architecture is available, the relentless pace of hardware innovation makes the tuning of numerical libraries a constant burden. This chapter presents an innovative approach to automating the process of producing such optimized kernels for various processor architectures.

Finally, many scientists and researchers increasingly tend nowadays to use simultaneously a variety of distributed computing resources such as massively parallel processors, networks and clusters of workstations and "piles" of PCs. This chapter describes the NetSolve software system that has been specifically designed and conceived to efficiently use such a diverse and lively computational environment and to tackle the problems posed by such a complex and innovative approach to scientific problem solving. NetSolve provides the user with a pool of computational resources. These resources are computational servers that provide run-time access to arbitrary optimized numerical software libraries. This unified, easy-to-access computational service can make enormous amounts of computing power transparently available to users on ordinary platforms.

1. Introduction

The increasing availability of advanced-architecture computers is having a very significant effect on all spheres of scientific computation, including algorithm research and software development in numerical linear algebra. Linear algebra—in particular, the solution of linear systems of equations—lies at the heart of most calculations in scientific computing. In this chapter, particular attention will be paid to dense general linear system solvers, and these will be used as examples to highlight the most important factors that must be considered in designing linear algebra software for advanced-architecture computers. We use these general linear system solving algorithms for illustrative purpose not only because they are relatively simple, but also because of their importance in several scientific and engineering applications [Ede93] that make use of boundary element methods. These applications include for instance electromagnetic scattering [Har90, Wan91] and computational fluid dynamics problems [Hes90, HS67].

This chapter discusses some of the recent developments in linear algebra software designed to exploit these advanced-architecture computers. Since most of the work is motivated by the need to solve large problems on the fastest computers available, we focus on three essential components out of which current and modern problem solving environments are constructed:

1. well-designed numerical software libraries providing a comprehensive functionality and confining most machine dependencies into a small number of kernels, that offer a wide scope for efficiently exploiting computer hardware resources,
2. automatic generation and optimization of such a collection of numerical kernels on various processor architectures, that is, software tools enabling well-designed software libraries to achieve high performance on most modern computers in a transportable manner,
3. software systems that transform disparate, loosely-connected computers and software libraries into a unified, easy-to-access computational service, that is, a service able to make enormous amounts of computing power transparently available to users on ordinary platforms.

For the past twenty years or so, there has been a great deal of activity in the area of algorithms and software for solving linear algebra problems. The linear algebra community has long recognized the need for help in developing algorithms into software libraries, and several years ago, as a community effort, put together a *de facto* standard identifying basic operations required in linear algebra algorithms and software. The hope was that the routines making up this standard, known collectively as the Basic Linear Algebra Subprograms (BLAS) [LHK+79, DDH+88, DDH+90], would be efficiently implemented on advanced-architecture computers by many manufacturers, making it possible to reap the portability benefits of having them efficiently implemented on a wide range of machines. This goal has been largely realized.

The key insight of our approach to designing linear algebra algorithms for advanced-architecture computers is that the frequency with which data is moved between different levels of the memory hierarchy must be minimized in order to attain high performance. Thus, our main algorithmic approach for exploiting both vectorization and parallelism in our implementations is the use of block-partitioned algorithms, particularly in conjunction with highly-tuned kernels for performing matrix-vector and matrix-matrix operations. In general, the use of block-partitioned algorithms requires data to be moved as blocks, rather than as vectors or scalars, so that although the total amount of data moved is unchanged, the latency (or startup cost) associated with the movement is greatly reduced because fewer messages are needed to move the data. A second key idea is that the performance of an algorithm can be tuned by a user by varying the parameters that specify the data layout. On shared-memory machines, this is controlled by the block size, while on distributed-memory machines it is controlled by the block size and the configuration of the logical process mesh.

Section 2. presents an overview of some of the major numerical linear algebra software library projects aimed at solving dense and banded problems. We discuss the role of the BLAS in portability and performance on high-performance computers as well as the design of these building blocks, and their use in block-partitioned algorithms.

The Linear Algebra PACKage (LAPACK) [ABB+95], for instance, is a typical example of such a software design, where most of the algorithms are expressed in terms of a reduced set of computational building blocks, in this case called the Basic Linear Algebra Subprograms (BLAS). These computational building blocks support the creation of software that efficiently expresses higher-level block-partitioned algorithms, while hiding many details of the parallelism from the application developer. These subprograms can be optimized for each architecture to account for the deep memory hierarchies [AD89, DMR91] and pipelined functional units that are common to most modern computer architectures, and thus provide a transportable way to achieve high efficiency across diverse computing platforms. For fastest possible performance, LAPACK requires that highly optimized block matrix operations be already implemented on each machine, that is, the correctness of the code is portable, but high performance is not—if we limit ourselves to a single source code.

Speed and portable optimization are thus conflicting objectives that have proved difficult to satisfy simultaneously, and the typical strategy for addressing this problem by confining most of the hardware dependencies in a small number of heavily-used computational kernels has limitations. For instance, producing hand-optimized implementations of even a reduced set of well-designed software components for a wide range of architectures is an expensive and tedious task. For any given architecture, customizing a numerical kernel's source code to optimize performance requires a comprehensive understanding of the exploitable hardware resources of that architecture. This primarily includes the memory hierarchy and how it can be utilized to maximize data-reuse, as well as the functional units and registers and how these hardware components can be programmed to generate the correct operands at the correct time. Clearly, the size of the various cache levels, the latency of floating point instructions, the number of floating point units and other hardware constants are essential parameters that must be taken into consideration as well. Since this time-consuming customization process must be repeated whenever a slightly different target architecture is available, or even when a new version of the compiler is released, the relentless pace of hardware innovation makes the tuning of numerical libraries a constant burden.

The difficult search for fast and accurate numerical methods for solving numerical linear algebra problems is compounded by the complexities of porting and tuning numerical libraries to run on the best hardware available to different parts of the scientific and engineering community. Given the fact that the performance of common computing platforms has increased exponentially in the past few years, scientists and engineers have acquired legitimate expectations about being able to immediately exploit these available resources at their highest capabilities. Fast, accurate, and robust numerical methods have to be encoded in software libraries that are highly portable and optimizable across a wide range of systems in order to be exploited to their fullest potential.

Section 3. discusses an innovative approach [BAC+97, WD97] to automating the process of producing such optimized kernels for RISC processor architectures that feature deep memory hierarchies and pipelined functional units. These research efforts have so far demonstrated very encouraging results, and have generated great interest among the scientific computing community.

Many scientists and researchers increasingly tend nowadays to use simultaneously a variety of distributed computing resources such as massively parallel processors, networks and clusters of workstations and "piles" of PCs. In order to use efficiently such a diverse and lively computational environment, many challenging research aspects of network-based computing such as fault-tolerance, load balancing, user-interface design, computational servers or virtual libraries, must be addressed. User-friendly, network-enabled, application-specific toolkits have been specifically designed and conceived to tackle the problems posed by such a complex and innovative approach to scientific problem solving [FK98]. Section 4. describes the NetSolve software system [CD95] that provides users with a pool of computational resources. These resources are computational servers that provide run-time access to arbitrary optimized numerical software libraries. The NetSolve software system transforms disparate, loosely-connected computers and software libraries into a unified, easy-to-access computational service. This service can make enormous amounts of computing power transparently available to users on ordinary platforms.

The NetSolve system allows users to access computational resources, such as hardware and software, distributed across the network. These resources are embodied in computational servers and allow users to easily perform scientific computing tasks without having any computing facility installed on their computer. Users' access to the servers is facilitated by a variety of interfaces: Application Programming Interfaces (APIs), Textual Interactive Interfaces and Graphical User Interfaces (GUIs). As the NetSolve project matures, several promising extensions and applications will emerge. In this chapter, we provide an overview of the project and examine some of the extensions being developed for NetSolve: an interface to the Condor system [LLM88], an interface to the ScaLAPACK parallel library [BCC+97], a bridge with the Ninf system [SSN+96], and an integration of NetSolve and ImageVision [ENB96].

Future directions for research and investigation are finally presented in Section 5.

2. Numerical Linear Algebra Libraries

This section first presents a few representative numerical linear algebra packages in a chronological perspective. We then focus on the software design of the LAPACK and ScaLAPACK software libraries. The importance of the BLAS as a key to (trans)portable efficiency as well as the derivation of block-partitioned algorithms are discussed in detail.

2.1 Chronological Perspective

The EISPACK, LINPACK, LAPACK and ScaLAPACK numerical linear algebra software libraries are briefly outlined below in a chronological order. The essential features of each of these packages are in turn rapidly described in order to illustrate the reasons for this evolution. Particular emphasis is placed on the impact of the high-performance computer architecture on the design features of these libraries.

2.1.1 The pioneers: EISPACK and LINPACK. The EISPACK and LINPACK software libraries were designed for supercomputers used in the seventies and early eighties, such as the CDC-7600, Cyber 205, and Cray-1. These machines featured multiple functional units pipelined for good performance [HJ81]. The CDC-7600 was basically a high-performance scalar computer, while the Cyber 205 and Cray-1 were early vector computers.

EISPACK is a collection of Fortran subroutines that compute the eigenvalues and eigenvectors of nine classes of matrices: complex general, complex Hermitian, real general, real symmetric, real symmetric banded, real symmetric tridiagonal, special real tridiagonal, generalized real, and generalized real symmetric matrices. In addition, two routines are included that use singular value decomposition to solve certain least-squares problems. EISPACK is primarily based on a collection of Algol procedures developed in the sixties and collected by J. H. Wilkinson and C. Reinsch in a volume entitled *Linear Algebra* in the *Handbook for Automatic Computation* [WR71] series. This volume was not designed to cover every possible method of solution; rather, algorithms were chosen on the basis of their generality, elegance, accuracy, speed, or economy of storage. Since the release of EISPACK in 1972, over ten thousand copies of the collection have been distributed worldwide.

LINPACK is a collection of Fortran subroutines that analyze and solve linear equations and linear least-squares problems. The package solves linear systems whose matrices are general, banded, symmetric indefinite, symmetric positive definite, triangular, and tridiagonal square. In addition, the package computes the QR and singular value decompositions of rectangular matrices and applies them to least-squares problems. LINPACK is organized around four matrix factorizations: LU factorization, pivoted Cholesky factorization, QR factorization, and singular value decomposition. The term LU factorization is used here in a very general sense to mean the factorization of a square matrix into a lower triangular part and an upper triangular part, perhaps with pivoting. Some of these factorizations will be treated at greater length later, but, first a digression on organization and factors influencing LINPACK's efficiency is necessary.

LINPACK uses column-oriented algorithms to increase efficiency by preserving locality of reference. This means that if a program references an item in a particular block, the next reference is likely to be in the same block. By column orientation we mean that the LINPACK codes always reference arrays down columns, not across rows. This works because Fortran stores arrays in column major order. Thus, as one proceeds down a column of an array, the memory references proceed sequentially in memory. On the other hand, as one proceeds across a row, the memory references jump across memory, the length of the jump being proportional to the column's length. The effects of column orientation are quite dramatic: on systems with virtual or cache memories, the LINPACK codes will significantly outperform codes that are not column oriented.

Another important influence on the efficiency of LINPACK is the use of the Level 1 BLAS [LHK+79]. These BLAS are a small set of routines that may be coded to take advantage of the special features of the computers on which LINPACK is being run. For most computers, this simply means producing machine-language versions. However, the code can also take advantage of more exotic architectural features, such as vector operations. Further details about the BLAS are presented below in Section 2.2.1.

2.1.2 LAPACK. The development of LAPACK [ABB+95] in the late eighties was intended to make the EISPACK and LINPACK libraries run efficiently on shared-memory vector supercomputers. LAPACK [Dem89] provides routines for solving systems of simultaneous linear equations, least-squares solutions of linear systems of equations, eigenvalue problems, and singular value problems. The associated matrix factorizations (LU, Cholesky, QR, SVD, Schur, generalized Schur) are also provided, along with related computations such as reordering of the Schur factorizations and estimating condition numbers. Dense and banded matrices are handled, but not general sparse matrices. In all areas, similar functionality is provided for real and complex matrices, in both single and double precision. LAPACK is in the public domain and available from *netlib* [DG87].

The original goal of the LAPACK project was to make the widely used EISPACK and LINPACK libraries run efficiently on shared-memory vector and parallel processors. On these machines, LINPACK and EISPACK are inefficient because their memory access patterns disregard the multilayered memory hierarchies of the machines, thereby spending too much time moving data instead of doing useful floating point operations. LAPACK addresses this problem by reorganizing the algorithms to use block matrix operations, such as matrix multiplication, in the innermost loops [AD90, Dem89]. These block operations can be optimized for each architecture to account for the memory hierarchy [AD89, DMR91], and so provide a transportable way to achieve high efficiency on diverse modern machines. Here we use the term "transportable" instead of "portable" because, for fastest possible performance, LAPACK requires that highly optimized block matrix operations be already implemented on each machine. In other words, the correctness of the code is portable, but high performance is not—if we limit ourselves to a single Fortran source code.

LAPACK can be regarded as a successor to LINPACK and EISPACK. It has virtually all the capabilities of these two packages and much more besides. LAPACK improves on LINPACK and EISPACK in four main respects: speed, accuracy, robustness and functionality. While LINPACK and EISPACK are based on the vector operation kernels of the Level 1 BLAS [LHK+79], LAPACK was designed at the outset to exploit the Level 3 BLAS [DDH+90] — a set of specifications for Fortran subprograms that do various types of matrix multiplication and the solution of triangular systems with multiple right-hand sides. Because of the coarse granularity of the Level 3 BLAS operations, their use tends to promote high efficiency on many high-performance computers, particularly if specially coded implementations are provided by the manufacturer.

2.1.3 ScaLAPACK. The ScaLAPACK [BCC+97] software library is extending the LAPACK library to run scalably on MIMD distributed-memory concurrent computers. For such machines the memory hierarchy includes the off-processor memory of other processors, in addition to the hierarchy of registers, cache, and local memory on each processor. Like LAPACK, the ScaLAPACK routines are based on block-partitioned algorithms in order to minimize the frequency of data movement between different levels of the memory hierarchy. The fundamental building blocks of the ScaLAPACK library are parallel (distributed-memory) versions of the BLAS (PBLAS) [CDO+95], and a set of Basic Linear Algebra Communication Subprograms (BLACS) [WD95] for communication tasks that arise frequently in parallel linear algebra computations. In the ScaLAPACK routines, all interprocessor communication occurs within the PBLAS and the BLACS, so that the source code of the top software layer of ScaLAPACK looks very similar to that of LAPACK.

The ScaLAPACK library contains routines for the solution of systems of linear equations, linear least squares problems and eigenvalue problems. The goals of the LAPACK project, which continue into the ScaLAPACK project, are efficiency so that the computationally intensive routines execute as fast as possible; scalability as the problem size and number of processors grow; reliability, including the return of error bounds; portability across machines; flexibility so that users may construct new routines from well designed components; and ease of use. Towards this last goal the ScaLAPACK software has been designed to look as much like the LAPACK software as possible.

Many of these goals have been attained by developing and promoting standards, especially specifications for basic computational and communication routines. Thus LAPACK relies on the BLAS [LHK+79, DDH+88, DDH+90], particularly the Level 2 and 3 BLAS for computational efficiency, and ScaLAPACK [BCC+97] relies upon the BLACS [WD95] for efficiency of communication and uses a set of parallel BLAS, the PBLAS [CDO+95], which themselves call the BLAS and the BLACS. LAPACK and ScaLAPACK will run on any machines for which the BLAS and the BLACS are available. A PVM [GBD+94] version of the BLACS has been available for some time and the portability of the BLACS has recently been further increased by the development of a version that uses MPI [MPI+94, SOH+96].

The underlying concept of both the LAPACK and ScaLAPACK libraries is the use of block-partitioned algorithms to minimize data movement between different levels in hierarchical memory. Thus, the ideas discussed in this chapter for developing a library for dense linear algebra computations are applicable to any computer with a hierarchical memory that imposes a sufficiently large startup cost on the movement of data between different levels in the hierarchy, and for which the cost of a context switch is too great to make fine grain size multithreading worthwhile. The target machines are, therefore, medium and large grain size advanced-architecture computers. These include respectively "traditional" shared-memory vector supercomputers, such as the Cray Y-MP and C90, and MIMD distributed-memory concurrent computers, such as massively parallel processors (MPPs) and networks or clusters of workstations.

The ScaLAPACK software has been designed specifically to achieve high efficiency for a wide range of modern distributed-memory computers. Examples of such computers include the Cray T3 series, the IBM Scalable POW-

ERparallel SP series, the Intel iPSC and Paragon computers, the nCube-2/3 computer, networks and clusters of workstations (NoWs and CoWs), and "piles" of PCs (PoPCs).

Future advances in compiler and hardware technologies in the mid to late nineties are expected to make multithreading a viable approach for masking communication costs. Since the blocks in a block-partitioned algorithm can be handled by separate threads, our approach will still be applicable on machines that exploit medium and coarse grain size multithreading.

2.2 Software Design

Developing a library of high-quality subroutines for dense linear algebra computations requires to tackle a large number of issues. On one hand, the development or selection of numerically stable algorithms in order to estimate the accuracy and/or domain of validity of the results produced by these routines. On the other hand, it is often required to (re)formulate or adapt those algorithms for performance reasons that are related to the architecture of the target computers. This section presents three fundamental ideas to this effect that characterize the design of the LAPACK and ScaLAPACK software.

2.2.1 The BLAS as the key to (trans)portable efficiency. At least three factors affect the performance of portable Fortran code:

1. **Vectorization.** Designing vectorizable algorithms in linear algebra is usually straightforward. Indeed, for many computations there are several variants, all vectorizable, but with different characteristics in performance (see, for example, [Don84]). Linear algebra algorithms can approach the peak performance of many machines—principally because peak performance depends on some form of chaining of vector addition and multiplication operations, and this is just what the algorithms require. However, when the algorithms are realized in straightforward Fortran 77 code, the performance may fall well short of the expected level, usually because vectorizing Fortran compilers fail to minimize the number of memory references—that is, the number of vector load and store operations.

2. **Data movement.** What often limits the actual performance of a vector, or scalar, floating point unit is the rate of transfer of data between different levels of memory in the machine. Examples include the transfer of vector operands in and out of vector registers, the transfer of scalar operands in and out of a high-speed scalar processor, the movement of data between main memory and a high-speed cache or local memory, paging between actual memory and disk storage in a virtual memory system, and interprocessor communication on a distributed-memory concurrent computer.

3. **Parallelism.** The nested loop structure of most linear algebra algorithms offers considerable scope for loop-based parallelism. This is the principal type of parallelism that LAPACK and ScaLAPACK presently aim to

exploit. On shared-memory concurrent computers, this type of parallelism can sometimes be generated automatically by a compiler, but often requires the insertion of compiler directives. On distributed-memory concurrent computers, data must be moved between processors. This is usually done by explicit calls to message passing routines, although parallel language extensions such as Coherent Parallel C [FO88] and Split-C [CDG+93] do the message passing implicitly.

The question arises, "How can we achieve sufficient control over these three factors to obtain the levels of performance that machines can offer?" The answer is through use of the BLAS. There are now three levels of BLAS:

Level 1 BLAS [LHK+79]: for vector-vector operations $(y \leftarrow \alpha x + y)$,
Level 2 BLAS [DDH+88]: for matrix-vector operations $(y \leftarrow \alpha A x + \beta y)$,
Level 3 BLAS [DDH+90]: for matrix-matrix operations $(C \leftarrow \alpha A B + \beta C)$.

Here, A, B and C are matrices, x and y are vectors, and α and β are scalars.

Table 2.1. Speed (Mflops) of Level 2 and Level 3 BLAS Operations on a CRAY Y-MP. All matrices are of order 500; U is upper triangular.

Number of processors:	1	2	4	8
Level 2: $y \leftarrow \alpha A x + \beta y$	311	611	1197	2285
Level 3: $C \leftarrow \alpha A B + \beta C$	312	623	1247	2425
Level 2: $x \leftarrow U x$	293	544	898	1613
Level 3: $B \leftarrow U B$	310	620	1240	2425
Level 2: $x \leftarrow U^{-1} x$	272	374	479	584
Level 3: $B \leftarrow U^{-1} B$	309	618	1235	2398
Peak	333	666	1332	2664

The Level 1 BLAS are used in LAPACK, but for convenience rather than for performance: they perform an insignificant fraction of the computation, and they cannot achieve high efficiency on most modern supercomputers. The Level 2 BLAS can achieve near-peak performance on many vector processors, such as a single processor of a CRAY X-MP or Y-MP, or Convex C-2 machine. However, on other vector processors such as a CRAY-2 or an IBM 3090 VF, the performance of the Level 2 BLAS is limited by the rate of data movement between different levels of memory. Machines such as the CRAY Y-MP can perform two loads, a store, and a multiply-add operation all in one cycle, whereas the CRAY-2 and IBM 3090 VF cannot. For further details of how the performance of the BLAS are affected by such factors see [DDS+91]. The Level 3 BLAS overcome this limitation. This third level of BLAS performs $O(n^3)$ floating point operations on $O(n^2)$ data, whereas the Level 2 BLAS perform only $O(n^2)$ operations on $O(n^2)$ data. The Level 3 BLAS also allow us to exploit parallelism in a way that is transparent to the software that calls them. While the Level 2 BLAS offer some scope for exploiting parallelism, greater scope is provided by the Level 3 BLAS, as Table 2.1 illustrates.

2.3 Block Algorithms and Their Derivation

It is comparatively straightforward to recode many of the algorithms in LIN-PACK and EISPACK so that they call Level 2 BLAS. Indeed, in the simplest cases the same floating point operations are done, possibly even in the same order: it is just a matter of reorganizing the software. To illustrate this point, we consider the LU factorization algorithm, which factorizes a general matrix A in the product of the triangular factors L and U.

Suppose the $M \times N$ matrix A is partitioned as shown in Fig. 2.1, and we seek a factorization $A = LU$, where the partitioning of L and U is also shown in Fig. 2.1. Then we may write,

$$L_{00}U_{00} = A_{00} \qquad (2.1)$$
$$L_{10}U_{00} = A_{10} \qquad (2.2)$$
$$L_{00}U_{01} = A_{01} \qquad (2.3)$$
$$L_{10}U_{01} + L_{11}U_{11} = A_{11} \qquad (2.4)$$

where A_{00} is $r \times r$, A_{01} is $r \times (N - r)$, A_{10} is $(M - r) \times r$, and A_{11} is $(M - r) \times (N - r)$. L_{00} and L_{11} are lower triangular matrices with ones on the main diagonal, and U_{00} and U_{11} are upper triangular matrices.

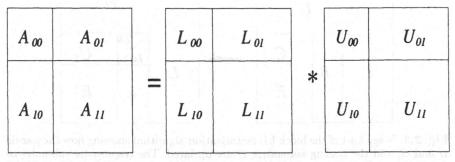

Fig. 2.1. Block LU factorization of the partitioned matrix A. A_{00} is $r \times r$, A_{01} is $r \times (N-r)$, A_{10} is $(M-r) \times r$, and A_{11} is $(M-r) \times (N-r)$. L_{00} and L_{11} are lower triangular matrices with ones on the main diagonal, and U_{00} and U_{11} are upper triangular matrices.

Equations 2.1 and 2.2 taken together perform an LU factorization on the first $M \times r$ panel of A (i.e., A_{00} and A_{10}). Once this is completed, the matrices L_{00}, L_{10}, and U_{00} are known, and the lower triangular system in Eq. 2.3 can be solved to give U_{01}. Finally, we rearrange Eq. 2.4 as,

$$A'_{11} = A_{11} - L_{10}U_{01} = L_{11}U_{11} \qquad (2.5)$$

From this equation we see that the problem of finding L_{11} and U_{11} reduces to finding the LU factorization of the $(M - r) \times (N - r)$ matrix A'_{11}. This can be done by applying the steps outlined above to A'_{11} instead of to A. Repeating these steps K times, where

$$K = \min([M/r], [N/r]), \tag{2.6}$$

and $[x]$ denotes the least integer greater than or equal to x, we obtain the LU factorization of the original $M \times N$ matrix A. For an in-place algorithm, A is overwritten by L and U – the ones on the diagonal of L do not need to be stored explicitly. Similarly, when A is updated by Eq. 2.5 this may also be done in place.

After k of these K steps, the first kr columns of L and the first kr rows of U have been evaluated, and the matrix A has been updated to the form shown in Fig. 2.2, in which panel B is $(M - kr) \times r$ and C is $r \times (N - (k - 1)r)$. Step $k + 1$ then proceeds as follows,

1. factor B to form the next panel of L, performing partial pivoting over rows if necessary. This evaluates the matrices L_0, L_1, and U_0 in Fig. 2.2,
2. solve the triangular system $L_0 U_1 = C$ to get the next row of blocks of U,
3. do a rank-r update on the trailing submatrix E, replacing it with $E' = E - L_1 U_1$.

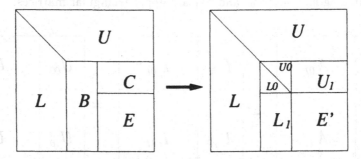

Fig. 2.2. Stage $k+1$ of the block LU factorization algorithm showing how the panels B and C, and the trailing submatrix E are updated. The trapezoidal submatrices L and U have already been factored in previous steps. L has kr columns, and U has kr rows. In the step shown another r columns of L and r rows of U are evaluated.

The LAPACK implementation of this form of LU factorization uses the Level 3 BLAS to perform the triangular solve and rank-r update. We can regard the algorithm as acting on matrices that have been partitioned into blocks of $r \times r$ elements. No extra floating point operations nor extra working storage are required for simple block algorithms [DDS+91, GPS90].

2.4 High-Quality, Reusable, Mathematical Software

In developing a library of high-quality subroutines for dense linear algebra computations the design goals fall into three broad classes: performance, ease-of-use and range-of-use.

2.4.1 Performance. Two important performance metrics are *concurrent efficiency* and *scalability*. We seek good performance characteristics in our algorithms by eliminating, as much as possible, overhead due to load imbalance, data movement, and algorithm restructuring. The way the data are distributed (or decomposed) over the memory hierarchy of a computer is of fundamental importance to these factors. Concurrent efficiency, ϵ, is defined as the concurrent speedup per processor [FJL+88], where the concurrent speedup is the execution time, T_{seq}, for the best sequential algorithm running on one processor of the concurrent computer, divided by the execution time, T, of the parallel algorithm running on N_p processors. When direct methods are used, as in LU factorization, the concurrent efficiency depends on the problem size and the number of processors, so on a given parallel computer and for a fixed number of processors, the running time should not vary greatly for problems of the same size. Thus, we may write,

$$\epsilon(N, N_p) = \frac{1}{N_p} \frac{T_{\text{seq}}(N)}{T(N, N_p)} \tag{2.7}$$

where N represents the problem size. In dense linear algebra computations, the execution time is usually dominated by the floating point operation count, so the concurrent efficiency is related to the performance, G, measured in floating point operations per second by,

$$G(N, N_p) = \frac{N_p}{t_{\text{calc}}} \epsilon(N, N_p) \tag{2.8}$$

where t_{calc} is the time for one floating point operation. Occasional examples where variation does occur are sometimes dismissed as "pathological cases". For iterative routines, such as eigensolvers, the number of iterations, and hence the execution time, depends not only on the problem size, but also on other characteristics of the input data, such as condition number.

Table 2.2 illustrates the speed of the LAPACK routine for LU factorization of a real matrix, SGETRF in single precision on CRAY machines, and DGETRF in double precision on all other machines. Thus, 64-bit floating point arithmetic is used on all machines tested. A block size of one means that the unblocked algorithm is used, since it is faster than – or at least as fast as – a block algorithm. In all cases, results are reported for the block size which is mostly nearly optimal over the range of problem sizes considered.

LAPACK [ABB+95] is designed to give high efficiency on vector processors, high-performance "superscalar" workstations, and shared-memory multiprocessors. LAPACK in its present form is less likely to give good performance on other types of parallel architectures (for example, massively

Table 2.2. SGETRF/DGETRF speed (Mflops) for square matrices of order n.

Machine (No. of processors)	Block size	Values of n				
		100	200	300	400	500
IBM RISC/6000-530 (1)	32	19	25	29	31	33
Alliant FX/8 (8)	16	9	26	32	46	57
IBM 3090J VF (1)	64	23	41	52	58	63
Convex C-240 (4)	64	31	60	82	100	112
CRAY Y-MP (1)	1	132	219	254	272	283
CRAY-2 (1)	64	110	211	292	318	358
Siemens/Fujitsu VP 400-EX (1)	64	46	132	222	309	397
NEC SX2 (1)	1	118	274	412	504	577
CRAY Y-MP (8)	64	195	556	920	1188	1408

parallel SIMD machines, or MIMD distributed-memory machines). LAPACK can also be used satisfactorily on all types of scalar machines (PCs, workstations, mainframes). The ScaLAPACK project, described in Section 2.1.3, adapts LAPACK to distributed-memory architectures.

A parallel algorithm is said to be scalable [GK90] if the concurrent efficiency depends on the problem size and number of processors only through their ratio. This ratio is simply the problem size per processor, often referred to as the granularity. Thus, for a scalable algorithm, the concurrent efficiency is constant as the number of processors increases while keeping the granularity fixed. Alternatively, Eq. 2.8 shows that this is equivalent to saying that, for a scalable algorithm, the performance depends linearly on the number of processors for fixed granularity.

Fig. 2.3 shows the scalability of the ScaLAPACK implementation of the *LU* factorization on the Intel XP/S Paragon computer. Fig. 2.3 shows the speed in Mflops per node of the ScaLAPACK *LU* factorization routine for different computer configurations. This figure illustrates that when the number of nodes is scaled by a constant factor, the same efficiency or speed per node is achieved for equidistant problem sizes on a logarithmic scale. In other words, maintaining a constant memory use per node allows efficiency to be maintained. This scalability behavior is also referred to as *isoefficiency*, or *isogranularity*.) In practice, however, a slight degradation is acceptable. The ScaLAPACK driver routines, in general, feature the same scalability behavior up to a constant factor that depends on the exact number of floating point operations and the total volume of data exchanged during the computation. More information on ScaLAPACK performance can be found in [BCC+97, BW98].

2.4.2 Ease-of-use. Ease-of-use is concerned with factors such as portability and the user interface to the library. Portability, in its most inclusive sense, means that the code is written in a standard language, such as Fortran, and that the source code can be compiled on an arbitrary machine to produce a program that will run correctly. We call this the "mail-order software" model of portability, since it reflects the model used by software

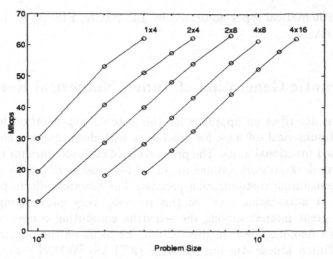

Fig. 2.3. LU Performance per Intel XP/S MP Paragon node.

servers such as *netlib* [DG87]. This notion of portability is quite demanding. It requires that all relevant properties of the computer's arithmetic and architecture be discovered at runtime within the confines of a Fortran code. For example, if it is important to know the overflow threshold for scaling purposes, it must be determined at runtime *without overflowing*, since overflow is generally fatal. Such demands have resulted in quite large and sophisticated programs [DP87, Kah87] which must be modified frequently to deal with new architectures and software releases. This "mail-order" notion of software portability also means that codes generally must be written for the worst possible machine expected to be used, thereby often degrading performance on all others. Ease-of-use is also enhanced if implementation details are largely hidden from the user, for example, through the use of an object-based interface to the library [DPW93]. In addition, software for distributed-memory computers should work correctly for a large class of data decompositions. The ScaLAPACK library has, therefore, adopted the block cyclic decomposition [BCC+97] for distributed-memory architectures.

2.4.3 Range-of-use. The range-of-use may be gauged by how numerically stable the algorithms are over a range of input problems, and the range of data structures the library will support. For example, LINPACK and EISPACK deal with dense matrices stored in a rectangular array, packed matrices where only the upper or lower half of a symmetric matrix is stored, and banded matrices where only the nonzero bands are stored. In addition, some special formats such as Householder vectors are used internally to represent orthogonal matrices. There are also sparse matrices, which may be stored in many different ways; but in this chapter we focus on dense and banded matrices, the mathematical types addressed by LINPACK, EISPACK, LAPACK and ScaLAPACK.

3. Automatic Generation of Tuned Numerical Kernels

This section describes an approach for the automatic generation and optimization of numerical software for processors with deep memory hierarchies and pipelined functional units. The production of such software for machines ranging from desktop workstations to embedded processors can be a tedious and time consuming customization process. The research efforts presented below aim at automating much of this process. Very encouraging results generating great interest among the scientific computing community have already been demonstrated. In this section, we focus on the ongoing Automatically Tuned Linear Algebra Software (ATLAS) [WD97] project developed at the University of Tennessee (see http://www.netlib.org/atlas/). The ATLAS initiative adequately illustrates current and modern research projects on automatic generation and optimization of numerical software such as PHiPAC [BAC+97]. After having developed the motivation for this research, the ATLAS methodology is outlined within the context of a particular BLAS function, namely the general matrix-multiply operation. Much of the technology and approach presented below applies to other BLAS and on basic linear algebra computations in general, and may be extended to other important kernel operations. Finally, performance results on a large collection of computers are presented and discussed.

3.1 Motivation

Straightforward implementation in Fortan or C of computations based on simple loops rarely achieve the peak execution rates of today's microprocessors. To realize such high performance for even the simplest of operations often requires tedious, hand-coded, programming efforts. It would be ideal if compilers where capable of performing the optimization needed automatically. However, compiler technology is far from mature enough to perform these optimizations automatically. This is true even for numerical kernels such as the BLAS on widely marketed machines which can justify the great expense of compiler development. Adequate compilers for less widely marketed machines are almost certain not to be developed.

Producing hand-optimized implementations of even a reduced set of well-designed software components for a wide range of architectures is an expensive proposition. For any given architecture, customizing a numerical kernel's source code to optimize performance requires a comprehensive understanding of the exploitable hardware resources of that architecture. This primarily includes the memory hierarchy and how it can be utilized to provide data in an optimum fashion, as well as the functional units and registers and how these hardware components can be programmed to generate the correct operands at the correct time. Using the compiler optimization at its best, optimizing the operations to account for many parameters such as blocking factors, loop unrolling depths, software pipelining strategies, loop ordering, register allocations, and instruction scheduling are crucial machine-specific factors affecting performance. Clearly, the size of the various cache levels, the latency of floating point instructions, the number of floating point units and other hardware constants are essential parameters that must be taken into consideration as well. Since this time-consuming customization process must be repeated whenever a slightly different target architecture is available, or even when a new version of the compiler is released, the relentless pace of hardware innovation makes the tuning of numerical libraries a constant burden.

The difficult search for fast and accurate numerical methods for solving numerical linear algebra problems is compounded by the complexities of porting and tuning numerical libraries to run on the best hardware available to different parts of the scientific and engineering community. Given the fact that the performance of common computing platforms has increased exponentially in the past few years, scientists and engineers have acquired legitimate expectations about being able to immediately exploit these available resources at their highest capabilities. Fast, accurate, and robust numerical methods have to be encoded in software libraries that are highly portable and optimizable across a wide range of systems in order to be exploited to their fullest potential.

For illustrative purpose, we consider the Basic Linear Algebra Subprograms (BLAS) described in Section 2.2.1. As shown in Section 2., the BLAS have proven to be very effective in assisting portable, efficient software for sequential, vector, shared-memory and distributed-memory high-performance computers. However, the BLAS are just a set of specifications for some elementary linear algebra operations. A reference implementation in Fortran 77 is publically available, but it is not expected to be efficient on any particular architecture, so that many hardware or software vendors provide an "optimized" implementation of the BLAS for specific computers. Hand-optimized BLAS are expensive and tedious to produce for any particular architecture, and in general will only be created when there is a large enough market, which is not true for all platforms. The process of generating an optimized set of BLAS for a new architecture or a slightly different machine version can be a time consuming and expensive process. Many vendors have thus invested considerable resources in producing optimized BLAS for their architectures. In many cases near optimum performance can be achieved for some operations. However, the coverage and the level of performance achieved is often not uniform across all platforms.

3.2 The ATLAS Methodology

In order to illustrate the ATLAS methodology, we consider the following matrix-multiply operation $C \leftarrow \alpha AB + \beta C$, where α and β are scalars, and A, B and C are matrices, with A an M-by-K matrix, B a K-by-N matrix and C an M-by-N matrix. In general, the arrays A, B, and C containing respectively the matrices A, B and C will be too large to fit into cache. It is however possible to arrange the computations so that the operations are performed with data for the most part in cache by dividing the matrices into blocks [DMR91]. ATLAS isolates the machine-specific features of the operation to several routines, all of which deal with performing an optimized "on-chip" matrix multiply, that is, assuming that all matrix operands fit in Level 1 (L1) cache. This section of code is automatically created by a code generator which uses timings to determine the correct blocking and loop unrolling factors to perform optimally. The user may directly supply the code generator with as much detail as desired, i.e. size of the L1 cache size, blocking factor(s) to try, etc; if such details are not provided, the code generator will determine appropriate settings via timings. The rest of the code produced by ATLAS does not change across architectures; it is presented in Section 3.2.1. It handles the looping and blocking necessary to build the complete matrix-matrix multiply from the on-chip multiply. The generation of the on-chip multiply routine is discussed in Section 3.2.2. It is obvious that with this many interacting effects, it would be difficult, if not impossible to predict a priori the best blocking factor, loop unrolling, etc. ATLAS provides a code generator coupled with a timer routine which takes in some initial information, and then tries different strategies for loop unrolling and latency hiding and chooses the case which demonstrated the best performance.

3.2.1 Building the general matrix multiply from the on-chip multiply. In this section, the routines necessary to build a general matrix-matrix multiply using a fixed-size on-chip multiply are described. Section 3.2.2 details the on-chip multiply and its code generator. For this section, it is enough to assume the availability of an efficient on-chip matrix-matrix multiply of the form $C \leftarrow A^T B$. This multiply is of fixed size, i.e. with all dimensions set to a system-specific value, N_B ($M = N = K = N_B$). Also available are several "cleanup" codes, which handle the cases caused by dimensions which are not multiples of the blocking factor.

The first decision to be taken by the general matrix multiply is whether the problem is large enough to benefit from our special techniques. The AT-LAS algorithm requires copying of the operand matrices; if the problem is small enough, this $O(N^2)$ cost, along with miscellaneous overheads such as function calls and multiple layers of looping, can actually make the "optimized" general matrix multiply slower than the traditional three do loops. The size required for the $O(N^3)$ costs to dominate these lower order terms varies across machines, and so this switch point is automatically determined at installation time. For these very small problems, a standard three-loop multiply with some simple loop unrolling is called. This code will also be called if the algorithm is unable to dynamically allocate enough space to do the blocking (see below for further details).

Assuming the matrices are large enough, ATLAS presently features two algorithms for performing the general, off-chip multiply. The two algorithms correspond to different orderings of the main loops. In the first algorithm, the outer loop is over M, i.e., the rows of A and the second loop is over N, i.e., the columns of B. In the second algorithm, this order is reversed. The common dimension of A and B (i.e., the K loop) is currently always the innermost loop. Let us define the input matrix looped over by the outer loop as the outer or outermost matrix; the other input matrix will therefore be the inner or innermost matrix. In the first algorithm, A is thus the outer matrix and B is the inner matrix. Both algorithms have the option of writing the result of the on-chip multiply directly to the matrix, or to an output temporary $\hat{C}$. The advantages to writing to $\hat{C}$ rather than C are:

1. address alignment may be controlled (i.e., one can ensure during the dynamic memory allocation that one begins on a cache-line boundary),
2. Data is contiguous, eliminating possibility of unnecessary cache-thrashing due to ill-chosen leading dimension (assuming the cache is non-write-through).

The disadvantage of using $\hat{C}$ is that an additional write to C is required after the on-chip operations have completed. This cost is minimal if many calls to the on-chip multiply are made (each of which writes to either C or $\hat{C}$), but can add significantly to the overhead when this is not the case. In particular, an important application of matrix multiply is the rank-K update, where the write to the output array C can be a significant portion of the cost of the algorithm. Writing to $\hat{C}$ essentially doubles the write cost, which is unacceptable. The routines therefore employ a heuristic to determine if the number of times the on-chip multiply will be called in the K loop is large enough to justify using $\hat{C}$, otherwise the answer is written directly to C.

Regardless of which matrix is outermost, the algorithms try to dynamically allocate enough space to store the $N_B \times N_B$ output temporary, $\hat{C}$ (if needed), one panel of the outermost matrix, and the entire inner matrix. If this fails, the algorithms attempt to allocate enough space to hold $\hat{C}$, and one panel from both A and B. The minimum workspace required by these routines is therefore $2KN_B$, if writing directly to C, and $N_B^2 + 2KN_B$ if not. If this amount of workspace cannot be allocated, the previously mentioned small case code is called instead. If there is enough space to copy the entire innermost matrix, we see several benefits to doing so:

- Each matrix is copied only one time,
- If all of the workspaces fit into L2 cache, we get complete L2 reuse on the innermost matrix,

- Data copying is limited to the outermost loop, protecting the inner loops from unneeded cache thrashing.

Of course, even if the allocation succeeds, using too much memory might result in unneeded swapping. Therefore, the user can set a maximal amount of workspace that ATLAS is allowed to have, and ATLAS will not try to copy the innermost matrix if this maximum workspace requirement is exceeded.

If enough space for a copy of the entire innermost matrix is not allocated, the innermost matrix will be entirely copied for each panel of the outermost matrix, i.e. if A is the outermost matrix, the matrix B will be copied $\lceil M/N_B \rceil$ times. Further, the usable size of the Level 2 (L2) cache is reduced (the copy of a panel of the innermost matrix will take up twice the panel's size in L2 cache; the same is true of the outermost panel copy, but that will only be seen the first time through the secondary loop). Regardless of which looping structure or allocation procedure used, the inner loop is always along K. Therefore, the operation done in the inner loop by both routines is the same, and it is shown in Fig. 3.1.

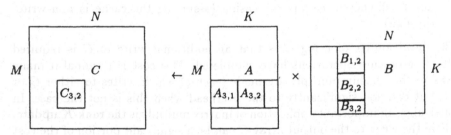

Fig. 3.1. One step of the general matrix-matrix multiply.

When a call to the matrix multiply is made, the routine must decide which loop structure to call (i.e., which matrix to put as outermost). If the matrices are of different size, L2 cache reuse can be encouraged by deciding the looping structure based on the following criteria:

- If either matrix will fit completely into L2 cache, put it as the innermost matrix (we get L2 cache reuse on the entire inner matrix),
- If neither matrix fits completely into L2 cache, put the one with the largest panel that will fit into L2 cache as the outermost matrix (we get L2 cache reuse on the panel of the outer matrix).

By default, the code generated by ATLAS does no explicit L2 blocking (the size of the L2 cache is not known anywhere in the code), and so these criteria are not presently used for this selection. Rather, if one matrix must be accessed by row-panels during the copy, that matrix will be put where it can be copied most efficiently. This means that if one has enough workspace to copy it up front, the matrix will be accessed column-wise by putting it as the innermost loop and copying the entire matrix; otherwise it will be placed as the outermost loop, where the cost of copying the row-panel is a lower order term. If both matrices have the same access patterns, B will be made the outermost matrix, so that C is accessed by columns.

3.2.2 Generation of the on-chip multiply. As previously mentioned, the ATLAS on-chip matrix-matrix multiply is the only code which must change depending on the platform. Since the input matrices are copied into blocked form, only one transpose case is required, which has been chosen as $C \leftarrow A^T B + C$. This case was chosen (as opposed to, for instance $C \leftarrow AB + C$), because it generates the largest (flops)/(cache misses) ratio possible when the loops are written with no unrolling. Machines with hardware allowing a smaller ratio can be addressed using loop unrolling on the M and N loops (this could also be addressed by permuting the order of the K loop, but this technique is not presently used in ATLAS.

In a multiply designed for L1 cache reuse, one of the input matrices is brought completely into the L1 cache, and is then reused in looping over the rows or columns of the other input matrix. The present ATLAS code brings in the array A, and loops over the columns of B; this was an arbitrary choice, and there is no theoretical reason it would be superior to bringing in B and looping over the rows of A. There is a common misconception that cache reuse is optimized when both input matrices, or all three matrices, fit into L1 cache. In fact, the only win in fitting all three matrices into L1 cache is that it is possible, assuming the cache is not write-through, to save the cost of pushing previously used sections of C back to higher levels of memory. Often, however, the L1 cache *is* write-through, while higher levels are not. If this is the case, there is no way to minimize the write cost, so keeping all three matrices in L1 does not result in greater cache reuse. Therefore, ignoring the write cost, maximal cache reuse for our case is achieved when all of A fits into cache, with room for at least two columns of B and one cache line of C. Only one column of B is actually accessed at a time in this scenario; having enough storage for two columns assures that the old column will be the least recently used data when the cache overflows, thus making certain that all of A is kept in place (this obviously assumes the cache replacement policy is least recently used). While cache reuse can account for a great amount of the overall performance win, it is obviously not the only factor. For the on-chip matrix multiplication, other relevant factors are outlined below.

Instruction cache overflow. Instructions are cached, and it is therefore important to fit the on-chip multiply's instructions into the L1 cache. This means that it won't be possible to completely unroll all three loops, for instance.

Floating point instruction ordering. When we discuss floating point instruction ordering in this section, it will usually be in reference to *latency hiding*. Most modern architectures possess pipelined floating point units. This means that the results of an operation will not be available for use until s

cycles later, where s is the number of stages in the floating point pipe (typically 3 or 5). Remember that the on-chip matrix multiply is of the form $C \leftarrow A^T B + C$; individual statements would then naturally be some variant of `C[i] += A[j] * B[k]`. If the architecture does not possess a fused multiply/add unit, this can cause an unnecessary execution stall. The operation `register = A[j] * B[k]` is issued to the floating point unit, and the add cannot be started until the result of this computation is available, s cycles later. Since the add operation is not started until the multiply finishes, the floating point pipe is not utilized. The solution is to remove this dependence by separating the multiply and add, and issuing unrelated instructions between them. This reordering of operations can be done in hardware (out-of-order execution) or by the compiler, but this will sometimes generate code that is not quite as efficient as doing it explicitly. More importantly, not all platforms have this capability, and in this case the performance win can be large.

Reducing loop overhead. The primary method of reducing loop overhead is through loop unrolling. If it is desirable to reduce loop overhead without changing the order of instructions, one must unroll the loop over the dimension common to A and B (i.e., unroll the K loop). Unrolling along the other dimensions (the M and N loops) changes the order of instructions, and thus the resulting memory access patterns.

Exposing parallelism. Many modern architectures have multiple floating point units. There are two barriers to achieving perfect parallel speedup with floating point computations in such a case. The first is a hardware limitation, and therefore out of our hands: All of the floating point units will need to access memory, and thus, for perfect parallel speedup, the memory fetch will usually also need to operate in parallel. The second prerequisite is that the compiler recognizes opportunities for parallelization, and this is amenable to software control. The fix for this is the classical one employed in such cases, namely unrolling the M and/or N loops, and choosing the correct register allocation so that parallel operations are not constrained by false dependencies.

Finding the correct number of cache misses. Any operand that is not already in a register must be fetched from memory. If that operand is not in the L1 cache, it must be fetched from further down the memory hierarchy, possibly resulting in large delays in execution. The number of cache misses which can be issued simultaneously without blocking execution varies between architectures. To minimize memory costs, the maximal number of cache misses should be issued each cycle, until all memory is in cache or used. In theory, one can permute the matrix multiply to ensure that this is true. In practice, this fine a level of control would be difficult to ensure (there would be problems with overflowing the instruction cache, and the generation of such precision instruction sequence, for instance). So the method used to control the cache-hit ratio is the more classical one of M and N loop unrolling.

3.3 ATLAS Performance Results

In this section we present double precision (64-bit floating point arithmetic) timings across various platforms. The timings presented here are different than many BLAS timings in that the cache is flushed before each call, and the leading dimensions of the arrays are set to greater than the number of rows of the matrix. This means that the performance numbers shown below, even when timing the same routine (for instance the vendor-supplied general matrix multiply routine) are lower than those reported in other papers. However, these numbers are in general a much better estimate of the performance a user will see in his application. More complete performance results and analysis can be found in [WD97].

Fig. 3.2 shows the performance of ATLAS versus the vendor-supplied matrix multiply (where available) for a 500 × 500 matrix multiply.

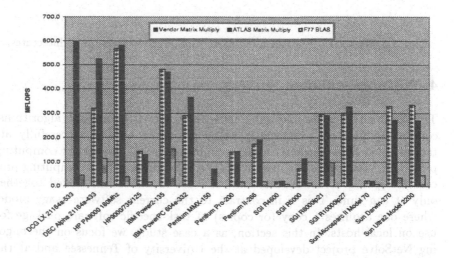

Fig. 3.2. 500x500 matrix multiply performance across multiple architectures.

Fig. 3.3 shows the performance of LAPACK's LU factorization. For each platform three results are shown in the figure: (1) LU factorization time linking to ATLAS matrix multiply, (2) LU factorization time linking to vendor supplied BLAS, (3) LU factorization time linking only to the reference Fortran 77 BLAS. These results demonstrate that the automatically generated ATLAS routine provide good performance in practice.

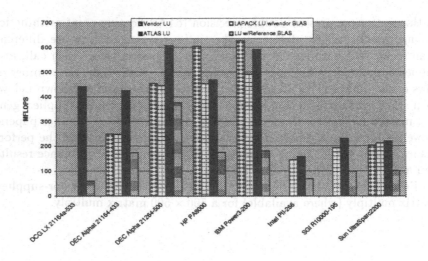

Fig. 3.3. 500x500 LU factorization performance across multiple architectures.

4. Network-enabled Solvers

Thanks to advances in hardware, networking infrastructure and algorithms, computing intensive problems in many areas can now be successfully attacked using networked, scientific computing. In the networked computing paradigm, vital pieces of software and information used by a computing process are spread across the network, and are identified and linked together only at run time. This is in contrast to the current software usage model where one acquires a copy (or copies) of task-specific software package for use on local hosts. In this section, as a case study, we focus on the ongoing NetSolve project developed at the University of Tennessee and at the Oak Ridge National Laboratory (see http://www.cs.utk.edu/netsolve). This project adequately illustrates the current and modern research initiatives on network-enabled solvers. We first present an overview of the NetSolve project and examine some extensions being developed for NetSolve: an interface to the Condor system [LLM88], an interface to the ScaLAPACK parallel library [BCC+97], a bridge with the Ninf System [SSN+96], and an integration of NetSolve and ImageVision [ENB96].

4.1 The NetSolve System

The NetSolve system uses the *remote computing* paradigm: the program resides on the server; the user's data is sent to the server, where the appropriate programs or numerical libraries operate on it; the result is then sent back to the user's machine.

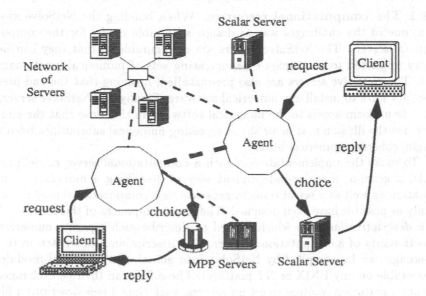

Fig. 4.1. NetSolve's organization.

Fig. 4.1 depicts the typical layout of the system. NetSolve provides users with a pool of computational resources. These resources are computational servers that have access to ready-to-use numerical software. As shown in the figure, the computational servers can be running on single workstations, networks of workstations that can collaborate for solving a problem, or Massively Parallel Processor (MPP) systems. The user is using one of the NetSolve client interfaces. Through these interfaces, the user can send requests to the Net-Solve system asking for a numerical computation to be carried out by one of the servers. The main role of the NetSolve agent is to process this request and to choose the most suitable server for this particular computation. Once a server has been chosen, it is assigned the computation, uses its available numerical software, and eventually returns the results to the user. One of the major advantages of this approach is that the agent performs load-balancing among the different resources.

As shown in Fig. 4.1, there can be multiple instances of the NetSolve agent on the network, and different clients can contact different agents depending on their locations. The agents can exchange information about their different servers and allow access from any client to any server if desirable. NetSolve can be used either via the Internet or on an intranet, such as inside a research department or a university, without participating in any Internet based computation. Another important aspect of NetSolve is that the configuration of the system is entirely flexible: any server/agent can be stopped and (re-)started at any time without jeopardizing the integrity of the system.

4.1.1 The computational resources. When building the NetSolve system, one of the challenges was to design a suitable model for the computational servers. The NetSolve servers are configurable so that they can be easily upgraded to encompass ever-increasing sets of numerical functionalities. The NetSolve servers are also pre-installed, meaning that the end-user does not have to install any numerical software. Finally, the NetSolve servers provide uniform access to the numerical software, in the sense that the end-user has the illusion that he or she is accessing numerical subroutines from a single, coherent numerical library.

To make the implementation of such a computational server model possible, a general, machine-independent way of describing a numerical computation as well as a set of tools to generate new computational modules as easily as possible have been designed. The main component of this framework is a *descriptive language* which is used to describe each separate numerical functionality of a computational server. The description files written in this language can be compiled by NetSolve into actual computational modules executable on any UNIX or NT platform. These files can then be exchanged by any institution wanting to set up servers: each time a new description file is created, the capabilities of the entire NetSolve system are increased.

A number of description files have been generated for a variety of numerical libraries: ARPACK, FitPack, ItPack, MinPack, FFTPACK, LAPACK, BLAS, QMR, Minpack and ScaLAPACK. These numerical libraries cover several fields of computational science; Linear Algebra, Optimization, Fast Fourier Transforms, etc.

4.1.2 The client interfaces. A major concern in designing NetSolve was to provide several interfaces for a wide range of users. NetSolve can be invoked through C, Fortran, Java, Matlab [Mat92] and Mathematica [Wol96]. In addition, there is a Web-enabled Java GUI. Another concern was keeping the interfaces as simple as possible. For example, there are only two calls in the MATLAB interface, and they are sufficient to allow users to submit problems to the NetSolve system. Each interface provides asynchronous calls to NetSolve in addition to traditional synchronous or blocking calls. When several asynchronous requests are sent to a NetSolve agent, they are dispatched among the available computational resources according to the load-balancing schemes implemented by the agent. Hence, the user—with virtually no effort—can achieve coarse-grained parallelism from either a C or Fortran program, or from interaction with a high-level interface. All the interfaces are described in detail in the "NetSolve's Client User's Guide" [CD95].

4.1.3 The NetSolve agent. Keeping track of what software resources are available and on which servers they are located is perhaps the most fundamental task of the NetSolve agent. Since the computational servers use the same framework to contribute software to the system (see Section 4.1.1), it is possible for the agent to maintain a database of different numerical functionalities available to the users.

Each time a new server is started, it sends an application request to an instance of the NetSolve agent. This request contains general information about the server and the list of numerical functions it intends to contribute to the system. The agent examines this list and detects possible discrepancies with the other existing servers in the system. Based on the agent's verdict, the server can be integrated into the system and available for clients.

The goal of the NetSolve agent is to choose the best-suited computational server for each incoming request to the system. For each user request, the agent determines the set of servers that can handle the computation and makes a choice between all the possible resources. To do so, the agent uses computation-specific and resource-specific information. Computation-specific information is mostly included in the user request whereas resource-specific information is partly static (server's host processor speed, memory available, etc.) and partly dynamic (processor workload). Rationale and further detail on these issues can be found in [BCD96], as well as a description of how NetSolve ensures fault-tolerance among the servers.

Agent-based computing seems to be a promising strategy. NetSolve is evolving into a more elaborate system and a major part of this evolution is to take place within the agent. Such issues as user accounting, security, data encryption for instance are only partially addressed in the current implementation of NetSolve and already is the object of much work. As the types of hardware resources and the types of numerical software available on the computational servers become more and more diverse, the resource broker embedded in the agent need to become increasingly sophisticated. There are many difficulties in providing a uniform performance metric that encompasses any type of algorithmic and hardware considerations in a metacomputing setting, especially when different numerical resources, or even entire frameworks are integrated into NetSolve. Such integrations are described in the following sections.

4.2 Integration of Computational Resources into NetSolve

In this section, we present how various computational resources can be integrated into NetSolve. As explained in Section 4.1.1, traditional software libraries are easy to integrate into the NetSolve system. We present however how four very different and more complex computational resources have been integrated. We selected a workstation manager environment, a parallel numerical library, a global-wide computing infrastructure similar to NetSolve itself, and finally a general purpose image processing application.

4.2.1 Interface to the Condor system. Condor [LLM88], developed at the University of Wisconsin, Madison, is an environment that can manage very large collections of distributively owned workstations. Its development has been motivated by the ever increasing need for scientists and engineers to exploit the capacity of such collections, mainly by taking advantage of otherwise unused CPU cycles. Interfacing NetSolve and Condor is a very natural idea. NetSolve provides remote easy access to computational resources through multiple, attractive user interfaces. Condor allows users to harness the power of a pool of machines while using otherwise wasted CPU cycles. The users at the consoles of those machines are not penalized by the scheduling of Condor jobs. If the pool of machines is reasonably large, it is usually the case that Condor jobs can be scheduled almost immediately. This could prove to be very interesting for a project like NetSolve. Indeed, NetSolve servers may be started so that they grant local resource access to outside users. Interfacing NetSolve and Condor could then give priority to local users and provide underutilized only CPU cycles to outside users.

A Condor pool consists of any number of machines, that are connected by a network. Condor daemons constantly monitor the status of the individual computers in the cluster. Two daemons run on each machine, the *startd* and the *schedd*. The *startd* monitors information about the machine itself (load, mouse/keyboard activity, etc.) and decides if it is available to run a Condor job. The *schedd* keeps track of all the Condor jobs that have been submitted to the machine. One of the machine, the *Central Manager*, keeps track of all the resources and jobs in the pool. When a job is submitted to Condor, the scheduler on the central manager matches a machine in the Condor pool to that job. Once the job has been started, it is periodically checkpointed, can be interrupted and migrated to a machine whose architecture is the same as the one of the machine on which the execution was initiated. This organization is partly depicted in Fig. 4.2. More details on the Condor system and the software layers can be found in [LLM88].

Fig. 4.2 shows how an entire Condor pool can be seen as a single NetSolve computational resource. The Central Manager runs two daemons in addition to the usual *startd* and *schedd*: the *negotiator* and the *collector*. A machine also runs a customized version of the NetSolve server. When this server receives a request from a client, instead of creating a local child process running a computational module, it uses the Condor tools to submit that module to the Condor pool. The negotiator on the Central Manager then chooses a target machine for the computational module. Due to fluctuations in the state of the pool, the computational module can then be migrated among the machines in the pool. When the results of the numerical computation are obtained, the NetSolve server transmits that result back to the client.

The actual implementation of the NetSolve/Condor interface was made easy by the Condor tools provided to the Condor user. However, the restrictions that apply to a Condor job concerning system calls were difficult to satisfy and required quite a few changes to obtain a Condor-enabled Net-Solve server. A major issue however still needs to be addressed; how does

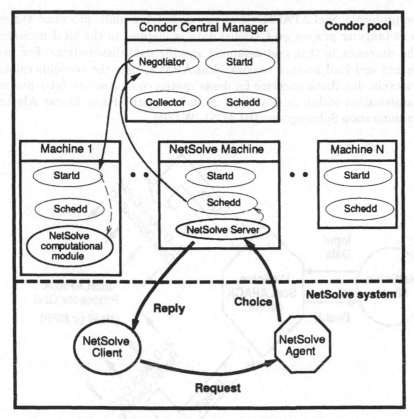

Fig. 4.2. NetSolve and Condor.

the NetSolve agent perceive a Condor pool as a resource? Finding the appropriate performance prediction technique is at the focus of the current NetSolve/Condor collaboration.

4.2.2 Integrating parallel numerical libraries. Integrating software libraries designed for distributed-memory concurrent computers into NetSolve allows a workstation's user to access massively parallel processors to perform large computations. This access can be made extremely simple via NetSolve and the user may not even be aware that he or she is using a parallel library on such a computer. As an example, we describe in this section, how the ScaLAPACK library [BCC+97] has been integrated into the NetSolve system.

As briefly described in Section 2.1.3, the Scalable Linear Algebra Package (ScaLAPACK) is a library of high-performance linear algebra routines for distributed-memory message-passing MIMD computers as well as networks or clusters of workstations supporting PVM [GBD+94] or MPI [SOH+96]. It is a continuation of the LAPACK [ABB+95] project, and contains routines for solving systems of linear equations, least squares problems, and eigenvalue problems. ScaLAPACK views the underlying multi-processor system as a rectangular process *grid*. Global data is mapped to the local memories of the processes in that grid assuming specific data-distributions. For performance and load balance reasons, ScaLAPACK uses the two-dimensional block cyclic distribution scheme for dense matrix computations. Inter-process communication within ScaLAPACK is done via the Basic Linear Algebra Communication Subprograms (BLACS) [WD95].

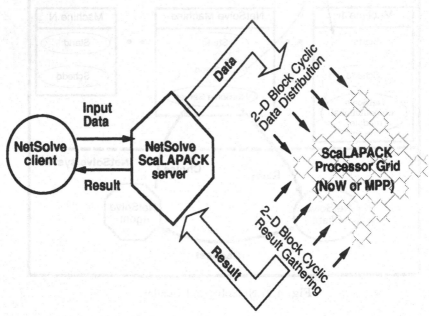

Fig. 4.3. The ScaLAPACK NetSolve Server Paradigm.

Fig. 4.3 is a very simple description of how the NetSolve server has been customized to use the ScaLAPACK library. The customized server receives data input from the client in the traditional way. The NetSolve server uses BLACS calls to set up the ScaLAPACK process grid. ScaLAPACK requires that the data already be distributed among the processors prior to any library call. This is the reason why each user input is first distributed on the process grid according to the block cyclic decomposition when necessary. The server can then initiate the call to ScaLAPACK and wait until completion of the computation. When the ScaLAPACK call returns, the result of the computation is distributed on the two-dimensional process grid. The server then gathers that result and sends it back to the client in the expected format. This process is completely transparent to the user who does not even realize that a parallel execution has been taking place.

This approach is very promising. A client can use MATLAB on a PC and issue a simple call like [x] = netsolve('eig',a) and have an MPP system use a high-performance library to perform a large eigenvalue computation. A prototype of the customized server running on top of PVM [GBD+94] or MPI [SOH+96] has been designed. There are many research issues arising with integrating parallel libraries in NetSolve, including performance prediction, choice of processor-grid size, choice of numerical algorithm, processor availability, accounting, etc.

4.2.3 NetSolve and Ninf. Ninf [SSN+96], developed at the Electrotechnical Laboratory, Tsukuba, is a global network-wide computing infrastructure project which allows users to access computational resources including hardware, software, and scientific data distributed across a wide area network with an easy-to-use interface. Computational resources are shared as Ninf remote libraries and are executable at remote Ninf servers. Users can build an application by calling the libraries with the Ninf Remote Procedure Call, which is designed to provide a programming interface similar to conventional function calls in existing languages, and is tailored for scientific computation. In order to facilitate location transparency and network-wide parallelism, the Ninf MetaServer maintains global resource information regarding computational server and databases. It can therefore allocate and schedule coarse-grained computations to achieve good global load balancing. Ninf also interfaces with existing network service such as the WWW for easy accessibility. Clearly, Net-Solve and Ninf bear strong similarities both in motivation and general design. Allowing the two systems to coexist and collaborate should lead to promising developments.

Some design issues prevent an immediate seamless integration of the two softwares (conceptual differences between the NetSolve agent and the Ninf Metaserver, problem specifications, user interfaces, data transfer protocols, etc.). In order to overcome these issues, the Ninf team started developing two *adapters*: a NetSolve-Ninf adapter and a Ninf NetSolve-adapter. Thanks to those adapters, Ninf clients can use computational resources administrated by a NetSolve system and vice-versa.

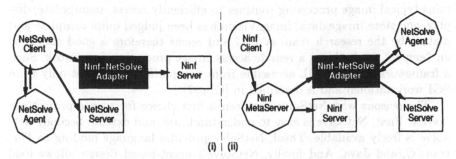

Fig. 4.4. Going (i) from NetSolve to Ninf and (ii) from Ninf to NetSolve.

Fig. 4.4(i) shows the Ninf-NetSolve adapter allowing access to Ninf resource from a NetSolve client. The adapter is just seen by the NetSolve agent as any other NetSolve server. When a NetSolve client sends a request to the agent, it can then be told to use the NetSolve adapter. The adapter performs protocol translation, interface translation, and data transfer, asks a Ninf server to perform the required computation and returns the result to the user.

In Fig. 4.4(ii), the NetSolve-Ninf adapter can be seen by the Ninf MetaServer as a Ninf server, but in fact plays the role of a NetSolve client. This is a little different from the Ninf-NetSolve adapter because the NetSolve agent is a resource broker whereas the Ninf MetaServer is a proxy server. Once the adapter receives the result of the computation from some NetSolve server, it transfers that result back to the Ninf client.

There are several advantages of using such adapters. Updating the adapters to reflects the evolutions of NetSolve or Ninf seems to be an easy task. Some early implementation evaluations tend to show that using either system via an adapter causes acceptable overheads, mainly due to additional data transfers. Those first experiments appear encouraging and will definitely be extended to effectively enable an integration of NetSolve and Ninf.

4.2.4 Extending ImageVision by the use of NetSolve. In this section, we describe how NetSolve can be used as a building block for a general purpose framework for basic image processing, based on the commercial ImageVision library [ENB96]. This project is under development at the ICG institute at Graz University of Technology, Austria. The scope of the project is to make basic image processing functions available for remote execution over a network. The goals of the project include two objectives that can be leveraged by NetSolve. First, the resulting software should prevent the user from having to install complicated image processing libraries. Second, the functionalities should be available via Java-based applications. The ImageVision Library (IL) [ENB96] is an object-oriented library written in C++ by Silicon Graphics, Inc. (SGI) and shipped with newer workstations. It contains typical image processing routines to efficiently access, manipulate, display, and store image data. ImageVision has been judged quite complete and mature by the research team at ICG and seems therefore a good choice as an "engine" for building a remote access image processing framework. Such a framework will make IL accessible from any platform (and not only from SGI workstations) and is described in [Obe97].

The reasons why NetSolve has been a first choice for such a project are diverse. First, NetSolve is easy to understand, use, and extend. Second, NetSolve is freely available. Third, NetSolve provides language binding to Fortran, C, and Java. And finally, NetSolve's agent-based design allows load monitoring and balancing among the available servers. New NetSolve computational modules corresponding to the desired image processing functionalities will be created and integrated into the NetSolve servers. A big part of the project at ICG is to build a Java GUI to IL.

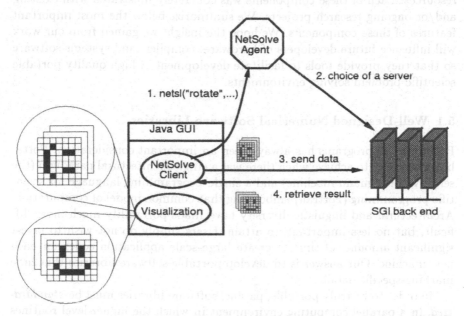

Fig. 4.5. ImageVision and NetSolve.

Fig. 4.5 shows a simple example of how ImageVision can be accessed via NetSolve. A Java GUI can be built on top of the NetSolve Java API. As shown on the figure, this GUI offers visualization capabilities. For computations, it uses an embedded NetSolve client and contacts SGI servers that have access to IL. The user of the Java GUI does not realize that NetSolve is the back end of the system, or that he or she uses a SGI library without running the GUI on a SGI machine! The protocol depicted in the figure is of course simplistic. In order to obtain acceptable levels of performance, the network traffic needs to be minimized. There are several ways of attacking this problem: keeping a "state" in the server, combine requests, reference images with URLs for instance, etc.

5. Conclusions

This chapter presented some of the recent developments in linear algebra software designed to exploit advanced-architecture computers. We focused on three essential components out of which current and modern problem solving environments are constructed: well-designed numerical software libraries, automatic generators of optimized numerical kernels and flexible, easy-to-access software systems enabling the hardware and software computational resources. Each of these components was concretely illustrated with existing and/or ongoing research projects. We summarize below the most important features of these components. We hope the insight we gained from our work will influence future developers of hardware, compilers and systems software so that they provide tools to facilitate development of high quality portable scientific problem solving environments.

5.1 Well-Designed Numerical Software Libraries

Portability of programs has always been an important consideration. Portability was easy to achieve when there was a single architectural paradigm (the serial von Neumann machine) and a single programming language for scientific programming (Fortran) embodying that common model of computation. Architectural and linguistic diversity have made portability much more difficult, but no less important, to attain. Users simply do not wish to invest significant amounts of time to create large-scale application codes for each new machine. Our answer is to develop portable software libraries that hide machine-specific details.

In order to be truly portable, parallel software libraries must be *standardized*. In a parallel computing environment in which the higher-level routines and/or abstractions are built upon lower-level computation and message-passing routines, the benefits of standardization are particularly apparent. Furthermore, the definition of computational and message-passing standards provides vendors with a clearly defined base set of routines that they can implement efficiently.

From the user's point of view, portability means that, as new machines are developed, they are simply added to the network, supplying cycles where they are most appropriate.

From the mathematical software developer's point of view, portability may require significant effort. Economy in development and maintenance of mathematical software demands that such development effort be leveraged over as many different computer systems as possible. Given the great diversity of parallel architectures, this type of portability is attainable to only a limited degree, but machine dependences can at least be isolated.

Like portability, *scalability* demands that a program be reasonably effective over a wide range of number of processors. The scalability of parallel algorithms, and software libraries based on them, over a wide range of architectural designs and numbers of processors will likely require that the fundamental granularity of computation be adjustable to suit the particular circumstances in which the software may happen to execute. The ScaLAPACK approach to this problem is block algorithms with adjustable block size.

Scalable parallel architectures of the present and the future are likely to be based on a distributed-memory architectural paradigm. In the longer term, progress in hardware development, operating systems, languages, compilers, and networks may make it possible for users to view such distributed architectures (without significant loss of efficiency) as having a shared-memory with a global address space. Today, however, the distributed nature of the underlying hardware continues to be visible at the programming level; therefore, efficient procedures for explicit communication will continue to be necessary. Given this fact, standards for basic message passing (send/receive), as well as higher-level communication constructs (global summation, broadcast, etc.), have become essential to the development of scalable libraries that have any degree of portability. In addition to standardizing general communication primitives, it may also be advantageous to establish standards for problem-specific constructs in commonly occurring areas such as linear algebra.

Traditionally, large, general-purpose mathematical software libraries have required users to write their own programs that call library routines to solve specific subproblems that arise during a computation. Adapted to a shared-memory parallel environment, this conventional interface still offers some potential for hiding underlying complexity. For example, the LAPACK project incorporates parallelism in the Level 3 BLAS, where it is not directly visible to the user.

When going from shared-memory systems to the more readily scalable distributed-memory systems, the complexity of the distributed data structures required is more difficult to hide from the user. One of the major design goal of *High Performance Fortran* (HPF) [KLS+94] was to achieve (almost) a transparent program portability to the user, from shared-memory multiprocessors up to distributed-memory parallel computers and networks of workstations. But writing efficient numerical kernels with HPF is not an easy task. First of all, there is the need to recast linear algebra kernels in terms of block operations (otherwise, as already mentioned, the performance will be limited by that of Level 1 BLAS routines). Second, the user is required to explicitly state how the data is partitioned amongst the processors. Third, not only must the problem decomposition and data layout be specified, but different phases of the user's problem may require transformations between different distributed data structures. Hence, the HPF programmer may well choose to call ScaLAPACK routines just as he called LAPACK routines on sequential processors with a memory hierarchy. To facilitate this task, an interface has been developed [BDP+98]. The design of this interface has been made possible because ScaLAPACK is using the same block-cyclic distribution primitives as those specified in the HPF standards. Of course, HPF can still prove a useful tool at a higher level, that of parallelizing a whole scientific operation, because the user will be relieved from the low level details of generating the code for communications.

5.2 Automatic Generation and Optimization of Numerical Kernels on Various Processor Architectures

The ATLAS package presently available on netlib is organized around the matrix-matrix multiplication. This operation is the essential building block of all of the Level 3 BLAS. Initial research using publicly available matrix-multiply-based BLAS implementations [KLV93, DDP94] suggests that this provides a perfectly acceptable Level 3 BLAS. As time allows, we can avoid some of the $O(N^2)$ costs associated with using the matrix-multiply-based BLAS by supporting the Level 3 BLAS directly in ATLAS. We also plan on providing the software for complex data types.

We have preliminary results for the most important Level 2 BLAS routine (matrix-vector multiply) as well. This is of particular importance, because matrix vector operations, which have $O(N^2)$ operations and $O(N^2)$ data, demand a significantly different code generation approach than that required for matrix-matrix operations, where the data is $O(N^2)$, but the operation count is $O(N^3)$. Initial results suggest that ATLAS will achieve comparable success with optimizing the Level 2 BLAS as has been achieved for Level 3 (this means that the ATLAS timings compared to the vendor will be comparable; obviously, unless the target architecture supports many pipes to memory, a Level 2 BLAS operation will not be as efficient as the corresponding Level 3 BLAS operation).

Another avenue of ongoing research involves sparse algorithms. The fundamental building block of iterative methods is the sparse matrix-vector multiply. This work leverages the present research (in particular, make use of the dense matrix-vector multiply). The present work uses compile-time adaptation of software. Since matrix-vector multiply may be called literally thousands of times during the course of an iterative method, run-time adaptation is also investigated. These run-time adaptations may include matrix dependent transformations [Tol97], as well as specific code generation.

ATLAS has demonstrated the ability to produce highly optimized matrix multiply for a wide range of architectures based on a code generator that probes and searches the system for an optimal set of parameters. This avoids the tedious task of generating by hand routines optimized for a specific architecture. We believe these ideas can be expanded to cover not only the Level 3 BLAS, but Level 2 BLAS as well. In addition there is scope for additional operations beyond the BLAS, such as sparse matrix-vector operations, and FFTs.

5.3 The NetSolve Problem Solving Environment

We have discussed throughout this chapter how NetSolve can be customized, extended, and used for a variety of purposes. We first described in Sections 4.2.1 and 4.2.2 how NetSolve can encompass new types of computing resources, resulting in a more powerful and flexible environment and raising new research issues. We next discussed in Section 4.2.3 how NetSolve and Ninf can be merged into a single metacomputing environment. Finally, in Section 4.2.4, we gave an example of an entire application that uses NetSolve as an operating environment to build general image processing framework. All these developments take place at different levels in the NetSolve project and have had and will continue to have an impact on the project itself, causing it to improve and expand.

The scientific community has long used the Internet for communication of email, software, and documentation. Until recently there has been little use of the network for actual computations. This situation is changing rapidly and will have an enormous impact on the future. Novel user interfaces that hide the complexity of scalable parallelism require new concepts and mechanisms for representing scientific computational problems and for specifying how those problems relate to each other. Very high level languages and systems, perhaps graphically based, not only would facilitate the use of mathematical software from the user's point of view, but also help to automate the determination of effective partitioning, mapping, granularity, data structures, etc. However, new concepts in problem specification and representation may also require new mathematical research on the analytic, algebraic, and topological properties of problems (e.g., existence and uniqueness).

5.4 Software and Documentation Availability

Most of the software mentioned in this document and the corresponding documentations are in the public domain, and are available from *netlib* (http://www.netlib.org/) [DG87]. For instance, the EISPACK, LINPACK, LAPACK, BLACS, ScaLAPACK, and ATLAS software packages are in the public domain, and are available from *netlib*. Moreover, these publically available software packages can also be retrieved by e-mail. For example, to obtain more information on LAPACK, one should send the following one-line email message to netlib@ornl.gov: send index from lapack. Information for other packages can be similarly obtained. Real-time information on the NetSolve project can be found at the following web address http://www.cs.utk.edu/netsolve.

References

[ABB+95]   Anderson E., Bai Z., Bischof C., Demmel J., Dongarra J., Du Croz J., Greenbaum A., Hammarling S., McKenney A., Ostrouchov S. and Sorensen D., *LAPACK User's Guide* (second edition), SIAM, Philadelphia PA, 1995.

[AD89]   Anderson E. and Dongarra J., Results from the Initial Release of LA-PACK, *LAPACK Working Note*, No. 16, Technical Report, University of Tennessee, Knoxville, TN, 1989.

[AD90]   Anderson E. and Dongarra J., Evaluating Block Algorithm Variants
            in LAPACK, *LAPACK Working Note*, No. 19, Technical Report, Uni-
            versity of Tennessee, Knoxville, TN, 1990.

[BAC+97]   Bilmes J., Asanović K., Chin C. W. and Demmel J., Optimizing Ma-
            trix Multiply Using PHiPAC: A Portable, High-Performance, ANSI C
            Coding Methodology, *Proceedings of the International Conference on
            Supercomputing*, ACM SIGARC, Vienna, Austria, 1997, 340-347.

[BCC+97]   Blackford L., Choi J., Cleary A., D'Azevedo E., Demmel J., Dhillon I.,
            Dongarra J., Hammarling S., Henry G., Petitet A., Stanley K., Walker
            D. and Whaley R. C., *ScaLAPACK Users' Guide*, SIAM, Philadelphia
            PA, 1997.

[BDP+98]   Blackford L., Dongarra J., Papadopoulos C., and Whaley R. C., In-
            stallation Guide and Design of the HPF 1.1 Interface to ScaLAPACK,
            SLHPF, *LAPACK Working Note*, No. 137, Technical Report UT CS-
            98-396, University of Tennessee, Knoxville, TN, 1998.

[BW98]   Blackford L. S. and Whaley R. C., ScaLAPACK Evaluation and Per-
            formance at the DoD MSRCs, *LAPACK Working Note*, No. 136, Tech-
            nical Report UT CS-98-388, University of Tennessee, Knoxville, TN,
            1998.

[BCD96]   Browne S., Casanova H. and Dongarra J., Providing Access to High
            Performance Computing Technologies, in: Wasniewski J., Dongarra J.,
            Madsen K. and Olesen D. (eds.), *Lecture Notes in Computer Science*
            No.1184, Springer-Verlag, Berlin, 1996, 123-133.

[CD95]   Casanova H. and Dongarra J., NetSolve: A Network Server for Solv-
            ing Computational Science Problems, Technical report UT CS-95-313,
            University of Tennessee, Knoxville, TN, 1995.

[CDO+95]   Choi J., Dongarra J., Ostrouchov S., Petitet A., Walker D. and Whaley
            R. C., A Proposal for a Set of Parallel Basic Linear Algebra Subpro-
            grams, *LAPACK Working Note*, No. 100, Technical report UT CS-95-
            292, University of Tennessee, Knoxville, TN, 1995.

[CDG+93]   Culler D., Dusseau A., Goldstein S., Krishnamurthy A., Lumetta S.,
            von Eicken T. and Yelick K., Introduction to Split-C: Version 0.9,
            Computer Science Division – EECS, University of California, Berkeley,
            CA 94720, 1993.

[DDP94]   Dayde M., Duff I. and Petitet A., A Parallel Block Implementation
            of Level 3 BLAS for MIMD Vector Processors, *ACM Transactions on
            Mathematical Software* 20, 1994, 178-193.

[Dem89]   Demmel J., LAPACK: A Portable Linear Algebra Library for Su-
            percomputers, *Proceedings of the 1989 IEEE Control Systems Society
            Workshop on Computer-Aided Control System Design*, 1989.

[Don84]   Dongarra J., Increasing the Performance of Mathematical Software
            through High-Level Modularity, *Proceedings Sixth Int. Symp. Comp.
            Methods in Eng. & Applied Sciences*, Versailles, France, North-
            Holland, 1984, 239-248.

[DDH+90]   Dongarra J., Du Croz J., Hammarling S. and Duff I., A Set of Level
            3 Basic Linear Algebra Subprograms, *ACM Transactions on Mathe-
            matical Software* 16, 1990, 1-17.

[DDH+88]   Dongarra J., Du Croz J., Hammarling S. and Hanson R., An Extended
            Set of Fortran Basic Linear Algebra Subroutines, *ACM Transactions
            on Mathematical Software* 14, 1988, 18-32.

[DDS+91]   Dongarra J., Duff I., Sorensen D. and Van der Vorst H., *Solving Lin-
            ear Systems on Vector and Shared Memory Computers*, SIAM Publi-
            cations, Philadelphia, PA, 1991.

[DG87]   Dongarra J. and Grosse E., Distribution of Mathematical Software via
           Electronic Mail, *Communications of the ACM* **30**, 1987, 403-407.
[DMR91]   Dongarra J., Mayes P. and Radicati di Brozolo G., The IBM RISC
           System 6000 and Linear Algebra Operations, *Supercomputer* **8**, 1991,
           15-30.
[DPW93]   Dongarra J., Pozo R. and Walker D., An Object Oriented Design for
           High Performance Linear Algebra on Distributed Memory Architec-
           tures, *Proceedings of the Object Oriented Numerics Conference*, 1993,
           257-264.
[DP87]   Du Croz J. and Pont M., The Development of a Floating-Point Valida-
           tion Package, *Proceedings of the 8th Symposium on Computer Arith-
           metic*, IEEE Computer Society Press, Como, Italy, 1987.
[ENB96]   Eckel G., Neider J. and Bassler E., ImageVision Library Programming
           Guide, Silicon Graphics, Inc., Mountain View, CA, 1996.
[Ede93]   Edelman A., Large Dense Numerical Linear Algebra in 1993: The Par-
           allel Computing Influence, *International Journal of Supercomputing
           Applications* **7**, 1993, 113-128.
[FO88]   Felten E. and Otto S., Coherent Parallel C, *Proceedings of the Third
           Conference on Hypercube Concurrent Computers and Applications*,
           ACM Press, 1988.
[FK98]   Foster I. and Kesselman C. (eds.), *The Grid – Blueprint for a New
           Computing Infrastructure*, Morgan Kaufmann Publishers, Inc., San
           Francisco, CA, 1998.
[FJL+88]   Fox G., Johnson M., Lyzenga G., Otto S., J. Salmon and D. Walker,
           Solving Problems on Concurrent Processors, Volume 1, Prentice Hall,
           Englewood Cliffs, N.J., 1988.
[GPS90]   Gallivan K., Plemmons R. and Sameh A., Parallel Algorithms for
           Dense Linear Algebra Computations, *SIAM Review* **32**, 1990, 54-135.
[GBD+94]   Geisti A., Beguelin A., Dongarra J., Jiang W., Manchek R. and Sun-
           deram V., *PVM : Parallel Virtual Machine. A Users' Guide and Tu-
           torial for Networked Parallel Computing*, The MIT Press Cambridge,
           Massachusetts, 1994.
[GK90]   Gupta A. and Kumar V., On the Scalability of FFT on Parallel Com-
           puters, *Proceedings of the Frontiers 90 Conference on Massively Par-
           allel Computation*, IEEE Computer Society Press, 1990.
[Har90]   Harrington R., Origin and Development of the Method of Moments
           for Field Computation, *IEEE Antennas and Propagation Magazine*,
           1990.
[Hes90]   Hess J., Panel Methods in Computational Fluid Dynamics, *Annal Re-
           views of Fluid Mechanics* **22**, 1990, 255-274.
[HS67]   Hess J. and Smith M., Calculation of Potential Flows about Arbitrary
           Bodies, in: Küchemann D., editor, *Progress in Aeronautical Sciences*,
           Volume 8, Pergamon Press, 1967.
[HJ81]   Hockney R. W. and Jesshope C. R., *Parallel Computers*, Adam Hilger
           Ltd., Bristol, UK, 1981.
[KLV93]   Kågström B., Ling P. and Van Loan C., Portable High Performance
           GEMM-based Level 3 BLAS, in: Sincovec R. F. et al., (eds.), *Parallel
           Processing for Scientific Computing*, SIAM, Philadelphia, 1993, 339-
           346.
[Kah87]   Kahan W., Paranoia, (See http://www.netlib.org/).
[KLS+94]   Koebel C., Loveman D., Schreiber R., Steele G., and Zosel M., *The
           High Performance Fortran Handbook*, The MIT Press, Cambridge,
           Massachusetts, 1994.

[LHK+79]   Lawson C., Hanson R., Kincaid D. and Krogh F., Basic Linear Algebra Subprograms for Fortran Usage, *ACM Transactions Mathematical Software* 5, 1979, 308-323.

[LLM88]   Litzkow M. and Livny M. and Mutka M. W., Condor - A Hunter of Idle Workstations, *Proceedings of the 8th International Conference of Distributed Computing Systems*, 1988, 104-111.

[Mat92]   The Math Works Inc., *MATLAB Reference Guide*, The Math Works Inc., 1992.

[MPI+94]   Message Passing Interface Forum, MPI: A Message-Passing Interface standard, *International Journal of Supercomputer Applications* 8, 1994, 159-416.

[Obe97]   Oberhuber M., Integrating ImageVision into NetSolve, see http://www.icg.tu-graz.ac.at/mober/pub, 1997.

[SSN+96]   Sekiguchi S., Sato M., Nakada H., Matsuoka S. and Nagashima U., Ninf : Network based Information Library for Globally High Performance Computing, *Proceedings of Parallel Object-Oriented Methods and Applications (POOMA)*, Santa Fe, 1996.

[SOH+96]   Snir M., Otto S., Huss-Lederman S., Walker D. and Dongarra J., *MPI: The Complete Reference*, MIT Press, Cambridge, Massachusetts, 1996.

[Tol97]   Toledo S., Improving Instruction-Level Parallelism in Sparse Matrix-Vector Multiplication Using Reordering, Blocking, and Prefetching, *Proceedings of the 8th SIAM Conference on Parallel Processing for Scientific Computing*, SIAM, 1997, ISBN 0-89871-395-1 (CD-ROM).

[Wan91]   Wang J., *Generalized Moment Methods in Electromagnetics*, John Wiley & Sons, New-York, 1991.

[WD95]   Whaley R. C. and Dongarra J., A User's Guide to the BLACS v1.1, *LAPACK Working Note*, No. 94, Technical Report UT CS-95-281, University of Tennessee, Knoxville, 1995, (See also http://www.netlib.org/blacs/).

[WD97]   Whaley R. C. and Dongarra J., Automatically Tuned Linear Algebra Software, *Proceedings of Supercomputing '98*, ACM SIGARCH and IEEE Computer Society, ISBN 0-89791-984-X (CD-ROM) (also *LAPACK Working Note*, No. 131, Technical Report UT CS-97-366, University of Tennessee, Knoxville, TN, 1997, (See also http://www.netlib.org/atlas/).

[WR71]   Wilkinson J., Reinsch C., *Handbook for Automatic Computation: Volume II - Linear Algebra*, Springer-Verlag, New York, 1971.

[Wol96]   Wolfram S., *The Mathematica Book*, (Third Edition), Wolfram Median, Inc. and Cambridge University Press, 1996.

XI. High-performance Computing in Molecular Sciences

Wojciech Cencek[1], Jacek Komasa[1], and Jacek Rychlewski[1,2]

[1] Quantum Chemistry Group, Department of Chemistry, Adam Mickiewicz University, Grunwaldzka 6, PL-60780 Poznań, Poland
[2] Poznań Supercomputing and Networking Center, Wieniawskiego 17/19, PL-61713 Poznań, Poland

Summary. A task which is very common in theoretical chemistry, physics, and engineering – solving the generalized symmetric eigenvalue problem – is discussed. In the considered examples modern quantum chemical methods are applied to solve the Schrödinger equation with a molecular Hamiltonian operator. The solution of the Schrödinger equation is of fundamental importance in quantum chemistry and molecular physics since it gives knowledge of the microscopic world. Two subproblems of completely different character – evaluating matrix elements (a scalar task) and solving the eigenequations (a vector task) are analyzed in terms of the overall computational cost, its scaling with the dimension of the algebraic space and with the size of the molecular system, and of the appropriateness of different computer architectures. The most logical way to achieve a good performance is to use distributed processing on heterogeneous (scalar-vector) systems employing message passing. Experiences in testing one of such systems are discussed and compared with speedups obtained on shared- and distributed-memory homogeneous machines.

1. Foreword

Molecular sciences belong to these sciences which have profited the most from modern high-performance computers, but their appetite seems to be growing faster and faster, which is clearly seen in computer resources consumption reports of almost every computing centre. One reason for this is the common use of such techniques as basis set expansions involving large matrices or random simulations with very large statistical populations. It emphasizes the need to search for new and more efficient programming methods, among which distributed and parallel computing seem very promising. Our quantum chemistry package CORREL represents, as we believe, a good example with which some of these methods can be illustrated.

This chapter is organized as follows. In the next section a minimal quantum chemistry background is sketched in order to give the reader some idea of what kind of problems CORREL is designed for. The general structure of the program is also discussed. Section 3. presents a computational cost analysis of CORREL's main building blocks, which is indispensable for developing an efficient distributed version and predicting its performance. Techniques used to parallelize the program on homogeneous multiprocessor systems and the results obtained are reported in Section 4. Section 5. deals with some general aspects of distributed heterogeneous systems and gives an example how a high performance can be gained thanks to the mixed scalar-vector character of the application and a skilful choice of computers used to build the heterogeneous machine.

The following symbols are used among others and retain their meanings throughout the chapter.

N Number of electrons in the investigated molecule

K Basis size of the algebraic expansion of the wave function; consequently, also the order of the resulting GSEP (general symmetric eigenvalue problem)

S $K \times K$ matrix containing overlap integrals s_{kl} between basis functions

H $K \times K$ matrix containing Hamiltonian integrals h_{kl} between basis functions

S The speedup

P Number of processors

The terms "execution time" or "elapsed time" should be understood as wall-clock time difference between the stop of the last processor and the start of the first processor, measured on a dedicated system.

2. Introduction

2.1 Quantum Chemistry Background

As it is commonly known, elementary particles and sufficiently small objects built out of them – such as atoms and molecules – cannot be described in terms of classical Newtonian mechanics, even when we neglect relativistic effects contained in Einstein theory. Instead of Newton's laws we have to deal with quantum mechanics and the famous Schrödinger equation

$$\hat{H}\Psi = \mathcal{E}\Psi, \tag{2.1}$$

where $\hat{H}$ is the so-called Hamiltonian operator (the total energy operator) modifying in some defined way the function Ψ following it. The construction of this operator for a given quantum system is usually a simple task. To solve the Schrödinger equation means to find both the *wave function*, Ψ, and the total energy of the system, $\mathcal{E}$. As follows from quantum mechanics, if we know Ψ we can easily calculate, apart from the energy, all static properties of the system. Unfortunately, from what the chemist may be interested in, namely atoms and molecules, only trivial one-electron cases such as the hydrogen atom can be directly solved. For larger systems the Schrödinger equation becomes so difficult to solve that one is forced to look for some approximations. One commonly used, called the Born-Oppenheimer approximation, treats the movements of the electrons independently of those of the nuclei, a model based upon the large mass ratio of the two types of particles. In the first step, the *electronic* Schrödinger equation at a number of different frozen nuclear configurations is solved, i.e. it is assumed that the nuclear masses in the Hamiltonian operator are infinite (the nuclei do not move) and the function Ψ depends only on the electronic coordinates (and – parametrically – on the nuclear positions). This is the subject of the *electronic structure theory*. The second step involves solving the equation for the nuclear motion. In this equation, the electronic energy as a function of the nuclear positions is a potential for the nuclear dynamics. Having completed both the tasks one can also subsequently compute the couplings between both the types of movements so that starting with the Born-Oppenheimer approximation does not exclude the calculation of quantum system properties with high accuracy.

The electronic problem, on which our interest will be henceforth focused, is very complicated but can be numerically solved in some indirect way, for example *variationally*. Such methods rely on the following theorem (variational principle)

$$\varepsilon = \frac{\int \Phi \hat{H} \Phi \, dV}{\int \Phi^2 \, dV} \geq E. \tag{2.2}$$

It states that taking *any* square-integrable function Φ and calculating the quantity ε according to Eq. (2.2) (where dV stands for the integration over all the electronic coordinates) one never gets a value lower than the true electronic energy E defined by an electronic analogue of Eq. (2.1). Consequently, among different trial functions the best one is that yielding the lowest value of ε. If these functions depend on some set of parameters, we treat ε as a function of these parameters and look for its minimum. It is particularly simple (see Section 2.2) if Φ is a linear combination

$$\Phi(\mathbf{r}_1, \ldots, \mathbf{r}_N) = \sum_{i=1}^{K} c_i \, \phi_i(\mathbf{r}_1, \ldots, \mathbf{r}_N). \tag{2.3}$$

In the above equation, $\mathbf{r}_i$ denotes the set of all the coordinates of the ith electron and ϕ_i are *basis functions* defining the K-dimensional space on which one projects the unknown function Ψ. A standard way in the electronic structure theory is to express the ϕ_i's as products of N one-electron factors, which is known as the method of configuration interaction (CI). It turns out, however, that the CI expansions are extremely slowly convergent, i.e. the value of ε in Eq. (2.2) is far above E (at least dozens of cm^{-1}, in comparison with accuracies of a small fraction of cm^{-1} reached by today's experimental methods) unless an astronomic (computationally not achievable) number of expansion terms, K, is used. Higher accuracy can be obtained if the ϕ_i's depend not only on the individual electron coordinates but also on interelectronic distances. These so-called *explicitly correlated* functions describe better the electron-electron Coulomb repulsions. Examples are the Kołos-Wolniewicz function [KW65] for the hydrogen molecule (one of the greatest achievements of the Polish chemistry) and the Gaussian-type function introduced in the 60's by Boys [Boy60] and Singer [Sin60]:

$$\phi_i = \hat{P} \exp\left(-\sum_{k=1}^{N} \alpha_{ik}|\mathbf{r}_k - \mathbf{A}_{ik}|^2 - \sum_{k>l=1}^{N} \beta_{ikl}|\mathbf{r}_k - \mathbf{r}_l|^2\right). \tag{2.4}$$

The first sum contains electron coordinates expressed as squared distances between the kth electron and the given point $\mathbf{A}_{ik}$. The second sum mixes the electron coordinates introducing explicit correlation of their movements. $\hat{P}$ is an operator ensuring that the total function has appropriate symmetry properties. Because of the symmetry requirements, in atoms all the N centers $\mathbf{A}_{ik}$ coincide usually with the position of the nucleus and need not to be determined, and in linear molecules they lie on the molecular axis and have one component to be optimized. Apart from these, the following variational parameters are associated with each ϕ_i term: one c_i (linear), N α_{ik}'s (nonlinear) and $\binom{N}{2}$ β_{ikl}'s (nonlinear). This type of wave function has been tried for thirty years, generally yielding significantly worse results than other explicitly correlated functions (e.g. the Kołos-Wolniewicz expansion). An opinion that it is inferior – when very high accuracy is desired – has been commonly accepted. A few years ago a large project was started in our group, which aimed at weakening this conviction and investigating what level of accuracy can be reached when large expansions with very carefully optimized nonlinear parameters are used in conjunction with high-performance and efficiently programmed computers. It should be noted that almost all of today's quantum chemical computations are restricted to the linear optimization because optimizing nonlinear variational parameters is usually extremely expensive. As a part of the project we developed a computer program named COR-REL which allows one to optimize all the parameters in the wave function of the type (2.4) for small atoms and molecules. The largest expansion used so far by us has been a 2400-term wave function for the lithium hydride LiH ($K=2400$, $N=4$). As follows from above, it contains 2400 linear and 33600 nonlinear parameters, all of them to be optimized. This already sheds some light on the difficulties arising from such extensive calculations and explains the need of high-performance computing.

Our method of exponentially correlated Gaussian (ECG) wave functions applies to few-electron systems. We have shown that it yields much higher accuracy than any other variational method. Quantum-chemical aspects of our computations can be found in Refs. [RCK94, KCR95, CKR95, CR95, KCR96, KR97, CRJ+98]. For an orientation, in the table below we compare best accuracies achieved so far with three mostly used variational quantum chemistry techniques, applied to homonuclear diatomic molecules with $N=2$, 3, and 4 electrons. HF stands for Hartree-Fock, a method which relies on a single term of the expansion (2.3) and is still considered standard in routine quantum chemical calculations. It is worth to mention here that the accuracy of today's spectroscopic measurements amounts to small fractions of cm^{-1}.

N	Molecule	HF	CI	ECG
2	H_2	$9 \cdot 10^3$	38	<0.0001
3	He_2^+	$15 \cdot 10^3$	78	~0.1
4	He_2	$18 \cdot 10^3$	300	<0.1

2.2 Optimization of the Linear Parameters

If one would like to optimize only the linear parameters c_i in (2.3), the problem is not theoretically difficult and has a general solution. Putting (2.3) into the expression for ε (2.2) and assuming $\partial\varepsilon/\partial c_i=0$ leads to

$$\mathbf{Hc} = \varepsilon\mathbf{Sc} \tag{2.5}$$

where $\mathbf{H}$ and $\mathbf{S}$ are symmetric $K \times K$ matrices defined by

$$h_{kl} = \int \phi_k \hat{H} \phi_l \, dV \tag{2.6}$$

$$s_{kl} = \int \phi_k \phi_l \, dV \tag{2.7}$$

and $\mathbf{c}$ is a $K \times 1$ vector of the parameters c_i (see any good textbook of quantum chemistry).

Equations of the type (2.5) are well known in linear algebra as the *general symmetric eigenvalue problem* (GSEP). Its solution presents no formal difficulties but becomes time-consuming for large matrices since its cost goes as K^3. On the other hand, the accuracy of the computed energy (and usually also of the other physical quantities) grows monotonically with K. Hence, it is often desirable to use as large matrices as possible.

It should be also noted that Eq. (2.5) has K solutions defined by the pairs $\{(\varepsilon, \mathbf{c})_l, \; l = 1, K\}$, each of them fulfilling the variational principle (2.2) for the lth quantum state of the system ($l=1$ for the ground state and $l \geq 2$ for excited states).

2.3 Optimization of All the Parameters

Unfortunately, it is not possible to obtain a compact equation for the best nonlinear parameters, analogous to (2.5). Instead one is forced to use some kind of nonlinear optimization. There are many such techniques but most of them consist in changing iteratively the values of the parameters according to some predefined strategy, testing values of the *objective function* (in our case – energy) after each step, and modifying the strategy in order to move in the direction where the energy diminishes faster. The process stops when no modification of the parameters leads to further energy improvement. In the CORREL program we have implemented the conjugate directions method introduced over thirty years ago by Powell [Pow64] and still considered as one of the most efficient despite its simplicity.

The whole algorithm of optimizing all the parameters in the wave function of the type (2.3) can be summarized as follows.

1. Choose starting values for the nonlinear parameters.
2. Compute $\mathbf{H}$ and $\mathbf{S}$ matrices.
3. Solve eigenvalue problem $\mathbf{Hc} = \varepsilon \mathbf{Sc}$.
4. Stop condition fulfilled?
   NO: change the values of the nonlinear parameters; go to 2.
   YES: stop.

One execution of steps 2 and 3 constitutes what is called the *optimization shot*, i.e. it gives one trial value of the energy, ε. As we can see, each single shot involves the full linear optimization (step 3). In practice a number of the shots which are necessary to reach the convergence turns out to be of the order of 100 times the number of the nonlinear parameters. Turning back to our 2400-term example LiH function, it means that following tasks have to be completed *a few million times*:

– computation of almost 3 million matrix elements h_{kl} and s_{kl}, each of them involving thousands of floating-point operations,
– solving general eigenvalue problem of the order $K=2400$.

It becomes clear that without efficient algorithms and powerful computers our method would be hopelessly time-consuming.

2.4 Algorithmic Details

2.4.1 Inverse iteration. Solving the eigenvalue problem (2.5) is crucial for the efficiency of our program. Even if, for some special cases, the computation of $\mathbf{H}$ and $\mathbf{S}$ matrices might be the slowest step, its time is only $\mathcal{O}(K^2)$. For high-accuracy quantum chemical calculations, in which we are ultimately interested, K has to be large and K^3-dependence of (2.5) will sooner or later become a bottleneck. We have used the inverse iteration method, known as fast and numerically stable. The vector $\mathbf{c}$, being the solution of Eq. (2.5), is found as the following limit

$$\mathbf{c} = \lim_{k \to \infty} \frac{\mathbf{c}_k}{\|\mathbf{c}_k\|}, \tag{2.8}$$

where the sequence $\{\mathbf{c}_k\}$ is defined by the recurrence relation

$$(\mathbf{H} - \varepsilon_0 \mathbf{S}) \, \mathbf{c}_{k+1} = \mathbf{S} \mathbf{c}_k \tag{2.9}$$

and $\mathbf{c}_0$ is an arbitrary starting vector. The norm $\|\mathbf{c}_k\|$ is defined with respect to the $\mathbf{S}$ matrix:

$$\|\mathbf{c}_k\| = \sqrt{\mathbf{c}_k^T \mathbf{S} \mathbf{c}_k}. \tag{2.10}$$

It is known that $\{\mathbf{c}_k\}$ converges to an eigenvector corresponding to this eigenvalue which is closest to the constant ε_0. Therefore, the eigenvalue (energy) has to be known approximately at the beginning. The exact value can be computed from the converged eigenvector:

$$\varepsilon = \frac{\mathbf{c}^T \mathbf{H} \mathbf{c}}{\|\mathbf{c}\|^2} \tag{2.11}$$

In practice, for a reasonably chosen ε_0, only a few iterations ($\sim$ 3–5) are needed to obtain 15 significant digits of ε.

That the computational effort involved in the inverse iteration procedure amounts to $\mathcal{O}(K^3)$ results from the necessity to solve (several times) the linear equation system (2.9). Fortunately, the matrix $\mathbf{H} - \varepsilon_0 \mathbf{S}$ remains constant throughout all the iterations. Hence, one can find its triangular (LU) decomposition with $\mathcal{O}(K^3)$ operations just once before the first iteration:

$$\mathbf{H} - \varepsilon_0 \mathbf{S} = \mathbf{L} \mathbf{U} \tag{2.12}$$

and replace in each iteration the system (2.9) with two simpler, $\mathcal{O}(K^2)$, triangular systems

$$\mathbf{L} \mathbf{y} = \mathbf{S} \mathbf{c}_k \tag{2.13}$$

$$\mathbf{U} \mathbf{c}_{k+1} = \mathbf{y} \tag{2.14}$$

In the above equations, $\mathbf{L}$ is a lower triangular matrix and $\mathbf{U}$ an upper triangular matrix. In most cases, one is interested in the ground electronic state and ε_0 can be chosen below the lowest root of Eq. (2.5). The matrix $\mathbf{H} - \varepsilon_0 \mathbf{S}$

is then positive definite and there exists its triangular decomposition of the simpler form $\mathbf{LL}^T$ which can be found by the well-known Cholesky algorithm.

In summary, the following matrix operations are necessary to find one solution of the GSEP:

Operation	Cost	How many times
Cholesky decomposition	$\mathcal{O}(K^3)$	1
Triangular system of equations	$\mathcal{O}(K^2)$	2× No. of iterations
Matrix-vector multiplication	$\mathcal{O}(K^2)$	2× No. of iterations

2.4.2 Updating the Cholesky decomposition. By using the matrix decomposition (2.12) to solve the system (2.9) it is possible to reduce the overall number of operations significantly, but the leading term in the cost expression remains K^3. It can be however noticed that the decomposition (2.12) is performed many times during the whole optimization process, namely once per each shot (see Section 2.3). If not all the elements of the $\mathbf{H}$ and $\mathbf{S}$ change from one shot to another, some operations in the Cholesky decomposition are repeated and could be avoided. Instead of performing the full decomposition one then has to compute merely its *update*. Since the $\mathbf{H}$ and $\mathbf{S}$ matrices depend on the basis functions ϕ_i, see Eqs. (2.6, 2.7), their smallest possible change takes place when only one ϕ_i changes from one shot to another and consists in a modification of one row and one column. A particularly simple situation occurs if it is the last basis function in the expansion (2.3) which is modified. The reason is the following property of the Cholesky decomposition: The ith row and column of the matrix $\mathbf{A}$ being decomposed do not influence the rows $1, 2, \ldots, i - 1$ of the computed factor $\mathbf{L}$. To update the decomposition of a matrix with modified last row and column it is therefore sufficient to recompute the last row of $\mathbf{L}$ which requires only $\mathcal{O}(K^2)$ operations.

2.4.3 Organization of the optimization process. To make use of the above idea we perform the optimization as follows:

- Only parameters belonging to a single expansion term ϕ_i in (2.3) are optimized simultaneously (with the Powell method), while the others are kept fixed. In this way only one row and column of the $\mathbf{H}$ and $\mathbf{S}$ matrices change which makes the decomposition update efficient. Additionally, K instead of $\mathcal{O}(K^2)$ integrals (2.6) and (2.7) have to be recomputed at each shot. After all the parameters in this expansion term have been optimized, the next term ϕ_{i+1} is optimized in the same way.
- Before we start the optimization of the given term ϕ_i we formally renumber the terms in (2.3) by swapping the ith with the Kth. Of course, it does not affect the solutions of (2.5). The first shot for the ϕ_i (now the ϕ_K) comprises the full GSEP with $\mathcal{O}(K^3)$ operations, the next shots – the updated GSEP with $\mathcal{O}(K^2)$ operations.

The optimization procedure is performed for each basis function ϕ_i from $i = 1$ up to $i = K$. We call this K-fold loop execution the *optimization cycle*. One such cycle is not sufficient in practice, since each optimized basis function is no longer optimal as soon as the next one is released and allowed to change. In order to find the true minimum of the energy with respect to all the nonlinear parameters it is necessary to make many cycles. The single cycle is, however, the largest computational unit discussed throughout this chapter. It is presented graphically in Fig. 2.1. Note that due to the symmetry of **H** and **S**, only their full upper triangles are stored and altered.

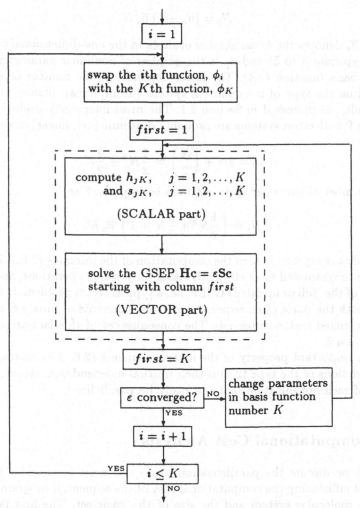

Fig. 2.1. General scheme of one optimization cycle in CORREL program. The dashed box denotes one optimization shot.

They must be already filled with the values corresponding to the starting nonlinear parameters before the first entry into the loop over i. It should be also noted that the full optimization of each basis function ("ε converged" as the condition to leave the inner loop) is too expensive and not really needed (it will be undertaken again in the next cycle). Usually we do just one iteration of the Powell algorithm which comprises one one-dimensional optimization per each nonlinear parameter plus one additional one-dimensional optimization along the *conjugate direction*. It makes possible to estimate the total number of shots per cycle N_s, which determines the cost of the cycle. Since the Powell optimization is done for each of the K basis functions, it can be expressed as

$$N_s = (n_p + 1)\,\bar{n}_s\,K, \qquad (2.15)$$

where $\bar{n}_s$ denotes the mean number of shots in the one-dimensional optimization (typically 3 to 5) and n_p is the number of nonlinear parameters in the single basis function (2.4). The latter depends on the number of electrons N and on the type of the quantum system (atom, linear, planar, or general molecule), as discussed in Section 2.1. The most intensively studied systems among few-electron systems are probably diatomic (i.e., linear) molecules for which

$$n_p = 2N + \binom{N}{2} = \frac{1}{2}N^2 + \frac{3}{2}N. \qquad (2.16)$$

The number of shots per cycle can then be expressed as

$$N_s = \left(\frac{1}{2}N^2 + \frac{3}{2}N + 1\right)\bar{n}_s\,K. \qquad (2.17)$$

Each shot comprises in turn the computation of the integrals (2.6, 2.7), which can be programmed most efficiently using only *scalar* operations, and the solution of the (full or updated) GSEP, i.e. a typical vector problem. It turns out that both the parts often require comparable amounts of time, i.e. one deals with a mixed scalar-vector job. The consequences of this fact are discussed in Section 5.

An important property of the matrix elements (2.6, 2.7) computed with the functions of the type (2.4) is their mutual independence. Hence, the first part of each optimization shot can easily be parallelized.

3. Computational Cost Analysis

Before we discuss the parallelization issues, we want to consider the main factors influencing the computational cost of the sequential program: the size of the molecular system and the size of the basis set. The first factor has only an effect on the matrix element section of the program. The second is important for both sections.

Benchmark results reported in this chapter were obtained on a set of computers currently available to us. The following list presents the specification of the computers, their operating systems, compilers and the linear algebra

libraries the program has been linked with. Each machine has been assigned
a label used throughout the chapter as a reference:

SGI R10000 Silicon Graphics Origin 200, processor MIPS R10000 180 MHz
Operating system: IRIX64 6.4
Compiler: Mongoose Fortran 7.11
Compiling command: f77 -64 -mips4 -O3 (Table 3.1 and 3.3)
f77 -64 -mips4 -O2 (Table 3.2)
Libraries: BLAS (libblas.a)

SGI R8000 Silicon Graphics Indigo 2, processor MIPS R8000 75 MHz
Operating system: IRIX64 6.2
Compiler: Mongoose Fortran 7.10
Compiling command: f77 -64 -mips4 -O3 (Table 3.1 and 3.3)
f77 -64 -mips4 -O2 (Table 3.2)
Libraries: BLAS (libblas.a)

NS-860 Microway Number Smasher, processor Intel 860-XR 40 MHz
Operating system: MSDOS 5.0
Compiler: Microway NDP Fortran-860 4.1d
Compiling command: mf860n -on
Libraries: Kuck & Associates Library (libkden.a, libkmath.a)

Pentium IBM PC compatible, processor Intel Pentium 100 MHz
Operating system: MSDOS 5.0
Compiler: Microway NDP Fortran-486 3.20
Compiling command: mf486 -n2 -n3 -on -OL
Libraries: none

Cray EL Cray Y-MP EL 33 MHz
Operating system: Unicos 8.0.4.2
Compiler: Cray Fortran CFT77 6.0.2.0
Compiling command: cf77 -dp -Ovector3 -Oscalar2 (Table 3.2,
3- and 4-electron integrals)
Compiling command: cf77 -dp -Ovector3 -Oscalar3 (the other
cases)
Libraries: Cray Research Scientific Library (libsci.a)

Cray J916 Cray J916 100 MHz
Operating system: Unicos 9.0.2.4
Compiler: Cray Fortran CFT77 6.0.4.24
Compiling command: cf77 -dp -Ovector3 -Oscalar2 (Table 3.2,
3- and 4-electron integrals)
Compiling command: cf77 -dp -Ovector3 -Oscalar3 (the other
cases)
Libraries: Cray Research Scientific Library (libsci.a)

Cray T3E Cray T3E-900, processors DEC Alpha 450 MHz
Operating system: Unicos/mk 1.5.2
Compiler: Cray Fortran CF90 3.0.1.0
Compiling command:

f90 -dp -Oaggress,pipeline3,scalar3,vector3
Libraries: Cray Research Scientific Library (libsci.a)

HP 715   Hewlett-Packard 715, processor PA-RISC 50 MHz
Operating system: HP-UX 10.20
Compiler: HP Fortran/S700 10.20.02
Compiling command: f77 +O3
Libraries: BLAS, Lapack (libblas.a, liblapack_hppa.a)

IBM SP2   IBM 9076 Scalable POWERparallel System,
processors POWER2 66 MHz
Operating system: AIX 4.1.4
Compiler: AIX XL Fortran 03.02
Compiling command: f77 -O2 (Table 3.2)
f77 -O3 (Table 3.3)
Libraries: BLAS (libblas.a)

3.1 Scaling of the Problem with the Size of the Molecular System

The size of the molecular systems of our interest is determined by the number of electrons, N. The number of electrons determines the cost of the evaluation of the matrix elements but does not affect the eigenvalue problem. Hence, this subsection concerns only the evaluation of the Hamiltonian and overlap matrix elements, Eq. (2.6) and (2.7). The number of nuclei in a molecule has a less significant effect on the cost of the matrix elements, therefore we limit our present discussion to homonuclear diatomics at the equilibrium internuclear distances, with $2 \leq N \leq 6$: H_2, He_2^+, He_2, Li_2^+, Li_2. At present, our method is effective for systems with up to 6 electrons.

We have developed two distinct routines for computing the matrix elements. The first one is general in the sense that it could be applied for any value of N. It involves compact expressions, mainly matrix operations of the order N. The other routine contains specialized expressions for each value of N, obtained by expanding and simplifying the general formulae. So far, the 2-, 3-, and 4-electron cases are implemented. The resulting expressions are very lengthy (a few hundreds lines of the code for $N = 4$) but perform much better than the general ones. They involve only scalar operations.

We analyse below the scaling of both of these routines. The behaviour of the general routine is important in predicting perspectives of the method, since developing specialized expressions becomes unfeasible for larger values of N. The specialized routine, on the other hand, is what we currently use in practice for 2-, 3-, and 4-electron systems and it is essential to know its benchmarks when developing distributed versions of the program and trying to predict their performance.

Table 3.1 lists results of benchmark calculations performed on a set of different machines for all five molecular systems from H_2 to Li_2. The matrix elements were evaluated using the general N-electron version of our program. The computers are ordered according to the growing speed. This order

Table 3.1. Time needed to evaluate one pair of the matrix elements, h_{kl} and s_{kl}, with the general integral routine (in milliseconds).

Machine	Number of electrons, N				
	2	3	4	5	6
Cray EL	1.49	9.81	74.5	661	6630
NS-860	0.930	6.73	48.9	473	4467
Cray J916	0.533	3.39	24.9	222	2227
Pentium	0.275	2.06	18.3	190	2289
HP 715	0.214	1.51	12.4	124	1343
SGI R8000	0.121	0.845	7.16	69.8	758
IBM SP2	0.0944	0.661	5.29	48.0	512
SGI R10000	0.0440	0.316	2.77	26.3	286
Cray T3E	0.0258	0.182	1.48	14.8	164

is independent of the number of electrons except for the case when vector properties of the Cray J916 predominate for $N = 6$ and it becomes faster than the next on the list – the Pentium.

Table 3.2. Time t^{intN} to compute one pair of N-electron matrix elements, h_{kl} and s_{kl}, with the specialized integral routine (in milliseconds).

Machine	t^{int2}	t^{int3}	t^{int4}
Cray EL	0.476	2.35	15.5
NS-860	0.356	1.79	13.1
Cray J916	0.178	0.924	6.11
Pentium	0.126	0.617	4.68
HP 715	0.104	0.439	2.68
SGI R8000	0.0522	0.242	1.52
IBM SP2	0.0496	0.227	1.51
Cray T3E	0.0174	0.0909	0.635
SGI R10000	0.0168	0.0727	0.464

Table 3.2 contains the benchmark results for the specialized routine. The main qualitative difference between these results and those in Table 3.1 is the improved relative performance of the general routine on vector machines for larger values of N. For example, while for the specialized (scalar) routine the Pentium is faster than the Cray J916 by an almost N-independent factor of 1.4–1.5, for the general (vector) one, it is two times faster for $N = 2$ but already slower for $N = 6$. The order of the processors in Tab. 3.2 is the same as in Table 3.1 except at the last two lines. On this purely scalar test the SGI R10000 reveals effectively its superscalar properties. The speedup, resulting from the conversion of the general matrix element subroutine to the specialized form, grows with N and ranges from 1.5 to 3.1 for 2-electron integrals and from 2.3 to 6.0 for $N = 4$.

Fig. 3.1 presents a general layout of the double loop filling the Hamiltonian, **H**, and overlap, **S**, matrices. When **k1=1**, the outer loop runs over all the columns, and the upper triangle of **H** and **S** is computed. Such a situation occurs once in the whole run – before the first entry into the optimization – and is irrelevant for the performance of the optimization cycle. For k1=K, the matrix elements are stored in the last columns only. This takes place while the matrices update, i.e. during the optimization itself.

```
do k=k1,K
  do l=1,k
    call matrix_element(k,l,Hkl,Skl)
    H(l,k)=Hkl
    S(l,k)=Skl
  enddo
enddo
```

Fig. 3.1. A general layout of the double do-loop filling up the upper triangles of the Hamiltonian and overlap matrices (k1=1) or the last columns of **H** and **S** (k1=K).

The number of floating point operations executed in the **matrix_element** subroutine depends on the number of electrons as $N!(a_4N^4 + a_3N^3 + a_2N^2 + a_1N + a_0)$. For the molecular systems of our current interest ($N = 2, \ldots, 6$) the evaluation of a matrix element involves $\sim 10^{N+1}$ operations. The basis set size may be of the order of 10^3, hence the entire optimization cycle would require 10^{11}–10^{16} operations involved in repeated evaluation of the matrix elements only. The family of curves shown in Fig. 3.2 represents the equation $t^m(N) = N!(a_4^m N^4 + a_3^m N^3 + a_2^m N^2 + a_1^m N + a_0^m)$. The coefficients a_i^m can be obtained from a fit to the data given in Table 3.1 for each machine m separately.

The leading $N!$ factor in the above equation is responsible for computational bottlenecks appearing when an N-electron system is modelled on the quantum mechanical level. It comes from the indistinguishability of electrons, so its origin is purely physical, and every high accuracy theory must take it into account. The scale of the problem connected with the $N!$ dependence of the matrix element cost is illustrated in Fig. 3.2. Tracing a line belonging to any machine, one can easily conclude that when increasing the size of the molecular system from 2 to 6 electrons, the cost of the matrix elements expands by a factor of 10^3–10^4. Indeed, while for H_2 ($N = 2$) extremely accurate results (12 significant figures of the energy) can be recovered within 24 hours on an average workstation, for He_2 ($N = 4$) the time needed to obtain 9 correct significant figures counts in weeks, whereas for $N = 6$ the achievable accuracy is directly limited by the performance of the present day supercomputers. It is therefore crucial to us, to put all the possible effort into improving the performance of the matrix element part of the program. A great hope is connected with the concurrent computing area, especially that the double do-loop of Fig. 3.1 undergoes parallelization perfectly because the matrix elements are mutually independent.

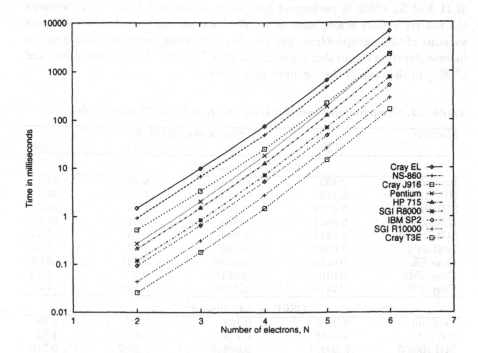

Fig. 3.2. Dependence of the computational cost (in milliseconds) of one matrix elements pair on the number of electrons, evaluated on various computers with the general integral routine.

3.2 Scaling of the Problem with the Size of the Basis Set

If in expansion (2.3) $K = \infty$, it could in principle describe an exact wave function. In real computations, however, only finite expansions ($K < \infty$) can be employed. It is, though, understandable that in search for high accuracy one tends to increase K as much as possible. In the last decade the computer memory ceased to be a real obstacle limiting the growth of the matrix size. It is rather the time in which the matrix can be built up which limits the calculation size to reasonable values of K. A common procedure in finite basis calculations is to extend the basis set size gradually, extrapolating the sequence obtained to infinity. Note that each K requires a separate run, which involves many optimization cycles. It makes this procedure quite time consuming. It is important then to know how the computation time distributes between the main parts of the algorithm when the wave function expands.

The choice of K affects both the matrix elements and the eigenvalue sections of the program. Its influence is different at the initial matrix setup and in the rest of the optimization. The initial generation of the upper triangles of H and S, which is performed just once, scales as $K^2/2 + K/2$, whereas the matrix update scales only as K. We have also to consider two different variants of the eigenproblem. The number of floating point operations in our inverse iteration eigenvalue algorithm is $\mathcal{O}(K^3)$ for the full eigenproblem and $\mathcal{O}(K^2)$ in the case of the eigenproblem update.

Table 3.3. Computational cost of solving the $K \times K$ GSEP (in seconds).

Machine	Size of the GSEP, K			
	128	256	512	1024
Full GSEP time, T^K				
Pentium	0.160	0.940	6.28	48.0
HP 715	0.113	0.759	5.03	35.9
SGI R8000	0.0250	0.184	1.45	16.7
NS-860	0.0664	0.313	1.91	13.1
SGI R10000	0.0112	0.0696	0.685	7.04
IBM SP2	0.0280	0.149	1.07	7.15
Cray EL	0.0205	0.0918	0.542	3.66
Cray J916	0.0108	0.0518	0.301	2.10
Cray T3E	0.0119	0.0527	0.239	1.27
GSEP update time, t^K				
Pentium	0.0366	0.132	0.538	2.48
HP 715	0.0316	0.114	0.434	1.72
SGI R8000	0.00277	0.00918	0.0967	0.716
NS-860	0.0174	0.0515	0.172	0.633
SGI R10000	0.00276	0.0131	0.0703	0.329
IBM SP2	0.00660	0.0208	0.0866	0.302
Cray EL	0.00699	0.0190	0.0604	0.212
Cray J916	0.00381	0.0122	0.0395	0.142
Cray T3E	0.00399	0.0137	0.0499	0.196

Let us now concentrate on a single optimization cycle as defined in Section 2.4.3. Assuming that $K \simeq 10^3$, we can estimate that an average optimization cycle requires $\sim 10^{12}$ flops spent in the eigenproblem section. If we recall that a single pair of the matrix elements requires $\sim 10^{N+1}$ flops, then for the same order of K we can estimate that the entire optimization cycle would require 10^{12}–10^{16} operations executed both in the matrix element and the GSEP section.

These estimates give a first insight into the distribution of the work between the matrix element and the eigenvalue sections. Such a distribution can be characterized in more detail by a ratio of the time the program spends in the matrix element routine, t_{mel}, to the time used by the eigenproblem routine, t_{eig}. From the model of the optimization cycle introduced in Section 2.4.3 we can predict the time spent on the evaluation of the matrix elements: $t_{\mathrm{mel}} = N_s K t_1$, where N_s is defined in Eq. (2.15)–(2.17) and t_1 is the time of the evaluation of h_{kl} and s_{kl} (see Table 3.1). The overall eigenproblem time in one optimization cycle can be modelled as $t_{\mathrm{eig}} = K T^K + (N_s - K) t^K$,

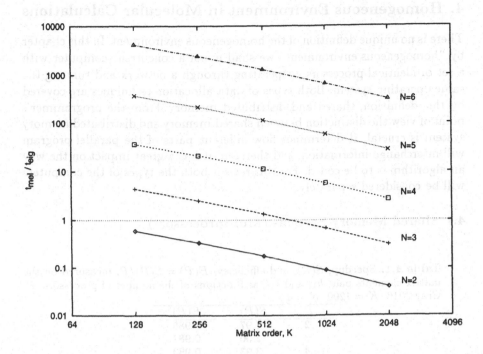

Fig. 3.3. Distribution of the computation time between matrix element and eigen-problem sections of the optimization cycle as functions of K (Cray T3E).

where T^K is the time needed to solve the full $K \times K$ GSEP, and t^K – the time of the corresponding GSEP update. The experimental values of T^K and t^K obtained on all our machines are collected in Table 3.3. The lower the machine lies in the table, the higher vector speed it exhibits. Note that the order in the table differs significantly from that in Tables 3.1 and 3.2. The experimental values of the fraction t_{mel}/t_{eig} computed as functions of K for different N are presented in Fig. 3.3. Several useful conclusions can be drawn from this picture when preparing for a new project. Suppose we have an access to a range of different types of computers, both scalar and vector oriented. For an N-electron system it allows one to choose an optimal K for a given computer type. It enables one to optimally distribute different calculations among different computers. It also provides hints on where to search for the most effective algorithm improvements.

The considerations presented in Sections 3.1 and 3.2 have motivated our interest in efficient eigenproblem methods and in parallel algorithms. Our experience in implementation of our quantum-chemical program on parallel computers is sketched in the next two sections.

4. Homogeneous Environment in Molecular Calculations

There is no unique definition of the homogeneous environment. In this chapter by "homogeneous environment" we shall mean a concurrent computer with a set of identical processors cooperating through a network and running the same operating system. Both types of data allocation techniques are covered by this definition, shared and distributed memory. From the programmer's point of view the distinction between shared memory and distributed memory system is crucial. It determines how different parts of the parallel program will interchange information, and therefore it has a great impact on the way an algorithm is to be coded. For this reason both the types of the computers will be considered separately.

4.1 Shared Memory Systems (Multiprocessors)

Table 4.1. Speedup, $S(P)$, and efficiency, $E(P) = S(P)/P$, measured on the matrix elements pair, h_{kl} and s_{kl}, as functions of the number of processors, P. Cray J916, $K = 1200$, $N = 4$.

P	$S(P)$	$E(P)$
2	1.97	0.985
3	2.96	0.987
4	3.93	0.983
5	4.73	0.946
6	5.83	0.971
7	6.45	0.921
8	7.65	0.956
9	8.51	0.946
10	8.87	0.887
11	9.90	0.900
12	10.91	0.909
13	11.40	0.877
14	11.83	0.845
15	12.89	0.859
16	13.40	0.838

Adaptation of a sequential code of the type displayed on Fig. 3.1 to the shared memory environment is not difficult. In principle, it involves placing pertinent compiler directives immediately before the parallelized loop. Most of the low level programming constructs enabling synchronization and interprocessor communication are hidden from the user.

The example presented in this subsection concerns a 16-processor Cray J916. Preparation of the code for autotasking is supported by the XBROWSE Cray tool, which generates proper compiler directives:

```
CMIC$ DO ALL SHARED  ( ...
CMIC$*         PRIVATE ( ...
```

They ascribe a scope, shared or private, to all the variables involved in the parallel work. This tool is particularly helpful when a large number of variables has to be listed in such directives.

The experiment of filling up the upper triangle of **H** and **S** matrices has been performed for $K = 1200$ and $N = 4$. The speedup and efficiency, computed as functions of the number of processors, P, are presented in Table 4.1 and Figures 4.1 and 4.2. It shows how the access to the parallel machine allows one to reduce the computation time with a minimum effort. The time needed to evaluate the matrix elements on this particular machine is one order of magnitude shorter than on a single processor. Also the rule saying that the efficiency decreases with the machine size is well illustrated by these results.

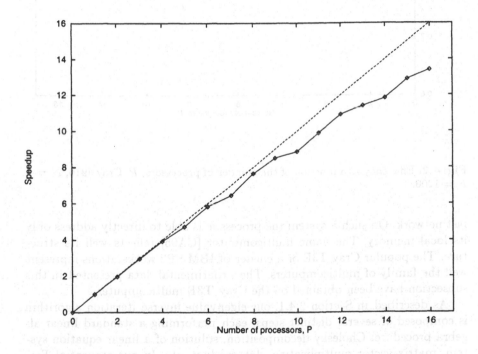

Fig. 4.1. Speedup as a function of the number of processors, P. Cray J916, $N = 4$, $K = 1200$.

4.2 Distributed Memory Systems (Multicomputers)

A distributed memory system can be viewed as a collection of individual computers, each built of a processor and memory and connected through a

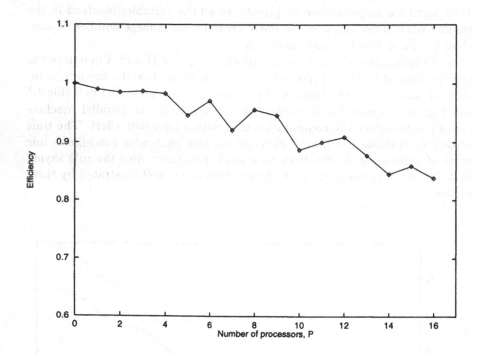

Fig. 4.2. Efficiency as a function of the number of processors, P. Cray J916, $N = 4$, $K = 1200$.

fast network. On such a system the processor is able to directly address only its local memory. The name multicomputer [CA95] reflects well its structure. The popular Cray T3E or a cluster of IBM SP2 workstations represent well the family of multicomputers. The experimental data presented in this subsection have been obtained on the Cray T3E multicomputer.

As described in Section 2.4.1, our eigenvalue inverse iteration algorithm is composed of several distinct steps, each performing a standard linear algebra procedure: Cholesky decomposition, solution of a linear equation system, matrix-vector multiplication, dot product, etc. In our sequential Fortran code, most of these procedures have been replaced by calls to the LAPACK [ABB+90, ABB+95, ABD+92] and BLAS routines [LHK+79, DDH+88a, DDH+88b, DDH+90]. Since 1995 a parallel version of the LA-PACK adapted to distributed memory architectures has been available. It is called ScaLAPACK for Scalable Linear Algebra PACKage [CDP+92b, BCC+97a, BCC+97b]. The ScaLAPACK is based on a distributed memory version of the BLAS library called PBLAS (for Parallel BLAS) [CDW94a, CDO+95]. The interprocessor communication is accomplished by the BLACS

(Basic Linear Algebra Communication Subprograms) library [ABD+91, DG91, DW95] – a message-passing library designed for linear algebra.

4.2.1 Data distribution. The main task for the programmer preparing an application for a multicomputer is to distribute data properly over the nodes of the concurrent machine. The ScaLAPACK and PBLAS subroutines assume that all the matrix operands involved in the parallel computations are distributed in so-called block-cyclic (or block-scattered) fashion. For the purpose of this article we give only a sketch of the block-cyclic data distribution. The details of this method of data allocation can be found for instance in [DGW92, CDP+92a].

First, a set of P processors is organized in a virtual $P_r \times P_c$ grid ($P = P_r \cdot P_c$), and each processor is given coordinates (p_r, p_c), where $0 \le p_r \le P_r - 1$ and $0 \le p_c \le P_c - 1$. Next, a $K' \times K''$ matrix is decomposed into blocks of $M_r \times M_c$ size, with possible exception of the blocks in the last row and column which can be smaller. Each block is then assigned to a processor and stored contiguously in its local memory (see Fig. 4.3).

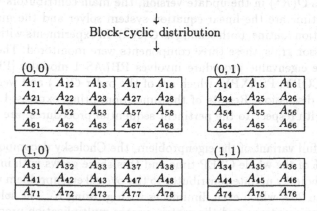

Fig. 4.3. An example of the block-cyclic decomposition of a 7×8 matrix **A** into blocks of the 2×3 size, followed by a distribution over a 2×2 virtual processor grid.

The block-cyclic data storage ensures good load balance and scalability in the frame of the ScaLAPACK routines. Additional advantages come from the fact that only $1/P$-th part of a distributed matrix has to be stored in local memory. First advantage is a better data locality which allows for more effective caching. Second – larger matrices can be used in case there are memory limitations. The choice of the optimal block size and the processor grid belongs to the user and depends mainly on the type and size of the problem and the number and type of the processors available. It is worth noting that nowadays most of a programmer's work connected with data distribution can be automated with the help of the High Performance Fortran compiling system [KLS+94, HPFF97].

4.2.2 The eigenvalue problem. As described in Sections 2.4.2 and 3.2 two variants of the GSEP procedure are employed: the full eigenproblem and the eigenproblem update. Both procedures are built of the same components with the only difference being the version of the Cholesky decomposition routine: full and update, respectively. The full Cholesky procedure is realized by PSPOTRF subroutine of the ScaLAPACK library [CDO+94]. The Cholesky update subroutine available in the ScaLAPACK is too general for our update scheme, in which only the last column of the upper triangle is updated. Therefore, our own subroutine has been constructed, relying on the BLAS 1, PBLAS 1 and SHMEM libraries. The SHMEM (logically shared, distributed memory access) routines are data passing library routines similar to message passing library routines. They lack in portability, as they are Cray specific, but their bandwidth and latency are close to the hardware peak performance. For this reason, the SHMEM routines have been used whenever an explicit communication between processing elements was needed.

Apart from the Cholesky decomposition, which scales as $\mathcal{O}(K^3)$ in the full, and as $\mathcal{O}(K^2)$ in the update version, the main contributors to the overall GSEP time are the linear equation system solver and the matrix-vector multiplication routine, both scaling as $\mathcal{O}(K^2)$. In experiments with block sizes and processor grids, these three components were monitored. The remaining part of the eigenvalue procedure involves PBLAS 1 modules [PBLAS]: PS-DOT, PSCOPY, PSAXPY, which are of the order $\mathcal{O}(K)$ and were neglected in further discussion. Results of the time monitoring, expressed in terms of speedup with respect to the pertinent sequential procedures, are collected in Table 4.2.

In the full variant of the eigenproblem, the Cholesky decomposition takes about 80% of the whole GSEP time and this share grows with increasing K. But the Cholesky update contributes to the overall eigenproblem update time in less than 20% which even diminishes with growing K. The solution of the set of linear equations and the matrix-vector multiplication procedures take ca. 40% of the GSEP update time each, with a tendency to grow with K. This superficial analysis gives information on which part of the algorithm should be decisive when analyzing speedups of different sections of the eigenproblem routine.

Table 4.2. The speedup of the GSEP components for different choices of the data distribution parameters. Cray T3E, $K = 2048$.

Processor grid		2 × 2			1 × 4
Block size	16 × 16	32 × 32	64 × 64	128 × 128	32 × 32
Full GSEP	2.60	3.12	**3.17**	2.41	2.67
PSPOTRF[a]	2.50	3.08	3.16	2.33	2.68
GSEP update	2.19	2.27	2.19	1.99	1.57
Cholesky update	0.50	0.50	0.50	0.50	0.30
PSTRSV[b]	3.05	3.39	3.45	3.25	2.44
PSSYMV[c]	2.14	2.13	1.94	1.65	1.53
Processor grid		4 × 1			
Block size	16 × 16	32 × 32	64 × 64	128 × 128	
Full GSEP	2.53	2.93	2.82	2.18	
PSPOTRF[a]	2.36	2.78	2.68	2.04	
GSEP update	3.12	**3.28**	3.03	2.48	
Cholesky update	0.95	0.94	0.94	0.92	
PSTRSV[b]	4.04	4.57	4.51	3.67	
PSSYMV[c]	2.94	2.92	2.50	1.95	

[a]The full Cholesky decomposition subroutine from the ScaLAPACK library.
[b]A double call to the ScaLAPACK subroutine solving a system of triangle linear equations.
[c]The matrix-vector multiplication subroutine of the ScaLAPACK.

Several factors affect the speedup achievable by parallelizing the GSEP procedure. If our goal is to compute just the energy from a given wave function, we shall be guided by the speedup of the full eigenproblem which, in turn, depends almost entirely on the speedup on the PSPOTRF subroutine. However, if we are going to run an optimization cycle, we should be concerned with the update variant of the GSEP, dominated by both the linear set solver, PSTRSV or PSPOTRS, and the matrix-vector multiplier PSSYMV [CDW94a, CDW94b, CDO+94]. The GSEP update case, as crucial for the whole optimization, requires careful analysis. First of all, the solution of Eq. (2.9) can be obtained either from the PSPOTRS or from two subsequent calls to the PSTRSV routine. In the case of the sequential job the LAPACK's STRSV subroutine gives better performance for $K \leq 1024$. The SPOTRS routine of LAPACK takes over for larger dimensions. The opposite was observed for the concurrent jobs and the ScaLAPACK library.

For the sake of example, suppose we have a 4-processor pool. The possible 2-dimensional grids are 2×2, 1×4, and 4×1. The results of numerical experiments performed on these three grids with the block size fixed at 32×32 are collected in Table 4.2. They point at the last grid as yielding the best speedup in the case of the optimization and at the first grid when just one energy evaluation is to be done.

Equally important is the choice of the block factors M_r and M_c. Because certain ScaLAPACK routines require their matrix operands to be decomposed into the square blocks, we limited our tests to the case $M_r = M_c = M$ with M equal to whole powers of 2. The outcome for the 2×2 and 4×1

grids illustrates a strong influence of the choice of M on the performance (see Table 4.2). The only exception is our hand-made Cholesky update procedure, which is less sensitive to the block size change. As already mentioned, the final effect on the performance of the GSEP update comes from the speedup of PSTRSV and PSSYMV subroutines. Curiously, their performance changes with M in different ways and the optimum choice is a result of a compromise. It should be taken into account, however, that for larger K the equilibrium between the routines may move towards larger M.

The final choice of the distribution parameters depends on whether we are going to compute just a single energy or to optimize it. The former case favours the 2×2 and 64×64 combination whereas the latter prefers 4×1 and 32×32 distribution (see the emboldened entries in Table 4.2).

One should note the very good performance of the PSTRSV subroutine on both processor grids mentioned above. A speedup larger than the number of processors can be explained by a better cache utilization in the case of the distributed matrices compared with the single processor matrix treatment. The speedups given in Table 4.2 were obtained by a direct comparison of the measured execution time of a LAPACK sequential subroutine with the corresponding ScaLAPACK subroutine without analyzing the internally coded algorithms. Therefore, these speedups do not reflect the absolute efficiency of the parallelization of the eigenproblem subroutines. They are merely relative measures guiding the user in the choice of the best distribution parameters.

Finally, Table 4.3 presents the experimental speedup measured on the GSEP components for a few different matrix sizes, K. This time the speedup is taken relative to the ScaLAPACK routines running on a single processor. These results support a known rule that the larger the problem, the more profitable are the parallel computations. Too small matrix size may cause a distributed subroutine to run even slower than the sequential one which is illustrated in Tables 4.2 and 4.3 by the entries less than 1. Several entries in the tables exceed the number of processors, $P = 4$. It is not an indication of any superlinear speedup, it is rather a matter of the speedup definition. There is no unique definition of the speedup (see i.e. [CA95]). For instance, one can define the speedup as the ratio of the execution time for the best serial program with that obtained for the parallel one. Another possible definition uses the ratio of the execution time measured for the same program running on one processor to the time on P processors. In our case, the former definition has been employed to compute the results listed in Table 4.2 – the sequential program uses the LAPACK subroutines and is dedicated to run on one processor. Table 4.3 has been constructed with the use of the latter definition of the speedup – the sequential reference program uses the parallel oriented ScaLAPACK library but runs on one processor. The last column of Tab. 4.3 can be directly compared with that labeled 4×1 and 32×32 in Tab. 4.2. Both columns correspond to the same experiment but use different speedup definitions.

Table 4.3. Speedup, $S(P)$, and efficiency, $E(P) = S(P)/P$, measured on the matrix elements pair, h_{kl} and s_{kl}, as functions of the number of processors, P. Cray J916, $K = 1200$, $N = 4$.

Matrices size, K	256	512	1024	2048
Full GSEP	1.78	2.15	2.74	3.27
PSPOTRF	0.67	1.90	2.37	2.89
GSEP update	1.21	1.78	3.49	5.90
Cholesky update	0.64	0.85	1.52	2.44
PSTRSV	1.04	1.67	3.57	5.80
PSSYMV	1.83	2.52	4.40	7.23

Of course, the above analysis is not to be generalized. It should be considered as a single case signalling the most important factors that influence the performance of the parallel eigenvalue problem. The performance will change not only with the factors mentioned above. The processor type, the underlying communication network, the communication software, etc. also influence the performance of the linear algebra routines and the optimal choice of the distribution parameters is likely to change with these factors. The above example shows that it is always worthwhile experimenting a bit with the data distribution before the bulk calculations are started.

4.2.3 Matrix elements. The square block-cyclic distribution is supposed to be the most efficient one for the ScaLAPACK routines operating on symmetric matrices. In our program we deal with symmetric matrices with at most the upper triangle in use. For evaluating matrix elements of such a triangle this type of distribution produces a significant load imbalance. The imbalance depends on the choice of the block size and the processor grid. In filling up the upper triangle of a matrix one would expect the matrix elements to be equally spread over all the processors. Let η be such an ideal number of matrix elements per processor, and η_i the number actually assigned to i-th processor, then $\sigma = \max_i \left(\left| \dfrac{\eta_i - \eta}{\eta} \right| \right)$ may be a measure of the imbalance in the matrix element distribution. For the whole triangle $\eta = (K + 1)K/(2P)$, for the last column $\eta = K/P$. In the former case, with $K = 1024$ and $M_r = M_c = 32$ for instance, $\sigma = 9.37\%$, 9.37%, and 6.34% for 1×4, 4×1, and 2×2 processor grids, respectively. This indicates that some processors are strongly underutilized. After several experiments we have chosen to distribute the matrix elements columnwise scattered, assigning a single matrix element, A_{lk}, to a single processor i according to the rule $i = l \bmod P$. It corresponds to the decomposition into the $1 \times K$ blocks over a column of processors ($P \times 1$). In this case the imbalance $\sigma = 0.29\%$.

A similar analysis can be performed for the fill-up of the last column of the matrix. The imbalance is much more evident in this case. Only the 4×1 grid and the columnwise scattered distributions give a good balance. For the 2×2

grid the column is distributed over only 2 processors leaving the remaining 2 unemployed. In the extreme case, the 1×4 grid employs only 1 processor.

In order to avoid the imbalance in the matrix element section, two separate distribution schemes were employed: one for the evaluation of the matrix elements and another for the eigenvalue problem of our program. Although it involved an additional cost for the conversion from one distribution type to the other, the gain from the better load balance was significantly larger than the overhead from the additional communication. In the example considered above ($K = 1024$), the overhead increased the matrix element time by merely 0.66%.

Table 4.4 contains sample results of the search for the most effective type of the decomposition. The first three lines present the speedup and the efficiency with growing number of processors. Note that for such a small P the efficiency remains constant. The last four lines in the table concern 4-processor jobs. The "scattered + conversion" variant, described above, yields the best speedup.

Table 4.4. The speedup and efficiency of the matrix element computation. Cray T3E, $N = 4$, $K = 2048$.

P, decomposition type	Speedup	Efficiency
2, scattered + conversion	1.93	0.966
3, scattered + conversion	2.90	0.966
4, scattered + conversion	3.86	0.966
2×2, block-cyclic	3.69	0.921
4×1, block-cyclic	3.63	0.908
1×4, block-cyclic	3.63	0.908

5. Heterogeneous Environment in Molecular Calculations

In this section we analyse the impact of the heterogeneity of a computer system on its performance. Section 5.1 is quite general and applies to any mixed (scalar-vector) job computed on a heterogeneous two-processor system, whereas Section 5.2 presents an implementation of our CORREL program on the Pentium-860 system.

5.1 Distribution Models and Their Performance Analysis

The computational procedure implemented in our package CORREL (see Fig. 2.1) represents an example of a rather typical situation in which in a single job both scalar and vector calculations have to be carried out, and each component requires a considerable effort. As follows from our discussion in Section 3., though with the advent of modern superscalar processors the traditional distinction between scalar and vector machines has been weakened, the relative performance of different computers still depends significantly on the type of calculations performed in a benchmark. It suggests that mixed (scalar-vector) applications should run efficiently on heterogeneous systems, where each architecture can be assigned the part of the job it is best suited to.

To illustrate this point, let us represent graphically our mixed-type application as a sequence of scalar (s_1, s_2, ...) and vector (v_1, v_2, ...) parts depicted as rectangles, where the area of each rectangle is proportional to the number of operations in the particular part and where one can imagine a horizontal axis denoting the total elapsed time. The height of each rectangle therefore corresponds directly to the speed of computation in the particular part. This application can be run sequentially on a scalar (S) or on a vector (V) machine (see Fig. 5.1). Which machines can be considered scalar and which vector is to a large extent merely intuitive, but a strict definition is not really needed in our present discussion and one may even think of S and V just as labels standing for two arbitrary computers. Let the label in the rectangle indicate that the given part of the job is executed on the pertinent machine.

Let $t_l(L)$ stand for the overall time spent in all the scalar (l = s) or vector (l = v) parts by the scalar (L = S) or vector (L = V) computer. The total time needed to solve the problem sequentially on the single processor is then expressed as

$$t(L) = t_s(L) + t_v(L). \tag{5.1}$$

To discuss how our problem can be solved in a distributed (we deliberately avoid here such notions as "parallel" or "concurrent") manner and in order not to complicate resulting expressions, we restrict ourselves to a model heterogeneous system consisting of just the two machines S and V. Firstly, since there are only two distinct types of parts with significantly different characters in our job, all the main ideas and effects resulting from the heterogeneity can be described in terms of such a model. Secondly, it can always be generalized by treating S and V as subsystems consisting of numbers of processors.

The simplest possibility, which can be used even when none of the parts s_i and v_i is parallelizable, consists in assigning each part entirely to the processor that executes it faster, for example the scalar parts to S and the vector parts to V, as seen in Fig. 5.2. We will call this **Model 1**. Its two main features are *full specialization* (each processor does only what it can do best) and *zero concurrency* (at no moment both processors run in parallel). The shortest time needed to finish the whole job on the system (when the communication time is negligible compared to the computations) is clearly

$$t = t_s(S) + t_v(V). \tag{5.2}$$

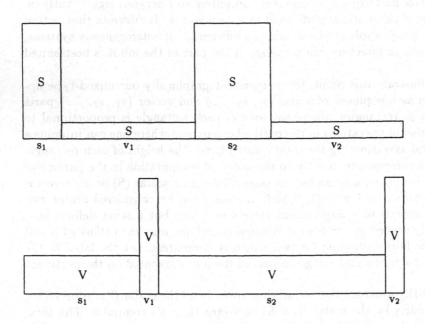

Fig. 5.1. A job running sequentially on a scalar (upper) machine S or a vector (lower) machine V.

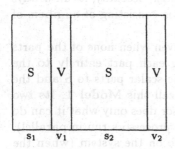

Fig. 5.2. Model 1 of the distribution.

Up to the end of this subsection we will ignore the impact of the communication, so that all our performance predictions should be understood as upper bounds to what can be really gained.

If, for example, $t_s(S) = 3$ seconds, $t_v(S) = 7$ seconds, $t_s(V) = 9$ seconds and $t_v(V) = 1$ second, (note that the times correspond precisely to our figures) then each of the two machines alone requires 10 seconds and the best time achievable by the whole system is only 4 seconds. This simple example illustrates two important facts: that the *superlinear speedup* (larger than the number of processors used – here 2.5 times faster on 2 processors) is not unusual on heterogeneous systems and that concurrency is not the only way to speed up the program execution. The reason is that the distribution of the job avoids the bottlenecks present in a single machine (the vector parts on S and the scalar parts on V).

One step further would be to parallelize the scalar parts leaving the vector ones to be executed sequentially on V (as seen in Fig. 5.3) or *vice versa*. In

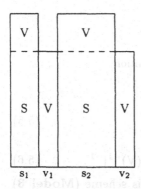

Fig. 5.3. Model 2 of the distribution.

this scheme, which we will call **Model 2**, processor V helps to execute the scalar parts which can be therefore finished faster than in Model 1. If the work is well load-balanced, i.e. each processor is assigned the fraction of each s_i which is proportional to its speed, then both finish the s_i's at the same time. The speed (reciprocal of time) of the heterogeneous system at the scalar parts is then the sum of the component speeds:

$$t_s^{-1} = t_s(S)^{-1} + t_s(V)^{-1} \tag{5.3}$$

and the total execution time is

$$t = [t_s(S)^{-1} + t_s(V)^{-1}]^{-1} + t_v(V). \tag{5.4}$$

Using the same values of $t_s(S)$, $t_s(V)$, $t_v(S)$, and $t_v(V)$ as in the previous example we get in this case $t = 3.25$ seconds. The improvement is achieved thanks to a significant degree of concurrency, though the specialization is not complete. The analogous reasoning can be made in the case where only the vector parts instead of the scalar parts are parallelized.

Note that the diagram in Fig. 5.3 and in subsequent figures in this sub-section can easily be constructed with the correct width (i.e., the correct total execution time) by complying with two simple rules. Firstly, the area of each s_i and v_i rectangle (number of operations) remains the same as in the sequential executions (Fig. 5.1). Secondly, the height of each sub-rectangle (the processor's speed), e.g. (V in s_1)-subrectangle, is the same as the height of the corresponding rectangle in Fig. 5.1.

Still better performance is possible if all the parts of our job are paral-lelized, as presented in Fig. 5.4. Ensuring good load balance also in the vector

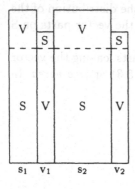

s_1 v_1 s_2 v_2

Fig. 5.4. Model 3 of the distribution.

parts one gets

$$t_v^{-1} = t_v(S)^{-1} + t_v(V)^{-1} \tag{5.5}$$

and

$$t = [t_s(S)^{-1} + t_s(V)^{-1}]^{-1} + [t_v(S)^{-1} + t_v(V)^{-1}]^{-1} \tag{5.6}$$

which amounts in our example to 3.125 seconds. This scheme (**Model 3**) exhibits full concurrency (neither of the two processors is ever idle) but only partial specialization. The degree of specialization can be augmented without destroying concurrency only at a coarser granularity of parallelism, i.e. if the scalar parts could be done in parallel with the vector ones (**Model 4**), as illustrated in Fig. 5.5. If $t_s(S)$ happens to be equal to $t_v(V)$, the scalar and vector parts are finished simultaneously, each done exclusively by "its" processor (full concurrency + full specialization). The execution time then is $t = t_s(S) = t_v(V)$. If one of the processors finishes its work first (like V in Fig. 5.5), it takes over the appropriate fraction of the work left to the second processor. In this case t can be expressed as

$$t = |t_s(S) - t_v(V)| \begin{cases} \times \frac{t_s(S)^{-1}}{t_s(V)^{-1} + t_s(S)^{-1}} + t_v(V) & \text{if } t_s(S) > t_v(V) \\ \times \frac{t_v(V)^{-1}}{t_v(S)^{-1} + t_v(V)^{-1}} + t_s(S) & \text{if } t_s(S) < t_v(V) \end{cases} \tag{5.7}$$

and amounts to only 2.5 seconds in our example. Model 4 is, however, not applicable if the scalar parts s_i depend on the results of the vector parts v_i or *vice versa*. In the CORREL program, for example, the solution of the matrix

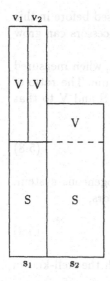

Fig. 5.5. Model 4 of the distribution.

eigenproblem (v_i) is possible only after the relevant matrix elements (s_i) are ready and it determines in turn the next set of trial parameters with which the new matrix elements will be computed (see Fig. 2.1). The order of the v_i's and s_i's cannot be changed and this makes parallelization on this level impossible.

In order to compare quantitatively the behaviour of all the models with one another and with homogeneous systems it is necessary to introduce appropriate performance measures. First of all let us note that "high performance" can be thought of, depending on one's needs, in at least two distinct – and in fact often mutually exclusive – ways. In the first sense, we can say that machine A has higher performance than B if some task is accomplished sooner on A. This definition is appropriate if the single task has to be finished as soon as possible, a classical example being a weather forecast. In the second sense, the performance means the ability of the system to accomplish as many tasks as possible within some period of time and can be expressed as "processing power", for instance in tasks/hour. As an illustration, let us imagine a large number of independent tasks, each one executing in one hour on a single (from 10 available) processor. The processors can work either separately or as a parallel system completing each task with the 50%-efficiency, i.e. within 1/5 hour. By letting the processors work concurrently we wait only 12 minutes for each task, but each hour brings only 5 completed tasks compared with 10 on *the set* of isolated processors. Someone involved in a long production effort and running a large number of tasks (such that each processor has always something to do) would clearly prefer to run each job on a single processor. If our second definition of performance, the "processing power", were the only criterion, it would make no sense at all to use homogeneous parallel computers, where the efficiency is always less than 100%.

This is no longer true in heterogeneous machines – as discussed before in this section, the overall processing power of a set of different processors can grow significantly when the computations are distributed.

The processing power expressed in tasks per unit of time, when measured for a single task, is simply the reciprocal of its execution time. The ratio of the processing power of the distributed system made up of S and V to that of the two components working separately is then

$$S'_H = \frac{t^{-1}}{t(S)^{-1} + t(V)^{-1}}, \qquad (5.8)$$

which is a possible definition of the speedup on the heterogeneous system. This expression, after normalizing to the number of processors,

$$S_H = \frac{2t^{-1}}{t(S)^{-1} + t(V)^{-1}} \qquad (5.9)$$

becomes in the special case $t(S) = t(V) = t_1$ equivalent with the well-known definition of the speedup on a homogeneous system

$$S = \frac{t_1}{t}. \qquad (5.10)$$

In the homogeneous case, the largest possible value of S is the number of processors, which case is referred to as the 100%-efficiency of parallelization (the processing power of the system working in parallel equals the sum of the processing powers of the components). S_H, however, can be larger than 2, which in the traditional language corresponds to an over-100% efficiency, or *superlinear speedup*.

There are other possibilities to define the speedup on a heterogeneous system, even with the restriction that in the special case of equal processors the expression should be equivalent with (5.10). This follows directly from the fact that the execution time on the single processor, t_1, is not uniquely defined, and illustrates difficulties connected with the performance analysis of such systems. Perhaps the most obvious solution is the use of the arithmetic mean of all the single-processor execution times as t_1 in (5.10), which in our two-processor case is given by

$$S_A = \frac{t(S) + t(V)}{2t}. \qquad (5.11)$$

Still another way to measure the speedup is to compare t with the time needed for the task by the fastest among the component processors [MFS94, ZY95]:

$$S_M = \frac{\min[t(S), t(V)]}{t}. \qquad (5.12)$$

It is easy to notice that S_H of Eq. (5.9) is the ratio of the harmonic mean of $t(S)$ and $t(V)$ to t. Since the harmonic mean of a set is never greater than its arithmetic mean, but never smaller than its smallest element, we have

$$S_M \leq S_H \leq S_A. \tag{5.13}$$

The differences among the three definitions are most easily seen when $t(V)$ and $t(S)$ differ strongly. For example, if $t(V) = 1$ s, $t(S) = 100$ s, and $t = 1$ s, one obtains $S_A = 50.5$, $S_H = 1.98$, $S_M = 1.0$. The first value is in clear disagreement with what we intuitively expect from a useful speedup definition, since it is too much influenced by the (less important) slower processor. The second number reflects correctly the fact that the processing power (in tasks per unit of time) of the system amounts to 1.98 times the arithmetic mean of the individual processing powers of the components. However, from the practical point of view another fact is more relevant, namely that the performance reached by the heterogeneous two-processor system could also be obtained by staying with just one processor, namely with V. Hence, speedup equal to 1 (i.e., no speedup) seems to be here the most acceptable value. A more detailed analysis confirms that S_M is the most reliable measure, while the other two expressions tend to overestimate what is intuitively acceptable as the speedup. Henceforth we will refer to the expression (5.12) simply as "speedup" and denote it by S.

By putting into (5.12) the expressions for $t(S)$ and $t(V)$ from (5.1) and for t from (5.2), (5.4), or (5.6), one can obtain the speedup S in each model[1] as functions of 4 variables: $t_s(S)$, $t_v(S)$, $t_s(V)$, and $t_v(V)$. These functions are homogeneous of the order zero, i.e. invariant with respect to the simultaneous multiplication of all the variables by the same constant (which is rather obvious, because the speedup does not depend on the units in which all the times are expressed). This means that 3 variables are also sufficient, the simplest choice being to set e.g. $t_s(S)$ to 1 and to express the others in units of $t_s(S)$. However, each of these variables depends on the properties of both the job and the processor and such functions would not be easy to interpret. A more useful set is:

$$\delta_s = \frac{t_s(V)}{t_s(S)}, \quad \delta_v = \frac{t_v(S)}{t_v(V)}, \quad x_s = \frac{t_s(S)}{t_v(S)}. \tag{5.14}$$

The term δ_s, which is the ratio of the scalar speed of S to the scalar speed of V, is to some extent independent of the job, as long as this job contains only scalar operations. Hence, it characterizes every pair of computers. For example, if V is the Number Smasher with the Intel 860 processor and S is the Intel Pentium 100 MHz (see Section 3. for details), this parameter measured on two-, three-, and four-electron integrals (three independent formula sets) amounts to 2.82, 2.90, and 2.80, respectively, as can be calculated from the data in Table 3.2. Analogously, δ_v is the ratio of the vector speed of V to the vector speed of S. It is, generally speaking, more dependent on the type of job than δ_s is, especially on the vector size. For the same (V=860, S=Pentium) pair, using the times to solve the full matrix eigenvalue problem

---

[1] We do not discuss in detail Model 4 which is not realizable in our CORREL program.

from Table 3.3, we get $\delta_v = 2.4, 3.0, 3.3$, and 3.7 for $K = 128, 256, 512$, and 1024, respectively (but note that this time it is the 860 which is faster). The reason is a higher efficiency of the cache and a faster memory access in the Number Smasher, that becomes relatively better and better for large vector problems, for which it was mainly designed. Nevertheless, δ_v can be a useful measure of the relative vector performance of a pair of computers, especially if one narrows the class of applications one is interested in.

The last variable, x_s, characterizes the job and takes values from $x_s = 0$ (purely vector jobs) up to $x_s = \infty$ (purely scalar jobs). Its concrete value depends also on the machine that plays the role of S, but for each choice of the (S,V)-pair it orders uniquely all the possible jobs according to the relative contribution of the vector and scalar operations. The speedup can now be expressed in terms of δ_s, δ_v, and x_s for each of the distribution models. In the following equations, $D = \delta_v \delta_s x_s - \delta_v x_s - \delta_v + 1$.

$$1: \quad S = \begin{cases} \delta_v(x_s + 1)(\delta_v x_s + 1)^{-1} & \text{if } D \geq 0 \\ (\delta_v \delta_s x_s + 1)(\delta_v x_s + 1)^{-1} & \text{if } D \leq 0 \end{cases} \tag{5.15}$$

$$2: \quad S = \begin{cases} \delta_v(\delta_s + 1)(x_s + 1)(\delta_v \delta_s x_s + \delta_s + 1)^{-1} & \text{if } D \geq 0 \\ (\delta_s + 1)(\delta_v \delta_s x_s + 1)(\delta_v \delta_s x_s + \delta_s + 1)^{-1} & \text{if } D \leq 0 \end{cases} \tag{5.16}$$

$$3: \quad S = \begin{cases} (\delta_v + 1)(\delta_s + 1)(x_s + 1)\left[(\delta_v + 1)\delta_s x_s + \delta_s + 1\right]^{-1} \\ \quad \text{if } D \geq 0 \\ (\delta_v + 1)(\delta_s + 1)(\delta_v \delta_s x_s + 1)\delta_v^{-1} \\ \quad \times \left[(\delta_v + 1)\delta_s x_s + \delta_s + 1\right]^{-1} \\ \quad \text{if } D \leq 0 \end{cases} \tag{5.17}$$

An interesting question is: What is the highest possible speedup (i.e. that achievable if the proportion of scalar to vector operations in the job is optimal) for a given pair of computers (and what is this ideal proportion)? To obtain the answer one has to solve the equations $\partial S/\partial x_s = 0$ for x_s, which is straightforward but must be done with some care due to the interval definitions of S. The results are collected in Table 5.1 and S_{max} as function of δ_s and δ_v is plotted in Fig. 5.6. In general, high speedup values are possible if both δ_v and δ_s are large (the upper right corners of the plots). This is easy to understand, because large δ_v and δ_s mean that each processor is significantly faster than its partner at this part of the job this processor is mainly assigned to. In Model 3 the lower left corner is equally good, because this model is invariant with respect to the exchange (V $\leftrightarrow$ S), or equivalently $(\delta_s \to \delta_s^{-1}, \delta_v \to \delta_v^{-1})$, which can be compensated by changing distribution ratios (relative areas of the S- and V-sub-rectangles in Fig. 5.4), whereas in the other two models the label V is always ascribed to the processor which alone computes the vector parts v_i.

Table 5.1. Maximal possible speedups and corresponding optimal values of the job characteristic x_s for given computer-pair-characteristics δ_v and δ_s. $D = (\delta_v - 1)(\delta_s - 1)$.

case	$S_{\max}$	optimal x_s
	MODEL 1	
$D > 0$	$\frac{\delta_v \delta_s - 1}{\delta_v + \delta_s - 2}$	$\frac{\delta_v - 1}{\delta_v(\delta_s - 1)}$
$D \leq 0$	1	$\begin{cases} 0 & \text{if } \delta_s < 1 \\ \infty & \text{if } \delta_v < 1 \\ \text{any} & \text{if } \delta_s, \delta_v \geq 1 \end{cases}$
	MODEL 2	
$\delta_s \leq 1$	$\delta_s + 1$	∞
$\delta_s > 1$ and :		
$\delta_s(1 - \delta_v) > -1$	$\frac{\delta_s + 1}{\delta_s}$	∞
$\delta_s(1 - \delta_v) < -1$	$\frac{(\delta_s + 1)(\delta_v \delta_s - 1)}{\delta_v \delta_s + \delta_s^2 - \delta_s - 1}$	$\frac{\delta_v - 1}{\delta_v(\delta_s - 1)}$
$\delta_s(1 - \delta_v) = -1$	$\delta_v = \frac{\delta_s + 1}{\delta_s}$	any $x_s \geq \frac{1}{(\delta_s - 1)(\delta_s + 1)}$
	MODEL 3	
$D > 0$	$\frac{(\delta_v + 1)(\delta_s + 1)(\delta_v \delta_s - 1)}{\delta_s(\delta_v^2 - 1) + \delta_v(\delta_s^2 - 1)}$	$\frac{\delta_v - 1}{\delta_v(\delta_s - 1)}$
$D = 0$	2	$\begin{cases} 0 & \text{if } \delta_v = 1 \\ \infty & \text{if } \delta_s = 1 \\ \text{any} & \text{if } \delta_v = \delta_s = 1 \end{cases}$
$D < 0$	$\begin{cases} \delta_{\min} + 1 & \text{if } \delta_v \delta_s \geq 1 \\ \frac{\delta_{\max} + 1}{\delta_{\max}} & \text{if } \delta_v \delta_s < 1 \end{cases}$ where : $\delta_{\min} = \min(\delta_v, \delta_s)$ $\delta_{\max} = \max(\delta_v, \delta_s)$	$\begin{cases} 0 & \text{if } |\log \delta_s| > |\log \delta_v| \\ \infty & \text{if } |\log \delta_s| < |\log \delta_v| \\ \text{any} & \text{if } |\log \delta_s| = |\log \delta_v| \end{cases}$

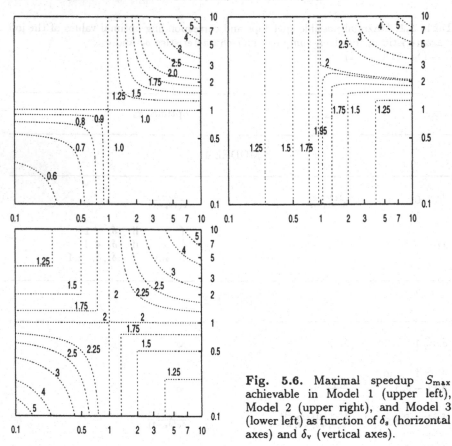

Fig. 5.6. Maximal speedup S_{max} achievable in Model 1 (upper left), Model 2 (upper right), and Model 3 (lower left) as function of δ_s (horizontal axes) and δ_v (vertical axes).

Table 5.2 contains the values of δ_v and δ_s for all the possible pairs of the computers benchmarked in Section 3., calculated from the data in Tables 3.2 and 3.3. As already noted, both parameters (especially δ_v) depend on the benchmark and should be measured, if possible, on routines and data similar to those contained in the job for which performance predictions are made. Hence, the numbers in Table 5.2 should be treated only as orientation values. They correspond to the computation of three-electron integrals (δ_s) and to the solution of the updated matrix eigenvalue problem of the size 512×512 (δ_v).

One could ask what values of δ_s and δ_v are sufficient to gain something really significant from the heterogeneity of our system. In Model 1 (without concurrency!) quite large values are necessary to obtain the superlinear (greater than 2) speedup. However, as seen on the first plot in Fig. 5.6, any pair of computers with $\delta_v > 1$ and $\delta_s > 1$ can execute the job faster than on the single processor, which is especially valuable if the parallelization of the individual vector and/or scalar parts of the job is not possible or prohibitively

Table 5.2. The values of δ_v (upper) and δ_s (lower) for different pairs of computers. δ_v corresponds to the solution of the updated 512×512 GSEP, δ_s to the computation of 3-electron matrix elements. For the detailed hardware and software descriptions see Section 3.

V: S:	(1)	(2)	(3)	(4)	(5)	(6)	(7)	(8)	(9)
(1) Cray T3E	1.0	0.79	1.2	1.3	1.9	3.4	1.7	8.7	11
	1.0	0.098	0.039	1.2	0.38	0.051	0.40	0.21	0.15
(2) Cray J916	1.3	1.0	1.5	1.6	2.4	4.4	2.2	11	14
	10	1.0	0.4	13	3.8	0.52	4.1	2.1	1.5
(3) Cray EL	0.82	0.65	1.0	1.0	1.6	2.8	1.4	7.1	8.8
	26	2.5	1.0	32	9.7	1.3	10	5.4	3.8
(4) SGI R10000	0.78	0.62	0.95	1.0	1.5	2.7	1.4	6.8	8.4
	0.80	0.079	0.031	1.0	0.30	0.041	0.32	0.17	0.12
(5) SGI R8000	0.52	0.41	0.63	0.66	1.0	1.7	0.90	4.2	5.2
	2.7	0.26	0.10	3.3	1.0	0.14	1.1	0.55	0.39
(6) NS-860	0.29	0.23	0.35	0.37	0.60	1.0	0.50	2.5	3.1
	20	1.9	0.76	25	7.4	1.0	7.9	4.1	2.9
(7) IBM SP2	0.58	0.46	0.70	0.74	1.1	2.0	1.0	5.0	6.2
	2.5	0.24	0.096	3.1	0.94	0.13	1.0	0.52	0.37
(8) HP 715	0.12	0.091	0.14	0.15	0.24	0.40	0.20	1.0	1.2
	4.8	0.48	0.19	6.0	1.8	0.24	1.9	1.0	0.71
(9) Pentium	0.093	0.073	0.11	0.12	0.19	0.32	0.16	0.81	1.0
	6.8	0.67	0.26	8.5	2.5	0.34	2.7	1.4	1.0

complicated. In the last of the three models, any such pair is already sufficient to obtain (at some class of jobs – remember the role of x_s) the superlinear speedup. As seen in Table 5.2, the case ($\delta_v > 1$, $\delta_s > 1$) is not uncommon and occurs often if V is one of the vector Cray machines and S is some RISC processor.

It is also instructive to imagine in the most important, upper-right corner on the first and third plots in Fig. 5.6 straight lines connecting points $(x,10)$ and $(10,x)$, i.e. the lines with constant values of $\delta_v \delta_s$. Each such line has common ends with some S_{max}=const contour but lies entirely above it, the distance being the largest in the middle of the line, i.e. for $\delta_v = \delta_s$. It means that in Models 1 and 3, among all the pairs with similar value of $\delta_v \delta_s$ (which should be large), the pair of machines with similar *average* (scalar+vector) speed is most preferable. Model 2 is slightly different, because it treats differently the scalar parts (which are parallelized) and the vector parts, which have to run efficiently on V alone. Hence, by $\delta_v \delta_s$=const the ratio δ_v / δ_s has its optimal value at $\delta_v > \delta_s$.

To conclude our discussion, let us recall that S_{max} represents the maximum value of the speedup, which can be achieved only for some concrete value of x_s. Of course, in practice, jobs which one computes are not constructed so as to suit one's computers, but rather reflect real problems to be solved and one has very little influence on what the value of x_s is. It is therefore interesting how sensitive the function $S(\delta_v, \delta_s, x_s)$ is to this parameter. Table 5.3 shows the speedups achievable in each model for some selected values of x_s on two different systems: V=Cray EL, S=HP 715 ($\delta_v=7.1$, $\delta_s=5.4$) and V=NS-860, S=Pentium 100 ($\delta_v=3.1$, $\delta_s=2.9$), computed from Eqs. (5.15–5.17). The bold face numbers denote the optimal value of x_s, i.e. $(\delta_v - 1)/[\delta_v(\delta_s - 1)]$.

Table 5.3. Dependence of the speedup S on the job parameter x_s.

x_s	$\delta_v=7.1$, $\delta_s=5.4$ S in Model:			$\delta_v=3.1$, $\delta_s=2.9$ S in Model:		
	1	2	3	1	2	3
0	1.00	1.00	1.14	1.00	1.00	1.30
0.01	1.29	1.31	1.48	1.06	1.07	1.40
0.05	2.15	2.24	2.48	1.26	1.30	1.66
0.10	2.83	3.02	3.28	1.45	1.54	1.93
0.15	3.27	3.56	3.80	1.60	1.75	2.13
0.1953	**3.56**	**3.91**	**4.15**	1.72	1.90	2.28
0.25	3.20	3.55	3.74	1.83	2.06	2.44
0.30	2.95	3.30	3.45	1.92	2.19	2.55
0.3668	2.69	3.04	3.16	**1.98**	**2.30**	**2.65**
0.40	2.59	2.93	3.04	1.94	2.26	2.59
0.50	2.34	2.67	2.75	1.82	2.16	2.44
1.0	1.75	2.03	2.07	1.51	1.88	2.03
2.0	1.40	1.64	1.66	1.29	1.66	1.73
10	1.09	1.28	1.29	1.07	1.42	1.43
100	1.01	1.20	1.20	1.01	1.35	1.35
∞	1.00	1.19	1.19	1.00	1.34	1.34

5.2 Practical Implementation

After extensive theoretical consideration it is now time to describe one of the working realizations of our two-processor scalar-vector machine. It is built up of two machines described in detail (along with the software) in Section 3.: a Microway Number Smasher with the Intel 860 40 MHz processor (V) and a PC with the Intel Pentium 100 MHz processor (S). Clearly, both components do not represent the highest level of what is today achievable in high-performance computing. Nevertheless, this combination is an excellent choice for performance experiments, because:

- the Number Smasher card can be placed directly into a free slot of any PC ensuring direct and sure communication,
- the whole system runs under the simple MSDOS operating system with negligible impact of system operations on the job execution times, which are therefore quite repeatable,
- both δ_v and δ_s parameters have relatively large values as seen in Table 5.2.

The job distribution in the system uses the master-slave paradigm. The master task starts on the Pentium motherboard and loads the slave task (both written in Fortran 77) into the 860 card. The communication is accomplished by the following simple message-passing routines

```
send860 (variable, num_of_bytes)
get860 (variable, num_of_bytes)
```
on the master side and
```
sendhost (variable, num_of_bytes)
gethost (variable, num_of_bytes)
```
on the slave (860) side. The routines send (or receive) num_of_bytes bytes starting from the address occupied by variable. Only the synchronous communication is supported, which means that the sending processor blocks until the receiving is complete and *vice versa*. The transfer is rather slow since it proceeds through a 16-bit ISA bus of the PC[2]. The time needed to transfer n bytes by a single routine call can be very well expressed by the traditional two-term formula

$$t(n) = t_{\mathrm{L}} + \frac{n}{v}, \qquad (5.18)$$

where t_{L} is the latency (the message-passing routine overhead) and v is the bandwidth (transfer speed). On our Pentium-860 system these parameters amount to

$$t_{\mathrm{L}} = 1.7 \cdot 10^{-4}\,\mathrm{s} \qquad (5.19)$$

$$v = \begin{cases} 5.6 \cdot 10^5 \text{ bytes/s} & (\text{Pentium} \to 860) \\ 5.3 \cdot 10^5 \text{ bytes/s} & (860 \to \text{Pentium}) \end{cases} \qquad (5.20)$$

The bandwidth is of the same order as in workstations connected by Ethernet $(8 \cdot 10^5$ bytes/s), but the latency is closer to such machines as n-CUBE-2 or Intel Paragon $(1.54 \cdot 10^{-4}\,\mathrm{s}$ and $1.21 \cdot 10^{-4}\,\mathrm{s}$, respectively, compared with $1.5 \cdot 10^{-3}\,\mathrm{s}$ on Ethernet[3]). The former follows from the small throughput of the ISA bus, the latter from the very simple communication model which can be efficiently implemented (full synchronization, no data buffering or conversion).

There exist so far two implementations of our package CORREL on the Pentium-860 machine, one exploiting Model 1 of the job distribution (Fig. 5.2) and one exploiting Model 2 (Fig. 5.3). The time needed to perform one cycle optimizing all the basis functions $(i = 1, 2, \ldots, K - 1, K$ in Fig. 2.1) can be in either case expressed as

$$t = t_{\mathrm{s}} + t_{\mathrm{v}} + t_{\mathrm{c}}, \qquad (5.21)$$

where t_{s} denotes the total time spent computing matrix elements (scalar operations), t_{v} – solving all the GSEP's (vector operations), and t_{c} – communicating. Note that if either processor is in one of the three states, the other one is either in same state or idle. In other words, the three parts of the program execution do not overlap and t_{s}, t_{v}, and t_{c} are uniquely defined.

---

[2] The 32-bit EISA version of the Number Smasher card is also available from Microway.

[3] All the times taken from Table 3.1 in [Fos95].

As discussed in Section 2., the cost of computations in the CORREL program depends on the number of electrons in the molecule N, on the basis set size (number of the basis functions) K, and on the number of optimization shots (calls to the "objective function" which computes the trial energy) N_s. In Model 2, which exhibits the concurrency, one has to take into account the fourth parameter, let's say x_{860}, denoting the fraction of each scalar part which is computed on the 860.

As explained in Section 2., each optimization shot involves recomputing one row (column) of symmetric $K \times K$ matrices $\mathbf{H}$ and $\mathbf{S}$ containing molecular integrals, and further solving either the full (for one shot per each of the K basis functions) or the updated (for all the other shots) matrix eigenvalue problem. The cost of the scalar operations during one optimization cycle is hence

$$t_s = N_s K \left[x_{860} t_{860}^{\text{int}N} + (1 - x_{860}) t_{\text{Pent}}^{\text{int}N} \right], \tag{5.22}$$

or, employing the relation (2.17) between N_s and the mean number of shots in one direction $\bar{n}_s$:

$$t_s = \bar{n}_s K^2 \left(\frac{1}{2}N^2 + \frac{3}{2}N + 1 \right) \left[x_{860} t_{860}^{\text{int}N} + (1 - x_{860}) t_{\text{Pent}}^{\text{int}N} \right] \tag{5.23}$$

where $t_{\text{M}}^{\text{int}N}$ is the time needed to compute one (h_{kl}, s_{kl})-pair of N-electron integrals on machine M (see Tab. 3.2).

The cost of the vector operations (which are done entirely on the 860) is

$$t_v = K T_{860}^K + (N_S - K) t_{860}^K, \tag{5.24}$$

where T_{860}^K and t_{860}^K are the times to solve the "large" (full) or the "small" (updated) eigenvalue problem of the size $K \times K$ on the 860. Using (2.17) one gets

$$t_v = K T_{860}^K + K \left[\left(\frac{1}{2}N^2 + \frac{3}{2}N + 1 \right) \bar{n}_s - 1 \right] t_{860}^K. \tag{5.25}$$

T_{860}^K goes theoretically as K^3 and can be very well fitted to a third-order polynomial using data from Table 3.3. Similarly, t_{860}^K can be fitted to a second-order polynomial yielding

$$t_v = W_{860}^4(K) + W_{860}^3(K) \left[\left(\frac{1}{2}N^2 + \frac{3}{2}N + 1 \right) \bar{n}_s - 1 \right], \tag{5.26}$$

where $W_{860}^n(K)$ is an n-th order polynomial of K.

The major part of the communication consists of matrix elements h_{kl} and s_{kl} which are computed on the Pentium and sent to the 860. Subsequently, the computed trial energy is sent back to the Pentium which controls the whole optimization process. Some number of auxiliary messages from the master (Pentium) to the slave (860) is also required to control the slave's work. In our implementations, the total number of messages per cycle amounts to

$$n_{\text{msgs}} = K \left[\left(4N^2 + 12N + 8 \right) \bar{n}_s + 3 \right] \tag{5.27}$$

in Model 1, and

$$n_{\text{msgs}} = K \left[\left(5N^2 + 15N + 10 \right) \bar{n}_s + 6 \right] \tag{5.28}$$

in Model 2. The total number of bytes sent amounts to

$$
\begin{aligned}
n_{\text{bytes}} &= K^2 \left[\left(8N^2 + 24N + 16 \right) \bar{n}_s + 4 \right] \tag{5.29} \\
&+ K \left[\left(14N^2 + 42N + 28 \right) \bar{n}_s + 8 \right] \tag{5.30}
\end{aligned}
$$

and

$$
\begin{aligned}
n_{\text{bytes}} &= K^2 \left[\left(8N^2 + 24N + 16 \right) \left(1 - x_{860} \right) \bar{n}_s + 12 \right] \tag{5.31} \\
&+ K \left[\left(N^2 + 3N + 8 \right) \left(2N^2 + 6N + 4 \right) \bar{n}_s + 12 \right] \tag{5.32}
\end{aligned}
$$

in Model 1 and 2, respectively. Hence, the communication cost is

$$t_c = n_{\text{msgs}} t_L + \frac{n_{\text{bytes}}}{v}, \tag{5.33}$$

where t_L and v are taken from (5.19, 5.20) (the first value of v is relevant because almost all the communication goes from the Pentium to the 860). Equations (5.21), (5.23), (5.26), and (5.33) enable one to estimate the total time of one optimization cycle on our heterogeneous distributed machine. The only operations not accounted for are the organization of the optimization process, whose cost, however, does not play a significant role except for small values of K. The same equations can be used to obtain the execution times on a single processor, in which case x_{860} has to be set to either zero or one in (5.23), t_c is always zero, and in Eq. (5.26) W_{Pent}^4 and W_{Pent}^3 have to be introduced for the Pentium processor. The speedup, S, as a function of K, N, $\bar{n}_s$, and x_{860} can then be calculated from Eq. (5.12).

Table 5.4 contains the execution times on the Pentium, the 860, and the Pentium-860 with the job distributed according to Model 1 (M1) and Model2 (M2), predicted in the described way for different numbers of electrons N and different basis sizes K. Additionally, the job parameters x_s (5.14) calculated from Eqs. (5.23) and (5.26) for the Pentium, the speedups in both models and the percentage of the total execution time taken by communication are listed. The given values of x_{860} (only relevant for Model 2) are chosen so that the ideal load-balance is achieved, i.e. both the processors finish their parts of the scalar computations simultaneously:

$$x_{860} = \frac{t_{\text{Pent}}^{\text{int}N}}{t_{\text{Pent}}^{\text{int}N} + t_{860}^{\text{int}N}}, \tag{5.34}$$

while the values of $\bar{n}_s$ are rather arbitrary, yet typical.

The cases yielding the highest speedups for $N=2$ and $N=3$ are emphasized by bold face type. One sees that the optimal value of x_s is in agreement with

Table 5.4. Performance predictions for the CORREL program (one optimization cycle). All the times in thousands of seconds, $t_c(M1)/t(M1)$ and $t_c(M2)/t(M2)$ in percents.

K	x_s	t(Pent)	t(860)	t(M1)	$\frac{t_c(M1)}{t(M1)}$	S(M1)	t(M2)	$\frac{t_c(M2)}{t(M2)}$	S(M2)
			$N=2$,	$x_{860}=0.262$,	$\overline{n}_s=4.0$				
100	0.487	0.0924	0.118	0.0729	14.3	1.26	0.0641	15.3	1.44
150	0.334	0.272	0.282	0.179	11.7	1.52	0.158	11.8	1.71
200	0.252	0.601	0.535	0.349	9.97	**1.53**	0.313	9.68	**1.71**
250	0.199	1.14	0.893	0.600	8.70	1.49	0.543	8.20	1.65
300	0.162	1.95	1.37	0.950	7.70	1.45	0.867	7.08	1.58
500	0.086	9.59	4.93	3.74	5.13	1.32	3.51	4.43	1.41
700	0.053	29.4	12.3	9.92	3.69	1.24	9.46	3.09	1.30
1000	0.031	101	34.6	29.8	2.46	1.16	28.9	2.00	1.20
			$N=3$,	$x_{860}=0.256$,	$\overline{n}_s=3.5$				
100	2.46	0.304	0.672	0.277	5.47	1.09	0.220	6.55	1.38
300	0.855	4.22	6.47	2.88	3.70	1.47	2.36	3.79	1.78
500	0.464	17.0	19.4	9.38	2.97	1.82	7.94	2.85	2.15
550	0.409	22.5	23.9	11.8	2.83	1.90	10.1	2.68	2.23
600	0.364	29.1	29.0	14.6	2.70	**1.98**	12.6	2.53	**2.31**
650	0.326	37.1	34.8	17.9	2.58	1.95	15.4	2.39	2.25
700	0.294	46.6	41.1	21.6	2.47	1.91	18.7	2.27	2.20
1000	0.174	146	95.3	55.3	1.93	1.72	49.6	1.69	1.92
			$N=4$,	$x_{860}=0.263$,	$\overline{n}_s=4.0$				
100	19.3	2.95	7.94	2.91	0.89	1.02	2.17	1.14	1.36
300	7.00	28.9	72.1	26.8	0.68	1.08	20.1	0.76	1.44
500	3.90	88.2	202	76.4	0.62	1.15	57.9	0.66	1.52
700	2.53	192	401	154	0.59	1.24	118	0.61	1.63
1000	1.53	464	834	330	0.55	1.41	256	0.55	1.81
1200	1.17	751	1217	492	0.53	1.53	385	0.52	1.95
1400	0.919	1150	1680	693	0.51	1.66	548	0.49	2.10
1600	0.743	1686	2228	939	0.49	1.80	749	0.47	2.25
1800	0.614	2393	2864	1234	0.47	1.94	993	0.44	2.41

that given in Table 5.3 (it is smaller for $N=2$, $K=200$, because for such small matrices δ_v has a lower value than 3.1 assumed in Table 5.3), but the speedup values are lower because those in Table 5.3 do not take into account the communication cost. The higher the number of electrons N, the higher is the basis size K at which the optimal value of x_s is reached (in fact, it cannot be reached at all for $N=4$ unless one uses very large matrices for which our polynomial fit (5.26) becomes problematic due to the long extrapolation). The reason is that the growing number of scalar operations must be compensated by the larger vector size in order to retain the given value of x_s.

An interesting fact which can be discovered in Table 5.4 is that the maximal speedup is reached when both the single-processor times t(Pent) and t(860) approach each other. Indeed, by inserting the definitions (5.14) into the equation $x_s(\text{opt}) = (\delta_v - 1)/[\delta_v(\delta_s - 1)]$ from Table 5.1, one arrives at

$$t_v(S) + t_s(S) = t_v(V) + t_s(V). \tag{5.35}$$

By combining this with our earlier observations, we can say that the gain from heterogeneity is the largest when both the processors perform equally well on the whole job, but as differently as possible on each of its parts.

The highest predicted speedup grows with the number of electrons which is directly related to the diminishing impact of the communication time (transmitting matrix elements becomes cheaper and cheaper in comparison with computing them). At some basis sizes for $N=3$ and $N=4$ the superlinear speedup is predicted.

Our predictions have been checked by using two "real life" wave functions (obtained by us even before we started developing the distributed code): a 150-term 2-electron function for H_2 (see Ref. [CK96]) and a 600-term 3-electron function for He_2^+. Table 5.5 presents timings from both the optimizations as well as the mean numbers of shots per Powell direction reported by the program after the completion (our choice of the $\bar{n}_s$ values in Table 5.4 becomes now clear).

Table 5.5. Benchmark calculations on the Pentium-860 system in Model 1 (M1) and Model2 (M2); $t(M)$ and $S(M)$ denote the execution time and the speedup on machine M, respectively.

N	K	$\bar{n}_s$	$t(\text{Pent})$	$t(860)$	$t(\text{M1})$	$S(\text{M1})$	$t(\text{M2})$	$S(\text{M2})$
2	150	4.0	259	297	195	1.33	173	1.50
3	600	3.5	30180	29030	16830	1.72	13650	2.13

In general, the measured execution times are a few percent larger than those in Table 5.4, the reason being, as already mentioned, additional operations such as the optimization control, which are not accounted for in our prediction scheme. The only exception is the 150-term H_2 function on the Pentium, which happens to run 5% faster than predicted. We did not investigate the reasons of this phenomenon but it can be caused by the sensitivity of the cache hit ratio to the program environment. Since the optimization control runs entirely on the Pentium (is not distributed), the obtained speedups are smaller than predicted by about 10%. Nevertheless, the optimization of the 600-term He_2^+ wave function runs on our heterogeneous system over 2 times faster than on either component machine, i.e. with the superlinear speedup. Remember that still larger speedup is possible by parallelizing the matrix eigenvalue problem, which is currently executed entirely on the 860.

Looking at Table 5.2 one can see that our Pentium-860 pair is not the only (and in fact not the best) combination for building heterogeneous systems. Significantly larger values of both δ_v and δ_s are exhibited by some pairs containing vector Cray processors. A large value of δ_s in such cases means that by running a mixed scalar-vector application on the Cray processor one does not use its power efficiently because the scalar parts of the job are a bottleneck and could be executed several times faster by assigning them to some other (scalar) processor. It would be, perhaps, an interesting idea to build workstations containing at least one vector processor and at least one scalar chip, with a fast internal communication ensuring independence from the external network load.

Finally, let us stress once more that the model two-processor machine discussed in this section is just an illustration of what can be gained from heterogeneity. All our qualitative and quantitative conclusions apply without changes to systems where both the scalar and the vector processing parts are massively parallel machines.

6. Conclusions

Our adventure with explicitly correlated Gaussian functions began in 1991 when we implemented this variational method on a PC 486/25. Our 2-electron program handled matrices of the order 100–200 in reasonable time. Encouraged by surprisingly good results we started to develop more and more efficient algorithms for the integrals and the optimization. Soon it turned out that the effectiveness of the optimization is the key to the success of our computation. The updating algorithm introduced to the matrix elements and the eigenproblem parts of the program was a milestone in the progress we made over those years. The speedup gained from the application of the updating (up to hundreds) enabled us to expand the basis set size by one order of magnitude and obtain the best variational energy for H_2 ever achieved. It has also finally opened the possibility of extending the highest accuracy calculations to systems with more than two electrons. Increased access to a variety of different machines with optimized, hardware-specific libraries added to the speedup on the eigenvalue routine. No less important was the progress in computer engineering. Faster clocks, pipelines, superscalar chips, etc. are only a few examples of what has happened in this area in last few years. Finally, the concurrent computers, both homo- and heterogeneous, allowed to extend our computations to systems with 6 electrons and to wave function expansions counted in thousands.

References

[ABB+90]   Anderson, E., Bai, Z., Bischof, C., Demmel, J., Dongarra, J., DuCroz, J., Greenbaum, S., Hammarling, A., McKenney, S., Sorensen, D., LA-PACK: A Portable Linear Algebra Library for High-Performance Computers, University of Tennessee, Technical Report CS-90-105, 1990.

[ABD+92]   Anderson, E., Bai, Z., Demmel, J., Dongarra, J., DuCroz, J., Greenbaum, S., Hammarling, A., McKenney, S., Ostrouchov, S., Sorensen, D., *LAPACK Users' Guide*, SIAM Press, Philadelphia, 1992.

[ABB+95]   Anderson, E., Bai, Z., Bischof, C., Demmel, J., Dongarra, J., DuCroz, J., Greenbaum, S., Hammarling, A., McKenney, S., Ostrouchov, S.,

Sorensen, D., *LAPACK User's Guide*, Second Edition, SIAM Press, Philadelphia, 1995.

[ABD+91]   Anderson, E., Benzoni, A., Dongarra, J., Moulton, S., Ostrouchov, S., Tourancheau, B., van de Geijn, R., Basic Linear Algebra Communication Subprograms, *Proc. of Sixth Distributed Memory Computing Conference*, IEEE Computer Society Press, 1991, 287-290.

[BCC+97a] Blackford, L. S., Cleary, A., Choi, J., Dongarra, J. J., Petitet, A., Whaley, R. C., Demmel, J., Dhillon, I., Stanley, K., Walker, D., Installation Guide for ScaLAPACK, LAPACK Working Note #93, University of Tennessee, Technical Report CS-95-280, 1997.

[BCC+97b] Blackford, L. S., Choi, J., Cleary, A., D'Azevedo, E., Demmel, J., Dhillon, I., Dongarra, J., Hammarling, S., Henry, G., Petitet, A., Stanley, K., Walker, D., Whaley, R. C., *ScaLAPACK Users' Guide*, Society for Industrial and Applied Mathematics, Philadelphia, 1997, (See http://www.netlib.org/scalapack/slug).

[Boy60]   Boys, S. F., The integral formulae for the variational solution of the molecular many-electron wave equation in terms of Gaussian functions with direct electronic correlation, *Proc. of the Royal Society* **A258**, 1960, 402-411.

[CA95]   Computer Architecture, A chapter in *Computational Science Education Project*, 1995, (See http://csep1.phy.ornl.gov/csep.html).

[CKR95]   Cencek, W., Komasa, J., Rychlewski, J., Benchmark calculations for two-electron systems using explicitly correlated Gaussian functions, *Chemical Physics Letters* **246**, 1995, 417-420.

[CK96]   Cencek, W., Kutzelnigg, W., Accurate relativistic corrections of one- and two-electron systems using Gaussian wave functions, *Journal of Chemical Physics* **105**, 1996, 5878-5885.

[CR95]   Cencek, W., Rychlewski, J., Many-electron explicitly correlated Gaussian functions. II. Ground state of the helium molecular ion He_2^+, *Journal of Chemical Physics* **102**, 1995, 2533-2538.

[CRJ+98]   Cencek, W., Rychlewski, J., Jaquet, R., Kutzelnigg, W., Sub-microhartree accuracy potential energy surface for H_3^+ including adiabatic and relativistic effects. I. Calculation of the potential points, *Journal of Chemical Physics* **108**, 1998, 2831-2836.

[CDO+94]   Choi, J., Dongarra, J., Ostrouchov, S., Petitet, A. P., Walker, D. W., Whaley, R. C., The Design and Implementation of the ScaLAPACK LU, QR, and Cholesky Factorization Routines, LAPACK Working Note #80, University of Tennessee, Technical Report CS-94-246, 1994.

[CDO+95]   Choi, J., Dongarra, J., Ostrouchov, S., Petitet, A., Walker, D., Whaley, R. C., A Proposal for a Set of Parallel Basic Linear Algebra Subprograms, LAPACK Working Note #100, University of Tennessee, Technical Report CS-95-292, 1995.

[CDP+92a] Choi, J., Dongarra, J., Pozo, R., Walker, D., ScaLAPACK: A Scalable Linear Algebra for Distributed Memory Concurrent Computers, LAPACK Working Note #55, University of Tennessee, Technical Report CS-92-181, 1992.

[CDP+92b] Choi, J., Dongarra, J. J., Pozo, R., Walker, D., ScaLAPACK: a scalable linear algebra library for distributed memory concurrent computers, *Proc. of the Fourth Symposium on the Frontiers of Massively Parallel Computation (FRONTIERS '92)*, IEEE Computer Society Press, 1992.

[CDW94a]   Choi, J., Dongarra, J. J., Walker, D. W., PB-BLAS: A set of parallel block basic linear algebra subprograms, Technical Report ORNL/TM-

12468, Oak Ridge National Laboratory, Mathematical Sciences Section, Oak Ridge, Tennessee, 1994.

[CDW94b] Choi, J., Dongarra, J. J., Walker, D. W., PB-BLAS: Reference manual, Technical Report ORNL/TM-12469, Oak Ridge National Laboratory, Mathematical Sciences Section, Oak Ridge, Tennessee, 1994.

[DDH+88a] Dongarra, J. J., DuCroz, J., Hammarling, S., Hanson, R. J., An extended set of FORTRAN basic linear algebra subprograms, *ACM Transactions on Mathematical Software* 14, 1988, 1-17.

[DDH+88b] Dongarra, J. J., DuCroz, J., Hammarling, S., Hanson, R. J., Algorithm 656. An extended set of basic linear algebra subprograms: model implementation and test programs, *ACM Transaction on Mathematical Software* 14, 1988, 18-32.

[DDH+90] Dongarra, J. J., DuCroz, J., Hammarling, S., Duff, I., A set of level 3 basic linear algebra subprograms, *ACM Transactions on Mathematical Software* 16, 1990, 1-17.

[DG91] Dongarra, J. J., van de Geijn, R. A., Two Dimensional Basic Linear Algebra Communication Subprogram, LAPACK Working Note #37, University of Tennessee, Technical Report CS-91-138, 1991.

[DGW92] Dongarra, J., van de Geijn, R., Walker, D., A Look at Scalable Dense Linear Algebra Libraries, LAPACK Working Note #43, University of Tennessee, Technical Report CS-92-155, 1992.

[DW95] Dongarra, J. J., Whaley, R. C., A User's Guide to the BLACS v1.0, LAPACK Working Note #94, University of Tennessee, Technical Report CS-95-281, 1995.

[Fos95] Foster, I., *Designing and Building Parallel Programs*, 1995, (See http://www.mcs.anl.gov/dbpp/).

[HPFF97] The High Performance Fortran Forum (HPFF), 1997, (See http://www.crpc.rice.edu/HPFF).

[KLS+94] Koelbel, C., Loveman, D., Schreiber, R., Steele Jr., G., Zosel, M., *The High Performance Fortran Handbook*, The MIT Press, Cambridge, MA, London, England, 1994.

[KW65] Kołos, W., Wolniewicz, L., Potential-energy curves for the $X\,^1\Sigma_g^+$, $b\,^3\Sigma_u^+$, and $C\,^1\Pi_u$ states of the hydrogen molecule, *Journal of Chemical Physics* 43, 1965, 2429-2441.

[KCR95] Komasa, J., Cencek, W., Rychlewski, J., Explicitly correlated Gaussian functions in variational calculations: The ground state of the beryllium atom, *Physical Review A* 52, 1995, 4500-4507.

[KCR96] Komasa, J., Cencek, W., Rychlewski, J., Application of explicitly correlated Gaussian functions to large scale calculations on small atoms and molecules, *Computational Methods in Science and Technology* 2, Scientific Publishers OWN, Poznań, 1996, 87-100.

[KR97] Komasa, J., Rychlewski, J., Explicitly correlated Gaussian functions in variational calculations: the ground state of helium dimer, *Molecular Physics* 91, 1997, 909-915.

[LHK+79] Lawson, C. L., Hanson, R. J., Kincaid, D., Krogh, F. T., Basic linear algebra subprograms for fortran usage, *ACM Transaction on Mathematical Software* 5, 1979, 308-323.

[MFS94] Mechoso, C. R., Farrara, J. D., Spahr, J. A., Achieving superlinear speedup on a heterogeneous, distributed system, *IEEE Parallel & Distributed Technology* 2, 1994, 57-61.

[PBLAS] An electronic PBLAS manual, 1999, (See http://www.netlib.org/scalapack/html/pblas_qref.html).

[Pow64]   Powell, M. J. D., An efficient method for finding the minimum of a function of several variables without calculating derivatives, *Computer Journal* **7**, 1964-1965, 155-162.

[RCK94]   Rychlewski, J., Cencek, W., Komasa, J., The equivalence of explicitly correlated Slater and Gaussian functions in variational quantum chemistry computations. The ground state of H_2, *Chemical Physics Letters* **229**, 1994, 657-660.

[Sin60]   Singer, K., The use of Gaussian (exponential quadratic) wave functions in molecular problems. I. General formulae for the evaluation of integrals, *Proc. of the Royal Society* **A258**, 1960, 412-420.

[ZY95]   Zhang, X., Yan, Y., Modelling and characterizing parallel computing performance on heterogeneous networks of workstations, *Proc. of the Seventh IEEE Symposium on Parallel and Distributed Processing*, 1995, 25-34.

XII. Multimedia Applications for Parallel and Distributed Systems

Giuseppe De Pietro

IRSIP - National Research Council of Italy
Via P. Castellino 111, Naples Italy
e-mail depietro.g@irsip.na.cnr.it

Summary. This Chapter deals with multimedia applications in parallel and distributed systems. After a brief introduction to the subject, several issues are discussed. They include at first an overall explanation of MPEG, the most popular digital audio-video standard. Next, the crucial networking topic is treated with particular attention paid to ATM networks. Later the CORBA standard and Java language are presented as the most accredited software environments for multimedia development in a typical heterogenous scenario. Finally, the last section presents the most diffused multimedia applications: the Video on Demand, the Digital Video Broadcasting, and the Multimedia Conferencing.

1. What Is Multimedia ?

Multimedia describes a new application-oriented technology based on the multisensory nature of humans and the evolving ability of computers to store and convey diverse types of information. It is the integration of storage, communication, and presentation mechanisms for diverse data types including text, images, audio, and video, to provide a single unified information system. We are already witnessing a growing need of such information systems in a variety of fields including medicine, sports, CAD/CAM, weather, entertainment such as Video-on-Demand , education., exploration, the arts, Virtual Reality, and so on. Such systems, in general, are concerned with manipulation, display, transport, synchronization, and integration. These systems must have considerably more functionalities and high performance capabilities than conventional database management systems.

An important feature of multimedia information is that it may not be confined to some central repository, rather it may have to be retrieved from distributed sources which may be spread geographically over wide areas. The main requirement for such information management is the integration of multimedia data retrieved from distributed data sources across high speed networks and presented to the end users in a meaningful way.

The development of multimedia applications and supporting environments is a difficult task because many different technologies must be developed and integrated. To support the diverse media, specialized hardware must also be used. Recent developments in these base technologies has driven the development of a large number of applications. Leading application areas are summarized in Table 1.1. These applications fall into various levels of system integration, the most notable being ones distinguished by the use of fully digital media, especially video. Some discussion about these applications is given below.

- There are many multimedia applications in medicine. These include telemedicine, medical instruction, remote diagnosis through videoconferencing, collaboration, and so on.
- Electronic document processing (EDP) is another important application of multimedia. Historically, EDP has been primarily concerned with office automation by providing data management of large volumes of textual and image data. By storing memos, receipts, invoices, photographs, etc., the goal of office automation and EDP is to facilitate a paperless office. There has not been a large demand for video service in this application.
- Network news, another multimedia application, provides a linear, non-interactive format of information presentation. Printed news is interactive and non-linear, allowing a reader to browse stories in any order or to jump to stories listed in the index. In the provision of on-line, multimedia stories including video clips, an interactive combination of these two media

is possible. This *Electronic Magazine* represents a hybrid of the television, computer and the magazine, and can incorporate advertisements.

- Another application of multimedia is in education. Interactive learning systems are designed to provide self-paced instructions with course materials replacing some of the interaction normally provided by a "live" instructor.
- Music has caught the wave of multimedia. Primary use of multimedia in music include music visualization, music composition, and music production. They provide a collection of papers on current trends in music and computer support for such applications.
- Perhaps the most important multimedia application is Videoconferencing. Videotelephony is the bi-directional, real-time communication analogous to telephony developed in the 60's. Low-cost, high-speed communications and video compression make video telephony affordable.
- Command and control applications exist both in industrial and government. In the military, the acquisition, processing and dissemination of intelligence information represents a typical multimedia application scenario.
- Multimedia mail is an extension of conventional, textbased electronic mail. With multimedia mail, a user can create messages containing voice, images, text, graphics, and video which can be transmitted to other users across a computer network.

Note that almost all multimedia applications "live" in a *Computer Supported Cooperative Work (CSCW)* environment. CSCW can be defined as the field concerned with the design of computer-based systems to support and improve the work of groups of users engaged in common tasks or objectives, and the understanding of the effects of using such systems. CSCW is concerned with all computer-based improvements to group communication, which includes modern multimedia applications of course, but also more conventional monomedia systems. CSCW is a field which has been studied since the early 1980s by pioneers such as Irene Greif and Paul Cashman. Its progress resulted from the combined efforts of computer technologists and social scientists [Gru91]. Below a non-exhaustive list of areas follows where significant research has been undertaken over the last decade. Note that so far only a few have given rise to production systems regularly used in professional environments.

- *Group decision and meeting support.* Pilot systems have been developed to assist in the decision-making process or to improve the efficiency of meetings. Examples are argumentation tools which record and help in classifying arguments. This remains an area for research.
- *Voting mechanisms.*
- *Idea generation.*
- *Co-authoring.*

Table 1.1. Multimedia Application and Characteristics.

Application	Media	Selected Function
Office Automation	Images, Text, Spreadsheets, Mail	Composition, Filing Communication
Medical Information Systems	Video (Telephony), Images, Text	Data Acquisition, Communication, Filing
Geography	Images, Graphics	Data Acquisition, Storage, Image
Education/Training	Audio, Video, Images, Text	Browsing, Interactivity
Command and Control	Audio, Images	Data Acquisition, Communication
Weather	Images, Numeric Data, Text	Data Acquisition, Simulation Data Integration
Banking	Numeric Data, Text, Images	Image Recognition
Travel Agents	Audio, Video Images, Text	Video Browsing, Communication
Advertising	Video, Images	Image Composition Enhancement
Electronic Mail	Audio, Images, Text	Communication
Engineering, CAD/CAM	Numeric Data, Text	Cooperative Work
Consumer Electronic Catalogs	Audio, Video, Text	Video Browsing
Home Video Distribution	Audio, Video	Video Browsing
Real Estate	Audio, Video, Image, Text	Video Browsing, Communication
Library	Image, Text	Database Browsing, Query
Legal Information Systems	Image, Text	Database Query
Tourist Information	Audio, Video, Text	Video Browsing
Newsprint Publication	Image, Text	Image, Text Composition
Dictionaries	Image, Text	Database Browsing, Query
Electronic Collaboration	Audio, Video, Text	Videoconferencing, Concurrency Control
Air Traffic Control	Audio, Text, Graphics	Concurrency Control, Communication

- *Collaborative design involving drawings or figures* (in computer-aided design: CAD). Examples of fields are mechanical and electrical design or architecture [CLF+93].
- *Education:* Lecturing.
- *Education:* Tutoring. The difference with the above is that interaction between the tutor and the student is mandatory.

Another important problem faced by multimedia application developers is the design of user interfaces. Tools for developing such interfaces include window systems and *applications programmer's interfaces* (APIs) which permit a developer a full range of access to the utilities available in a multimedia information system. These tools allow the rapid development of user interfaces for any application, often use an object oriented approach [Bar86], and are becoming standards de facto. New approaches to accessing information have also been developed that facilitate operations by untrained users.

Multimedia requires integration of text, images, audio, and video in a variety of application environments. Generally, such integration is due to the temporal relational constraints among these data which can be heavily time-dependent, such as audio and video in a movie, and can require time-ordered presentation during use. The task of coordinating of these data in time in order to compose objects is called multimedia synchronization. Synchronization can be applied to the playout of concurrent or sequential streams of data, and also to the external events generated by a human user. Temporal relationships between the media may be implied, as in the simultaneous acquisition of voice and video, or may be explicitly formulated, as in the case of a multimedia document which possesses voice annotated text. In either situation, the characteristics of each medium, and the relationships among them must be established in order to provide synchronization in the presence of vastly different presentation requirements. Consider a mulimedia slide presentation in which a series of verbal annotations coincides with a series of images. The presentation of the annotations and the slides is sequential. Points of synchronization correspond to the change of an image and the end of a verbal annotation, representing a coarse-grain synchronization between objects. A multimedia system must preserve the timing relationships among the elements of the object presentation at these points of synchronization by the process of temporal integration.

In addition to simple linear playout of time-dependent data sequences, other modes of data presentation are also desirable, and should be supported by a multimedia database management system. These include reverse, fast-forward, fast-backward, and random access. Although these operations are quite common in existing technologies (e.g., VCRs), when nonsequential storage, data compression, data distribution, and random communication delays are introduced, the provision of these capabilities can be very difficult.

The multimedia synchronization problem for time-dependent media can be described at three levels. These are the physical level, the service level, and the human interface level [Sve87]. At the physical level, data from different media are multiplexed over single physical connections or are arranged in physical storage. The service level is concerned with the interactions between the multimedia application and the various media, and among the elements of the application. This level deals primarily with intermedia synchronization necessary for presentation or playout. The human interface level describes the random user interaction to a multimedia information system such as viewing a succession of database items, also called browsing.

Another problem concerning multimedia application development is related to the storage of data and, consequently, to the database organization. For database applications, the trend is to move away from traditional relational query-type interfaces that require substantial knowledge of the content and structure of the stored information. One of the important features of multimedia database systems is that they need a data model more powerful than the relational model, without compromising its advantages. The relational model exhibits limitations in managing complex objects. Another major issue is going to be system performance as more functionality is added. Distributed environments will make the problems even more difficult. In addition, the issues of data dictionary management and distributed object management have to be dealt with. Exploiting the parallelism through multiprocessor computers is one promising way to provide high performance.

Many data structures have been proposed for storing images in a database system. These include pixel-oriented, quad-trees, R-trees or vector based. However, irrespective of the representation, the storage of this type of data is essentially in a digital form with the indexing scheme to provide 2-dimensional browsing. The digital information is stored in a compressed form using well known data compression techniques. Since the data is highly structured and formatted, high speed retrieval and storage techniques can also be employed in this case.

The Full-Motion Video Data are unique in their nature in the sense that they can be totally in analog form containing both video frames and associated audio signals. The information can be stored in the same way as in video cassettes with the functions of replay, freezing frame, advancing etc. However, in order to integrate this information with other data they must be digitalized in order to prepare composite digital data packets carrying requested multimedia object information for the user. Therefore, analog to digital conversion and compression of video data needs to be carried out by the server. The equivalent inverse function needs to be performed at the user end. This signal processing can be avoided if the video information is pre-stored in a digital compressed form. In digital form data manipulation is much more flexible as compared to analog form. However, irrespective of the nature of information, this service requires an enormous capacity for storage and very high access rate.

In the next three sections, the basic aspects for multimedia development are discussed. In particular, the Section 2. gives an overall explanation about MPEG, the most popular digital audio-video standard. Nowadays, MPEG is the standard de facto for digital representation and stream compression , and is largely used in several type of applications such as Video on Demand, Digital Video Broadcast, and so on. First, the MPEG1 standard is discussed, focusing the video and audio compression techniques adopted, and after, the improvements provided by MPEG2, MPEG4 and MPEG7, are presented.

In Section 3., the multimedia computing systems are discussed. Initially, an overall presentation about the multimedia environments and their related topologies is given. Next, the crucial networking topic is treated with particular attention paid to ATM networks. In fact, the ATM network protocol is considered nowadays the best solution because it satisfies the most important requirements for multimedia delivery such as dynamic bandwidth allocation, quality of service definition, and variable bit-rate management. Finally, the CORBA standard and the Java language are presented as the most accredited software environments for multimedia development in a typical heterogeneous scenario.

The last Section 4. presents the most diffused multimedia applications: the Video on Demand, the Digital Video Broadcasting, and the Multimedia Conference. While the last two applications are nowadays largely diffused, the Video on Demand represents the challenge for the near future. The considerable economical implications foretold for the availability of this new service leads to a more and more growing interest by different market players. Some international organizations have proposed specific standards (such as the DAVIC specification and the ISO/IEC DSM-CC) in order to prevent a confused growth of no-interoperable VoD systems. For these reasons, the last section gives a quite general VoD architecture, a brief explanation of the most accredited standards, and a description of the possible market players that will participate in the VoD diffusion.

2. Digital Audio and Video Compression Techniques

At present, most national and local TV stations still broadcast video in analogue format. Typically the professional broadcasting industry is conservative about adopting new technology; but the picture is changing with the marriage of computer networking and digital video: the ability to provide digital video from a telephone line or from a satellite is being a scientific fact. Finally, the attractions offered by digital video lead on to a growing interest in using digital networks to broadcast digital video.

Digital video has several advantages over its analogue counterpart:

- It is easy to copy and reproduce without losing or degrading quality.
- It is easy to manipulate in digital format: for example, morphing requires the video to be in digital format before processing.
- It is possible to use compression techniques in order to reduce the bandwidth to deliver the stream.
- It is possible to incorporate additional information of different nature such as subtitles, alternative language soundtracks, and informative warnings of what you are going to see.

However, digital video and the communication infrastructure for transmitting do have some technological complications:

- Encode and decode video stream requires a lot of processing power.
- The storage medium and the encoder/decoder hardware are still too much expensive.
- Much of video material available today is still in the analogue format.
- Because video delivery is time dependent, the broadcast will be distorted if the video transmission has to wait for other traffic to go through first.

MPEG is a data compression standard for storage and transmission of digital audio/video streams. It is based on complex mathematical algorithms that define a compressed bit stream, which implicitly defines a decoder. The basic idea is to transform a stream of discrete samples into a bit-stream which takes less space as compared with direct PCM (pulse code modulation), while preserving a high level of perceived quality. This improved representation is realized through video coding, audio coding, and system management and multiplexing defined into respective parts.

The Video Part (referred as ISO/IEC-11172-1) defines the syntax and semantics of the compressed video bit-stream. The Audio Part (referred as ISO/IEC-11172-2) defines the same for the audio bit-stream, while the Systems Part (referred as ISO/IEC-11172-3) addresses the problem of multiplexing the audio and video streams into a single system stream with all the necessary timing information. The standard keeps the data types synchronized and multiplexed in a common serial bit-stream.

MPEG, as a compression standard for audio and video, was established by the International Telecommunications Union (ITU) and International Standards Organization (ISO). The MPEG standard was developed by the Moving Pictures Experts Group with the aim of defining standards for digital compression for audio-visual signals. MPEG is part of a broader effort to standardize image and video compression. Related to MPEG are the ITU-T Standard for videoconferencing and video-telephony now known as H.261 and the JPEG Standard based in a DCT algorithm for still picture. MPEG standard has followed five main stages of development: MPEG1, MPEG2, MPEG3, MPEG4 and MPEG7 with the characteristics shown in Table 2.1.

Table 2.1. Basic characteristics about the MPEG standards.

MPEG standard	Characteristics
MPEG1	Medium Bandwith (up to 1.5Mbits/sec) 1.25Mbit/sec video 352 x 240 x 30 Hz 250Kbit/sec audio (two channels) Non-interlaced video Optimized for CD-ROM
MPEG2	Higher Bandwidth (up to 40Mbits/sec) Up to 5 audio channels (i.e. surround sound) Wider range of frame sizes (including HDTV) Can deal with interlaced video
MPEG3	MPEG3 was for HDTV application with dimensions up to 1920 x 1080 x 30 Hz, however, it was discovered that the MPEG2 and MPEG2 syntax worked very well for HDTV rate video. Now HDTV is part of MPEG2 High-1440 Level and High Level tool kit.
MPEG4	Very Low Bandwith (64Kbits/sec) 176 x 144 x 10 Hz Optimized for videophones
MPEG7	Content based multimedia information retrieval

2.1 MPEG1

The standard [ISO93] for audio and video compression, established in 1992, is an international open standard developed by the Motion Picture Expert Group, in order to provide a compression method for high quality audio and video. One of the most important advantages of MPEG1 is the fact that it is an official ISO standard. This means that MPEG digital video is a cross platform; therefore it can play back across different components and systems. MPEG1 can be played back on TV monitors, video-CD players, CD-i players, CD-ROM drives and PCs. Thus, it is the best digital video format for the home and business environment.

MPEG1 video compression typically compresses a SIF (Standard Interchange Format) picture of 352 pixels by 240 lines at 30 frames per second (when the format used is the US NTSC format) or 352 pixels by 288 lines at 25 frames per second (when the format uses is the Europe an PAL format). Note that both the formats have the same number of bits per frame; in fact the number of pixels per second for both formats is:

$$352x240x30 = 352x288x25 = 5068800$$

The whole data bit-stream is designed for a bandwidth of 1.5 Mbits per second, which is the data transfer rate from a single speed CD-ROM drive: therefore the rate of 1.5 Mbits per second must be shared between audio and video. Since the rate of MPEG1 video is typically about 1.25 Mbits per second, 250 Kbits per second of bandwidth stay for the audio compression.

Video compression is basically a process by which the information content of an image or image sequences is reduced by eliminating redundancy in video signals (temporal and spatial redundancies). Compression techniques generally attempt to identify this redundancy and expel a significant amount of it from the bit-stream. MPEG1 adopts two compression techniques simultaneously. The first is the motion estimation used to eliminate the temporal redundancy which means that, for a given image sequence, the picture generally varies little from frame to frame. The second is the discrete cosine transform (DCT) used in order to eliminate the spatial redundancy present in each frame of video.

Audio compression can be obtained using and combining different approaches: reducing the sampling rate (and then the bandwidth of the audio signal) in accordance with the characteristic of the human ear, reducing the sample size (for example using 8 bits to represent a sample instead 16 bits), and using coding techniques to eliminate redundancy inside the data representation. The MPEG1 audio compression process adopts the sample size reducing based on the psycho-acoustic model and the Huffman encoding to further compress the audio data.

2.1.1 The video compression process. Depending on the originating format, the first step is to convert the video picture into the analogue format that MPEG expects: this is the 4:2:0 YCrCb format. Since the incoming data is typically in the RGB format, it needs to be converted. In 4:2:0 sampling, chrome samples from two adjacent lines in a field are interpolated to produce a single chrome sample, which is spatially located halfway between one of the original samples and the location of the same line but the opposite field. The line from the other field is that which falls between the two lines where samples are located (cf. Fig. 2.1). Therefore, this format involves sub-sampling and some data loss, then compression.

The first step in most compression systems is to identify the spatial redundancy present in each frame of video. This is done by three sequential steps: applying the Discrete Cosine Transform (DCT) throughout the image, quantizing the DCT coefficients and finally coding the DCT coefficients using some data reduction codes.

The DCT is a lossless, reversible, mathematical process, which converts spatial amplitude data into spatial frequency data. For video compression, this calculation is made on 8 by 8 blocks of luminance samples and the corresponding blocks of color difference samples. It is the nature of video that a DCT-based transformation often results in very small and invariable values for many higher spatial frequency coefficients, while the significant information is placed into lower frequency coefficients. This means that the bulk of the information is often grouped in the top corner of each converted block, and therefore an opportune strategy can be adopted to reduce the

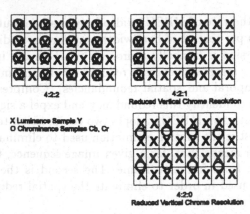

Fig. 2.1. 4:0:2 Chrome Sub-sampling.

existing spatial redundancy in the video representation. The DCT does not reduce the data. In fact, to be properly reversible and lossless, more significant bits must actually be carried to ensure that there are no rounding errors in the calculations.

The actual compression begins with a clever quantization of the DCT coefficients. Quantizing is simply the process of reducing the number of bits, which represent each coefficient. Quantization may use up to 11 bits to carry the DCT coefficient but significantly fewer bits are used to carry the higher order coefficients. A different quantizing scale may be specified for each macro-block (16 x 16 pixels) or for large groups of macro-blocks.

Following quantization, lossless data reduction is applied using VLC (variable length coding) and RLC (run length coding). The order in which the coefficients are sent optimizes the efficiency of this encoding process. Processing the 64 coefficients in the 8X8 blocks using a zigzag pattern (see Fig. 2.2) maximizes runs of zero values for more efficient compression.

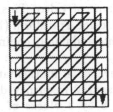

Fig. 2.2. Zigzag path.

Variable length encoding is a process that identifies common patterns (or words) in the data and uses fewer bits to code frequently occurring values and more words to code less frequently occurring values. Morse code is a form of

VLC using very short sequences for frequently occurring letters such as "e" (one dot). Like quantization, VLC coding produces tables to map patterns to codes. These tables, combined with the mapped codes, generally take much less data than the original data patterns. Run length encoding is a process by which a unique code word represents a repeating pattern. For example, a string of 20 zero values can be represented by the ESC character followed by the value 20 (number of zeros) followed by the value zero. Thus, 20 bytes are compressed to only 3 bytes. Note that VLC and RLC are lossless encoding processes.

The second and last step consists of eliminating temporal redundancy by the motion estimation. This compression process is based on the property of video signals that generally vary little from frame to frame. Based on this property, the motion estimation consists of determining the current frame by the knowledge of the objects movement respect the previous frame (forward prediction) or the next frame (backward prediction).

The calculation of the relative picture content position changes (motion) between frames is an important part of inter-frame (between frame) compression. The motion estimation process in MPEG consists of dividing the picture into macro-blocks which are 16 by 16 pixels (four 8x8 blocks) and a search carried out to determine its location in a subsequent frame. Although the samples in the macro-block may have changed somewhat, correlation techniques are used to determine the best location match down to one-half pixel. A successful search will result in a motion vector for that macro- block.

Inter-frame compression works on the uncompressed picture and is essentially lossless. Since the frames may be different in various manners and only macro-block vectors are allowed, the prediction may not be perfect. The predicted frame holds the predicted present frame which has been constructed using the previous frame and the motion vector information. The predicted present picture is then subtracted from the actual present picture and the difference is the output. If there was no motion and no other changes (for example a repeated frame), the present frame could be perfectly predicted and the difference frame output would be zero (very easy to compress). When the two frames aren't the same, the difference frame can still have much less information and be easier to compress.

The motion estimation processing produces three types of frames: I-frame, B-frame, and P-frame (cf. Fig. 2.3)

The I-frame (or intra-frame) does not require the knowledge of other frames to decode it. That is, the motion estimation processing has not been performed on this type of frame. I-frames are periodically present inside a sequence of frames in order to re-establish the quality of the stream. I-frames are often used for particular play mode not directly contemplated by MPEG such as fast-forward and back-forward play. This particular play modes may be simulated by parsing the bit-stream and displaying only the I-frames in one of the two desired directions.

Fig. 2.3. Motion estimation.

The P-frame (or predicted frame) uses the preceding I-frame or P-frame as its reference for motion estimation processing. Each macro-block in the frame is supplied as both vector and difference with respect to a previous frame or, if no match was found, as a completely encoded macro-block (as is the case with the I-frame). The decoder must retain the I-frame information (or the P-frame previously decoded) to allow this frame to be decoded.

The B-frame (or bi-directional frame) uses the nearest preceding I or P-frame and the next I or P-frame. When compressing data, the encoder tries to do a backward prediction using the next I or P-frame. If this does not give a good match, the encoder tries to do a forward prediction using the preceding I or P-frame. If also this attempt gives bad result, the encoder tries to do a bi-directional estimation (that is the arithmetic average of forward and backward predictions). If all else fails, the encoder produces an intra-coded macro-block (as is the case with the I-frame). Generally, the B-frame requires two frames (I or P frames) to be decoded.

A sequence of frames is typically referred to as a group of pictures (GOP for short). A GOP is formed by a variable number of frames with a prefixed order (see Fig. 2.4). That is GOP starts with an I-frame and goes on alternating two B-frames and one P-frame. During the compression the encoder terminates the current GOP when the predicted frames do not give a good compression quality, starting with a new GOP and therefore with a new I-frame: this is the reason of a variable GOP length. If the last GOP frame is a B-frame then the decoder uses the I-frame of the next GOP to decode it: in this case the GOP is known as an open GOP. Conversely, if the GOP terminates with a P-frame, the decoder doesn't need the frame of the next GOP: in this case, the GOP is referred as a closed GOP. The real order of frames inside the GOP is different respect to the time order of the frames displayed. The reason is that a B-frame generally needs next I or P-frame to be decoded. Therefore the storage order of frames anticipates the I and P frames with respect to the B-frames. For example, if the displayed frame sequence is IBBP, the real storage order is IPBB. In this way the decoder first encounters and displays the I-frame, while the next P-frame is not displayed but used to decode the next two B-frames. After displaying them, the decoder displays the P-frame. In this case the I and P frames are called anchor-frames for decoding of the two B-frames. Timing information to help the decoder is added when the transport stream is developed (known as the presentation time stamp).

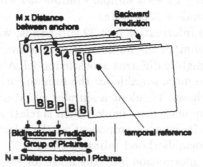

Fig. 2.4. GOP structure.

2.1.2 The audio compression process.

The MPEG1 audio compression process uses the sample size reducing based on the masking effect. This is a phenomenon where noise (as high frequency hiss) is not perceived from a listener because it is masked by other sounds. This effect also appears when the audio contains a very loud sound at a certain frequency: this sound will reduce the perceived amplitude of sounds at the near frequencies. The idea behind the MPEG1 audio compression process is to use a worse quantization for these masked frequencies: this means a lower sample size and then compression. This idea exploits the fact that the human ear will not tend to listen these frequencies because of the masking effect. The audio compression process exploits another two masking effects: the non-linear sensitivities and the pre-and post-masking effect. The first is because the human ear is prevalently sensitive to the 2-4 kHz frequency range, for which the less sensitive frequencies are more easily to be masked. The second effect occurs before and after strong sounds: pre-masking occurs for about 5 miliseconds before the strong sound is perceived by the listener, while the post-masking effect lasts for about 100 miliseconds after the sound. Therefore, this masking effect could be exploited to achieve compression.

The MPEG1 standard defines three audio compression standards named Audio Level I, II and III. The first level is the simplest compression process, while the third is the most advanced. The three levels aim to supply respectively the next bit rates per channel: above 128 kbits, about 128 kbits, and about 64 kbits.

All three levels support various sample rates: 48kHz for use in professional sound equipment, 44.1 kHz as used in CD-audio and 32 kHz for communication. Two audio channels are provided, which can either be used such as single mono channels or as a stereo channel. The steps of compression process are quite similar for the three levels:

- Convert the sampled audio into the frequency domain using the fast Fourier transform (FFT) algorithm. The range of the sample window varies for the levels: typically Level I uses a sample window 384 wide, while Level II and III use a sample window 1024 wide.
- Divide the spectral information into 32 sub-bands, where each band is 625 Hz wide. The dividing of the audio spectrum allows each sub-band to be processed using a slightly different acoustic model. Although a non-uniform sub-bands could be more suitable for the human ear, a fixed width for the sub-band has be chosen to adopt a simpler situation. The sub-bands are created using a polyphase filter bank, which is relatively fast. However, due to quantization, a frequency component at the edge of one sub-band can also appear in its neighborhood (aliasing effect).
- Extract the audio information from the noise for each sub-band and apply noise masking across the neighboring sub-bands.
- Determine the value at which noise is masked calculating the masking threshold for each sub-band.
- Calculate the required signal to noise ratio from the masking thresholds. This information is exploited to determine the number of bits that will be use to encode each sample.
- Encode the bitstream using the Huffman encoding algorithm to achieve a further data compression.

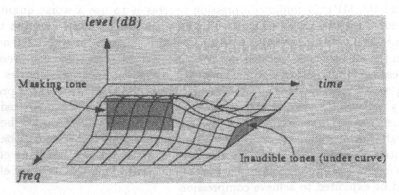

Fig. 2.5. The masking effect.

2.1.3 The system part. The MPEG system specification defines how to combine a plurality of coded audio and video streams into a single data stream. The specification provides a fully synchronized audio and video and facilitates the possible further transmission of the combined information through a variety of digital media.

This system coding includes necessary and sufficient information in the bit stream to provide the system-level functions of synchronization of decoded audio and video, initial and continuous management of coded data buffers to prevent overflow and underflow, random access start-up, and absolute time identification. The coding layer specifies a multiplex data format that allows multiplexing of multiple simultaneous audio and video streams as well as privately defined data streams.

The basic principle of MPEG System coding is the use of positional time stamps (PST) which specify the decoding and display time of audio and video and the time of reception of the multiplexed coded data at the decoder, all in terms of a single 90kHz system clock. This method allows a great deal of flexibility in such areas as decoder design, the number of streams, multiplex packet lengths, video picture rates, audio sample rates, coded data rates, digital storage medium or network performance. It also provides flexibility in selecting which entity is the master time base, while guaranteeing that synchronization and buffer management are maintained. Variable data rate operation is supported. A reference model of a decoder system is specified which provides limits for the ranges of parameters available to encoders and provides requirements for decoders.

2.2 MPEG2

MPEG2 is the natural consequence of the success achieved by MPEG1. It was released in 1994, with the aim to improve the compression of algorithms used by MPEG1 and extend it to new multimedia technologies such as high definition television (HDTV). The MPEG2 standard [ISO94] retains compatibility with its predecessor MPEG1: this means that every MPEG2 compatible decoder can decode a valid MPEG1 bitstream.

One of the major restriction of the MPEG1 standard was that it didn't directly support broadcast television picture as in the CCIR 601 specification: that is the standard video input format for MPEG1 was non- interlaced. MPEG2 overcomes this restriction introducing the concept of frame pictures and field pictures.

MPEG2 introduces the new concepts of profiles and levels. Each profile defines a new set of algorithms added to the algorithms used by the profile below, while a level specifies a range of parameters used by the implementation (i.e. image size and bit rate). Permitted combinations of profiles and levels open the standard to applications that do not support the full syntax. This means that MPEG2 covers, for example, both PAL and HDTV systems.

Others fascinating features offered by MPEG2 standard are the scalability mode provided, for example, to support a graceful quality degradation in presence of transmission errors, and the spatial scalability.

2.2.1 Field and frame pictures. The standard video input format for MPEG1 is non-interlaced. However, coding of interlaced color television standard such as NTSC and PAL is possible using a pre-processing step for encoding and a post-processing step for decoding. In essence, during the coding process, only one horizontally sub-sampled field of each interlaced video input frame is encoded, i.e. the sub-sampled top field. During the decoding process, the decoder generates the bottom field by interpolating the lines of the last decoded top field. Unfortunately, this trick impacts the motion estimation process and reduces the image quality.

MPEG2 overcomes this MPEG1 restriction introducing the concept of frame and field pictures coupled to the frame and field prediction modes. A field picture consists of either a series of odd lines (top field) or a series of even lines (bottom field) of a frame picture. When an interlaced input video sequence is adopted, the field picture coding is used and the field prediction method is employed. This is similar to the frame prediction, with an exception that the prediction is made by using data from one or more previous fields. This means that a top field, for example, may be obtained from either a previous top field or a previous bottom field.

2.2.2 Profiles and levels. The MPEG2 specification defines multiple configurations to provide a set of configurations for including various types of applications. Each configuration is obtained by choosing a supported combination of *profiles* and *levels*. Four profiles and four levels are defined, and ten combinations are supported.

The profile is used to fix the compression algorithm. The profiles available are:

- **Simple:** this profile does not use the B-frames for encoding. It is oriented to software decoding.
- **Main:** this profile is similar to the previous profile except that the B-frames are used for the encoding.
- **Main+:** this profile is the same as the Main profile, but adds encoding information for spatial and SNR scalability.
- **Next:** it works in the same manner of the Main+ profile using the 4:2:2 YcrCb sampling to encode the macroblocks.

The level defines the parameters (sample rates, frame dimensions, coded bit-rates, etc.) that may be used within the chosen profile. The levels available are:

- **Low:** the constrained parameters fixed by this level are tailored for NTSC and PAL formats. A bit rate of up to 4 Mbits per second is achieved.

- **Main:** this supports the CCIR-601 specification, where the maximum frame size is 720 by 480 at 30 frames per second. A bit rate of up to 15 Mbits per second is achieved.
- **High 1440:** this supports the HDTV standard, for which the maximum frame size is 1440 by 115 at 30 frames per second (four times the frame size used by the main level). A bit rate of up to 60 Mbits per second is achieved.
- **High:** this supports the SMPTE 240M specification with a maximum frame size of 1920 by 1080 at 30 frames per seconds. A bit rate of up to 80 Mbits per second is achieved.

Both, Video Main Profile and Main Level normalize complexity within feasible limits of 1994 VLSI technology (0.5 micron), yet still meet the needs of the majority of application users.

2.2.3 MPEG2 scalability modes. The MPEG2 scalability modes are supported only in the Main+ and Next profiles. For these profiles the MPEG2 video bitstream is broken into layers with different priorities. The high priority layers contain the essential coding information that are sufficient to display the video stream. The less priority layers carry the additional coding information to achieve the prefixed quality. This separation of coding information gives several potential advantages.

One of these is a graceful quality degradation in the presence of transmission errors. In fact, with an information separation, the receiver is able to display the images also with only the high priority coding data. Therefore the loss of some less important information does not prevent the stream displaying, but only reduces the quality.

Another use for scalability is to support the simultaneous broadcasting (*simulcast*) of images with different resolutions (*spatial scalability*). This spatial domain method codes a base layer at lower sampling dimensions, while the upper layers contain the information needed to create the higher resolution images from the base layer. This means that information of various resolutions are multiplexed into a single bit-stream. When the bit-stream is simultaneously transmitted on the network, each system uses only the needed information: for example a cable TV simply extracts the low resolution image discarding the additional information, while the HDTV uses all information. The up-sampled reconstructed lower (base) layers are then used as a prediction for the higher layers.

2.2.4 MPEG2 audio. MPEG2 has developed the MPEG2 audio standard for high bit rate coding of multi-channel audio (indicated by 5.1). MPEG2 audio coding will supply up to five full bandwidth channels (left, right, center, and two surround channels), plus an additional 100 Hz special effects channel (the ".1" is referred to this optional channel). The MPEG2 audio standard will also extend the stereo and mono coding of the MPEG1 Audio Standard to half sampling-rates (16 kHz, 22.05 kHz, and 24 kHz), for improved quality for bit-rates at or below 64 kbits/s per channel.

However, the MPEG2 audio multi-channel coding standard will provide backward-compatibility with the existing MPEG1 audio standard. The main channels (left and right) in MPEG2 audio will remain backward compatible, whereas new coding methods and syntax will be used for the surround channels.

2.2.5 MPEG2 system. The MPEG2 system standard specifies the coding formats for multiplexing audio, video, and other data into a form suitable for the transmission or storage. There are two data stream formats defined: the Transport Stream, which can carry multiple programs simultaneously, and which is optimized for the use in applications where data loss may be likely, and the Program Stream, which is optimized for multimedia applications, for performing system processing in software, and for MPEG1 compatibility. Both streams are designed to support a large number of known and anticipated applications, and they retain a significant amount of flexibility such as may be required for such applications, while providing interoperability between different device implementations.

The Transport Stream is well suited for transmission of digital television and video telephony over fiber, satellite, cable, ISDN, ATM, and other networks, and also for storage on digital video tape and other devices. It is expected to find widespread use for such applications in the very near future.

The Program Stream is similar to the MPEG1 system standard. It includes extensions to support new and future applications.

Both the Transport Stream and Program Stream are built on a common *Packetized Elementary Stream* (PES) packet structure, facilitating common video and audio decoder implementations and stream type conversions. This is well-suited for the use over a wide variety of networks with ATM/AAL and alternative transports. Among other items, the Transport Stream packet length was fixed at 188 bytes, including the 4-byte header. This length is suited for the use with ATM networks, as well as a wide variety of other transmission and storage systems.

2.3 MPEG4

The growing success in the fields of digital television, interactive multimedia and interactive graphics applications has pointed out the need to use new standardized technological elements. MPEG4 [MP98a] proposes a new approach for efficiently coding multimedia data, based on the object-oriented system design paradigm. MPEG4 is not focused on the efficient coding of images frames or fields and the associated audio but on the efficient coding and representation of the objects (visible,audible,control objects) that constitute the information to be presented. Those objects are then combined, based on a timeline, to build composite scenes, that can be bi-directionally interpolated.

The MPEG4 standard, currently under development, aims to provide a standardized way to:

- represent ≪ *mediaobjects* ≫, which are units of audio, visual or audiovisual content. These media objects can be of natural or synthetic origin;
- give the composition rules for these objects in order to realize audiovisual scenes made out of elementary or compound media objects;
- multiplex and synchronize the data associated with media objects, so that they can be transported over network channels providing a QoS appropriate for the nature of the specific media objects;
- interact with the audiovisual scene generated at the receiver's end.

An MPEG4 media object or audio/visual object (AVO) is an entity that can be viewed, heard, or experienced as a part of a presentation. For example, the background of a scene can be an object or a composition of objects (audible sounds, visible images, control icons, etc) independent of whatever objects might be seen or heard in the foreground of the same scene. Depending on the particular characteristics of each AVO, optimal coding algorithms and delivery schemes can be used. For example, one could use JPEG for static objects, fractal or wavelet transforms for background objects, MPEG2 for moving foreground objects, MIDI for background music, etc. MPEG4 also provides an approach to the composition of scenes. It allows to:

- modify the AVO attributes (e.g. surface textures of moving objects, physical appearance information and animation parameters of moving heads) by applying data streams to AVOs;
- put AVOs in any place of the scene, including placing the user as an additional object capable to interact with other objects;
- group primitive AVOs to create compound AVOs ;
- interactively change the viewing position and listening point anywhere in the scene.

Media objects are delivered through data stream, that can be composed of one or more elementary streams. Each stream is described by a set of descriptors that hold configuration information to indicate, for example, the required decoder resources and the precision of encoded timing information.

Data streams are of two types: TransMux stream and FlexMux stream. TransMux (Transport Multiplexing) streams are MPEG4 object data streams taken from a telecommunications or computer data network (ATM, frame relay, ISDN, LAN,etc.), or from mass storage devices. FlexMux streams are demultiplexed from a TransMux stream, and sent to right demultiplexers that retrieve elementary streams, which are then decoded, decompressed, and parsed. The resulting AVOs are then rebuilt to be composed and rendered onto appropriate presentation devices (audio speakers, visual displays, etc.); the final scene is composed by using the scene description information. According to the permissions of the application authors, the user can interact with the scene object, that can be local (AVOs on the user terminal) or placed on the remote server.

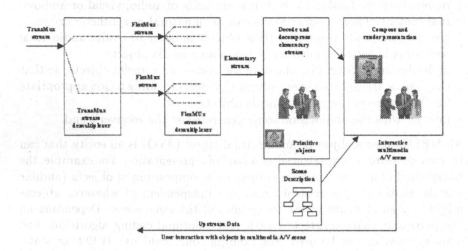

Fig. 2.6. Main subsystems in an MPEG4 user terminal.

Synchronization of elementary streams is achieved through time stamping of individual access units within elementary streams. The identification of such access units and the time stamping is accomplished by the synchronization layer. The synchronized delivery of streaming information from source to destination, exploiting different QoS as available from the network, is specified in terms of synchronization layer and a delivery layer containing a two-layer multiplexer. The first multiplexing layer may be embodied by the MPEG-defined FlexMux tool, which allows grouping of Elementary Streams (ESs) with a low multiplexing overhead. Multiplexing at this layer may be used, for example, to group ES with similar QoS requirements, reduce the number of network connections or the end to end delay. The "TransMux" layer models the layer that offers transport services matching the requested QoS. Only the interface to this layer is specified by MPEG4 while the concrete mapping of the data packets and control signaling must be done in collaboration with the bodies that have jurisdiction over the respective protocol.

Operation of multimedia applications over interactive data networks is addressed by the delivery multimedia integration framework (DMIF). DMIF is a session protocol for the management of multimedia streaming over generic delivery technologies. In principle it is similar to FTP. The only (but essential) difference is that FTP returns data, DMIF returns pointers to where to get (streamed) data [Ric98].

The functionality provided by DMIF are expressed by an interface called DAI (DMIF-Application Interface), and translated into protocol messages.

These protocol messages may differ based on the network on which they operate.

An application accesses data through the DMIF-Application Interface, irrespectively whether such data comes from a broadcast source, from local storage or from a remote server. In all scenarios the Local Application only interacts through a uniform interface (DAI). Different DMIF instances will then translate the Local Application requests into specific messages to be delivered to the Remote Application, taking care of the peculiarities of the involved delivery technology. Similarly, data entering the terminal (from remote servers, broadcast networks or local files) is uniformly delivered to the Local Application through the DAI.

The DMIF architecture is built in such a way that applications which rely on DMIF for communication do not have to be concerned with the underlying communication method. The implementation of DMIF takes care of the delivery technology details presenting a simple interface to the application. Using the DMIF interface, a MPEG4 application can establish multiple-peer application sessions. Each peer is identified by a unique address. A peer can be online and can interact over a network, or it can be prerecorded (on broadcast or storage media). An interactive peer can select a service, a scene description, and specific data streams for AVOs in the scene to be transmitted, and can request the quality of service to match the receiving system's limitations. The MPEG4 DMIF session and resource management (SRM) functionality includes the MPEG2 digital storage media command and control (DSM-CC) SRM functionality. In addition to the SRM capabilities specified for MPEG2, MPEG4 allows application developers the option of whether or not to employ SRM.

2.4 MPEG7

One of the main problems related to the enormous availability of information stored in different digital format in many sites around the world is to be able to efficiently retrieve the information that the end user really needs. Today, textual information can be easily accessible through the available research engines, capable also to perfrom context dependent search. For multimedia objects, the possibility to find the requested information based on particular features of the object (e.g. a picture with a red car or a song with a specific refrain) is still an open problem, even if multimedia databases on the market provide searching tools for images using characteristics like colour, texture and information about the shape. Moreover, it is worth remembering that, at present, there is no unique standard to store images, videos and sound, and this complicates the information retrivial phase.

As the description of multimedia data is related to the characteristics of a multimedia system, i.e. computer-controlled, integrated production, manipulation, presentation, storage and communication of independent information, different aspects for generating and using content descriptions of multimedia data can be viewed as a sequence of events:

1. Extracting of features describing the content.
2. Describing the logical organization of the described multimedia data and placing the extracted values in the framework specifying this structure.
3. Manipulating such description frameworks to accommodate them to different needs.
4. Manipulating instantiated description frameworks to make the description more accessible for human or machine usage.

In 1996, MPEG started a new work item to provide a solution to the questions described above. The main goal of MPEG7 [MP98f] (formally called Multimedia Content Description Interface) is to propose a standardized description of various types of multimedia information. The standard does not comprise the (automatic) extraction of descriptions/features, nor does it specify the search engine (or any other program) that can make use of the description. MPEG7 will also standardize ways to define descriptors as well as structures (Description Schemes) for the descriptors by means of a Description Definition Language (DDL). To provide an effective and efficient search of the material requested by the user, this description (i.e. the combination of descriptors and description schemes) shall be associated with the content itself. Audio/Video (AV) material that has MPEG7 data associated with it, can be indexed and searched for. This 'material' may include: still pictures, graphics, 3D models, audio, speech, video, and information about how these elements are combined in a multimedia presentation ('scenarios', composition information). Special cases of these general data types may include facial expressions and personal characteristics.

MPEG7 descriptors, however, do not depend on the ways the described content is coded or stored. Even though the MPEG7 description does not depend on the (coded) representation of the material, the standard in a way is built on MPEG4, which provides the means to encode audio-visual material as objects having certain relations in time (synchronization) and space (on the screen for video, or in the room for audio). Using MPEG4 encoding, it will be possible to attach descriptions to elements (objects) *within* the scene, such as audio and visual objects.. MPEG7 will allow different granularity in its descriptions, offering the possibility to have different levels of discrimination.

The level of abstraction is related to the way the features can be extracted: many low-level features can be extracted in fully automatic ways, whereas high level features need (much) more human interaction.

Next to having a description of the content, it may also be required to include other types of information about the multimedia data:

- *The form* - An example of the form is the coding scheme used (e.g. JPEG, MPEG2), or the overall data size. This information helps determining whether the material can be read by the user.
- *Conditions for accessing the material* - This could include copyright information, and price.
- *Classification* - This could include parental rating, and content classification into a number of pre-defined categories.
- *Links to other relevant material* - The information may help the user speeding up the search.
- *The context* - In the case of recorded non-fiction content, it is very important to know the occasion of the recording (e.g. Olympic Games 1996, final of 200 meter hurdles, men).

MPEG7 data may be physically located with the associated AV material, in the same data stream or on the same storage system, but the descriptions could be placed somewhere else. When the content and its descriptions are not located in the same place, mechanisms that provide bi-directional links between AV material and their MPEG7 descriptions have to be used.

2.4.1 The Description Definition Language DDL. This is the language in which description schemes are specified. The DDL will allow the creation of new description schemes and descriptors and the extension of existing description schemes.

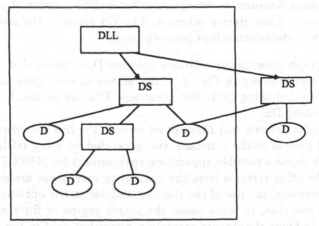

Fig. 2.7. An abstract representation of possible relations between Ds and DSs.

This section describes the terminology used by MPEG7 as described in [MP98c]:

- **Data** AV information that will be described using MPEG7, regardless of the storage, coding, display, transmission, medium, or technology. This definition is intended to be sufficiently broad to encompass graphics, still images, video, film, music, speech, sounds, text and any other relevant AV medium. Examples for MPEG7 data are : a MPEG4 stream, a video tape, a CD containing music, sound or speech, a picture printed on paper, or an interactive multimedia installation on the web.

- **Feature** A feature is a distinctive part or characteristic of the data which stands to somebody for something in some respect or capacity. Some examples are: color of an image, pitch of a speech segment, rhythm of an audio segment, camera motion in a video, style of a video, the title of a movie, the actors in a movie etc.
- **Descriptor** A Descriptor (D) defines the syntax and semantics of a representation entity for a feature. The representation entity is composed out of an identifier of the feature and a datatype. An example might be: Color: string. However, the datatype can be composite, meaning that it may be formed by a combination of datatypes. An example might be: RGB-Color: [int,int,int]. It is possible to have several descriptors representing a single feature, i.e. to address different relevant requirements. Examples for descriptors are: a time-code for representing duration, color moments and histograms for representing color, and a character string for representing a title.
- **Descriptor Value** An instantiation of a descriptor is a value assigned to the feature as pertaining to the data. Descriptor values are combined via the mechanism of a description scheme to form a description.
- **Description Scheme** A description scheme (DS) consists of one or more descriptors and description schemes. The DS specifies the structure and semantics of the relationships between them.

A typical graph showing the relations between Descriptors (Ds), Descriptor Schemes (DSs) is shown in Fig. 2.7 ; the arrows in this figure indicate that DSs are generated using DDL. Note that new DSs can be also built starting from an existing DS.
The Descriptor Scheme and Descriptors outside the box are user-defined elements not present in the standard, and generated by using DDL.

Fig. 2.8 shows a possible application environment for MPEG7. Note that there can be other streams from the content to user; these are not depicted here. Furthermore, the use of the encoder and decoder is optional. It should be pointed out that, in some cases, the search engine or filter agents (user side) need to know the feature extraction algorithm used in the description generation process. Nevertheless, the specific extraction algorithm employed is out of the scope of MPEG7 standards. However, MPEG7 may provide the facility for the DDL to allow a code to be embedded or to be referenced in description schemes.
Moreover, how to use data to answer user queries is not defined by the standard: any type of AV material may be retrieved by means of any type of query material. In other words, video material may be queried using video,

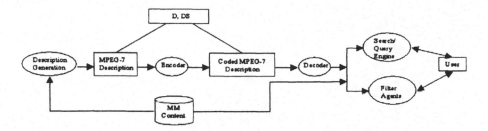

Fig. 2.8. An abstract representation of possible applications using MPEG7.

music, speech, etc. It is a job of the search engine to retrieve data comparing the query data and the MPEG7 AV description. For query examples see [MP98d].

2.4.2 MPEG7 application fields. MPEG7 can be profitably used in many applications and application domains. A few application examples are [MP98d]:

– Digital libraries (image catalogue, musical dictionary,...)
– Multimedia directory services (e.g. yellow pages)
– Broadcast media selection (radio channel, TV channel,...)
– Multimedia editing (personalized electronic news service, media authoring)

The potential applications are spread over the following application domains:

– Education,
– Journalism (e.g. searching speeches of a certain politician using his name, his voice or his face),
– Tourist information,
– Cultural services (history museums, art galleries, etc.),
– Entertainment (e.g. searching a game, karaoke),
– Investigation services (human characteristics recognition, forensics),
– Geographical information systems,
– Remote sensing (cartography, ecology, natural resource management, etc.),
– Surveillance (traffic control, surface transportation, non-destructive testing in hostile environments, etc.),
– Bio-medical applications,
– Shopping (e.g. searching for clothes that you like),
– Architecture, real estate, and interior design,
– Social (e.g. dating services), and
– Film, Video and Radio archives.

Table 2.2. Typical feature types, features and descriptors.

Feature types	Descriptor Feature	Datatype
Annotation		text, etc.
N-dimensional spatio-temporal structure	duration of music segments	time code, etc.
	trajectory object	chain code, etc.
Statistical information	color	color histogram, etc.
	audio frequency content	average of frequency components, etc.
Objective features	color of an object	color histogram, text, etc.
	shape of an object	a set of polygon vertices, a set of moments, etc.
	texture of an object	a set of wavelet coefficients, a set of contrast, coarseness and directionality quantities, etc.
Subjective features	emotion (happiness, anger, sadness, etc.)	a set of eigenface parameters, text, etc.
	style	text, etc.
Production features	author	text, etc.
	producer	text, etc.
	director, etc.	text, etc.
Composition information	scene composition	tree graph, etc.
Concepts	event	text, etc.
	activity	text, etc.

3. Parallel and Distributed Systems for Multimedia

3.1 Multimedia Computing System

A multimedia platform is a computer system capable of supporting multimedia applications. The required hardware for such systems depends on the role that the resulting multimedia systems is due to play. Multimedia platforms may simply serve for the presentation (or delivery) of multimedia information. Others may be required in addition to capture in real-time multimedia information, such as in videoconferencing. Others may support multimedia authoring tools, for the asynchronous development of multimedia documents. Finally, multimedia systems must provide multimedia information to remote client over a network: in this case, these systems are referred as multimedia servers.

Recent advanced in computing and communication make on-line access to multimedia information both possible and cost effective. The architecture for these services consists of multimedia storage servers connected to client sites through high-speed networks. Client can retrieve multimedia objects from the server for real-time playback. Furthermore, this access is often interactive because client can stop, pause and resume playback and, in some cases, perform fast-forward and rewind operations.

Some media, such as audio and video are classified as continuos because they consist of a sequence of media quanta (such as audio samples or video frames), which can convey meaning only when presented in time. The design of services to support continuous media (CM) differs significantly from services that support only traditional textual and numeric data because of two fundamental characteristics:

- **Real-time storage and retrieval.** CM recording devices (such as video cameras) generate a continuous media stream of media quanta that must be stored in real-time. CM playback is essentially recording in reverse: the media quanta must be presented using the same timing sequence with which they were captured. Any deviation from this timing sequence can lead to artifacts such as jerkiness in video motion and pops in audio. Furthermore, media components can be combined in a fashion requiring synchronization. For example, a slide presentation must synchronize audio with images.
- **High data transfer rate and large storage space.** Digital video and audio playback demand a high data transfer rate, so storage space is rapidly filled. Thus, a multimedia service must efficiently store, retrieve and manipulate data in large quantities at a high speed.

Consequently, the critical components in the design of multimedia services are multimedia storage servers that support continuous media storage and retrieval network subsystems that synchronously deliver media information on time to the client sites.

To facilitate shared access to multimedia data, multimedia servers need to control three architectural components: large volume of continuous data, data storage devices, and the networks and communications that deliver the data to and from the subscribers in real-time. Digital multimedia server let users incrementally add, delete, or edit stored multimedia content through digital video editing techniques. Digital servers also let multiple clients concurrently access the same media devices.

In recent years, there were very big technological improvements for processors, memories, networks and I/O devices. This race is still ongoing, specially for CPU which clock rate is continuously increased. However, single CPU systems usually are not capable to meet advanced multimedia application requirements. The 'natural' solution to satisfy these requirements is to use parallel and distributed computing systems. It should be noted that there is not a clear borderline for classifying a computing system as parallel or distributed. Roughly speaking, parallel computing systems consists of several processors that are located within a small distance of each other. They are mainly designed for cooperating in executing a computational task; communication between processors can be considered reliable and predictable. In distributed computing systems, processors may be far apart, and inter-processor communication is more problematic. Communication delays may be unpredictable and the communication links themselves may be unreliable. Distributed computing systems are usually loosely coupled with, in some cases, a light central coordination and control. When operating over a communiaction network, the above mentioned systems may interact together in a symmetrical manner. Consider for example two mutlimedia systems each provided with TV camera, microphone, and speakers to support bilateral videoconferencing. They will interact remotely and symmetrically, as neither has a privilidged role - except that of possibly initiating the conference. Each system is at the same time the source and the destination of all multimedia information involved in the interaction.

However, strictly symmetrical computing systems where all resources are equally distributed over a network are often uneconomical. The natural tendency has always been to pool resources which can be shared remotely onto bigger or specialized systems where an economy of scale in hardware and operation will be possible. Resources which can be pooled include storage capacity such as magnetic disks or magnetic tapes, software applications such as database management or computer-aided design, and more recently processing power. This old idea was adapted and relabeled in the 1980s the *client-server* paradigm. Thus, distributed computing architecture refers to disc or tape servers, application servers, or central processing unit servers, which are accessed remotely by client computers. Client computers of a given service may themselves act as servers for other services. Multimedia is no exception and the client-server paradigm applies equally. Indeed, the nature of multimedia information - which often requires large storage capacity or high processing power - leads naturally to its implementation. A *multimedia server* is therefore a computer system which will provide multimedia services to other systems which in turn act as *multimedia clients*. The servers will in general pool *multimedia storage* capacity, or *multimedia capture* facilites, and may be dedicated to a specific medium. They may also act as shared gateways between the networing infrastructure local to an organization, and external networing or broadcast services. Examples include:

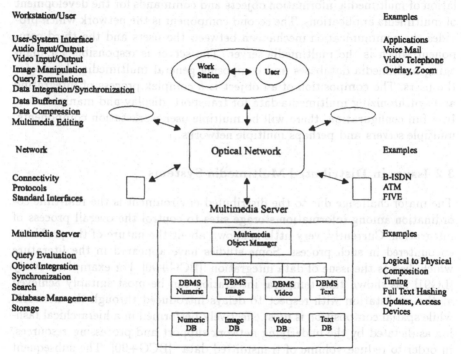

Workstation/User

User-System Interface
Audio Input/Output
Video Input/Output
Image Manipulation
Query Formulation
Data Integration/Synchronization
Data Buffering
Data Compression
Multimedia Editing

Examples

Applications
Voice Mail
Video Telephone
Overlay, Zoom

Network

Connectivity
Protocols
Standard Interfaces

Examples

B-ISDN
ATM
FIVE

Multimedia Server

Query Evaluation
Object Integration
Synchronization
Search
Database Management
Storage

Examples

Logical to Physical
Composition
Timing
Full Text Hashing
Updates, Access
Devices

Fig. 3.1. Composition Architectures for DMIS.

- **Image server.** A computer provided with large magnetic or optical storage capacity to hold databases of recorded images; clients are delivery systems which may display images without having to store them on local devices.
- **Motion video server.** It is similar to image server but with sufficient processing power to output multiple sustained streams of motion video; clients are delivery systems playing back stored video (or animated) sequences over the local-area network.
- **Scan server.** A single or a set of shared scanning stations; typical clients are the users of regular desktop computers.
- **TV broadcast server.** A gateway between TV broadcasts and the local-area network of an organization; clients will be delivery systems displaying

TV broadcasts without TV tuner equipment. The TV video streams are
carried by the local-area network.
- **Facsimile server.** A gateway between the public telefax service and the
  local-area network.

A general configuration of a *Distributed Multimedia Information System*
(DMIS) consists of three components as shown in Fig. 3.1. The user workstation component deals with the issues related to presentation and manipulation of multimedia information objects and commands for the development
of multimedia applications. The second component is the network which provides the communication mechanism between the users and the third component which is the multimedia server. The server is responsible for managing multimedia databases and composing general multimedia objects for
the users. The composition of an object is a complex process of integrating
and synchronizing multimedia data for transport, display and manipulation.
In a full configuration, there will be multiple user workstation components,
multiple servers and perhaps multiple networks.

3.2 Issues in Distributed Multimedia Systems

The major challenge due to the distributed environment is the real-time coordination among information storage sites to control the overall process of
integration. Currently, very little is known about the nature of the problems
encountered in such process. Some studies have appeared in the literature
which discuss the issue of data integration [BCG+90]. For example, a study
[LG91] has shown that temporal integration can be most suitably achieved
at the workstation with respect to delays introduced through the network,
while spatial composition is most effectively performed in a hierarchical fashion as dictated by the underlying network support and processing resources,
in order to reduce volume of transmitted data [BCG+90]. The subsequent
composition methodology is unique in its combination of both spatial and
temporal integration and can be viewed as a network service.

Almost every distribution of multimedia data can be organized as the centralized, master-slave, and federated types. In the simplest case, a multimedia
information system resides on a single server system incorporating DBMS
functionality, for each medium. In this case, any data integration is done
entirely at the server. However, information sources can be distributed and
connected via high-speed networks. The architecture of coordination among
these sites can be viewed either as a master-slave type or in a more general
form of federated type. In either case the role of a data server needs to be
expanded beyond a conventional database management system.

After data elements for desired multimedia information are identified and
sites are located, the spatial and temporal integration of accessed data can be
performed by multiple servers in order to reduce the load on the destination

workstation as well as the required network bandwidth for object communication. In particular, spatial operations such as generation of mosaics, cropping, and color conversions, which are common in window-based environments, can significantly reduce superfluous data transfer when performed at the server sites. The same benefit is not exhibited by integration at remote servers when temporal integration is considered, since no data reduction occurs between source and destination. For strictly temporal composition, without spatial integration requirements, a point-to-point virtual connection between source and destination is most suitable for maintaining synchronization for continuous communication and presentation of objects. No additional processing can be performed within the network at some intermediate site. Based on the assumption of a distributed DBMS organization, four types of point-to-point connection for object retrieval and composition in a DMIS can be identified. These composition architectures include:

1. single source to single destination,
2. single source to multiple destinations,
3. multiple sources to single destination,
4. multiple sources to single destination using an intermediate site, and
5. multiple sources to multiple destinations.

Case (1) is a point-to-point connection for which a client-server relationship exists between a single multimedia server and the workstation. Case (2) represents a shared object architecture in which a single object is displayed simultaneously to various users via multicasting. This mode is necessary to enable Computer Supported Cooperative Work (CSCW) via teleconferencing [PGC+85]. Additional requirements include concurrency and consistency control mechanisms for shared objects. Case (3) represents a distributed object environment, for which complete composition is performed at the sink in a multidrop fashion. This case can be handled by independent network connections between the sink and each source and poses a challenge to control intermedia synchronization by the workstation. Case (4) shows a scenario in which objects are composed at an intermediate site after arriving from distributed sources and are sent via a single connection to the final destination. By using a single connection, data sequencing ensures strict ordering and thereby provides intermedia synchronization. Case (5) defines the general multicast and multidrop case of distributed object composition in a shared object environment. As mentioned above, the process of data composition can be distributed within the network to minimize various system costs. In particular, the criteria for the selection of composition locus is a funtion of various system costs including communication, storage processing, and the desired performance characteristics of the system such as reliability and quality of communication service. The problem is analogous to optimization of queries in a distributed DBMS.

In a general scenario, multiple data servers (DS) and intermediate sites (called *composition servers* (CS)), will collaborate to compose the requested multimedia objects in a hierarchical fashion, both spatially and temporally. Generally, an object model consists of information describing the various operations necessary for spatial composition and intermedia timing and is stored at a central site in the network. At the time a session is established by a user, this information is identified from the central site, and the object hierarchy is decomposed and mapped onto the set of servers (i.e., DSs, CSs, and the workstation). The problem of assignment of composition locus for a given multimedia object can be viewed as analogous to query optimization for distributed databases.

Temporal composition always requires control by the workstation since independent media cannot be combined in any reasonable manner at intermediate sites in the network and routed to the playout destination, except to provide sequencing. On the other hand, spatial composition can be performed at either the composition servers or at the destination workstation. The choice is dependent on the characteristics of the objects to compose, the workstation storage and computational capability, and the bandwidth of the network. If remote composition is dictated, the composition is delegated to at least one CS, which is known as primary CS. The secondary servers consist of data sources. The choice of primary server and overall allocation of DMIS resources should take into account many considerations, such as the locality of objects, the amount of spatial processing required on the selected objects, the spatial composition capability of each CS in terms of raw processing power, the loading on each CS, the overall data transfer cost, etc.

Object locality is an important consideration and affects the choices of the rest of the parameters, since the composition server with the closest proximity to the largest percentage of data can be an optimal choice and is therefore most suitable to be the primary server. Similarly, the spatial processing consideration can be weighed in determining the primary server. Also, the load on a CS can affect the primary server selection. With respect to the workstation and network components, the assignment of spatial operations must consider the utilization of bandwidth in an optimal way. Clearly, there is a tradeoff between traffic on the network, computation at the workstation, and user control over presentation. When objects are composed at the CSs, the user loses the ability to control the assembly of data since this operation is performed prior to the reception of the data. A compromise solution is to allow specification of the object hierarchy such that some objects must be assembled at the WS and others can be distributed to various CSs.

3.3 Networking

Distributed multimedia applications, such as multimedia mail, conferencing, virtual desktop, video on demand, and so on, are imposing new requirements on data transmission:

- **High data throughput.** The delivery of audio-video streams demands high data throughput. Even if compression techniques are used (e.g. MPEG1 or MPEG2) streams can require up to 20 Mbit/second.
- **Fast transfer rates.** Different applications "living" in the same system impose transmission requirements varying from error-free to time constrained.
- **Time and space guarantees.** User will be judging the new applications against the high standards quality set by radio, television.

All these requirements involve a multidimensional resource management (time, space and frequency). Because of the heterogeneous of requirements from different applications, multimedia services are parameterized. Parameterization allows for flexibility and customization of services, so that each application does not implement a new set of system services. The International Standards Organization (ISO) uses quality of service (QoS), a concept for specifying how "good" networking services are, to define parameterization. Researchers have yet to determine the "best" set of QoS parameters for multimedia systems (or benchmark to compare the different approaches); Table 3.1 show QoS parameters that are common in the multimedia community.

Existing operating systems and communication protocols present many limitations for multimedia transmission. Continuous media transmission is constrained by the end-system architecture. Typically, data is obtained from a source (microphone, camera or video adapter) and forwarded to a sink (speaker, display, network adapter, or video adapter). One possibility for satisfying delivery requirements with current systems is to take the "shortest possible path" through the system and move the data from adapter to adapter. The application sets the correct switches for the data flow, but it never really touches the data as in the traditional processing. This approach is fast, but it is does not provide the necessary resource control and adaptability.

The layered architecture of communication systems implies considerable data movement in the protocols. Because of the expense of physically copying data, virtual copying mechanisms are used. One approach, integrated layer processing, is based on the concept of application level framing. It structures protocols into one or two integrated processing loops that operate over a single, common data unit instead over different data units in the various layers of the communication protocol stack. Layering is also used to compress and store data; examples include MPEG system's seven layers and data stored in a CD-ROM/XA format.

Different communication-systems layers may also have different protocol data-unit size. If the upper layer wants to transmit a large data size, the data unit must be broken into the size required by the underlying layer (for example, ATM cell-sized data units). This segmentation is performed at sender, and the underlying layer's data units must be reassembled at the

Table 3.1. Example of possible quality of service (QoS) parameters.

Medium Type	QoS Parameter	Range	Characterization of Quality
Audio (application QoS)	Sample size	8-bit	Telephone voice quality (Intermediate delay 125μs)
	Sample rate	8kHz	
	Sample size	16-bit	CD audio
	Sample rate	44.1 kHz	(Intermediate delay 22.7μs)
	Playback point	$\approx$ 100 to 150 ms	Depends on network delay
Audio (network QoS)	End-to-end delay	0 to 150 ms	Acceptable for most user apps
		150 to 400 ms	May impact some apps
		Above 400 ms	Unacceptable
	Round-trip delay	Up to 800 ms	Acceptable for conversations
	Packet loss	$\leq 10^{-2}$	Telephone quality
	Bandwidth	16Kbps	Telephone speech
		32Kbps	Audio-conferencing speech
		64Kbps	Near-CD-quality audio
		128Kbps	CD-quality audio
Video (application QoS)	Frame rate	30 fps	NTSC format
		25 fps	PAL format
		60 fps	HDTV format
	Frame width	$\leq$ 720 pixels	Video signal MPEG coded
	Frame height	$\leq$ 576 pixels	Vertical size
	Color resolution	8 bit/pixels	Gray-scale resolution of 256 colors
		16 bit/pixels	65,536 possible colors
	Aspect ratio	4:3	NTSC,PAL TV format
		16:9	HDTV format
	Compression ratio	2:1	Lossless compression of HDTV
		50:1	Lossy compression of HDTV
Video (System QoS)	Decoder buffer	$\leq$ 376,832 bits	MPEG related parameters
Video (Network QoS)	Bandwidth	$\leq$ 1.86 Mbps	MPEG encoded video
		64 Kbps to 2 Mbps	H.261 encoded video
		1,544 Kbps to 2 Mbps	H.120
		140 Mbps	TV, PCM coding
		Over 1 Gbps	HDTV uncompressed quality
		$\approx$500 Mbps	HDTV lossless compression
		20 Mbps	HDTV lossy compression
	Bit error rate	$\leq 10^{-6}$	Long-term bit error rate
	Packet loss	$\leq 10^{-2}$	Uncompressed video
		$\leq 10^{-11}$	Compressed video
	End-to-end delay	$\approx$ 250 ms	
Audio/Video	Sync skew	+/-80 ms	Lip synchronization
Audio/image	Sync skew	+/-5 ms	Music with notes
Audio/pointer	Sync skew	+750 ms	(+) audio-ahead pointer
		-500 ms	(-) pointer-ahead audio
Data (Network QoS)	Bandwidth	0.2 to 10 Mbps	File transfer
	End-to-end delay	$\approx$ 1 sec.	
	Packet loss	10^{-11}	

receiver. Some protocols use a retransmission mechanism to achieve reliable data delivery, but this requires additional buffer space for queues and increases end-to-end delays.

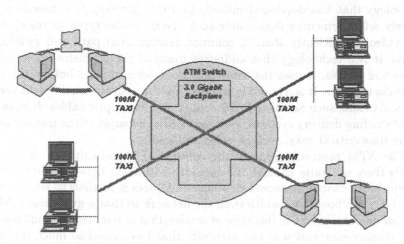

Fig. 3.2. Typical ATM Network.

For multimedia applications, it is important that bandwidth is available and guaranteed so that data stream can be maintained. With Ethernet, this is not the case, and depending on the loading (and hence the number of collisions on the network) the time taken for a data packet to be successfully transmitted can vary. For an audio-video display reliant on data from a hard disc on the network, this can cause problems when the data is needed and not available. To solve this, buffering is used to provide a reservoir in case packets are delayed. The buffer can hold many packets (the number being dependent on the worst case delay that the system must tolerate and the resulting delay in starting the playback) and only the start the playback once the buffer is full. If packets are regularly received, the buffer stays full until the end packet is received. If a packet is not received when expected, all that happens is that the buffer is emptied by one packet. Various handshaking protocols can be added to this basic mechanism to ensure that the data supply to the playback system is maintained.

This method appears fine, but the delay in filling the buffer can be inconvenient if it is too long and, more importantly, it is a major issue with interactive or synchronized multimedia, such as video conferencing. Imagine trying to hold a simple telephone conversation with a two second delay between the two parties. In practice an acceptable delay for a good video conferencing is about 150-200 ms.

To prevent this problem bandwidth must be guaranteed or some method for sending priority data needs to be used to ensure that the buffers can be kept to as small as possible. As a result, many development in the LAN Ethernet world are now focusing on supporting these requirements as well as providing QoS.

Asynchronous Transfer Mode (ATM) is a networking and communication technology that was developed initially in 1982 [DeP93]. It is based on an entirely set of principles that enable such diverse traffic types as voice, data and video to efficiently share a common transmission path and switching points. It is a technology that addresses many of the problems facing both LANs and WANs. It uses the same protocols, which makes linking the two networks together. It is a scalable architecture that can run on different speed physical media, such as twisted pair copper and fiber optic cables. It runs on top of existing delivery systems, such as ADSL, and support the transmission of the time critical data, such as video and audio.

The ATM protocol supports the concept of "bandwidth on demand"; clearly there is a finite amount of bandwidth within the network and delivery system which cannot be exceeded. What ATM does is to allow to request and effectively pre-book bandwidth from the network so that a guaranteed delivery can be obtained. It is this type of service that is required for multimedia data transmission and it is this attribute that has caused so much interest. The basic principles behind ATM are as follows.

ATM devices are connected directly to an ATM switch. This is typical in the telecommunications arena with a single wire per subscriber but is less common within the LAN arena. Coax based Ethernet links effectively share a cable between many nodes and thus share the bandwidth.

All data in ATM is handled in containers, known as cells, that carry a fixed number of bytes. This principle has two important benefits. First, control queueing delay is greatly improved, as the largest component of a queueing delay is caused by variation in data element size and ATM makes all data elements of the same size. Second, equipment that processes fixed size data units is simpler than for variable-sized units.

Each ATM cell has a header containing information that each ATM switching point uses in combination with previously stored routing information to determine where to send the ATM cell and thus transfer its information. This previously stored routing information is determined by the process of establishing a virtual connection or circuit. There is an entire set of machinery that maintains these virtual connections by manipulating the stored information at co-operating switching points. This machinery operates over the same network as the data, using its own virtual connections.

While the cells are little workers carrying information in their payload bit-times, some will get lost due to noise or equipment failure, others due to congestion. Therefore, various types of traffic generators with their different requirements have to carefully prepare or 'adapt' their messages for travel over the ATM network. This is done in each case by a piece of software or firmware called ATM *Adaptation Layer* (AAL). The AAL has two stages:

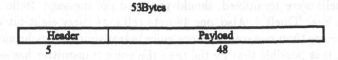

Fig. 3.3. ATM Cell Structure.

- A service (or traffic type) dependent sublayer called *Convergence Sublayer* (CS) and
- A service independent *Segmentation And Reassembly* (SAR) sublayer.

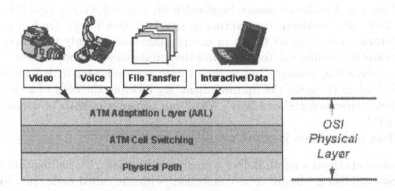

Fig. 3.4. Different Data Traffic over ATM.

The CS assures the necessary error control and sequencing as well as the sizing of information. The SAR then chops the CS message into the 48-byte payload packets and attaches them to the five-byte header. There are five types of adaptation layer services, designated AAL1, AAL 2, etc. At the transmission node AAL1 prepares voice traffic, AAL2 prepares video traffic, AAL3 and AAL5 prepare connection-oriented data (TCP-like data) and AAL4 prepares connectionless data (SMDS or LAN-like) for cell relay switching. After the preparation stage, the message is delivered to the segmentation layer, where the cells are created and sent.

At the receiving side the cells go through the re-assembly layer and then they pass to AAL1, 2, 3, 4, or 5 for the recreation of the original message. This message is then delivered to the video monitor, the voice receiver or the data process expecting it.

AAL1 is intended for voice traffic. Since voice traffic is error tolerant, no error control (CRC) is required. However, what is important in the case of voice transmission is that cells are received in the exact sequence in which they were sent, and that they arrive at a constant rate. AAL1 assures sequence numbers. (If cells were scrambled, should you send the message 'Hello', the receiver might hear 'Ohell'.). Also, one 48 byte cell may carry eight-bit voice samples from more than one source. Since voice is transmitted synchronously without delay, it is possible that by the time the voice transmitter has sent a few samples, the cell must leave partially empty. This type of service is called 'Streaming Mode Service'. AAL1 is designed to handle this: it inserts sequence numbers in cells and identifies what portion of the cell carries voice and what portion carries nothing. With video, not only do we need synchronization and sequencing, but we also need error checking codes (CRCs). And, since a screen may have a lot of pixel information, many cells may have to be used to transmit the whole screen; so we need to know where the screen starts and where it ends. That's why the cells are labelled as 'the first' or 'intermediate one' or 'the last'.

This way AAL2 can assure bandwidth-on-demand with a variable rate. Think of video conferencing. Normally, speakers aren't very fond of public appearances and they sit frozen in one position moving only their lips. Occasionally something excites them and they make sudden body moves - then entire screen may change - but in their frozen position, very little bandwidth is required to transmit the lip movement. By labeling the cells of a message as 'first', 'intermediate' and 'last', AAL2 can transmit as little or as much as is needed.

Data transmission is of two kinds:

- **Connection-oriented.** Before actually sending data, the calling side must first establish a 'circuit' or a 'connection' with the called node (just like in telephony); and
- **Connectionless.** A piece of data is 'thrown' in the network with a destination address in it and, magically, it arrives at the destination. This kind of service is also known as 'datagram' service and is like the letter delivery performed by the postal service.

AAL3 and 5 are designed for connection-oriented service, and AAL4 for datagrams. Like AAL2 for video, both data services require error checking (CRC), sequencing, and identification of the cells as part of the message. In addition, some sort of indication has to be given to the receiver about the total length of the message, so an appropriate buffer size can be reserved for the message. AAL3 is very similar to AAL2. The difference is in timing (AAL3 does not require synchronism between receiver and transmitter). AAL4, in addition, must identify each cell as belonging to one datagram. So each cell is given a 'Multiplex Identifier' (a ten-bit field) for this purpose. AAL5 does not bother to insert all this extraneous information into each cell. Instead, before the TCP or some other data message is chopped into cells, a 'trailer' is appended to that message, containing a 'length' indicator of two bytes (TCP segments can be 65,536 bytes long), a CRC error checking code for the whole message, and some bits signaling user-to-user (end-to-end) what this message is about (this is still under study and is to be used by each user equipment as it sees a fit). Then this 'adapted' message is put through the chopper and the cells are sent.

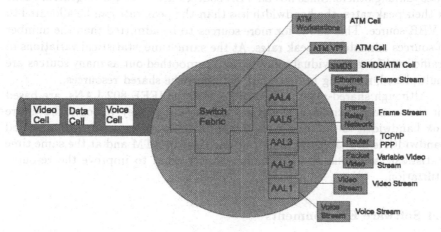

Fig. 3.5. ATM Integrated Services.

Each switching point queues ATM cells for outbound transmission in a logical scheduling structure that allows control over such parameters as delay, delay variation and cell loss, based on the needs of the application, as expressed when the virtual connection is established. For example, a data file transfer is much more sensitive to cell loss than to delay, whilst a voice connection is more sensitive to delay and video to delay variation. This is referred to as Quality of Service (QoS).

Scalability is one of the most valuable properties of ATM. The key factors contributing to the scalability are a switch based architecture and the common cell structure across all ATM system components. Conventional LAN technologies (Ethernet, FDDI, etc) are limited by the propagation delays involved in coordinating the sharing of the link bandwidth. For example, increasing Ethernet speed reduces efficiency due to correspondingly long collision detection/resolution times. User can access ATM networks via a variety of physical connections irrespectively of media types and applications. Within the limit of the physical bandwidth, an arbitrary bit rate can be allocated to a user. Furthermore, the bandwidth remains allocated for the entire connection. At the same time, from the viewpoint of systems, the network bandwidth can be provisioned in a scaled manner with the switch-based configuration.

An important topic for multimedia network traffic is how the network itself manages variable bit-rate. A *variable bit-rate* (VBR) source is characterized by having different degrees of activities during a connection. ATM networks exhibit such behavior. A VBR video source, for example, has a peak rate at scene changes but a significantly lower rate as temporal and spatial compressions are performed after a scene change (as a matter of fact, many times video streams are compressed at a constant bit rate). Characteristics of VBR traffic may be represented by long-term average and peak cell emission rates, among others. Since not all VBR sources are expected to generate cells at their peak rates, the bandwidth less than the peak rate can be allocated to a VBR source. This allows for more sources to be admitted than the number of sources admitted by peak rates. At the same time, statistical variations in traffic load from individual sources can be smoothed out as many sources are multiplexed, resulting in better utilization of the shared resources.

Although shared-medium networks , such as IEEE 802 LANs, are based on the same principle of statistical multiplexing, they allocate the entire link bandwidth to one user on a temporal basis. In contrast, the allocated bandwidth is available to the user all the time in ATM and at the same time statistical variations in VBR traffic are exploited to improve the resource utilization.

3.4 Software Environments

Introduction

An important aspect of distributed applications based on large computer network is the heterogeneity. Even if the union of different structures of networks, operating systems and applications may appear a more complex way to develop a wide system, the heterogeneity is a necessary requirement justified by several factors:

- **Engineering trade-off.** A complex problem doesn't have a single acceptable solution, but developers and users must often choose between diverse approaches basing their choice on numerous trade-offs. This situation appears often when a well-suited application is needed, and then a more general and diffused solutions cannot be taken into consideration.
- **Cost factor.** The competitiveness of the technology business presses the vendors to produce increasingly efficient systems at the lowest cost. If this implies a frantic growth of new alluring technologies, the compatibility requirement becomes always more complicated.
- **Legacy systems.** When systems become obsolete, their substitution with systems based on newest technologies may be too much expensive and critical. In this situation, the tendency is to upgrade the systems without replacing them. Over the time, this approach drives to the necessity of coexistence between systems of different technological generations.
- **Distributed behavior.** Some applications, like the Video on Demand, needs to be broken in several components characterized by different functions and requirements. Typically, such components require suitable environments in order to satisfy the necessity of high performance and security. Therefore, distributed applications usually run in a heterogeneous

environment and need an appropriate communication system that grants the interoperability.

Ideally, the use of heterogeneous and true open systems enables to achieve the best combination of hardware and software for each specific problem. Unfortunately, dealing with heterogeneous distributed systems is rarely easy especially for software development. In recognition of these problems, several new paradigms have been introduced. One of these is the client-server paradigm where the overall application is divided in two monoliths: one on the server side which provides services for the incoming requests, and one on the client side for delivering requests and manipulating results. Although this organization permits a clear task separation between clients and server, unfortunately it tends to a centralization of the load onto a single power server. A more general architecture is provided by the client-server based on distributed objects, where the applications are distributed on several machines and encapsulated as objects available to the external world. In this scenario each machine can act both as client of remote applications and server for external requests. The distributed objects paradigm represents the ultimate form of the client-server distribution and it isn't far the moment when millions of machines will strictly interact both as clients and servers.

However, the scenario involved by the distributed objects paradigm implies many critical problems for managing heterogeneous environments. For this reason, many organizations work to promote standards for the development of this type of applications. One of these is the *Object Management Architecture* (OMA) proposed by the Object Management Group (OMG). OMG was formed in 1989 and nowadays it is the largest software consortium in the world with over 700 members (developers, vendors, and end users). These members participate to the standards development, replying to Request For Proposals (RFP) issued by the OMG. The OMG uses these responses for defining the standard specifications basing their choices on commercially available object technologies. The next two sections give a brief description of the OMA model and subsequently a more detailed explanation of the *Common Object Request Broker Architecture* (CORBA) specification that is the principal component of the OMA. The CORBA standard [Pop97] defines a truly open object infrastructure, where the development process start from the use of a neutral object-oriented definition language (the IDL) and relies on a common software communication bus (the ORB) which grants a transparent communication environment between heterogenous client and server machines. CORBA extends the object-oriented development to a distributed environment achieving the hardware, network, and operating system independence.

Finally, a brief introduction to Java language environment is given in the last section, in order to present a new object-oriented language well-suited for a very flexible development of architecture neutral application. Java has been thought especially to develop downloadable and secure applications from remote sites without worrying about platform dependencies. This result has been reached because the Java compiler maps the applications into an intermediate code (named bytecode); to effectively execute the bytecode a Java virtual machine must be present on every platforms for its on-fly translation to machine code. Java doesn't constitute an alternative to object distributed application development, but certainly is the best candidate for object distributed applications based on CORBA standard.

3.4.1 The Object Management Architecture (OMA). The aim of the OMA model is to define an architecture, based on heterogeneous systems with distributed objects and services available on the network. Each application that contains objects acts as server for replying to requests issued by clients. On the other hand, the application can behave as client for other distributed applications. Details on how the distributed objects are implemented or where they are located are hidden from the requesting clients; each client locates and invokes the remote entities exploiting general and common services present in OMA.

The OMA is composed of an Object Model (for defining how the distributed objects can be described) and a Reference Model (for describing how the objects interact). In the Object Model, an object is an encapsulated entity, viewed by the external world through well-defined interfaces. The object users (clients) issue requests to perform services on their behalf, ignoring the implementation and location of the objects exploited. The Reference Model defines four fundamental categories of services covering the needs of a distributed component. The four objects interface categories are:

- **Basic Object Services:** these interfaces form a collection of basic object services that most applications need. Detailed specifications for many of these services are complete. An example of service is the Naming Service, used to find distributed objects exploiting names associated to them. Other fundamental services specified are Implementation Repository, Interface Repository, Trading, Life Cycle, Events Notification, Transactions, and Security.
- **Common Facilities:** this collection of object services provides general-purpose capabilities, useful in many applications. Unlike the Basic Object Services, these interfaces are oriented towards end user applications. An example of such services is the RFP1 that covers compound document presentation and interchange resulting in a Distributed Document Component Facility (DDCF) based on OpenDoc.
- **Domain Interfaces:** these interfaces are oriented towards specific application domains. The OMG has created a Domain Technical Committee to oversee the work of a new series of Task Forces in domain vertical areas such as Finance, Manufacturing, Healthcare, Business Objects, Analysis and Design, Multimedia and Electronic Commerce.
- **Application Objects:** these are specific to particular end-user applications and are not subject to standardization.

Application Objects Domain Interfaces

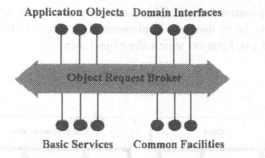

Basic Services   Common Facilities

Fig. 3.6. OMA Reference Model Interface Categories.

These services use the *Object Request Broker* (ORB) component to facilitate the communication between the clients and the objects, as shown in Fig. 3.6. The ORB provides a message passing bus for transporting requests and responses in a distributed environment. The ORB is the most important component in the OMA model and for this reason, much of the OMG's attention was focused on it. The next paragraph deals with the *Common Object Request Broker Architecture* (CORBA).

3.4.2 The Common Object Request Broker Architecture (CORBA).
The CORBA specification describes the interfaces and services that must be provided by compliant ORBs. The last major update of the CORBA specification was in 1995 when the OMG published the revision 2.0. The main features of CORBA 2.0 are (cf. Fig. 3.7):

- ORB Core
- OMG Interface Definition Language (IDL)
- Interface Repository (IR)
- Language Mappings
- Stubs and Skeletons
- Dynamic Invocation and Dispatch
- Object Adapters
- Inter-ORB Protocols

The Fig. 3.7 shows how each component interacts with one another. A brief description of each component is given below.

The ORB has the fundamental role of delivering requests issued by client applications and returning the responses to them. The ORB contains the essential functionality to perform its role, in order to keep it as simple as possible. Other functions are pushed to other OMA components. The key feature of the ORB is the transparency given to client applications for using remote services. The ORB hides the following aspects:

- **Object location.** The client does not know where the needed object (referred as target object) is located. The client perceives the remote object as a local object, without knowing where it really is located.

- **Object implementation.** The client does not know what programming language has been used to implement the target object, nor operating systems and platform on which the object runs.

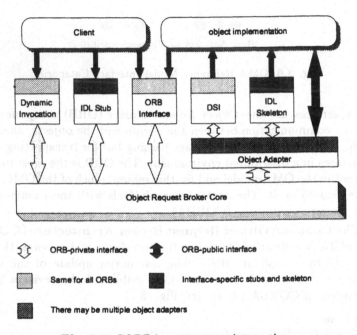

Fig. 3.7. CORBA components interaction.

- **Object execution state.** The client must not worry if the target object is running on remote machine and ready to accept the requests. The ORB controls if the object is activated, starting it if necessary.
- **Object communication mechanism.** The client does not know what communication mechanism the ORB uses. Even if the target object is locally (in the same process or in the same machine) or remotely located, the client adopts the same mechanism to invoke its services. To make a request to a desired target object, the client must first obtain its object reference and then can use it to invoke the object methods as if the object were local. Object references can have a standard format (such as the OMG IIOP standard format, see below) or a proprietary format, depending on the software application implementing the CORBA standard. However, the tendency is to adopt the IIOP standard format. Client can obtain object references in several different ways. The first way consists of making a creative invocation to a factory object: this is not a CORBA standard object, but a user's object responsible for creating objects and

returning them references. Another way is to use dedicated service such as the Naming Service, which gives a directory structure (name space) where the objects are logically associated to symbolic names. The client user can browse the name space using the available methods in order to choose the desired object and get the reference. The last way is to exploit the string-fied reference service that ORB offers: the service consists of translating the reference in to a unique string that can be stored into a file or database. When the object reference is required, the client asks ORB to converse the stringfied reference into a real object reference.

The common starting point for all CORBA developers is the IDL definition of the target objects. The IDL is a declaration language, not a programming language, used to produce a common definition for distributed objects. A mapping from IDL definition to the specific syntax of the chosen language is needed. Typically, this is performed automatically by an IDL compiler. The key entity definable in IDL is the interface that is very similar to class in C++ and interface in Java. An example of IDL interface is shown below:

```
// OMG IDL - Note: this comment is just like C++
// An example of a grid interface
interface Grid {
        exception NotValidIndex {string reason; };

        readonly attribute short height;
        readonly attribute short width;

        void set(in short n, in short m, in long value);
              raises (NotValidIndex);
        long get(in short n, in short m);
              raises (NotValidIndex);
};
```

The definition specifies an interface named Grid that has two attributes (height and width) and two operations (set and get). The attributes are declared as readonly attributes: this means that attributes are not directly accessible by external clients, but they can be modified only by using the methods offered by the interface. The IDL provides the common types present in the most diffused languages:

- **Basic types:** long, short, unsigned long, and unsigned short as integer types; float and double as floating point type; char and octet (an 8-bit quantity that is guaranteed not to undergo any conversion during transmission) for char types; boolean type that can be have only two values (true and false); any that allows the specification of values that can express an arbitrary IDL type.
- **Constructed types:** struct for data aggregation; union for the definition of variable type data based on discrimination; enum that allows the definition of a set of values.

Template types: string for the definition of bounded or unbounded sequence of characters; sequence that consists of a dynamic-length container of same type values.

- **Object reference types:** the IDL provides the Object type as a reference to the basic CORBA object from which each interface implicitly inherits. However, reference to a previously defined interface can be used specifying the name of the interface. This possibility is clarified in the example shown below. The interface GridFactory offers the create method for asking the server application to create a new Grid object with the specified numbers of rows and columns. Instead, the delete method releases the resources (memory allocated for the matrix and resources associated to the object instance) associated to the specified Grid object.

```
// OMG IDL
module GridApplication {
        interface Grid {
                // ...interface definitions
        };

        // An example of a factory interface

        interface GridFactory {
                Grid create (in short rows, in short columns);
                void delete (in Grid grid_to_delete);
        };
};
```

The methods take a syntax very similar to their counterpart in C++, except for the fact that for each parameter the passage direction (in, out, and inout) is specified. To define exceptional conditions, the IDL provides **exception** definitions. The exception can be associated with the methods using the **raise** clause that gives the possibility to the target object to throw the exception caused by anomalous situations. The **module** construct is used to limit the definition visibility to prevent name clashes.

The IDL supports the interface inheritance. This makes possible the reuse of previously developed interfaces. All the user-developed interfaces implicitly inherit from the **Object** interface defined in the **CORBA module**: the adverb implicitly means that this necessary inheritance need not be declared because it occurs automatically. The next example shows how the **SpreadSheet** interface inherits from the previous **Grid** interface specifying it after the name declaration and a colon.

```
// OMG IDL
module GridApplication {
```

```
interface Grid {
      // ...interface definitions
};
// An example of inheritance
interface SpreadSheet : Grid {
          void GridInitialization (in long value);
          long AddColumn (in short column);
};
};
```

As mentioned above, the IDL is only used as common definition language, therefore no implementation details are specified. This is performed in a successive step where the developers add the implementation to the previous definitions. OMG had defined precise mapping rules from the IDL language to many diffused languages such as C, C++, Java and SmallTalk. Typically, the mapping is performed by an IDL compiler that produces the needed structure (skeletons and stubs, see below) to develop the required implementation. To understand how the language mapping functions, consider the C++ mapping for the interfaces. The IDL interfaces map to C++ classes and the IDL interface methods map to the member functions of the classes. Typically, the IDL attributes don't directly map to the class members, but some member functions for the attributes access are generated, depending on the fact whether they are read-only or not. The object references are mapped to objects that support the operator →. Therefore, when a client application gets in some way the object reference of a desired target object, it can invoke the member functions with the usually C++ syntax, as shown in the next example:

```
// C++ client application example

// ...

main() {
      // ...define the Grid object reference Gptr in some way

      // ...obtain the Gptr in some way

      //invoke the set method
      //for setting the (2,4) grid element
      //with the 123 value        Gptr->set(2,4,123);

      //invoke the get method
      //for getting the (2,4) grid element
      //previously set
      Gptr->get(2,4);
```

}

In addition to generating the interface mapping, the IDL compilers also generate client-side stubs and server-side skeletons. A stub (sometimes referred to as surrogate or proxy) is an object that interacts with the client application to effectively create and issue the client requests through the ORB. Instead, the skeleton is the object that gets the client requests from the ORB and delivers them to the target object implementation. When a client application invokes a method of a target object, the request is marshaled by the stub in order to convert the parameters to a suitable data representation for transmission in accordance with underlying ORB. Once the request arrives at the target object, the server ORB and the skeleton object cooperate to unmarshal the data representation in one suitable to the server application. When the target object has performed the request, the response is sent back the way it came. This communication mechanism is shown in Fig. 3.8.

Stubs and skeletons are produced at IDL compile time based on the knowledge of the interfaces: for this reason, this dispatching mechanism is often called *Static Invocation Interface* (SII). Other two mechanisms are provided by CORBA in order to support generic stub and generic skeleton. They are respectively known as *Dynamic Invocation Interface* (DII) and *Dynamic Skeleton Interface* (DSI).

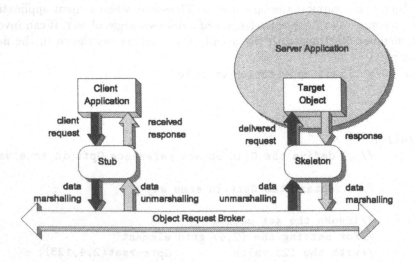

Fig. 3.8. Client Request Dispatching.

Applications for which the SII are too limited and DII must be used are for example browsers and gateways. These types of client application programs require that they can use an indeterminate range of interfaces:

using the SII limits these applications to contemplate only a fixed set of pre-defined interfaces. In fact, when a new interface must be added to the set, the client application needs to be recompiled. To overcome this general problem, the DII allows invocations to be constructed by specifying, at runtime, the target object reference, the operation/attribute name and the parameters to be passed. Such calls are termed dynamic because the IDL interfaces used by a program do not have to be statically determined at the time the program is designed and implemented. The server need not consider whether the client uses the DII or the SII.

The DSI is the server-side equivalent of the DII. It allows a server to receive an operation or attribute invocation on any object, even one with an IDL interface unknown at compile time. The server does not need to be linked with the skeleton code for an interface to accept operation invocations on it. Instead, a server can define a function that will be informed of an incoming operation or attribute invocation: that function can determine the identity of the object being invoked; the name of the operation and the types and values of each argument must be provided by the user. It can then carry out the task that is being requested by the client, and construct and return the result. The client is not aware that the server is in fact implemented using the DSI; it simply makes IDL calls as normal.

We have seen that dynamic invocation mechanisms (DII and DSI) are the only way to handle particular types of applications such as browsers and gateways. However, the possibility to use dynamically unknown interfaces rises the necessity to discover what effectively the interfaces do. For this purpose the CORBA standard provides the Interface Repository (IR) that acts as a container of IDL interface definitions. The IR is itself a CORBA object whose operations can be invoked just like any other CORBA object. Many methods to navigate the hierarchy of IDL interfaces are provided.

On the server-side, the target objects interact with the ORB using the Object Adapter (OA). In general, an object adapter has the role of adapting the interface of an object to the interface expected by a caller. Since in a CORBA environment more languages and different programming tools are allowed to develop server applications, an OA is needed to interface them to the same ORB. Therefore, the CORBA Object Adapter acts as a glue between the target objects implementation and the ORB itself. The lack of an object adapter would mean that the target object would need to connect them to the ORB to receive the requests, seriously complicating the application development. Moreover, in order to keep the ORB as simple as possible, many responsibilities are entrusted to the OA:

- **Object registration:** the OA supplies operations that allow target object implementations to be registered as CORBA objects.
- **Object reference creation:** the OA creates and interprets object references for the CORBA objects.

- **Server process activation:** when a client request arrives, the OA activates the server containing the target object required if it is not already running. When the server is no longer needed, the OA deactivates it according to the timeout setting.
- **Object activation:** the OA activates the requested target objects if they are not already activated.

Though the CORBA standard contemplates the existence of multiple OA, it actually only specifies one named Basic Object Adapter (BOA).

In a large CORBA environment, there are many motivations to partition it into different ORBs. Apart from the implementation diversity due to many ORB vendors, a valid motivation may be the necessity to restrict a part of the CORBA environment for security and management needs. It is in fact undesirable that malicious external people get reserved information, by simply accessing them via the CORBA communication mechanism. For these reasons the ORB boundaries are fixed by the concept of domain: a domain is a distinct scope, within which certain common characteristics are exhibited and common rules are observed. Domains are generally identified by their administrative (e.g. security needs) or technological (e.g. network domain or different ORB implementation) nature. Before the last release, the CORBA specification did not fix any particular information on how the ORBs should interoperate. The CORBA 2.0 specifications introduce a general ORB interoperability architecture that establishes the rules of how the interoperability must be achieved in the same domain or between different domains. In particular, when a request must leave its domain, it must traverse an inter-ORB bridge which ensures that content and semantics are mapped to the correct form of receiving ORB.

The ORB interoperability architecture is fundamentally based on the General Inter-ORB Protocol (GIOP). The GIOP specifies the transfer syntax and a standard set of messages for ORB interoperation over any connection-oriented transport. The transfer syntax, known as Common Data Representation (CDR), establishes the encoding for all the IDL data types. A common message header is defined for all messages, which includes the message size, a version number indicating the version of GIOP being used, the byte ordering and the message type. Messages are exchanged between clients and servers. In this context, a client is an agent that opens connections and originates requests. A server is an agent that accepts connections and receives requests.

As mentioned, the GIOP specifies a general protocol for the ORB to ORB interactions over any connection-oriented transport protocol. The Internet Inter-ORB Protocol (IIOP) specifies the GIOP implementation for TCP/IP protocol. Any CORBA compliant implementation must support the GIOP and IIOP architectures. An object accessible via IIOP is identified by an interoperable object reference (IOR). An IOR stores information needed to locate and communicate with the target object such as its Internet host address and its port number. An IOR is managed internally by the ORB; therefore, it is not necessary for an application programmer to know its structure.

3.4.3 The Java language environment.

Java is an object-oriented programming language. It was created in early 1990 by James Gosling, a SUN software developer, during a research project inherent to the development of advanced software for heterogeneous network environment. Initially, this research group adopted C++ such as development language. However, over time, portability and robustness problems addressed the group to develop an entirely new language platform. The aim of this challenge was to design an ideal language for the development of secure, distributed, and easy portable applications.

The most attractive innovation introduced by Java is the total portability feature. This means that each application produced can be executed on an unlimited variety of hardware platforms and operating systems, without recompiling it for the specific environment. This result is possible because the Java compiler produces an intermediate code (named bytecode) that is architecture neutral. The generated bytecode is not directly interpretable by the processors, but a real time translator (the Java Virtual Machine) is needed for each specific platform. In this way, although each specific platform must have the appropriate Java Virtual Machine, we have the assurance that Java applications can be executed everywhere. The presence of a further step of interpretation may appear as a cause of a performance worsening. This is not entirely true due to several factors. For example, the Java Virtual Machine is optimized to operate during idle moments, when the user is thinking on what he has to do, in order to use the wasted time. Besides, Java was thought to reduce as much as possible the run time controls. However, when high performance is required, a Just In Time (JIT) compiler can be used to translate on the fly (at a run time) the Java bytecodes into machine code for the specific processor on which the application is running. Performance of bytecodes converted to machine code is roughly the same as native C++.

As mentioned, Java has been designed as an easy and secure language. Although many constructs in Java are borrowed from the C++ (and other languages), many programming aspects have been eliminated because they have been considered redundant or possible cause of development errors. In the optic to make Java application as much simple as possible, the typedef and define constructs, for example, have been removed because they often complicate the program legibility. Besides, pointers, that are the primary way to inject bugs into their code, have been eliminated: thus, the programmers are got nothing to do with pointers arithmetic, dangling pointers and memory trashing due to the use of incorrect pointers. In fact, Java completely removes the memory management load from the programmer providing an automatic garbage collection integrated in the Java Virtual Machine. This means that the programmer must only specify the need to allocate the object; at run time the Java memory manager evaluates when the object resources are no more needed and then the object becomes a candidate for garbage collection. Finally, while C++ is a hybrid object-oriented language because it is developed to be entirely compatible with its predecessor C (remember that C is a procedural language), Java is a pure object-oriented language. This means that functions, structures, strings, arrays and so on, become common objects.

As the most popular object-oriented languages, Java supports the *class* constructor in order to define an entity characterized by *members*, which are *fields* (that define the state of the entity) and *methods* (that define the behavior of the entity). The example below shows a simple Java class which represents the geometric point entity:

```
Class Point extends Object {

        private static int numpoints = 0;
        /* how many Point object
        have been instantiated */
        private double x; /* horizontal coordinate */
        private double y; /* vertical coordinate */

        Point () {
                /* constructor to initialize
                the point to the origin */
                        x=0.0;
                        y=0.0;
                        numpoint++;
        }

        Point (double x, double y) {
                /* constructor to initialize
                the point to the specified coordinates */
                        this.x=x;
                        this.y=y;
                        numpoint++;
        }

        protected void finalize () {
                /* destroyer to decrement
                the number of points instantiated */
                numpoint--;
        }

        public static int HowMany () {
                /* return the number
                of points instantiated */
```

```
        return numpoint;
    }

    public void set (double x, double y) {
        /* set the point to the (x,y) position */
        this.x=x;
        this.y=y;
    }

    public double getX () {
        /* get the x-coordinate */
        return x;
    }

    public double getY () {
        /* get the y-coordinate */
        return y;
    }
}
```

The first particularity to note is that the Point class inherits from the Object class. The latter is a standard base-class from which all the user-defined classes must directly or indirectly inherit. The inheritance is specified by the extends clause. The designers of Java considered that multiple inheritance created too many problems for programmers and compiler writers. Therefore, Java implements the single-inheritance model: this implies that a class can inherit only from a class at once. However, Java offers the concept of *interface* in order to enhance the adopted single-inheritance model. An interface is a collection of specifications of methods that some classes implement. The implementation code is hidden within the class definition. Thus, inheriting from an interface, a class may share the methods of multiple classes.

Continuing the example analysis, we find the fields declaration of the class. For each of these there is specified the *access control* that establishes its scope. The access control must be specified also for the methods. Four types of access control exist:

- public. A public member is available to any other class anywhere.
- protected. A protected member is accessible only by classes that inherit from the class, which the member belongs to.
- private. This means that the member is accessible only within the class. For example, a private method can be used only by other methods within the same class.
- friendly. A member is said friendly, when no control access is specified (therefore "friendly" is not a keyword). A friendly member is accessible

to all classes within the same package. A package is a collection of classes and interfaces that are related to each other and need to work very closely. Typically, the package's classes need to access each other's instance members directly. The source file of the classes belonging to a package must be stored in the same directory in the file system. The primary utility of packages consists of grouping many class definitions in a single unit.

Java, like C++ and other object-oriented languages, allows the definition of instance members and class members. An instance member is duplicated for each instance of the class, while the class member is the same for all the instances. The class members are specified by using the **static** keyword. In the example above, the **numpoints** field is used to count how many Point objects have been instanced. When the class is defined **numpoints** is set to zero, and every time a Point object is instanced, **numpoints** is incremented by one by the *constructor*. Finally, when one object is released **numpoints** is diminished by one by the *destroyer*. In the example the **HowMany** method is a class method that returns the **numpoints** value.

The constructor is a special method that is automatically invoked when an instance of the object is made: its name is the same as that of the class. We see that more constructors may be specified in a single class, but they must have different parameters in order to discriminate them. The first constructor in the example, does not take parameters and implicitly sets the coordinates to zero. Instead, the second constructor takes a couple of parameters that specify the values, which the parameters must be set to. After the constructors, a destroyer is defined. For every class, it is identified by the reserved word **finalize**. The destroyer is automatically invoked when its master object is released. For the given example, the destroyer decrements the **numpoint** value by one. Probably, you should have noted the presence of the **this** variable used into the second constructor. Well, the **this** variable refers to the receiving object and is used to clarify which variable you are referring to. For instance, the second constructor takes two parameters that must not be confused with the class field. For this reason, to refer to the **x** and **y** fields, the **this** variable is used. Finally, the last four methods specify the behavior of the **Point** class.

We have already discussed about the architecture neutrality and portability of Java. But this is not all. Java was developed with particular attention to the security and safe-concurrency problems. The first is a dramatic problem for a language such as Java, that aims to produce application to download everywhere from the network. For this reason, Java was provided with many security functions, without decreasing its performance. The strategy of defense conduced by Java is articulated through four layers:

- **Language and Compiler.** We have already seen that by eliminating pointers, the Java developers can't directly manipulate the memory but can only refer to the objects by symbolic handles. This implies the malicious programmers cannot infer the physical memory layout, as is possible in C++ by an explicit usage of pointers.

- **Bytecode Verifier.** When the Java bytecode is loaded from a remote system, nothing about the remote Java compiler adopted is known. This means that possible hostile Java compiler may have been exploited to produce an illegal bytecode, in order to injure the safety of the remote client which will load it. For this reason, the Java runtime system performs a verification of the bytecode that must be executed. One of these checks, for instance, consists of verifying if the bytecode forges pointers to manipulate objects outside the virtual machine. These runtime checks together with the underlying Java language model make unnecessary many other traditional language controls such as the stack overflow check. Therefore, the computational load due to the bytecode verification is partially balanced by the lack of no more necessary controls.

- **Class Loader.** While a Java application is running, it may request that a class or a set of classes be loaded from the local system (built-in class) or from across the network (imported class). For further security, each class is associated to a specific namespace referred to as the class source. Thus, when a built-in class references to another class belonging to the same namespace, an imported class cannot intrude between them because it belongs to a different namespace. If the built-in class needs to refer to an imported class, it must specify such class explicitly.

- **Interface-specific Security.** Java offers a networking package that provides interfaces to standard networking protocols such as HTTP, FTP, and so on. This package can be set to four different security levels:

  1. Disallow all network accesses.
  2. Allow network accesses to only the hosts from which the code was imported.
  3. Allow network accesses only outside the firewall if the code came from outside.
  4. Allow all network accesses.

The Java security system was submitted to a Princeton University team for a complete examination. Some security bugs were found, but they were essentially due to implementation errors, not conceptual errors in Java's underlying security model. These bugs were examined by Sun's Java team and fixed in the recent release.

The last aspect of Java that we are going to explain is the *multithreading* support. What's a multithread ? It is the capacity, supported by the operating system, to concurrently run some pieces (*threads*) of an application. A multithreaded application is needed, for instance, when it must interact with the user and simultaneously execute the command previously issued by the user. In fact, if the user requires a file search, he hopes to do something else without waiting during the time of a boring search. The threads share the variables belonging to the application and need of an appropriate management for their consistence. This means, for example, that if a thread relies on an index to do an iteration, nothing else must change the index until the end of the iteration. Many languages such as C++ give the possibility to write multithreaded applications using a proper library, but the level of difficulty goes up by orders of magnitude. Java offers a powerful, safe, and very easy to use multithreading support based on the *monitor* paradigm. The Java library provides a **Thread** base class that offers many methods to manage threads. When a user-defined class inherits from the **Thread** class, its methods are able to run concurrently. If a method needs to run alone it must be declared as **synchronized**. In this way, the method waits until all the other methods from this class terminate, and immediately after it obtains the leadership until its end.

3.4.4 Comparison. CORBA provides an infrastructure that enables invocations of operations on objects located anywhere on a network as if they were local to the application using them. Java introduces platform-independent low-level code which, when integrated with World Wide Web protocols and browser, results in what are known as *applets*. In this approach instead of invoking a method on a remote object, the code for the class providing the method is transferred across the network, run locally, and then the method is invoked on a local object instance. As a matter of fact, Java provides also the *Remote Method Invocation* (RMI) approach for distributed object computing; however, this approach has several disadvantages with respect to CORBA, which represents a more robust, flexible, complete environment for distributed object computing. Just to give an idea, RMI is a Java-only solution, whereas CORBA provides access to objects implemented in different programming languages (C++, Java, Smalltalk, etc).

These differences between Java and CORBA lead to different use of these computing environments in the multimedia world. Java is most popular for lightweight multimedia internet applications, for which the key factors are: the easiness of use, portability, low cost servers and clients. On the other hand, for high-end multimedia applications like Video on Demand, high-quality videoconferencing, digital video broadcast, and so on, CORBA provides more safe and complete environment to meet most of the requirements of these applications. At present, the main problem of CORBA is related to the communication efficiency, in particular for applications that require efficient streaming services. Enhancement in this direction are currently in progress [MSS99]. The present trend is to develop interactive multimedia applications by using Java and CORBA together [VD98] (there are now many Java ORBs available), with CORBA providing the distributed object infrastructure and Java providing a strong mobile code system [Lew98].

4. Multimedia Applications

4.1 Video on Demand

Nowadays, almost every household has a television. The quick diffusion of television system was due to several factors:

- The capacity to broadcast together audio and video signals that resulted in a very expressive mean for divulging the information.
- The very accessible cost for the end-user.
- The typically large availability of different channels.
- The limited knowledge about the system while using it.

However, the television has a big limit: it isn't interactive! This implies, albeit the user can change the channel, that he or she must see the desired program when and how the broadcasting stations decide to do. Moreover, the television system is limited to provide only audio and video streams. No integration with other types of information is possible! Although these limitations don't burden on the utility of the actual television, the possible diffusion of an interactive and multimedia television system opens new interesting economic prospective for producers and end users. For this reason, many telecommunication industries and research groups are employing a lot of their resources to study the feasibility of this new video service, nowadays known as Video on Demand (VoD). The *Video on Demand* has been defined as a collection of services like [Fre89]

- **Movies on Demand.** Customers can select and play movies with full and more VCR capabilities.
- **Interactive News Television.** Customers navigate inside a virtual newspaper selecting and deepening only the desired news.
- **Distance Learning.** Customers subscribe to courses being taught at remote sites. Students tailor courses to individual preferences and time constraints.
- **Video Conferencing.** Customers can negotiate with each other. This service can integrate audio, video, text, and graphics.

One of these services on which more research efforts are lavished is the *Movie on Demand* (MoD). It can be defined as the service of *interactive* delivery of a video-program chosen from a *large* set of available programs [FKK+95]. This brief definition sins of various ambiguous aspects that need to be clarified.Interactive delivery has to imply the ability to control the stream flow through VCR-type control (i.e. stop, start, rewind, fast forward, pause); besides, the waiting time between the control request and the reaction, must be limited to a prefixed range of time. When this range is not longer than few seconds, the MoD is said *pure* MoD, otherwise *near* MoD. The waiting time will largely determine the take-up of the service. About the available set of programs, to be successful, a MoD services must give the appearance of an infinite availability of programs (the ideal case). However, the MoD system can exploit statistical information to offer at last the most popular videos of the moment; alternative storing techniques may be adopted for less required videos. Finally, a MoD service should support different audio and video resolution in according with the user-bandwidth requirement. The fundamental innovation of this new service is that it will allow users to select the programs they want to view at the time they want to view them. The programs are provided on demand by the video server and distributed to the requesting user through a broadband switching and access network. MoD is fundamentally different from broadcast video, cable television, or even Pay Per View (PPV) television. In these forms of television, the user's only choice is to select a channel from a number of "pre-programmed" channels, which are oriented towards the *average user* at an *average time* of the day for watching television.

4.1.1 VoD architecture. Depending on several factors (such as the reuse of existing networks, the type of services to offer, and so on) many VoD architectures have been proposed in literature. A largely accepted VoD scenario is shown in Fig. 4.1.

The VoD's subsystems are briefly described below:

– **Service Consumer.** Usually, as a *service consumer* the device is meant from which the people can access the VoD service providers, rather than the effective final users. It is placed at the subscriber premises and contains the access network termination, the video and audio decoders, and a television interface for the connection to common television. The service-consumer role is usually absolved by a set-top unit (STU) also known as set-top box. A set-top unit is very similar to a VCR unit, and can be accessed by a powerful and complete remote control handset. It is provided with the only necessary hardware for VoD applications, like for example electronic device for the hardware decompression of digital encoded streams (typically MPEG2 streams). In order to produce a cheap device, a STU is frequently discless and equipped with a small central memory. The software for the overall management is usually taken on removable smart card, or loaded from a remote machine. In this perspective, the STU often supplies a hardware chip that works as Java interpreter, for efficient execution of remote loaded Java applications.

– **Service Provider.** The *service provider* is the bridge element of a VoD system. Its task consists in interaction with both the service consumers and the content providers. The service provider represents the interface of the VoD system to the real users, and it plays the key-role in controlling and reacting to the user requests. A group of core services must be supplied by a service provider in order to control and manage the overall flow of the remote user accesses. Some of the most important charges for a service provider are

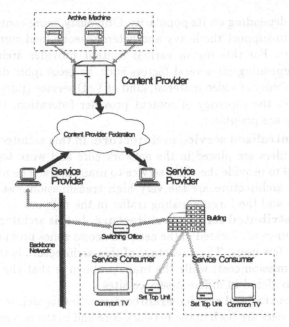

Fig. 4.1. VoD system: a very general architecture.

- **Acknowledgement and admission of user requests.** For example, when a user desires to open a new work session with the VoD system, he must forward the appropriate request to a service provider specifying clearly its identity. In reaction to this request, the service provider will try to identify the user and admit it if it is subscribed.
- **Core Services.** The service providers must supply to the remote user at least the basic functions to interact with the VoD system. These are browsing service to discover other services, stream service to control the stream flow, and so on.
- **Billing Service.** The service provider must also invoice the services provided depending on the several factors such as the quality of service, the kind of contract, and so on.
- **Regulation and assignment of resources.** Because of the time variation of the user requests, the service provider must dynamically manage the network resources according to the user subscriptions and must be able to balance the load between the content providers.

Content Provider. The *content provider* is the repository of information provided by the VoD system to the customers such as the video material. It has to perform many functions, such as admission control, request handling, data retrieval, guaranteed stream transmission, and support of functions found in VCRs including pause, rewind, and fast forward. Usually these systems are equipped with different storage media such hard disc arrays, optical discs, and magnetic tapes on which the video material is distributed depending on its popularity. Obviously, more content providers are needed to support the heavy and heterogeneous load coming from the user requests. For this reason various content provider architectures are proposed depending on several factors such as geographic distribution of users, availability of video material, kind of VoD service (pure or near) and so on. About the topology of content provider federation, three kinds of architecture are possible:

- **Fully centralized service architecture.** In this architecture the content providers are placed in the network core and work together at the same level to provide the video service to many users. The main problems with this architecture are the very high transmission cost to transport the video and the large signaling traffic in the network.
- **Fully distributed service architecture.** In this architecture the content providers are located in the network access zones providing the video service to few users. The advantage of this architecture is that it reduces the transmission cost, while the main problem is that the same movies must be buffered in different service sites.
- **Quasi-centralized service architecture.** In this architecture the content providers are both in the network core and in the access zone, named respectively *Core Service Center* (CSC) and *User Service Center* (USC). The less frequently requested movies are stored in the CSCs. When a user requests to access to one of these movies, the movie will be transferred, first to USC and then to the user: therefore the access delay is high. Because of this, the popular movies are buffered in USC. In this case the number of user connections to the service center is not very large, some copies of the same movie are buffered, and then the access delay is not high. The Quasi-centralized architecture seems to be the more adaptable architecture for variable situations of the load than a pure VoD service presents. This architecture can be also extended into more hierarchical levels. This means that the video material can be distributed on different levels each corresponding to a different geographic type of nodes.
- **Network.** The *network* acts as a glue for all the elements described above. It represents one of the most critical components for the entire VoD system. Due to the real-time characteristics of video delivery, the network must assure quality of service, dynamic balancing of network resources, and so on. Beyond performance requirements, further economical and political problems are represented by the installation and distribution of network cables underground through the cities to reach all the final users. Usually, the network is subdivided into different strategic components. Generally speaking, two sub-components are identified:
    - **Switching office.** The switching office means both the telephone companies central office and the cable companies head-end. It is the place where services are fed and distributed to individual subscribers.

- **Backbone network.** Outside of the local switching office, the backbone network connects it to the other video servers which are not in the local switching office and provide some national or specialized information. Currently, the high speed backbone network uses fiber cable with ATM technology.

4.1.2 Parallel video server. Parallel architectures have been introduced for VoD applications in order to overcome problems related to the lack of performance, fault tolerance, and efficient mass storage systems. The main work of a VoD server is to *pump* data streams from a mass storage system and to deliver these data to the final clients through a communication network. In a parallel video server, the data streams are stripped across discs that usually belong to the same file system. The data stripping can be either provided as a facility of the operating system running on the machine, or by special devices (e.g. disc arrays) or it can be managed at a higher abstraction level by programmers. A combination of these three approaches is also possible. Clearly, in order that the video client displays the original video stream, the data split across the discs has to be re-ordered and merged for the final destination. This work is performed by software or hardware module called *proxy*, which knows the system's configuration (number and address of data servers, data locations, and stripping policy). There are three main solutions to implement the proxy [Lee98]:

1. At the server computer - proxy at server
2. At an independent computer - independent proxy
3. At the client computer - proxy at client

Note that in this context the term computer refers to the hardware performing the proxy function that may not be a computer in the general sense. In the following, we describe these three approaches.

Proxy-at-server

In this architecture, one proxy is placed on each storage server. All servers are locally connected through an interconnection network (see Fig. 4.2). Each proxy manages the data retrieved from its storage system and requests to the other proxies the data placed elsewhere.

Finally, the proxy combines the gathered data, and delivers them to the connected client. Clearly, in this approach, clients know nothing about system configuration and do not play any role in the data-retrieving phase: therefore, a client transparency is obtained.

Two main drawbacks are related to proxy-at-server solution. First, because the same processor is shared by the proxy and retrieve processes, there is an overhead due the competition for the same resource. Second, there is a communication overhead whenever data do not reside on the local storage; in this case, the required data have to be read from other server's local storage,

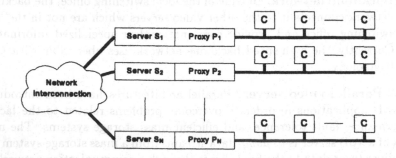

Fig. 4.2. Proxy-at-server architecture: the proxies are placed on each storage server.

processed and then transmitted to the client. Therefore, the data transmission requires in general a double step to reach the destination, and then a double bandwidth is needed.

Independent-Proxy

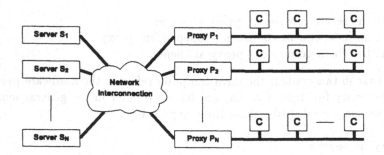

Fig. 4.3. Independent-proxy architecture: the proxies are placed on different machines with respect to the storage servers.

In this case, proxies run on different processors with respect to the storage server processes. The back-end storage servers and proxy processors are connected through an internal interconnection network (see Fig. 4.3), while the clients are connected to the proxies by another external network, usually with different characteristics from the internal one. The main advantage of this approach with respect to proxy-at-server solution is the reduction of the processing overhead. Clearly, this approach requires additional hardware (processors and communication links); moreover, the concept of data locality is lost, because storage server are anonymous for a proxy (as matter of fact, the topology of the internal communication network, whenever is not bus oriented, can strongly influence the time spent from retrieve data from a given server). Like the proxy-at-server solution, the independent-proxy architecture requires a double bandwidth.

Proxy-at-client In this third architecture, all the proxy functions are moved to the client side (see Fig. 4.4). Clients need to be equipped with additional software modules and/or hardware in order to combine data coming from storage servers into a single video stream suitable for the video-client application. In this case, there is a reduction of communication overhead with respect to the proxy-at-server and independent-proxy architectures, because data are directly transmitted to the client. Another advantage is that a proxy failure involves only one client, while in the other approaches it involves all the clients connected to that proxy.

However, this approach presents some disadvantages related to the absence of client transparency. First, there is a processing overhead for the client: this implies that the client hardware must provide suitable hardware and software to satisfy additional requirements due to the implementation of proxy functions. Second, while the proxy-at-server and independent-proxy architectures essentially require the client to be able to decode a video stream compressed in a standard format (e.g. MPEG2) and do not care about what is the client's hardware (a PC or a Set Top Box), for the client-at-proxy architecture the proxy implementation is strongly related to the particular client hardware and, in general, there is no portability among different clients.

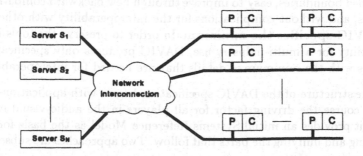

Fig. 4.4. Proxy-at-client architecture: the proxies are placed directly on the clients' videos.

4.1.3 Standards. The rapid development of digital video and audio technologies is creating isolated areas of market activity. Achieving critical mass of hardware creation and service development have led the market to confusion and users to wrong decisions. For this reason some international standard organizations are working to produce preventive standards for tracing the guidelines for the VoD system development. One of these is the Digital Audio Visual Council (DAVIC) that is a non-profit standard organization which aims are to produce enduring cross-industry specifications and make the development of widely supported VoD systems easy. DAVIC specifications aim to achieve the following goals:

- **Openness of the specification process.** When a specification process must be started, DAVIC issues Call for Proposals (CFP), in order to allow anybody to propose solutions and strategies to produce it. The responses to a CFP are sifted by the DAVIC members and taken into consideration when producing a largely accepted specification.
- **Specification of tools.** In its specification, DAVIC defines "tools" that tend to be *non-system-specific* because they have to be usable by different industries in different systems. Typically the process of tool specification is carried out in the following steps:
  - Analysis of target systems
  - Breakdown of systems into components
  - Identification of common components across systems
  - Specification of all necessary components (tools)
  - Verification whether tools defined in the above way can be used to assemble the target systems.
- **Relocation of tools.** In order to make tools usable in a variety of different systems, DAVIC defines its tools in such a way that they can be relocated, whenever this relocation is technically possible and practically meaningful.
- **One Functionality One Tool.** Each tool is conceived to implement only one functionality. This adopted strategy aims to produce tools with well defined boundaries, easy to improve through new backward compatible versions, and without complications for the interoperability with other tools.
- **DAVIC specifies the minimum.** In order to preserve the tools interoperability for a multi-industry use, DAVIC produces only specifications of tools with the minimum of details that are needed for interoperability.

The structure of the DAVIC specification begins with applications, which are of course the driving factor for all players in the audio-visual industry. Then it provides an initial Systems Reference Model as the basis for understanding and unifying the parts that follow. Two approaches are subsequently developed:

- Functional blocks and interfaces of the three major components of the audio-visual system (Service Provider System, Content Provider System, and Service Consumer System) are described.
- A toolbox composed of high and mid-layer protocol stacks, modulation, coding, and signaling techniques, and a set of protocol walk-through, or "Application Notes", that rehearse both the steady state and dynamic operation of the system at relevant reference points using specified protocols, are explained.

Two other self-contained parts deal with a representation of the audio-visual information and a usage information gathering.

About the end-to-end interface for the interaction between the service consumer and the service provider, DAVIC adopts the *Digital Media Command and Control* (DSM-CC) user-to-user specification (ISO/IEC 13818-6). The DSM-CC standard essentially defines the core interfaces for the user-to-user communication at the ISO-OSI layer 7 (application-specific). The DSM-CC primitives are based on the MPEG delivery system, and works are in progress to make the DSM-CC as an integral part of the MPEG2 standard. The interfaces are described by the OMG IDL (ISO/IEC 14750) in the perspective of using the CORBA standard as the development environment, in order to produce interoperable applications in a client-server scenario. The most important interfaces defined are:

- **Service gateway interface.** This service provides the methods for browsing and discovering other services, authentication of an end-user, registration of a new service and new users, resolution of the connection between clients and servers, and managing of session opening and resuming.
- **Directory interface.** This service provides the methods for the management of a name space where objects and data are registered and subsequently retrieved.
- **Stream interface.** This interface defines the essential methods for controlling continuous media stream playing. The methods extend the typical commands offered by a VCR.
- **File interface.** This interface provides storage and retrieval of data to applications.

4.1.4 Market players. The participation in the VoD market will be initially limited to those players who can provide the widespread infrastructure needed to reach residential users. For this reason telecommunication operators (TO) and cable TV companies (CATV) will be competing for the same market and the outcome will largely depend on the regulation. Because several scenarios are possible, each player tends to exploit the own infrastructures already developed. Therefore, the services offered to the end users will essentially depend on the different marketing strategies that these players will adopt. Below, a possible future market situation is explained:

- **Telecommunication Operators.** Telecommunication operators have ambitions to provide the full infrastructure up to the end user exploiting their telephone network. They are therefore particularly interested in methods of providing VoD that would allow them to capitalize on this advantage to provide new services. The use of the twisted pairs at higher speed, made possible by digital line coding techniques such as ADSL, is thus particularly appealing to them. Because several telecommunication operators are actively upgrading their access infrastructure by installing widespread optical fiber, much interests is also oriented to this solution. In a futuristic scenario, the access network will include the set-top units terminating the access network in the customer premises, and the set-top units will most probably be rented to the end user by the telecommunication operator as a part of its service offer. However, although no serious technical problems seem to appear, country specific regulations can restrict this development.

- **Cable TV Companies.** CATV companies also have to adapt themselves to regulatory changes allowing for open competition with their telecommunication operator counterparts. The deregulation could offer them the opportunity to provide switched services like telephony on their network, but it could also allow the telecommunication operators to offer video services. CATV companies are likely to react to this situation by upgrading their coax network to offer interactive services. Countries with high CATV penetration (like the USA and the Benelux countries) are good candidates for the introduction of VoD through the coax cable.

4.2 Multimedia Conferencing

The aim of the multimedia conferencing is to furnish the ability of interactively communicate using audio, video, and information by means of the use of telecommunication and computer technologies. With regard to the traditional telephone system, the multimedia conferencing adds the ability of seeing the interlocutors and interchanging data. The telephone is based on a world standard, therefore any end-user adopts the same procedure for talking with any other end-user in the world, without worrying about the equipment that the other part has. Unfortunately, the situation is more complex for the multimedia conferencing because of the variable standards of the computer technology. To unify the approach, the International Telecommunication Union (ITU) defined the H.320 standard to provide video conferencing compatibility between any H.320 compliant terminal, irrespective of what system it is based on.

4.2.1 The H.320 standard. The H.320 video conferencing protocol defines a standard for video conferencing over ISDN and other narrow-band transmission media (less then 2 Mbits per second). In essence, the H.320 is an umbrella document in the sense that it refers to others ITU standards for data and video compression, control, and communication.

H.320 actually calls on three protocol groups, each addressing a different aspect of low bandwidth video conferencing. The first group contains the ITU video compression standards H.261 and H.263, which define the compression algorithms and video resolutions used in video conferencing. The second group focuses on the diverse audio need of video conferencing applications and includes the audio encoding algorithm G.711, G.722, and G.728. The third and the last group deals with the transmission and control issues surrounding video conferencing and contains the specifications H.221, H.230, H.231, H.242, H.243, H.233, and T.120.

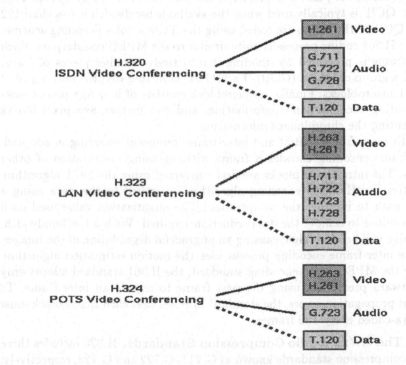

Fig. 4.5. The H-series of ITU videoconferencing standards.

In the following sections, most of these protocol standards will be examined (cf. Fig. 4.5).

4.2.2 The H.261 video compression standard. H.261 is a video compression standard designed to provide different compression bit rates 64 Kbps through 2 Mbps. This standard is also known as px64 where p is in the range of 1 to 30 (multiples of the bandwidth provided by a single ISDN B-Channel).

Two picture size are supported. The larger size is called CIF (Common Image Format) and has a size of 352 by 288 pixels for PAL format while for the NTSC format the size is 352 by 240 pixels. The smaller picture is called QCIF (quarter SIF) and is a quarter of the CIF size: i.e. 176 by 144 for PAL format. QCIF is typically used when the available bandwidth is less than 192 Kbps. QCIF/CIF images are coded using the YCbCr color encoding scheme.

The H.261 coding process is quite similar to the MPEG counterpart. Each video frame is processed by dividing it into twelve smaller pieces of frame named a group of blocks (GOB). Each GOB is further divided into a grid of 3 by 11 macroblocks. Finally, a macroblock consists of four 8x8 pixel blocks representing the luminance information, and two further 8x8 pixel blocks representing the chrominance information.

Both intra-frame spatial and inter-frame temporal encoding is adopted. Intra-frame encoding encodes a frame without using information of other frames. The intra-frame blocks are first converted using the DCT algorithm, and after the Huffman encoding algorithm is applied to the data using a zigzag path to improve the compression. The quantization value used each time is suited to achieve the data reduction required. With a low bandwidth, this value will be often high, causing an ungraceful degradation of the images.

The inter-frame encoding process uses the motion estimation algorithm. Unlike the MPEG video encoding standard, the H.261 standard adopts only the forward prediction, using the past frame to encode an inter-frame. To prevent propagation errors, the standard imposes that each macroblock must be intra-coded every 132 frames.

4.2.3 The G.7xx Audio Compression Standards. H.320 includes three audio compression standards known as G.711, G.722 and G.728, respectively. They were designed to handle the diverse audio needs that arise in video conferencing.

G.711 supports 3.1 kHz audio at 64 or 56 kbits per second. It's the worst audio standard supported and it is initially used to establish the H.230 call before moving on to more efficient audio algorithms. G.722 is similar to G.711 but produces 7 kHz stereo quality audio using 64 Kbps of bandwidth. G.728 provides a 3 kHz near telephone quality audio using only 16 Kbps of bandwidth. Because of its low bandwidth requirement, typically it can be multiplexed with the video on a single 64 kbits/sec channel.

G.711 employs the Pulse Code Modulation (PCM) audio encoding. The PCM is a waveform coding scheme in which samples are quantized to one of a finite set of reconstruction levels using logarithmic quantization (U-law in the US or A-law in Europe). The G.711 standard specifies 8-bit PCM as the standard method for coding telephone speech. PCM has enjoyed widespread use in phone systems because of its ability to endure several encoding and decoding stages and its low encoding delay (low delay allows some analog stages to be used in the phone network).

G.728 employs the Code Excited Linear Prediction (CELP). It is a more complicated speech encoding scheme. CELP compares speech with an analytical model of the vocal tract and computes the errors between the original speech and the model. Then it transmits the characteristic parameters of the model and the errors. CELP encoders have more overhead but produce higher quality speech.

4.2.4 ISDN. The H.320 standard supports multiple channels communication to provide the data delivery. The most standard communication for teleconferencing in use today is ISDN. For this reason, before study the control protocols, a brief explanation of ISDN is given.

ISDN stands for Integrated Services Digital Networks, and it's an ITU term for a relatively new telecommunication service package. ISDN aims to integrate audio, video and data information exploiting the existing switches and wiring of the telephone network. More telephone channels (each one with a bandwidth of 64 kbits per second) are used together to obtain bigger bandwidth. ISDN defines a basic network configuration known as Basic Rate Interface (BRI). The BRI is based on two 64K bearer (B) channels and a single delta (D) channel. The B channels are used for voice or data, and the D channel is used for signaling. For this reason, the BRI is often referred to as 2B+D. Equipment known as a Terminal Adapter (TA) can be used to adapt these channels to existing terminal equipment standards such as RS-232 and V.35.

ISDN supports several call modes where the most popular are:

- Voice: it is the regular 3.1 kHz analogue voice service used for telephone calling. Data and fax transmissions are excluded.
- Speech: this mode is the analogous to the voice mode, but allows for the use of fax and data transmission.
- Data: for this mode, the data rate is specified separately. This is the mode used for a H.320 call.

4.2.5 The H.221 Framing Protocol. The H.221 standard defines the protocol to multiplex together the audio and video bit-streams. H.221 organizes data into fixed sized frames that are 80 octets (eight bits) in length. Each octet contains multiplexed audio, video, data, and alignment information signals generated by the other protocols in H.320. The less significant bit is used to send these signals. The first four octets of a H.221 frame contain the Frame Alignment Signal (FAS) indicating the start of a frame. Another very important signal is the Bit-rate Allocation Signal (BAS) used to adjust the characteristics of the call as bandwidth allocation, start capability exchanges, and so on. The BAS octets are positioned in the second four octets of H.221 frame. The last signal inside the frame is the Encryption Control Signal (ECS) used to control the encrypted information. The ECS octets are sent in the third four octets. When no more signal octets are needed, the less significant bit is used for video information sending.

Depending on how many channels are used to transmit the frames, the H.221 standard allocates the information inside the frame. The next examples show how the information are marshaled when one or two channels are used:

- 1B audio visual call: the frames are transmitted over a single B channel every ten milliseconds. When the call starts, the G.711 audio protocol is used: therefore, the entire frame carries the G.711 encoded audio. Subsequently the audio encoding will be switched to G.728, freeing space for the video and data allocation. When this occurs, approximately one quarter of the channel is allocated for audio, one quarter for data, and approximately half (less the bits for frame signals) of the channel is dedicated to the video transmission.

- 2B audio visual call: in this case two B channels are used, where the second channel is exploited entirely for carrying video information. In this way, one quarter of the bandwidth is allocated for audio and data, while the rest is allocated for the video transmission (about 96 kbits per second). However, the frames coming from the two separate channels, must be synchronized using the FAS code.

When more than two channels are used, the H.221 standard combines the frames to form logically a sub-multiframe. This comprises a couple of adjacent frames for each B channel used. For each couple an expanded FAS code is used to identify them. Eight sub-multiframes, in turn, can be combined to form a bigger structure named multiframe.

4.2.6 The H.231 Multipoint Control Protocol. H.231 defines the standards for multipoint videoconference (MVC) where more people are involved. MVC is accomplished using a special type of bridge called a Multipoint Control Unit (MCU). When two or more people wish to hold a multipoint videoconference each connects to the MCU. The MCU exchanges then capability information with the VTC equipment of each participant using the H.242 protocol. During this communication the MCU collects information about the video format (CIF or QCIF), audio capabilities and data rates supported by each videoconference endpoint. Once the MCU has complied a database of the capabilities available at each endpoint, it negotiates the capabilities of all endpoint systems and sets the conference at the lowest common denominator so that everyone can participate.

5. Conclusions

The growth in the development of multimedia applications has been essentially related to the initial linkage with low cost hardware products (e.g. personal computers, entry-level workstation). However, the great impact that multimedia technologies have in many fields of everyday's life, results in generating a growing request for more sophisticated and innovative applications. In order to fully satisfy the requirements related to the present and next generation of high-end multimedia applications, more powerful computing systems, programming environments and data compression algorithms have to be used and developed.

The need of computing power lead to the utilization of parallel and distributed systems: as a matter of fact, these systems are not only required to supply CPU time but also high network communication throughput and huge and safe mass storage systems.

With particular reference to distributed systems, distributed object technology is becoming the most used approach: CORBA and Java seem to be accepted as the standard for building distributed applications outside the Microsoft world.

It should be noted that the impact of object oriented technologies is not only on the software development environment, but extends its influence also in multimedia compression standards (e.g. MPEG4).

Almost all multimedia applications deal with the concept of interactivity; generally speaking each application which allows the end-user to modify its behavior and/or the data to be provided can be defined as 'interactive'. However, the key point of most of the new multimedia applications is interactivity between remote users and service providers; Video on Demand, high-quality teleconferencing are the two useful examples of applications for which the "appeal" for the end-user is strongly connected with the ability to provide interactivity.

References

[Bar86]   Barth, P.S., An object-oriented approach to graphical interfaces, *ACM Trans. on Graphics* 5, 1986, 142-172.

[BB96]   Bernhardt, C., Biersack, E.W., *The Server Array: A Scalable Video Server Architecture. High-Speed Networking for Multimedia Applications*, Kluwer, Amsterdam, 1996.

[BCG+90]   Berra, P.B., Chen, C.Y.R., Ghafoor, A., Lin, C.C., Little, T.D.C., Shin, D., An architecture for distributed multimedia database systems, *Computer Communications* 13, 1990, 217-231.

[BRG88]   Bertino, E., Rabitti, R., Gibbs, S., Query processing in a multimedia document system, *ACM Trans. on Office Information, Systems* 6, 1988, 1-41.

[CLF+93]   Craighill, E., Lang,R., Fong, M., Skinner,K., CECED: A system for informal multimedia collaboration, *Proc. of ACM Multimedia 93*, Anaheim, California, 1993, 437-445.

[DeP93]   De Prycker, M., *Asynchronous Transfer Mode, Solution For Broadband ISDN*, E. Horwood, Chichester, 1993.

[Fre89]   Frenkel, K.A., The next generation of interactive technologies, *Communications of the ACM* **32**, 1989, 872-881.

[FKK+95]   Fuhrt, B., Kalra, D., Kitson, F.L., Rodriguez A., Wall, Designs issues for interactive television systems, *IEEE Computer* **28**, 1995, 25-39.

[GWB98]   Gafsi,J., Walter, U., Biersack, E.W., Design and implementation of a scalable, reliable, and distributed VOD-server, *Proc. of the 5th joint IFIP-TC6 and ICCC Conference on Computer Communications*, 1998, (See http://fantasia.eurecom.fr/~erbi/Bib/bib.html).

[Gru91]   Grudin, J., On computer supported collaborative work, collaborative computing, *Communication of the ACM* **34**, 1991, 30-34.

[ISO93]   *ISO/IEC DIS 13818-2: Generic Coding of Moving Pictures and Associated Audio for Digital Storage Media at up to about 1.5 Mbit/s-Part2: Video*, International Standard Organisation, 1993.

[ISO94]   *ISO/IEC11172-2: Coding of Moving Pictures and Associated Audio Information Part 2: Video*, International Standard Organisation, 1994.

[Koh89]   Kohli, J., Medical imaging applications of emerging broadband networks, *Communications Magazine* **27**, 1989, 8-16.

[LP91]   Lazar, A.A., Pacifici, G., Control of resources in broadband networks with quality of service guarantees, *IEEE Transactions on Communications* **29**, 1991, 66-73.

[Lee98]   Lee, J., Parallel video servers, *IEEE Transactions on Multimedia* **5**, 1998, 20-28.

[Lew98]   Lewandowski, S.M., Frameworks for component-based client/server computing, *ACM Computing Surveys* **30**, 1998, 3-27.

[LL97]   Liao, W., Li, V., The split and merge protocol for interactive video on demand, *IEEE Transactions on Multimedia* **4**, 1997, 51-62.

[LG91]   Little, T.D.C., Ghafoor, A., Spatio-temporal composition of distributed multimedia objects for value-added networks, *Computer* **24**, 1991, 42-50.

[MD89]   Mackay, W.E., Davenport, G., Virtual video edit in interactive multimedia applications, *Communications of the ACM* **32**, 1989, 802-810

[MP91]   Mathews, M.V., Pierce, J.R., (eds.), *Current directions in computer music research*, MIT Press, Cambridge, 1991.

[Mcg90]   McGarty, T.P., Image processing in full multimedia communications, *Advance Imaging* **5**, 1990, 28-33.

[Mil98]   Milonkevic, M., Delivering interactive services via digital TV infrastructure, *IEEE Transactions on Multimedia* **5**, 1998, 34-43.

[MP98a]   *MPEG4 Standard promoted to Final Committee Draft*, Document Number ISO/IEC JTC1/SC29/WG11 N2166, 1998.

[MP98b]   *MPEG4 Overview*, Koenen, R., (ed.), Document Number ISO/IEC JTC1/SC29/WG11 N2196, 1998.

[MP98c]   *MPEG Requirements Group, MPEG7 Requirements Document*, Doc. ISO/MPEG N2461, MPEG Atlantic City Meeting, 1998.

[MP98d]   *MPEG Requirements Group, Applications for MPEG7*, Doc. ISO/MPEG N2462, MPEG Atlantic City Meeting, 1998.

[MP98e]   *MPEG Requirements Group, MPEG7 Evaluation Procedure*, Doc. ISO/MPEG N2463, MPEG Atlantic City Meeting, 1998.

[MP98f]   *MPEG Requirements Group, MPEG7 Proposal Package Description (PPD)*, Doc. ISO/MPEG N2464, MPEG Atlantic City Meeting, 1998.

[MSS99]   Mungee,S., Surendran, N., Schmidt, D., The design and performance of a CORBA audio/video streaming service, *Proc. of the HICSS-32 International Conference on System Sciences, Multimedia DBMS and the WWW*, Hawaii, 1999, 312-319.

[PE90]   Patterson, J.F., Egido, G., Three keys to the broadband future: a view of applications, *IEEE Network Magazine*, 1990, 41-47.

[PGC+85]   Poggio, A., Garcia Luna Aceves, J.L., Craighill, E.F., Tivioran, D., Aguilar, L., Worthington, D., Hight, CCWS: a computer-based multimedia information system, *Computer*, 1985, 92-103.

[Pop97]   Pope, A., *The CORBA Reference Guide*, Addison Wesley, 1997.

[PFK+88]   Postel, J., Finn, G., Katz, A., Reynolds, L., An experimental multimedia mail system, *ACM Trans. on Office Information Systems* 6, 1988, 63-81.

[Pre90]   Press, L., Computervision or teleputer, *Communications of the ACM* 33, 1990, 29-36.

[Ric98]   Riccomi, A., MPEG4: Object oriented coding of multimedia data, *Multimedia System Design* 3, 1998, (see www.msdmag.com/frameindex.htm?98/9807art3.htm).

[Rub87]   Rubenstein, W.B., A database design for musical information, *Proc. ACM SIG-MOD Conference on Management of Data*, San Francisco, 1987, 479-490.

[Spr91]   Special report on gigabit networks, *IEEE Computer* 24, 1991.

[Sve87]   Sventek, J.S., An architecture for supporting multi-media integration, *Proc. IEEE Computer Society Office Automation Symposium*, 1987, 46-56.

[TFC+85]   Thomas, R.H., Forsdick, H.C., Crowley, T.R., Schaaf, R.W., Toinlinson, R.S., Travers, V.M., Robertson, G.G., Diamond: a multimedia message system built on a distributed architecture, *Computer*, 1985, 65-78.

[VD98]   Vogel, A., Duddy, K., *Java Programming with CORBA*, J.Wiley, 1998.

[WSM91]   Watabe, K., Sakata, S., Maeno, K., Fukuoka, H., Ohmori, T., Multimedia desktop conferencing system: MERMAID, *NEC Research and Development* 32, 1991, 158-167.

[WLK87]   Woelk, D., Luther, W., Kim, W., Multimedia applications and database requirements, *Proc. IEEE Office Automation Symposium*, 1987, 180-189.

Index

List of Contributors

Selim G. Akl
Department of Computing and Information Science
Queen's University
Kingston, Ontario
Canada K7L 3N6

Jacek Błażewicz
Institute of Computing Science
Poznań Universtiy of Technology
ul.Piotrowo 3a, 60-965 Poznań
Poland

H. Casanova
University of Tennessee
Knoxville, TN 37996
U.S.A.

Wojciech Cencek
Quantum Chemistry Group
Department of Chemistry
Adam Mickiewicz University
ul.Grunwaldzka 6, 60-780 Poznań,
Poland

J. Dongarra
Oak Ridge National Laboratory,
Oak Ridge, TN 37831
and
University of Tennessee,
Knoxville, TN 37996,
U.S.A.

Maciej Drozdowski
Institute of Computing Science,

Poznań University of Technology,
ul.Piotrowo 3a, 60-965 Poznań,
Poland

Klaus Ecker
Institut für Informatik
Technische Universität Clausthal
Clausthal-Zellerfeld
Germany

Ian Foster
The University of Chicago, and
Mathematics & Computer Science
Argonne National Laboratory
Argonne, IL 60439
U.S.A.

João Garcia
IST/INESC, Lisbon, Portugal

Leana Golubchik
University of Maryland at College
Park and
University of California at Los Angeles
U.S.A.

Paulo Guedes
IST/INESC, Lisbon
Portugal

Paulo Ferreira
IST/INESC, Lisbon
Portugal

Jacek Komasa
Quantum Chemistry Group
Department of Chemistry
Adam Mickiewicz University
ul.Grunwaldzka 6, 60-780 Poznań
Poland

D. Litaize
Institut de Recherche en Informatique de Toulouse
Université Paul Sabatier
Toulouse
France

Allen D. Malony
Department of Computer and Information Science
307 Deschutes Hall, University of Oregon
1477 E. 13th, Eugene, OR 97403-1202
U.S.A.

Richard R. Muntz
University of Maryland at College Park, and
University of California at Los Angeles
U.S.A.

A. Mzoughi
Institut de Recherche en Informatique de Toulouse
Université Paul Sabatier
Toulouse
France

Jarek Nabrzyski
Poznań Supercomputing and
Networking Center,
ul.Wieniawskiego 17/19,
61-713 Poznań
Poland

A. Petitet
University of Tennessee
Knoxville, TN 37996
U.S.A.

Giuseppe De Pietro
IRSIP - National Research Council of Italy,
Via P. Castellino 111, Naples
Italy

Brigitte Plateau
Institut National Polytechnique de Grenoble
ID - IMAG, BP 53
F-38041 Grenoble Cedex
France

Y. Robert
Ecole Normale Supérieure de Lyon,
69364 Lyon Cedex 07
France

C. Rochange
Institut de Recherche en Informatique de Toulouse
Université Paul Sabatier
Toulouse
France

Jacek Rychlewski
Quantum Chemistry Group
Department of Chemistry
Adam Mickiewicz University
ul.Grunwaldzka 6, 60-780 Poznań
and Poznań Supercomputing and
Networking Center
ul.Wieniawskiego 17/19
61-713 Poznań
Poland

P. Sainrat
Institut de Recherche en Informatique de Toulouse
Université Paul Sabatier

Toulouse
France

Maciej Stroiński
Poznań Supercomputing and
Networking Center
ul.Wieniawskiego 17/19
61-713 Poznań
Poland

Denis Trystram
Institut National Polytechnique de
Grenoble
ID - IMAG, BP 53
F-38041 Grenoble Cedex
France

Jan Węglarz
Poznań Supercomputing and
Networking Center
ul.Wieniawskiego 17/19
61-713 Poznań
Poland

R. C. Whaley
University of Tennessee
Knoxville, TN 37996
U.S.A.